1,001
BEST
GRILLING
RECIPES

**DELICIOUS, EASY-TO-MAKE
RECIPES FROM
AROUND THE WORLD**

1,001
BEST
GRILLING
RECIPES

DELICIOUS, EASY-TO-MAKE
RECIPES FROM
AROUND THE WORLD

RICK BROWNE

SURREY
BOOKS

CHICAGO

Printed in the United States of America

The Library of Congress Cataloging-in-Publication Data

Browne, Rick, 1946-
1,001 best grilling recipes : delicious, easy-to-make recipes from around the world / by Rick Browne.
      p. cm.
Summary: "Over 1,000 grilling recipes from around the world for everything from appetizers to desserts. Includes sauces, marinades, and rubs"--Provided by publisher.
Includes index.
 ISBN-13: 978-1-57284-116-1 (pbk.)
 ISBN-10: 1-57284-116-8 (pbk.)
 1. Barbecuing. 2. International cooking. 3. Cookbooks. I. Title. II. Title: One thousand and one best grilling recipes. III. Title: One thousanda one best grilling recipes.
 TX840.B3B759 2011
 641.7'6--dc22

                          2011006340

14 13 12 11 10   10 9 8 7 6 5 4 3 2 1

Surrey Books is an imprint of Agate Publishing, Inc.
Agate and Surrey books are available in bulk at discount prices. For more information, go to agatepublishing.com.

DEDICATION

This book is dedicated to and honors Chef Mike Barret, an incredibly dedicated husband; a proud father of four beautiful children; an honest, decent, humble, and caring man; an extremely talented executive chef; as he called himself on his business card, the "Superior Intergalactic Grand Chef of the Universe"; and, to me, a dear, dear friend.

He loved his family, his church, his friends, his coworkers, and life itself. We'll miss his smile, his wry sense of humor, his passion for excellence, his zest for life, and, of course, his remarkable talents in the kitchen.

CONTENTS

ACKNOWLEDGMENTS

While traveling around the U.S. and through 26 countries during the past 9 years, I've met hundreds of people who I'd like to thank for helping my barbecue pilgrimage along and for their help in writing this barbecue tome. The following list contains but a few of the folks to whom I'm indebted for their help, cooking tips, support, recipes, advice and friendship.

Al Roker, *Today*
Anne & Terry Callon
Anne & Kary Goodwin
Ardie Davis, aka Remus Powers
"Aunt" Linda Doden
Barb, Jim, Abby, Anthony, Tyler & Betsy Smith
Barbara Johnson & Tom Ryll
Bruce Jacobson, Canadian Barbecue Smokers Association
Bruce & Pam Paris
Campbell Brown, *Today*
Carlene & Mitch Phelps, barbecuenews.com
Carol Ladd, Portland
Carolyn Wells, Kansas City Barbecue Society
Dan Macey, Philadelphia
Dave DeWitt, fiery-foods.com
Dave Hentosh, Smoldering Lake Outfitters
Dennis Hayes
Donna Myers, Hearth, Patio & Barbecue Association
Dorothy & Arnold Browne
Doug & Joyce Spittler
Doug Mosley, National Barbecue News
Doug Seibold, Agate Publishing

Eileen Johnson, Agate Publishing
Garrett Bess, Two River Pictures
Geoff Latham, NickyUSA
Grant & June Browne
Greg & Susan Gilbert
Jack and Cheryl Lawrence
Jack Rogers, Jim Minion, The Car Dogs
Jamie Gwen, Chef
Jamieson Fuller
Jennifer Lyons
John Davis
Jordan Asher
Kara & Stephen Petersen
Kate & Chris Browne
Katie Couric, *Today*
Kim Hemphill & Kim Schafer
Karen Adler, Pig Out Publications
Kelly Ripa
Linda & Bob Buckley
Lisa Miller
Lois Manno, |fiery-foods.com
Lyn Johnson
Lynn & Jeff Shivers, IBCA
Kevin, Amber & Stephen Lynch
Marie Haycox, New York City
Mark Mathias, Beaches
Marsha Matta, Baxter's Mom

Martin Yan
Matt Lauer, *Today*
Michael Gelman
Michelle Rousseau
Nathan Wu & Karen Kulm
Patty Anderson Browne
Perrin Davis, Agate Publishing
Peter Reinhart
Regis Philbin
Richard & Amanda, Little House Digital
Rick & Jennifer Browne
Robert & Marti Browne
Rocky Danner, National Barbecue News
Rubie Lloyd, ChefWear
Sandy & Ken Calllon
Scott Mendel
Scott Stewart, The High Lonesome Ranch
Smudge Browne
Stephen Marsden
Suzanne Rousseau-Bernard
Terry Browne
Tony Lyons
Tricia & Reed Kawahara
The Columbian Photogs: Milan Chuckovich, Kim Blau, Jerry Coughlan, Linda Lutes, Dave Olson, Janet Mathews, and Steve Lane
Zoe Miller, Oregon Spice Company

INTRODUCTION

This book is a collection of recipes I've gathered over ten years of roaming around the United States, Canada, Mexico, and twenty-three other countries. It has been an endless pursuit of the world's best barbecue and grilling recipes—terms, by the way, that I use interchangeably, much to the chagrin of some barbecue purists. But to me, if you cook food outdoors using wood, charcoal, natural gas, propane, or just about any other combustible materials, you're barbecuing. The only measure of success or failure is how the end product—that steak, chicken breast, fish fillet, side dish, or even dessert—tastes when you've finished your culinary endeavors.

I wish to extend my thanks to the hundreds of wonderful people I've met in my travels who freely shared their ideas, cooking and barbecuing tips, techniques, experiences, and recipes so I could to pass them on to others. To all I've met, worked with, worked for, cooked with, and cooked for, I say a big and hearty . . . ThankQUE!

—*Rick Browne, PhB (Doctor of Barbecue)*

GRILLING GUIDELINES

Indirect Cooking

A technique that many barbecue chefs use, and that I use throughout this book, is to cook everything with indirect heat—thereby cooking everything "low and slow." This technique uses a temperature of 180°F (85°C) to 240°F (115°C) for the "low" part of the equation and a cooking time of 2 to 24 hours for the "slow" part. Obviously, the 2 hours is for pork ribs, fish, or small roasts, and the 24 hours is for tough beef briskets, large roasts, and whole birds.

The best way to do this is to use a combination of direct grilling over the hottest part of the grill and indirect grilling, moving the food to an unheated or cooler part of the grill and cooking it slowly, thereby keeping it juicy, tender, and loaded with taste. To create the indirect heat effect when using coals, briquettes, or wood pieces, place them on one side only on the bottom of the barbecue. Leave the other half of the bottom empty (for now) and start your fire as you normally would.

When the barbecue is up to temperature (and the coals are covered with a thin film of white ash), place a 9 × 12-inch (22.5 × 32.5-cm) metal or foil pan on the empty side of the grill, then fill the pan with 1 to 2 inches (2.5 to 5 cm) of water. Refill the pan as the water evaporates during cooking.

I recommend starting meat, poultry, and fish on the direct, hot side of the grill. This way, you can sear the food over high heat, trapping in its natural juices. Depending on the type of food, its thickness, and the fire temperature, you should only need to cook the food for a short time—2 to 10 minutes, on average—on each side.

Then again, depending on the recipe, you may need to move the food to the unheated cooler side of the grill. ("Cooler" is a relative term here; the "hot" side of the grill may be at 600°F [315°C] to 700°F [370°C] while the "cool" side may be as high as 400°F [200°C] to 500°F [260°C], or thereabouts.) In most cases, a temperature of 200°F (100°C) to 250°F (120°C) is a good target for the unheated side.

The pan of water under the unheated side of the grill captures any fat dripping down, keeping flames from shooting up and burning the food. Also, the water evaporates during the cooking process, and the steam helps keep the food above it moist, juicy, and tasty.

If you have a gas grill, the process is much the same, only the placement of the water pan is different. Most gas barbecues have at least two burners, some have three, and a few have four or more burners. It really doesn't matter, as long as there are at least two. On a two-burner grill, turn on only one burner. Place your water pan over the unlit burner, and you're good to go. Depending on the height of your burners, you may have to put bricks on both sides of the unlit burner to support the water pan. To cook indirectly on a gas barbecue, first place the food on the hot side to sear it, and then transfer it to the cool side for the rest of the cooking time, just as when cooking with charcoal.

If you've got more burners, you can be a bit more creative. With a three-burner setup, you can turn on the two outside burners only (to the same temperature; otherwise you'll cook one side of your food faster than the other). Then place the water pan over the middle burner, again under the grill rack. As with charcoal cooking, sear what you're cooking on one or both of the hot sides, and follow up by cooking for the remaining time on the cool side.

We've used indirect cooking to make soufflés, breads, custards, cakes, and pies and perfectly cooked what might have burned or overcooked if grilled for the full time over direct heat.

Okay, future grill masters—armed with this tidbit of grilling savvy, you can cook "cool" and never have to scrape the burned flesh from a roast, chicken wing, or T-bone steak again.

Cooking to Temperature Versus Cooking to Time

As we traveled the country making notes, testing recipes, and learning barbecue tips from chefs, we settled on a new method that we recommend to all barbecue cooks. We believe that *cooking to temperature* rather than old-fashioned *cooking to time* is a much better method for grilling, smoking, and barbecuing.

First, if you don't have a meat thermometer, get one. It is invaluable and takes the guesswork out of every barbecue outing. Second, when we remove meat or poultry from the grill, we almost always cover it with foil and let it rest for 5 to 20 minutes to (a) let the natural juices reabsorb into the meat (as the heat has driven the internal juices to the top of whatever we were cooking) and (b) let the temperature rise 5°F (1°C) to 15°F (3°C). So if you've cooked a steak to a perfect 155°F (68°C) medium-rare on the grill, by the time it gets to the table it will have reached 160°F (71°C) to 165°F (74°C), or medium.

If, instead, you follow someone's direction to cook a steak, for "4 to 5 minutes," it can go wrong in many ways. That 4 to 5 minutes entirely depends on each steak being the same thickness and maintaining the same temperature for the entire cooking time. It allows for no variation in the temperature inside the barbecue, in the fuel you are using, or in the outside temperature or humidity. It accounts for no heat loss from the barbecue itself when lifting the lid to check on the food. Because of these variables, cooking by time can lead to raw or overcooked food and other assorted culinary disasters.

We prefer to give you a much more accurate means of checking the doneness of the food you are cooking. Time is only a guideline; it's temperature that really rules in barbecue. The following are meat-cooking temperatures provided by the USDA, and while they are quite conservative, they are good guidelines to follow.

- Cook beefsteak to medium-rare (145°F [63°C]), medium (160°F [71°C]), medium well (170°F [77°C]), or your preferred temperature.
- Pork should be cooked to medium pink (155°F [168°C]), medium (160°F [71°C]), or your preferred temperature. Why "medium pink" instead of rare? Because there's something about using the word "rare" while discussing pork that scares people silly; today, pork is perfectly safe served with the center of the meat slightly pink—and much better tasting, too.
- Lamb should be prepared to medium-rare (145°F [63°C]), medium (160°F [71°C]), medium well (170°F [77°C]), or your preferred temperature.
- Poultry (chicken, turkey, duck, game hen, etc.) should be cooked until a meat thermometer inserted in the breast reads 165°F (74°C) and in the thigh, 180°F (82°C).

Grilling Tips
- Preheat your barbecue, whether it's a charcoal, wood, gas, or even electric grill. Most charcoal briquettes need up to 45 minutes to heat to the right temperature, lump charcoal takes an average of 30 minutes, and raw wood logs take about the same length of time as the briquettes to form the right kind of coals. Even instant-flame gas and electric grills need time to reach temperature, so give them 15 minutes to fire up.
- Use the right equipment. Don't use short kitchen tongs, table forks and spoons, or small, kitchen-size oven potholders. Use the proper tools for a safe and enjoyable barbecue. Here are some suggested items you should have if you love to barbecue:
  - Long tongs with rubber grips and clamshell jaws
  - Long-handled barbecue spatula
  - Dripless, heat-resistant silicone basting brush with a shield that prevents dripping sauce from reaching your hands
  - Barbecue gloves or silicone potholders
  - Good set of stainless-steel kebab skewers
  - Top-quality brass grill-cleaning brush

- A 17-inch meat-turning hook
- Instant-read digital thermometer

- Marinating in liquid has become very popular and is an efficient and tasty way to add flavor, promote tenderness, and give a personal touch to an otherwise ordinary chicken, brisket, or other meat. But, for heaven's sake, don't immediately use the marinade as a basting sauce or—horror of horrors—a sauce base. *You must boil the marinade for 10 minutes before using it as a basting or serving sauce!*
- Do not apply sugar-based sauces to any food earlier than the last 10—or, even better, 5—minutes of cooking. Since 90 percent of all commercially bottled barbecue sauces, and most homemade ones, contain sugar, molasses, maple syrup, corn syrup, or tomato sauce, they can burn or char very easily. We have experienced the tragedy of a chicken with a crisply inciner-ated exterior and a bright pink, raw interior. A raw chicken meteorite is not a good thing.

GRILLING TIMES & TEMPERATURES FOR FRESH FRUIT

FRUIT, HOW BEST TO COOK	TIME, TEMPERATURE ON GRILL
Apples, whole	35 to 40 minutes (indirect, medium)
Apples, cut into ½-inch (1-cm) thick rounds	4 to 6 minutes (direct, medium)
Apricots, halved and pitted	6 to 8 minutes (direct, medium)
Bananas, halved lengthwise	6 to 8 minutes (direct, medium)
Cantaloupes, cut into wedges	6 to 8 minutes (direct, medium)
Nectarines, halved and pitted	8 to 10 minutes (direct, medium)
Peaches, halved and pitted	8 to 10 minutes (direct, medium)
Pears, halved lengthwise	10 to 12 minutes (direct, medium)
Pineapple, peeled and cored, cut crosswise into ½-inch (1-cm) thick rings or lengthwise into 1-inch (2.5-cm) thick wedges	5 to 10 minutes (direct, medium)
Strawberries, whole	4 to 5 minutes (direct, medium)

ONE

Appetizers

Grilled Pepper Poppers
Yield: 16–18 appetizers

If jalapeño peppers are too fiery for you, you can substitute milder poblanos, which are the peppers used in chilies rellenos.

Dipping Sauce
1 (16-ounce [454-g]) bottle ranch dressing
Juice of 1 lemon
1 tablespoon (15 mL) ground paprika
1 tablespoon (15 mL) minced fresh parsley

Peppers
1 pound (454 g) hickory-smoked bacon
8 ounces (227 g) cream cheese, at room temperature
1 cup (236 mL) shredded provolone cheese
½ cup (118 mL) shredded cheddar cheese
1 tablespoon (15 mL) garlic powder
2 teaspoons (10 mL) ground cumin
1 teaspoon (5 mL) freshly ground black pepper
16–18 large jalapeño peppers

1. Preheat the barbecue to medium high (350°F [180°C] to 400°F [200°C]).

2. To make the dipping sauce, in a medium bowl, mix together the ranch dressing, lemon juice, paprika, and parsley. Cover and refrigerate.

3. Fry the bacon, drain it on paper towels, and let it cool to room temperature.

4. With your hands, crumble the bacon into a separate medium bowl. Add the cream cheese, provolone cheese, cheddar cheese, garlic powder, cumin, and black pepper. Mix well.

5. Spoon the cream cheese mixture into a pastry bag or a 1-quart (0.95-L) food storage bag. (If using a storage bag, cut the tip off one of the corners so you can squeeze the mixture into the peppers.)

6. Cut a small cap (about ¼ inch [0.5 cm]) off the top of each pepper and set the tops aside. Squeeze the cream cheese mixture into each pepper and replace the caps. Wrap each pepper tightly in foil.

7. Place the wrapped peppers on the grill over direct heat and cook them for 10 to 12 minutes, turning frequently.

8. Remove the peppers from the grill, remove the foil, and let them cool. Serve with the dipping sauce, which will help cool down the spicy peppers.

Dragon Eggs

Yield: 36 appetizers

You can fill these with just about any type of meat, fish, or poultry on the planet.

Peppers

36 large jalapeño peppers, roasted and peeled
½ cup (118 mL) minced cooked chicken or shrimp
2 teaspoons (10 mL) mayonnaise
2 teaspoons (10 mL) bottled chili sauce
2 teaspoons (10 mL) minced green onions
2 teaspoons (10 mL) minced fresh parsley
½ teaspoon (2.5 mL) hot mustard
½ teaspoon (2.5 mL) grated fresh horseradish
¼ teaspoon (1.25 mL) paprika
¼ teaspoon (1.25 mL) cayenne pepper
Salt, to taste
Freshly ground black pepper, to taste
Peanut or vegetable oil, for frying

Batter

1¾ cups (413 mL) all-purpose flour
¾ cup (177 mL) (177 mL) beer, at room temperature
2 eggs, beaten
3 tablespoons (45 mL) minced green onions, green and white parts
2 tablespoons (30 mL) olive oil
1 tablespoon (15 mL) ketchup
2½ tablespoons (37.5 mL) Worcestershire sauce
1½ teaspoons (7.5 mL) lemon juice
1½ teaspoons (7.5 mL) baking powder
1 teaspoon (5 mL) salt
1 teaspoon (5 mL) cayenne pepper

1. Preheat the barbecue to medium high (350°F [180°C] to 400°F [200°C]).

2. Using a sharp knife, cut a slit along the length of each pepper. Wearing rubber or plastic gloves, carefully scrape out the seeds and rinse out the peppers, and then drain them on paper towels.

3. In a medium bowl, mix together the chicken or shrimp, mayonnaise, chili sauce, green onions, parsley, mustard, horseradish, paprika, cayenne pepper, salt, and black pepper. Spoon 1 to 2 teaspoons (5 to 10 mL) of the filling into each pepper, being careful not to knock off the top cap of the pepper. Arrange the peppers on a plate and refrigerate.

4. Pour ¾ inch (1.5 cm) oil into a skillet (a cast-iron skillet is perfect) and set it on the barbecue grill or on a side burner until the temperature of the oil reaches 350°F (180°C).

5. In a large bowl, combine the flour, beer, eggs, green onions, olive oil, ketchup, Worcestershire sauce, lemon juice, baking powder, salt, and cayenne pepper. Dip each pepper in the batter, coating it completely.

6. Add four or five of the peppers to the heated oil in the skillet and fry until golden brown, turning once, for a total of about 5 minutes. Repeat with the remaining peppers. Drain on paper towels and serve.

Cheesy Zukes
Yield: 24 appetizers

Any leftovers can be refrigerated, covered, and eaten later; just bring them back to room temperature before serving. I've also chopped up leftover pieces and used them to stuff a chicken. You can use this as a side dish with a meat and a second vegetable.

3 cups (708 mL) thinly sliced zucchini, skin left on
1 cup (236 mL) Bisquick baking mix
½ cup (118 mL) grated Parmesan cheese
½ cup (118 mL) finely chopped yellow or Spanish onion
1 clove garlic, peeled and finely minced
4 large eggs, beaten
½ teaspoon (2.5 mL) seasoned salt
2 tablespoons (30 mL) minced fresh parsley
½ teaspoon (2.5 mL) dried oregano
Freshly ground black pepper, to taste
1 cup (236 mL) vegetable oil

1. Preheat the barbecue to medium high (350°F [180°C] to 400°F [200°C]).

2. Grease or spray with nonstick cooking spray a 9 × 13-inch (22.5 × 32.5 cm) glass baking pan.

3. In a large bowl, mix together the zucchini, Bisquick, Parmesan cheese, onion, garlic, eggs, seasoned salt, parsley, oregano, and black pepper. Spread the mixture in the prepared pan.

4. Bake in the barbecue until golden brown, about 20 to 25 minutes.

5. Cut the zucchini loaf into 2 × 3-inch (5 × 7.5-cm) rectangles and serve warm.

Bacon-Wrapped Chicken Livers
Yield: 24 appetizers

If you want to make these into world-class appetizers, spend a few extra bucks and buy Whole Foods Black Forest bacon. You will never again look at regular bacon the same way.

Livers

12 chicken livers
6 slices bacon
24 crackers of your choice or small toast rounds

Dip

½ cup (118 mL) prepared mustard
½ cup (118 mL) honey
1 tablespoon (15 mL) ketchup
1 pinch salt
Freshly ground black pepper, to taste

1. Make sure the grill is clean and generously sprayed with nonstick grilling spray. Preheat the barbecue to medium high (350°F [180°C] to 400°F [200°C]).

2. In a nonstick skillet, quickly sauté the livers until they are just firm enough to hold together.

3. Cut the bacon slices and livers in half and wrap each liver half with half a slice of bacon, skewering each with a toothpick to hold them together.

4. Place the bacon-wrapped livers on the grill and grill for several minutes, turning once or twice, until the bacon is browned and crisp.

5. Meanwhile, make the dip by combining the mustard, honey, ketchup, salt, and pepper in a small bowl. Stir well and set aside.

6. Serve the cooked livers immediately on crackers or small toast rounds, accompanied by the dip.

Barbecued Whole Garlic

Yield: 24 appetizers

Never store garlic in the refrigerator. Instead, keep it in a cool, dry place. Americans consume 300 million pounds (136 million kg) of garlic a year—that's why there are no vampires here!

4–6 heads garlic
¼ cup olive oil, for drizzling
1 pound (454 g) butter, melted
2 tablespoons (30 mL) minced fresh parsley
1 teaspoon (5 mL) celery salt
1 teaspoon (5 mL) paprika
24 or more toast rounds, for serving

1. Preheat the barbecue to medium high (350°F [180°C] to 400°F [200°C]).

2. Remove the papery outer covering from the garlic heads, but do not separate or peel the cloves. Using a sharp knife, cut off and discard the top ¼ inch (0.5 cm) of each bulb.

3. Place the garlic on a 12-inch (30-cm) square sheet of heavy-duty aluminum foil. Then drizzle the olive oil over the entire heads. Fold the foil over the garlic to seal it in

4. Bake in the preheated barbecue for 45 minutes.

5. While the garlic bakes, in a small bowl, mix together the butter, parsley, celery salt, and paprika. Brush this mixture on the toast rounds and keep them warm.

6. Serve the whole heads of garlic with a basket of the buttered toast.

7. To eat, pick out individual cloves with a small cocktail fork or toothpick, drop them onto the toast, and spread with a butter knife.

Robbie's Barbecue Baked Brie
Yield: 12–14 servings

Brie cheese gets its name from the French province of the same name. Like wine, Brie gets stronger in flavor and taste as it ages. This recipe comes from Robbie Buckley of Orlando, FL.

1 (8-ounce, 227 g) wheel Brie cheese
2 tablespoons (30 mL) butter
1 cup (236 mL) raspberry or apricot jam
½ cup (118 mL) slivered almonds
French bread, for serving

1. Preheat the barbecue to medium high (350°F [180°C] to 400°F [200°C]).

2. Place the Brie cheese in an ovenproof baking dish or roasting pan. Dot it with the butter.

3. Spread the jam over the top of the cheese and sprinkle it with the almonds. Place the pan in the heated barbecue and bake until the Brie cheese begins to bulge and the jam is bubbling, about 20 minutes.

4. Serve as an appetizer with fresh or toasted French bread or toasted cocktail rye bread rounds.

Chiles Rellenos Squares
Yield: 16 appetizers

Anaheim chili peppers, also called California green or long chilies, are a mild variety that is perfect for this dish. You can use a commercial "Mexican cheese" blend instead of the individual cheeses listed here.

4 large eggs, beaten
½ cup (118 mL) half-and-half
2 tablespoons (30 mL) all-purpose flour
8 ounces (227 g) grated Monterey Jack cheese
8 ounces (227 g) grated cheddar cheese
2 tablespoons (30 mL) finely chopped yellow or Spanish onion
12 Anaheim chili peppers, charred, peeled, stem and seeds removed,
    chopped into 2-inch (5-cm) pieces

1. Preheat the barbecue to medium high (350°F [180°C] to 400°F [200°C]).

2. Grease or spray a 9-inch (22.5-cm) square baking pan with nonstick spray and set it aside.

3. Beat the eggs in a medium bowl. Add the half-and-half and flour and stir until smooth.

4. Mix in the cheeses, onions, and peppers. Pour the mixture into the prepared pan.

5. Bake 30 to 40 minutes, or until a knife inserted into the center comes out clean.

6. Remove the pan from heat and cool for 10 minutes. Using a sharp knife, cut into 2-inch (5-cm) squares. Serve warm.

Great Balls O' Ham

Yield: 20 appetizers

These can be made using ground beef, turkey, chicken, lamb, or pork, but the ham provides a nice texture and color that makes it my favorite ingredient for these snacks.

1½ pounds (681 g) cooked ham, ground
2 large eggs
1 cup (236 mL) fresh breadcrumbs
2 tablespoons (30 mL) minced green onions, green and white parts
1 tablespoon (15 mL) minced fresh parsley
1 teaspoon (5 mL) prepared mustard
½ teaspoon (2.5 mL) granulated garlic
½ teaspoon (2.5 mL) seasoned salt
½ teaspoon (2.5 mL) freshly ground black pepper
1 (10-ounce [280-g]) jar apricot jam
½ cup (118 mL) barbecue sauce of your choice
½ teaspoon (2.5 mL) ground cumin

1. Make sure the grill is clean and generously sprayed with nonstick grilling spray. Preheat the barbecue to medium high (350°F [180°C] to 400°F [200°C]).

2. In a large bowl, combine the ham, eggs, breadcrumbs, green onions, parsley, mustard, garlic, salt, and pepper, stirring until well combined.

3. With your hands, roll the meat into 1½- to 2-inch (3.5- to 5-cm) balls. Put the finished balls on a plate as you work.

4. Carefully place the meatballs on your grill and cook them for 15 to 20 minutes, rolling them around to cook on all sides. When they are finished, remove them from grill and set them aside. Keep the grill flame medium high.

5. While the meat is cooking, in a medium saucepan, combine the jam and barbecue sauce. Stir well, add the cumin, and stir again. Cook until the sauce bubbles and remove the pan from the heat. Add the meatballs and return the pan to the burner or grill. Cook for an additional 5 minutes, or until sauce is bubbling.

6. Serve in a casserole or chafing dish, or serve individual portions of 3 to 4 meatballs per person.

Bleu Bayou Cheesecake

Yield: 12–14 appetizers

This recipe also works as a side dish to a grilled steak dinner. As a side dish, it serves 4 or 5.

½ cup (118 mL) packed blue cheese
4 tablespoons (60 mL) butter, softened
½ cup (118 mL) cream cheese
6 large eggs, beaten
5 tablespoons (75 mL) sour cream
2 tablespoons (30 mL) finely minced chives
1 tablespoon (15 mL) granulated sugar
½ teaspoon (2.5 mL) ground white pepper
¼ teaspoon (1.25 mL) seasoned salt

1. Preheat the barbecue to medium high (350°F [180°C] to 400°F [200°C]).

2. Butter or spray with nonstick spray a 9 × 13-inch (22.5 × 32.5-cm) baking dish.

3. In a large bowl with an electric mixer or in a food processor, cream the blue cheese with the butter, mixing until very smooth. Add the cream cheese and blend thoroughly.

4. Add the eggs one at a time, mixing until smooth after each addition. Add the sour cream, chives, sugar, pepper, and salt, and blend until smooth.

5. Pour the cheesecake batter into the prepared dish and place this dish in larger pan. Fill the larger pan with enough hot water to come 1½ to 2 inches (3.5 to 5 cm) up the sides of the cheesecake pan.

6. Place the cheesecake in the barbecue and bake in the water bath for 30 to 35 minutes, until the mixture is firm and pulls away from the sides of dish. A knife inserted into the center of the cake should come out clean.

7. Remove the dish and cool the cheesecake to room temperature. Cut it into squares to serve as an appetizer. You can serve it as individual squares on small plates or as a spread with crackers.

Pesto and Steak Toasts
Yield: 8–16 appetizers

These appetizers are super on a cold fall day while watching a football game with friends. Serve them with a cold adult beverage for a festive indoor tailgate party.

Pesto Sauce

1 cup (236 mL) fresh basil leaves
½ cup (118 mL) grated Parmesan cheese
¼ cup (59 mL) pine nuts
2 cloves garlic, peeled
Salt, to taste
Freshly ground black pepper, to taste
½ cup (118 mL) olive oil

Toasts

2 tablespoons (30 mL) minced garlic, divided
1 teaspoon (5 mL) red pepper flakes
½ teaspoon (2.5 mL) freshly ground black pepper
4 (¼-inch [0.5-cm] thick) beef steaks, trimmed of most of the fat
¼ cup (59 mL) butter, very soft
1 tablespoon (15 mL) finely minced fresh cilantro or parsley
1 (1-pound, 454-g) loaf French bread (or sourdough)

1. Place all of the pesto ingredients except the olive oil in a food processor and process briefly. With the processor running, slowly drizzle in the olive oil and continue to process until fully incorporated. Cover and set aside.

2. Make sure the grill is clean and generously sprayed with nonstick grilling spray. Preheat the barbecue to medium high (350°F [180°C] to 400°F [200°C]).

3. Mix 1 tablespoon (15 mL) of the garlic with the red pepper flakes and black pepper to make a loose paste.

4. Rub this paste on both sides of the steaks. Grill the steaks until they are done to your taste. (We prefer medium-rare, 3 to 4 minutes per side.)

5. In a small bowl, combine the soft butter, ¼ cup (118 mL) of the pesto, the cilantro, and the remaining garlic and mix together.

6. Cut 4 (1-inch [2.5-cm] thick) slices of bread on a sharp diagonal. Grill the bread alongside the steaks just long enough to toast both sides.

7. Remove the steaks and bread from the grill. Spread the pesto–butter mixture over the toasted bread and top with the steaks. Cut each steak and toast into halves or quarters for appetizer-size treats.

Grilled Porky Dates
Yield: 4–6 servings

If you want to make these even better, add a small cooked shrimp to each date before adding the bacon and cook for the same length of time.

12 large pitted dates
12 slices uncooked bacon

1. Make sure the grill is clean and generously sprayed with nonstick grilling spray. Preheat the barbecue to medium high (350°F [180°C] to 400°F [200°C]).

2. Roll each date in a strip of uncooked bacon and fasten with a toothpick.

3. Broil on one side until the bacon is brown and crispy, and then turn over and broil the other side. Let the bacon-wrapped dates rest for 2 to 3 minutes on paper towels.

4. Serve as is or on crackers.

Muffin Tin Burger Biscuits
Yield: 10 appetizers

1 pound (454 g) ground beef
½ cup (118 mL) barbecue sauce of your choice
¼ cup (59 mL) minced onion
2 tablespoons (30 mL) brown sugar
1 teaspoon (5 mL) ground oregano
1 (10-ounce [280-g]) can refrigerated biscuit dough
¼ cup (59 mL) shredded cheddar or American cheese

1. Preheat the barbecue to medium high (475°F [250°C] to 525°F [275°C]).

2. Grease or spray with nonstick spray 10 of the cups in a muffin pan. Set aside.

3. Brown the ground beef in a cast-iron or nonstick skillet. Drain the pan and then add the barbecue sauce, onion, brown sugar, and oregano and cook, stirring often, for 2 to 3 minutes to blend the flavors.

4. Separate the dough into 10 biscuits. Place 1 biscuit in each greased muffin cup; firmly press the dough into the bottom of the cup and up all sides, forming a ¼-inch (0.5-cm) rim. Spoon about ¼ cup (59 mL) of the meat mixture into each biscuit-lined cup and sprinkle with the cheese.

5. Bake in the grill for 10 to 12 minutes or until the edges of the biscuits are golden brown. Let the biscuits cool in the pan for 1 minute, and then remove them from the pan and serve.

Corned Wiener Dogs

Yield: 36 appetizers

You can use Vienna sausage in this recipe instead, but you'll probably need to reduce the cooking times by half.

1 pound (454 g) wieners
½ (12-ounce [336-g]) package corn muffin mix
½ cup (118 mL) whole or skim milk
½ teaspoon garlic powder
1 small egg, beaten
Fat, for deep frying
Ketchup and mustard, for serving

1. With a sharp knife, cut each wiener into four pieces and set the pieces aside.

2. In a medium bowl, mix together the corn muffin mix, milk, garlic powder, and egg to form a thick batter.

3. Drop the wiener pieces into the batter and stir to coat well.

4. On a barbecue side burner or stovetop burner, heat the fat in a deep pan to 375°F (190°C).

5. Drop the battered dogs one at a time into the hot fat and cook until the batter is browned, about 1 minute, turning with a fork or spoon while cooking.

6. Transfer the wieners to paper towels to drain and then serve with ketchup, mustard, or any other dipping sauce you like.

Nacho Hardest Appetizer

Yield: 8–10 servings

If you wish you can use refried black beans instead of the pinto beans and replace the olives with a couple of minced jalapeño or green peppers.

1½ pounds (681 g) ground beef
1 large yellow or Spanish onion, peeled and diced
1 (20.5-ounce [574-g]) can refried pinto beans
1 (7-ounce [196-g]) can diced green chilies
1½ cups (354 mL) shredded Jack cheese
1½ cups (354 mL) shredded cheddar cheese
1 cup (236 mL) taco sauce
1 container guacamole
½ cup (118 mL) sour cream
½ cup (118 mL) minced onions, for sprinkling
1 cup (236 mL) sliced or chopped pitted olives, for sprinkling (optional)
6–8 cups tortilla chips

1. Preheat the barbecue to medium high (350°F [180°C] to 400°F [200°C]).

2. In a large cast-iron or nonstick skillet, fry the ground beef and onions until the meat has turned light brown.

3. Spread the refried beans in a 9 × 13-inch (22.5 × 32.5-cm) pan. Cover the beans evenly with the ground beef mixture, chilies, and shredded cheeses. Drizzle taco sauce over the top and bake uncovered for 25 minutes.

4. Remove the pan from the barbecue and let it cool for no more than 4 to 5 minutes.

5. Dollop guacamole and sour cream on top and sprinkle with the minced onions and olives, if using. Serve with the tortilla chips.

Orange and Lemon MiniRibs

Yield: 16 appetizers

4 pounds (1.8 kg) pork spareribs (cut the rack of ribs in half horizontally)
1 (6-ounce [168-g]) can frozen orange juice concentrate, thawed
2 tablespoons (30 mL) fresh lemon juice
1½ teaspoons (7.5 mL) Worcestershire sauce
½ teaspoon (2.5 mL) garlic salt
¼ teaspoon (1.25 mL) freshly ground black pepper
1 generous pinch ground cinnamon
1 generous pinch ground nutmeg

1. Preheat the barbecue to medium high (350°F [180°C] to 400°F [200°C]).

2. Cut the rack of ribs into individual ribs and place them in a large Dutch oven or roasting pan with enough water to cover them completely. Bring to a boil on a grill side burner, cover, reduce the heat, and simmer for 1 hour. Drain the ribs, return them to the pan, and set it aside.

3. Combine the juices, Worcestershire sauce, garlic salt, pepper, cinnamon, and nutmeg and stir to mix well. Brush the ribs generously with the sauce and bake, uncovered, for 30 to 40 minutes, basting and turning occasionally.

Corn Cheddar Biscuits

Yield: 6 appetizers

You can add finely chopped shrimp, crab meat, or chicken to the batter if you wish. Double the recipe for more appetizer fritters or to use them as a main course for a luncheon.

⅔ cup (158 mL) yellow cornmeal
½ cup (118 mL) grated cheddar cheese
3 tablespoons (45 mL) all-purpose flour
1 tablespoon (15 mL) fresh minced garlic
¼ teaspoon (0.5 mL) seasoned salt
⅛ teaspoon (0.6 mL) baking soda
½ cup (118 mL) whole milk
1 large egg, beaten
1 tablespoon (15 mL) pure maple syrup
⅔ cup (158 mL) frozen or (well-drained) canned corn
⅓ cup (79 mL) olive oil

1. In a large bowl, whisk together the cornmeal, cheese, flour, garlic, salt, and baking soda.

2. In a small bowl, whisk together the milk, egg, and maple syrup. Pour this mixture into the cornmeal mixture and stir just until moistened (do not over mix). Gently incorporate the corn into the batter.

3. Heat the olive oil in a large nonstick or well-sprayed skillet over medium-low heat on a side burner or stovetop.

4. Spoon 1 heaping tablespoon (22.5 mL) batter per fritter into the skillet. Cook 4 or 5 fritters at a time until they are lightly browned on the bottom, about 2 minutes.

5. With a spatula, turn the fritters over and cook until lightly browned on the second side, approximately another 2 minutes.

6. Transfer the fritters to paper towels to drain, and serve warm.

Popeye Loaf

Yield: 16 appetizers

Do not use frozen spinach in this recipe. It will not produce good results, as it's too watery and lacks the character of fresh spinach.

3 cups (708 mL) fresh spinach, chopped
4 large eggs, beaten
1 cup (236 mL) Bisquick baking mix
½ cup (118 mL) finely chopped yellow or Spanish onion
½ cup (118 mL) grated Parmesan cheese
2 tablespoons (30 mL) minced fresh parsley
½ teaspoon (2.5 mL) kosher salt
½ teaspoon (2.5 mL) dried oregano
½ teaspoon (2.5 mL) paprika
½ teaspoon (2.5 mL) dried thyme
¼ teaspoon (1.25 m) garlic powder
1 dash cayenne pepper
½ cup (118 mL) olive or vegetable oil

1. Make sure the grill is clean and generously sprayed with nonstick grilling spray. Preheat the barbecue to medium high (350°F [180°C] to 400°F [200°C]) for indirect heating, putting a water pan under the unheated side of the grill.

2. Grease an 8-inch (20-cm) square glass dish or spray it with nonstick spray.

3. In a large bowl, mix together the spinach, eggs, Bisquick, onion, cheese, parsley, salt, oregano, paprika, thyme, garlic powder, and cayenne pepper. Add the oil and stir well.

4. Pour the mixture into the prepared dish and place it in the barbecue. Cook for 25 to 30 minutes, or until the top of the loaf is golden brown.

5. Remove the dish from the grill and let cool slightly. Cut the loaf into 2-inch (5-cm) squares for serving as appetizers.

Three Cheese Pepperoni Biscuits
Yield: 20 appetizers

Please use Parmigiano-Reggiano cheese for this dish. It's a bit pricier than other varieties, but the flavor, consistency, and texture make it the king of Parmesan cheeses, and certainly your guests are worth it!

1 cup (236 mL) ricotta cheese
½ cup (118 mL) shredded mozzarella cheese
¼ cup (59 mL) freshly grated Parmigiano-Reggiano cheese
1 (10-ounce [280-g]) package refrigerated flaky biscuits
20 thin slices pepperoni
1 (24-ounce) jar marinara sauce of your choice, at room temperature, for dipping (optional)

1. Preheat the barbecue to medium high (350°F [180°C] to 400°F [200°C]).

2. Lightly grease a baking sheet or coat it with nonstick spray.

3. In a medium bowl, combine the cheeses and stir to mix well. Set aside.

4. Separate each biscuit into 2 layers. Roll or shape each half into 2 × 4-inch (5 × 10-cm) ovals and set aside.

5. Place 1 slice of pepperoni and 1 tablespoon (15 mL) of the cheese mixture on each oval. Moisten the edges with water, and fold the dough ovals in half (making a crescent-moon shape). Press the edges firmly together and use a fork to seal.

6. Transfer the biscuits to the prepared baking sheet and bake them in the barbecue for 18 to 20 minutes or until the tops of the biscuits are golden brown.

7. Serve the biscuits warm, either as they are or with small bowls of warm marinara sauce for dipping.

Edible Firecrackers
Yield: 25 appetizers

These yummy treats can be refrigerated for two weeks, or frozen for as long as six months, as long as they are tightly sealed in plastic wrap. Thaw them to room temperature before cooking.

2½ cups (591 mL) all-purpose flour
1 teaspoon (5 mL) garlic salt
1 teaspoon (5 mL) cayenne pepper
1 teaspoon (5 mL) hot paprika
1 cup (236 mL) grated cheddar cheese
½ pound (227 g) unsalted butter, at room temperature
1 cup (236 mL) finely chopped pecans or walnuts

1. In a medium bowl, sift together the flour, garlic salt, cayenne pepper, and paprika.

2. In a separate bowl, cream together the cheese and butter. Gradually add the flour mixture, stirring to mix thoroughly. Stir in the nuts. Divide the dough in half and roll each half into a log 1½ inches (3.5 cm) wide and 8 inches (20 cm) long.

3. Wrap each log in plastic wrap and refrigerate for at least one day before baking.

4. Preheat the barbecue to medium high (350°F [180°C] to 400°F [200°C]).

5. Grease a large baking sheet or coat it with nonstick spray.

6. With a sharp knife, cut the logs into ¼-inch (0.5-cm) thick slices. Arrange the slices about ½ inch (1 cm) apart on the prepared baking sheet.

7. Bake for 15 to 20 minutes, or until the slices are a light golden brown.

8. Remove them from the cookie sheet and cool completely. You can serve them right away, or store them for several days in airtight containers.

Blue Cheese and Chicken Turnovers
Yield: 8 appetizers

If you're not a blue cheese fan, you can use Swiss, cheddar, Monterey Jack, or just about any other variety you like. This is a great recipe to use up that barbecued chicken you have in the refrigerator.

2 tablespoons (30 mL) butter
1 cup (236 mL) chopped onion
1½ cups fresh crimini mushrooms (or another mushroom of your choice)
½ cup (118 mL) chicken broth
1 teaspoon (5 mL) dried rosemary, crushed
½ teaspoon (2.5 mL) dried thyme
½ teaspoon ground cumin
2¼ cups (531 mL) diced smoked chicken
½ cup (118 mL) crumbled blue cheese
2 (8-ounce [227-g]) cans refrigerated crescent dinner roll dough

1. Preheat the barbecue to medium high (350°F [180°C] to 400°F [200°C]).

2. In a 10-inch (25-cm) nonstick skillet, melt the butter over medium heat on the grill or side burner. Add the onion and cook for 5 minutes, stirring occasionally. Add the mushrooms and cook, stirring occasionally, until both the onions and mushrooms are tender.

3. Reduce the heat to medium low. Add the broth, rosemary, thyme, and cumin and cook 4 to 5 minutes, stirring occasionally, until the liquid has evaporated. Remove the pan from the heat; stir in the chicken and blue cheese.

4. Separate the dough into 8 rectangles and press or roll each into a 5-inch (12.5-cm) square, firmly pressing down the perforations to seal the pastry. Spoon about ½ cup (118 mL) of the chicken mixture onto center of each dough square, and then bring all 4 corners of the square up over the filling, pinching the seams to seal.

5. Place the turnovers on an ungreased baking sheet and bake in the barbecue for 11 to 14 minutes, until the crust turns golden brown.

Sausage and Corn Fritters

Yield: 24 appetizers

If you use fresh corn, cutting it off the cob as suggested here, run the back of the knife along the cob after you've cut off the kernels, pressing into the cob as you drag the knife from top to bottom all the way around the cob. This will draw out the corn "milk" that is in the cob, a sweet, flavorful liquid that will help the flavor of this dish.

1 cup (236 mL) all-purpose flour
1 tablespoon (15 mL) baking powder
1 tablespoon (15 mL) garlic salt
1 teaspoon (5 mL) dried rosemary
¼ teaspoon (0.5 mL) paprika
⅛ teaspoon (0.6 mL) freshly ground black pepper
1 cup (236 mL) cooked and crumbled pork sausage
1 cup (236 mL) fresh corn kernels
2 egg yolks, beaten
2 tablespoons (30 mL) milk or heavy cream
Oil, for frying
2 egg whites, beaten until stiff

1. In a medium bowl, sift together the flour, baking powder, garlic salt, rosemary, paprika, and pepper. Add the sausage, corn, egg yolks, and milk and mix until blended.

2. Add the oil to a skillet. On a barbecue side burner or a stovetop burner, heat the oil until a deep-frying thermometer reads 350°F (180°C).

3. Fold the stiffly beaten egg whites into the batter. Slide heaping table-spoons of the batter into the oil and cook for 3 to 5 minutes, or until the fritters turn brown, turning once.

4. Drain the fritters on paper towels and serve warm.

Shrimp Biscuits

Yield: 3–4 dozen appetizers

Scallops, crab, or flaked salmon, trout, or swordfish can be substituted for the shrimp in these appetizers.

⅔ cup (158 mL) Bisquick baking mix
2 tablespoons (30 mL) water
1 teaspoon (5 mL) chopped fresh dill, divided
4 ounces (112 g) chopped cooked shrimp, rinsed and dried
2 tablespoons (30 mL) cream cheese, softened
1 tablespoon (15 mL) mayonnaise
1 tablespoon (15 mL) finely minced red bell pepper
1 teaspoon (5 mL) Dijon mustard
1 teaspoon (5 mL) fresh lemon juice
¼ teaspoon onion powder
⅛ teaspoon (0.6 mL) freshly ground black pepper

1. Preheat the barbecue to medium high (350°F [180°C] to 400°F [200°C]).

2. In a medium bowl, mix together the Bisquick, water, and half of the dill until a dough forms. Turn the dough onto a floured cloth and knead until smooth, 12 to 15 times.

3. Roll out the dough ⅛-inch (0.25-cm) thick. Cut out rounds with a 1-inch (2.5-cm) biscuit cutter or a shot glass dipped in dry baking mix. Place the rounds about 1 inch (2.5 cm) apart on an ungreased baking sheet.

4. Bake the biscuits until they are lightly brown, 6 to 8 minutes. Remove the baking sheet from the barbecue and set aside.

5. In a clean medium bowl, mix together the remaining dill, shrimp, cream cheese, mayonnaise, red pepper, mustard, lemon juice, onion powder, and pepper until thoroughly incorporated. Spoon 1 teaspoon (5 mL) of this mixture onto each baked biscuit.

6. Return the baking sheet to the barbecue and bake 4 minutes longer.

7. Remove the baking sheet from the heat. Transfer the biscuits to a plate or platter and serve immediately.

Smoked Sausage and Mushrooms

Yield: 12 appetizers

The Beaumont Inn in Harrodsburg is Kentucky's oldest B&B, welcoming guests since it opened in 1919. Meals are served in the luxurious main dining room, where you can order this dish, and in the adjoining and very atmospheric Old Owl Tavern. This recipe comes from the Beaumont Inn.

24 large button mushrooms, cleaned, stems removed
½ pound (226 g) ground smoked sausage, cooked and drained
8 ounces (226 g) cream cheese
1 ounce (28 g) freshly grated Parmesan cheese

1. Make sure the grill is clean and generously sprayed with nonstick grilling spray. Preheat the barbecue to medium high (350°F [180°C] to 400°F [200°C]).

2. Cook the mushrooms on the grill for 7 to 9 minutes. Remove from the grill and and allow them to cool.

3. In a small bowl, mix together the cooked sausage, cream cheese, and Parmesan cheese. Fill each mushroom cap with 1 teaspoon (5 mL) of the filling. Bake for another 7 to 9 minutes.

4. Remove the stuffed mushrooms from the heat and let cool for 2 to 3 minutes. Serve.

Marinated Lamb Kebabs

Yield: 12–15 servings

Lamb is gaining fans in America as young chefs learn how to cook it properly and also because an influx of Middle Eastern immigrants, who have always enjoyed great lamb dishes, are increasing U.S. availability.

Marinade

⅓ cup (79 mL) cider vinegar
¼ cup (59 mL) balsamic vinegar
1 tablespoon (15 mL) fresh thyme
1 tablespoon (15 mL) fresh rosemary
1 tablespoon (15 mL) dried oregano
2 bay leaves
1 teaspoon (5 mL) freshly ground black pepper
3 tablespoons (45 mL) minced garlic
1 tablespoon (15 mL) Dijon mustard
¼ cup (59 mL) minced fresh parsley
3 tablespoons (45 mL) minced green onions, green and white parts
1½ cups (354 mL) olive oil

Lamb

8 pounds (3.6 kg) boneless leg of lamb or lamb shoulder
3 bell peppers, cut into 2-inch (5-cm) squares
3 large onions, cut into 2-inch (5-cm) squares
Salt, to taste
Freshly ground black pepper, to taste

1. To make the marinade, in a food processor, combine the vinegars, thyme, rosemary, oregano, bay leaf, pepper, garlic, and mustard; process until blended.

2. Add the parsley and green onions and pulse until mixed in. Continue running the food processor and add the oil in a thin and steady stream. Process until the mixture has thickened. Cover and set aside.

3. Cut the lamb into 1-inch (2.5-cm) squares.

4. Place the meat, bell peppers, and onions in a large container or plastic garbage bag and pour in the marinade. Refrigerate for 8 to 24 hours—the longer, the better.

5. Make sure the grill is clean and generously sprayed with nonstick grilling spray. Preheat the barbecue to high (400°F [200°C] to 450°F [240°C]).

6. Remove the meat and vegetables from the marinade and alternately thread the lamb, peppers, and onions onto 4-inch [10 cm] bamboo skewers. Transfer the remaining marinade to a saucepan and bring it to a boil. (After boiling the marinade for 12 minutes, you can use it to baste the kebabs.) Season the kebabs with salt and additional black pepper.

7. Grill the kebabs over high heat about 20 minutes, turning often and basting with the marinade.

8. Remove the meat and vegetables from the skewers and serve.

Mini Calzones

Yield: 8 to 10 servings

Serve these pastries with a bowl of marinara sauce—either your own or a commercial product—for dipping.

2 (8-ounce [227-g]) cans Pillsbury Pizza Crust Dough
8 ounces (227 g) ricotta cheese
¾ cup (177 mL) grated mozzarella cheese
½ cup (118 mL) grated Parmesan cheese
1 large bunch fresh spinach, stems removed, cleaned, and roughly chopped
¾ cup (177 mL) chopped onion
¾ cup (177 mL) chopped red and green bell peppers
2 tablespoons (30 mL) dried oregano
10–12 slices pepperoni
1 cup (236 mL) melted butter
1 tablespoon (15 mL) garlic granules

1. Make sure the grill is clean and generously sprayed with nonstick grilling spray. Preheat the barbecue to medium high (350°F [180°C] to 400°F [200°C]). If you have a pizza stone, place it on the grill to heat.

2. Fold out the pizza dough and use a cookie cutter to cut it into 3-inch (7.5-cm) circles.

3. In a large bowl, mix together the ricotta, mozzarella, and Parmesan cheeses, spinach, onion, bell peppers, and oregano.

4. Place 1 tablespoon (15 mL) of the mixture on one half of each dough round, add 2 slices of pepperoni, and then fold the dough over the filling, forming a half moon. Moisten the edges with a brush dipped in water and press the edges together. Press with a fork to seal.

5. Combine the melted butter and the garlic granules. Place the calzones on a baking sheet and brush them with the butter mixture. Bake in the barbecue for about 30 minutes, until the pastry is golden on top. Remove and let cool slightly, and then serve.

Parmesan–Caraway–Poppy Seed Appetizers

Yield: 6 dozen appetizers

Warning: Folks who wear dentures should pass on these tasty treats, because a caraway seed under the dentures can be very painful to the wearer.

2 cups (473 mL) Bisquick baking mix
1 cup (236 mL) freshly grated Parmesan cheese
⅓ cup (79 mL) heavy cream
1 tablespoon (15 mL) caraway seeds
1 tablespoon (15 mL) poppy seeds
1 tablespoon (15 mL) parsley flakes
2 tablespoons (30 mL) vegetable oil
½ teaspoon (2.5 mL) garlic powder
½ teaspoon (2.5 mL) salt
1 large egg, beaten

1. Preheat the barbecue to medium high (350°F [180°C] to 400°F [200°C]).

2. In a medium bowl, mix together all the ingredients to form a stiff dough.

3. Drop generous tablespoonfuls about 1 inch (2.5 cm) apart onto an ungreased baking sheet.

4. Place the baking sheet in the barbecue and bake, turning once, until they begin to lightly brown, about 8 minutes.

5. Remove the baking sheet from the grill, cool slightly, and serve.

Yakitori (Grilled Chicken and Chicken Livers)
Yield: 6 to 8 servings

For those not offal-y inclined, you can replace the chicken livers with pieces of bamboo shoot, but the dish won't be the same. Yaki *means grilled, and* tori *means bird or fowl.*

2 tablespoons (30 mL) dry sherry
2 tablespoons (30 mL) chicken broth
2 tablespoons (30 mL) teriyaki sauce
1 small clove garlic, peeled and very thinly sliced
1 (1½-inch [3.5-cm]) piece fresh ginger root, peeled and very thinly sliced
1 whole chicken breast, skinned and boned, cut into 1-inch pieces
8 ounces (227 g) fresh chicken livers, washed and trimmed
8 small button or crimini mushrooms, cleaned, stems removed
4 green onions, green and white parts, cut into 1-inch (2.5-cm) pieces

1. In a small glass mixing bowl, combine the sherry, chicken broth, teriyaki sauce, garlic, and ginger and mix well. Add the chicken breast and livers and toss to coat them with the marinade. Cover with plastic wrap and refrigerate for at least 2 or 3 hours.

2. Preheat the barbecue to medium high (350°F [180°C] to 400°F [200°C]), covering the grill with a sheet of heavy-duty aluminum foil that you've sprayed generously with nonstick grilling spray.

3. Thread the yakitori onto soaked bamboo or metal skewers, starting with a mushroom cap; add a piece chicken, a piece of green onion, and a chicken liver, and end with another mushroom cap.

4. Pour the remaining marinade into a saucepan and boil for 12 minutes. Use a spoon to scoop out and discard the garlic and ginger slices.

5. Grill the skewers on the aluminum foil, turning once and brushing frequently with the boiled marinade, until the livers are browned and firm and the chicken is tender and the edges are browned, 2 to 3 minutes on each side.

6. Arrange the skewers on a serving plate and brush the remaining marinade or drippings from the foil sheet over them.

Ham 'N' Cheese Tartlets

Yield: 24 appetizers

For variety, you can also make these tartlets with diced roast beef and Cheddar cheese.

½ cup (118 mL) butter, softened
1 (3-ounce [84-g]) package cream cheese, softened
1 cup (236 mL) all-purpose flour
½ cup (118 mL) diced smoked ham
⅓ cup (79 mL) shredded Swiss cheese
¼ cup (59 mL) crumbled, crisp-cooked bacon (about 4 slices)
2 tablespoons (30 mL) finely minced green onion, green and white parts
2 large eggs, beaten
½ cup (118 mL) milk
½ teaspoon (2.5 mL) paprika
½ teaspoon (2.5 mL) salt
Freshly ground black pepper, to taste
1 dash ground nutmeg

1. Preheat the barbecue to medium high (350°F [180°C] to 400°F [200°C]).

2. In a bowl, whip together the softened butter and cream cheese until blended. Add the flour and mix well. Cover the bowl and chill the pastry mixture for at least 1 hour.

3. Cut the dough into 24 equal-sized pieces. With your hands, shape each piece into a small ball. Place each ball into an ungreased mini muffin cup. Press the dough onto the bottom and sides of the cups, so that it lines the entire cup. Cover the muffin pan and chill the dough for 30 minutes.

4. In a medium bowl, mix together the ham, cheese, bacon, and green onion. Divide this mixture equally among the pastry-lined cups.

5. In a separate bowl, combine the eggs, milk, paprika, salt, pepper, and nutmeg, and stir to mix. Place about 2 teaspoons (10 mL) of this mixture into each muffin cup over the ham and cheese mixture.

6. Bake in the barbecue for 18 to 20 minutes, or until muffins are browned on top and the mixture is bubbling.

7. Remove the pan from the barbecue and cool for 5 minutes before removing the pastries. Serve warm or chilled, but freshly warmed from the barbecue is best.

Pesto-Filled Mushrooms

Yield: 24 appetizers

If you want to make pesto the traditional way, use a mortar and pestle to grind everything together. I use a modified method: I grind the garlic the old-fashioned way and then put it into the mortar and pestle of today—a food processor—to finish puréeing the sauce.

3 large cloves garlic, peeled
2 cups (473 mL) fresh basil leaves, chopped
½ cup (118 mL) plus 2 tablespoons (30 mL) grated Parmesan cheese, divided
½ cup (118 mL) pine nuts, minced
¼ cup (59 mL) minced fresh parsley
¼ cup (59 mL) olive oil
Freshly ground black pepper, to taste
24 fresh button, brown, or crimini mushrooms, stems removed, cleaned

1. Make sure the grill is clean and generously sprayed with nonstick grilling spray. Preheat the barbecue to medium high (350°F [180°C] to 400°F [200°C]).

2. Place the garlic in a mortar and grind the cloves to a fine paste. Set aside.

3. To make the pesto, in a food processor, combine the mashed garlic, the basil, ½ cup (118 mL) of the Parmesan cheese, the pine nuts, the parsley, and the oil and process until smooth. Add the pepper to taste.

4. Spoon a rounded teaspoon (7.5 mL) of pesto into each mushroom cap and sprinkle with the remaining Parmesan cheese.

5. Place the mushrooms directly on the grill (or you may wish to line the grill with a sheet of aluminum foil first) and bake about 10 minutes, or until bubbling and browned on top.

6. Remove the mushrooms from the grill with tongs and drain them on a paper towel. Serve warm.

Dungeness Crab Muffins

Yield: 24 appetizers

If you can't find Dungeness crab locally, feel free to use King crab, blue crab, coconut crab, peekytoe crab, rock crab, snow crab, or pretty much any of the other 4,400 varieties of crab available around the world.

1 (12 ounce [354 mL]) jar port wine cheese spread of your choice
½ cup (118 mL) butter, softened
1½ teaspoons (7.5 mL) mayonnaise
1 teaspoon (5 mL) fresh lime juice
½ teaspoon (2.5 mL) garlic salt
½ teaspoon (2.5 mL) seasoned salt
8 ounces (227 g) fresh crabmeat
6 English muffins, split in half
Paprika, to taste (optional)
Minced fresh parsley, to taste (optional)

1. Make sure the grill is clean and generously sprayed with nonstick grilling spray. Preheat the barbecue to medium high (350°F [180°C] to 400°F [200°C]).

2. In a medium bowl, mix together the cheese spread, butter, mayonnaise, lime juice, garlic salt, and seasoned salt; stir in the crabmeat. Spread this mixture on the muffin halves.

3. Place the muffin halves on the grill and cook for 2 to 3 minutes, until the bottoms begin to brown and the topping is bubbling.

4. Remove the muffins from the grill and cool slightly. Cut each muffin into quarters and sprinkle with paprika and/or parsley. Serve hot.

'Shroom Turnovers

Yield: 2–3 dozen appetizers

These may be made ahead and frozen, vacuum-sealed, for up to a month. Merely bring them to room temperature and proceed from Step 5 when you are ready to cook and serve them.

Dough

1 (8-ounce [227-g]) package cream cheese, softened
½ cup (118 mL) butter, softened
1½ cups (354 mL) all-purpose flour

Filling

3 tablespoons (45 mL) butter
1 large onion, finely minced
8 ounces (227 g) mushrooms, finely minced
2 tablespoons (30 mL) all-purpose flour
1 tablespoon (15 mL) seasoned salt
½ teaspoon (2.5 mL) dried thyme
½ teaspoon (2.5 mL) dried oregano
½ teaspoon (2.5 mL) dried mint
⅓ cup (79 mL) sour cream

Egg Wash

1 egg yolk, beaten
1 teaspoon (5 mL) water

1. To make the dough, in a medium bowl, whip the dough ingredients together thoroughly. Refrigerate while you prepare the filling.

2. Make sure the grill is clean and generously sprayed with nonstick grilling spray. Preheat the barbecue to medium high (400°F [200°C] to 450°F [240°C]).

3. For the filling, in a cast-iron or nonstick skillet on the grill or a side burner, melt the butter over medium heat. Add the onion and mushrooms and sauté until the onions are translucent, about 4 minutes. Add the flour, seasoned salt, thyme, oregano, and mint and cook until thickened. Stir in the sour cream. Cover and set aside to cool.

4. Divide the dough in half and roll out each half to ⅛ inch (0.25 cm) thickness. Using a 3- or 4-inch (7.5- or 10-cm) round cookie cutter, cut the dough into circles. Place 1 to 2 teaspoons (5 to 10 mL) of filling on each pastry. Brush the edges with cold water and then fold the rounds over to make half-moons. Seal with your fingers or a fork.

5. Mix together the egg yolk and the water. Using a sharp knife, cut three small slits in the top of each pastry. Brush each with the egg wash and arrange them on an ungreased baking sheet. Bake in the barbecue for 12 to 15 minutes, or until the pastries are golden.

My HoneYaki Wings
Yield: 24 appetizers

This recipe hails from north of the border—it's from Grant Browne of Kimberley, British Columbia.

Wings
24 chicken wings (4 pounds [1.8 kg] total)
2 tablespoons (30 mL) garlic powder
1 tablespoon (15 mL) kosher salt
1 teaspoon (5 mL) freshly ground black pepper
¼ cup (59 mL) teriyaki sauce

Honey Glaze
1 cup (236 mL) bottled chili sauce
½ cup (118 mL) butter
½ cup (118 mL) honey
6 tablespoons (90 mL) lemon juice
¼ cup (59 mL) minced chives or green onions
3 tablespoons (45 mL) lime juice
1 tablespoon (15 mL) Dijon mustard
Several generous grinds black pepper

1. Make sure the grill is clean and generously sprayed with nonstick spray. Preheat the barbecue to medium high (350°F [180°C] to 400°F [200°C]).

2. With a sharp knife, cut each chicken wing into three sections, discarding the tips (or saving them for stock). Place the remaining sections in a large plastic bag and sprinkle in the garlic powder, salt, and pepper. Shake the bag to coat all the wings and then pour the wings onto a baking sheet. Drizzle the teriyaki sauce over the wings.

3. Place the wings in the barbecue and bake for 20 minutes.

4. While the wings are cooking, combine the Honey Glaze ingredients in a small saucepan. Heat the glaze over medium-high heat until it bubbles, stirring occasionally to mix well.

5. After the wings have cooked for 20 minutes, brush each section with glaze. Bake an additional 20 minutes, basting two or three times, and then remove wings from the barbecue and serve.

BBQ Yogurt Wings
Yield: 36 appetizers

I like to use lime yogurt for this recipe, but some find flavored yogurts too sweet. You can substitute any flavor you wish, or just use plain yogurt instead. Alternatively, you can substitute sour cream.

18 chicken wings (3 pounds [1.4 kg] total)
1½ cups (354 mL) Italian seasoned breadcrumbs
2 teaspoons (10 mL) finely chopped chives
1¼ teaspoon (6.25 mL) salt
¾ teaspoon (3.75 mL) ground ginger
¾ teaspoon (3.75 mL) paprika
¼ teaspoon (1.25 mL) sesame seeds
⅛ teaspoon (0.6 mL) cayenne pepper
1 cup (236 mL) lime yogurt
1 stick butter, melted
3 tablespoons (45 mL) pure maple syrup

1. Make sure the grill is clean and generously sprayed with nonstick grilling spray. Preheat the barbecue to medium high (350°F [180°C] to 400°F [200°C]).

2. With a sharp knife, cut each chicken wing at the joint into three sections, discarding the wing tips (or reserve them for stock). Set aside.

3. In a wide, flat dish, mix together the breadcrumbs, chives, salt, ginger, paprika, sesame seeds, and cayenne pepper.

4. In a deeper wide dish, mix together the yogurt, butter, and maple syrup.

5. Place the two dishes side by side. Dip each wing section into the sweetened yogurt, then into the crumbs, making sure the wings are well coated.

6. Place the chicken wings on a broiler rack in a large roasting pan.

7. Bake in the barbecue for 15 minutes, then turn the wings and bake for 10 to 15 minutes longer, or until they are browned and tender.

Grilled Chicken Enchiladas
Yield: 6 appetizers

Did you know there are over 500 varieties of avocado? The most popular are the Hass, Bacon, and Fuerte varieties. Each has its own unique flavor characteristic: Hass has a rich taste, Bacon has a lighter taste, and Fuerte has a very creamy flavor.

Chicken

1 cup (236 mL) dark beer
2 tablespoons (30 mL) olive oil
1 tablespoon (15 mL) finely chopped garlic
1 teaspoon (5 mL) dried oregano
1 teaspoon (5 mL) ground cumin
1 teaspoon (5 mL) seasoned salt
½ teaspoon (2.5 mL) freshly ground black pepper
¼ teaspoon (1.25 mL) cayenne pepper
6 boneless chicken breasts

Guacamole

2 ripe avocados, pits removed, peeled
1 tablespoon (15 mL) finely minced onion
1 tablespoon (15 mL) lime juice
¼ teaspoon (1.25 mL) salt

To Finish

6 (8-inch) flour tortillas, wrapped in foil
¼ cup (59 mL) sour cream
Paprika, for garnish

1. In a small bowl, mix together the beer, oil, garlic, oregano, cumin, salt, pepper, and cayenne pepper. Place the chicken breasts in a 1-gallon (3.8 L) resealable plastic bag and pour the marinade over the chicken. Seal the bag and turn it over several times to coat all of the breasts. Refrigerate the chicken for 4 to 6 hours, rotating the bag several times to distribute the marinade.

2. Make sure the grill is clean and generously sprayed with nonstick grilling spray. Preheat the barbecue to medium high (350°F [180°C] to 400°F [200°C]).

3. To make the guacamole, in a medium bowl, combine the avocado flesh, minced onions, lime juice, and salt. Mix thoroughly, cover, and refrigerate the guacamole until 20 minutes before serving. Do not make the guacamole more than 1 hour ahead of when you'll use it as it can begin to turn brown if done too far in advance.

4. Remove the chicken from the bag and discard the marinade. Grill the chicken 12 to 14 minutes, or until the skin is browned and crunchy, the meat is firm, and the juices run clear, turning once halfway through the grilling time. Remove the guacamole from the refrigerator and let it warm up.

5. Remove the chicken from the barbecue, throw the foil-wrapped tortillas on the hot grill, and cut the breasts crosswise into thin strips. Remove the tortillas from the barbecue and unwrap the foil. Spread the warm tortillas on a cutting board. Using tongs, place 4 or 5 strips of chicken on each tortilla, top each with a generous tablespoon of the guacamole, and roll them up. Cut each tortilla in half, top with a teaspoon (5 mL) of sour cream and a sprinkle of paprika, and serve on a warmed platter.

Baby Porcupine Balls

Yield: 12–14 appetizers

No, these don't come from baby porcupines! These appetizers also work as a main dish; just double the recipe and serve them with pasta or mashed potatoes and grilled corn or mixed vegetables, pouring the remaining sauce over the meatballs on the plate.

Meatballs

¾ pound (336 g) ground beef
½ pound (227 g). ground pork
½ cup uncooked white rice
1 large egg, beaten
2 tablespoons (30 mL) finely minced green bell pepper
1 tablespoon (15 mL) minced garlic
1 tablespoon (15 mL) minced onion
1 teaspoon (5 mL) celery salt

Sauce

2 cups (473 mL) Bloody Mary mix
2 tablespoons (30 mL) Worcestershire sauce
2 whole cloves garlic, peeled and mashed
½ teaspoon (2.5 mL) dried oregano
½ teaspoon (2.5 mL) ground ginger

1. Preheat the barbecue to medium high (350°F [180°C] to 400°F [200°C]) or turn a side burner to medium.

2. In a large bowl, combine the ground meats, rice, egg, green bell pepper, garlic, onion, and celery salt and mix well.

3. With your hands form the mixture into 1½-inch (3.5-cm) diameter balls (golf-ball size) and place them in a saucepan on the grill or side burner.

4. In a small bowl, stir together the Bloody Mary mix, Worcestershire sauce, garlic, oregano, and ginger. Add the sauce to the meatballs, cover, and simmer for 45 to 50 minutes.

5. Remove from the heat and serve with toothpicks.

Crunchy Sweet Potato Bites

Yield: 3½–4 dozen appetizers

Sweet potatoes are often confused with yams, but yams are large, starchy roots grown in Africa and Asia, while sweet potatoes are Native American plants with a much higher nutritional value.

3 cups (708 mL) cooked and mashed sweet potatoes
⅓ cup (79 mL) packed brown sugar
¼ cup (59 mL) chopped pecans
2 tablespoons (30 mL) all-purpose flour
1 tablespoon (15 mL) butter
1 teaspoon (5 mL) vanilla extract
¼ teaspoon (1.25 mL) ground cinnamon
¼ teaspoon (1.25 mL) ground nutmeg
1 large egg
3 cups (708 mL) crushed Frosted Flakes

1. Preheat the barbecue to medium high (350°F [180°C] to 400°F [200°C]).

2. Spray a baking sheet with nonstick cooking spray.

3. In a large bowl, combine the sweet potatoes, brown sugar, pecans, flour, butter, vanilla, cinnamon, and nutmeg and mix well. Add in the egg and stir to incorporate it into the mix.

4. With your hands, form the mixture into bite-size balls (about 1½ inches [3.5 mL] in diameter) and roll the balls in the crushed Frosted Flakes.

5. Place the sweet potato balls on the prepared baking sheet and bake them in the barbecue for about 20 minutes, until the crust is barley charred, turning once or twice with tongs or a long spoon.

6. Remove the balls from the barbecue and serve with toothpicks.

Escargots on Mushroom Caps

Yield: 18 appetizers

Two popular brands of canned snails to look for: Escal French Burgundy Escargots (18 per can) or Helix Snails Escargots (24 per can). I've used both with great success, and both can be ordered online if your local grocery store can't provide them.

1 (18–24 count) can escargots (snails)
1 cup (236 mL) dry white wine
2 tablespoons (30 mL) finely minced onion
4 whole cloves garlic, peeled and crushed
1 teaspoon (5 mL) dark soy sauce
1 bay leaf
2–3 grinds sea salt
1 dash allspice
½ cup (118 mL) butter
2 tablespoons (30 mL) finely minced fresh parsley
2 tablespoons (30 mL) finely minced green onions
⅛ teaspoon freshly ground nutmeg
18–24 mushroom caps (the same quantity as the escargots)

1. Open the can of snails and rinse them in cold water. Drain and set aside.

2. In a saucepan on a barbecue grill or side burner, combine the wine, onion, garlic, soy sauce, bay leaf, salt, and allspice. Stir, then add the snails and cook over low heat 10 minutes.

3. Remove and drain the snails, reserving the liquid. Return the liquid to the saucepan. Add the butter, parsley, and green onions to the pan and cook, stirring, for 2 to 3 minutes. Add the nutmeg and stir once more.

4. Make sure the grill is clean and generously sprayed with nonstick grilling spray. Preheat the barbecue to medium high (350°F [180°C] to 400°F [200°C]).

5. Place the mushroom caps in a baking dish or mini-muffin pan and top each cap with a snail. Pour the butter mixture over the caps and bake in the barbecue for 7 minutes.

6. Serve immediately on small plates with sliced French bread, pouring butter sauce over each serving.

Quick Sausage Nibbles
Yield: 30–40 appetizers

You can combine ¼ cup (118 mL) Dijon mustard with 2 tablespoons (30 mL) honey to make a sweet and tangy second dip for these sausages.

Meatballs

1 pound (454 g) raw pork sausage
2 cups (473 mL) Bisquick baking mix
½ cup (118 mL) grated cheddar (or blue) cheese
1 teaspoon (5 mL) dried oregano
½ teaspoon (2.5 mL) freshly ground black pepper

Dip

¼ cup (59 mL) marmalade
1 tablespoon (15 mL) curry powder

1. Make sure the grill is clean and generously sprayed with nonstick grilling spray. Preheat the barbecue to medium high (350°F [180°C] to 400°F [200°C]).

2. Spray a baking sheet with cooking spray or line the grill with aluminum foil.

3. In a medium bowl, mix together all the meatball ingredients together. With your hands, form the mixture into balls 1½ inches (3.5 cm) in diameter. Place the meatballs on the prepared baking sheet or aluminum foil.

4. Bake in the barbecue for 16 to 20 minutes, turning once, until the balls are browned on top.

5. To make the dip, combine the marmalade and curry powder.

6. Remove the balls from the heat and serve with toothpicks to dip the balls into the curried marmalade.

BBQ Cornflake Chicken Strips
Yield: 6 servings

To crush cornflakes, put them in a resealable plastic bag and roll over them with a rolling pin or wine bottle until they are finely ground. You can also buy prepared cornflake crumbs from the grocery store.

4 cups (0.95 L) crushed plain cornflakes
½ cup (118 mL) all-purpose flour
1 teaspoon (5 mL) seasoned salt
1 teaspoon (5 mL) poultry seasoning
½ teaspoon (2.5 mL) freshly ground black pepper
½ teaspoon (2.5 mL) onion powder
2 large eggs, beaten
2 tablespoons (30 mL) heavy cream
4 boneless, skinless chicken breast halves, cut into thin strips

1. Preheat the barbecue to medium high (350°F [180°C] to 400°F [200°C]).

2. Spray a baking sheet or roasting pan well with nonstick cooking spray.

3. In a medium bowl, combine the cornflakes, flour, salt, poultry seasoning, pepper, and onion powder and stir to mix well.

4. In a wide, flat bowl or pan, whip the eggs and cream together. Dip the chicken strips in the egg mixture, and then roll them in the cornflakes, pressing the meat firmly to coat each strip in crumbs.

5. Place the strips on the prepared baking sheet or roasting pan and place them in the barbecue to bake for 10 minutes. Turn the strips over and cook another 5 minutes, until the crumbs begin to brown.

6. Serve warm on a platter with a bowl of your favorite barbecue sauce for dipping.

Evan's Eggplant
Yield: 12 appetizers

Eggs aren't purple, and neither were the first varieties of eggplant. They looked like long, white eggs. Only later did the purple varieties become popular. Now, the white (egg-colored ones) are as scarce as (sorry for this) hen's teeth.

1 large eggplant
Salt, to taste
1 cup (236 mL) all-purpose flour
5 large eggs, beaten, divided
1 cup (236 mL) seasoned breadcrumbs
Freshly ground black pepper, to taste
¼ cup (59 mL) olive oil
¼ cup (59 mL) freshly grated Parmesan cheese
¼ cup (59 mL) chopped fresh parsley
1 tablespoon (15 mL) chopped fresh basil
10–12 slices Muenster or smoked Gouda cheese
2 cups (473 mL) tomato sauce

1. Make sure the grill is clean and generously sprayed with nonstick grilling spray. Preheat the barbecue to medium high (350°F [180°C] to 400°F [200°C]).

2. Spray a 9 × 13-inch (22.5 × 32.5-cm) baking pan with nonstick cooking spray.

3. Peel and cut the eggplant into ¼-inch (1.25 cm) slices. Place the slices in a colander, salting each layer, and set aside for 1 hour. Quickly rinse the slices and pat dry with paper towels.

4. Put the flour in a shallow bowl, 2 of the eggs in a second shallow bowl, and the breadcrumbs in a third shallow bowl. Dip the dried eggplant slices in the flour, then the eggs, then the breadcrumbs. Sprinkle them lightly with pepper. On a flat griddle (or large skillet) on the grill or a side burner, heat the olive oil. Add the breaded eggplant slices and sauté them until the slices begin to brown.

5. Remove the slices from the grill and drain on paper towels.

6. Beat the remaining 3 eggs with the Parmesan cheese, parsley, and basil and set aside.

7. Place a layer of the eggplant slices in the prepared pan, followed by a layer of cheese slices. Then pour one third of the egg mixture over the top. Repeat these steps until all the eggplant, cheese slices and egg mixture are used, ending with a final layer of egg mixture on the top. Pour the tomato sauce over the assembled dish.

8. Cover and place in the barbecue for 25 to 30 minutes, or until the egg mixture is set and a knife inserted in the center comes out clean.

9. Cut into small squares and serve warm or cold, but warm is better.

Ham and Swiss Croissants
Yield: 6 appetizers

For a more pungent and savory variety of this dish, use Huntsman (sometimes called Stilchester) cheese instead of the Swiss. Huntsman is a combination of several layers of Stilton and English Double Gloucester.

3 tablespoons (45 mL) butter
3½ cups (826 mL) sliced mushrooms
3 tablespoons (45 mL) minced green onions, white and green parts
3 tablespoons (45 mL) all-purpose flour
1 cup (236 mL) milk
¼ teaspoon salt
Freshly ground black pepper, to taste
6 large croissants, top and bottom separated
12 slices smoked or honey-baked deli ham
12 slices Swiss cheese

1. Preheat the barbecue to medium high (350°F [180°C] to 400°F [200°C]).

2. In a saucepan, melt the butter. Add the mushrooms and onions and sauté over medium heat until both are tender and all the mushroom liquid has evaporated.

3. Stir in the flour, then the milk. Bring to a boil over medium heat, stirring often. Reduce the heat and simmer the sauce until it thickens. Add salt and pepper.

4. Arrange the bottom halves of the croissants in a large baking pan. Place 2 slices of ham and 2 slices of cheese on each croissant. Pour the mushroom sauce over the cheese and cover with the tops of the croissants.

5. Bake in the barbecue for about 15 minutes, or until the croissants are heated through and the sauce is bubbling. Slice to serve in appetizer portions.

Herbed Tater Wedgies

Yield: 20 appetizers

Most of the potatoes grown in the state of Idaho are Russet Burbanks—what we normally call Russets—which were originally grown mainly to feed the hungry and poor gold miners who flocked to Idaho in 1860. This recipe comes from Tom Eldsmore from Santa Cruz, CA.

6 medium Russet or Yukon gold potatoes
1 cup (236 mL) butter
1 tablespoon (15 mL) onion powder
1 teaspoon (5 mL) seasoned salt
1 teaspoon (5 mL) ground cumin
1 teaspoon (5 mL) dried parsley
1 teaspoon (5 mL) paprika
Freshly ground black pepper, to taste

1. Make sure the grill is clean and generously sprayed with nonstick grilling spray. Preheat the barbecue to medium high (350°F [180°C] to 400°F [200°C]).

2. Scrub the potatoes, leaving the skins on, then quarter them lengthwise. Place the potatoes skin side down on the grill and cook for 30 minutes, turning often with tongs.

3. While the potatoes are cooking, heat the butter in a small saucepan. Add the onion powder, salt, cumin, parsley, paprika, and pepper and stir until the butter is melted. Remove from the heat and keep warm.

4. Turn the potatoes skin side down and, using a long barbecue brush, slather the flesh sides with the spiced butter. Bake for another 20 to 25 minutes.

Snack-Size Pizzas

Yield: 16 appetizers

These are great make-ahead appetizers, which you can assemble and freeze to reheat in the oven or microwave later.

½ cup (118 mL) butter, very soft
1 teaspoon (5 mL) garlic powder
8 English muffins
1 pound (454 g) ground chuck
2 tablespoons (30 mL) minced onions
2 tablespoons (30 mL) tomato paste
1 teaspoon (5 mL) savory
1 teaspoon (5 mL) tarragon
Salt, to taste
Freshly ground black pepper, to taste
½ cup (118 mL) freshly grated Parmesan cheese

1. Preheat the barbecue to medium high (350°F [180°C] to 400°F [200°C]).

2. Mix together the softened butter and the garlic powder. Split and toast the muffins and generously cover them with the garlic butter.

3. In a large cast-iron or nonstick skillet, sauté the ground chuck and onions for 10 minutes, until all the meat has browned. Add the tomato paste, savory, tarragon, salt, and pepper and cook, stirring, for another 2 to 3 minutes to incorporate the flavors.

4. Spoon the mixture onto the muffin halves, spreading it edge to edge.

5. Cover the meat mixture with generous sprinkles of the cheese and bake the muffins in the barbecue for 10 minutes, or until the meat and cheese are bubbling and cheese is beginning to brown.

6. Remove the muffins, cool for 1 to 2 minutes, and serve.

Greek-Style Triangles

Yield: 4 dozen appetizers

2 cups (473 mL) Bisquick baking mix
1 cup (236 mL) buttermilk
2 large eggs, beaten
¼ cup (59 mL) butter, melted
1 cup (236 mL) crumbled Feta cheese
2 tablespoons (30 mL) chopped fresh Italian parsley
1 teaspoon (5 mL) garlic salt
Olive oil, for brushing
Minced fresh rosemary, to taste

1. Preheat the barbecue to medium high (350°F [180°C] to 400°F [200°C]).

2. Grease or spray with nonstick cooking spray a 9 × 13-inch (22.5 × 32.5-cm) baking pan.

3. In a large bowl, mix together the Bisquick, buttermilk, and eggs. Pour this mixture into the prepared pan. Drizzle with the melted butter, then sprinkle with the cheese, parsley, and garlic salt. Bake in the barbecue until deep golden brown, 30 to 35 minutes.

4. Cool for 8 to 10 minutes then cut into 2-inch (5-cm) squares. Cut the squares diagonally into triangles, brush them with olive oil, and sprinkle lightly with rosemary.

Honey-Roasted Peanuts
Yield: 4 cups (0.95 L)

We use Virginia peanuts in this recipe, but you could use the smaller Spanish varieties—the small, round ones with the brown, papery skin. You can also fire these up by sprinkling them with cayenne pepper after you add the salt.

4 cups (0.95 L) raw, unsalted peanuts
¼ cup (59 mL) butter
¼ cup (59 mL) honey
1 teaspoon (5 mL) ground nutmeg
1 teaspoon (5 mL) fine sea salt

1. Preheat the barbecue to medium high (350°F [180°C] to 400°F [200°C]).

2. Spray a baking sheet with nonstick cooking spray.

3. Place the peanuts in a medium bowl.

4. In saucepan over medium heat, melt the butter. Add the honey and nutmeg and stir well.

5. Pour the honey-butter over the peanuts and stir well.

6. Pour the peanuts onto the prepared baking sheet, sprinkle with the sea salt, and bake in the barbecue for 5 to 10 minutes, or until the peanuts are golden brown.

Orange You a Dog?
Yield: 32 appetizers

These are perfect appetizers, or a light lunch, for a children's party. Some adults will find these a little too sweet.

½ cup (118 mL) sugar
3 tablespoons (45 mL) cornstarch
1½ cups (354 mL) orange juice
¼ cup (59 mL) cider vinegar
¼ teaspoon (1.25 mL) ground cloves
¼ teaspoon (1.25 mL) ground cinnamon
1 (8-count) package hot dogs of your choice, each dog quartered

1. Preheat the barbecue to medium high (350°F [180°C] to 400°F [200°C]) for direct and indirect heating.

2. In a wide, flat roasting pan, combine the sugar and cornstarch; stir in the orange juice, vinegar, cloves, and cinnamon, then place the pan on the heated side of the grill.

3. When sauce begins to bubble move the pan to the unheated side of the grill, add the hot dogs, and cook for 10 to 12 minutes, stirring often, to thicken.

Barbecued Rumaki
Yield: 24 appetizers

Chicken liver–water chestnut–bacon skewers. These traditional Japanese kebabs are perfect for serving as appetizers, and you can substitute 2 tablespoons (30 mL) of brown sugar for the maple syrup if you wish.

Marinade
½ cup (118 mL) maple syrup
⅓ cup (79 mL) soy sauce
2 tablespoons (30 mL) cider vinegar
1 tablespoon (15 mL) sherry
½ teaspoon salt
Freshly ground black pepper, to taste

Appetizers
12 chicken livers
18 bacon slices, halved crosswise
2 (5-ounce [140-g]) cans water chestnuts, drained

1. In a small bowl, mix together the maple syrup, soy sauce, cider vinegar, sherry, salt, and pepper and set aside.

2. Clean and trim the chicken livers and dry them with paper towels. Cut each in half and set aside. Cut the water chestnuts into ¼-inch (0.25-cm) thick slices and set those aside.

3. Take a piece of liver and a slice of chestnut and wrap them together in a half-slice of bacon. Secure with a toothpick. Repeat until all the livers have been wrapped.

4. Put the rumaki into a resealable plastic bag—carefully, so those toothpicks don't puncture the sides—and pour in the marinade. Seal the bag and refrigerate for several hours or overnight.

5. Make sure the grill is clean and generously sprayed with nonstick grilling spray. Preheat the barbecue to medium high (350°F [180°C] to 400°F [200°C]).

6. Remove the rumaki from the marinade, reserving the liquid, and place them directly on the well-sprayed grill rack. Grill for about 15 to 20 minutes, turning once or twice as needed.

7. While they are cooking boil the remaining marinade, then use it to baste the rumaki.

8. Using tongs, remove the rumaki from the grill. Serve warm.

Mexican Grilled Potato Skins
Yield: 8 appetizers

If you wish, substitute chopped sun-dried tomatoes or chopped, drained pimientos for the red bell peppers in this recipe

4 large baking potatoes
1 tablespoon (15 mL) butter, melted
1 cup (236 mL) diced red bell pepper
½ cup (118 mL) chopped green onions, white and green parts
1½ cups (354 mL) fresh corn kernels (cut from 3 or 4 cobs)
2 teaspoons (10 mL) chili powder
½ teaspoon garlic salt
1 cup (236 mL) light sour cream
¼ cup minced fresh cilantro
Olive or vegetable oil, for frying
2 cups (473 mL) Sargento Mexican 4-cheese mix
Chopped fresh cilantro, for garnish

1. Make sure the grill is clean and generously sprayed with nonstick grilling spray. Preheat the barbecue to medium high (350°F [180°C] to 400°F [200°C]).

2. Scrub and dry the potatoes. Prick each one several times with a fork. Bake for 1 hour, or until the potatoes are tender.

3. In a large skillet over medium high heat, melt the butter. Add the red bell pepper and green onions and sauté for 3 to 4 minutes, or until the peppers are tender. Stir in the corn, chili powder, and salt and sauté for another 3 to 4 minutes. Remove the pan from the heat, pour the mixture into a bowl, and let cool.

4. Stir in the sour cream and minced cilantro and set aside.

5. Once the potatoes are cool enough to handle comfortably, cut them in half lengthwise. Carefully, use a spoon to scoop out the flesh, leaving a shell about ⅛ inch (0.25 cm) thick. Reserve the potato flesh for use in another recipe.

6. Pour 2 to 3 inches of oil into a Dutch oven or deep roasting pan and heat it until a deep-frying thermometer reads 375°F (190°C). Fry the shells in the hot oil for 1 to 2 minutes, or until they are browned. Invert the shells and drain them well on paper towels.

7. Place the shells, skin side down, on an ungreased baking sheet. Spoon the corn mixture evenly into the shells, then sprinkle with the cheese. Grill for 2 to 3 minutes, just until the cheese melts and begins to brown.

8. Remove the potato skins from the grill and cool for 4 to 5 minutes. Garnish with cilantro and serve.

Prosciutto Wraps

Yield: 24 appetizers

These aren't cooked, grilled, smoked, or barbecued, but they sure are refreshing for the cook who's cooking, grilling, smoking, or barbecuing.

12 thin slices prosciutto, cut in half
24 bite-size pieces of cantaloupe, peaches, and/or figs
24 (1-inch [2.5-cm]) cubes Fontina and/or Swiss cheese
Fresh lettuce leaves, for serving
Lemon and lime wedges, for serving

1. Cut the sliced prosciutto into 1-inch (2.5-cm) strips.

2. Wrap one piece of fruit and one piece of cheese in a prosciutto strip and secure with a toothpick. Repeat until all the fruit, cheese, and prosciutto is used.

3. Arrange the appetizers on a lettuce-lined plate.

4. Serve with the lemon or lime wedges.

Piglets in Blankets

Yield: 32 appetizers

If you can't find cocktail franks, you can either cut regular hot dogs into four sections or use canned Vienna hot dogs.

1 (8-ounce [227-g]) can Pillsbury Refrigerated Dinner Rolls
32 cocktail franks

1. Preheat the barbecue to medium high (350°F [180°C] to 400°F [200°C]).

2. Cut each dinner roll in quarters and use a rolling pin to roll them out to 2- to 2½-inch (5- to 6-cm) circles.

3. Wrap each cocktail frank in a circle of dough. Place the wrapped franks on an ungreased baking sheet.

4. Bake in the barbecue for 15 minutes, or until the pastries are golden brown.

5. Use a spatula to remove the piglets from the grill. Serve warm with ketchup and mustard or your favorite condiments.

Chicken Flautas

Yield: 32 appetizers

You may substitute corn tortillas in this recipe without changing the cooking method or time. I prefer the lighter flour variety, but some like the heavier, more flavorful corn tortillas.

2 cups (473 mL) finely shredded or chopped cooked chicken
⅔ cup (158 mL) picante sauce, plus more for serving
¼ cup (59 mL) sliced green onions, green and white parts
¾ teaspoon (3.75 mL) ground cumin
½ teaspoon (2.5 cm) chili powder
Vegetable oil, for frying
32 (6-inch [15-cm]) flour tortillas
2 cups (473 mL) shredded Monterey Jack cheese
1 cup (236 mL) shredded cheddar cheese
Guacamole, for serving
Fresh salsa, for serving
Picante sauce, for serving

1. Preheat the barbecue to medium high (350°F [180°C] to 400°F [200°C]).

2. In a large bowl, combine the chicken, the ⅔ cup picante sauce, onion, cumin, and chili powder and mix well.

3. In a small skillet, heat ½ inch (1 cm) of oil until very hot. Quickly fry each tortilla until soft (about 5 seconds on each side), then drain the tortillas on paper towels.

4. Mix together the two shredded cheeses.

5. Spoon 1 tablespoon (15 mL) of the spiced chicken mixture and 1 tablespoon (15 mL) of the mixed cheeses down the center of each tortilla. Roll each very tightly and secure with 1 or 2 wooden toothpicks.

6. Place the rolled tortillas seam side down on a baking sheet and bake in the barbecue for 18 to 20 minutes, until the tortillas are crisp and beginning to brown.

7. Serve warm with guacamole, fresh salsa, and picante sauce.

Pita Crisps

Yield: 24 appetizers

These can also be made with rye cocktail toasts, English muffins, or thin slices of breads, such as sourdough, limpa, or dark rye.

6 (6-inch [15-cm]) pita breads
½ cup (118 mL) butter or margarine, at room temperature
¼ cup (59 mL) freshly grated Parmesan cheese
2 tablespoons (30 mL) sesame seeds
1½ tablespoons (22.5 mL) granulated garlic
1 tablespoon (15 mL) dried oregano
Paprika, for garnish

1. Make sure the grill is clean and generously sprayed with nonstick grilling spray. Preheat the barbecue to medium high (350°F [180°C] to 400°F [200°C]).

2. Split the pitas horizontally into two halves. Butter the inside surfaces and arrange the pitas on a baking sheet, butter side up.

3. In a small bowl, mix together the Parmesan cheese, sesame seeds, garlic, and oregano and sprinkle it over the butter. Sprinkle with paprika for color.

4. Place the bread rounds on the barbecue grill and cook for about 2 minutes, until the pitas are browned and crunchy. Watch closely, as they can easily and quickly burn.

Green Onion and Bacon Potato Cakes
Yield: 12–20 appetizers

Instead of bacon, you can use chopped ham, shrimp, chicken, pork sausage, or any other protein.

4 cups (0.95 L) mashed potatoes
1 cup (236 mL) crumbled crisp bacon
2 large eggs, beaten
¼ cup (59 mL) all-purpose flour
3 tablespoons (45 mL) chopped green onions, green and white parts
½ teaspoon (2.5 mL) garlic salt
Freshly ground black pepper, to taste
Olive oil, for frying
Sour cream, for serving
Applesauce, for serving
Parsley, for garnish

1. Preheat the barbecue to medium high (350°F [180°C] to 400°F [200°C]). Place a barbecue griddle on the burners or grill. If you don't have a griddle, you can use a cast-iron or nonstick skillet.

2. In a medium bowl, combine the potatoes, bacon, eggs, flour, onions, garlic salt, and pepper. Set aside.

3. Oil the griddle or skillet. Spoon about 2 tablespoons (30 mL) of potato mixture for each cake onto the griddle.

4. Cook the cakes until they are nicely browned on the bottom, then turn them over with a spatula and cook the other side until brown, about 5 to 6 minutes total.

5. Transfer the potato cakes to a heated plate and keep them warm until all the cakes are done and you are ready to serve.

6. Serve with bowls of sour cream and applesauce. Garnish with parsley.

Barbecued Artichoke Heart Casserole

Yield: 16–20 appetizers

A variety of chili pepper, pimientos are fleshy, aromatic, and sweet. They are often sold roasted and bottled, and may be most familiar as the stuffing in green olives. Most of the pimiento crop is dried and powdered to make paprika.

2 (6-ounce [168-g]) jars marinated artichoke hearts, drained and chopped
1 cup (236 mL) grated cheddar cheese
4 large eggs, beaten
1 bunch green onions, green and white parts, chopped
¼ cup (59 mL) chopped bottled pimientos
2 teaspoons (10 mL) minced fresh parsley
1 clove garlic, peeled and minced
3–5 drops hot pepper sauce of your choice

1. Preheat the barbecue to medium high (300°F [150°C] to 350°F [180°C]) for indirect heating.

2. Grease a 9-inch (22.5-cm) square baking pan.

3. In a medium bowl, mix together the artichoke hearts, cheese, eggs, green onions, pimentos, parsley, and garlic. Bake in the prepared baking pan on the unheated side of the grill for 35 to 40 minutes, or until the top is brown and the mixture is firm and set.

4. Cool for 10 to 15 minutes, then cut into 2-inch (5-cm) squares and serve.

Slammin' Salmon Cakes

Yield: 8 appetizers

For a taste twist, use salmon you've smoked yourself, increasing the milk by 1 tablespoon (15 mL).

1½ cups (354 mL) coarsely crushed Toll House (or other favorite) crackers, divided
1 large egg, beaten
2 tablespoons (30 mL) minced fresh dill
2 tablespoons (30 mL) minced green onion, green and white parts
2 tablespoons (30 mL) milk
¼ teaspoon (1.25 mL) freshly ground black pepper
¼ teaspoon (1.25 mL) A1 steak sauce
1 (16-ounce [454-g]) can sockeye salmon, drained
2 cups (473 mL) extra-sharp cheddar cheese
3 tablespoons (45 mL) butter, melted

1. Preheat the barbecue to medium high (300°F [150°C] to 350°F [180°C]).

2. In a medium bowl, combine ¾ cup (177 mL) of the cracker crumbs with the egg, dill, onion, milk, pepper, and A1 sauce and stir. Add the salmon and cheese and mix with a fork.

3. With your hands, shape the mixture into eight small cakes.

4. Brush the cakes with the melted butter, then press them into the remaining crumbs, coating each patty on both sides.

5. Arrange the salmon cakes on an ungreased baking sheet and place it in the barbecue. Cook, turning once, for 10 to 12 minutes, or until the crumb topping browns on both sides.

6. Remove the salmon cakes from the barbecue and serve warm.

Grilled Clams on the Half-Shell
Yield: 36 appetizers

Eastern clams, such as Cherrystone and Littlenecks, and Pacific clams, such as Manila, Butter, Pismo, and, again, Littlenecks, are the most popular, readily available, and best clams for this recipe.

8 strips (4 ounces [112 g]) hickory-smoked bacon, roughly chopped
2 tablespoons (30 mL) minced garlic
1½ teaspoons (7.5 mL) sweet red pepper flakes
¼ cup (59 mL) finely chopped mushrooms
3 tablespoons (45 mL) minced fresh parsley
2 tablespoons (30 mL) olive oil
Freshly ground black pepper, to taste
36 clams, cleaned and scrubbed
2 ounces (56 mL) fresh lemon juice

1. Make sure the grill is clean and generously sprayed with nonstick grilling spray. Preheat the barbecue to medium high (350°F [180°C] to 400°F [200°C]).

2. In a cast-iron or nonstick skillet, cook the bacon on the grill or on a side burner until golden brown, 5 to 6 minutes, turning the bacon once. Add the garlic and red pepper flakes and cook for another minute. Remove the pan from the heat and stir in the olive oil, parsley, and mushrooms. Season with pepper and set aside.

3. Place the clams directly on the grill, close the cover, and cook until all the clams have opened, 3 to 4 minutes. Discard any that do not open.

4. Transfer the clams to a platter and top each with the bacon mixture. Drizzle with the lemon juice just before serving.

Toad-in-the-Hole
Yield: 8–10 appetizers

For a bit of spice, add 1 teaspoon (5 mL) of a Dijon-style mustard to the batter before pouring it over the sausages.

1 cup (236 mL) all-purpose flour
2 large eggs
1 cup (236 mL) milk
½ teaspoon (2.5 mL) salt
Freshly ground black pepper, to taste
1 pound (454 g) pork sausage links, cut into 1-inch (2.5-cm) long pieces

1. In a medium food processor bowl, combine the flour, eggs, milk, salt, and pepper. Process on high for 2 to 3 seconds. Remove the bowl from the processor, cover, and chill for at least an hour.

2. Make sure the grill is clean and generously sprayed with nonstick grilling spray. Preheat the barbecue to medium high (350°F [180°C] to 400°F [200°C]).

3. Place the cut sausages in a cast-iron or nonstick skillet, add 2 tablespoons (30 mL) water, cover, and cook over medium-high heat for about 3 minutes to extract the fat. Uncover, raise the heat to high, and cook until the sausages begin to brown.

4. Pour the batter over the sausages and place the skillet in the barbecue. Bake for about 30 to 35 minutes, or until the dough has risen and the top has browned.

5. Remove the pan from the grill and cool slightly, then cut the "toads" into pie-shaped wedges and serve with your favorite mustards or other condiments.

Pacific Salmon Tartare

Yield: 10–12 appetizers

You can also blend 4 ounces (112 g) cream cheese with the other ingredients for a smoother tartare.

½ pound (227 g) lightly smoked salmon (lox)
1 tablespoon (15 mL) finely chopped onion
1 tablespoon (15 mL) capers
1 teaspoon (5 mL) lemon juice
Salt, to taste
Freshly ground black pepper, to taste

1. Chop the salmon to the consistency of ground beef and put it in a medium bowl. Add the onion, capers, lemon juice, salt, and pepper and mix. Refrigerate for 20 minutes.

2. Serve with crackers or toast points.

Grilled Vanilla Shrimp Toast

Yield: 24 appetizers

Vanilla? In a savory shellfish dish? Yup, the vanilla adds an unusual and very complementary flavor to the melted cheese and spices. Ask your guests to identify the "key flavor" of these toasts; I'll bet no one guesses correctly.

1 baguette
2 ounces (56 g) Gruyere or Pecorino cheese, chilled
4 tablespoons (60 mL) butter, divided
1 pound (454 g) large uncooked shrimp, peeled and deveined
½ cup (118 mL) dry white wine
2 tablespoons (30 mL) chopped fresh basil
2 teaspoons (10 mL) pure vanilla extract
½ teaspoon (2.5 mL) kosher salt
¼ teaspoon (1.25 mL) cayenne pepper
Minced fresh chives, for garnish
1 lemon, quartered

1. Make sure the grill is clean and generously sprayed with nonstick grilling spray. Preheat the barbecue to medium high (350°F [180°C] to 400°F [200°C]).

2. Cut the baguette diagonally into ¼-inch (0.5-cm) thick, oval-shaped slices. Grill the slices directly on the gill until they are lightly toasted.

3. Using a vegetable peeler, or a very sharp knife, shave the cheese into very thin slices. Set aside.

4. In a nonstick or cast-iron skillet, melt 2 tablespoons (30 mL) of the butter over medium-high heat. Add the shrimp and sauté. Add the wine, basil, vanilla, salt, and cayenne pepper and cook for 2 to 4 minutes, or until the shrimp are pink. Remove the shrimp from the pan with a slotted spoon and keep warm.

5. Bring the remaining sauce to a boil, then remove the pan from the heat and whisk in the remaining butter, 1 tablespoon (15 mL) at a time. The idea is to melt the butter slowly to form a creamy sauce.

6. Brush the toasted baguette ovals with the warm butter from the skillet. Top each with one or two thin slices of cheese, then add a shrimp or two and brush with additional sauce. Garnish with a sprinkle of chives and a squeeze of fresh lemon and serve.

Breaded and Grilled BBQ Wings
Yield: 15–20 servings

These wings are mildly hot, but you can increase their fire by doubling the cayenne pepper or adding minced Scotch bonnet or habañero peppers to the breading, or by serving them with a hot, spicy dipping sauce.

½ cup (118 mL) cornmeal
½ cup (118 mL) all-purpose flour
2 tablespoons (30 mL) barbecue rub of your choice
2 teaspoons (10 mL) salt
½ teaspoon (2.5 mL) cayenne pepper
1 large egg
1½ cups (354 mL) milk
24–30 frozen chicken wings, thawed, tips removed, separated into two sections
Ranch or blue cheese dressing, for serving

1. In a shallow bowl, combine the cornmeal, flour, rub, salt, and cayenne pepper. In a separate bowl, mix together the egg and milk. Dip each wing part in the egg mixture, then coat it in the breading mixture. Arrange the wing parts in a pan, cover, and refrigerate for about an hour.

2. Make sure the grill is clean and generously sprayed with nonstick grilling spray. Preheat the barbecue to medium high (350°F [180°C] to 400°F [200°C]) for indirect heating. Place a pan of water pan under the unheated side of the grill.

3. Remove the wings from the refrigerator and place them on the unheated side of the grill. Close the lid and cook for about 30 minutes. Turn the chicken pieces and cook for another 20 minutes. When wings are a nice golden brown color, carefully remove them from the grill.

4. Serve with ranch or blue cheese dressing for dipping.

Smoked Sausage Bites

Yield: 12–14 servings

You can make these hotter by adding one or two minced jalapeño peppers, 1 teaspoon (5 mL) cayenne pepper, and/or ½ teaspoon (2.5 mL) of your favorite hot sauce.

1 (1 pound [454 g]) package miniature smoked sausages
¾ pound (336 g) cooked bratwurst links, cut into ½-inch (1-cm) slices
¾ pound (336 g) Polish sausage, cut into ½-inch (1-cm) slices
1 (18-ounce [504-g]) bottle smoky barbecue sauce
⅔ cup (158 mL) orange marmalade
½ teaspoon (2.5 mL) dry mustard
⅛ teaspoon (0.6 mL) ground allspice
1 (20-ounce [560-g]) can pineapple chunks, drained

1. Preheat the barbecue to medium high (350°F [180°C] to 400°F [200°C]) for indirect heating. Place a pan of water under the cold side of the grill.

2. Spray a Dutch oven or roasting pan with nonstick cooking spray.

3. Place the sausages, bratwurst, and Polish sausage in the prepared pan. Add the barbecue sauce, marmalade, dry mustard, allspice, and pineapple and stir to mix well.

4. Cover and cook on the grill for 1½ to 2 hours, or until the meat is heated through. Serve with toothpicks.

Bratwurst in Dark Beer Sauce

Yield: 8 servings

You could also use hot dogs, other varieties of sausage, or Vienna wieners in this dish.

8 fresh bratwurst
1 tablespoon (15 mL) all-purpose flour
2 teaspoons (10 mL) vegetable oil
⅛ teaspoon (0.6 mL) caraway seeds
1 cup (236 mL) dark beer

1. Preheat the barbecue to medium high (350°F [180°C] to 400°F [200°C]).

2. Place the bratwurst in the center of grill and cook approximately 20 minutes, or until the brats are no longer pink in the middle, turning several times to brown on all sides.

3. In a small saucepan over low heat, heat the flour and oil. Stir frequently until the sauce is light brown. Add the caraway seed, stir in the dark beer, and bring the sauce to a boil. Reduce the heat and simmer, stirring frequently, until the sauce is slightly thickened.

4. Cut each bratwurst into four pieces and place them in the pan of sauce. Stir to coat each piece.

5. Pour the bratwurst and sauce into a serving dish. Provide toothpicks for picking up the brat pieces.

Pineapple and Coconut Lollipops

Yield: 4–8 servings

With just a hint of rum, this is a grilled dish for adults—but if you're serving kids, omit the rum and it will still be quite tasty. You can toast the coconut on a baking sheet or piece of aluminum foil just until it begins to brown before sprinkling it on the pineapple, if you wish. This recipe is from Patti Anderson Browne of Campbell River, British Columbia.

2 tablespoons (30 mL) honey
2 tablespoons (30 mL) dark rum
1 teaspoon (5 mL) lemon juice
4–5 (1-inch [2.5-cm] thick) slices fresh pineapple
1 cup (236 mL) flaked coconut

1. In a side dish, whisk together the honey, rum, and lemon juice. Add the pineapple and coat well with coconut. Allow the pineapple to marinate for at least an hour in the refrigerator and serve at room temperature.

Sweet Grilled Potato Cakes

Yield: 12–14 cakes

You can serve sour cream, blue cheese, or creamy ranch dressing as dips for these cakes.

½ teaspoon (2.5 mL) freshly ground black pepper
½ teaspoon (2.5 mL) ground cinnamon
½ teaspoon (2.5 mL) ground cumin
¼ teaspoon (1.25 mL) ground cloves
2 cups (473 mL) cooked sweet potatoes
½ cup (118 mL) chickpea flour
¼ cup (59 mL) chopped fresh cilantro leaves
2 tablespoons (30 mL) Greek yogurt
1 tablespoon (15 mL) grated fresh ginger
1 teaspoon (5 mL) garlic salt
2 tablespoons (30 mL) olive or peanut oil

1. Preheat the barbecue to medium high (350°F [180°C] to 400°F [200°C]) for direct heating.

2. Mix together the pepper, cinnamon, cumin, and cloves.

3. In a bowl, mash the sweet potatoes. Add the flour, cilantro, yogurt, ginger and garlic salt, and 1 teaspoon (5 mL) of the spice mix. Mix well and form this mixture into patties about 2 inches (5 cm) in diameter.

4. In a well-oiled, cast-iron skillet or on a barbecue griddle, heat the oil. Cook the patties in batches, allowing plenty of room between them, for about 2 minutes on each side, or until they are golden, crisp, and cooked through.

TWO

Beef

Eisenhower Steak

Yield: 4 servings

This technique works well for any relatively tender steak or chop of a uniform thickness. Branch out and try thick pork chops or even a thick tuna steak.

4 (8-ounce [227-g]) beef ribeye, sirloin, T-bone, or strip steaks, cut 1 inch (2.5 cm) thick, at room temperature
Kosher salt, to taste
Freshly ground black pepper, to taste
½ cup (118 mL) unsalted butter
1 lemon, quartered (optional)

1. Sprinkle both sides of the steaks liberally with salt and pepper. Set aside.

2. Fill a charcoal chimney with charcoal briquettes. Set the chimney on the bottom grill grate and light. When the coals are ready, dump them into the bottom of your grill. Cover half of your bottom grate with briquettes.

3. When the briquettes are grayed over, use long-handled tongs or a fork to place each steak directly onto the hot coals. Leave the steaks on the coals for 2 minutes. Turn them over and grill for another 2 to 3 minutes for rare (125°F [52°C] on a meat thermometer). For medium-rare (135°F [57°C]) to medium (140°F [60°C]), leave the steaks on the coals for 1 to 2 minutes longer.

4. Remove the steaks from the coals and brush off the ashes. Put steaks on a heated plate and add a pat of butter to each, if desired. Cover the steaks with aluminum foil and wait 5 minutes for the meat juices to resettle. Serve lemon wedges on the side to squeeze over hot steaks if desired.

Salt-Encrusted Prime Rib

Yield: 6–8 servings

The salt in this recipe not only seals in all the moisture—notice how much drips out onto the grill or into a pan when you roast in the barbecue or oven—it also prevents the meat from charring at this high heat. The meat will have no extra salty taste as long as you brush off any salt crystals that stick to it. You'll need a disposable aluminum pan just large enough to hold the roast for this recipe. Be careful not to burn yourself on the salt. It will be very hot. You can also cook this directly on the grill if you can maintain 500°F (260°C). You almost can't mess this one up.

1 (6–7 pound [2.7–3.2 kg] beef prime rib roast
Worcestershire sauce for coating
2 tablespoons (30 mL) granulated garlic
1 tablespoon (15 mL) freshly ground black pepper
Coarse kosher salt, to taste

1. Preheat the barbecue to medium high (500°F [260°C]).

2. Completely rub the outside of the prime rib with Worcestershire sauce, covering it well. Sprinkle with the granulated garlic and black pepper.

3. Put a layer of kosher salt in the pan about 1-inch (2.5-cm) deep. Lay the prime rib on the salt. Cover the prime rib completely with salt, wetting your hands and packing so the salt sticks to the rib and is completely covered.

4. Place the pan in the barbecue and cook 12 minutes per pound.

5. Take the pan out of the barbecue and let the roast rest for 10 minutes. Use a hammer to break the salt covering. The beef will be rare to medium-rare. Lift the roast out of the salt, wiping off any crystals that stick to the meat. Cover the meat with foil and let it rest for 10 more minutes.

6. Carve the roast at the table and serve generous slices on warmed plates.

Fired-Up BBQ Pot Roast

Yield: 6–8 servings

For a whole meal in a pot, you can add root vegetables such as turnip or parsnips and vegetables such as Brussels sprouts and whole carrots when you add the potatoes.

1 (1–2 pound [454–908 g] beef boneless chuck roast
1 cup (236 mL) diced carrots
1 cup (236 mL) diced onions
1 cup (236 mL) diced celery
2 cups (473 mL) beef broth
3 tablespoons (45 mL) ketchup
2 tablespoons (30 mL) cider vinegar
1 teaspoon (5 mL) balsamic vinegar
¼ teaspoon (1.25 mL) ground cinnamon
¼ teaspoon (1.25 mL) ground cloves
¼ teaspoon (1.25 mL) minced fresh ginger
6 Yukon gold potatoes, peeled and halved
2 tablespoons (30 mL) cornstarch
¼ cup (59 mL) dry red wine

1. Preheat the barbecue to medium high (300°F [150°C] to 325°F [165°C]) for indirect cooking.

2. In a large roasting pan or Dutch oven placed on the barbecue side burner or a stovetop burner, brown the beef on all sides, turning occasionally.

3. Remove the beef from the pot and set aside. Add the carrots, onions, and celery to the pot. Cook, stirring, for 2 minutes, then add the beef broth, stirring to loosen the brown bits.

4. Stir in the ketchup, vinegars, cinnamon, cloves, and ginger. Return the beef to the pot and bring to a boil, then place the covered pot in the barbecue over the unheated part of the grill and simmer for 1 hour.

5. Uncover the pot and add the potatoes. Replace the lid and cook for another 30 minutes.

6. Remove the beef and potatoes and set them aside. Return the pot to the burner.

7. In a small bowl, mix the cornstarch and wine until smooth. Add it to the pot, stirring constantly, bring to a boil, and boil for 1 minute. Return the beef and potatoes to the pot and cook another 5 minutes.

8. Carve the roast into thick slices. Serve with the cooked potatoes and several generous tablespoons of the gravy.

Korean Bulgogi (Barbecued Beef)

Yield: 4 servings

In Korea, this dish, like most, would be served with kimchi, which consists of fermented vegetables such as cabbage, Chinese turnips, garlic, and cucumbers. It is sealed in jars and either buried or stored in underground cellars for up to a month, giving it a strong, heady flavor.

1 pound (454 g) boneless beef top loin or sirloin steak
¼ cup (59 mL) soy sauce
3 tablespoons (45 mL) sugar
2 tablespoons (30 mL) vegetable oil
¼ teaspoon (1.25 mL) freshly ground black pepper
3 green onions, finely chopped, green and white parts
2 cloves garlic, peeled and finely minced

1. Trim the fat from the beef and cut the meat diagonally, across the grain, into ⅛-inch (0.25 cm) thick slices.

2. In a medium bowl, mix together the soy sauce, sugar, oil, pepper, onions, and garlic. Stir in the beef until all the slices are well coated. Cover and refrigerate for 2 to 4 hours.

3. Make sure the grill is clean and generously sprayed with nonstick grilling spray. Preheat the barbecue to medium high (350°F [180°C] to 400°F [200°C]).

4. Drain the beef. Cook the slices directly on the grill, 1 to 2 minutes per side, until they get a light char, then transfer them to a heated platter until you finish cooking all of the meat. Serve with steamed or fried rice and grilled vegetables.

Tang-y Grill-Roast Prime Rib

Yield: 8–10 servings

A powdered breakfast drink developed for the first U.S. astronauts provides the secret citrus flavor to this beef; Tang is used liberally in the rub applied to the roast before cooking.

1 (12–15 pound [5.4–6.8 kg]) beef prime rib with bone-in, cap off
1 cup (236 mL) kosher salt
1 cup (236 mL) coarse cracked black pepper
½ cup (118 mL) Tang powdered breakfast drink
¼ cup (59 mL) granulated garlic
5 cloves garlic, peeled and thinly sliced
Creole-butter injector marinade (or your favorite flavor) as needed
1 cup (236 mL) port
1 cup (236 mL) barbecue sauce

1. Make sure the grill is clean and generously sprayed with nonstick grilling spray. Preheat the barbecue to medium high (350°F [180°C] to 400°F [200°C]).

2. Stir together the salt, pepper, Tang, and granulated garlic; rub over the prime rib.

3. With a sharp knife, cut slits in the meat and insert slices of garlic in each slit.

4. Fill a kitchen injector syringe with the marinade and inject the liquid deeply into the sides and ends of the roast in multiple locations.

5. In a large kettle grill, mound charcoal well over to one side. Place a 9 × 12-inch (22.5 × 30-cm) aluminum pan on other side of coal bed. When the coals are glowing, place the prime rib on the grill on the side opposite the coals, being careful that no part of the rib is directly over the coals. Put the lid on the kettle with the vents one-quarter open. Cook for approximately 2 hours, adding a handful of fresh charcoal every 30 minutes or so.

6. If using a gas grill, place the meat over indirect heat and rotate the meat several times while it is cooking.

7. At the 2-hour point, check the prime rib with a meat thermometer to determine doneness. Remove it from the fire at 110° F (43°C) for very rare, 115° F (46°C) for rare, 120° (49°C) for medium-rare, and so on, adding 4°F (2°C) for each degree of doneness. Remember, the temperature will rise approximately 10°F (3°C) while it is resting.

8. Allow the roast to rest, covered with aluminum foil, for 20 minutes before slicing.

9. In a small saucepan, mix together the port and barbecue sauce. Warm over medium heat while the meat is resting. Serve in a sauce boat beside the meat.

Bing Cherry-Yaki Beef
Yield: 4–6 servings

I prefer to use Bing cherries in this dish, but you could substitute Lambert, Rainer, or even the blush-yellow Royal Ann varieties. This recipe comes from Cam Kellett from Camas, Wash.

1 (3½-pound [1.6-kg]) lean beef chuck steak, cut into 1½-inch (3.5-cm) cubes
1½ cup cherry juice
¼ cup (59 mL) dry sherry
1 (1 5/8-ounce [45.5-g]) packet teriyaki sauce mix
1 clove garlic, peeled and minced
1 tablespoon (15 mL) finely chopped candied ginger
1 tablespoon (15 mL) cornstarch
1 pint (454 g) black sweet cherries, cleaned, and pitted
Cooked white rice, for serving
2 tablespoons (30 mL) blanched slivered almonds
Chopped fresh parsley, for garnish

1. Make sure the grill is clean. Preheat the barbecue to medium high (350°F [180°C] to 400°F [200°C]) for direct and indirect heating.

2. In a cast-iron skillet over high heat, brown the beef cubes on all sides in small amount of fat trimmed from the beef. Remove from the heat when all pieces are nicely browned.

3. In a small bowl, blend ¼ cup (59 mL) of the cherry juice with the sherry, teriyaki sauce mix, garlic and, ginger and pour it over the beef in the skillet.

4. Cover the skillet and bake in the center of the grill for 2 to 2½ hours, stirring occasionally, until the beef is fork-tender.

5. Transfer the beef cubes to the center of large platter and cover with aluminum foil.

6. Blend the cornstarch with the remaining cherry juice and stir this mixture into the liquid remaining in skillet. Cook over medium high heat until the sauce thickens. Add the pitted cherries and stir until heated through.

7. Uncover the beef, surround it with mounds of white rice, spoon the cherry sauce over the beef and rice, sprinkle everything with slivered almonds and chopped parsley, and serve.

Brazilian Marinated Steaks with Chile-Lime Sauce
Yield: 4 servings

Churrascaria restaurants in Brazil vary from those that use eight-foot-tall stainless rotisserie racks over gas flames and waiters who bring huge joints of meat to carve tableside to pits dug in the earth, framed by wooden logs, where the meat is cooked on wooden skewers placed across the logs.

5 jalapeño peppers, stemmed, seeded, and chopped
2 teaspoons (10 mL) flake salt, divided
2 white onions, peeled and chopped
12 cloves garlic, peeled and chopped
4 (½-pound [227-g]) beef sirloin steaks, 1½ inches (3.5 cm) thick
½ cup (118 mL) fresh-squeezed lime juice (from about 3 limes)
⅓ cup (79 mL) dry red wine
2 teaspoons (10 mL) dried oregano
1 bay leaf
1 teaspoon (5 mL) freshly ground black pepper
1 cup (236 mL) loosely packed, coarsely chopped fresh Italian parsley

1. In a food processor, combine the jalapeño peppers, 1 teaspoon (5 mL) of the salt, half the onions, and one-third of the garlic, and process until a paste is formed. You should have about ½ cup (118 mL) of sauce. Refrigerate until ready to use.

2. Place the steaks in a large baking dish. In a small bowl, whisk together the lime juice, the wine, the remaining minced onion and garlic, the oregano, the bay leaf, the remaining 1 teaspoon (5 mL) salt, and the pepper. Pour this marinade over the steaks, turning to coat each steak evenly. Cover and refrigerate, turning every couple of hours, for 4 to 6 hours.

3. Make sure the grill is clean and generously sprayed with nonstick grilling spray. Preheat the barbecue to high (450°F [240°C] to 500°F [260°C]).

4. Remove the jalapeño–onion–garlic sauce from the refrigerator to bring it to room temperature.

5. Remove the steaks from the marinade and wipe off the excess. Transfer the steaks to the grill over direct heat and cook for 5 to 6 minutes per side, to an internal temperature of 145°F (63°C) for medium-rare.

6. Transfer the steaks to a heated platter, sprinkle with the parsley, cover them with foil, and let stand for 5 minutes. Serve with the sauce on the side.

Sir Brucie's Meat Loaf

Yield: 8 servings

You can change this recipe by using 1½ pounds (680 g) beef and ½ pound (227 g) pork, ground turkey, sausage, chicken, or lamb. All other ingredients stay the same. This recipe comes from Sir Bruce Paris from Nairobi, Kenya.

1 cup (236 mL) soft breadcrumbs
½ cup (118 mL) milk
2 pounds (908 g) ground beef
2 tablespoons (30 mL) minced onion
1½ teaspoons (7.5 mL) salt
1 large egg, beaten
½ cup (118 mL) barbecue sauce or ketchup
3 (½-inch [1-cm]) thick slices cheddar cheese
Minced fresh parsley, for garnish

1. Preheat the barbecue to medium high (350°F [180°C] to 400°F [200°C]).

2. Lightly grease a loaf pan.

3. Soak the breadcrumbs in the milk.

4. In a medium bowl, mix together the ground beef, onions, soaked bread, salt, and egg. Scoop half of the mixture into the prepared loaf pan and add the cheese. Cover with the remaining mixture.

5. Mix the barbecue sauce (or ketchup) with ½ cup (118 mL) water and pour half of this mixture over the meat. Bake in the center of the barbecue for 1 hour, basting often with the remaining sauce.

6. Remove the meat from the barbecue, let cool, and cut into slices or spoon onto plates. Sprinkle with minced parsley and serve.

Thweet Tooth Thirloin Thteaks

Yield: 6 servings

Thith ith a fun way to cook thteaks. The thugar doesn't burn, it merely carmelithez on the meat, adding a thugary, thweet tasthe.

¾ cup (177 mL) packed dark brown sugar
1 tablespoon (15 mL) cracked black peppercorns
1 tablespoon (15 mL) paprika
1 tablespoon (15 mL) granulated garlic
1 teaspoon (5 mL) kosher salt
1 teaspoon (5 mL) onion powder
1 teaspoon (5 mL) dried rosemary
6 (1-inch [2.5-cm] thick) beef sirloin steaks

1. Make sure the grill is clean and generously sprayed with nonstick grilling spray. Preheat the barbecue to high (400°F [200°C] to 450°F [240°C]).

2. In a medium bowl, combine the sugar, peppercorns, paprika, garlic, salt, onion powder, and rosemary and set aside. Pat the steaks dry with a paper towel and coat both sides of the steaks with the dry mixture, pressing the steaks deeply into the sugary rub.

3. Grill the steaks directly over high heat for about 2 minutes per side, until they are well-marked and seared. Move the steaks to the indirect side of the grill for about 3 minutes per side, cooking until the steaks are done to your liking. If you prefer them medium-rare, take them off the grill when a meat thermometer inserted into the center of a steak sideways registers 135°F (57°C).

4. Transfer the steaks to a heated platter and let them rest, covered, for 10 minutes before serving. The temperature will rise to 145°F (63°C), perfect for medium-rare. Medium would be 10°F (6°C) higher.

5. Don't ask about well-done or I'll thmack you.

Cow-Stuffed Pig Roast

Yield: 6–8 servings

I tasted this roast at a barbecue festival in Charlotte, North Carolina, as an entry submitted in the "Backyard BBQ" category, and I never forgot how good it was. This approximation of that recipe comes from Robert Krumbine from Charlotte, N.C.

1 (3-pound [1.3-kg]) boneless pork loin roast
1 cup (236 mL) barbecue sauce of your choice, divided
½ pound (227 g) ground beef
¼ cup (59 mL) chopped onion
1 small clove garlic, peeled and minced
¼ teaspoon (1.25 mL) salt
Freshly ground black pepper, to taste
8 ounces (227 g) mushrooms, stems removed, coarsely chopped
¼ cup (59 mL) seasoned breadcrumbs
¼ cup (59 mL) freshly grated Parmesan cheese
1 tablespoon (15 mL) chopped fresh basil

1 teaspoon (5 mL) ground cumin
Parsley sprigs, for garnish
Mixture of 1 cup (236 mL) apple juice and 1 tablespoon (15 mL) olive oil in a spray bottle

1. Make sure the grill is clean and generously sprayed with nonstick grilling spray. Preheat the barbecue to medium high (300°F [150°C] to 350°F [180°C]).

2. To butterfly the loin, split it lengthwise almost all the way to opposite side, then spread it open flat and pound with a meat-tenderizing mallet to spread the meat out to a rectangle about 10 × 15 inches (25 × 37.5 cm) and ¾-inch (0.75-cm) thick. Brush the surface with ¼ cup (59 mL) of the barbecue sauce.

3. In a large bowl, combine the ground beef, onion, garlic, salt, pepper, and ¼ cup (59 mL) of the remaining barbecue sauce and mix thoroughly. Spread this mixture evenly over the top of the pork roast.

4. Press the chopped mushrooms into the ground beef, then sprinkle the breadcrumbs and Parmesan cheese over the meat. Sprinkle with the basil and cumin. Starting at one side, roll up and tie the pork roast into a large round shape. Place it on a rack in a shallow roasting pan.

5. Place pan in the barbecue and roast, uncovered, for about 2½ hours, spraying 3 or 4 times with the apple juice mixture.

6. During the last 10 to 15 minutes of the cooking time, baste the roast with the remaining barbecue sauce. Serve roast on heated platter, and garnish with fresh parsley.

Coffee-and-Pepper-Crusted New York Steaks

Yield: 4 servings

If you love the smell of roasting coffee beans and the smell of steaks on a charcoal fire, stand back, Bubba you're gonna love this recipe. I prefer ribeye steaks, but this New York version is as good as it gets.

2 tablespoons (30 mL) whole coffee beans
2 tablespoons (30 mL) whole black peppercorns
4 (¾-pound [336-g]) New York strip steaks, 1–1½-inches (2.5–3.5 cm) thick
Vegetable oil grilling spray
Kosher salt, to taste

1. Make sure the grill is clean and generously sprayed with nonstick grilling spray. Preheat the barbecue to medium high (450°F [240°C] to 500°F [260°C]).

2. In a food processor or coffee grinder, coarsely grind the coffee beans and peppercorns. Pour the grounds into a wide, flat pan.

3. Press the steaks heavily into the coffee-peppercorn mixture, making sure the steaks are evenly covered on both sides.

4. Spray the steaks lightly with the oil and grill them over direct heat for 4 to 5 minutes per side, or until they reach desired doneness, turning once.

5. Remove the steaks from the grill. Sprinkle both sides with the kosher salt, cover, and allow to rest for 4 to 5 minutes before serving.

Jack Daniel's Old No. 7 Flank Steak
Yield: 4 serving

Of course, you could use just about any whiskey or Scotch in this recipe, but I'm partial to Old Jack because they sponsor the annual "World Cup" of barbecue: the Jack Daniel's World Championship Invitational Barbecue contest.

1 (1½-pound [681-g]) beef flank steak, ½-inch (1-cm) thick
1 clove garlic, peeled and minced
2 teaspoons (10 mL) dry mustard
¼ cup (59 mL) Jack Daniel's whiskey
2 tablespoons (30 mL) butter
Kosher salt, to taste
Freshly ground black pepper, to taste

1. Score the flank steak with a sharp knife, about ⅛ inch (0.25 cm) deep, in a diamond pattern, and set aside.

2. In a small bowl, mash the garlic with the mustard. Stir in the whiskey, pour the mixture over the steak, cover with plastic wrap, and refrigerate overnight.

3. Remove the steak from the refrigerator and bring it to room temperature. (This should take about 1 hour.) Remove the steak from the marinade and discard the liquid.

4. Make sure the grill is clean and generously sprayed with nonstick grilling spray. Preheat the barbecue to medium high (350°F [180°C] to 400°F [200°C]).

5. Grill the steak for 3 to 5 minutes per side.

6. Transfer the steak to a hot plate, drop the butter on top, cover with aluminum foil, and let rest for 4 minutes.

7. Sprinkle the steak with salt and pepper. Cut it across the grain into ¼-inch (0.5-cm) thick slices. Serve hot.

Browne-Bagged Sirloin Steaks
Yield: 4–6 servings

I developed this recipe while fooling around with a similar recipe (Mojo Pork Butt in a Bag, page 516). I also like to use brown paper bags for Dirty Bag Shrimp (page 331), Ribs in a Bag (page 465), and Apple Pie Baked in a Bag (page 720).

1 (2–3 pound [908 g–1.3 kg]) beef top sirloin steak, cut 2½ inches (6 cm) thick
¼ cup (60 mL) butter, melted
¼ cup (60 mL) olive oil
1 tablespoon (15 mL) dried savory
1 tablespoon (15 mL) freshly ground black pepper
2 teaspoons (10 mL) seasoned salt
1 teaspoon (5 mL) minced garlic
1 cup (236 mL) soft breadcrumbs
1 cup (236 mL) shredded sharp cheddar cheese
Butter, for garnish

1. Make sure the grill is clean and generously sprayed with nonstick grilling spray. Preheat the barbecue to medium high (350°F [180°C] to 400°F [200°C]).

2. With a sharp knife, trim the excess fat from the steak and set the steak aside.

3. In small bowl, mix together ¼ cup butter, the olive oil, the savory, the black pepper, the salt, and the garlic until well blended. Brush both sides of the steak with this mixture.

4. In a wide, flat pan or bowl, combine the breadcrumbs and cheese and stir to mix well. Press both sides of the steaks into the breadcrumb-cheese mixture to coat.

5. Place the steak in a brown paper bag. Fold the end over twice and staple or paperclip the bag shut.

6. Place the bag on a rimmed baking sheet and cook the steak for 30 minutes. Increase the temperature to 425°F (220°C) by adding more lit coals or turning up the gas, and cook for 15 minutes longer.

7. Remove the steak from the bag. Add a pat of butter to each steak, cover with foil, and let rest for 4 to 5 minutes.

8. With a sharp knife, carve the steak into thin slices across the grain and serve.

Fabiano's Italian-Style Short Ribs
Yield: 4–6 servings

You can also cook this dish with full-sized beef ribs or with ribs cut in the South American "asado" style, in 1-inch (2.5-cm) pieces across the bones the width of the beef rack. This recipe comes from Fabiano Domenico from Preci, Italy.

3½–4 pounds (1.6–1.8 kg) beef short ribs, cut into serving pieces
1 cup (236 mL) ketchup
½ cup (118 mL) Italian salad dressing
½ cup (118 mL) chopped onion
¼ cup (59 mL) firmly packed brown sugar
2 tablespoons (30 mL) Worcestershire sauce
1 tablespoon (15 mL) prepared mustard
Red leaf lettuce, for serving
Parsley, for garnish
Orange slices, for garnish

1. Preheat the barbecue to medium high (250°F [120°C] to 300°F [150°C]).

2. Place the ribs in a Dutch oven, add water to cover, cover tightly, and cook on a stovetop or barbecue side burner over medium heat for 1½ to 2 hours.

3. While the ribs are cooking, combine the ketchup, salad dressing, onion, brown sugar, Worcestershire sauce, and mustard in a medium bowl and stir well. Set aside.

4. Drain the fat from the ribs and return the ribs to the Dutch oven. Pour the barbecue sauce over the ribs, cover tightly, and cook in the barbecue grill for 50 to 60 minutes, basting and turning the ribs frequently.

5. Remove the cover during last 20 minutes to reduce and thicken the sauce.

6. Transfer the ribs to a large platter. Skim the fat from the sauce and pour the sauce over the ribs.

7. Serve on red leaf lettuce, garnished with parsley sprigs and orange slices.

Old Fashioned Beef Short Ribs

Yield: 4–6 servings

Instead of beef ribs, you could use buffalo short ribs in this recipe. They are very flavorful and contain less cholesterol, fat, and saturated fat compared with beef, pork, chicken, and even most fish.

2 tablespoons (30 mL) vegetable oil
3 pounds (1.3 kg) beef short ribs
3 tablespoons (45 mL) all-purpose flour
2 cups (473 mL) beef broth
1 cup (236 mL) dried apricots
3 tablespoons (45 mL) brown sugar
1 tablespoon (15 mL) cider vinegar
½ teaspoon (2.5 mL) salt
¼ teaspoon (1.25 mL) ground cinnamon
¼ teaspoon (1.25 mL) ground cloves
¼ teaspoon (1.25 mL) ground allspice

1. Preheat the barbecue to medium high (350°F [180°C] to 400°F [200°C]).

2. In a cast-iron skillet or Dutch oven on a side burner or stovetop burner, heat the oil. Dust the ribs with the flour and brown them well in the oil.

3. Drain off the excess fat. Add the remaining ingredients to the ribs and bring everything to a boil.

4. Place the skillet in the center of the grill, cover, and let the ribs bake for 2½ hours, turning and basting occasionally until they are done.

5. Using long barbecue tongs, remove the ribs and place them on a serving dish. Cover and set aside.

6. Skim the fat from the surface of the sauce, reheat it, and pour over the ribs on the platter.

Mustard-Butter Steaks

Yield: 2–4 servings

For a zippier butter mixture, use Dijon-style or hot mustard, or add a teaspoon of bottled horseradish to ignite your taste buds.

1 stick butter, softened, divided
2 (¾-inch [1.5-cm] thick) beef ribeye steaks
1½ teaspoons (7.5 mL) lemon juice
1½ teaspoons (7.5 mL) prepared mustard

1. Preheat the barbecue to medium high (350°F [180°C] to 400°F [200°C]).

2. Place a 10-inch (25-cm) cast-iron skillet on the barbecue grill. Add 3 tablespoons (45 mL) of the butter. When the butter has melted, add the steaks to the pan and cook them until browned on both sides, about 8 minutes for rare, or until they reach your desired doneness.

3. In small bowl, combine the remaining butter, the lemon juice, and the mustard and mix well. When the steaks are done, top them with mustard-butter, cover with foil and let rest for 5 to 8 minutes.

Santa Maria Tri-Tip
Yield: 8–10 servings

This is by far the most popular cut of meat barbecued in California's Central coast area, from Santa Barbara north to San Louis Obispo, and in parts of Oregon and Washington. Unfortunately, the rest of the country ignores the bottom part of the sirloin, often using it for sirloin tips, a poor second choice to the juicy, flavorful tri-tip roast itself.

1 (4–5 lb. [2.2–2.7 kg]) beef tri-tip roast
1 cup (236 mL) teriyaki sauce
1 cup (236 mL) Chianti
1 large onion, peeled and chopped
¼ cup (59 mL) melted clarified butter
¼ cup (59 mL) olive oil
¼ cup (59 mL) A1 steak sauce
3 tablespoons (45 mL) minced garlic
Several long rosemary branches, tied at one end to form a basting brush

1. Put the roast in a resealable plastic bag. In a large bowl, combine the teriyaki sauce, Chianti, onion, butter, olive oil, steak sauce, and garlic and stir well. Pour the mixture into the bag over the roast and marinate overnight in the refrigerator.

2. Make sure the grill is clean and generously sprayed with nonstick grilling spray. Preheat the barbecue to medium high (400°F [200°C] to 450°F [240°C]) for direct and indirect heating.

3. Remove the meat from the marinade and set it aside. Pour the reserved marinade into a small saucepan and bring it to a boil. Boil for at least 10 minutes so it will be safe to use as a brush-on marinade, then let it cool.

4. Place the tri-tip over direct heat for 5 minutes a side, then transfer it to an unheated side of the barbecue and cook for 1 to 1½ hours, until the meat is evenly browned and has an internal temperature of 130°F (54°C) to 135°F (57°C). Use the rosemary brushes to baste the meat once every half hour as it cooks, leaving the brush standing in the marinade between basting sessions.

5. Seal the meat in foil for 15 to 20 minutes. The meat's internal temperature should reach 145°F (63°C; medium-rare) in that time. Slice thinly and serve on toasted sourdough bread or crusty rolls. Bring any remaining marinade to the table to pour over the meat.

Citrus-Grilled Steak

Yield: 2 servings

An unusual but delicious combination of orange juice and meat makes a tangy, sweet steak sauce that goes well with the charred strip steaks.

1 cup (236 mL) frozen orange juice concentrate, thawed
½ cup (118 mL) A1 Steak sauce
¼ cup (59 mL) dry sherry
Juice of 1 lemon
1 clove garlic, peeled and minced
2 (8-ounce [227-g]) beef strip steaks, about 1 inch (2.5 cm) thick

1. In a small bowl, combine the orange juice concentrate, steak sauce, sherry, lemon juice, and garlic. Place the steaks in a flat glass baking dish and pour in half of the orange juice mixture. Cover and refrigerate for 1 hour, turning the meat occasionally.

2. Make sure the grill is clean and generously sprayed with nonstick grilling spray. Preheat the barbecue to medium high (350°F [180°C] to 400°F [200°C]).

3. In a small saucepan over medium heat, cook the remaining orange juice mixture until it is reduced by half. Turn off the burner and keep the sauce warm.

4. Remove the steaks from the marinade and grill them over direct heat for 4 minutes on each side until they get a light char, or until done to your liking, turning once.

5. Serve the steaks with the warm orange sauce on the side.

Peppercorn Beef Kebabs

Yield: 4 servings

Try sprinkling the meat with brown sugar just before it goes on the grill. The sugar quickly caramelizes, giving the kebabs a sweet, charred flavor.

1 (1-pound [454-g]) beef sirloin steak, cut 1 inch (2.5 cm) thick
1 teaspoon (5 mL) black peppercorns, freshly cracked
½ teaspoon (2.5 mL) salt
½ teaspoon (2.5 mL) paprika
1 clove garlic, peeled and mashed
1 medium onion, peeled and cut into 12 wedges

1. Make sure the grill is clean and generously sprayed with nonstick grilling spray. Preheat the barbecue to medium high (450°F [240°C] to 475°F [250°C]).

2. With a sharp knife, cut the steak into 1-inch (2.5-cm) pieces, place the pieces in a shallow dish, and set aside.

3. In a small bowl, mix together the peppercorns, salt, paprika, and garlic. Pour this mixture over the beef and toss to coat. Let marinade for 30 minutes to 1 hour, covered, at room temperature.

4. Thread an equal number of beef pieces onto each of 4 (12-inch [30-cm]) skewers, separated by onion wedges. Place the kebabs on the grill and cook for 8 to 10 minutes, turning often, for rare to medium-rare.

5. Remove the kebabs from grill and serve one per person.

Smokin' Sirloins
Yield: 4 servings

The reason we suggest letting steaks rest after cooking is the physics of cooking: Fire drives moisture to the top surface of steaks and roasts, and when you turn the meat over, the process repeats. If you serve meat right away, only the top portion is juicy. When you let meat rest, the juices recirculate throughout the meat and your whole steak is juicy.

4 (2-inch [5-cm] thick) beef top sirloin or ribeye steaks
1 tablespoon (15 mL) garlic salt
½ teaspoon (2.5 mL) freshly ground black pepper, plus more, to taste
1 (6-ounce [168-g]) can tomato paste
¾ cup (177 mL) Worcestershire sauce
¼ cup (60 mL) butter
Juice of 2 lemons
¼ teaspoon (1.25 mL) garlic powder
Olive oil, for brushing

1. Make sure the grill is clean and generously sprayed with nonstick grilling spray. Preheat the barbecue to medium high (450°F [240°C] to 500°F [260°C]) for direct and indirect cooking.

2. Soak 1 to 2 pounds (454 to 908 g) hickory chips in water.

3. Lightly season the steaks with garlic salt and a few healthy grinds of pepper on both sides. Cover and set aside.

4. In a small saucepan, combine the tomato paste, Worcestershire sauce, butter, lemon juice, garlic powder, and ½ teaspoon (2.5 mL) pepper and bring to a boil. Lower the heat and simmer for 20 minutes, stirring several times.

5. Lightly brush olive oil on the steaks and place them on the grill to quickly sear the meat on both sides, about 1 minute per side, then remove the steaks from the grill.

6. Place the well-drained hickory chips in an aluminum foil packet and poke holes in the top only. Place the foil directly on the coals or on a gas flame and return the steaks to the unheated side of the grill. Baste the steaks with the sauce, cover, and close all vents. Turn the steaks over every 5 minutes and baste; cooking approximately 15 to 20 minutes for medium-rare and 20 to 25 for medium-rare to medium.

7. When the steaks reach your preferred doneness remove the cover of the bbq and baste the meat one more time. Serve the steaks on very hot plates.

Peppercorn Rib Eyes
Yield: 4–6 servings

You can buy cracked peppercorns or, better yet, crack your own. Put green, red, white and black peppercorns in a dish towel on a marble or stone countertop and lightly hit with a hammer to just crack them, not pulverize them.

½ cup unsalted butter, at room temperature
¼ cup (60 mL) crumbled blue cheese
½ teaspoon (2.5 mL) finely minced shallots
2 teaspoons (10 mL) brandy
1 sprinkle sea salt
4 (10–12 ounce [280–336 g]) beef ribeye steaks
½ cup (118 mL) cracked black, red, white, and green peppercorns
1 tablespoon (15 mL) coarse French sea salt
3 tablespoons (45 mL) extra virgin olive oil

1. In a small bowl, mash together the warm butter, crumbled blue cheese, shallots, and brandy. Lightly season with salt, stir, and set aside.

2. Make sure the grill is clean and generously sprayed with nonstick grilling spray. Preheat the barbecue to medium high (350°F [180°C] to 400°F [200°C]).

3. Rub the peppercorns into both sides of each steak, pressing them into the meat with your hands. Sprinkle with the salt.

4. Place steaks on the very hot grill and cook until well browned on one side, 2½ minutes. Turn the steaks and place them on the cooler side of grill for an additional 2½ minutes.

5. Transfer the steaks from the grill to an oiled cast-iron skillet on the unheated side of the grill. Cook for an additional 6 to 7 minutes for rare (120°F [49°C] on an instant-read thermometer); 8 to 9 minutes for medium-rare (125°F [52°C]); or 9 to 10 minutes for medium (130°F [54°C]), remembering the temperature will rise between 5° to 15°F (3° to 9°C) while resting, if covered.

6. Remove the steaks from the pan and place them on a heated platter. Top each cooked steak with a generous 1 tablespoon (15 mL) mound of the flavored butter, cover with foil, and let the meat rest for 5 to 10 minutes.

Smoked Beef Brisket

Yield: 8–10 servings

Some say cooking brisket is like cooking a snow tire, but with this method, the results will be mouthwateringly moist, even though the outside of the brisket may look like a meteorite or a charred hunk of rubber.

3 tablespoons (45 mL) brown sugar
2 tablespoons (30 mL) cayenne pepper
1 tablespoon (15 mL) paprika
1 tablespoon (15 mL) salt
1 tablespoon (15 mL) onion powder
1 tablespoon (15 mL) freshly ground black pepper
2 teaspoons (10 mL) granulated garlic
1 teaspoon (5 mL) ground cumin
¼ cup (59 mL) prepared yellow mustard
2 tablespoons (30 mL) Worcestershire sauce
1 teaspoon (5 mL) hot sauce of your choice
1 (8–10 pound [3.6–4.4 kg]) beef brisket

1. Preheat the smoker to 220°F (105°C) and add your favorite wood chips.

2. In a small bowl, combine the brown sugar, cayenne pepper, paprika, salt, onion powder, black pepper, garlic, and cumin and set aside.

3. In another bowl, mix together the yellow mustard, Worcestershire sauce, and hot sauce. Spread this mixture all over the brisket, massaging it into the meat.

4. Sprinkle the dry rub onto the mustard base and, again, massage it into the meat.

5. Place the brisket in the smoker, fat cap on top, and cook for 10 hours. Keep the smoker temperature at about 220°F (105°C) at all times. You only need the wood chips and the smoke they produce for about 30 minutes; after that the meat can't absorb any more smoke flavor.

6. To increase tenderness, take the brisket out of the smoker, wrap it in several layers of clear plastic wrap and then in aluminum foil, and return it to the smoker, and smoke it at 180° to 200°F (80 to 95°C) for 2 more hours.

7. Take the brisket out of the smoker and allow it to sit for 20 minutes, then unwrap the foil and plastic wrap and present it at the table. Using a sharp knife, slice the meat across the grain.

Phyllo Phillet (aka Phyllo Dough–Wrapped Filet Mignon)
Yield: 8 servings

Frozen phyllo dough should be brought to room temperature slowly before using, then carefully unfolded and kept covered with a damp cloth until you are ready to brush each sheet with butter.

1 (3-pound [1.3-kg]) beef filet mignon, trimmed
1 teaspoon (5 mL) kosher salt
2 tablespoons (30 mL) butter
1 tablespoon (15 mL) olive oil
1 teaspoon (5 mL) balsamic vinegar
8 ounces (227 g) mushrooms, coarsely chopped
4 large shallots, peeled and chopped
1 (1-pound) package phyllo pastry
½ cup (1187 mL) melted butter
Paprika, for garnish

1. Make sure the grill is clean and generously sprayed with nonstick grilling spray. Preheat the barbecue to medium high (350°F [180°C] to 400°F [200°C]).

2. Grease or spray a baking sheet generously with cooking spray.

3. Sprinkle the filet with the salt. In a large cast-iron skillet over high heat, combine the butter, olive oil, and balsamic vinegar. Add the filet and sear on all sides. Remove the filet from the pan, cover it with foil, and set aside.

4. Add the mushrooms and shallots to the skillet and sauté them in the steak juices for 2 to 3 minutes, until they soften and begin to brown. Set aside.

5. On a cutting board or other flat surface, stack 14 sheets of phyllo on top of one another, brushing each layer with melted butter as you stack.

6. Spread the mushroom mixture in the center of the stack of phyllo and then place the filet on top of the mushrooms. Fold the phyllo dough carefully around the beef. Seal all the edges with additional sheets of pastry and brush the seams with butter. (You may have extra sheets left over.)

7. Place the dough-encased filet meat side down carefully onto the prepared baking sheet. Cook the filet in the barbecue for 45 minutes, or until the pastry is golden and flaky.

8. Remove the wrapped steak from the pan and let it rest for 5 minutes, covered. Sprinkle the top of the pastry with paprika, then cut into portions to serve.

Planked Porterhouse
Yield: 4 servings

There are several kinds of planks made for barbecuing on the grill, but I prefer oak planks for steaks, cedar planks for salmon and pork, and alder planks for halibut and other fish. If you can't find them at your local supermarket, www.tailgating-planks.com carries several varieties, including a new "beer-butt chicken" plank.

1 (2-inch [5-cm] thick) beef porterhouse steak
Olive oil, as needed
Seasoned salt, to taste
Freshly ground black pepper, to taste
4 cups (0.95 L) garlic mashed potatoes
½ cup (118 mL) melted butter, divided
¼ cup (59 mL) minced fresh parsley

1. Soak an oak plank overnight in water, weighted down with cans of vegetables or a pitcher filled with water so the wood is completely submerged under the water.

2. Preheat the barbecue to medium high (450°F [240°C] to 500°F [260°C]).

3. With a sharp knife, cut the excess fat from the steak and score any edge fat you leave on the meat. Set aside at room temperature until you are ready to grill the steak.

4. Remove the plank from the water, briefly wipe the surface, and brush it with olive oil. Place the steak on the plank, season it with the salt and pepper, and put the plank in the center of the grill. Keep a spray bottle of water handy; if the plank begins to ignite around the edges, merely spray the flames down with the water and continue cooking.

5. After 10 minutes, open the barbecue and carefully spoon the mashed potatoes around the steak, making small indentations all around the top of the potatoes. Drizzle the potatoes with half of the melted butter.

6. Close the lid and continue cooking the steak for 5 to 7 minutes, again watching the oak plank for flare-ups, spray bottle in hand.

7. When the steak is cooked to your desired doneness (this is not a good method for medium or well-done meat), remove the plank and steak from the barbecue, drizzle the potatoes with the remaining butter, sprinkle with parsley, and serve at once on a large platter.

Apple Cider–Marinated Sirloin Tip
Yield: 8–10 servings

You can, of course, make your own concentrated beef stock, boiling bones, vegetables, and beef trimmings for hours, then reducing the liquid to concentrate it. Or you can purchase any number of concentrated beef stock products online or at your local grocery store. I've used and like Savory Choice, Kikkoman Soup Base, and especially the More Than Gourmet Pro Reduced Veal and Beef Stock, all of which are available online.

1 (5–pound [2.3-kg]) beef sirloin tip roast
1½ cups (354 mL) apple cider
¼ cup (59 mL) vegetable oil
3 tablespoons (45 mL) apple cider vinegar
1 tablespoon (15 mL) balsamic vinegar
1 tablespoon (15 mL) chopped green onion, green and white parts
2 cloves garlic, peeled and crushed
2 bay leaves
½ teaspoon (2.5 mL) kosher salt
¼ teaspoon (1.25 mL) ground thyme
Freshly ground black pepper, to taste
5 slices bacon
1 teaspoon (5 mL) instant beef bouillon
1 cup (236 mL) boiling water
2 tablespoons (30 mL) all-purpose flour
1 tablespoon (15 mL) milk

1. Place the beef in a 2-gallon (7.6-L) resealable plastic bag and set aside.

2. In a large bowl, combine the cider, oil, vinegars, onion, garlic, bay leaf, salt, thyme, and pepper and mix well. Pour this mixture over the beef in the plastic bag and seal it shut. Place the bag a shallow dish (just in case the bag leaks) and refrigerate for at least 12 hours.

3. Preheat the barbecue to medium high (350°F [180°C] to 400°F [200°C]).

4. Fry the bacon in a Dutch oven or roasting pan until crisp, then remove and drain the bacon. Remove the beef from the marinade and brown the meat in the remaining bacon fat in the Dutch oven over medium heat for about 20 minutes.

5. Dissolve the beef bouillon in the boiling water, then pour it and the reserved marinade into the Dutch oven. Add the crumbled bacon, cover, and cook in the barbecue for 2½ hours, or until an instant-read meat thermometer reads 160°F (71°C).

6. Place the beef roast on a warm platter, cover, and let stand for 10 to 15 minutes before slicing.

7. While the meat is resting, whisk together the flour and milk, then add it to the liquid in the Dutch oven, which you've returned to the grill or a side burner. Stir with a whisk until the liquid thickens, then pour the gravy into a pitcher and put it on the table.

8. Slice and serve the sirloin tip roast.

Roquefort Ribeyes

Yield: 4–6 servings

You can make this recipe with several kinds of steak, but nothing beats a well-marbled, bone-in ribeye steak for tenderness, juiciness, and intense beef flavor that lasts until the last bite.

4 or 6 (8–10 ounce [224–280 g]) bone-in beef ribeye steaks, 1–1¼ inches (3 cm) thick
1 tablespoon (15 mL) extra virgin olive oil
Kosher salt, to taste
Freshly ground black pepper, to taste
½ cup unsalted butter, at room temperature
4–6 tablespoons (60–90 mL) crumbled Roquefort cheese
2 teaspoons (10 mL) brandy
½ teaspoon (2.5 mL) finely minced shallots

1. Make sure the grill is clean and generously sprayed with nonstick grilling spray. Preheat the barbecue to medium high (350°F [180°C] to 400°F [200°C]).

2. Rub olive oil onto both sides of steak, generously sprinkle each side of each steak with salt and pepper, and set aside.

3. Place the steaks on the grill and cook for 2½ minutes per side. Turn the steaks and place them on the cooler side of grill for 5 to 6 minutes for rare (120°F [49°C] on an instant-read thermometer), 7 to 8 minutes for medium-rare (130°F [54°C]); or 8 to 9 minutes for medium (135 to 140°F [57 to 63°C]).

4. While the steaks are cooking, mash together the butter, crumbled Roquefort cheese, brandy, and shallots. Season with salt and pepper.

5. Remove the steaks from the pan and place them on a heated platter. Top each cooked steak with a generous portion of the Roquefort-brandy butter, cover the steaks with foil, and let the meat rest for 5 minutes.

6. Serve with green salad and large baked potatoes.

Battered Beef

Yield: 4–6 servings

While the beef is cooking, the batter rises up and surrounds the meat, sort of like a shepherd's pie. You could also substitute 1 pound (454 g) lamb and 1 pound (454 g) beef for a more rustic pie.

2 cups cooked beef cut in 1-inch (2.5-cm) cubes
1 cup (236 mL) cooked carrots cut in chunks
1 cup (236 mL) cooked potatoes cut in chunks
½ cup (118 mL) sautéed onions
½ cup (118 mL) chopped celery
1 cup (236 mL) beef gravy
2 tablespoons (30 mL) butter
1½ cups (354 mL) milk
1 cup (236 mL) grated extra-sharp cheddar cheese
½ cup (118 mL) chopped fresh parsley
1½ cups (354 mL) all-purpose flour
2 teaspoons (10 mL) baking powder
1 tablespoon (15 mL) sugar
1 teaspoon (5 mL) salt
1 teaspoon (5 mL) garlic powder
Paprika, for garnish

1. Preheat the barbecue to medium high (350°F [180°C] to 400°F [200°C]).

2. Grease an 8-inch (20-cm) baking dish or coat with nonstick spray.

3. In a large bowl, combine the beef, carrots, potatoes, onions, and celery, then stir in the gravy. Set aside.

4. Melt the butter in a microwave oven. In a mixing bowl, combine the melted butter with the milk, cheddar cheese, and parsley. Stir in the flour, sugar, baking powder, salt, and garlic powder. Stir until blended and then pour into the prepared baking dish.

5. Spoon the beef and vegetables on top of the batter, but do not stir.

6. Bake in the barbecue for 60 minutes.

7. Remove from the barbecue, let cool slightly, sprinkle with paprika, and serve.

Beef and Brie Skillet Pie

Yield: 4–6 servings

I invented this meal while driving an RV 36,000 miles around the country promoting my Barbecue America *TV series with my wife, Kate. We used what we had in the refrigerator and came up with a unique way to make a savory beef pie.*

1 pound (454 g) ground beef
1 cup (236 mL) smoky barbecue sauce of your choice
5 strips cooked bacon, crumbled
½ cup (118 mL) minced onions
½ cup (118 mL) cooked minced carrots
½ teaspoon (59 mL) dried oregano
½ teaspoon (59 mL) dried thyme
1 (8-ounce [227-g]) can refrigerated crescent rolls
1 (8-ounce [227-g]) wheel Brie cheese, sliced

1. Make sure the grill is clean and generously sprayed with nonstick grilling spray. Preheat the barbecue to medium high (350°F [180°C] to 400°F [200°C]).

2. In a cast-iron skillet, brown the ground beef. Drain off the grease, then add the barbecue sauce, bacon, onions, carrots, oregano, and thyme and stir to mix well. Cool the pan to room temperature by placing it in the refrigerator for 12 to 15 minutes.

3. Completely cover the cooled meat with slices of the Brie cheese.

4. Roll out the crescent roll dough into a 13 × 15-inch (32.5 × 37.5-cm) rectangle and lay it over the top of the cast-iron skillet, folding the edges underneath. Using a sharp knife, cut 3 vents in the pastry to let steam escape.

5. Bake in the barbecue for 20 to 25 minutes or until the crescent roll dough is nicely browned. Let cool for 3 to 4 minutes.

6. With a sharp knife and a pie spatula, remove slices of the pie and serve.

Honey-Mustard Grilled Steaks

Yield: 4 servings

The pat of butter melted on each steak seems excessive, but several very expensive steak restaurants use this trick, and I promise it will make people rave about your steaks.

4 (1½-inch [3.5-cm]) (thick) beef ribeye (or sirloin) steaks
1 cup (236 mL) prepared yellow mustard
2 tablespoons (30 mL) honey
2 tablespoons (30 mL) water
1½ tablespoons (22.5 mL) cider vinegar
1 tablespoon (15 mL) dried rosemary leaves, crushed
1 tablespoon (15 mL) dried thyme, crushed
1½ teaspoons (7.5 mL) Worcestershire sauce
1 tablespoon (15 mL) chopped fresh parsley
½ teaspoon (2.5) Frank's Red Hot sauce
¼ teaspoon (1.25 mL) coarsely ground black pepper
4 pats butter

1. Make sure the grill is clean and generously sprayed with nonstick spray. Preheat the barbecue to medium high (350°F [180°C] to 400°F [200°C]).

2. Put the steaks in a flat baking dish. In a small bowl, mix together the mustard, honey, water, vinegar, rosemary, thyme, Worcestershire sauce, hot sauce, parsley, and black pepper and pour it over the steaks. Marinate for 1 to 2 hours in the refrigerator, poking the steaks with a fork and turning them over several times so the marinade gets into the center of the steaks.

3. Either discard the marinade or put it in a saucepan and boil it while steaks are warming to use it as a baste.

4. Wipe off the excess marinade and let the steaks come to room temperature, then cook them on a hot grill for 4 to 5 minutes per side for medium-rare. Brush the boiled marinade, if using, on the steaks near the end of the cooking time on each side.

5. Remove the steaks from the grill and place a small pat of butter on top of each steak. Cover with aluminum foil and let the steaks rest for 5 minutes, then serve.

Salisbury Steaks

Yield: 6 servings

This recipe recreates a very popular but almost-forgotten cooking method from the 1950s and '60s that my mother loved. I think you will like it as well.

2 pounds (908 g) lean ground beef
2 large eggs, slightly beaten
1 teaspoon (5 mL) salt
¼ teaspoon (1.25 mL) freshly ground black pepper
⅓ cup (79 mL) fine fresh breadcrumbs
3 tablespoons (45 mL) butter or margarine, divided
1½ cups (354 mL) thinly sliced fresh mushrooms
1⅓ cups (315 mL) beef broth
2 tablespoons (30 mL) all-purpose flour

1. Preheat the barbecue to medium high (350°F [180°C] to 400°F [200°C]).

2. In a large bowl, mix together well the beef, eggs, salt, and pepper. Using your hands, shape the meat into 6 oval hamburger steaks about ½ inch (1 cm) thick and 5 inches (12.5 cm) long.

3. Put the breadcrumbs into a wide, flat pan and press the hamburger steaks into the crumbs to get a good coating on both sides. Cover and chill the steaks in the refrigerator.

4. In a cast-iron skillet on the grill, melt 2 tablespoons (30 mL) of the butter, then add the mushrooms and sauté, stirring occasionally, for 3 to 4 minutes or until the mushrooms are nicely browned and soft.

5. In another skillet, melt the remaining butter. Add the steaks and bake them in the barbecue for 5 to 6 minutes, until the steaks are browned and charred crisp on top, then remove them from the grill. Put the steaks on a plate, cover, and keep warm.

6. Add the beef broth to the pan drippings, stirring to scrape up the browned bits left behind. Mix the flour with 2 to 3 tablespoons (30 to 45 mL) water, stir to a smooth paste, and add it to the broth in the skillet. Bring to a boil and cook, stirring, until the gravy is smooth and thickened.

7. Stir in the mushrooms, then add the steaks and simmer them in the gravy to heat through.

8. Serve each person a steak and several tablespoons of gravy.

Chef Mike's Teriyaki Tidbits
Yield: 6–8 servings

Cut from the pointed (tail) end of the tenderloin, these tasty chunks of meat are tender and delicious and soak up this flavorful marinade like a sponge. Beaches Restaurants in Vancouver, Wa., serves these both as appetizers and, for those who ask, as an entrée with garlic mashed potatoes. I always ask. This recipe makes 1½ gallons (5.7 L) of sauce, a lot to be sure, but you can use it on just about anything you cook, and it is worth the trouble to make up a large batch like this. This is probably the best teriyaki sauce I've tasted anywhere in the world! No kidding! This recipe comes from Chef Mike Barret from Camas, Wash.

Kal-bi Sauce
3¾ pounds (1.7 kg) sugar
8 cups (1.9 L) low-sodium soy sauce
1¼ pounds (568 g) minced garlic
1 cup (236 mL) minced green onion
3 tablespoons (45 mL) sesame seeds
1¼ tablespoons (19 mL) coarsely ground black pepper
1 tablespoon plus (15 mL) ¼ teaspoon (1.25 mL) crushed red pepper flakes
1 tablespoon (15 mL) freshly grated ginger
1 cup (236 mL) canola oil
1 cup (236 mL) sesame oil

Tenderloin
2⅓ pounds (1 kg) tenderloin tips, cut into ¾–1 inch (1.5–2.5 cm) pieces
1 cup (236 mL) Kal-bi sauce

Garnish
2 teaspoons (3.75–5 mL) shredded green onion, green part only
2 teaspoons (3.75–5 mL) sesame seeds

1. In a large pot over medium high heat, combine the sugar, soy sauce, garlic, green onion, sesame seeds, black pepper, red pepper flakes, and ginger, and cook, stirring until the sugar has completely dissolved. Take the pot off the heat and add the canola and sesame oils. Stir well, cover, and set aside, or divide into several containers you can seal.

2. Place the tenderloin tips in a 1- to 2-gallon (3.8- to 7.6-L) resealable plastic bag. Pour 1 cup (236 mL) of the Kal-bi sauce into the bag, seal, and shake the bag to distribute the marinade. Refrigerate overnight or as long as 16 hours.

3. Remove the meat from the marinade; pour the marinade into a measuring cup, and add enough fresh sauce to make 1 full cup (236 mL). Pour the sauce into a saucepan and boil for 10 minutes while the meat comes to room temperature.

4. Preheat the barbecue to medium high (400°F [200°C] to 450°F [240°C]).

5. In a large, oiled cast-iron skillet on the grill, sauté the meat. Add the boiled Kal-bi sauce and cook until the largest piece of meat is medium-rare and the sauce is reduced by one-fourth, about 5 minutes. Remove the skillet from the grill, garnish the meat with the shredded onion and sesame seeds, and serve with garlic mashed potatoes and/or thick slices of sourdough bread to soak up the sauce.

Counter Kappo Teriyaki Kebabs
Yield: 4–6 servings

Popular in Japan, eateries called Counter Kappo—meaning "cut and grill"—feature sit-down counters like those in American diners. This recipe was inspired by a day spent with Chef Shin-Ichiro Takagi in Kanazawa City, Ishikawa Prefecture, one of the richest experiences in my most recent visit to Japan.

1 pound (454 g) beef flank steak
½ cup (118 mL) teriyaki sauce
¼ cup (59 mL) beef broth
¼ cup (59 mL) vegetable oil
1 teaspoon (5 mL) minced fresh ginger
12 green onions, white parts only, cut into 2-inch (5-cm) long pieces
2 medium red bell peppers, cut into 1½-inch (3.5-cm) squares

1. Soak 12 to 15 bamboo skewers in water for 2 hours.

2. Freeze the beef for 1 hour.

3. In a medium bowl, combine the teriyaki sauce, beef broth, oil, and ginger and stir to combine.

4. Remove the beef from freezer and, using a sharp knife, cut it across the grain into ⅛-inch (0.25-cm) thick slices. Place the beef strips in a 1- to 2-gallon (3.8- to 7.6-L) resealable plastic bag, pour in the marinade, and refrigerate for 1 to 2 hours.

5. Make sure the grill is clean and generously sprayed with nonstick spray. Preheat the barbecue to medium high (350°F [180°C] to 400°F [200°C]).

6. Working with one strip of marinated beef at a time, roll the green onions up in slices of beef and skewer them on the bamboo skewers, alternating with pieces of red pepper.

7. Pour the remaining marinade into a saucepan and boil for 10 minutes.

8. Using a pastry brush, lightly coat each kebab with the marinade, placing the kebabs directly on the grill to cook for 2 to 3 minutes per side, turning once.

9. Remove the kebabs and place one on a plate of grilled vegetables and rice for each person.

Country-Fried Coffee Steaks
Yield: 6 servings

This method of cooking steaks has always been very popular in the South and usually involves coating and pan-frying. Coffee-flavored gravy turns this into a traditional redeyed meal.

3 tablespoons (45 mL) heavy cream
2 egg whites
1 cup (236 mL) very strong black coffee
½ cup (118 mL) beef broth
1 teaspoon (5 mL) used coffee grounds
⅓ cup (79 mL) plus 2 tablespoons (30 mL) all-purpose flour, divided
1 teaspoon (5 mL) dried oregano
½ teaspoon (5 mL) granulated garlic
½ teaspoon (5 mL) kosher salt
¼ teaspoon (1.25 mL) freshly ground black pepper
6 (5–7 ounce [140–196 g]) cube steaks
2 tablespoons (30 mL) bacon grease
1 tablespoon (15 mL) butter
2 tablespoons (30 mL) minced green onion, green part only
1 teaspoon (5 mL) brown sugar

1. Preheat the barbecue to medium high (350°F [180°C] to 400°F [200°C]).

2. In a medium bowl, whisk together the cream and egg whites. Set aside.

3. In a small bowl, combine the coffee, beef broth, and grounds. Set aside.

4. In a wide, flat baking dish, combine ⅓ cup (79 mL) of the flour with the oregano, garlic, salt, and pepper and stir to fully incorporate. Dip each steak into the egg mixture, then into the flour mixture, coating both sides well, and shake off excess. Repeat for all the steaks.

5. In a large cast-iron skillet placed directly on the grill or on a lit side burner, heat the bacon grease until a drop of water dropped in it sizzles. Using long barbecue tongs, add the steaks, 1 or 2 at a time, and cook for 3 minutes on each side or until nicely browned. Transfer the steaks to a heated platter, cover with aluminum foil, and keep warm.

6. When all steaks have been cooked, stir the remaining flour and butter into the pan drippings. Pour in the coffee-broth, green onion, and brown sugar, whisk together, and bring the gravy to a boil.

7. Remove the foil covering the steaks and spoon the hot gravy over the meat. Serve immediately.

Greek BBQ Kasseri Beef

Yield: 6–8 servings

If you can't find Greek Kasseri cheese, you can substitute provolone, mozzarella or kaser cheese instead, although nothing is quite like the salty, tangy sheep's milk flavor of the Kasseri.

2 large eggs, lightly beaten
¼ cup (60 mL) olive oil
⅔ cup (158 mL) seasoned dry breadcrumbs
2 pounds (908 g) rare roast beef, thinly sliced
1⅓ cups (315 mL) beef broth
1 cup (236 mL) tomato paste
2 teaspoons (10 mL) dried oregano
2 cloves garlic, peeled and minced
2 cups (473 mL) grated Greek Kasseri cheese

1. Preheat the barbecue to medium high (420°F [215°C] to 475°F [250°C]).

2. Spray a baking sheet with a lip or a large roasting pan with nonstick cooking spray.

3. In a wide, flat baking pan, whisk the eggs and oil together. Set aside.

4. Pour the breadcrumbs into another wide, flat pan and set aside.

5. Dip the roast beef slices into the egg, then into the breadcrumbs, coating both sides. Shake off the excess and put the breaded slices on the prepared baking sheet or roasting pan.

6. Place the pan in the center of the barbecue and cook for 8 to 10 minutes, until the slices are golden and nicely crisped. While the meat is cooking, in a small bowl combine the broth, tomato paste, oregano, and garlic and stir to mix. Set aside.

7. When the meat is ready, open the barbecue and spoon the sauce over the slices, then sprinkle on the cheese. Cook until the cheese bubbles, about 4 to 5 minutes.

8. With a spatula, transfer the slices from the pan to a platter or individual plates and serve.

Beer Brisket Beef Buns

Yield: 4–6 servings

If you don't want the corned variety of beef brisket, you can buy a whole brisket point cut, usually about 8 to 10 pounds (3.6 to 4.4 kg) and cut it into smaller pieces to use in this recipe and others.

3 pounds (1.3 kg) corned beef brisket
1–2 large Bermuda onions, peeled and thinly sliced
1 (12-ounce [336-mL]) can beer
¾ cup (177 mL) ketchup
¼ cup (59 mL) bottled chili sauce
8 Kaiser rolls or large onion hamburger rolls

1. Make sure the grill is clean and generously sprayed with nonstick grilling spray. Preheat the barbecue to medium high (350°F [180°C] to 400°F [200°C]).

2. Place the corned beef on the grill and cook for 1 hour, turning several times.

3. Transfer the beef from the grill to a roasting pan and top with the onion slices. In a bowl, mix together the beer, ketchup, and chili sauce. Pour this mixture over the beef and onions.

4. Return the beef to the barbecue and bake, uncovered, for about 2 hours, spooning the sauce over the beef several times.

5. Split the rolls and grill them face down until they are nicely browned. Remove them from the grill and top them with slices of the beef and onions.

Smoked Sauerbraten Steak

Yield: 6–8 servings

The essential ingredients of this dish are the cloves, vinegar, and gingersnap cookie crumbs. If you want to make this dish, you will need to start two to four days in advance, depending on how saur you like your braten.

2 cups (473 mL) water
1½ cups (354 mL) cider vinegar
1 cup (236 mL) cola
¼ cup (59 mL) balsamic vinegar
3 onions, peeled and thinly sliced
2 stalks celery, chopped
2 carrots, chopped
10 whole black peppercorns
10 whole cloves
1 bay leaf
3 tablespoons (45 mL) brown sugar
1½ teaspoons (7.5 mL) salt
1 teaspoon (5 mL) paprika
1 (4–5 pound [1.8–2.3 kg]) boneless beef sirloin roast, or a less expensive beef roast
1 cup (236 mL) plus 5 tablespoons (75 mL) gingersnap crumbs
7 tablespoons (105 mL) all-purpose flour, divided
3 tablespoons (45 mL) vegetable oil
5 tablespoons (75 mL) gingersnap crumbs
2 cups (473 mL) golden raisins

1. To make the marinade, in a large, resealable plastic bag, combine the water, cider vinegar, cola, balsamic vinegar, onion, celery, carrot, peppercorns, cloves, bay leaf, sugar, salt, and paprika, and shake well to combine. Add the meat, seal the bag tightly, pressing out the air, and lay it in a large, flat pan. Refrigerate, turning the bag each day. If you like a sour sauerbraten, let the meat soak in the bag for 4 days; if not, 2 days will suffice.

2. When you're ready to grill, place 1 cup (236 mL) fruitwood chips (such as peach, pear, apple, or cherry wood) in a bowl or can, cover with water, and soak for at least 2 hours.

3. Make sure the grill rack is clean and oil it thoroughly with nonstick cooking spray. Preheat a charcoal or gas barbecue to 375°F (190°C).

4. Remove the meat from the bag and pour the marinating liquid (with the vegetables) into a small saucepan. Pat the meat dry with paper towels and set aside. Boil the marinade for 12 minutes and set aside.

5. Put the soaked wood chips on a piece of heavy-duty aluminum foil and fold it over like an envelope to enclose the wood. Using a pencil, poke 3 or 4 holes in the top of the foil envelope (don't poke all the way through). Place the foil directly on the coals or gas jets. When the wood inside starts to smoke, place the meat on the grill rack over direct heat. Cook for 5 minutes per side to sear the meat and give it nice grill markings. Remove the meat from the heat and immediately sprinkle 2 tablespoons of the flour (30 mL) over it.

6. Place a Dutch oven on the grill over direct heat, heat the oil, and add the meat. Cover the pot and lower the grill lid. Cook for 10 minutes, then add 1 cup (236 mL) of the marinade with the reserved vegetables. Move the Dutch oven to the indirect side of the grill and cook, uncovered, on the barbecue with the lid lowered over indirect heat for 3 to 4 hours, until the meat is fork-tender and it has an internal temperature of 145°F (63°C). Keep at least ½ inch (1 cm) of liquid in the Dutch oven during cooking, adding more marinade as needed.

7. Remove the meat and keep it warm until ready to slice. Strain the drippings into a small bowl, then transfer them to a gravy separator to remove the fat.

8. In the Dutch oven over medium heat on a side burner, make the gravy by combining the strained drippings, the remaining flour, the cookie crumbs, and the raisins. Cook, stirring, for about 5 to 7 minutes, until the gravy is thickened and has picked up any bits stuck to the bottom of the Dutch oven.

Beef Paprikash
Yield: 2 servings

If you can find Hungarian paprika cream in a tube, please use it. It's more flavorful than the powdered variety and keeps much longer without losing its potency.

¾ pound (336 g) beef sirloin steak
1 tablespoon (15 mL) vegetable oil
1½ teaspoons butter (7.5 mL)
½ cup (118 mL) chopped onion
1 clove garlic, peeled and minced
2 cups (473 mL) beef stock
½ cup (118 mL) sliced mushrooms
2 tablespoons (30 mL) Hungarian paprika
Salt, to taste
Freshly ground black pepper, to taste
1 tablespoon (15 mL) all-purpose flour
½ cup (118 mL) sour cream
1½ teaspoons (7.5 mL) lemon juice

1. Preheat the barbecue to medium high (350°F [180°C] to 400°F [200°C]) for direct and indirect cooking.

2. Chill the beef until very firm but not frozen. Slice it into thin strips about 3 inches (7.5 cm) long, then grill them on the barbecue for 1 minute per side. Remove the meat from the grill and set it aside.

3. In a cast-iron skillet, melt the oil and butter. Add the onion and garlic and sauté until tender, but not browned.

4. Add the beef slices to the skillet, then add the beef stock, mushrooms, and paprika and season with salt and pepper. Place the skillet on the grill over direct heat. Bring the mixture to a boil, then move the pan to the unheated side of the grill, cover it with a lid or aluminum foil, and simmer until the meat is tender, about 45 minutes to an hour.

5. When the beef is tender, stir the flour into the sour cream and add it to the beef mixture. Bring to a boil and cook, stirring, until thickened. Stir in the lemon juice.

6. Remove the pan from the heat. Serve the meat at once over hot noodles.

Stuffed Green Peppers

Yield: 6 servings

You can use green, yellow, and orange bell peppers for a more colorful dish, serving each person two different color peppers. You may also wish to substitute lamb, pork, ground turkey or chicken, or ground game meats in this dish.

6 large bell peppers
1 teaspoon (5 mL) salt
1 pound (454 g) ground beef
½ pound (227 g) ground pork
1 cup (236 mL) instant rice
1 small onion, peeled and diced
1 large egg, beaten
1 teaspoon (5 mL) minced garlic
¼ teaspoon (2.5 mL) dried oregano
¼ teaspoon (2.5 mL) dried basil
¼ teaspoon (2.5 mL) ground cumin
1 (16-ounce [454-g]) can tomato sauce
¼ cup (59 mL) barbecue sauce
¼ cup (59 mL) minced parsley, for garnish

1. Preheat the barbecue to medium high (350°F [180°C] to 400°F [200°C]).

2. Seed the peppers and split them lengthwise. Boil the peppers with the salt just until their color changes, then drain.

3. In a small bowl, combine the beef, pork, rice, onion, egg, garlic, oregano, basil, and cumin and mix thoroughly.

4. In a separate small bowl, mix the tomato and barbecue sauces and stir to combine.

5. Pour half the sauce into the beef mixture and stir well, then spoon the meat into the bell pepper halves. Place the peppers in a Dutch oven or roasting pan, put the pan in the grill, and cook for 8 to 9 minutes.

Note: You could also just cut off the top of each pepper, remove membrane and seeds, and fill with the meat mixture, then stand upright to cook. If using this method add water until it reaches up about 1 to 2 inches on the peppers.

Veronica's Grilled Veal Steaks

Yield: 4 servings

This recipe was inspired by the chef at Casa Veronica in Montevideo, Uruguay, who gave me a turn at the grill in the tiny but bustling restaurant. Now I remember why I'm glad I'm a writer, TV host, and photographer. It was like working inside a blast furnace, and we were there in their cool fall season!

1 large tomato, seeded and diced
3 tablespoons (45 mL) chopped, pitted green olives
3 tablespoons (45 mL) chopped, pitted black olives
1 clove garlic, peeled and minced
Juice and zest of 1 lemon
2 tablespoons (30 mL) chopped fresh parsley, plus more for garnish
4 tablespoons (60 mL) olive oil, divided
2 (½ pound [227 g]) veal steaks
Salt, to taste
Freshly ground black pepper, to taste

1. In a medium bowl, combine the tomato, green and black olives, garlic, lemon juice, lemon zest, parsley, and 2 tablespoons (30 mL) of the oil. Mix well and set aside.

2. Place the veal steaks side by side on a large piece of aluminum foil. Using your fingers, rub the remaining 2 tablespoons (30 mL) oil into the steaks on both sides and season generously with salt and pepper. Wrap the foil around the steaks, and let them marinate for 1 hour at room temperature.

3. Make sure the grill rack is clean and oil it thoroughly with nonstick spray. Preheat a charcoal or gas grill to high (400°F [200°C] to 450°F [240°C]).

4. Remove the steaks from the foil package and transfer them to the grill over direct heat. Cook for 3 minutes, then rotate the steaks 90 degrees to make criss-cross grill marks, and cook for 3 minutes longer.

5. Flip the steaks over and cook for 5 to 7 minutes longer, until the internal temperature reaches 145°F (63°C) for medium-rare. Transfer the steaks to a plate, grill-marked side up, and let stand, covered, for 5 minutes.

6. To serve, top each steak with 1 to 2 tablespoons (15 to 30 mL) of the olive-tomato sauce and garnish with chopped parsley.

Dr. Bill's Burnt Ends

Yield: 4–6 servings

This is my favorite doctor's favorite dish, and since literally I owe him my life, I felt that a small way of saying thanks would be to publish his recipe for Kansas City–style burnt ends. This recipe comes from Bill Supplitt, M.D., from Vancouver, Wash.

2 tablespoons (30 mL) paprika
2 tablespoons (30 mL) granulated garlic
2 tablespoons (30 mL) salt
2 tablespoons (30 mL) brown sugar

1 tablespoon (15 mL) ground cumin
1 tablespoon (15 mL) chili powder
1 tablespoon (15 mL) onion powder
1 tablespoon (15 mL) freshly ground black pepper
1 teaspoon (5 mL) dry yellow mustard
½ teaspoon (2.5 mL) cayenne pepper
1 (8–10 pound [3.6–4.4 kg]) beef brisket
8 ounces (227 g) barbecue sauce of your choice

1. Make sure the grill is clean and generously sprayed with nonstick spray. Preheat the barbecue smoker to medium high (200°F [100°C] to 230°F [115°C]).

2. To make the spice rub, combine the paprika, garlic, salt, sugar, cumin, chili powder, onion powder, black pepper, mustard, and cayenne pepper. Massage the rub well into both sides of the meat and then place it in the smoker.

3. Smoke for 8 hours. Transfer the brisket to a platter and leave the smoker on.

4. Cut the burnt ends (the blackened portions) from the lean section of smoked brisket and chop those pieces into cubes. Place the chopped pieces in a large pan with holes in the bottom and smoke for 1½ hours more, or until the meat is dried out. You can also cut off more of the point or lean end and add to the pan, thereby making more "burnt ends."

5. Remove the pan from the smoker and transfer the brisket cubes to a frying pan or roasting pan and stir in the barbecue sauce. Return the pan to the smoker for an additional 1½ hours.

6. Burnt ends may be combined with baked beans or served on a sandwich.

Victor's Dominating Meatballs
Yield: 10–12

If these are too sweet for you, eliminate the apricot preserves or, better yet, add 1 large, finely chopped jalapeño pepper and ½ teaspoon (2.5 mL) cayenne pepper to the meatball mix. This recipe comes from Victor Domine from New York City.

1 pound (454 g) ground beef
1 pound (454 g) ground turkey
2 cups (473 mL) fresh breadcrumbs
½ cup (118 mL) chopped onion
2 eggs, beaten
2 tablespoons (30 mL) chopped parsley
2 teaspoons (10 mL) salt
2 tablespoons (30 mL) margarine
1 (10-ounce [280-g]) jar apricot preserves
1 teaspoon (5 mL) ground cumin
½ cup barbecue sauce

1. Preheat the barbecue to medium high (350°F [180°C] to 400°F [200°C]).

2. In a large bowl, combine the beef, turkey, breadcrumbs, onions, eggs, parsley, and salt. Mix lightly, then use your hands to form this mixture into 2½ to 3-inch (6 to 7.5 cm) meatballs.

3. Place a cast-iron pan on the grill and add the margarine. When the margarine has melted, add the meatballs, placing them so they do not touch each other.

4. In a small bowl, stir together the preserves, cumin, and barbecue sauce. Pour this sauce over the meatballs, close the lid, and cook for 30 minutes, stirring occasionally.

San Antonio Meatballs
Yield: 6–8 servings

These are pungent and fiery and will test even those who like hot sauces. You should definitely provide an alternative, milder sauce for those who don't normally carry fire extinguishers with them to lunch or dinner.

Pecos River Barbecue Sauce

2 tablespoons (30 mL) butter
¼ cup (59 mL) finely chopped yellow onion
¼ cup (59 mL) finely chopped bell pepper, any color
½ jalapeño pepper, finely minced
1½ cups (354 mL) ketchup
1 teaspoon (5 mL) chili powder
2½ tablespoons (37.5 mL) cider vinegar
1 tablespoon (15 mL) Worcestershire sauce
¼ cup (59 mL) bottled chili sauce
1 teaspoon (5 mL) hot pepper sauce

Meatballs

1 pound (454 g) lean ground beef
½ pound (227 g) Italian or pork sausage
1 (16-ounce [454-g]) can evaporated milk
3 tablespoons (45 mL) onion soup mix
2 tablespoons (30 mL) Worcestershire sauce

1. Make sure the grill is clean and generously sprayed with nonstick spray. Preheat the barbecue to medium high (350°F [180°C] to 400°F [200°C]).

2. In a medium saucepan, melt the butter over medium heat. Add the onion and peppers and cook until the onion becomes translucent; do not brown. Add the ketchup, chili sauce, vinegar, Worcestershire sauce, chili powder, and hot pepper sauce and simmer, stirring often, for about 10 minutes, or until the sauce is heated through and the seasonings are blended.

3. In a large bowl, combine the ground beef, sausage, evaporated milk, soup mix, and Worcestershire sauce and mix well. Shape the mixture into balls, using 4 heaping tablespoons (60 mL) of meat mixture for each ball.

4. Cook the meatballs directly on the grill, carefully turning several times with long tongs, about 10 to 12 minutes.

5. Remove the meatballs from the grill and serve with Pecos River BBQ sauce on the side so folks can pour it themselves.

Little Beef Barbecues
Yield: 4 servings

Brazilians have the fourth highest consumption of beef per capita of any country on earth, behind Argentina, the United States, and New Zealand. So this appetizer, served with cold beer, is right up their alley.

1 pound (454 g) beef tenderloin
2 tablespoons (30 mL) olive oil
2 tablespoons (30 mL) fresh lemon juice
1 tablespoon (15 mL) minced fresh parsley
1 tablespoon (15 mL) minced onion
Kosher salt, to taste
Freshly ground black pepper, to taste
½ pound (227 g) bacon
Cooked rice, to serve

1. Cut the beef tenderloin into 1-inch (2.5-cm) slices, then into cubes about 1-inch (2.5 cm) square. Put the cubes in a 1- to 2-quart (0.95- to 1.9-L) resealable plastic bag, then add the olive oil, lemon juice, parsley, onion, salt, and pepper. Seal the bag, pressing out any air. Refrigerate for at least 4 and no more than 12 hours.

2. Make sure the grill is clean and generously sprayed with nonstick spray. Preheat the barbecue to medium high (350°F [180°C] to 400°F [200°C]).

3. Cut the bacon slices in half crosswise and wrap each piece of beef with a half-slice of the bacon. Thread the meat onto steel kebab skewers, spacing them ½ inch (1 cm) apart.

4. Place the skewers directly on the grill and cook, turning often, for 7 to 8 minutes, or until the meat is browned on all sides.

5. Remove the skewers from the grill and serve over rice.

Hickory-Grilled Beef Fajitas
Yield: 4–6 servings

I actually prefer to use mesquite chips and would recommend them if you can find them, but hickory chips provide a nice, smoky flavor and are much more readily available.

2 pounds (908 g) beef skirt steaks
⅔ cup (158 mL) dark soy sauce
¼ cup (59 mL) lime juice
10 flour tortillas
2 tablespoons (30 mL) vegetable oil
2 medium red onions, sliced ¼ inch (0.5 cm) thick
1 red bell pepper, cut into ¼-inch (0.5-cm) strips
1 green bell pepper, cut into ¼-inch (0.5-cm) strips
2 tablespoons (30 mL) teriyaki sauce
Sour cream, for serving

1. Make sure the grill is clean and generously sprayed with nonstick grilling spray. Preheat the barbecue to medium high (350°F [180°C] to 400°F [200°C]). Soak a handful of hickory chips in a bowl of hot water.

2. Cut the steaks into slices ⅛ to ¼ inch (0.25 to 0.5 cm) thick and 4 to 5 inches (6 to 7.5 cm) long. Place the meat in a 1- to 2-gallon (3.8- to 7.6-L) resealable plastic bag.

3. In a small bowl, combine the soy sauce and lime juice. Pour this mixture into the bag over the meat, then shake the bag to coat all the slices, and marinate for 30 to 45 minutes.

4. Prepare a smoking package by putting a handful of soaked hickory chips onto a 12-inch (30-cm) square sheet of heavy-duty aluminum foil, folding it shut then poking holes in the top only. Set the package on the coals or gas flame, replace the grill grate and place the meat on the grill to cook for 3 to 4 minutes on each side for rare. Wrap the tortillas in aluminum foil and place this package on the grill while the meat cooks, until warm.

5. Pour the vegetable oil into a large cast-iron skillet and add the onion slices and pepper strips. Cook on the heated grill for 2 to 3 minutes, or until the peppers and onions begin to soften and brown at the edges. Remove the pan from the heat and sprinkle the vegetables with the teriyaki sauce. Stir and set aside, keeping the vegetables warm.

6. Remove the meat and tortillas from the grill and place both in on serving platters. Pour the peppers and onions in a bowl, and add smaller bowls for the sour cream. If you like, serve guacamole as well.

Beefy BBQ Cups

Yield: 4–6 servings

For a more substantial meal, you can add ¼ cup (118 mL) each of cooked rice, chopped celery, and frozen peas to the meat mixture.

2 cups (473 mL) Bisquick baking mix
½ cup (118 mL) cold water
1 pound (454 g) ground beef
½ cup (118 mL) chopped onions
¼ cup (59 mL) minced, cooked carrots
1 clove garlic, peeled and crushed
½ cup (118 mL) barbecue sauce
¼ teaspoon (0.25 mL) hot sauce
½ cup (118 mL) shredded cheddar cheese

1. Make sure the grill is clean and generously sprayed with nonstick grilling spray. Preheat the barbecue to medium high (350°F [180°C] to 400°F [200°C]).

2. In a medium bowl, mix the Bisquick with the water until a soft dough forms. Beat vigorously with a spoon for 20 strokes. Drop by spoonfuls into 12 ungreased standard muffin cups. With floured hands, press the dough into the bottom and up the sides of each cup.

3. In a saucepan over medium heat, cook the ground beef, onions, carrots, and garlic until the beef is browned. Drain the fat from the meat, stir in the barbecue and hot sauces, and heat through.

4. Spoon the cooked beef mixture into the muffin cups, sprinkle with cheese, and bake in the barbecue until the crust is golden brown, about 15 minutes.

Beef Empanadas

Yield: 6 to 8 servings

Empanadas are individual turnovers with pastry crusts filled with chicken, meat, seafood, vegetables, or fruit. This recipe calls for lard, which is richer than many other fats and makes superbly tender, flaky pastry. You can substitute solid vegetable shortening, but the taste will not be the same.

Pastry

2 cups (473 mL) all-purpose flour
2 teaspoons (10 mL) baking powder
½ teaspoon (2.5 mL) salt
2 tablespoons (30 mL) cold lard
1 large egg
½ cup (118 mL) milk, plus more, for brushing the pastry

Filling

1–2 large onions, peeled and coarsely chopped
1 pound (454 g) ground beef
3 tablespoons (45 mL) lard
1 tablespoon (15 mL) sweet paprika
¼ teaspoon (1.25 mL) crushed red pepper flakes
½ teaspoon (2.5 mL) ground cumin
Salt, to taste
Freshly ground black pepper, to taste
2 hard-boiled eggs, chopped
¼ cup (59 mL) dark or golden raisins
¼ cup (59 mL) chopped green or black olives

1. To make the crust, sift together the flour, baking powder, and salt in a large bowl. Add the lard and crumble between your fingers to combine. In a small bowl, beat the egg, add the milk, and add both to the flour mixture. Mix with a wooden spoon until the dough forms a ball. Divide the dough into 8 parts, form each part into a ball, and roll the balls out on a floured surface into 3- to 4-inch (7.5- to 9-cm) circles, each about 1 inch (2.5 cm) thick. Set aside.

2. To make the filling, combine the onions and ground beef in a large bowl and set aside. In a saucepan, heat the lard, paprika, and red pepper flakes, stirring constantly, until well-mixed. Remove the pan from the heat and let stand a minute, then stir in the lard until melted. Add the cumin, salt, and pepper and stir to combine. Let cool completely.

3. Preheat the barbecue to medium high (350°F [180°C] to 400°F [200°C]) for indirect heating.

4. To form the empanadas, place 1 to 3 heaping tablespoons (22.5 to 67.5 mL) of filling onto each dough round. Divide the hard-boiled egg, raisins, and olives evenly among the rounds.

5. Wet the edges of the dough with cold water. Fold each round in half over the filling, sealing with the tines of a fork. Brush the edges with milk.

6. Transfer the pastries to a sheet pan and place the pan on the barbecue over indirect heat for 20 minutes, turning once so the pastry doesn't burn, or until the empanadas are just turning brown on the edges. Remove from the barbecue and serve.

Surf IN Turf Pt. 2
Yield: 6–8 servings

You've heard of surf and turf, where a whole lobster or lobster tail is served alongside a sizzling steak. We've gone them one better with lobster meat stuffed inside a succulent beef tenderloin. This recipe comes from Susan Gilbert from La Center, Wash.

1 (3–4 pound [1.3–1.8 kg]) whole beef tenderloin
2 (4-ounce [112-g]) fresh (or frozen) lobster tails
1 tablespoon (15 mL) butter, melted
1½ teaspoons (7.5 mL) fresh lemon juice
½ cup (118 mL) butter
½ cup (118 mL) sliced green onions, green and white parts
½ cup (118 mL) dry white wine
¼ teaspoon (1.25 mL) garlic salt
Freshly ground black pepper, to taste

1. Make sure the grill is clean and generously sprayed with nonstick spray. Preheat the barbecue to medium high (425°F [220°C] to 450°F [240°C]).

2. With a sharp knife, slice the beef tenderloin lengthwise to within ½ inch (1 cm) of the bottom to butterfly, then repeat with both new sections, making two more cuts. With a tenderizing hammer, pound all four sections lightly to spread the meat out as much as possible. Set aside.

3. Place the lobster tails in boiling salted water to cover. Return to a boil, then reduce the heat and simmer 5 to 6 minutes. Remove the lobster meat from the shells and cut it in half lengthwise. Place the lobster tail sections end to end on the flattened beef. Combine the melted butter and lemon juice and brush it on the lobster.

4. Roll the meat around the lobster and tie the roast together with butcher's twine at 3-inch (7.5-cm) intervals. Place the meat in a shallow roasting pan and roast in the barbecue for 45 to 50 minutes for medium-rare. Increase the time by 5 to 10 minutes for medium.

5. Meanwhile, in a small saucepan, melt the ½ cup (118 mL) butter. Add the green onion and cook over low heat until the onions are tender, about 3 to 4 minutes, stirring frequently. Add the wine, garlic salt, and pepper and heat through, stirring frequently. Do not let the mixture boil.

6. Remove the roast from the barbecue, cover it with foil, and let it rest for 10 minutes. Cut the strings and slice the tenderloin in 1-inch (2.5-cm) thick slices. Put the butter-wine sauce in a sauce boat to serve at the table.

BBQ Beef Ribs with Molasses-Bourbon Sauce
Yield: 4–6 servings

There is a controversy about how to prepare beef ribs. Some folks say the membrane on the back of the ribs needs to be removed, while others claim it's there to keep moisture in the meat. I subscribe to the latter mode of thinking and have cooked ribs for years without removing the membrane—with very good results, I might add.

1½ cups (354 mL) water
1 (12-ounce [336-g]) bottle IPA-style beer
¼ cup (59 mL) molasses
1 tablespoon (15 mL) brown sugar
1 tablespoon (15 mL) salt
5 fresh thyme sprigs
1 teaspoon freshly ground black pepper
16 beef short ribs or 8 whole beef ribs
1 tablespoon (15 mL) olive oil
1 small onion, peeled and finely diced
1 cup (236 mL) red wine vinegar
2 cups (473 mL) ketchup
1 cup (236 mL) bourbon
½ cup (118 mL) molasses
½ teaspoon seasoned salt, to taste
¼ teaspoon white pepper, to taste

1. In a large saucepan, combine the water, beer, molasses, brown sugar, salt, thyme, and pepper and bring to a boil. Remove the marinade from the heat and cool completely in the refrigerator or by placing the bowl of marinade in a larger bowl of ice.

2. When the marinade has cooled, put the ribs in a 1- to 2-gallon (3.8- to 7.6-L) resealable plastic bag and pour the marinade in over it. Seal the bag and turn several times to coat the ribs. Refrigerate overnight, turning the bag occasionally.

3. Make sure the grill is clean and generously sprayed with nonstick grilling spray. Preheat the barbecue to medium high (250°F [120°C] to 300°F [150°C]) for indirect heating, piling charcoal on one side of the barbecue only, and place a filled water pan on the other side of the barbecue.

4. Place the ribs on the grill above the water pan. Cover the barbecue and cook the ribs for about 2½ to 3 hours, maintaining a temperature between 250°F (120°C) and 300°F (150°C) by opening the vents wider to increase the heat and closing them to decrease the heat. Check the temperature frequently with a meat thermometer.

5. While the ribs are cooking, heat the olive oil in a large saucepan over medium high heat. Add the onion and sauté until golden brown, about 5 to 6 minutes, then add the vinegar and bring to a boil. Reduce the heat and simmer until the sauce reduces by one-fourth, then remove the saucepan from the heat. Stir in the ketchup, bourbon, and molasses and stir to blend. Return the pan to the heat, add the salt and pepper, and simmer for 10 to 12 minutes to blend the flavors.

6. Cook the ribs for about 3 hours, or until the meat is very tender when pierced with a knife, turning occasionally and basting generously with sauce only during the last 10 minutes of cooking. Transfer the ribs to a heated platter, brush with more sauce, and serve.

Corned Beef with Apricots and Mustard Sauce
Yield: 6- 8 servings

Corned beef really has nothing to do with corn. Rather, the term refers to a very coarse salt used by early English cooks to cure and preserve meat. Today corned beef is cured in a brine solution.

1 (3–4 pound [1.3–1.8 kg]) corned beef
1 (15½-ounce [440-g]) can halved apricots in heavy syrup
¾ cup (177 mL) packed brown sugar
2 tablespoons (30 mL) prepared yellow mustard
1 tablespoon (15 mL) Dijon mustard
1 (18-ounce [504-g]) jar apricot jam
1 (16–ounce [454-g]) can apricot nectar
¼ cup (59 mL) dark rum (optional)
Minced fresh parsley, for garnish

1. Rinse the corned beef in water and rub it with your hands to remove all the seasonings and seeds, then place the beef in a large pot and cover with water. Bring to a boil and simmer for 3 hours.

2. Spray a Dutch oven or a deep roasting pan with nonstick cooking spray.

3. Preheat the barbecue to medium high (350°F [180°C] to 400°F [200°C]).

4. In a bowl, mix together the syrup from the can of apricots, the brown sugar, and the two mustards. Set aside.

5. Transfer the cooked beef from the pot to the prepared Dutch oven or roasting pan. Spread half the apricot jam over the top of the roast, then pour the mustard-apricot juice over the covered meat. Arrange the apricot halves around the meat. Cover the Dutch oven with a lid or with tin foil and bake in the barbecue for 45 minutes.

6. In a small bowl, mix together the remaining apricot jam, the apricot nectar, and the rum, if using. Use this mixture to baste the meat several times while it's cooking.

7. Remove the corned beef from the pan, reserving the juices and apricot halves, and place it on a large heated platter. Pour some of the apricot juices over the meat and the rest into a sauce boat. Arrange the apricot halves around the bottom of the platter, sprinkle parsley over the roast, and serve.

Bangkok Beef Satay

Yield: 4–6 servings

Although recipes and ingredients vary, satay usually consists of chunks or slices of meat on skewers that are grilled over wood or charcoal fires. Satay is usually served with a spicy peanut sauce or peanut gravy and accompanied by slivers of onion and cucumber in vinegar.

6 tablespoons (90 mL) dark soy sauce, divided
6 tablespoons (90 mL) freshly squeezed lime juice (from about 3 limes), divided
6 tablespoons (90 mL) smooth or chunky peanut butter
3 tablespoons (45 mL) chopped fresh cilantro leaves
2 tablespoons (30 mL) brown sugar, divided
1 tablespoon (15 mL) sweet rice vinegar
2 teaspoons (10 mL) Sriracha or other Asian hot chili sauce, divided
3 green onions, white and green parts, minced
1 (1-inch [2.5-cm]) piece fresh ginger, peeled and chopped
2 cloves garlic, peeled and minced
Zest of 1 lime
1 tablespoon (15 mL) vegetable oil
1 (1½-pound [681-g]) beef steak (round, sirloin, rib-eye, or chuck)

1. Soak about 18 wooden or bamboo skewers in water for 1 hour.

2. In a medium bowl, combine 4 tablespoons of the soy sauce, 4 tablespoons of the lime juice, the peanut butter, the cilantro, 1 tablespoon of the sugar, the vinegar, and 1 teaspoon (5 mL) of the chili sauce, and 1 tablespoon (15 mL) of the sugar, stirring until it reaches a smooth, thick, gravy-like consistency. Cover and set aside.

3. To make the marinade, combine the remaining 2 tablespoons (30 ml) of the soy sauce, the remaining 2 tablespoons (30 mL) of the lime juice, the remaining 1 tablespoon of the sugar, the remaining 1 teaspoon (5 mL) of the chili sauce, the onions, ginger, garlic, lime zest, and oil. Process until puréed and set aside.

4. Cut the beef against the grain into pieces 6 inches (15 cm) long and ½ inch (1 cm) wide. Thread the beef lengthwise, piercing it in several places in an accordion fold, on the prepared skewers. Transfer the skewers to a large, shallow pan and pour the marinade over the meat. Cover and refrigerate for 3 to 4 hours.

5. Make sure the grill is clean and generously sprayed with nonstick grilling spray. Preheat the barbecue to medium high (350°F [180°C] to 400°F [200°C]).

6. Place a strip of heavy-duty aluminum foil across the front 3 to 4 inches of the grill. The bottom part of the satay skewers can rest on this, protecting the part you handle from burning.

7. Remove the skewers from the marinade and drain, discarding the marinade. Place the skewers on the grill over direct heat for 2 minutes per side, or until cooked through. Meanwhile, warm the peanut sauce in a small saucepan over low heat until it just barely begins to bubble.

8. Serve the satay on the skewers with small bowls of the warmed peanut sauce on the side, for dipping.

Uncle Jim's Sesame Beef

Yield: 4 servings

Sesame seeds have a nutty, sweet aroma with a milky, buttery taste. When toasted, their flavor intensifies, yielding an almost almond- or peanut butter-like flavor. This recipe comes from Jim Smith from Southington, Conn.

1 pound (454 g) beef flank steak
¼ cup (59 mL) toasted sesame seeds
3 tablespoons (45 mL) all-purpose flour
¾ teaspoon (3.75 mL) ground coriander
¾ teaspoon (3.75 mL) ground ginger
¾ teaspoon (3.75 mL) chili powder
1 cup (236 mL) beef broth
3 tablespoons (45 mL) vegetable oil
1 teaspoon (5 mL) sesame oil

1. Make sure the grill is clean and generously sprayed with nonstick grilling spray. Preheat the barbecue to medium high (350°F [180°C] to 400°F [200°C]).

2. Slice the beef thinly across the grain and set aside.

3. In shallow bowl, mix together the sesame seeds, flour, coriander, ginger, and chili powder. Dip the beef strips into the broth; then toss them in the flour mixture.

4. In a cast-iron skillet on the grill, heat the two oils until hot. Add the beef and ¼ cup (59 mL) of the broth and cook, stirring constantly, for about 2 minutes. When the beef is cooked, add the remaining broth and stir constantly, until the liquid is thickened and heated through.

Braised Sweet and Sour Short Ribs

Yield: 4 servings

Short ribs must be braised, as the tough meat is too tough to chew and barely edible otherwise. We braise them for 4 to 4½ hours here, which we feel is an optimum time for this meat. Braise them for a shorter time and they're too tough, much longer and they fall off the bone in the pan.

¼ cup (59 mL) all-purpose flour
¼ cup (59 mL) packed brown sugar
1 teaspoon (5 mL) ground cumin
½ teaspoon (2.5 mL) garlic salt
¼ teaspoon (1.25 mL) freshly ground black pepper
2½ pounds (1.1 kg) beef short ribs
1 cup (236 mL) sliced onion
2 tablespoons (30 mL) chopped garlic
½ cup (118 mL) bottled chili sauce
½ cup (118 mL) ginger ale
¼ cup (59 mL) cider vinegar
¼ cup dark sesame oil
2 tablespoons (30 mL) dark soy sauce
1 tablespoon (15 mL) Worcestershire sauce

1. Preheat the barbecue to medium high (350°F [180°C] to 400°F [200°C]).

2. Grease a Dutch oven or roasting pan.

3. Cut the beef short ribs into 3-inch (7.5-cm) lengths. In a wide, flat dish, combine the flour, brown sugar, cumin, garlic salt, and pepper. Roll the ribs in this mixture, coating them on all sides, and shake off the excess.

4. Arrange the ribs in a single layer in the prepared Dutch oven or roasting pan. Place the sliced onions over the ribs and sprinkle with the garlic.

5. In a small bowl, combine the chili sauce, ginger ale, vinegar, sesame oil, soy sauce, and Worcestershire sauce, stir together, and pour over the ribs. Braise the ribs, covered, in the barbecue for 2½ to 3 hours, basting occasionally with the barbecue and pan sauce. Uncover and continue cooking for 1½ hours longer, or until the ribs are browned on top and are very tender.

6. Transfer the ribs from the pan to a serving platter, pouring the sauce over the ribs after you've spooned off any accumulated fat, and serve.

Barbecued King of Beef

Yield: 12 servings

A ribeye roast, also called a prime rib roast (if the meat is prime grade, that is), is the best that you can ever buy, cook, or eat. The meat is well marbled and, properly cooked, comes out juicy, buttery, and extremely tender. Please do not cook to anything beyond medium, or you'll ruin the best cut of meat on the planet.

Roast

3 pounds (1.3 kg) white onions
1 cup (236 mL) kosher salt
1 (15–20 pound [6.8–9.1 kg]) beef ribeye roast, bone in
6 cloves garlic, peeled and thinly sliced

Rub

¼ cup (59 mL) salt
¼ cup (59 mL) dried marjoram
2 tablespoons (30 mL) ground cumin
2 tablespoons (30 mL) freshly ground black pepper
1 tablespoon (15 mL) dried thyme
1 teaspoon (5 mL) brown sugar

1. Preheat the barbecue to medium high (425°F [220°C] to 450°F [240°C]) for direct and indirect heating.

2. Cut the onions ¾ inch (1.5 cm) thick and spread them across the bottom of a large Dutch oven or roasting pan, then sprinkle on the kosher salt.

3. Prepare the roast by cutting small slits all over it and inserting the thin slices of garlic into each slit. Mix together the rub ingredients and rub the meat all over with the mixture.

4. Lay the ribeye on top of the salted onions. Sear the roast for 1 hour over direct heat, then open up the barbecue vents to lower the heat to about 350°F (180°C). Move the roast to the unheated side of the grill. Cook to medium-rare, about 1½ to 2 hours.

5. Use a meat thermometer to determine when the roast is done: 125 degrees (52°C) for rare, 130 (54°C) for medium-rare, or 135 to 140 (57 to 60°C) for medium.

Charred Teriyaki Porterhouse Steak
Yield: 4–6 servings

Both porterhouse and T-bone steaks are cut from the short loin, but the porterhouse has a larger portion of tenderloin than the T-bone. Both are wonderful barbecued, but if they are priced the same buy the porterhouse for the larger, more tender portion of meat it carries.

1½ cups (354 mL) dark soy sauce
¼ cup (59 mL) extra virgin olive oil
⅓ cup (79 mL) packed brown sugar
¼ cup (59 mL) granulated sugar
¼ cup (59 mL) minced green onions, green and white parts
3 large garlic cloves, peeled, mashed, and minced
2 tablespoons (30 mL) finely minced fresh ginger
4–6 (10-ounce [280-g]) prime or choice aged beef porterhouse steaks, or 1
(4–5 pound [1.8–2.3 kg]) steak
1 teaspoon (5 mL) lemon pepper
4–6 pats butter
Minced fresh parsley, for garnish

1. In a small bowl, combine the soy sauce, olive oil, sugars, onions, garlic, and ginger and stir. Pour into a 1- to 2-gallon (3.8- to 7.6-L) resealable plastic bag and add the steaks, turning to coat all sides. Marinate for 2 hours.

2. Make sure the grill is clean and generously sprayed with nonstick grilling spray. Preheat the barbecue to medium high (500°F [260°C] to 600°F [315°C]) for direct and indirect heating.

3. Drain the steaks. Pour the marinade into a small microwave-safe dish and microwave on high for 4 to 5 minutes, or until the liquid boils. Cover and set aside.

4. Sprinkle the steaks with the lemon pepper and place them on the grill over the hot fire. Cook for 2 minutes per side, then move the steaks to a cooler part of the grill and cook for approximately 3 minutes more per side for medium-rare.

5. Just before serving the steaks place, them on a very hot platter. Slip a pat of butter on each steak, drizzle the top of the steaks with the remaining teriyaki sauce, cover with foil, and (here's the hardest part of this recipe) wait 5 minutes.

6. Sprinkle with parsley and serve immediately.

Rockin' Rib Roast

Yield: 4–6 servings

Dale's Seasoning has been a favorite in the South for a half-century and is available at most grocery stores in that part of the country. For the rest of us, fortunately, it's readily available from dozens of websites including, of course, amazon.com.

¼ cup (59 mL) Dale's Seasoning (or favorite steak seasoning)
½ cup (118 mL) corn oil
1 (5–6 pound [2.3–2.7 kg]) beef rib roast, bone in
2 scoops (4–6 tablespoons [60–90 mL]) powdered lemonade mix
1 tablespoon (15 mL) garlic salt
1 tablespoon (15 mL) paprika
1 tablespoon (15 mL) dried oregano
1 teaspoon (5 mL) freshly ground black pepper
1 cup (236 mL) Cabernet Sauvignon or Pinot Noir

1. Make sure the grill is clean and generously sprayed with nonstick grilling spray. Preheat the barbecue to medium high (350°F [180°C] to 400°F [200°C]).

2. In a small bowl, combine the Dale's Seasoning with the corn oil and stir. Pour this mixture onto the beef and massage it in.

3. In a separate small bowl, combine the lemonade mix, garlic salt, paprika, oregano, and pepper and stir well. Rub this mixture well into the surface of the ribeye and set the roast aside, covered, at room temperature for an hour.

4. Place the beef directly on the grill and sear for 2 to 3 minutes, turning frequently, until all sides are beginning to char. Remove the roast from the barbecue.

5. Lay two 12 × 24-inch (30 × 60-cm) pieces of aluminum foil one on top of the other to make a cross. Place the ribeye roast in the center of the foil, then pour the wine over the roast. Immediately close up the foil, one sheet at a time and seal completely with several folds.

6. Place the foil-wrapped roast in the barbecue and roast to your preferred doneness, about 1 to 1½ hours for medium-rare. Remember, the meat will rise 10 to 20°F (3 to 6°C) while it rests.

7. Remove the meat from the barbecue and let it rest for 20 minutes, then remove the foil and serve, carefully pouring the wine and meat juices into a gravy boat to serve at the table.

Barbecue Beef Ribs

Yield: 4–6 servings

Hoisin sauce is one of the most popular condiments in Chinese cooking. Though its name actually means "seafood," this sauce has no fish or shellfish in its ingredients. Instead, it contains sweet potatoes, wheat, soybeans, vinegar, chili peppers, salt and garlic.

2 pounds (908 g) beef ribs
½ cup (118 mL) dry or sweet white wine
¼ cup (59 mL) water
1 cup (236 mL) honey
½ cup (118 mL) melted butter
½ cup (118 mL) hoisin sauce
1½ teaspoons (7.5 mL) grated fresh ginger
1 cup (236 mL) minced green onions, white and green parts

1. Preheat the barbecue to medium high (350°F [180°C] to 400°F [200°C]).

2. Trim the excess fat from the ribs and put them in a roasting pan or Dutch oven. Pour in the wine and water. Cover and cook for 2 hours.

3. In a small bowl, whisk together the honey, melted butter, hoisin sauce, ginger and half of the green onions. Pour this mixture over the ribs. Cover the pan and return it to the barbecue 1 hour.

4. Remove the cover, baste the ribs with the sauce, and return the ribs to the barbecue for 30 minutes to brown them up, turning them several times.

5. Transfer the ribs to a warmed platter, cover, and let them rest for 5 to 10 minutes. Sprinkle with the remaining green onions and serve.

Coca-Cola Beef Brisket

Yield: 10–12 servings

It is very important to boil any marinade you've used on meat, poultry, fish, or game, as the uncooked protein can leave bacteria in the liquid and, if you use it as a baste, it can introduce dangerous bacteria into your food. Especially if you're adding the marinade at the last minute, the heat isn't enough to destroy those nasty critters. So boil for 10 to 12 minutes, cool, and then use for a marinade.

2 cans Coca-Cola
12 ounces (336 g) barbecue sauce of your choice
2 beef bouillon cubes dissolved in 4 ounces (112 mL) water
4 cloves garlic, peeled and minced
2 tablespoons (30 mL) lime juice
1 tablespoon (15 mL) Worcestershire sauce
Lawry's seasoned salt, to taste
Freshly ground black pepper, to taste
1 (10–12 pound [4.5–5.4 kg]) brisket

1. Combine the cola, barbecue sauce, dissolved bouillon, garlic, lime juice, Worcestershire sauce, salt, and pepper and pour the mixture into a 2-gallon (7.6-L) resealable plastic bag. Add the brisket and marinate for 24 hours, turning the bag several times.

2. Early in the morning of the day you are going to cook, remove the brisket from the marinade and let it sit at room temperature while you prepare the fire. Pour the remaining marinade into a saucepan and boil for at least 10 minutes. Cool and transfer to a sealable bottle.

3. Make sure the grill is clean and generously sprayed with nonstick grilling spray. Preheat the barbecue smoker to medium (275°F [140°C] to 325°F [165°C]).

4. Place the brisket in the smoker, fat side up, and cook for about 12 to 14 hours. (I usually start about 7:00 or 8:00 a.m. and take the meat off the smoker at about 10:00 or 11:00 p.m.). Baste several times with the marinade while the meat is cooking.

5. Remove the brisket from the smoker and wrap it in clear plastic wrap, then in two layers of heavy-duty foil. Lower the smoker temperature to 150 to 160°F (65 to 71°C). Return the brisket to the smoker or place it in the oven (set to the same temperature) and let it cook overnight.

6. At about 1:00 or 2:00 the next afternoon, remove the brisket, unwrap the foil and plastic wrap, and slice thinly across the grain for the best-tasting, juiciest, most tender brisket you have ever eaten.

Old Fashioned Cube Steaks

Yield: 4 servings

Cube steaks used to be very popular, as they're inexpensive, easy to cook, and have a nice flavor. Cooked properly, they are very tender; undercooked, they are way too chewy for most folks.

1½ pounds (681 g) beef cube steaks
3 tablespoons (45 mL) all-purpose flour
1 (10½–ounce) can condensed beef broth or beef consommé
2 medium onions, peeled and thinly sliced
½ cup (118 mL) water
2 tablespoons (30 mL) bottled chili sauce
2 tablespoons (30 mL) vegetable oil
1 teaspoon (5 mL) salt
¼ teaspoon (1.25 mL) dried thyme
Freshly ground black pepper, to taste
1 cup (236 mL) sour cream
Paprika, for garnish
Minced fresh parsley, for garnish

1. Make sure the grill is clean and generously sprayed with nonstick grilling spray. Preheat the barbecue to medium high (350°F [180°C] to 400°F [200°C]) for direct and indirect heating.

2. Flour both sides of the steaks with the flour, shaking off the excess.

3. Grill the steaks for about 10 minutes, turning often, until the meat is nicely browned on both sides

4. Remove the steaks from the heat and cut them into 1-inch (2.54-cm) wide strips.

5. To a large cast-iron skillet, add the beef broth, onion, water, chili sauce, and oil. Add the beef strips and place the skillet in the barbecue over direct until the liquid boils. Move the pan to the unheated side of the grill and sprinkle the mixture with the salt, thyme, and pepper. Cover the pan and simmer for 45 to 50 minutes.

6. Uncover the pan and stir in the sour cream. Cook for 5 more minutes. Remove the pan from the heat, sprinkle the meat with paprika and parsley, and serve.

Grilled Spicy Stroganoff

Yield: 6 servings

For a more tender stroganoff, use 1½ pounds (681 g) of beef tenderloin or top sirloin, sliced in thin strips. If you want an authentic stroganoff, use Hungarian paprika in the sour cream.

1½ pounds (681 g) beef chuck steak, cut into ⅛-inch (0.25-cm) slices
Oil olive, for brushing
2 tablespoons (30 mL) butter
1½ cups (354 mL) beef broth, divided
2 tablespoons (30 mL) ketchup
¼ teaspoon (1.25 mL) hot sauce
1 clove garlic, peeled and finely chopped
1 teaspoon (5 mL) celery salt
⅛ teaspoon (0.6 mL) cayenne pepper
8 ounces (227 g) sliced mushrooms
1 medium onion, peeled and chopped
2 large shallots, peeled and diced
2 tablespoons (30 mL) all-purpose flour
1 tablespoon (15 mL) heavy cream
1 cup (236 mL) sour cream
1 tablespoon (15 mL) paprika

1. Make sure the grill is clean and generously sprayed with nonstick grilling spray. Preheat the barbecue to medium high (350°F [180°C] to 400°F [200°C]) for direct and indirect heating.

2. Brush the beef strips with olive oil and quickly grill them until both sides begin to char, about 2 minutes per side. Remove and set aside.

3. In a roasting pan, melt the butter. Add the cooked beef strips to the pan. Add 1¼ cups (295 mL) of the beef broth, the ketchup, hot sauce, garlic, celery salt, and cayenne pepper and place the pan in the barbecue over direct heat. Cook until the liquid boils, then move the pan to the indirect side of the grill. Cover the pan and simmer until the beef is tender, 1 to 1½ hours.

4. Remove the lid and stir in the mushrooms, onions, and shallots. Replace the cover and cook for about 5 minutes more.

5. Pour the remaining ¼ cup (59 mL) broth into a plastic container or empty bottle. Add the flour and cream and shake until completely mixed. Move the pan back to the direct heat and add the flour mixture to the beef. Cook, stirring constantly, until the liquid boils. Mix together the sour cream and paprika and add it to the pan. Stir to incorporate, then remove the pan from the barbecue.

6. With a large ladle or spoon, serve the stroganoff over hot noodles, wild rice, or mashed potatoes.

Scottish Steak Auld Reekie
Yield: 4 servings

Auld Reekie was the name given to Edinburgh in the days when open coal fires filled the skies with smoke and smog. The addition of whisky gives this recipe an added kick.

4 (8-ounce [227-g]) Aberdeen Angus steak fillets, or your favorite fillet
4 tablespoons (60 mL) Scotch whisky
1½ cups (354 mL) heavy cream
½ cup (118 mL) grated smoked Gouda or cheddar cheese
Salt, to taste
Freshly ground black pepper, to taste
2 tablespoons (30 mL) butter

1. Make sure the grill is clean and generously sprayed with nonstick grilling spray. Preheat a charcoal or gas barbecue to 500°F (260°C) to 600°F (315°C).

2. Grill the steaks over direct heat until the internal temperature reaches 145°F (63°C) for medium-rare. Transfer to a warmed plate, cover, and let stand.

3. Add the whisky to a cast-iron skillet set over medium-high heat on the stove. Using an extra-long barbecue match or lighter, quickly but carefully ignite the whisky (always ignite the alcohol fumes at the edge of the pan, not the liquid itself).

4. Add the cream and cheese and bring the mixture slowly to a simmer. Simmer gently, stirring from time to time, until the sauce is reduced by half. Season with salt and pepper and whisk in the butter.

5. Transfer the steaks to serving plates and pour the sauce over them.

Greek-Style Green Onion Beef
Yield: 4 servings

If you wish, you can add a cup (236 mL) of crumbled feta cheese or ½ cup (118 mL) chopped, peeled, and cooked cucumbers just before serving.

⅓ cup (79 mL) dry white wine
3 tablespoons (45 mL) teriyaki sauce
1 clove garlic, peeled and minced
½ teaspoon (2.5 mL) Greek seasoning
1 pound (454 g) boneless beef (chuck or round steak), sliced ⅛ inch (0.25 cm) thick, brushed with olive oil
2 teaspoons (10 mL) cornstarch
2 tablespoons (30 mL) olive oil
10–12 green onions, sliced into 1-inch (2.5-cm) long pieces
Steamed rice, for serving

1. Preheat the barbecue to medium high (350°F [180°C] to 400°F [200°C]) for direct and indirect heating.

2. In a 1-gallon (3.8-L) resealable plastic bag, combine the wine, teriyaki sauce, garlic, and Greek seasoning. Add the beef and shake to coat well. Marinate at room temperature for 30 minutes or covered in the refrigerator for 2 hours.

3. Drain the meat, reserving ¼ cup (59 mL) of the marinade. Discard remaining marinade. Add enough water to the marinade to make ⅔ cup (158 mL) liquid, then stir in the cornstarch and set aside.

4. Preheat a large cast-iron skillet on the grill. Add the oil and green onions and stir-fry for 1 minute. Remove the onions from the pan and set aside.

5. Add the beef to the hot oil and place the skillet in the barbecue for 15 minutes, stirring several times. Cover the pan, move it to the unheated side of the grill and cook for another 15 minutes.

6. When the beef is tender, stir in the green onions. Add the cornstarch liquid and stir over heat for 5 minutes to thicken the sauce. Serve over cooked or steamed rice.

Cheryl's Brunswick Stew

Yield: 10–12 servings (at least)

Cheryl picked up this recipe on a trip to Virginia, where Brunswick stew is almost a religion. She sometimes substitutes okra for the lima beans, but you can add which-ever you like, or use both. This recipe comes from Cheryl Lawrence from La Center, Wash.

2 pounds (908 g) pork butt (shoulder)
2 pounds (908 g) boneless chicken breasts
1 (2-pound [908-g]) beef chuck roast
4 (16-ounce [454-g]) cans whole, peeled tomatoes
1 (32-ounce [908-g]) bottle ketchup
1 (18-ounce [504-g]) bottle spicy barbecue sauce
1 (18-ounce [504-g]) bottle hickory-flavored barbecue sauce
1 (10-ounce [280-g]) package frozen lima beans
3 medium onions, peeled and chopped
4 cloves garlic, peeled and mashed
2 tablespoons (30 mL) chili powder
1 tablespoon (15 mL) Worcestershire sauce
4 (17-ounce [476-g]) cans creamed corn
4 (17-ounce [476-g]) cans whole kernel corn

1. Preheat the barbecue to medium high (350°F [180°C] to 400°F [200°C]).

2. Using two large pots or Dutch ovens, place the pork in one pot and the beef and chicken in another. Add water to cover to each pot and set them in the barbecue to boil until the meat and chicken are tender, about 35 to 45 minutes. Remove the meat, pat dry, and set aside. Discard the water.

3. In a large pot over medium heat on a side burner or stovetop burner, cook the tomatoes, ketchup, barbecue sauces, lima beans, onions, garlic, chili powder, and Worcestershire sauce for 1 hour, lowering the heat to a simmer once it boils.

4. Tear or roughly chop the chicken, beef, and pork. Add them to the stew, along with the two kinds of corn, and simmer for 30 more minutes.

Grilled Boerwors Sausage

Yield: 6–8 servings

Boerwors is a very popular sausage in South Africa. The name is Afrikaans—boer means "farmer" and wors means "sausage." The coriander seeds and their bitter taste are a critical part of the recipe.

3–3½ ounces (84–98 g) sausage casings
3 tablespoons (45 mL) whole coriander seeds
1 teaspoon (5 mL) whole cloves
3 pounds (1.3 kg) coarsely ground beef (chuck or round steak)
3 pounds (1.3 kg) coarsely ground pork (loin or Boston butt)
1 pound (454 g) bacon
½ cup (118 mL) red wine vinegar
¼ cup (60 mL) Worcestershire sauce
2 tablespoons (30 mL) brown sugar
1 clove garlic, peeled and finely minced
2 tablespoons (30 mL) salt
1 teaspoon (5 mL) freshly ground black pepper
½ teaspoon (2.5 mL) freshly grated nutmeg
½ teaspoon (2.5 mL) dried thyme
½ teaspoon (2.5 mL) ground allspice

1. In a small skillet over high heat on a side burner, brown the coriander and cloves, shaking the pan gently from time to time, being careful not to burn them, about 5 minutes. Grind the spices with a mortar and pestle and strain with a fine-mesh sieve to remove the husks.

2. In a large bowl, combine the meat, spice mixture, Worcestershire sauce, brown sugar, garlic, salt, pepper, nutmeg, thyme, and allspice and mix thoroughly with your hands.

3. Make sure the grill is clean and generously sprayed with nonstick grilling spray. Preheat the barbecue to medium high (350°F [180°C] to 400°F [200°C]). Soak the sausage casings in warm water for 20 minutes.

4. Drain the casings and place one over the mouth of a sausage mill. Gather enough of the casing so that about 3 inches (7.5 cm) is ready to be filled, and tie a knot at that point An extra pair of hands makes this step much easier; have an assistant hold the casing and guide the meat, while you feed the meat into the casing Add the meat mixture to the mill in small amounts, lightly pushing on the stopper, to control the flow of the meat into the casings. Form and shape each boerwors with your hands so that it is equally thick all over. Don't overfill the casings, as this can cause the sausages to explode when cooking. Try to eradicate as many air bubbles as possible. Once the casing is full, remove it from the machine. Continue to push the rest of the mixture out of the mill and into the casings. Knot the casings and set the sausages aside.

5. Grill the sausages over a hot fire until the skin is nicely browned but the inside is still moist, turning often, about 12 to 14 minutes. Serve with fried potatoes and grilled ears of corn.

Saucy Skillet-Cooked Steak

Yield: 4 servings

This one-skillet meal is perfect for a cold fall or winter day. If it's too rainy or snowy, you can use your stovetop and oven. Or brush off the snow and cook on the barbecue anyway.

1 pound (454 g) boneless beef round steak, cut into 1-inch (2.5-cm) chunks
¼ cup (59 mL) all-purpose flour
1 tablespoon (15 mL) vegetable oil
1 large onion, peeled and chopped (about 1 cup [236 mL])
1 cup (236 mL) beef broth or unsalted beef stock
¼ cup (59 mL) ketchup
1 tablespoon (15 mL) Worcestershire sauce
1 small Anaheim pepper, finely minced
1 teaspoon (5 mL) garlic salt
½ teaspoon (2.5 mL) dried marjoram leaves
¼ teaspoon (1.25 mL) freshly ground black pepper
1 (16-ounce [454-g]) can sliced whole potatoes, drained
1 (10-ounce [280-g]) package frozen Italian green beans, thawed and drained
1 (3-ounce [84-g]) jar julienned sun-dried tomatoes, drained

1. Preheat the barbecue to medium high (350°F [180°C] to 400°F [200°C]) for direct and indirect heating.

2. In a flat pan, coat the steak pieces with flour, massaging the flour well into the beef. In a cast-iron skillet, brown the beef in the oil over direct heat in the barbecue. Remove the beef with a slotted spoon and set aside.

3. Add the onion to the oil in the pan and cook, stirring often, until the onions are tender, about 10 minutes. Return the beef to the skillet, stir, and set the skillet aside.

4. In a medium bowl, mix together the beef broth, ketchup, Worcestershire sauce, Anaheim pepper, garlic salt, marjoram, and pepper. Add this mixture to the beef and onions. Bring to a boil and reduce the heat to a simmer. Cover and simmer until the beef is tender, 1¼ to 1½ hours.

5. Add the potatoes, green beans, and sun-dried tomatoes to the skillet and stir well. Return the skillet to the grill and cook until the liquid boils, then move the skillet to the unheated side of the grill. Cover and simmer until the beans are tender, 10 to 15 minutes.

6. Remove from the heat and serve the steak directly from the skillet or transfer it to a large serving dish.

Grilled Flat Iron Steak with Chimichurri Sauce
Yield: 6–8 servings

You can also use flank steaks in this recipe; or, if you'd rather spend the money, ribeye, sirloin strip, and New York strip steaks are great with the herby, garlicky chimichurri sauce.

1 handful (⅔ cup [158 mL]) wood chips (oak, hickory, or cherry)
1 cup (236 mL) extra virgin olive oil
15 cloves garlic, peeled
⅓ cup (79 mL) sherry vinegar
¼ cup (59 mL) loosely packed chopped fresh parsley
¼ cup (59 mL) loosely packed chopped fresh cilantro
¼ cup (59 mL) loosely packed fresh oregano
3 tablespoons (45 mL) fresh thyme
1 teaspoon (5 mL) salt, plus more to taste
½ teaspoon (2.5 m) freshly ground black pepper, plus more to taste
2 (1½-pound [681-g]) flat iron steaks
¼ cup (59 mL) butter

1. Place the wood chips in a large bowl or can, cover them with hot water, and soak for at least 2 hours.

2. In a food processor, combine the olive oil, garlic, vinegar, parsley, cilantro, oregano, thyme, salt, and pepper. Process until smooth, scrape into a bowl, cover, and set aside.

3. Make sure the grill is clean and generously sprayed with nonstick spray. Preheat the barbecue to medium high (350°F [180°C] to 400°F [200°C]).

4. In a cast-iron saucepan over direct heat on the grill, melt the butter until it begins to turn brown, about 2 minutes. Add the chimichurri sauce and cook, stirring, for 2 to 3 minutes, until it's bubbling. Remove the pan from the heat and keep the sauce warm.

5. Sprinkle the steaks with salt and pepper and let stand at room temperature for 5 minutes.

6. Meanwhile, put a handful of soaked wood chips on a piece of heavy-duty aluminum foil and fold it over like an envelope to enclose the wood. Using a pencil, poke 3 to 4 holes in the top of the foil envelope (don't poke all the way through). Place the foil directly on the coals or gas jets. When the wood inside starts to smoke, transfer the steaks to the grill over direct heat, cover the grill, and cook until juices form on the top of the steaks, flip, and cook the other side (about 4 minutes per side for medium-rare). Remove the steaks from the grill, drop a pat of butter on each steak, cover with foil, and let stand for 5 minutes.

7. To serve, slice the steaks thinly across the grain and drizzle with the chimichurri sauce. Serve with extra sauce on the side.

Quickie Cube Steaks
Yield: 4 servings

If you aren't a mushroom fan, you can substitute cream of celery, cream of onion, or tomato soup in this recipe.

2 tablespoons (30 mL) all-purpose flour
¾ teaspoon (3.75 mL) salt
¼ teaspoon (1.25 mL) dried oregano
⅛ teaspoon (0.6 mL) garlic powder
⅛ teaspoon (0.6 mL) pepper
1¼ pounds (566 g) beef cubed steaks
2 tablespoons (30 mL) olive oil
8 ounces [227 g]) sliced mushrooms
1 small green bell pepper, diced
1 small red bell pepper, diced
⅔ cup (158 mL) dry white wine
⅓ cup (79 mL) barbecue sauce
1 teaspoon (5 mL) instant beef soup base or bouillon
1 (10½-ounce) can cream of mushroom soup
¼ cup (59 mL) chopped fresh parsley

1. In a shallow dish, combine the flour, salt, oregano, garlic powder, and pepper. Dredge the steaks in the seasoned flour, then brown them in the olive oil in a cast-iron skillet over medium heat on the barbecue side burner for about 3 minutes on each side.

2. Remove the steaks with tongs and set aside, leaving the liquid in the skillet. Add the mushrooms, bell peppers, wine, barbecue sauce, and instant beef base to the skillet and stir to combine.

3. Return the steaks to the skillet, cover, and cook for 7 to 9 minutes, turning the meat several times.

4. Place the steaks on a warm platter and cover them. Add the soup to the gravy in the skillet and stir to heat through. Pour the gravy over the steaks, sprinkle with parsley, and serve.

Cabernet-Mushroom Beef Tenderloin

Yield: 6–8 servings

This recipe uses some of the more flavorful (and unfortunately expensive) mushroom varieties, but the cost is worth it as these mushrooms impart flavors that you cannot achieve with more common varieties. This recipe comes from Carson and Nicki Davis from Chicago.

½ ounce (14 g) dried morels
½ ounce (14 g) dried shiitakes
½ ounce (14 g) dried chanterelles
1½ cups (354 mL) hot water
½ teaspoon (2.5 mL) garlic salt
½ teaspoon (2.5 mL) freshly ground black pepper
½ teaspoon (2.5 mL) ground ginger
¼ teaspoon (1.25 mL) ground coriander
¼ teaspoon (1.25 mL) ground cumin
¼ teaspoon (1.25 mL) ground nutmeg
⅛ teaspoon (0.6 mL) ground cinnamon
4 tablespoons (60 mL) olive oil, divided
1 (3–4 pound [1.3–1.8 kg]) beef tenderloin
¼ cup (59 mL) butter, divided
1 cup (236 mL) minced shallots
¼ cup (59 mL) balsamic vinegar
1½ cups (354 mL) beef broth
1 cup (236 mL) Cabernet Sauvignon
Salt, to taste
Freshly ground black pepper, to taste
¼ cup (59 mL) chopped fresh parsley

1. Make sure the grill is clean and generously sprayed with nonstick grilling spray. Preheat the barbecue to medium high (475°F [250°C] to 500°F [260°C]).

2. In a 1-gallon (3.8-L) resealable plastic bag, hydrate the mushrooms in the hot water, for at least 20 minutes. Drain well, reserving the liquid, mince the mushrooms, and set aside.

3. In a small bowl, combine the garlic salt, pepper, ginger, coriander, cumin, nutmeg, and cinnamon.

4. Massage 3 tablespoons (45 mL) of the olive oil into the meat, then rub on the spice mixture, patting it into all sides of the meat. Place the meat on a rack in a roasting pan and cook in the barbecue for 25 to 30 minutes, or until a meat thermometer registers 135°F (57°C) degrees for a medium-rare roast.

5. While the meat cooks, heat the remaining olive oil and 1 tablespoon (15 mL) of the butter in a skillet over low heat on the side burner. Add the shallots and sauté, stirring, until they are wilted and soft. Add the vinegar and boil until the liquid is almost evaporated, about 3 to 4 minutes.

6. Add the mushrooms, their reserved soaking water, the beef broth, and the Cabernet. Bring to a boil, then lower the heat to a simmer and cook until the sauce is reduced by half, to about 2 cups (473 mL). Season with salt and pepper.

7. When the meat is fully cooked, remove it from the heat and transfer it to a heated platter. Cover it loosely with foil and let it stand for 15 to 20 minutes.

8. Whisk the pan juices into the reduced sauce, and then whisk in the remaining 3 tablespoons (45 mL) of butter until it's fully incorporated. Transfer the sauce to a heated sauce pitcher.

9. Slice the tenderloin in 1-inch (2.5-cm) slices. Serve with a tablespoon of the mushroom sauce on each slice, sprinkled with the parsley.

Grilled Delmonico Steaks with Mango Salsa
Yield: 4 servings

New York steak, New York strip, Delmonico steak, Kansas City steak, Kansas City strip, shell steak, sirloin club steak, and strip steak are all basically the same cut of meat, it just goes by different names in different parts of the country.

Steaks

¼ cup (59 mL) Worcestershire sauce
¼ cup (59 mL) dark soy sauce
¼ cup (59 mL) lemon or lime juice
2 tablespoons (30 mL) vegetable oil
2 cloves garlic, peeled, mashed, and diced
1 tablespoon (15 mL) chili powder
1 tablespoon (15 mL) brown sugar
4 (¾-inch [0.75-cm] thick) Delmonico steaks

Salsa

2 cups (473 mL) diced tomatoes
1 fresh mango, peeled, pitted, and diced
1 green bell pepper, seeded and diced
6 green onions, green and white parts, diced
1 large jalapeño pepper, seeded and diced
½ cup (118 mL) chopped fresh cilantro
¼ cup (59 mL) fresh lime juice

1. Make sure the grill is clean and generously sprayed with nonstick spray. Preheat the barbecue to medium high (400°F [200°C] to 450°F [260°C]).

2. In a small bowl, mix together the Worcestershire sauce, soy sauce, lemon or lime juice, oil, garlic, chili powder and sugar. Put the steaks in a wide, flat baking pan and pour the marinade over it. Prick the steaks all over with a meat fork, cover, and marinate for 25 to 30 minutes.

3. In a medium bowl, combine the tomatoes, mango, green bell pepper, green onions, jalapeño pepper, cilantro, and lime juice and mix well. Cover and set aside at room temperature.

4. Grill steaks on the heated grill for 8 to 10 minutes (4 to 5 minutes per side), turning once.

5. Serve the steaks with the mango salsa on the side.

Hong Kong Pepper Steak

Yield: 4–6 servings

This dish was prepared for me by photographer, Neil Farrin, during a three-month stay in Hong Kong working on my Hong Kong: Here Be Dragons *books. I discovered that Neil was as good a cook as he was a photographer, and he's a very good photographer.*

¼ cup (59 mL) soy sauce
1 tablespoon (15 mL) dark sesame oil
½ teaspoon (2.5 mL) freshly ground black pepper
1 (1½-pound [681-g]) boneless beef round steak, cut into ¼-inch (0.5-cm) slices
1 tablespoon (15 mL) vegetable oil
1 teaspoon (5 mL) grated fresh ginger
1 clove garlic, peeled and minced
1 medium green bell pepper, sliced
1 medium red bell pepper, sliced
2 cups (473 mL) sliced mushrooms
6 green onions, cut into ½-inch (1-cm) pieces, green and white parts
½ cup (118 mL) beef broth
1 tablespoon (15 mL) cornstarch
1 tablespoon (15 mL) sesame seeds

1. Preheat the barbecue to medium high (350°F [180°C] to 400°F [200°C]).

2. In a large bowl, combine the soy sauce, sesame oil, and pepper. Stir, then add the beef. Toss to coat each slice well, then let stand several hours in the refrigerator. Drain the beef, reserving the marinade. Boil the marinade for 10 minutes and set it aside.

3. In a cast-iron skillet or wok on the side burner over medium heat, heat the vegetable oil. Add the ginger, garlic, and beef and stir-fry until beef is browned, about 4 minutes.

4. Remove the beef with a slotted spoon and set it aside. Add the bell peppers, mushrooms, and green onions to the skillet and cook, stirring, until the vegetables are getting soft but still have a crunch to them, about 2 minutes.

5. Return the beef to the skillet. To the boiled marinade, add the beef broth and cornstarch. Stir well, then pour this mixture over the beef mixture and cook, stirring, until the sauce thickens and bubbles.

6. Place the skillet in the barbecue, cover, and cook for 15 minutes. Remove it from the barbecue, cool slightly, sprinkle with sesame seeds, and serve.

Barbecued London Broil

Yield: 6 servings

Contrary to popular belief, London Broil is not a cut of meat. Rather, it's a method of broiling or grilling a flank steak after marinating it.

⅓ cup (79 mL) cider vinegar
⅓ cup (79 mL) vegetable oil
3 tablespoons (45 mL) packed brown sugar
3 tablespoons (45 mL) soy sauce
2 medium onions, cut into 1-inch (2.5-cm) thick rings
1 clove garlic, peeled and crushed
1 teaspoon (5 mL) dried rosemary
½ teaspoon (2.5 mL) coarsely ground black pepper
1 (1½-pound [681-g]) beef flank steak

1. Make sure the grill is clean and generously sprayed with nonstick spray. Preheat the barbecue to medium high (350°F [180°C] to 400°F [200°C]).

2. In a medium bowl, mix together the vinegar, oil, brown sugar, soy sauce, onions, garlic, rosemary, and pepper. Put the beef into a 1-gallon (3.8-L) resealable plastic bag and pour the marinade in over it. Seal and refrigerate for 4 to 6 hours, turning the bag 3 times.

3. Remove the beef slices and onions, cover them, and set aside. Transfer the marinade to a saucepan and boil for 10 minutes.

4. Grill the beef, turning and brushing 2 or 3 times with the boiled marinade until it reaches desired doneness, 10 to 12 minutes for medium. Grill the onions alongside the beef for about 5 minutes, turning often.

5. Cut the beef diagonally across the grain into very thin slices and place them on a heated platter, topped with the onions.

Dinosaur Ribs

Yield: 6–8 servings

No, they aren't really dinosaur ribs, but a full rack of beef ribs looks pretty impressive on a platter. For a flavorful variation next time, brush them with melted butter or hoisin sauce instead of the barbecue sauce and then serve with barbecue sauce on the side.

2 cups (473 mL) orange juice
1 cup (236 mL) extra virgin olive oil
1 cup (236 mL) balsamic vinegar
1 cup (236 mL) dark soy sauce
½ cup (118 mL) Worcestershire sauce
2 tablespoons (30 mL) garlic salt
2 tablespoons (30 mL) dry mustard
1 tablespoon (15 mL) brown sugar
1 teaspoon (5 mL) paprika
1 teaspoon (5 mL) chili powder
1 teaspoon (5 mL) freshly ground black pepper
1 teaspoon (5 mL) hot sauce
1 cup (236 mL) barbecue sauce of your choice
2–3 racks beef ribs

1. Make sure the grill is clean and generously sprayed with nonstick grilling spray. Preheat the barbecue to medium high (350°F [180°C] to 400°F [200°C]) for direct and indirect heating.

2. In a medium bowl, mix together the orange juice, olive oil, vinegar, soy sauce, Worcestershire sauce, garlic salt, mustard, brown sugar, paprika, chili powder, black pepper, and hot sauce. Place the ribs in a 2-gallon (7.6-L) resealable plastic bag and pour the marinade over the ribs. Refrigerate for 4 to 6 hours or overnight, turning the bag occasionally.

3. Drain the ribs, reserving the marinade, and set aside until they come to room temperature. Pour the marinade into a saucepan, boil for 10 minutes, and set aside to use for basting.

4. Place the ribs directly on the hot grill and cook for 1 hour, basting frequently.

5. Place the ribs on a double layer of heavy-duty aluminum foil and baste lavishly with the marinade. Seal the foil and set the package on the unheated side of the barbecue to bake for 3 hours. Remove the ribs and brush them with the barbecue sauce. Completely wrap them in two layers of clear plastic wrap, then place the wrapped ribs in another double layer of foil and seal the foil. Cook for another 2 hours.

6. Open the foil, remove the plastic wrap, and place the ribs on a heated platter. Drizzle the remaining marinade over the meat and serve with more barbecue sauce on the side.

Cattle Country Tri-Tip

Yield: 4–6 servings

This cut of meat, from the tip of the sirloin, is sometimes mistakenly called California cut, Newport steak, sirloin tip, sirloin butt, culotte, and bottom sirloin.

3 tablespoons (45 mL) chili powder, divided
2 tablespoons (30 mL) ground cumin
1 tablespoon (15 mL) seasoned pepper
1 tablespoon (15 mL) onion powder
1 tablespoon (15 mL) garlic powder
1 teaspoon (5 mL) fresh rosemary leaves
½ teaspoon (2.5 mL) fresh thyme
1 (1½-pound [681-g]) beef tri-tip roast
1 (26-ounce [728-g]) jar spaghetti sauce
3 tablespoons (45 mL) marmalade
2 tablespoons (30 mL) Worcestershire sauce
1 tablespoon (15 mL) honey
2 teaspoons (10 mL) dry mustard
1 teaspoon (5 mL) kosher salt

1. Make sure the grill is clean and generously sprayed with nonstick grilling spray. Preheat the barbecue to medium high (350°F [180°C] to 400°F [200°C]).

2. In a small bowl, combine 2 tablespoons (30 mL) of the chili powder, the cumin, pepper, onion and garlic powders, rosemary, and thyme. Rub this mixture on all the meat surfaces. Collect any remaining rub and pour into the spaghetti sauce. Cover the meat and set it aside.

3. In a large saucepan, whisk together the spaghetti sauce, remaining chili powder, marmalade, Worcestershire sauce, honey, mustard and salt. Bring to a boil. Reduce the heat and simmer for 15 minutes. Set aside.

4. Grill the roast for 40 to 50 minutes for medium-rare (a meat thermometer should read 135°F (57°C) to 140°F [60°C]). Brush generously with the sauce during the last 5 minutes of cooking.

5. Cover the roast with foil and let it sit for 10 to 12 minutes to let the juices re-circulate.

6. To serve, cut the roast into thick slices diagonally across the grain. Serve with the remaining barbecue sauce on the side.

Scottish Steak Balmoral

Yield: 4 servings

I tried this steak at the Witchery Restaurant in Edinburgh, Scotland, and pried the recipe out of one of the chefs. They serve the steak with roasted potatoes and turnips and a glass of local Scotch whisky. Unless you're very brave, don't do this indoors— you'll set off the smoke alarm.

4 (10–12 ounce [280–336 g]) Aberdeen Angus ribeye or sirloin steaks
6 tablespoons (90 mL) Scotch whisky
1 cup (236 mL) heavy cream
½ cup (118 mL) beef stock
½ cup (118 mL) sliced crimini or button mushroom caps
1 teaspoon (5 mL) coarse-grain mustard
Salt, to taste
Freshly ground black pepper, to taste
1 tablespoon (15 mL) butter

1. Make sure the grill is clean and generously sprayed with nonstick spray. Preheat the barbecue to medium high (400°F [200°C] to 450°F [260°C]).

2. Grill the steaks over direct heat until the internal temperature reaches 145°F (163°C) for medium-rare, about 8 to 10 minutes. Transfer the steaks to a warmed plate, cover, and let them rest.

3. Add the whisky to a cast-iron skillet set over high heat on the barbecue side burner. Using an extra-long barbecue match or lighter, quickly but carefully ignite the whisky (always ignite the alcohol fumes at the edge of the pan, not the liquid itself). Add the cream, stock, mushrooms, and mustard and bring to a boil. Decrease the heat and simmer gently until the sauce is reduced by half, stirring occasionally, about 10 to 12 minutes.

4. Season the steaks with salt and pepper and pour a generous amount of the sauce over the meat.

Lone Tree Ranch Pan-Broiled T-Bones

Yield: 4 servings

If you can get them (and I know this is the beef chapter), use buffalo T-bone steaks in this recipe. Buffalo fat is similar to the omega oil-rich fats of salmon and cold water fish and is actually good for you. So don't trim off the fat; cook it and be healthy.

4 (10-ounce [280-g]) beef or buffalo T-bone steaks
4 cloves garlic, peeled and thinly sliced
2 tablespoons (30 mL) kosher salt
½ cup (118 mL) butter, melted
1 tablespoon (15 mL) bacon fat
4 large mushrooms, sliced
1 splash Worcestershire sauce

1. Generously spray a cast-iron griddle with nonstick grilling spray. Preheat the barbecue to medium high (550°F [290°C] to 600°F [315°C]).

2. Using a small, sharp knife, make small cuts in the steaks and insert garlic slices in the cuts.

3. On the grill, heat the prepared cast-iron griddle to very hot. Sprinkle the kosher salt on the griddle and heat for another 2 to 3 minutes. Place the steaks on the griddle. (The salt prevents the steaks from sticking to the hot griddle.)

4. As soon as the steaks are well-seared on one side, turn them over. Brush the top with melted butter. When the bottom is seared, turn the steaks over one more time, brush butter on the second side, and cook for 1 minute.

5. Wrap the steaks in aluminum foil and seal. Let them rest in a warm oven or on a baking sheet in the barbecue for 10 minutes. They will be medium-rare.

6. In a cast-iron skillet, heat the bacon fat and any remaining butter. Add the sliced mushrooms and cook until soft and browned. Add the Worcestershire sauce and stir.

7. Serve each steak with 1 to 2 tablespoons (15 to 30 mL) of the mushrooms scattered on top.

Sage Brush Beef and Onion Casserole

Yield: 8 servings

If you can't find boiling onions, you can use double the number of cocktail onions, but you must soak them in milk for an hour to get rid of the pickled taste, then rinse them in cold water and pat dry. If you don't like onions, skip this dish, as it uses five members of the onion/garlic family.

⅓ cup (79 mL) all-purpose flour
1 tablespoon (15 mL) ground sage
½ teaspoon (2.5 mL) paprika
¼ teaspoon (1.25 mL) freshly ground black pepper
1 (2-pound [908-g]) beef round steak, cut into ¾-inch (0.75-cm) cubes
¼ cup (59 mL) olive oil
1 beef bouillon cube
1½ cups (354 mL) hot water
1 tablespoon (15 mL) minced garlic
16 small boiling onions
1 medium white onion, sliced into ½-inch (1-cm) rings
1 (10¾-ounce [301-g]) can condensed cream of mushroom soup
1 cup (236 mL) dry white wine, warmed
¼ cup (59 mL) minced green onions, green parts only
2 cups (473 mL) biscuit mix
1 teaspoon (5 mL) dry onion flakes
1 teaspoon (5 mL) poppy seeds
1 teaspoon (5 mL) ground sage
¼ teaspoon (1.25 mL) celery salt
⅔ cup (158 mL) milk
2 tablespoons (30 mL) minced chives, for garnish

1. Preheat the barbecue to medium high (350°F [180°C] to 400°F [200°C]). Spray a 4-quart (3.8-L) Dutch oven or a deep roasting pan with nonstick spray.

2. In a shallow dish, combine the flour, sage, paprika, and pepper. Dredge the beef cubes in the seasoned flour and then put them into a cast-iron or nonstick skillet with the olive oil. Brown on all sides. Dissolve the bouillon cube in the hot water and add the minced garlic. Add this mixture to the beef in the skillet. Cover and simmer for 30 minutes.

3. Add the boiling onions and continue simmering for 30 minutes longer, until the beef is tender. Transfer a third of the beef and onions to the prepared Dutch oven or deep roasting pan. Layer on half of the onion rings and spoon in half of the mushroom soup. Add another layer of the beef and onions, the rest of the onion rings; and the remaining mushroom soup, in that order. Pour in the white wine, but do not stir. Sprinkle with the minced green onions.

4. Place the Dutch oven in the barbecue and cook for 5 minutes, uncovered.

5. To make the dumplings, combine the biscuit mix, poppy seeds, ground sage, and celery salt in a medium bowl. Stir well. Add the milk and stir until a soft dough forms. Drop the dough by tablespoonfuls into the Dutch oven and bake for 20 to 25 minutes, or until the casserole is bubbling and the dumplings are nicely browned. Garnish with the minced chives and serve.

Teriyaki Steak and Spring Onion Rolls
Yield: 4 servings

Teriyaki is a sweet glaze applied to fish, meat, or fowl in the final stages of grilling or pan-frying. It is based on a trio of classic Japanese ingredients: soy sauce, sake, and mirin. These spring rolls make a nice appetizer, but they would also work for lunch or a light supper with fried rice and stir-fried asparagus, yellow string beans, and strips of red bell pepper.

½ cup (120 mL) water
6 tablespoons (90 mL) sugar
¼ cup (59 mL) dark soy sauce
¼ cup (59 mL) sake
2 tablespoons (30 mL) mirin (sweet rice wine)
¼ teaspoon (1.25 mL) minced garlic
1 pinch grated fresh ginger
3 (8-ounce (227-g)) boneless sirloin or ribeye steaks
6 whole green spring onions, cut in 3-inch (7.5-cm) pieces
Steamed rice, for serving

1. Make sure the grill is clean and generously sprayed with nonstick grilling spray. Preheat the barbecue to medium high (350°F [180°C] to 400°F [200°C]).

2. In a small saucepan over medium heat, combine the water, sugar, soy sauce, sake, mirin, garlic, and ginger. Heat, stirring, until the sugar has dissolved. Set aside.

3. Cut the steaks into 3-inch (7.5-cm) wide strips, each the length of the steak, then cut each piece in half across the grain so you have 3 × 4-inch (7.5 × 9-cm) pieces. Place the steak strips between sheets of waxed paper and, using a tenderizing mallet pound to a ¼-inch (0.5-cm) thickness.

4. Arrange one green onion piece in the center of each piece of meat, then brush with some of the teriyaki sauce. Starting with the long end, roll the steak into a tight cylinder. Secure with a toothpick. Repeat with the remaining ingredients.

5. Spray the rolls with grilling spray and place them on the grill. Grill for 3 minutes. Using tongs, turn them over, brush with teriyaki sauce, and grill on the other side for 3 minutes longer.

6. Transfer the rolls to a cutting board and remove the toothpicks. Cut the rolls in half and stand each piece on end on serving plates, surrounded by steamed rice. Drizzle the remaining teriyaki sauce on the meat and rice and serve.

Herb-Crusted Prime Rib Roast

Yield: 8–10 servings

Don't throw away the drippings from the cooked roast. Use them to make Yorkshire pudding (p. 601) or gravy or brush the fat on a pan of roasted potatoes 10 minutes before taking them out of the oven.

1 (9–10 pound [4.1–4.5 kg]) 4- or 5-rib prime rib roast, trimmed, chine bone removed
1 tablespoon (15 mL) salt
1 tablespoon (15 mL) dried rosemary
1 tablespoon (15 mL) dried savory
½ teaspoon (2.5 mL) freshly ground black pepper
4 tablespoons (60 mL) extra virgin olive oil, divided
1½ cups (354 mL) fresh breadcrumbs
½ cup (118 mL) chopped fresh rosemary
1 tablespoon (15 mL) dried oregano
1 tablespoon (15 mL) granulated garlic
1 tablespoon (15 mL) minced lemon zest
1 teaspoon (5 mL) dried thyme
½ teaspoon (2.5 mL) fresh lemon juice
¼ cup (59 mL) prepared yellow mustard
Fresh rosemary sprigs, for garnish

1. Make sure the grill is clean and generously sprayed with nonstick grilling spray. Preheat the barbecue to medium high (450°F [240°C] to 500°F [260°C]) for direct and indirect heating.

2. In a small bowl, mix together the salt, dried rosemary, savory, and pepper to make a rub. Place the roast in a medium size roasting pan, fat side up. Brush all surfaces with 3 tablespoons (45 mL) of the olive oil and sprinkle the rub on all sides of the roast, patting it into the meat as you turn the roast.

3. In a separate small bowl, mix together remaining olive oil, breadcrumbs, fresh rosemary, oregano, garlic, lemon zest, thyme, and lemon juice and set aside.

4. Place the prime rib in the roasting pan into the barbecue over direct heat and cook for 45 minutes. Remove the roast from the barbecue and roasting pan and generously brush the mustard over the entire roast. Gently press the bread mixture onto the mustard-coated roast.

5. Return the roast to the pan and place the pan on the unheated side of the barbecue. Cook for 1½ to 1¾ hours, or until the coating is golden and a meat thermometer inserted into the center of roast, not touching a bone, registers 130°F (54°C).

6. Remove the pan from the grill and transfer the meat to a heated platter. Cover the roast with aluminum foil and let it rest for 10 minutes so the juices redistribute throughout the roast. The internal temperature of meat will then rise to 140 to 145°F (60 to 63°C) for medium-rare upon standing.

7. Garnish with the rosemary sprigs and slice at the table.

Pineapple-Peach Barbecued Beef Ribs
Yield: 4–6 servings

For a variation on this recipe, substitute apricot jam, rhubarb preserves, or orange marmalade for the peach preserves and, instead of the pineapple, use stewed prunes, chopped nectarines, or chopped fresh plums.

3–4 pounds (1.3–1.8 kg) lean beef ribs
1 cup (236 mL) pineapple chunks
½ cup (118 mL) peach preserves
½ cup (118 mL) water
Juice of 1 lemon
2 tablespoons (30 mL) A1 steak sauce
1½ tablespoons (22.5 mL) brown sugar
1 tablespoon (15 mL) ground cumin
1 tablespoon (15 mL) white vinegar
1 teaspoon (5 mL) granulated garlic
½ teaspoon (2.5 mL) paprika
Freshly ground black pepper, to taste

1. Preheat the barbecue to medium high (450°F [240°C] to 500°F [260°C]) for direct and indirect heating.

2. Place the beef ribs on a rack in a deep roasting pan or Dutch oven and roast them in the barbecue for 30 minutes.

3. In a medium saucepan, combine the pineapple, peach preserves, water, lemon juice, steak sauce, brown sugar, cumin, vinegar, garlic, paprika, and pepper. Cook over medium heat until thickened, stirring constantly. Set aside.

4. Remove the ribs and rack from the pan. Pour off the fat. Cut the ribs into individual ribs Open vents in the barbecue to lower the temperature to 350°F (180°C).

5. Arrange the ribs in the pan, in a single layer, then pour the sauce over them. Cover and bake, basting occasionally until ribs are tender; about 1½ to 2 hours.

Beef Bourguignon
Yield: 6 servings

This is a long, involved process, to be sure, but it guarantees one of the best beef dishes you have ever served or eaten. This classic dish makes other beef stews taste like dog food.

2½ pounds (1.1 kg) boneless beef chuck, cut into 1½-inch (3.5 cm) cubes
¾ cup (177 mL) butter or margarine, divided
3 tablespoons (45 mL) brandy, divided
8 ounces (227 g) small white onions, peeled
8 ounces (227 g) small mushrooms
2½ tablespoons (22.5 mL) potato flour
2½ teaspoons (12.5 mL) meat extract paste
2 tablespoons (30 mL) tomato paste
1½ cups (354 mL) burgundy
1 (10-ounce [280-g]) can condensed beef broth
¾ cup (177 mL) dry sherry
¾ cup (177 mL) ruby port
½ teaspoon (2.5 mL) freshly ground black pepper
1 bay leaf

1. Preheat the barbecue to medium high (350°F [180°C] to 400°F [200°C]).

2. In a 4-quart (3.8-L) Dutch oven, slowly heat ¼ cup (56.7 g) of the butter. Add the beef in batches (about ¼ of the beef at a time) and brown well, removing the beef as it browns and adding ¼ cup more butter as needed. Return all of the beef to the Dutch oven.

3. In a large cast-iron skillet, heat 2 tablespoons (30 mL) of the brandy just until vapor rises. Ignite the brandy and pour it over the beef. As the flames die, remove the beef and set it aside. Add the remaining butter. When the butter has melted, add the onions. Cook over low heat, covered, until the onions brown slightly. Add the mushrooms and cook for 3 to 4 minutes until they are tender, and remove the pan from the heat. Stir in the flour, meat extract paste, and tomato paste until well blended. Add the burgundy, broth, sherry, and port, return the Dutch oven to the grill, and bring to a boil, stirring. Remove the pot from the heat.

4. Add the beef, pepper, and bay leaf and mix well. Cover the Dutch oven and return it to the barbecue. Cook for 1½ hours, or until the beef is tender, stirring a few times and adding the remaining brandy a little at a time.

Mini-Que Reubens

Yield: 4–6 servings

The Reuben sandwich is alleged to have been invented by several individuals, including a New York deli owner, two grocers in Nebraska, and a hotel waitress. By the way, Russian dressing originally contained caviar, but the cost of these treasured sturgeon eggs quickly made that version too pricey.

1 (12-ounce [354 mL]) can corned beef
½ cup (118 mL) Russian dressing
2 loaves party rye bread slices
1 (8-ounce [227-g]) can sauerkraut
1 (8-ounce [227-g]) package Swiss cheese

1. Preheat the barbecue to medium high (350°F [180°C]).

2. In a saucepan, combine the corned beef and Russian dressing and mix well. Cook over low heat on barbecue side burner and keep warm.

3. Spread the corned beef mixture on slices of the party rye. Add 1 teaspoon (5 mL) of sauerkraut to each slice.

4. Cut each slice of cheese into four. Place two small slices of cheese on top of each Reuben.

5. Bake the Reubens in the barbecue for 10 minutes, or until the cheese melts and barely begins to brown.

6. Serve with chilled adult beverages.

RBQ's Smoked Meatloaf

Yield: 4–6 servings

We call the process of adding smoke while meat is baking in the barbecue either "smilling" or "groking"—merely a combination of grilling and smoking, taking advantage of the best of both barbecue methods. This dish goes well with grilled corn and baked potatoes.

3 pounds (1.3 kg) ground beef
3 red Anaheim peppers, seeded and chopped
¾ cup (177 mL) whole-wheat breadcrumbs
¼ cup (59 mL) Parmigiano-Reggiano cheese, grated or shredded
¼ cup (59 mL) Asiago cheese
¼ cup (59 mL) pure maple syrup
¼ cup (59 mL) red wine vinegar
¼ teaspoon (1.25 mL) balsamic vinegar
2 large eggs, beaten
¼ teaspoon (1.25 mL) seasoned salt
¼ teaspoon (1.25 mL) freshly ground black pepper
1 cup (236 mL) smoky barbecue sauce

1. Soak a handful of hickory or oak chips in hot water for 3 hours.

2. Preheat the barbecue to medium high (350°F [180°C] to 400°F [200°C]).

3. Spray a 2-quart (1.9-L) Dutch oven with nonstick cooking spray.

4. In a large bowl, combine the ground beef and red peppers and stir well. Add the breadcrumbs, cheeses, maple syrup, vinegars, eggs, salt, and pepper, and mix well with your hands.

5. Place the soaked wood chips on a 12-inch (30-cm) square of heavy-duty foil and fold over the edges to make an envelope. Poke 3 or 4 holes in the top of the packet only and place it directly on the coals or gas flame to smoke the meatloaf while you are baking it.

6. Add the meat mixture to the prepared Dutch oven, pressing it down lightly to avoid air pockets. Place the Dutch oven in the barbecue and cook for 1 to 1½ hours, or until the internal temperature of the meat is 170°F (77°C)°.

7. Open the barbecue and pour the barbecue sauce over the top of the meatloaf. Lower the lid and cook for another 5 minutes.

8. Remove the meatloaf, cover it in foil, and let rest for 10 to 12 minutes. Cut it into 2-inch (5-cm) thick slices and serve.

Hungarian Goulash with Sauerkraut

Yield: 8 servings

Paprika, the backbone of true Hungarian goulash, is a red powder made from grinding the dried pods of bell or mild chili peppers. It comes in hot, medium, and mild varieties.

¼ cup (59 mL) vegetable or olive oil
3 pounds (1.3 kg) boneless beef chuck, cut into 1½-inch (3.5-cm) cubes
3 cups (708 mL) sliced onions
1 tablespoon (15 mL) mild Hungarian paprika (or Hungarian paprika cream)
1½ teaspoons (7.5 mL) salt
⅛ teaspoon (0.6 mL) freshly ground black pepper
1 cup (236 mL) water
1 beef bouillon cube
2 (14-ounce [392-g]) cans sauerkraut
3 tablespoons (45 mL) vegetable shortening
½ cup (118 mL) chopped onion
2 cups (473 mL) boiling water
1 large potato, peeled and grated
2 tablespoons (30 mL) brown sugar
1 teaspoon (5 mL) caraway seeds
3 tablespoons (45 mL) cornstarch
1 cup (236 mL) sour cream

1. Preheat the barbecue to medium high (350°F [180°C] to 400°F [200°C]).

2. In a 4-quart (3.8-L) Dutch oven or roasting pan, heat the oil. Add the beef cubes in single layers (this will take several batches) and brown them on all sides. As each batch browns up, transfer the cubes with a slotted spoon to a large bowl. Browning the beef should take about 20 minutes total. Leave the drippings in the pan.

3. Add the sliced onions to the drippings and cook until tender and golden, then return the beef to the Dutch oven. Add the paprika, salt, and pepper and stir until well blended. Add the water and bouillon cube. Place the Dutch oven in the barbecue, bring the mixture to a boil, and turn down the gas (or close down the vents if using charcoal) to reduce the heat. Simmer, covered, for 2 hours, until the meat is tender.

4. While the meat cooks, prepare the sauerkraut by rinsing it, then squeezing it dry. In a large skillet, heat the shortening. Add the chopped onion and sauté until golden. Add the sauerkraut, water, potato, brown sugar, and caraway seed, and boiling water and bring everything to a boil. Reduce the heat and simmer, uncovered, stirring occasionally, for 20 minutes, or until most of the liquid has evaporated.

5. Blend the cornstarch in ¼ cup (59 mL) water and gradually add it to the beef mixture. Stir well, then continue cooking, uncovered, for 15 minutes longer.

6. In a small bowl, stir ½ cup (118 mL) of the gravy from the Dutch oven into the sour cream, then add the sour cream slowly to the beef mixture, stirring to blend.

7. Scoop the sauerkraut mixture into a large serving bowl, pour the beef mixture over the sauerkraut, and serve.

Miso Barbecue Short Ribs with Ginger-Teriyaki Sauce
Yield: 6 servings

Miso, made from fermented soybeans, rice, or barley, gives this marinade a rich, salty-sweet, earthy flavor. Very popular in Japan (over 1,400 companies manufacture it there) miso is catching on in the United States as a healthy, protein-rich addition to any diet.

3 tablespoons (45 mL) mirin (sweet rice wine)
3 tablespoons (45 mL) good-quality sake
3 tablespoons (45 mL) dark soy sauce
1½ tablespoons (22.5 mL) red miso
1 tablespoon (15 mL) sugar
1 tablespoon (15 mL) distilled white vinegar
2 teaspoons (10 mL) toasted sesame oil
2½ pounds (1.1 kg) beef short ribs, well trimmed
1¼ cups (295 mL) teriyaki sauce
½ teaspoon (2.5 mL) finely minced fresh ginger
Cooked noodles or steamed white rice, for serving

1. In a small bowl, combine the mirin, sake, soy sauce, miso, sugar, vinegar, and sesame oil to make a marinade. Place the ribs in a resealable plastic bag and add the marinade. Shake the bag and massage each rib to coat. Refrigerate for 4 to 6 hours.

2. Prepare a charcoal or gas barbecue for direct and indirect cooking, placing a drip pan under the cool side of the grill rack. Preheat to 400°F (200°C). Make sure the grill rack is clean, and oil it thoroughly with nonstick spray.

3. Remove the ribs from the marinade and wipe off the excess. Pour the remaining marinade into a small saucepan, add the teriyaki sauce and ginger, and boil over high heat for 12 minutes, then cool it to use for basting. (Alternatively, you can baste with a favorite teriyaki sauce.)

4. Transfer the marinated ribs to the prepared grill rack over direct heat and cook for 1½ to 2 minutes per side to sear. Move the ribs to the indirect side of the grill and cook for 20 to 25 minutes, turning often and basting frequently with the miso-teriyaki sauce.

5. Serve hot over the noodles or rice with the remaining miso-teriyaki sauce on the side.

Beef, Bacon, and Beans Dinner
Yield: 4–6 servings

Perhaps the oldest cultivated food on earth, beans have been around since man first put a stick in the ground to plant a seed. I use Bush's because they offer dozens of varieties and are available everywhere.

1 (28-ounce [784 g]) can Bush's Black Bean Fiesta Grillin' Beans
1 (21-ounce [588-g]) can Bush's pinto beans, drained
1 (17-ounce [482-g]) can Bush's cannellini beans, drained
1 (15½-ounce [440-g]) can Bush's kidney beans, drained
1 cup (236 mL) chopped mushrooms
1 cup (236 mL) ketchup
⅔ cup (158 mL) barbecue sauce
1 teaspoon (5 mL) dry marjoram
1 teaspoon (5 mL) dry oregano
½ teaspoon (2.5 mL) ground ginger
½ pound (227 g) bacon, chopped
1½ pounds (681 g) ground beef
1 cup (236 mL) chopped onions
¼ cup (59 mL) chopped fresh parsley, for garnish

1. Preheat the barbecue to medium high (350°F [180°C] to 400°F [200°C]).

2. Spray a Dutch oven or a large heatproof casserole with nonstick cooking spray.

3. In a large skillet, cook the bacon until it's crisp. Remove the bacon from the pan, leaving the grease, drain bacon, break it into bite-sized pieces, and set aside.

4. Brown the ground beef and onion together in the bacon grease, then drain.

5. In the prepared Dutch oven or casserole, combine the beef, onions, and bacon pieces. Fold in the beans, mushrooms, ketchup, barbecue sauce, marjoram, oregano, and ginger and mix together.

6. Bake in the barbecue for 1 hour.

7. Remove from the barbecue, garnish with chopped parsley, and serve.

Bourbon-Marinated Steaks

Yield: 6 servings

Marinades need to contain an oil, an acid, and seasonings. If you want to use any marinade to baste the meat while it's on the grill, you must boil it for at least 10 minutes to kill any bacteria introduced to the liquid by the raw meat.

6 (1½-inch [3.5 cm] thick) beef T-bone or New York strip steaks
¾ cup (177 mL) olive oil
⅓ cup (79 mL) Maker's Mark (or your favorite brand) bourbon
¼ cup (59 mL) steak sauce
Juice of 2 lemons
6 cloves garlic, peeled and finely minced
Freshly ground black pepper, to taste

1. Place the steaks in a 1- to 2-gallon (3.8- to 7.6-L) resealable plastic bag.

2. In a small bowl, whisk together the olive oil, bourbon, steak sauce, lemon juice, minced garlic, and black pepper. Pour this mixture over the steaks, seal the bag, and marinate the steaks for 2 to 3 hours in the refrigerator.

3. Remove the marinating meat from the refrigerator 20 to 30 minutes before cooking. Take the steaks out of the bag and set them aside to warm to room temperature. Pour the marinade into a saucepan and boil it for 10 minutes.

4. Make sure the grill is clean and generously sprayed with nonstick grilling spray. Preheat the barbecue to medium high (400°F [200°C] to 450°F [240°C]).

5. Cook the steaks directly on the hot grill, 2 minutes on each side for rare, 3 minutes on each side for medium. Brush frequently with the boiled marinade.

Tennessee Mountain Beef Brisket

Yield: 8–10 servings

Although I specify certain brands in this recipe because I've used them several times and love the results, you can use your favorite brands instead, if you like. I'm not a spokesman for any of these; I merely like what happens when I use them.

1 (8–10 pound [3.6–4.5 kg]) fresh beef brisket, with deckle
½ cup (118 mL) prepared yellow mustard, divided
1 (8-ounce [227-g]) shaker Tony Chachere's Cajun Seasoning, divided
1 (1-pound [454-g]) bag dark brown sugar, divided
1 (8-ounce [227-g]) bottle Italian dressing
1 teaspoon (5 mL) Spice Barn hickory smoke powder

1. Make sure the grill is clean and generously sprayed with nonstick grilling spray. Preheat the barbecue to medium high (275°F [140°C] to 300°F [150°C]) for direct and indirect heating.

2. Place the raw brisket directly on the grill and cook for 20 minutes per side to sear the meat. Transfer the meat from the barbecue to a large sheet of heavy-duty aluminum foil.

3. Squirt about ¼ cup (59 mL) of the prepared mustard on one side of the brisket and, wearing plastic gloves, massage the mustard well into the meat. Sprinkle half the Cajun seasoning onto the mustard and rub it in with your hands. Turn the brisket over and repeat with the remaining mustard and Cajun seasoning on the other side.

4. Apply half of the brown sugar to the brisket so that it completely covers one side with a layer that is about ⅛ inch (0.25 cm) thick. Flip the brisket over and repeat on other side.

5. Place the brisket fat side up on the foil and pour the whole bottle of Italian dressing over it, trying not to melt off the sugar. Sprinkle with the hickory smoke powder and seal tightly in the aluminum foil. Wrap in a second layer of foil and seal.

6. Cook the foil-wrapped brisket in the barbecue for 6 hours.

7. Open the foil, exposing the meat, and cook for another hour.

8. Remove the meat from the barbecue, set it on a cutting board or serving platter, cover it with a tent of foil, and let it rest for 10 to 15 minutes. Pour the drippings into a gravy boat and keep warm.

9. With a sharp knife, slice the brisket across the grain and serve immediately.

Boeuf Bordelaise à la Barbecue
Yield: 5–7 servings

This recipe can only be prepared on a gas grill as you have to turn off the heat after 1 hour, and that's impossible with charcoal, unless you remove the meat and grates, shovel out the hot coals, replace the grates, and put the meat back into the barbecue. Nope—not worth trying! Start this recipe in the morning to have it ready in time for dinner.

1 (5–6 pound [2.3–2.7 kg]) beef standing rib roast
Salt, to taste
Freshly ground black pepper, to taste
2 tablespoons (30 mL) extra virgin olive oil, divided
3 shallots, peeled and minced
1 tablespoon (15 mL) all-purpose flour
1 cup (236 mL) beef stock
1 cup (236 mL) dry red wine
½ teaspoon (2.5 mL) Bovril beef extract, or a good-quality beef base concentrate, such as Penzey's
½ cup (118 mL) sliced mushrooms
1 teaspoon (5 mL) lemon juice

1. Take roast from the refrigerator in the afternoon and let it sit at room temperature for 1 hour, covered.

2. Preheat a gas barbecue to high (400°F [200°C]).

3. Season the meat with salt and pepper, then place the meat, fat side up, in a shallow roasting pan. Do not cover and do not add water. Put the roast in the barbecue and cook for 1 hour. Turn off the gas. Do not open the barbecue lid until ready to serve. (The meat can safely sit on the unlit grill for 3 hours.)

4. 30 to 40 minutes before you plan to eat, turn on the gas, again to 400°F (200°C), and cook for 40 minutes, still keeping the barbecue door (or lid) closed. The roast will be crusty on the outside and perfectly medium-rare on inside.

5. While the roast is cooking its last 40 minutes, heat 1 tablespoon (15 mL) of the olive oil in a large, nonstick skillet and sauté the shallots, stirring often. Blend in the flour, and slowly add the beef stock, wine, and Bovril (or beef base concentrate) and bring to a boil, stirring constantly.

6. Reduce the heat and keep on a high simmer until the sauce is reduced by one-third.

7. In another skillet, heat the remaining olive oil and sauté the sliced mushrooms. Add the lemon juice and cook until the mushrooms are soft. Add the cooked mushrooms to the wine sauce and keep warm.

8. Open the oven, remove the roast, and cover it with foil. Let it rest for 10 to 15 minutes.

9. Add the pan juices from the roast to the wine sauce. Slice the roast and serve with gravy boats of sauce on the side.

Kate's Kurried Kranberry Meatloaf
Yield: 4 servings

Many folks think that all the cranberries in the United States are grown in the bogs of Massachusetts, but nay, nay. The bitter fruit is also grown in Washington, Oregon, New Jersey, and Wisconsin. In fact, Wisconsin produces almost 4 million barrels of berries a year—more than all the other states combined!

½ cup (118 mL) whole cranberry sauce
¾ cup (177 mL) packed dark brown sugar, divided
2 tablespoons (30 mL) bottled chili sauce
1 teaspoon (5 mL) mild curry powder
2½ pounds (1.1 kg) ground beef chuck
½ cup (118 mL) milk
1 medium onion, peeled and finely diced
½ cup (118 mL) plain breadcrumbs
¼ cup (59 mL) ketchup
2 large eggs, beaten
½ teaspoon (2.5 mL) dried thyme
½ teaspoon (2.5 mL) dried basil
½ teaspoon (2.5 mL) garlic salt
¼ teaspoon (1.25 mL) freshly ground black pepper
¼ teaspoon freshly ground nutmeg

1. Preheat the barbecue to medium high (350°F [180°C] to 400°F [200°C]).

2. Spray a 9 × 5-inch (22.5 × 12.5-cm) loaf pan with nonstick spray.

3. In a small bowl, mix together the cranberry sauce, ½ cup (118 mL) of the brown sugar, the chili sauce, and the curry powder. Stir well to incorporate.

4. Spoon the cranberry mixture into the bottom of the prepared loaf pan and set aside.

5. In a large bowl, combine the ground chuck, milk, onion, breadcrumbs, ketchup, eggs, thyme, basil, garlic salt, and pepper and mix well with your hands. Spoon the meat mixture into the loaf pan on top of the cranberry sauce. Scatter the remaining ¼ cup (59 mL) brown sugar over the meat, sprinkle with the nutmeg, and place the pan in the barbecue to cook for 1½ hours or until done.

6. Allow the meatloaf to cool, covered, for 20 minutes. Then carefully turn the loaf onto a serving plate so that the sauce side is on top, drizzle the meat with any pan juices, slice, and serve.

Grill-Roasted Traditional Beef Wellington

Yield: 4–6 servings

It's fairly easy to make a perfect sauce for this dish by combining 1 cup (236 mL) of red wine and 2 cups (473 mL) of real beef stock (not consommé or bouillon) in a saucepan, bringing the liquid to a boil, simmering for 20 to 25 minutes until the sauce is reduced to a syrupy consistency, and whisking a tablespoon (15 mL) cold butter into the sauce. This recipe comes from Doug Spittler from Kalama, Wash.

1 (5–6 pound [2.3–2.7 kg]) prime beef tenderloin
5 tablespoons (75 mL) butter, melted, divided
Salt, to taste
Freshly ground black pepper, to taste
1 tablespoon (15 mL) olive oil
1 cup (236 mL) minced crimini mushrooms
2 tablespoons (30 mL) Madeira
1 teaspoon (5 mL) dried thyme
1 teaspoon (5 mL) minced shallots
1 (17.4-ounce [487-g]) package frozen puff pastry
½ pound (227 g) goose liver *foie gras*, best quality
1 large egg
2 teaspoons (10 mL) milk

1. Make sure the grill is clean and generously sprayed with nonstick grilling spray. Preheat the barbecue to medium high (375°F [190°C] to 400°F [200°C]) for direct and indirect heating.

2. Using butcher's twine, tie the tail of the tenderloin under the meat so that the roast has an even-diameter end to end. Brush the meat with 3 tablespoons (45 mL) of the melted butter, then season lightly with salt and pepper. Place the meat directly in the center of the grill and roast for 30 to 40 minutes, or until it reaches an internal temperature of 120°F (49°C) for very rare.

3. Remove the tenderloin from the grill and let stand, covered, for 30 minutes.

4. On barbecue side burner, heat the remaining butter and the olive oil in a nonstick skillet. Add the mushrooms, Madeira, thyme, and shallots and sauté, stirring, until the liquids evaporate and the mushrooms are soft.

5. On a floured cutting board, roll out 2 sheets of the pastry dough to a 14 × 12-inch (35 × 30-cm) rectangle, large enough to enclose the entire tenderloin. Set 1 sheet aside and cover it with a damp (not wet) towel.

6. Place the other sheet of dough on a clean, flat baking sheet, and place the meat lengthwise in the center of the dough. With a rubber spatula, spread the goose liver *foie gras* (don't pay the rent that month) on top of the tenderloin, then spoon on the mushroom mixture, gently packing it into the pâté with the spatula or your hands.

7. In a small bowl, beat together the egg and milk. Brush the edges of the pastry with the egg wash, then cover the meat with the second sheet of puff pastry, leaving a 1-inch (2.5-cm) border all around the meat and cutting off any excess pastry. Dip a fork into cold water and press down along the edges to seal completely all around the roast.

8. Brush the top and four sides of the pastry with the egg wash, tent the roast loosely with foil, and place the baking sheet in the center of the barbecue. Cook for 10 minutes, then lower the temperature to about 375°F (190°C) by closing the vents, lowering the gas flames, or cracking open the lid, and cook for an additional 20 to 25 minutes, until the pastry crust is golden.

9. Remove the baking sheet from the barbecue, carefully slide the meat onto a large serving platter, cover it with foil, and let it rest for 15 minutes

10. With a very sharp knife, slice the Wellington at the table into 3-inch (7.5-cm) thick slices. Use a long, thin spatula to transfer the slices to individual plates, being careful not to break the pastry around the meat.

Guinness Barbecued and Brewed Sirloin
Yield: 4–6 servings

You can make this recipe with a milder beer, but the rich, creamy, caramel malt flavor with a somewhat bitter finish works wonders for beef, whether you cook the meat in the beer or drink a brew along with your stew or steak.

3–4 pounds (1.3–1.8 kg) beef roast, either rump or sirloin
Salt, to taste
Freshly ground black pepper, to taste
2 medium onions, peeled and sliced
1 (1–1½-ounce [42-grams]) package onion soup mix
1 cup (236 mL) smoky barbecue sauce
¾ cup (177 mL) water
1 (14.9-ounce [441-mL]) can Guinness draught beer
Minced fresh parsley, for garnish

1. Preheat the barbecue to medium high (400°F [200°C] to 425°F [220°C]).

2. Spray a roasting pan with nonstick spray.

3. Season the beef with salt and pepper and put it in the prepared roast roasting pan. Cook in the barbecue for 30 minutes.

4. Remove the pan from the barbecue and scatter the onions over the meat, then pour the onion soup over the onions. Mix together the barbecue sauce and water and pour this mixture into the pan around the meat, not on top of it.

5. Lower the temperature by turning down the gas, or, if using charcoal, closing the vents by half. Cover the pan and return it to the barbecue. Continue cooking for 2 to 2½ hours.

6. Lift the lid and pour the beer over the meat. Cover and cook for 1 hour.

7. Remove the pan from the barbecue and let it sit, covered, for 15 minutes. Uncover the pan, transfer the meat to a platter, and slice, sprinkling the slices with the parsley. Pour the liquid and onions in the pan into a sauce boat and serve at the table.

Sear-Roasted Filet Mignon with Pinot–Black Pepper Sauce
Yield: 2–4 servings

To add even more decadence to this dish, while the steaks are cooking, melt butter in a saucepan on a side burner, add ¼ pound (112 g) of fresh, sliced morel mushrooms, a dash of lemon juice, and a pinch of salt, and cook until the morels are soft. Pour the mushrooms over the steaks or add them to the reduced Pinot Noir sauce.

2 (8–10 ounce [224–280 g]) filet mignon steaks, about 2–2½ inches (5–6 cm) thick
¼ cup olive oil
½ cup (118 mL) heavy cream
2 teaspoons (10 mL) Dijon mustard
½ cup (118 mL) Pinot Noir
2 tablespoons (30 mL) cracked black peppercorns
3 tablespoons (45 mL) cold butter

1. Preheat the barbecue to high (500°F [260°C] to 550°F [290°C]).

2. Place a well-seasoned cast-iron skillet in the barbecue and heat for 10 minutes. Carefully pull the skillet out of the barbecue and put it on a side burner or stovetop burner over high heat. Add the two filets to the dry pan, making sure they do not touch the edge of the pan or each other. Cook the steaks without touching them for 2 to 3 minutes, then turn them over with tongs (never, ever use a fork on cooking steaks) and sear the second side for 2 minutes.

3. Using oven mitts put the skillet back in the barbecue and roast for 5 to 6 minutes with the lid closed.

4. Use an instant-read meat thermometer to check on the internal temperature for the proper doneness. Rare = 120°F (49°C); medium-rare = 125°F (52°C); medium = 130°F (54°C). Remember that the temperature will rise 10 to 15°F (6 to 9°C) as the meat rests.

5. Remove the meat from the skillet and transfer it to a warmed platter, immediately returning the skillet to the hot barbecue and closing the lid. Wrap the steaks with foil and let them rest for 10 to 15 minutes to let the juices re-circulate.

6. To make the sauce, open the barbecue lid and add the olive oil and butter to the very hot pan. Add the cream and mustard, stirring to deglaze the pan. Add the wine, stir, and cook over high heat, stirring often, until the sauce reduces by a third, about 10 minutes, then add the cracked black peppercorns (do not cook them). Pour into a sauce boat to serve alongside the steaks.

Barbecue Beef Biscuits
Yield: 4 servings

You can make your own biscuit dough; however, being pastry-impaired, I prefer to let someone else do the work. There are literally dozens of varieties of premade refrigerated or frozen biscuits available, so why not?

1 teaspoon (5 mL) olive oil
1 small onion, peeled and minced
1 pound (454 g) ground beef
¼ cup (59 mL) barbecue sauce, or less as needed
1 (10.8-ounce [306-g]) package Pillsbury Grands refrigerated buttermilk biscuits
4 slices cheddar cheese, quartered

1. Preheat the barbecue to medium high (375°F [190°C] to 400°F [200°C]).

2. In a cast-iron skillet, heat the olive oil. Add the onions and sauté until tender, then add the ground beef and cook until all the meat is browned, stirring often.

3. Drain off the grease and add just enough barbecue sauce to moisten the beef, about ¼ cup (59 mL), stirring it in through the meat.

4. Place one biscuit in each of 8 muffin cups, pressing the dough into the bottom and ½-inch up the side of each cup.

5. To each biscuit cup, add 1 to 2 tablespoons (15 to 30 mL) of the beef-onion mixture. Bake in the barbecue until the tops of the biscuits begin to brown

6. Place two small squares of cheese on top of each biscuit and return the pan to the barbecue until the cheese begins to melt. Serve 2 biscuits per person.

Skillet Swiss Steak

Yield: 4–6 servings

The name "Swiss" steak has nothing to do with tiny Switzerland. Rather, it refers to "swissing"—a manufacturing process in which cloth or fibrous material is run through rollers or pounded to soften it, hence the process used here to pound and tenderize the meat.

2 tablespoons (30 mL) all-purpose flour
1 teaspoon (5 mL) garlic powder
¾ teaspoon (3.75 mL) seasoned salt
½ teaspoon (2.5 mL) freshly ground black pepper
1 (1 pound [454 g]) beef boneless bottom or top round steak, 1½ inches (3.5 cm) thick
1 tablespoon (15 mL) vegetable shortening or olive oil
1 (8-ounce [227-g]) can diced tomatoes
1 cup (236 mL) diced carrots
½ cup diced celery
1 medium onion, peeled and chopped
½ small red bell pepper, finely chopped
Mashed potatoes, for serving

1. Preheat the barbecue to medium high (350°F [180°C] to 400°F [200°C]) for direct and indirect heating.

2. In a wide, flat baking dish, mix together the flour, garlic powder, salt, and pepper.

3. With the back of a chef's knife or the side of a sturdy plate, tenderize the entire surface of the steak so it ends up looking like a waffle. Dredge both sides of the meat in the seasoned flour and set aside.

4. In a large cast-iron skillet, melt the shortening or heat the olive oil. Add the beef, slip the skillet into the barbecue, and brown both sides over direct heat, about 15 to 20 minutes total.

5. Mix together the tomatoes with their liquid, carrots, celery, onions, and bell pepper, then pour this mixture over the beef. Cover and simmer in the barbecue until the beef is tender, about 1½ to 2 hours.

6. Remove the steak from the pan and cut it into 4 pieces. Serve with mashed potatoes, pouring the remaining tomato gravy over the meat and potatoes.

Temple Street Night Market Baby Beef Ribs

Yield: 4–6 servings

This recipe was obtained through the use of a very patient interpreter talking to a street vendor at Hong Kong's (actually Kowloon's) Temple Street Night Market a few years ago. With her help, I pieced together a recipe that approximates the vendor's, coming pretty close to duplicating the best beef ribs I'd ever tasted. It's close. Not exact, but close.

3 pounds (1.3 kg) veal ribs
¼ cup (118 mL) water
½ cup (118 mL) honey
¼ cup (118 mL) lemon juice
¼ cup (118 mL) ketchup
3 tablespoons (89 mL) soy sauce
2 tablespoons (59 mL) sesame oil
4 cloves garlic, peeled and minced
1 (1-inch [2.5-cm]) piece ginger, peeled and grated
1 teaspoon (5 mL) Chinese five-spice powder

1. Make sure the grill is clean and generously sprayed with nonstick grilling spray. Preheat the barbecue to medium high (350°F [180°C] to 400°F [200°C]).

2. Grill the ribs directly on the heated grill for 10 minutes per side.

3. In a small saucepan, combine the water, honey, lemon juice, ketchup, soy sauce, oil, garlic, ginger, and five-spice powder. Stirring often, bring to a boil, then simmer for 5 minutes.

4. Remove the ribs from the grill and cut them into individual portions. Arrange them in the bottom of a Dutch oven or roasting pan and barbecue for 25 minutes, turning several times.

5. Pour the sauce into the pan, cover, and cook for 1½ hours, until done.

Lisbon-Style Steak and Eggs

Yield: 4 servings

Flambé cooking is best done outdoors. You must be careful when pouring the liquor into the pan that there is no open flame nearby, as this can cause an explosion of fire to envelop the pan, the barbecue, and you. Use a long charcoal lighter or a foot-long fireplace match to light the fumes at the edge of the pan, not the middle. Shake the pan back and forth until the flames go out; then proceed with the recipe.

2 tablespoons (30 mL) melted butter
1 tablespoon (15 mL) olive oil
1 (1½–2 pound [681–908 kg]) aged beef sirloin steak
Salt, to taste
Freshly ground black pepper, to taste
1 tablespoon (15 mL) minced garlic
¼ cup (60 mL) cognac
¼ cup (60 mL) red wine
¼ cup (60 mL) low-sodium beef broth
¼ cup (60 mL) crème fraîche
4 very thin slices Spanish-style ham
4 large eggs
Butter, for frying

1. Make sure the grill is clean and generously sprayed with nonstick spray. Preheat the barbecue to medium high (350°F [180°C] to 400°F [200°C]).

2. Place a Dutch oven over the hottest pat of the barbecue for 5 minutes, then add the butter and oil. Season the steak with salt and pepper and place it in the pan.

3. Add the garlic. Pour the cognac into the pan, swirl it around quickly, and immediately light the liquor with a long charcoal lighter. When the flames die down, transfer the steak to a plate with barbecue tongs, cover the meat, and let it rest.

4. Pour in the red wine and stir with a wooden spoon to pick up the browned bits. Add the beef broth and cook until the liquid is reduced by a quarter. Add the crème fraîche and reduce by another quarter, then remove the pan from the heat and set aside.

5. Return the steak to the pan, along with any juices it released while resting, and cook over direct heat until a meat thermometer inserted sideways into the center of the steak reads 135°F (57°C) for medium-rare, about 6 to 8 minutes.

6. Place the ham slices on the hot side of the grill and cook until the edges are crisp and browned, about 1 minute per side.

7. In a large nonstick skillet, quickly fry the eggs in a little butter, making sure the yolks are still runny.

8. Transfer the steak to a cutting board and cut it into quarters. Divide it among 4 serving plates, cover each piece of steak with a cooked piece of ham, and top each with a fried egg. Drizzle each plate with some of the gravy. Serve immediately.

Grilled Chateaubriand with Jalapeño–Lime–Mushroom Sauce

Yield: 4–6 servings

Chateaubriand is actually a method of cooking, but the term is usually used to refer to thick steaks cut from the center of a beef tenderloin. Many consider these the best steaks to grill.

½ cup (118 mL) red currant jelly
½ cup (118 mL) freshly squeezed lime juice
¼ cup (59 mL) chopped, seeded jalapeño peppers
2 tablespoons (30 mL) chopped fresh cilantro
1 teaspoon (5 mL) salt, plus more to taste
¼ teaspoon (1.25 mL) ground allspice
1 clove garlic, minced
2 (1–1½ pound [454–681 g]) center-cut beef fillet steaks
Freshly ground black pepper, to taste
2 tablespoons (30 mL) olive oil
2 tablespoons (30 mL) cold butter
2 large Portobello mushroom caps, washed and sliced ½ inch (1 cm) wide

1. In a small saucepan over high heat, melt the jelly, stirring it after 30 seconds. Add the lime juice, jalapeno peppers, cilantro, salt, allspice, and garlic and stir to combine. Set aside to cool.

2. Place the steaks in a 1-gallon (3.8-L) resealable plastic bag and pour in the marinade. Seal the bag and refrigerate for 2 to 3 hours. About 30 minutes before you wish to begin cooking the steaks, remove the bag from the refrigerator and drain the steaks, reserving the marinade. Let the meat warm to room temperature.

3. Make sure the grill is clean and generously sprayed with nonstick grilling spray. Preheat the barbecue to 450°F [240°C] to 475°F [250°C]). While the barbecue is heating, pour the reserved marinade into a saucepan, boil for 10 minutes, and set aside.

4. Generously season the meat with the black pepper. Put a cast-iron skillet on a side burner or stove top burner, add the oil, turn to high and allow the pan and oil to heat up until the oil just starts to smoke. Keeping the heat on high, add the beef fillets to the pan and quickly sear them on one side and then the other, about 1 minute per side. Wearing barbecue gloves, put the skillet into the barbecue and roast the meat for 10 to 15 minutes depending on how rare you like it. This time will give you beautifully medium-rare steaks.

5. When the chateaubriands are ready, remove the skillet from the barbecue and carefully transfer the steaks to a warmed plate, covering them loosely with foil. Let them rest for 15 minutes.

6. Place the skillet with the drippings over a medium-high flame or burner and add the boiled marinade. When the mixture bubbles, swirl in the cold butter until it melts. Add the sliced mushrooms and a seasoning of salt and freshly ground black pepper. Cook the mushrooms for about 2 minutes, turning frequently.

7. Cut each of the steaks in half and place each portion on a heated plate. Pour the lime-jalapeño-mushroom sauce over the steaks and serve immediately.

High Plains Fajitas
Yield : 4–6 servings

For a more colorful dish use 1 red bell pepper, 1 green bell pepper, 1 yellow or orange bell pepper, 2 yellow onions, and 1 red onion.

1 (0.6-ounce [17-g]) envelope of Good Seasons Zesty Italian dressing mix
1 (12-ounce [355-mL]) can beer
½ cup (118 mL) tarragon vinegar
½ cup (118 mL) Worcestershire sauce
¼ cup (59 mL) vegetable oil
Zest and juice of 2 limes, plus 2 additional limes, halved
3 bell peppers, stemmed, seeded, and sliced into ¼-inch (0.5-cm) strips
3 onions, peeled and sliced
3 pounds (1.3 kg) beef flank steak, cut into ½-inch (1-cm) wide strips
1 (14–16-ounce [392–448-g]) package flour tortillas, for serving

1. Make sure the grill is clean and generously sprayed with nonstick grilling spray. Preheat the barbecue to medium high (350°F [180°C] to 400°F [200°C]).

2. In a medium bowl, combine the the dressing mix with beer, vinegar, Worchestershire sauce, oil, and the lime juice and zests. Place the pepper strips in a 1-gallon (3.8-L) resealable plastic bag. Add the sliced onions, then pour in half the marinade and refrigerate the vegetables for 12 to 24 hours, turning the bag occasionally.

3. Meanwhile, place the beef strips in a separate 1-gallon (3.8-L) resealable plastic bag and pour in the rest of the marinade. Seal the bag, shake it to distribute the marinade, and refrigerate for the same amount of time as the peppers, turning the bag occasionally.

4. Remove the beef and peppers from their bags and discard the marinade. Grill the beef directly on the hot grill until it's browned and tender, turning often with tongs, about 8 to 10 minutes. After 4 to 5 minutes, put the drained peppers and onions in a grilling or vegetable basket and cook until tender and browned at the edges.

5. With tongs, transfer the meat from the grill to a large bowl, squeeze the juice from the 2 remaining limes over the meat, add the cooked peppers and onions, and stir.

6. Warm the tortillas in the microwave or oven and place them on serving plates beside the bowl of beef, onions and peppers. Serve with your favorite condiments, such as guacamole, sour cream, salsa, hot sauce, and grated cheddar cheese.

Barbecued Calf's Liver and Onions

Yield: 4 servings

When buying calf's liver at the store or butcher shop, check for the following: The liver should be shiny in appearance, should have a pleasant smell, and should come from an organically-raised animal. Refrigerate the liver immediately and use it within one day, two at the most.

1 (1½-pound [681 g]) calf's liver, cut into 4 pieces
3 cups (708 mL) whole milk
8 slices bacon, halved
1 tablespoon (15 mL) butter
3½ cups (826 mL) sliced yellow or Spanish onions
1 cup (236 mL) all-purpose flour for dredging
1 teaspoon (5 mL) dried rosemary
½ teaspoon (2.5 mL) dried oregano
½ teaspoon (2.5 mL) ground cumin
½ teaspoon (2.5 mL) salt
Freshly ground black pepper, to taste
½ cup (118 mL) Marsala

1. Preheat the barbecue to medium high (300°F [150°C] to 350°F [180°C]).

2. Soak the liver in the milk for 1 to 2 hours. Remove the liver, pat it dry, and discard milk.

3. Spray a casserole or a 2-quart (1.9-L) Dutch oven with nonstick cooking spray.

4. Fry bacon until crisp, then remove it from the skillet and set it aside to drain on paper towels. When the bacon is cool, crumble it into a small bowl. Pour half of the bacon fat into a separate small bowl and set aside.

5. Add the butter to the remaining fat in the skillet. Add the onions and sauté until they just begin to brown, then remove them from the pan and set aside. Do not drain.

6. In a shallow dish, stir together the flour, rosemary, oregano, and cumin. Sprinkle the liver with salt and pepper, then dredge it in the flour mixture. Add the reserved bacon fat to a nonstick skillet, then add the liver pieces and brown them lightly on both sides. Transfer the liver to a plate and add the Marsala to the pan, stirring and scraping up the browned bits.

7. Place the pieces of liver in the bottom of the prepared casserole or Dutch oven. Cover the liver with the onions, then with the crumbled bacon.

8. Pour the Marsala from the skillet over the liver and onions. Cover and bake in the barbecue for 15 to 20 minutes.

9. Transfer the liver to a warm platter, pour the onions and bacon over the liver, and serve.

Lemon-Lime Pepper Steaks
Yield: 4 servings

For the best results make your own cracked peppercorns by buying quality whole black peppercorns (not brined or water-packed peppercorns), pouring them whole onto a hard wooden cutting board, and using a skillet to crack them, pressing down firmly on the peppercorns by rocking the pan back and forth. Continue until all the peppercorns are cracked.

¼ cup (59 mL) dry white wine
¼ cup (59 mL) fresh lemon juice
⅛ cup (30 mL) fresh lime juice
2 tablespoons (30 mL) dark or light sesame oil
1 teaspoon (5 mL) chopped fresh rosemary
¼ teaspoon (1.25 mL) seasoned salt
1 (1¼-pound [567-g]) beef chuck steak, 1 inch (2.5 cm) thick
2 teaspoons (10 mL) grated lemon zest
½ teaspoon (2.5 mL) grated lime zest
2 tablespoons (30 mL) butter, softened
1 tablespoon (15 mL) cracked black peppercorns
1 tablespoon (15 mL) chopped fresh parsley, for garnish

1. In a small bowl, combine the wine, lemon and lime juices, sesame oil, rosemary, and salt. Place the chuck steak in a 1-gallon (3.8-L) resealable plastic bag. Pour in the marinade, seal the bag, and turn several times to coat the meat. Marinate in the refrigerator for 6 to 8 hours, turning several times.

2. In a small bowl, whip together the lemon and lime zests and butter until completely incorporated. Cover and refrigerate.

3. Make sure the grill is clean and generously sprayed with nonstick grilling spray. Preheat the barbecue to medium high (350°F [180°C] to 400°F [200°C]).

4. Remove the steak from the marinade, briefly drain, and pat dry. Firmly press the cracked peppercorns into both sides of the meat. Place the steak directly on the grill and cook for 8 to 10 minutes per side, turning several times.

5. Transfer the steak to a cutting board and, with a sharp knife, carve the meat into thin slices. Place a pat of citrus butter on each steak, sprinkle with parsley and serve immediately.

Braised and Grilled Filipino Oxtails
Yield: 4–6 servings

In the Philippines, "adobo" refers to an indigenous cooking process that involves stew-ing meat with vinegar, which makes it very flavorful and tender.

2–3 pounds (908 g–1.3 kg) oxtails
½ cup (118 mL) cider vinegar
½ cup (118 mL) soy sauce
¼ cup (59 mL) vegetable oil
8 whole cloves garlic, peeled and mashed
1 tablespoon (15 mL) whole black peppercorns
2–3 bay leaves
Salt, to taste
Freshly ground black pepper, to taste
Fresh basil leaves, finely julienned, for garnish

1. In a large pot on a barbecue side burner or propane burner, combine the oxtails, vinegar, soy sauce, oil, garlic, peppercorns, and bay leaves. Add water to completely cover the oxtails.

2. Bring to a boil and lower the heat to maintain a gentle simmer. Cover and cook for about 2 hours, replenishing the water as necessary to keep the oxtails fully covered. Using a long spoon, occasionally skim off the rendered fat.

3. Make sure the grill is clean and generously sprayed with nonstick grill-ing spray. Preheat the barbecue to medium high (350°F [180°C] to 400°F [200°C]).

4. Remove the oxtails from the broth and briefly drain them. Grill the oxtails until they are well-browned and slightly crisp. Season lightly with salt and pepper.

5. Using tongs, place the oxtails on a warmed serving platter over several cups of cooked black beans, and serve them surrounded by steamed rice and garnished with the basil leaves. Provide a small bowl of the *adobo* (cooking) broth on the side, for dipping.

THREE

Burgers

Pesto Turkey Burgers

Yield: 4 servings

You can also use ground chicken to make these into light and flavorful main-dish burgers, or roll them into small meatballs to add to spaghetti, macaroni, or other pasta.

1 large egg
¼ cup (59 mL) seasoned dry breadcrumbs
3 tablespoons (45 mL) chicken or turkey stock
3 tablespoons (45 mL) chopped fresh basil
3 tablespoons (45 mL) grated Parmesan cheese
2 tablespoons (30 mL) chopped yellow onion
2 tablespoons (30 mL) pine nuts
Salt, to taste
Freshly ground black pepper, to taste
1½ pounds (681 g) ground turkey
2 tablespoons (30 mL) extra virgin olive oil

1. Make sure the grill is clean and generously sprayed with nonstick grilling spray. Preheat the barbecue to medium high (350°F [180°C] to 400°F [200°C]).

2. In a large mixing bowl, beat the egg. Add the breadcrumbs, chicken or turkey stock, basil, cheese, onion, pine nuts, salt, and pepper. Using your (well-cleaned or gloved) hands, incorporate the ground turkey into the mix, and form it into 4 thick (or 6 thin) patties.

3. Grill the burgers for 4 to 5 minutes on each side. The meat inside should not be pink.

4. Serve on grilled onion rolls or Kaiser rolls with your favorite condiments.

Spicy Chicken Burgers

Yield: 4 servings

To really spice these up, you can double the amount of red pepper flakes or substitute ½ teaspoon (2.5 mL) of cayenne pepper.

1 large egg
¼ cup (59 mL) grated Parmesan cheese
¼ cup (59 mL) seasoned dry breadcrumbs
3 green onions, green & white parts, finely sliced
1 tablespoon (15 mL) half-and-half (or non-fat milk)
2 teaspoons (10 mL) Dijon mustard
½ teaspoon (2.5 mL) ground cumin
¼ teaspoon (1.25 mL) garlic salt
¼ teaspoon (1.25 mL) red pepper flakes
1¼ pounds (567 g) ground chicken

1. Make sure the grill is clean and generously sprayed with nonstick spray. Preheat the barbecue to medium high (350°F [180°C] to 400°F [200°C]).

2. In a large mixing bowl, beat the egg. Add the cheese, breadcrumbs, green onions, half-and-half, mustard, cumin, garlic salt, and red pepper flakes. Add the chicken and mix together with your hands. Shape the mixture into 4 thick (or 6 thin) patties.

3. Grill for 4 to 5 minutes on each side. The meat inside should not be pink.

4. Serve on toasted buns with garlic aioli.

Crab Open-Faced Burgers

Yield: 4–6 servings

You can use any cheese you like on these, but I prefer the mild taste of Swiss with the subtle taste of the crab.

2 large eggs, hard-boiled and chopped
1 cup (236 mL) Dungeness crabmeat (or your favorite variety)
½ cup (118 mL) grated Swiss cheese
2 green onions, white and green parts, grated
½ cup (118 mL) mayonnaise
3 tablespoons (45 mL) ginger ale
2 tablespoons (30 mL) yellow mustard barbecue sauce
¼ teaspoon (1.25 mL) garlic pepper
¼ teaspoon (1.25 mL) curry powder
⅛ teaspoon (0.6 mL) celery salt
Butter as needed
6 plain bagels, split
Paprika or chopped fresh parsley, for garnish

1. Make sure the grill is clean and generously sprayed with nonstick grilling spray. Preheat the barbecue to medium high (350°F [180°C] to 400°F [200°C]).

2. In a large mixing bowl, use a spoon to mix the eggs, crabmeat, cheese, onions, mayonnaise, ginger ale, barbecue sauce, garlic pepper, curry powder, and celery salt. Butter each bagel half.

3. Using your hands, form 12 thin crab patties. Place each patty on a bagel half, then grill for 5 to 7 minutes. Close the lid and cook until the crab mixture starts to brown.

4. Sprinkle with paprika or chopped parsley and serve with a green salad and fresh lemonade or limeade.

Festive Burgers à la Reuben

Yield: 6 servings

The best flavor is achieved with fresh deli sauerkraut. If you can't get that, buy sauer-kraut packaged in a jar, which tastes much better than canned.

2 pounds (908 g) ground corned beef or ground turkey
¼ cup (59 mL) finely minced yellow onion
¼ teaspoon (1.25 mL) salt
2 cloves garlic, finely minced
¼ teaspoon (1.25 mL) dry yellow mustard
¼ teaspoon (1.25 mL) freshly ground black pepper
10 ounces (280 g) deli or jarred sauerkraut, drained
6 slices Swiss or Emmentaler cheese

1. Make sure the grill is clean and generously sprayed with nonstick grill-ing spray. Preheat the barbecue to medium high (350°F [180°C] to 400°F [200°C]).

2. In a large bowl, mix together the ground corned beef or turkey, onion, salt, garlic, dry mustard, and pepper. With your hands, form the mixture into 6 patties (about ¾ inch [1.5 cm] thick).

3. Grill the patties for about 5 minutes per side, or until the inside is barely pink, turning once. Top each patty with a slice (or two) of Swiss cheese, then top that with 2 tablespoons (30 mL) of sauerkraut and cook until cheese begins to melt.

4. Serve on toasted pumpernickel or rye hamburger buns (or rolls) or toasted slices of marbled rye bread. Accompany with an ice-cold beer or iced tea.

Tasty Ahi Burgers

Yield: 8 servings

Instead of tuna, you can use other fish, such as salmon, crab, or even lobster.

1 (7-ounce [189-g]) can tuna fish, drained
¼ cup (59 mL) minced onion
¼ cup (59 mL) chopped sweet pickles (or sweet pickle relish)
¼ cup (59 mL) ketchup or barbecue sauce
¼ cup (59 mL) mayonnaise
¼ cup (59 mL) chopped tomatoes
½ teaspoon (2.5 mL) freshly ground black pepper
¼ teaspoon (1.25 mL) garlic salt
8 slices cheddar or Swiss cheese
8 hamburger buns

1. Make sure the grill is clean and generously sprayed with nonstick grill-ing spray. Preheat the barbecue to medium high (350°F [180°C] to 400°F [200°C]).

2. In a large bowl, combine the tuna, onion, pickles, ketchup, mayonnaise, tomatoes, pepper, and garlic salt and mix thoroughly. Using a spoon, divide the mixture among the bottoms of the hamburger buns. Cover each with a slice of cheese, then add the bun top.

3. Wrap each bun in aluminum foil and grill for 20 minutes. Unwrap the burgers and serve.

Wowee Maui Onion Burgers

Yield: 6 servings

If you can't find Maui onions, you can substitute Vidalia or Walla Walla.

1 pound (454 g) ground beef
1 (1-ounce [28-g]) envelope dry onion soup mix
1 tablespoon (15 mL) chopped fresh parsley
1 teaspoon (5 mL) paprika
½ teaspoon (2.5 mL) garlic powder
1 large sweet onion, cut into 6 (¼-inch [0.5-cm]) slices
Olive oil as needed
6 slices extra-sharp cheddar cheese
6 hamburger buns

1. Make sure the grill is clean and generously sprayed with nonstick grilling spray. Preheat the barbecue to medium high (350°F [180°C] to 400°F [200°C]).

2. In a large bowl, mix together the beef, soup mix, parsley, paprika, and garlic powder. Form the mixture into 6 patties and grill to your preference. Brush the onion slices with olive oil and grill them alongside the burgers, 3 minutes per side.

3. When burgers are done, top them with the cheese and onion and place them on hamburger buns. Serve hot, with tomatoes, mustard, ketchup, steak sauce or other favorite condiments.

Pacific Salmon Burgers

Yield: 4 servings

Try this recipe with catfish, tuna, or trout instead. You can also substitute regular mustard for the Dijon.

1 (1-pound [454-g]) salmon fillet, skin removed
3 tablespoons (45 mL) lemon juice
1 tablespoon (15 mL) Dijon mustard
1 teaspoon (5 mL) honey
¼ teaspoon (1.25 mL) curry powder
4 green onions, sliced, green and white parts
¾ cup (177 mL) seasoned dry breadcrumbs
2 large eggs

1. Make sure the grill is clean and generously sprayed with nonstick grilling spray. Preheat the barbecue to medium high (350°F [180°C] to 400°F [200°C]).

2. In a large bowl, break up the salmon with a fork, then add the lemon juice, mustard, honey, curry powder, green onions, breadcrumbs, and eggs, and mix well.

3. Using your clean hands, form the mixture into 4 patties. Cover and refrigerate for at least 2 hours to firm up the patties.

4. Bring the patties to room temperature. Grill until golden brown on both sides, about 3 to 4 minutes per side, turning only once.

5. Serve on buns with lettuce and sliced tomato.

Grilled Lamb Burgers

Yield: 4 servings

This is a great way to use leftover lamb roast or leg of lamb from a dinner party.

¼ cup (59 mL) minced fresh cilantro
3 tablespoons (45 mL) crumbled feta cheese
2 teaspoons (10 mL) minced red onion
¼ teaspoon (1.25 mL) garlic salt
¼ teaspoon (1.25 mL) ground tarragon
¼ teaspoon (1.25 mL) cayenne pepper
¼ teaspoon (1.25 mL) freshly ground black pepper
1½ pounds (681 g) cooked ground lamb

1. Make sure the grill is clean and generously sprayed with nonstick grilling spray. Preheat the barbecue to medium high (350°F [180°C] to 400°F [200°C]).

2. In large bowl, combine the cilantro, feta, onion, garlic salt, tarragon, cayenne pepper, black pepper, and lamb. Mix well. With your hands, divide the lamb mixture into 4 equal portions and shape each into a ¾ inch (1.5 cm) thick patty.

3. Place the patties on the grill and cook for 4 minutes on each side, or until done.

4. Serve on buns with your favorite burger toppings.

Kate's Teriyaki Burgers

Yield: 6 servings

These are great topped with a slice of fresh pineapple. Better yet, quickly grill the pineapple slices before you add them.

1 (8-ounce [224-g]) can water chestnuts, drained and finely chopped
⅓ cup (79 mL) teriyaki sauce
2 cloves garlic, peeled and minced
3–4 green onions, green and white parts, chopped
Salt, to taste
Freshly ground black pepper, to taste
1½ pounds (681 g) ground beef or ground turkey
6 hamburger buns

1. Make sure the grill is clean and generously sprayed with nonstick grilling spray. Preheat the barbecue to medium high (350°F [180°C] to 400°F [200°C]).

2. In a large bowl, combine the water chestnuts, teriyaki, garlic, and onions. Season with the salt and pepper. Add the ground beef, mix together, and shape into 6 patties.

3. Grill for 6 to 10 minutes on each side, or until the inside is no longer pink and reach the desired doneness.

4. Serve on grilled or toasted buns with tomato, sliced onion, and lettuce.

Spam Spam Burgers

Yield: 4–6 servings

A great favorite in Hawaii, Spam is great grilled. I like to add a dollop of mustard mixed with brown sugar.

1 pound (454 g) mild cheddar or Swiss cheese, shredded
1 (12-ounce [336-g]) can Spam, finely chopped
1 (10¾-ounce [301-g]) can condensed cream of mushroom soup
¼ cup (59 mL) finely chopped onion

1. Preheat the barbecue to medium high (350°F [180°C] to 400°F [200°C]).

2. In a large bowl, mix together all the ingredients. Spread the mixture on hamburger buns and wrap the buns in foil.

3. Grill the Spam burgers for 12 to 15 minutes, turning once, or until the meat is hot and the buns are slightly toasted.

Pizza-Man Burgers

Yield: 8–10 servings

These burgers make a great meal for watching baseball or football games. They're quick to fix and filling, and kids love them, too.

1 pound (454 g) ground beef (chuck)
1 (26-ounce [728-g]) jar spaghetti sauce
4 slices American cheese
8–10 hamburger buns
2 cups (473 mL) shredded mozzarella cheese
2 cups (473 mL) shredded cheddar cheese

1. Make sure the grill is clean and generously sprayed with nonstick grilling spray. Preheat the barbecue to medium high (350°F [180°C] to 400°F [200°C]) for indirect heating, and place a water pan under the unheated side of the grill.

2. Brown the hamburger and pour off the excess grease. Add the spaghetti sauce and bring to a hard simmer.

3. Add the American cheese slices and cook, stirring, until the cheese melts. Turn the heat to low and simmer for about 10 to 15 minutes, or until the mixture thickens.

4. When meat mixture is done simmering, spoon the mixture onto the hamburger buns (tops and bottoms) spreading it over the entire surface.

5. Sprinkle each with shredded cheddar and mozzarella cheeses to your personal preference.

6. Place in the barbecue over the unheated side of the grill, and cook for 10 to 15 minutes, or until the cheese has melted and slightly browned and the hamburger bun has become crispy and lightly browned.

Beer Burgers
Yield: 4 servings

Use your favorite beer in this recipe. For more kick, use a porter or other dark beer.

¼ cup (59 mL) steak sauce
¼ cup (59 mL) beer
1½ pounds (681 g) ground beef
1 large Vidalia onion, peeled and sliced
4 slices Swiss cheese
4 hamburger buns
Tomato slices, for serving
Lettuce, for serving

1. Make sure the grill is clean and generously sprayed with nonstick grilling spray. Preheat the barbecue to medium high (350°F [180°C] to 400°F [200°C]).

2. In a 1-cup (236-mL) glass measuring cup, combine the steak sauce and beer. Microwave on high for 1 to 1½ minutes. Alternatively, heat the sauce in a saucepan until bubbly. Set aside.

3. Shape the ground beef into ¾-inch (1.5-cm) thick patties.

4. Place the onion slices on the grill and cook, uncovered, for 3 to 4 minutes.

5. Add the patties to the grill and cook for 5 to 6 minutes per side, or until the burger centers are done to your preference, turning occasionally. Season, to taste.

6. Approximately 2 minutes before the burgers are done, brush them generously with the sauce mixture, reserving some for the table, and add a slice of cheese to each patty. When the cheese begins to melt, remove the burgers from the grill.

7. Place the burgers on buns and top with beer sauce, tomato slices, and lettuce.

Mushroom Burgers
Yield: 6 servings

You can also use rehydrated dried or fresh mushrooms if you wish.

1½ pounds (681 g) lean ground beef
1 (10-ounce [280-g]) can mushroom stems and pieces, drained and finely chopped
1 tablespoon (15 mL) minced onion
1 tablespoon (15 mL) soy sauce
¼ teaspoon (1.25 mL) freshly ground black pepper

1. Make sure the grill is clean and generously sprayed with nonstick grilling spray. Preheat the barbecue to medium high (350°F [180°C] to 400°F [200°C]).

2. In a large bowl, combine all the ingredients. Shape the mixture into 6 (1½-inch [3.5-cm]) thick patties.

3. Place the patties on the grill or in a pan, and cook for 5 to 7 minutes on each side.

4. Toast the buns on the grill and serve the burgers on the toasted buns.

Burgundy Burgers
Yield: 4–6 servings

You can also use Cabernet, Pinot Noir, or another hearty red wine.

1½ pounds (681 g) ground beef (round)
¼ cup (59 mL) Burgundy
¼ cup (59 mL) finely diced onion
1 tablespoon (15 mL) Worcestershire sauce (or your favorite steak sauce)
1 teaspoon (5 mL) seasoned salt
¼ teaspoon (1.25 mL) freshly ground black pepper
⅛ teaspoon (0.6 mL) garlic powder
4–6 slices Swiss or Jack cheese (optional)

1. Make sure the grill is clean and generously sprayed with nonstick grilling spray. Preheat the barbecue to medium high (350°F [180°C] to 400°F [200°C]).

2. In a large bowl, mix together the ground beef, Burgundy, onion, Worcestershire sauce, seasoned salt, pepper, and garlic powder. Shape the mixture into 4 to 6 patties, each about 1 inch (2.5 cm) thick.

3. Grill the burgers over direct flame or charcoal, turning once, to the desired doneness, about 8 to 10 minutes. When turning, do not flatten the burgers, this presses out the juices and will dry out the burgers.

4. Served on toasted buns, topped with the cheese slices and sautéed mushrooms or sweet onions.

Kangaroo Burgers
Yield: 8–10 servings

Kangaroo meat, like the meat of many game animals, is very lean, so you must not overcook these burgers or they will taste like cardboard.

2 pounds (908 g) ground kangaroo or ground beef
2 large eggs, beaten
1 cup (236 mL) soft breadcrumbs
1 tablespoon (15 mL) minced garlic
1 large onion, peeled and finely diced
¼ cup (59 mL) steak sauce
¼ cup (59 mL) ketchup
2 teaspoons (10 mL) dried thyme
1 teaspoon (5 mL) dried oregano
½ teaspoon (2.5 mL) freshly ground black pepper
10–14 drops hot sauce of your choice

1. Make sure the grill is clean and generously sprayed with nonstick spray. Preheat the barbecue to medium high (350°F [180°C] to 400°F [200°C]).

2. In a large bowl, thoroughly mix together the ground meat, eggs, breadcrumbs, garlic, onion, steak sauce, ketchup, thyme, oregano, pepper, and hot sauce.

3. Form the mixture into 8 to 10 burgers and grill until the meat is done to your preference, turning several times. This is a lean, low-fat burger that can fall apart easily, so be careful when turning.

4. Serve on grilled hamburger bun with your favorite condiments, sliced tomatoes, onions, and lettuce.

Buffalo (Bison) Burgers
Yield: 4 servings

More and more supermarkets, and websites like www.nickyusa.com, are making buffalo meat available to the public. It's a super meat, that's lean, loaded with vitamins, and contains beneficial omega-fats.

1 pound (454 g) ground buffalo meat
¼ red onion, peeled and finely diced
2 cloves garlic, peeled and finely diced
2 tablespoons (30 mL) Worcestershire or steak sauce
1 teaspoon (5 mL) dried oregano
1 pinch sea or kosher salt
Freshly ground black pepper, to taste

1. Make sure the grill is clean and generously sprayed with nonstick spray. Preheat the barbecue to medium high (350°F [180°C] to 400°F [200°C]).

2. In a large bowl, combine the buffalo, onion, garlic, Worcestershire sauce, oregano, salt, and pepper. Form the mixture into 1-inch (2.5 cm) thick patties.

3. Grill the burgers for 3 to 4 minute per side, or until they reach your desired doneness, but do not cook them beyond medium.

4. Serve on thick slices of grilled or toasted Texas toast or large hamburger buns.

Bella Portobello Burgers
Yield: 4 servings

This recipe is a lot of work, but it's well worth the effort. It takes burgers to a new height and complexity.

Mushrooms
¼ cup (59 mL) Zinfandel wine
2 tablespoons (30 mL) olive oil
1 tablespoon (15 mL) dried thyme
1½ teaspoons (7.5 mL) dried basil
½ teaspoon (2.5 mL) garlic salt
½ teaspoon (2.5 mL) grated fresh ginger
½ teaspoon (2.5 mL) freshly ground black pepper
4 Portobello mushrooms, stems removed

Burgers
1½ pounds (681 g) ground beef (chuck)
3 tablespoons (45 mL) Zinfandel or any red wine
2 green onions, finely chopped, green and white parts
1 tablespoon (15 mL) dried thyme
1½ teaspoons (7.5 mL) dried basil
1 teaspoon (5 mL) ground cumin
½ teaspoon (2.5 mL) garlic salt
½ teaspoon (2.5 mL) freshly ground black pepper
2 tablespoons (30 mL) mayonnaise
4 hamburger buns or onion rolls

1. Make sure the grill is clean and generously sprayed with nonstick grilling spray. Preheat the barbecue to medium high (350°F [180°C] to 400°F [200°C]).

2. To make the mushrooms, in a small bowl, combine the wine, olive oil, thyme, basil, garlic salt, ginger, black pepper and blend well. Put the mushrooms in a 1- or 2-gallon (3.8- or 7.6-L) resealable plastic bag. Pour in the marinade; seal the bag, shake to mix, and set aside.

3. To make the burgers, in a large bowl, combine the ground chuck, wine, green onions, thyme, basil, cumin, garlic salt, and black pepper and mix well. Using your hands, gently form 4 (1–1½-inch [2.5–3.5 cm] thick) patties, trying not to handle them too much.

4. Drain the mushrooms, reserving the marinade for basting the mushrooms during grilling. Place the burgers and mushrooms on the grill and cook, turning only once, until the patties are cooked to your preference

(5 to 6 minutes per side for medium) and the mushrooms are tender (6 to 9 minutes), basting the mushrooms with the marinade.

5. To assemble, spread the mayonnaise on the hamburger buns or rolls. Top each bun with a patty and a grilled mushroom.

English Stilton Burgers
Yield: 4 servings

You can use any strong, rich cheese here. One of my favorites is Huntsman, a blend of Stilton and double-cream Gloucester.

1½ pounds (681 g) ground beef
1 onion, peeled and finely diced
Salt, to taste
Freshly ground black pepper, to taste
1 teaspoon (5 mL) dried oregano
1 teaspoon (5 mL) dried savory
1 teaspoon (5 mL) dry mustard
½ cup (118 mL) English Stilton cheese, crumbled
4 hamburger buns, toasted bread, or focaccia rolls

1. Make sure the grill is clean and generously sprayed with nonstick spray. Preheat the barbecue to medium high (350°F [180°C] to 400°F [200°C]).

2. In a large bowl, combine the beef and onion. Season with salt and pepper.

3. Stir in the oregano, savory, and mustard and mix well. Divide the mixture into 8 equal portions. With your hands, form 8 thin patties of equal diameter.

4. Place 4 of the patties on a plate, flatten them slightly, and slightly indent the center of each with a large mixing spoon. Fill each depression with 1 to 2 tablespoons (15 to 30 mL) of the crumbled cheese.

5. Place the remaining 4 patties on top of the first 4, crimping the edges to fold in the cheese.

6. Grill for 10 minutes, turning once.

7. Serve the burgers on buns, toasted bread, or focaccia rolls.

Veggie Beef Burgers
Yield: 4–6 servings

This makes a great lunch for kids or adults on a cold, wet, windy, winter day.

½ cup (118 mL) diced onion
1 (14-ounce [392-g]) can diced tomatoes with their juice
2 (10-ounce [280-g]) cans condensed vegetable beef soup
½ cup (118 mL) frozen mixed peas and carrots, thawed and drained
1½ pounds (681 g) ground beef, divided into 4 or 6 patties
4–6 cups (0.95–1.4 L) hot mashed potatoes

1. Make sure the grill is clean and generously sprayed with nonstick grilling spray. Preheat the barbecue to medium high (350°F [180°C] to 400°F [200°C]).

2. In a large saucepan, grill onions until translucent and just beginning to brown. Add the tomatoes with their juice, then add the condensed soup. Bring to a boil.

3. Transfer the mixture to a small saucepan and simmer, covered, for about 30 to 40 minutes, stirring every few minutes.

4. During the last 10 minutes of cooking, stir in the peas and carrots.

5. Grill the burgers to your preferred doneness, 4 to 5 minutes per side for medium-rare.

6. Place each burger on a plate next to a dollop of potatoes, cover both with soup-sauce, and enjoy.

Porky Extreme Burgers
Yield: 4 servings

The bacon is the crowning touch, especially if you have hickory-smoked or maple-smoked bacon.

1 pound (454 g) ground pork
1 pound (454 g) spicy sausage, crumbled out of casings
3 strips bacon, cooked and crumbled
1 teaspoon (5 mL) garlic powder
1 teaspoon (5 mL) ground thyme
¼ teaspoon (1.25 mL) seasoned salt
⅛ teaspoon (0.6 mL) freshly ground black pepper
4 onion rolls, toasted

1. Make sure the grill is clean and generously sprayed with nonstick grilling spray. Preheat the barbecue to medium high (350°F [180°C] to 400°F [200°C]).

2. In a large bowl, combine the pork, sausage, bacon, garlic powder, thyme, salt, and pepper.

3. Form the mixture into 4 patties, each about ¾ inch (1.5 cm) thick. Grill for 5 to 6 minutes per side.

4. Serve on the onion rolls.

Venison Burgers

Yield: 4–6 servings

Venison, like most game meats, is very lean, and it needs a little help to prevent it from becoming dry and tasteless. You could use ½ pound (227 g) ground beef and ½ pound (227 g) ground pork instead of the beef for even more moisture and richness. These burgers can be served on buns with your favorite toppings or with a green salad and freshly grilled corn on the cob.

1 pound (454 g) ground beef
1 pound (454 g) ground venison
1 large egg, beaten
2 tablespoons (30 mL) minced onion
2 tablespoons (30 mL) barbecue sauce
1½ teaspoons (7.5 mL) Italian seasoning
1–2 teaspoons (5–10 mL) minced garlic
Salt, to taste
Freshly ground black pepper, to taste

1. Make sure the grill is clean and generously sprayed with nonstick grilling spray. Preheat the barbecue to medium high (350°F [180°C] to 400°F [200°C]).

2. In a large bowl, mix together the beef, venison, egg, onion, barbecue sauce, Italian seasoning, and garlic. Generously season with salt and pepper, and stir well.

3. Form the mixture into 4 to 6 patties, as thin or as thick as you want. Refrigerate for at least an hour so the burgers firm up and the flavors blend.

4. Cook the burgers for 4 to 6 minutes per side, or until they reach your desired doneness.

DogGone Burgers

Yield: 4–6 servings

My family loves this as a quickie meal when the grandkids come to visit, alongside a plate of baked beans.

3 hot dogs, thinly sliced
1 pound (454 g) ground beef
⅓ cup (79 mL) evaporated milk
¼ cup (59 mL) crushed Ritz crackers
1 teaspoon (5 mL) salt
1 teaspoon (5 mL) dried oregano
1 dash pepper
Butter as needed, at room temperature

1. Make sure the grill is clean and generously sprayed with nonstick grilling spray. Preheat the barbecue to medium high (350°F [180°C] to 400°F [200°C]).

2. In a large bowl, mix together the hot dogs, beef, milk, crackers, salt, oregano, and pepper. With your hands, shape the mixture into 6 (1-inch [2.5-cm] thick) patties. Spread both sides of the patties with the butter.

3. Broil over hot coals, turning once, about 5 to 7 minutes per side.

4. Serve on toasted buns with thin slices of onion, ketchup, mustard, and sweet pickle relish.

Cowpoke Burgers
Yield: 4–5 servings

These can be prepared with half sausage and half ground beef, and you can use spicy or mild sausage or salsa to liven up the burgers.

1 pound (454 g) spicy or mild sausage, crumbled out of the casings
¼ cup (59 mL) salsa
2 tablespoons (30 mL) diced red onions
2 tablespoons (30 mL) chopped fresh cilantro
½ teaspoon (2.5 mL) chili powder
½ teaspoon (2.5 mL) ground cumin
Freshly ground black pepper, to taste
4–5 slices cheese of your choice
4–5 hoagie or Kaiser rolls

1. Make sure the grill is clean and generously sprayed with nonstick grilling spray. Preheat the barbecue to medium high (350°F [180°C] to 400°F [200°C]).

2. In a large bowl, combine the sausage, salsa, onions, cilantro, chili powder, cumin, and pepper. With your hands, form the mixture into 4 or 5 (depending on the size desired) long, oval patties.

3. Cook the burgers until the are no longer pink in the middle, about 5 to 7 minutes per side.

4. Just before you take the burgers off the grill, add the cheese slices and cook until melted.

5. Serve on hoagie or Kaiser rolls with salsa, your favorite condiments, and baked beans or a side salad.

Beer Burgers with Beer-Braised Onions
Yield: 4 servings

These make a super meal to serve your buddies while you watch the World Series, Super Bowl, or Stanley Cup.

Onions
1 tablespoon (15 mL) olive oil
1 teaspoon (5 mL) butter
1 large onion, peeled and thinly sliced
1 cup (236 mL) dark beer, divided
1 teaspoon (5 mL) brown sugar
½ teaspoon (2.5 mL) garlic salt

Burgers

1½ pounds (681 g) ground beef (chuck)
2 tablespoons (30 mL) dark beer
½ teaspoon (2.5 mL) hot sauce
¼ teaspoon (1.25 mL) steak sauce
Salt, to taste
Freshly ground black pepper, to taste
4 hamburger buns or onion rolls
4 slices sharp cheddar or Pepper Jack cheese (or your favorite cheese)

1. Make sure the grill is clean and generously sprayed with nonstick grilling spray. Preheat the barbecue to medium high (350°F [180°C] to 400°F [200°C]).

2. In a saucepan on the grill, heat the oil and butter. Add the onions and sauté, stirring frequently, until tender, about 5 to 6 minutes.

3. Add ¾ cup (177 mL) of the beer, the brown sugar, and the garlic salt. Cook until all the beer has been absorbed by the onions and they begin to brown slightly, about 15 to 20 minutes. Add the remaining beer and bring to a simmer. Keep the onions warm.

4. In a large bowl, thoroughly combine the ground chuck, beer, hot sauce, steak sauce, salt, and pepper. Gently form this mixture into 4 patties, handling them as little as possible so as not to make the burgers tough.

5. Grill burgers to your desired doneness. During the last few minutes of grilling, toast the buns on the grill.

6. Serve the burgers on the toasted buns topped with the braised onions, cheese slices, and your favorite condiments.

Green Dragon Burgers
Yield: 4–6 servings

Jalapeño peppers liven up this burger. If you really like fire, leave in the seeds. Just get the fire extinguisher ready.

2 jalapeño peppers, seeded and finely chopped
2 tablespoons (30 mL) minced fresh cilantro
2 tablespoons (30 mL) beer
2 garlic cloves, peeled and minced
½ teaspoon (2.5 mL) freshly ground black pepper
¼ teaspoon (1.25 mL) salt
¼ teaspoon (1.25 mL) hot sauce
1½ pounds (681 g) lean ground turkey
4–6 slices Monterey Jack cheese
4–6 hamburger buns
Fresh salsa, for serving
Sour cream, for serving
Shredded lettuce, for serving

1. Make sure the grill is clean and generously sprayed with nonstick grilling spray. Preheat the barbecue to medium high (350°F [180°C] to 400°F [200°C]).

2. In a large bowl, combine the jalapeño peppers, cilantro, beer, garlic, pepper, salt, and hot sauce. Crumble turkey over this mixture and mix well. Shape into 4 to 6 patties.

3. Place the burgers on the grill, lower the lid, and grill for 4 to 5 minutes on each side, or until no longer pink.

4. Top with cheese, lower the barbecue lid, and grill 1 to 2 minutes longer, or until the cheese is melted.

5. Serve on the buns with the salsa, sour cream, and lettuce.

Havana-Style Burgers

Yield: 4 servings

You can add dill pickle slices to these burgers while they are cooking, as well as thinly sliced onion rounds.

1 pound (454 g) ground beef
½ pound (227 g) thinly sliced ham
½ pound (227 g) sliced cheese (Swiss or provolone preferred)
4 hamburger buns or hoagie rolls

1. Make sure the grill is clean and generously sprayed with nonstick grilling spray. Preheat the barbecue to medium high (350°F [180°C] to 400°F [200°C]).

2. Wrap bricks in heavy-duty aluminum foil and place them on grill to get them hot.

3. Form the beef into 4 patties. Grill the burgers for about 3 to 4 minutes per side, or until they are rare.

4. Spread the condiments of your choice on both sides of the buns or rolls.

5. Put slices of cheese on the tops and bottoms of the buns, place a burger on each bottom bun, then cover them with the top buns. Wrap each burger in aluminum foil.

6. Place the wrapped burgers on the grill and, wearing barbecue mitts, carefully place one foil-covered brick on each sandwich. Cook for an additional 2 to 3 minutes.

7. Wearing the mitts, remove the bricks. Unwrap the aluminum foil and enjoy.

Two-Times Pork and Double-Cheese Burgers

Yield: 4 servings

If you wish, you can use chopped Canadian bacon instead of regular bacon. The result will be a heavier burger with a subtle pork taste.

½ cup (118 mL) finely chopped bacon
1½ pounds (681 g) ground pork
1 teaspoon (5 mL) minced garlic
1 teaspoon (5 mL) dried thyme
1 teaspoon (5 mL) garlic salt
½ teaspoon (2.5 mL) freshly ground black pepper
4 (½-inch [1-cm] thick) slices sweet onion
Extra virgin olive oil, for brushing
4 hamburger buns or onion rolls
4 (¼-inch [0.5-cm] thick) slices Camembert cheese
4 (¼-inch [0.5-cm] thick) slices Stilton cheese
Lettuce, for serving
Tomato slices, for serving

1. Make sure the grill is clean and generously sprayed with nonstick grilling spray. Preheat the barbecue to medium high (350°F [180°C] to 400°F [200°C]).

2. Cook the bacon on the stovetop or a side burner until just beginning to crisp up, then transfer it to paper towels to drain and let cool.

3. In a large bowl, mix together the bacon, ground pork, garlic, thyme, garlic salt, and pepper.

4. Shape this mixture into four (1–1½ inch [2.5–3.5 cm] thick) patties.

5. Brush the onion slices with olive oil and grill them until lightly charred, about 2 minutes per side.

6. Grill the burgers until charred outside and cooked through, about 3 to 4 minutes per side.

7. Arrange the Camembert and Stilton slices on each burger and cook until the cheese is melted, 1 minute.

8. Brush the buns with olive oil and grill them until they just begin to brown. Add the burgers to the buns and layer with lettuce, tomato, and grilled onion.

Lemongrass and Lime Chicken Burgers
Yield: 4–6 servings

Australian chef Bill Granger shared this recipe with me when I visited his Sydney restaurant while filming an episode of Barbecue America.

Burgers

1½ pounds (681 g) ground chicken
1 onion, peeled and finely grated
3 ounces (84 g) fresh white breadcrumbs
1 clove garlic, peeled and crushed
1 stalk lemongrass, white part only, finely chopped
2 tablespoons (30 mL) chopped fresh cilantro
1 tablespoon (15 mL) fish sauce
2 teaspoons (10 mL) finely grated lime zest
2 teaspoons (10 mL) superfine sugar

Sweet Chili Dressing

2 long red chilies, seeded and finely chopped
2 tablespoons (30 mL) fish sauce
1 tablespoon (15 mL) rice vinegar, mirin, or distilled
white vinegar
1½ tablespoons (30 mL) lime juice
1 tablespoon (15 mL) superfine sugar
½ teaspoon (2.5 mL) salt

For Serving

4–6 soft rolls
Lettuce
Sliced onion
Mint leaves
Cilantro leaves
Chili sauce

1. In a large bowl, combine the ground chicken, onion, breadcrumbs, garlic, lemongrass, cilantro, fish sauce, lime zest, and sugar. Mix together well with your hands.

2. Shape the mixture into six patties. Cover and refrigerate for 30 minutes.

3. In a separate bowl, mix together all the dressing ingredients and stir until the sugar has dissolved.

4. Make sure the grill is clean and generously sprayed with nonstick grilling spray. Preheat the barbecue to medium high (350°F [180°C] to 400°F [200°C]).

5. Grill the patties for 4 minutes on each side, or until cooked through.

6. Serve the patties on soft rolls, topped with lettuce, mint, coriander leaves, and chili sauce, with a helping of coleslaw on the side.

Teriyaki Chicken Burgers
Yield: 4 servings

These are super to eat without a bun. Serve with wild rice and a grilled vegetable, such as carrots or zucchini.

Burgers

1½ pounds ground chicken breast
1 medium onion, peeled and finely diced
½ red bell pepper, finely diced
½ cup (118 mL) fresh breadcrumbs
1 jalapeño pepper, seeded and finely diced
2 tablespoons (30 mL) teriyaki sauce
2 tablespoons (30 mL) extra virgin olive oil
1 tablespoon (15 mL) minced garlic
1 tablespoon (15 mL) A1 steak sauce
1 teaspoon (5 mL) poultry seasoning
1 large egg

Mushroom Sauce

1 tablespoon (15 mL) extra virgin olive oil
12 crimini or brown mushrooms, sliced
Salt, to taste
Freshly ground black pepper, to taste
1 cup (236 mL) chicken stock
½ cup (118 mL) dry white wine
¼ cup (59 mL) teriyaki sauce
1 tablespoon (15 mL) butter

1. Make sure the grill is clean and generously sprayed with nonstick grilling spray. Preheat the barbecue to medium high (350°F [180°C] to 400°F [200°C]).

2. In a large bowl, mix together the ground chicken, onion, bell pepper, breadcrumbs, jalapeño pepper, teriyaki sauce, oil, garlic, steak sauce, poultry seasoning, and egg. If the mixture feels too moist, add in a bit more breadcrumbs.

3. Form the mixture into 4 patties and grill until golden brown on each side, turning once.

4. In a cast-iron skillet over a side burner, heat the olive oil. Add the mushrooms and sauté until browned. Season with salt and pepper.

5. Add the chicken stock and wine and scrape up all the brown bits from the bottom of the pan, then add the teriyaki sauce. Heat until sauce is reduced by a third.

6. Just before serving the sauce, add the butter and stir until melted.

7. Place the burgers on heated plates and spoon mushroom sauce over the patties.

Maui Mahi Mahi Burgers
Yield: 4–6 servings

You can substitute shark, salmon, swordfish or any other firm-fleshed fish in this recipe.

1 (1½–2 pound [681–908 g]) mahi mahi fillet, cut into chunks
¼ cup (59 mL) fresh cilantro leaves
¼ cup (59 mL) sliced green onions
2 tablespoons (30 mL) hoisin sauce
2 tablespoons (30 mL) mayonnaise
2 teaspoons (10 mL) minced fresh ginger
½ teaspoon (2.5 mL) minced garlic
Salt, to taste
Freshly ground black pepper, to taste
2 tablespoons (30 mL) vegetable oil (optional)
2 teaspoons (10 mL) light sesame or walnut oil (optional)

1. In a food processor, combine the fish, cilantro, onions, hoisin, mayonnaise, ginger, garlic, salt and pepper and pulse until finely chopped. Form this mixture into 4 patties and chill, covered, for 3 to 4 hours.

2. Make sure the grill is clean and generously sprayed with nonstick grilling spray. Preheat the barbecue to medium high (350°F [180°C] to 400°F [200°C]).

3. Grill the patties for 2 to 3 minutes per side, or until they are just beginning to brown. Or, in a large cast-iron skillet on a side burner, heat the vegetable oil and sesame or walnut oil over medium heat. Add the fish burgers and cook for 3 minutes per side, or until just cooked through.

4. Serve burgers the on toasted buns with mayonnaise, topped with lettuce and tomato, with hoisin sauce or teriyaki sauce on the side.

Eggplant and Portobello Burgers
Yield: 4 servings

Vegetarians delight with this burger. If you are indeed serving vegetarians, you can use a vegetarian Worcestershire sauce or substitute a top-quality soy sauce.

Salt as needed
4 very thin slices eggplant
4 large Portobello mushrooms, cleaned, gills scraped off
4 hamburger or focaccia buns
4 thin slices cheese of your choice
Worcestershire sauce, to taste
1 tablespoon (15 mL) garlic mayonnaise
1 large tomato, sliced

1. Salt the eggplant slices and let them rest for 30 minutes. Rinse them quickly and blot dry.

2. Make sure the grill is clean and generously sprayed with nonstick grilling spray. Preheat the barbecue to medium high (350°F [180°C] to 400°F [200°C]).

3. Grill mushrooms over the coals for 4 to 5 minutes total, turning once halfway through.

4. Put the bun bottoms on a baking sheet and top each with a slice of cheese. Place the baking sheet in the barbecue and cook until the cheese melts. Remove the buns from the grill and the baking sheet.

5. Spray both sides of the eggplant with grilling spray, brush them with Worcestershire sauce, and place them on the baking sheet. Barbecue them for 5 minutes on one side, then turn them. Add the bun tops to the baking sheet and cook the eggplant and buns for an additional 5 minutes. Remove the pan from the barbecue when the eggplant is tender and the bun tops are golden.

6. Spread a small amount of mayo on each bun bottom. Layer a slice of tomato, a slice of eggplant, and a whole mushroom cap on each bottom and top with the bun top.

Tofu Chicken Burgers
Yield: 4 servings

I'm not a huge fan of tofu, but these burgers are delightful—light, fresh, and a nice change from beef, pork, and even chicken burgers. I think people who try them will be surprised how much they like them.

1 pound (454 g) extra-firm tofu
¼ cup (59 mL) Miracle Whip or vegan mayonnaise
Seasoned salt, to taste
Freshly ground black pepper, to taste
¼ cup (59 mL) cornmeal
¼ cup (59 mL) all-purpose flour
1 teaspoon (5 mL) vegetable bouillon powder
½ teaspoon (2.5 mL) dried parsley
2 tablespoons (30 mL) vegetable oil
4 hamburger buns

1. Drain the tofu and freeze it for at least 24 hours to firm it up and make it easier to cut.

2. Let the tofu thaw. To remove excess moisture, press it for 10 to 20 minutes by placing a plate on top of it and some heavy books on top of that.

3. Make sure the grill is clean and generously sprayed with nonstick grilling spray. Preheat the barbecue to medium high (350°F [180°C] to 400°F [200°C]).

4. Slice the tofu into burger-sized rounds or squares.

5. Spread the Miracle Whip on a plate and dredge the tofu slices in it. Sprinkle both sides of each slice with the seasoned salt and a few grinds of black pepper.

6. On a plate, mix together the cornmeal, flour, bouillon powder, and parsley. Dredge the tofu slices in this mixture.

7. Coat a heavy pan with the oil. Add the tofu and fry it on the grill or side burner for 10 minutes, covered, turning every few minutes.

8. Serve on a bun with fresh tomato and onion slices and your favorite toppings, or provide soy or teriyaki dipping sauces.

Cheddar Beef Sliders

Yield: 4–6 servings

You can also sandwich two of these patties together with a slice of cheddar or blue cheese between them and serve on the buns.

1¼ pounds (567 g) ground beef
2 tablespoons (30 mL) sweet pickle relish
2 tablespoons (30 mL) steak sauce
1 tablespoon (15 mL) garlic salt
1 teaspoon (5 mL) sweet paprika
½ cup (118 mL) ranch dressing
½ cup (118 mL) ketchup
1 teaspoon (5 mL) freshly ground black pepper
1 pinch salt
10 soft dinner rolls, split
Lettuce, for serving
1 yellow onion, peeled and finely diced, for serving
Dill pickle slices, for serving
4 slices extra-sharp cheddar cheese, for serving

1. Make sure the grill is clean and generously sprayed with nonstick grilling spray. Preheat the barbecue to medium high (350°F [180°C] to 400°F [200°C]).

2. In a large bowl, mix together the meat, pickle relish, steak sauce, garlic salt, and paprika. Divide the meat in half and score each half into 5 pieces. Roll each piece into a golf ball–sized ball, then flatten each into a small, thin patty about 3 inches (7.5 cm) across (for a total of 10 to 14 patties).

3. Cook the burgers on the grill for about 2 to 3 minutes on each side for medium doneness.

4. While burgers are cooking, make the Slida' Sauce: in a small bowl, combine the ranch dressing, ketchup, black pepper, and salt.

5. Serve the burgers on dinner rolls with the lettuce, chopped onion, dill pickle slices, cheese slices, and Slida' Sauce.

Mazatlan Taco Burgers

Yield: 4–6 servings

1½ pounds (681 g) ground beef
1 small green bell pepper, finely diced
1 large egg
2 tablespoons (30 mL) water
¼ cup (59 mL) soft breadcrumbs
½ (1¼-ounce [35-g]) packet taco seasoning mix
1 teaspoon (5 mL) chili powder
4–6 slices Swiss or Monterey Jack cheese
4–6 hamburger buns
10 ounces (280 g) salsa

1. Make sure the grill is clean and generously sprayed with nonstick spray. Preheat the barbecue to medium high (350°F [180°C] to 400°F [200°C]).

2. In large bowl, combine the beef, bell pepper, egg, water, breadcrumbs, taco seasoning mix, and chili powder and mix well. If the mixture is too moist, add breadcrumbs, a tablespoon (15 mL) at a time.

3. Form the mixture into 4 to 6 patties, whatever size you wish.

4. Grill the patties until they are done to your preference, 5 to 6 minutes per side for medium-rare.

5. Add a slice of cheese to each burger during the last 2 minutes of grilling.

6. Serve on a hamburger bun, with a spoonful of salsa on top of each burger.

Ham and Cheese Burgers

Yield: 4 servings

1 ounce (28 g) pancetta (about 2 slices), chopped into ¼-inch (0.5-cm) pieces
⅓ cup (79 mL) diced onion
2 cloves garlic, peeled and minced
½ teaspoon (2.5 mL) freshly ground black pepper
¼ teaspoon (1.25 mL) salt
¼ teaspoon (1.25 mL) Italian seasoning
1 pound (454 g) ground beef (round)
½ cup (118 mL) shredded reduced-fat Swiss cheese (such as Sargento)
3 tablespoons (45 mL) light mayonnaise
1 tablespoon (15 mL) commercial pesto sauce
4 hamburger buns

1. Make sure the grill is clean and generously sprayed with nonstick spray. Preheat the barbecue to medium high (350°F [180°C] to 400°F [200°C]).

2. Coat a nonstick skillet or pan with grilling spray. Add the pancetta to the pan and cook for 4 to 5 minutes, or until crisp. Remove the pancetta from the pan, leaving the drippings in the pan.

3. Add the onion and garlic to the pan. Cook for 5 minutes, or until softened, stirring frequently. Transfer the mixture to a large bowl and add the pepper, salt, seasoning, and beef.

4. Shape the beef mixture into 8 (¼-inch [0.5-cm] thick) patties. Top 4 patties with pancetta and 2 tablespoons (30 mL) Swiss cheese, leaving a ¼-inch (0.5-cm) border around the edge. Top each of these patties with another patty and pinch the edges to seal.

5. Place the patties on the grill rack coated with cooking spray and cook for 5 minutes. Turn and cook for another 5 minutes, or until a meat thermometer inserted in the center measures 160°F (71°C).

6. Combine the mayonnaise and pesto. Spread about 1 tablespoon (15 mL) of the mayonnaise mixture on the bottom half of each bun. Top each serving with 1 patty and the top half of the bun.

Grill-Fired Bacon Burgers
Yield: 4 servings

This is a basic bacon cheeseburger that is accented by a chopped chipotle, lime juice, cumin, and Monterey Jack cheese.

½ chipotle pepper, minced to a paste
10–12 slices bacon
2–3 small shallots, peeled and finely chopped
2 tablespoons (30 mL) Worcestershire sauce
2 tablespoons (30 mL) dark brown sugar
2 tablespoons (30 mL) fresh lime juice
1 (15-ounce [420-g]) can tomato sauce
Salt, to taste
Freshly ground black pepper, to taste
1⅓ pounds (605 g) ground beef (sirloin or chuck)
1 tablespoon (15 mL) finely chopped garlic
1 tablespoon (15 mL) ground cumin
2 teaspoons (10 mL) chili powder
1 teaspoon (5 mL) barbecue rub of your choice
1 teaspoon (5 mL) dried savory
4 Kaiser or onion rolls, split and toasted
4 slices Monterey Jack cheese
3 tablespoons (45 mL) chopped fresh cilantro, for serving
Thinly sliced red onion, for serving

1. Make sure the grill is clean and generously sprayed with nonstick grilling spray. Preheat the barbecue to medium high (350°F [180°C] to 400°F [200°C]).

2. Spray a medium nonstick skillet with nonstick cooking spray. Heat the skillet over medium high heat and add the bacon. Cook for 5 to 6 minutes per side, or until crispy. Remove the bacon from the pan and drain it on paper towels, leaving about 2 tablespoons (30 mL) of fat in the skillet.

3. With the skillet still over medium high heat, add the shallots and cook for about 2 to 3 minutes, or until they are slightly translucent. Add the Worcestershire sauce, brown sugar, and lime juice and cook for about 1 to 2 minutes. Add the tomato sauce and bring to a simmer. Season the sauce with salt and pepper and cook for about 10 minutes.

4. In a medium bowl, combine the meat with the cumin, chili powder, barbecue rub, and dried savory and mix well. Divide the mixture into 4 patties about 1 inch (2.5 cm) thick.

5. Place the patties on the grill and cook for 5 to 6 minutes on each side. Baste them with some of the sauce during the last 2 minutes of cooking.

6. Place each burger on a Kaiser or onion roll. Top with sauce, bacon slices, and a slice of the cheese.

7. Garnish with the cilantro and red onion.

Apple and Brie Birdburgers
Yield: 8 servings

This tangy, satisfying, and unique way to serve ground turkey will surprise your luncheon or dinner guests. The basil adds a zesty touch to the milder Brie cheese and apple.

2½ pounds (1.1 kg) ground turkey
Seasoned or sea salt, to taste
Freshly ground black pepper, to taste
½ teaspoon (2.5 mL) garlic powder
2 large Granny Smith apples, cored and sliced into ½-inch (1-cm) rounds
2 tablespoons (30 mL) olive oil
16 (½-inch [1-cm] thick) slices French bread (about 1 loaf)
8 (¼-inch [0.5-cm] thick) slices Brie cheese
2 cups (473 mL) chopped fresh basil

1. Make sure the grill is clean and generously sprayed with nonstick grilling spray. Preheat the barbecue to medium high (350°F [180°C] to 400°F [200°C]).

2. In a large bowl, mix together the ground turkey, salt, pepper, and garlic powder. Shape the mixture into 8 round patties about 1½ inches (3.5 cm) thick.

3. Grill until cooked through, about 4 minutes per side for medium burgers.

4. While the burgers are cooking, brush the apple slices on both sides with olive oil and grill the slices until golden, about 2 minutes per side.

5. Toast the bread on the grill until golden, about 30 seconds per side.

6. Place each burger on a slice of toasted bread. Cover each burger with a slice of Brie cheese and a slice of cooked apple. Sprinkle some fresh basil on each, cover with a second slice of bread, and serve.

Buffalo Turkey Burgers

Yield: 6 servings

These are like eating buffalo wings on a bun with no bones, and they have less fat than chicken wings. You can make these as spicy as you like. To liven things up, brush garlic oil or garlic butter on the insides of the buns prior to setting them on the hot grill.

1 tablespoon (15 mL) butter
1 small yellow onion, peeled and finely diced
1 stalk celery, finely diced
2 tablespoons (30 mL) minced garlic
1½ pounds (681 g) ground turkey
1 teaspoon (5 mL) chili powder
½ teaspoon (2.5 mL) freshly ground black pepper
½ teaspoon (2.5 mL) seasoned salt
½ teaspoon (2.5 mL) cayenne pepper
½ cup (118 mL) crumbled blue cheese
4 large hamburger rolls or potato buns, split
Lettuce, for serving
Tomato slices, for serving
Your favorite hot sauce, to taste
1 cup (236 mL) ranch dressing, for serving

1. Make sure the grill is clean and generously sprayed with nonstick grilling spray. Preheat the barbecue to medium high (350°F [180°C] to 400°F [200°C]).

2. In a skillet, melt the butter over medium to low heat. Add the chopped onion and sauté until it begins to brown, approximately 5 to 7 minutes. Add the celery and garlic 2 minutes before the onion is done.

3. In a medium bowl, use your hands to mix together the ground turkey, sautéed onion mixture, chili powder, black pepper, seasoned salt, and cayenne pepper. Shape into 6 (1-inch [2.5-cm] thick) patties.

4. Grill the turkey patties for 5 minutes, or just until the meat loses its pink color throughout, turning once. (Burgers should reach an internal temperature of 160°F [71°C]). Just before you remove the patties from the grill (about the last 1½ minutes) sprinkle each with blue cheese. Remove the burgers just as the cheese starts to melt.

5. Toast the buns or rolls on the grill.

6. To serve, place lettuce and tomato slices on each roll or bun bottom, add a burger to each, and drizzle the hot sauce and a spoonful of ranch dressing over each burger. Cover with the roll or bun tops.

Gobbler Patties with Seasoned Onion Gravy
Yield: 4 servings

These are super served over noodles or wild rice—or, if you want to indulge a little bit, garlic mashed potatoes—and are very low in fat.

2 pounds (908 g) ground turkey breast
Salt, to taste
Freshly ground black pepper, to taste
1 tablespoon (15 mL) olive oil
1–2 chicken bouillon cubes
1 large onion, peeled and finely diced
1 cup (236 mL) sliced mushrooms
1 teaspoon (5 mL) poultry seasoning
½ teaspoon (2.5 mL) dried parsley
1½ cups (354 mL) warm water
1 tablespoon (15 mL) cornstarch
¼ cup (59 mL) dry white wine

1. Make sure the grill is clean and generously sprayed with nonstick grilling spray. Preheat the barbecue to medium high (350°F [180°C] to 400°F [200°C]).

2. Season the meat with salt and pepper, to taste. Divide the meat into 4 equal portions and shape each portion into a patty. Cover and refrigerate the patties to firm them up.

3. In large frying pan on the grill or on a side burner, heat the oil. Add the bouillon cubes, onions, and mushrooms. Sauté, stirring often, until the onions are translucent and the bullion cube dissolves, then lower heat to a simmer. Add the poultry seasoning and parsley. Stir in the water and cook until you have about 2 cups (473 mL) of gravy.

4. Gently place the burgers in the pan. Cook them for about 5 to 7 minutes on each side, until the meat juices run clear. Transfer the cooked burgers to a plate, cover with foil, and keep warm. Return the sauce to a boil and add more water if it is too thick.

5. In a small cup, whisk together the cornstarch and wine. Slowly pour this mixture into the sauce in the pan and cook until it is thick enough to coat the back of a spoon.

6. Spoon cooked rice or noodles onto a heated plate, place two burgers on top, and pour the gravy over the burgers.

Veal and Gorgonzola Burgers with Seasoned Onions
Yield: 4 servings

A light and tasty lunch, or a barbecue treat for the whole family, these have half the fat of a beef burger. The cheese and spiced onions bring the veal to a new taste dimension.

2 tablespoons (30 mL) olive oil
1 large white or yellow onion, peeled and sliced into rings
1 teaspoon (5 mL) ground sage
¼ cup (59 mL) dry white vermouth or wine
¼ teaspoon (1.25 mL) dried thyme
1 pinch sea salt
1 large egg
1 clove garlic, peeled and minced
¼ cup (59 mL) chopped fresh Italian parsley
3 tablespoons (45 mL) crushed tomatoes, drained
½ teaspoon (2.5 mL) salt
¼ teaspoon (1.25 mL) freshly ground black pepper
1 dash hot sauce
1 pound (454 g) ground veal
4 ounces (112 g) Gorgonzola or other blue cheese, divided

1. Make sure the grill is clean and generously sprayed with nonstick grilling spray. Preheat the barbecue to medium high (350°F [180°C] to 400°F [200°C]).

2. In a frying pan, heat the oil over medium-high heat. Add the onions and sauté for 2 minutes, until just wilting.

3. Add the sage and sauté until the onions are golden, stirring occasionally, about 20 minutes. Lower the heat if necessary.

4. Pour in the vermouth, thyme, and the pinch of sea salt and cook until the liquid is evaporated, 2 to 3 minutes. Cover and set aside.

5. In a large bowl, beat together the egg, garlic, parsley, tomatoes, the ½ teaspoon salt, the pepper, and the hot sauce. Mix in the veal.

6. Shape this mixture into 4 balls, press a quarter of the cheese into the center of each ball, seal well, and flatten into 1–1½ inch (2.5–3.5 cm) thick patties.

7. Grill the patties, turning once, until they are no longer pink inside, about 12 to 14 minutes total.

8. Place the patties on toasted, buttered buns and serve with a large spoonful of sautéed onions over each patty.

Waaaasssaaabbbiii Tuna Burgers

Yield: 4 servings

Low in calories, fat, and cholesterol, these burgers are high in flavor and offer a mouth-tingling surprise.

¾ cup (177 mL) coarsely chopped fresh parsley
½ cup (118 mL) coarsely chopped fresh cilantro
½ cup (118 mL) chopped onion
1½ tablespoons (22.5 mL) low-sodium soy sauce
1 teaspoon (5 mL) minced garlic
1 teaspoon (5 mL) sweet rice vinegar
2 tablespoons (30 mL) sesame seeds
1 pound (454 g) sashimi-grade tuna steak, cut into chunks
2 tablespoons (30 mL) wasabi paste

1. In a food processor or mini chopper, combine the parsley, cilantro, onion, soy sauce, garlic, and rice vinegar. Pulse for about 20 to 30 seconds, or until the mixture is blended and the herbs are finely chopped.

2. Transfer the herb mixture to a mixing bowl, add the sesame seeds and set aside.

3. Put the tuna into the food processor and pulse 6 to 8 times, until the tuna is ground up but not yet a paste.

4. Scrape the tuna out into the mixing bowl with the herb mixture. Add the wasabi paste.

5. Using a large fork or spoon, mix everything well. If you prefer to mix with your hands, wear rubber or disposable plastic gloves.

6. Divide the mixture into four portions and then form each portion into a patty about 1 inch (2.5 cm) thick. Put the patties on a plate, cover the plate with plastic wrap, and refrigerate for 30 minutes.

7. Remove the burgers from the refrigerator and let them stand until they reach room temperature, about 30 minutes.

8. Preheat the barbecue to medium high (350°F [180°C] to 400°F [200°C]).

9. Heat a nonstick or well-sprayed frying pan on the grill or over a side burner until it is hot. Add the patties and cook for about 4 minutes on each side, or until the middle is just beginning to firm up.

10. Serve on toasted English muffins or bagels.

Chicken Teriyaki Burgers with Pineapple

Yield: 4 servings

I first tasted burgers like these on Maui, and I fell in love with the marriage between pineapple and grilled meats. You can also make these with beef, fish, or turkey.

1 cup (236 mL) panko
3 tablespoons (45 mL) teriyaki sauce
1½ pounds (681 g) ground chicken
1 teaspoon (5 mL) light sesame oil
3 tablespoons (45 mL) finely diced onions
1 clove garlic, minced
1 teaspoon (5 mL) chopped fresh parsley
2 teaspoons (10 mL) prepared mustard
1 large egg, lightly beaten
½ teaspoon (2.5 mL) sea salt
½ teaspoon (2.5 mL) freshly ground black pepper
½ teaspoon (2.5 mL) ground ginger
¼ teaspoon (1.25 mL) ground nutmeg
1 pinch ground cloves
4 slices pineapple
1 teaspoon (5 mL) black or pink peppercorns, freshly crushed
1 teaspoon (5 mL) brown sugar
¼ teaspoon (1.25 mL) salt

1. Make sure the grill is clean and generously sprayed with nonstick grilling spray. Preheat the barbecue to medium high (350°F [180°C] to 400°F [200°C]).

2. In a large bowl, combine the panko with the teriyaki sauce. Stir and let rest for 5 minutes. Fold in the ground chicken.

3. In a small pan on the grill or on a side burner, heat the sesame oil. Add the onions, garlic, and parsley and sauté for 1 minute, then add this mixture to the ground meat mixture and mix thoroughly. Add the mustard, egg, salt, pepper, ginger, nutmeg, and cloves and mix well. Mold this mixture into 4 thick patties and refrigerate, covered, for 1 hour.

4. Place the pineapple slices on paper towels to drain. In a small bowl, mix together the crushed peppercorns, sugar, and salt, then sprinkle this mixture over the fruit slices. Spray lightly with grilling spray and set aside.

5. Grill the burgers for 5 to 6 minutes, or until the internal temperature reaches 160°F [71°C], turning once halfway through grilling time. Grill the pineapple for 1 to 2 minutes, turning only once. Toast the buns on the grill at the same time.

6. Place burgers on the toasted buns, top with pineapple, and serve.

Jerked Bird Burgers with Fruit Salsa
Yield: 4 servings

Hey, mon! These are cool and fiery at the same time, and the cool fruit salsa smooths out the spice for a light and refreshing burger. Serve with an ice-cold Jamaican beer, such as Red Stripe.

1 cup (236 mL) diced mango
¾ cup (177 mL) finely diced red onion, divided
½ cup (118 mL) diced papaya
½ cup (118 mL) finely diced green pepper, divided
2 tablespoons (30 mL) chopped fresh cilantro
2 tablespoons (30 mL) freshly squeezed lime juice
1 teaspoon (5 mL) sweet rice vinegar
1 pinch onion powder
½ cup (118 mL) uncooked quick oats
⅓ cup (79 mL) ketchup
1–2 tablespoons (15–30 mL) Caribbean jerk seasoning
1 large egg, beaten
1½ pounds (681 g) ground turkey or chicken

1. To prepare the salsa, in a medium bowl, combine the mango, ¼ cup (59 mL) of the red onion, papaya, ¼ cup (59 mL) of the green pepper, the cilantro, the lime juice, the vinegar, and the garlic powder. Stir well, cover with plastic wrap, and set aside.

2. In a large bowl, combine the remaining red onion, the remaining green pepper, the oats, the ketchup, the jerk seasoning, and the egg and mix well. Add the turkey or chicken and mix thoroughly. Shape this mixture into 4 (1-inch [2.5-cm] thick) patties; cover with plastic wrap, and refrigerate for 20 to 30 minutes.

3. Make sure the grill is clean and generously sprayed with nonstick grilling spray. Preheat the barbecue to medium high (350°F [180°C] to 400°F [200°C]).

4. Grill the burgers until done, flipping once, about 10 to 12 minutes total. The temperature inside the burgers should be 160°F (71°C).

5. Serve each burger on a toasted bun, topped with 1 to 2 heaping tablespoons (22.5 to 45 mL) of salsa on top of each patty.

Chicken Burgers with Satay Sauce
Yield: 4 servings   Satay Sauce

Most folks like satay pork, chicken or beef in Thai restaurants. Well, we just serve the same kind of sauce with a chicken (or turkey) burger for a tangy change.

Sauce
¼ cup (59 mL) chunky peanut butter
¼ cup (59 mL) chicken or vegetable broth
1 tablespoon (15 mL) brown sugar
1 teaspoon (5 mL) red pepper flakes
1 teaspoon (5 mL) garlic salt
¼ teaspoon (1.25 mL) ground cumin

Burgers

2 tablespoons (30 mL) smooth peanut butter
2 teaspoons (10 mL) brown sugar
2 teaspoons (10 mL) hot sauce
¼ cup (59 mL) chicken broth
1 pound (454 g) ground chicken
1 tablespoon (15 mL) minced garlic
½ teaspoon (2.5 mL) ground cumin
½ teaspoon (2.5 mL) ground ginger
½ cup (118 mL) chopped fresh parsley
½ teaspoon (2.5 mL) salt
4 hamburger buns with sesame seeds, toasted

1. Make sure the grill is clean and generously sprayed with nonstick grilling spray. Preheat the barbecue to medium high (350°F [180°C] to 400°F [200°C]).

2. In a medium bowl, prepare the satay sauce by mixing together the peanut butter, broth, brown sugar, red pepper flakes, garlic salt, cumin, and ginger until smooth. Set aside.

3. In a large bowl, whisk together the creamy peanut butter, brown sugar, hot sauce, and chicken broth until blended, then set aside.

4. In a separate bowl, mix together the chicken, garlic, cumin, parsley, and salt.

5. Stir half the creamy peanut butter mixture into the bowl of chicken and blend until smooth, then form this mixture into 4 patties about 1½ to 2 inches (3.5 to 5 cm) thick.

6. Grill the patties for about 4 to 5 minutes on each side, or until they are cooked to your desired doneness.

7. Serve the burgers on the toasted hamburger buns with the satay sauce on the side.

Ginger Salmon Burgers with Hoisin

Yield: 6–8 servings

We like to grill these, but instead of putting the patties right on the grill, we put down a sheet of heavy-duty aluminum foil, spray it well with nonstick spray, and cook the patties on the foil.

2 pounds (908 g) salmon fillets, boned and skinned
¼ cup (60 mL) hoisin sauce
⅓ cup (79 mL) chopped green onion, green and white parts
¼ cup (59 mL) reduced-fat mayonnaise
3–4 tablespoons (45–60 mL) minced fresh ginger
3 tablespoons (45 mL) finely chopped fresh parsley
2–3 cloves garlic, minced
1½ teaspoons (7.5 mL) salt
Freshly ground black pepper, to taste

1. Make sure the grill is clean. Preheat the barbecue to medium high (350°F [180°C] to 400°F [200°C]).

2. In a food processor, combine the salmon, hoisin and mayo. Pulse just until coarsely ground.

3. Transfer the salmon mixture to a large bowl and add the onions, mayo, ginger, parsley, salt, and pepper. With a spatula, mix to fully combine. Shape the mixture into 6 to 8 patties.

4. Place the salmon patties on a plate, cover with plastic wrap, and refrigerate for 3 to 4 hours. (This is an important step.)

5. Grill the patties on heavy-duty foil or in a large nonstick skillet for about 3 to 4 minutes on each side. You do not want to overcook these. The insides of the patties should be slightly pink.

Apricot and Mint Lamb Burgers with Mint Mayonnaise
Yield: 4 servings

If you don't like apricots, try using minced golden raisins.

Burgers
1 pound (454 g) ground lamb
⅓ cup (79 mL) minced red onion
3 tablespoons (45 mL) minced dried apricots
2–3 cloves garlic, finely minced
1 teaspoon (5 mL) brown sugar
½ teaspoon (2.5 mL) salt
½ teaspoon (2.5 mL) freshly ground black pepper

Mayonnaise
1 egg yolk
1 teaspoon (5 mL) sugar
½ teaspoon (2.5 mL) salt
½ teaspoon (2.5 mL) dry mustard
½ teaspoon (2.5 mL) freshly ground black pepper
⅔ cup (158 mL) olive oil
2 tablespoons (30 mL) fresh lemon juice
2 green onions, white and green parts, chopped
2 tablespoons (30 mL) chopped fresh parsley
2 tablespoons (30 mL) chopped fresh mint

Serving
4 hamburger buns
Lettuce

1. In a food processor, combine the egg yolk, sugar, salt, mustard, and pepper. Process on low, adding the oil in a slow stream and scraping down the sides to make sure the mayonnaise is smooth. When all oil has been added, add the lemon juice, green onion, parsley, and mint and process once or twice to blend. Do not over process.

2. Refrigerate the mayonnaise until the burgers are done.

3. Make sure the grill is clean and generously sprayed with nonstick grilling spray. Preheat the barbecue to medium high (350°F [180°C] to 400°F [200°C]).

4. In a large bowl, combine the lamb, onion, apricots, garlic, brown sugar, salt, and pepper and mix well.

5. Form this mixture into 4 patties. Grill for about 3 to 4 minutes per side.

6. When burgers are done, place each patty on a bun with lettuce, add a dollop of the mint mayonnaise, and serve.

Shrimp and Swordfish Burgers with Tartar Sauce
Yield: 4 servings

These work well using crab or lobster instead of the shrimp.

Burgers
8 ounces (227 g) medium shrimp, peeled, deveined, cut into chunks
10 ounces (280 g) swordfish steaks, cut into chunks
¾ cup (177 mL) panko
3 medium green onions, white and green parts, thinly sliced
¼ cup (59 mL) fresh lemon juice (from 1–2 large lemons)
2 tablespoons (30 mL) chopped fresh Italian parsley
½ teaspoon (2.5 mL) paprika
¼ teaspoon (1.25 mL) dried savory
1¼ teaspoons (6.25 mL) kosher salt
½ teaspoon (2.5 mL) freshly ground black pepper
4 hamburger buns or onion rolls

Tartar Sauce
1 cup (236 mL) olive oil mayonnaise
3 tablespoons (45 mL) sweet pickle relish
1 tablespoon (15 mL) fresh lemon juice (from 1 large lemon)
1 teaspoon (5 mL) finely minced onion
1 teaspoon (5 mL) seasoned salt
⅛ teaspoon (0.6 mL) freshly ground black pepper

1. In a food processor, combine the shrimp, swordfish, panko, green onions, lemon juice, parsley, paprika, savory, salt, and pepper and pulse until just combined.

2. Shape this mixture into 4 (1½–2 inch [3.5–5 cm] thick) patties.

3. Cover with plastic wrap and refrigerate for at least 1½ hours (or overnight).

4. Make sure the grill is clean and generously sprayed with nonstick grilling spray. Preheat the barbecue to medium high (350°F [180°C] to 400°F [200°C]).

5. Grill the burgers, turning once, until cooked through, about 3 minutes per side.

6. In a medium bowl, combine the tartar sauce ingredients and stir well to thoroughly incorporate.

7. Serve the burgers on toasted buns with a dollop tartar sauce, lettuce, tomato, sliced onion, or other favorite toppings.

Bean–Sunflower Seed Burgers

Yield: 6 servings

I'm not a vegetarian, but these burgers are delicious. They take a bit of work to be sure, but they are a refreshing change from beef, pork, or chicken burgers. You can find amaranth flour in health food shops or in the health food section of a major grocery store.

1 cup (236 mL) cooked black beans
1 cup (236 mL) steamed carrots
½ cup (118 mL) ground raw sunflower seeds
½–¾ cup (118–177 mL) amaranth flour
½ cup (118 mL) finely chopped onion
1 tablespoon (15 mL) dried parsley
1 tablespoon (15 mL) soy sauce
½ teaspoon (2.5 mL) dried basil
½ teaspoon (2.5 mL) dried oregano
½ teaspoon (2.5 mL) kosher salt
⅛ teaspoon (0.6 mL) cayenne pepper

1. In a food processor, combine the beans and carrots and pulse just until mixed. Transfer the mixture to a large bowl.

2. Add all the remaining ingredients and blend, adding more flour if the mix is too damp.

3. Form the mixture into 6 burgers about ½ inch (1 cm) thick. Cover and refrigerate for at least 2 hours.

4. Make sure the grill is clean and generously sprayed with nonstick grilling spray. Preheat the barbecue to medium high (350°F [180°C] to 400°F [200°C]).

5. Cook on the barbecue for 8 to 10 minutes on one side and 5 to 8 minutes on the other, or bake in a well-sprayed cast-iron pan in the barbecue for 25 to 30 minutes.

6. Serve on whole wheat hamburger buns or toasted thick slices of multigrain bakery bread.

Bacon and Blue Cheese Burgers

Yield: 4 servings

For a tasty new treat, add a thin slice of your favorite eating apple on top of the cheese and bacon burger. It adds a crunch and a nice sweetness that goes well with the bacon.

8 slices smoked bacon
2 pounds (908 g) ground beef (chuck)
2 teaspoons (10 mL) dried savory or oregano
1 teaspoon (5 mL) garlic salt
1 teaspoon (5 mL) freshly ground black pepper
1 teaspoon (5 mL) dried marjoram
½ cup (118 mL) crumbled blue cheese
4 sesame seed or onion hamburger rolls, toasted

1. Make sure the grill is clean and generously sprayed with nonstick grilling spray. Preheat the barbecue to medium high (350°F [180°C] to 400°F [200°C]).

2. Cook the bacon in a dry skillet over medium heat until it's as crispy as you desire. Drain the slices on paper towels and set aside.

3. In a medium bowl, mix together the ground beef, savory or oregano, garlic salt, pepper, and marjoram. Form the mixture into 8 thin patties.

4. Place a heaping tablespoon or two (22.5 to 45 mL) of the cheese in the center of one patty, leaving an edge of about ½ inch (1 cm) all the way around. Top with another patty and pinch the seams together to make sure the cheese won't leak out during cooking. Repeat with the remaining patties and cheese.

5. Cook the burgers until medium-rare, about 4 minutes per side.

6. Serve the burgers, topped with bacon, on the toasted rolls.

Fiery Pork Burgers with Cheese
Yield: 4 servings

You can fire these up even more by using Scotch bonnet or habañero peppers, adding cayenne pepper, or substituting a favorite hot sauce for the ketchup. Keep a fire extinguisher handy!

1 cup (236 mL) mayonnaise
1 teaspoon (5 mL) chili powder
1 teaspoon (5 mL) garlic powder
1 teaspoon (5 mL) fresh lemon juice
¼ teaspoon (1.25 mL) ground white pepper
1 dash cayenne pepper
½ pound (227 g) hot Italian sausage
½ pound (227 g) ground pork
½ cup (118 mL) shredded smoked cheddar cheese
½ cup (118 mL) diced yellow onion
¼ cup (59 mL) ketchup
2 tablespoons (30 mL) finely chopped fresh cilantro
2 tablespoons (30 mL) chopped fresh parsley
1 tablespoon (15 mL) finely chopped jalapeño pepper
1 tablespoon (15 mL) Worcestershire sauce
1 teaspoon (5 mL) red pepper flakes
4 sourdough rolls

1. In a small bowl, combine the mayonnaise, chili powder, garlic powder, lemon juice, white pepper and cayenne pepper and stir to mix well. Cover and refrigerate at least 1 hour, or until ready to use.

2. Make sure the grill is clean and generously sprayed with nonstick grilling spray. Preheat the barbecue to medium high (350°F [180°C] to 400°F [200°C]).

3. Remove the sausage casings. In a large bowl, mix together the sausage meat and the ground pork. Add the cheese, onion, ketchup, cilantro, parsley, jalapeño pepper, Worcestershire sauce, and red pepper flakes and mix until the ingredients are well incorporated.

4. Form this mixture into 4 patties of equal size (about 1½ to 2I inches [3.5 to 5 cm]).

5. Grill the burgers, turning them only once, until the juices run clear, about 4 to 5 minutes per side, or until they are cooked to your desired doneness.

6. Serve on sourdough rolls with generous dollops of the spicy mayonnaise.

Marrakech Lamb Burgers
Yield: 4 servings

The Grand Souk of Marrakech comes alive at night with dozens of food vendors selling everything from boiled sheep's heads to escargot. These burgers were inspired by some delicious pita burgers I enjoyed there.

1 large shallot, peeled and minced
2 tablespoons (30 mL) chopped fresh cilantro
1 jalapeño pepper, seeded and minced
1 clove garlic, peeled and minced
1¼ teaspoons (6.25 mL) salt
¾ teaspoon (3.75 mL) freshly ground black pepper
¾ teaspoon (3.75 mL) ground cumin
½ teaspoon (2.5 mL) paprika
1 pound (454 g) ground lamb
4 hamburger buns or pocket pitas
Lettuce, for serving
Olive oil mayonnaise, for serving

1. Preheat the barbecue to medium high (350°F [180°C] to 400°F [200°C]).

2. In a large bowl, combine the shallots, cilantro, jalapeño pepper, garlic, salt, black pepper, cumin, and paprika and mix well.

3. Add the lamb and, using a large fork or spoon, mix gently to combine.

4. Shape the mixture into 4 (½-inch [1-cm] thick) patties.

5. Grill the burgers until slightly charred and cooked to your desired doneness, about 4 minutes per side for medium-rare.

6. While the burgers are cooking, use part of the grill to toast the buns, cut side down, until golden brown, about 2 minutes.

7. Put lettuce on the bottom buns, add the burger, top each burger with a tablespoon (15 mL) of mayonnaise and serve.

L'il Walt's Sausage and Beef Burgers

Yield: 6 servings

Since sausage has more than enough fat for these burgers, buy extra-lean ground beef to mix with it, or you'll have a huge amount of grease dripping into the fire—and probably immolating your burgers. This recipe comes from Walter I. Kawahara of Walnut Creek, Calif.

1 pound (454 g) Italian sausage
1 pound (454 g) extra-lean ground beef
½ cup (118 mL) freshly grated Parmigiano-Reggiano cheese
¼ cup (59 mL) chopped green onion, white and green parts
2 tablespoons (30 mL) A1 steak sauce
½ teaspoon (2.5 mL) seasoned salt
¼ teaspoon (1.25 mL) freshly ground black pepper
6 sliced and toasted hoagie rolls

1. Make sure the grill is clean and generously sprayed with nonstick spray. Preheat the barbecue to medium high (350°F [180°C] to 400°F [200°C]).

2. In a large bowl, combine the sausage, beef, cheese, onion, A1 sauce, salt, and pepper. Form this mixture into 6 long, flattened, sausage-shaped patties.

3. Cook the patties on each side until done (no longer pink), approximately 4 to 5 minutes per side.

4. Serve on hoagie rolls with your favorite toppings.

Gilberto's Mexican Burgers with Lime and Cilantro Sauce

Yield: 8 servings

The black beans, corn, and rice make these protein-loaded burgers very hearty. You can use chilies as hot as you like to warm them up.

1 pound (454 g) ground beef
¾ cup (177 mL) cooked brown rice
½ cup (118 mL) frozen corn kernels, thawed and drained
½ cup (118 mL) black beans, mashed
1 tablespoon (15 mL) chili powder
1 tablespoon (15 mL) mayonnaise
2 teaspoons (10 mL) ground cumin
1 cup (236 mL) minced fresh cilantro
1 cup (236 mL) sour cream
Mexican hot sauce of your choice, to taste
Juice of 1 large lime

1. Make sure the grill is clean and generously sprayed with nonstick spray. Preheat the barbecue to medium high (350°F [180°C] to 400°F [200°C]).

2. In a large bowl, combine the beef, rice, corn, beans, chili powder, mayonnaise, and cumin, mixing well to distribute the spices, and form into 4 large, extra-thick patties.

3. Grill the burgers to your desired doneness.

4. While the burgers are cooking, whisk together the cilantro, sour cream, hot sauce, and lime juice in a small bowl.

5. Serve the bean burgers in hamburger buns topped with a generous tablespoon of lime-cilantro sauce or spoon the sauce over patties you've inserted into warmed pita pockets. You can also top with sliced chilies, as hot as you like them.

Sour Cream Sloppy Joes
Yield: 6–8 servings

If you don't want the chili sauce, which doesn't add much heat but provides good flavor, use ketchup instead and omit the hot sauce.

1 medium onion, peeled and chopped
1 tablespoon (15 mL) olive oil
1 ½pounds (681 g) ground beef
1 tablespoon (15 mL) minced fresh basil leaves
1 cup (236 mL) sour cream
6 tablespoons (90 mL) hamburger-style chili sauce
2 tablespoons (30 mL) prepared yellow mustard
1 tablespoon (15 mL) soy sauce
¼ teaspoon (1.25 mL) hot sauce
Seasoned salt, to taste
Freshly ground black pepper, to taste

1. Make sure the grill is clean and generously sprayed with nonstick spray. Preheat the barbecue to medium high (350°F [180°C] to 400°F [200°C]).

2. In a cast-iron skillet or heavy saucepan, sauté the onions in the olive oil until they just begin to turn translucent. Add the ground beef and basil and cook on a barbecue grill or side burner until the meat is done to your preference, about 10 minutes for medium.

3. Mix in the sour cream, chili sauce, mustard, soy sauce, and hot sauce, and stir well. Season with the salt and pepper.

4. Serve on buttered and grilled hamburger buns or hoagie rolls.

Apple and Ginger Pork Burgers
Yield: 4 servings

Although it sounds strange, a delicious substitute for the apples is finely diced prunes. Just don't tell anyone until after they've eaten.

1 pound (454 g) ground pork
¼ cup (60 mL) finely diced peeled red apples
1½ tablespoons (22.5 mL) grated fresh ginger
1 tablespoon (15 mL) minced onion
½ teaspoon (2.5 mL) dried parsley
¼ teaspoon (1.25 mL) garlic powder
¼ teaspoon (1.25 mL) ground cumin

1. Preheat the barbecue to medium high (350°F [180°C] to 400°F [200°C]).

2. In a medium bowl, combine all the ingredients and mix well.

3. Divide the mixture into 4 equal-sized portions, then form each portion into a patty.

4. Grill the burgers for about 6 minutes per side, until the patties have no pink in the center.

5. Serve with thin slices of cheddar or Swiss cheese.

Stuffed Buffalo "Buffalo" Burgers
Yield: 6 servings

It these appear too dry when you mix them up, you can add 1 tablespoon (15 mL) olive oil to the mix. Buffalo is very dry, and you don't want dry burgers.

¼ cup (60 mL) cold butter, cut in small pieces
⅓ cup (79 mL) mild (or hot) hot sauce
½ cup (118 mL) finely crumbled blue cheese
1 tablespoon (15 mL) minced fresh garlic
2 pounds (908 g) ground buffalo
½ cup (118 mL) finely chopped green onion, white and green parts
½ teaspoon (2.5 mL) dried oregano
½ teaspoon (2.5 mL) celery seeds
6 hamburger buns or 6 (2-inch [5-cm] thick) slices French bread

1. In a small saucepan, melt the butter. Whisk in the hot sauce and set aside to cool.

2. In a small bowl, mix together the blue cheese and garlic and set aside.

3. In a large bowl, mix together the buffalo meat, onion, oregano, celery seeds, and ¼ cup (59 mL) of the hot sauce mixture until thoroughly blended. Divide into 12 portions and form each portion into a patty no more than ½ inch (1 cm) thick.

4. Spoon 1 tablespoon (15 mL) of the cheese-garlic mixture into the centers of 6 of the patties, then top with the remaining patties and gently press the edges together, sealing them so cheese won't melt out of your double burgers.

5. Cover the patties with plastic wrap and refrigerate until ready to grill.

6. Make sure the grill is clean and generously sprayed with nonstick spray. Preheat the barbecue to medium high (350°F [180°C] to 400°F [200°C]).

7. Grill the burgers for about 4 to 5 minutes on each side, or until they are cooked to your preference. Baste generously with the remaining hot sauce mixture during the last 1 to 2 minutes of cooking.

8. Toast the buns (or bread) until lightly browned and add the double patties to the buns.

9. Serve with fresh lettuce leaves and a bowl of ranch dressing on the side.

Tailgate Party Meatloaf Burgers
Yield: 8–10 servings

These are great served on a plate covered with gravy alongside heaps of mashed pota-toes and creamed corn.

5 pounds (2.3 kg) lean ground beef
2 large eggs
1 large bell pepper, any color, seeded and minced
1 large onion, peeled and minced
1 cup (236 mL) seasoned dry breadcrumbs
¼ cup (59 mL) ketchup
3 tablespoons (45 mL) Worcestershire sauce
2 tablespoons (30 mL) olive oil
1 tablespoon (15 mL) kosher salt
1 tablespoon (15 mL) dried savory
3 cloves garlic, peeled and minced
1 teaspoon (5 mL) freshly ground black pepper
½ cup (118 mL) melted butter
1 teaspoon (5 mL) garlic powder
Hamburger buns or toasted Texas toast

1. Preheat the barbecue to medium high (350°F [180°C] to 400°F [200°C]) for direct and indirect heating and put a water pan under the unheated side of the grill.

2. Spray a loaf pan well with nonstick cooking spray.

3. In a large bowl, mix together the beef, eggs, bell pepper, onion, bread-crumbs, ketchup, Worcestershire sauce, olive oil, salt, savory, garlic, and black pepper. Pack into the prepared loaf pan.

4. Cook over indirect heat on for 30 to 40 minutes until medium inside, or until your desired doneness. Let the meatloaf cool slightly to firm it up.

5. Mix together the melted butter and garlic powder. Spread the garlic but-ter on the bun halves or toast and grill until lightly browned.

6. Slice the meatloaf into ½-inch (1-cm) slices and place the slices on the buns or toast. Serve with your favorite toppings.

Greek Lentil Burgers with Tzatziki Sauce

Yield: 8 servings

Some folks like to add chopped kalamata olives to this recipe. Not being an olive person, I don't, but if you like them, by all means add 2 to 3 tablespoons (30 to 45 mL) to the mix.

Burgers

½ cup (118 mL) dried lentils
3 tablespoons (45 mL) extra virgin olive oil
3 medium shallots, peeled and chopped
1 red bell pepper, seeded and finely minced
4 cloves garlic, peeled and minced
1 (15-ounce [420 g]) can chickpeas, rinsed and drained
1 cup (236 mL) fresh Italian parsley leaves
2 large eggs, beaten
2 teaspoons (10 mL) ground cumin
1 teaspoon (5 mL) ground coriander
1 teaspoon (5 mL) salt
½ teaspoon (2.5 mL) freshly ground black pepper
1 cup (236 mL) soft breadcrumbs
¾ cup (177 mL) finely grated carrots

Tzatziki Sauce

2 cups (473 mL) plain low-fat yogurt
1 medium cucumber, peeled, seeded, and finely minced
2 cloves garlic, peeled and minced
2 teaspoons (10 mL) minced lemon zest
Juice of 1 medium lemon
1 teaspoon (5 mL) finely minced fresh mint
1 teaspoon (5 mL) chopped fresh Italian parsley

1. Cook the lentils according to the package directions, drain, and set aside.

2. In a skillet over medium heat on a side burner or barbecue grill, heat the oil. Add the shallots and bell pepper and sauté for 5 to 6 minutes. Stir in the garlic.

3. In a blender or food processor, combine the chickpeas, Italian parsley, eggs, cumin, coriander, salt, and pepper and purée. Scoop the chickpea mixture into a large bowl, then add the breadcrumbs, shallot mixture, carrots, and lentils. Mix well and divide into 8 portions.

4. Shape each portion into a patty. Wrap each patty in plastic wrap and freeze them for at least 4 to 5 hours.

5. In a large bowl, combine the tzatziki ingredients, mix well, cover, and set aside.

6. Make sure the grill is clean and generously sprayed with nonstick grilling spray. Preheat the barbecue to medium high (350°F [180°C] to 400°F [200°C]).

7. Remove the plastic wrap from the still-frozen patties and spray them with nonstick grilling spray. Grill for about 5 to 6 minutes per side.

Onion and Mushroom Open-Faced Burgers

Yield: 4 servings

I like white onions in this dish. Sweeter varieties like Walla Walla, Vidalia, and Maui are masked by the sweetness of the mushrooms.

2 teaspoons (10 mL) olive oil
1 medium yellow onion, peeled, thickly sliced, and separated into rings
8 ounces (227 g) button or crimini mushrooms, sliced
½ teaspoon (2.5 mL) garlic salt
2 teaspoons (10 mL) balsamic vinegar
1½ tablespoons (22.5 mL) paprika
½ teaspoon (2.5 mL) dried savory
½ teaspoon (2.5 mL) dried basil
¼ teaspoon (1.25 mL) cayenne pepper
¼ teaspoon (1.25 mL) freshly ground black pepper
1½ pounds (681 g) ground beef (round)
2 English muffins or bagels, split and toasted

1. Make sure the grill is clean and generously sprayed with nonstick grilling spray. Preheat the barbecue to medium high (350°F [180°C] to 400°F [200°C]).

2. In a large nonstick skillet, heat the oil over medium-high heat. Add the onion and cook for 5 minutes, or until golden. Add the mushrooms and garlic salt and cook for 5 minutes, stirring constantly. Add the vinegar and stir to incorporate. Transfer the mixture to a bowl and set aside.

3. In a small bowl, combine the paprika, savory, basil, cayenne pepper, and black pepper.

4. Divide the ground round into 4 equal portions and shape each into a ½-inch (1-cm) thick patty. Sprinkle both sides of each patty with the spice mixture. Grill the patties for 4 minutes on each side, or until done to your liking.

5. Place the patties on the toasted muffin or bagel halves and top each burger with 2 to 3 tablespoons (30 to 45 mL) of the onion-mushroom mixture.

Savory Bacon-Cheese Burgers

Yield: 4 servings

Worcestershire sauce was the result of a mistake. When they first developed it, the folks at Lea & Perrins thought it tasted terrible and resigned the barrel to the basement. Two years later, someone opened the barrel, tried the sauce, and loved the new taste.

1½ pounds (681 g) ground beef (round or sirloin)
½ cup (118 mL) crumbled blue cheese or shredded extra-sharp cheddar cheese
¼ cup (59 mL) Worcestershire sauce
¼ cup (59 mL) chopped, slightly crisp, cooked bacon (about 5 pieces)
4 (¼-inch [0.5-cm] thick) slices sweet onion

1. Make sure the grill is clean and generously sprayed with nonstick spray. Preheat the barbecue to medium high (350°F [180°C] to 400°F [200°C]).

2. In medium bowl, combine the beef, cheese, Worcestershire sauce, and bacon. Shape this mixture into 4 patties.

3. Grill or broil the burgers until they are cooked to your preference. (These may also be pan-fried in a cast-iron or nonstick skillet on a side burner.)

4. Top with your favorite steak sauce or more Worcestershire and a slice of onion.

Kasha and 'Shroom Burgers with Fiery Mayo

Yield: 4 servings

This recipe comes from Cam Kellett from Portland, Ore.

⅔ cup (158 mL) vegetable stock or broth
⅓ cup (79 mL) coarse kasha
3 tablespoons (45 mL) unsalted butter
1 cup (236 mL) finely chopped onion
1 cup (236 mL) finely chopped green or red bell pepper
1 pound (454 g) Portobello mushrooms, finely chopped
2 cloves garlic, minced
1 teaspoon (5 mL) salt
½ teaspoon (2.5 mL) freshly ground black pepper
2 tablespoons (30 mL) finely chopped fresh parsley
1 teaspoon (5 mL) soy sauce
½ teaspoon (2.5 mL) dried thyme
1½ cups (354 mL) fine dry breadcrumbs, divided
1 large egg, lightly beaten
3 tablespoons (45 mL) olive oil
½ cup (118 mL) mayonnaise
1 tablespoon (15 mL) Tabasco or your favorite hot sauce
4 sesame-seed hamburger buns

1. Preheat the barbecue to medium high (350°F [180°C] to 400°F [200°C]).

2. In a large saucepan, bring the stock to a boil. Stir in the kasha, then cover and reduce the heat to low. Cook until the kasha is tender and the water is all absorbed, about 10 minutes. Transfer the cooked kasha to a bowl, cover and let cool.

3. In a large, heavy skillet, melt the butter over medium heat. Add the onion and bell peppers and sauté, stirring occasionally, until the vegetables are softened, about 5 minutes.

4. Add the chopped mushrooms, garlic, salt, and pepper and cook over medium-high heat, stirring occasionally, until the mixture is dry and the mushrooms begin to brown, 8 to 10 minutes. Transfer the mixture to a large bowl, then add in the kasha, parsley, soy sauce, thyme, and ½ cup (118 mL) of the breadcrumbs. Stir until well mixed. Cover and cool to room temperature.

5. Add the beaten egg and stir well, then form mixture into 4 (¾-inch [1.5-cm] thick) patties. Pour the remaining breadcrumbs into a shallow dish and dredge both sides of the patties in the breadcrumbs, shaking off any excess. Transfer the breaded patties to a plate. Cover and freeze for 20 to 25 minutes to firm up the patties.

6. On a flat griddle or in a large nonstick frying pan, heat the olive oil. Add the patties and cook for about 3 minutes per side, turning once, until they are deep golden brown. Whip together the mayonnaise and Tabasco sauce, spread 2 tablespoons (30 mL) of this mixture on the bottom of each bun, add a burger patty and the bun top, and serve.

Chi Chi's Chipotle Cheeseburgers
Yield: 6 servings

Chipotle peppers are really just the jalapeño peppers that are the last to be harvested after losing their bright red color and beginning to shrivel and are then smoked and dried and shipped off to market.

2 pounds (908 g) lean ground beef
3 tablespoons (45 mL) Tabasco Chipotle Pepper Sauce, divided
1 teaspoon (5 mL) garlic salt
½ cup (118 mL) mayonnaise
6 slices Monterey Jack or cheddar cheese
6 onion hamburger buns
Sweet onion slices, for serving
Beefsteak tomato slices, for serving
Fresh lettuce leaves, for serving

1. Make sure the grill is clean and generously sprayed with nonstick grilling spray. Preheat the barbecue to medium high (350°F [180°C] to 400°F [200°C]).

2. In a large bowl, combine the ground beef, 2 tablespoons (30 mL) of the chipotle sauce, and the garlic salt and mix well. Shape the mixture into 6 patties.

3. In a small bowl, mix together the mayonnaise with the remaining 1 tablespoon (15 mL) chipotle sauce and stir until well mixed, then set aside.

4. Grill or broil the hamburger patties to your desired doneness. Place a cheese slice on each burger, close the lid of the barbecue, and continue grilling just until the cheese melts.

5. Spread 1 to 2 teaspoons (5 to 10 mL) of the chipotle mayonnaise on the buns and top with the burgers, onion, tomato, and lettuce, and your favorite condiments.

Smoky Burgers with Pepper Jack Cheese and Bacon
Yield: 4 servings

To get the clever "smoke bombs" listed here go to www.tailgatingplanks.com/bombs or ask at your local barbecue or hardware store. They come in cedar, apple, cherry, mesquite, alder and hickory flavors and are easy to use and add distinctive smoky flavors to your meats. This recipe comes from Kim Hemphill from Spokane, Wash.

8 slices hickory-smoked bacon
1½ pounds (681 g) ground beef
2 tablespoons (30 mL) hot sauce, divided
1 teaspoon (5 mL) seasoned salt
1 teaspoon (5 mL) McCormick's Grill Mates Mesquite Seasoning
½ teaspoon (2.5 mL) freshly ground black pepper
4 slices Pepper Jack cheese
4 hamburger rolls

1. Make sure the grill is clean and generously sprayed with nonstick grilling spray. Preheat the barbecue to medium high (350°F [180°C] to 400°F [200°C]).

2. Place bacon strips on the grill or on a grill pan and cook until crisp, about 8 minutes. Drain and set aside.

3. Take a Chef Locke Smoke Bomb (either apple or cherry flavor), soak for 10 minutes in water, then place directly on coals, or if using gas barbecue, place in a sheet of aluminum foil which you've folded into an envelope and poked holes in the top.

4. In a medium bowl, combine the beef, 1 tablespoon (15 mL) of hot sauce, the seasoned salt, the Mesquite Seasoning, and the pepper and mix well. Form this mixture into 4 patties and grill or broil to your desired doneness, about 4 minutes per side for medium.

5. Baste burgers with the remaining hot sauce and top each with a slice of the Pepper Jack cheese.

6. Serve the burgers topped with the bacon on the rolls.

Taco Festival Burgers
Yield: 4 servings

This recipe is quick to fix and goes well with beans (baked, pinto, or refried) and French fries for a quick party meal. You can add cayenne pepper if you want to fire them up.

1 pound (454 g) ground beef
¼ cup (59 mL) finely minced onion
2½ tablespoons (45 mL) taco seasoning
2 teaspoons (10 mL) hot sauce
½ teaspoon (2.5 mL) freshly ground black pepper
¼ teaspoon (1.25 mL) ground cumin
4 slices Jack cheese

1. Make sure the grill is clean and generously sprayed with nonstick grilling spray. Preheat the barbecue to medium high (350°F [180°C] to 400°F [200°C]).

2. In a large bowl, combine the beef, onion, taco seasoning, hot sauce, pepper, and cumin and mix well. Cover and refrigerate for at least 30 to 40 minutes to incorporate the flavors. Shape into 4 patties.

3. Cook the patties for 4 to 5 minutes on each side or until the meat is cooked to your liking. Add the cheese slices and continue to grill until the cheese has melted. Remove the burgers and serve on buns with salsa, guacamole, and sour cream on the side.

Coke in a Burger
Yield: 4–6 servings

This burger recipe uses Coca-Cola to give it a sweet and juicy flavor, but you can also try other varieties of soda, such as Dr. Pepper, root beer, or another brand of cola. Do not use diet sodas, as they turn bitter when cooked.

1 large egg
½ cup (118 mL) Coke, divided
½ cup (118 mL) crushed Ritz crackers
6 tablespoons (90 mL) French salad dressing, divided
3 tablespoons (45 mL) minced fresh chives
2 tablespoons (30 mL) freshly grated Parmesan cheese
1½ pounds (681 g) ground beef

1. Make sure the grill is clean and generously sprayed with nonstick grilling spray. Preheat the barbecue to medium high (350°F [180°C] to 400°F [200°C]).

2. In a medium bowl, mix together the egg, ¼ cup (59 mL) of the Coke, the crackers, 2 tablespoons (30 mL) of the French dressing, the chives, and the cheese. Add the ground beef to the bowl and mix well to thoroughly blend.

3. In a small bowl, combine the remaining Coke and French dressing, mix well, and set aside.

4. Grill the burgers for about 4 to 5 minutes per side, brushing the patties several times with the dressing-Coke mixture, until they reach your desired doneness.

Stuffing-Stuffed Burgers

Yield: 8 servings

These burgers are delicious without any condiments on top, because they are all on the inside.

2 tablespoons (30 mL) melted butter
1 cup (236 mL) very moist prepared seasoned stuffing
1 large egg, beaten
1 (4-ounce [112-g]) can chopped mushrooms, drained
¼ cup (59 mL) beef broth
¼ cup (59 mL) thinly sliced green onion, green and white parts
1 teaspoon (5 mL) lemon juice
3 pounds (1.3 kg) ground beef
1 teaspoon (5 mL) seasoned salt

1. Make sure the grill is clean and generously sprayed with nonstick grilling spray. Preheat the barbecue to medium high (350°F [180°C] to 400°F [200°C]).

2. In a mixing bowl, combine the melted butter, stuffing, egg, mushrooms, broth, green onion, and lemon juice. Set aside.

3. In a separate bowl, sprinkle the beef with the salt, stir to mix, and form into 16 patties.

4. Top 8 of the patties with 2 tablespoons (30 mL) of the stuffing mixture. Cover with the 8 remaining patties, pinching the edges together to seal. Place the stuffed patties on the grill and cook for 6 to 7 minutes per side, turning several times.

5. Remove the burgers from the grill, cover with foil, and let rest for 5 minutes before serving.

Fired-Up Blue Cheese Burgers

Yield: 4–6 servings

You can use other cheeses (cheddar, Monterey Jack, Swiss, Gruyere, etc.) in these burgers, and, to decrease the heat, you can use fewer jalapeño peppers.

2 pounds (908 g) ground beef
6 jalapeño peppers, seeded and chopped
1 cup (236 mL) crumbled blue cheese
2 tablespoons (30 mL) dark soy sauce
1 tablespoon (15 mL) onion powder
1 tablespoon (15 mL) garlic powder
¼ teaspoon (1.25 mL) dried tarragon
Thick tomato slices, for serving
4 thick slices Texas toast, toasted

1. Make sure the grill is clean and generously sprayed with nonstick grilling spray. Preheat the barbecue to medium high (350°F [180°C] to 400°F [200°C]).

2. In a large bowl, combine the ground beef, jalapeño peppers, blue cheese, soy sauce, onion powder, garlic powder, and tarragon. Shape this mixture into 4 large or 6 small burgers.

3. Cook the burgers on the grill for about 4 to 5 minutes per side, or until done to your preference.

4. Serve on Texas toast with tomato slices and your favorite condiments.

Thai Maple-Soy Pork Patties
Yield: 4 servings

This recipe calls for Thai basil leaves, which have a stronger flavor than other basil varieties. You can use sweet basil if you don't like the anise flavor of the Asian variety.

1¼ pounds (567 g) ground pork
4 green onions, white and green parts, finely chopped
¼ cup (59 mL) dark soy sauce, divided
2 tablespoons (30 mL) finely chopped roasted unsalted peanuts (or cashews)
2 tablespoons (30 mL) finely chopped fresh cilantro
3 large Thai basil leaves, finely chopped
1 tablespoon (15 mL) grated fresh ginger
1 tablespoon (15 mL) maple syrup, divided
Grated zest of 1 lemon
¼ teaspoon (1.25 mL) red pepper flakes
1 tablespoon (15 mL) peanut or corn oil
4 onion or ciabatta rolls, split and toasted
Sriracha or hoisin sauce, for serving
Sliced tomatoes, cooked beets, or yellow onions, for serving

1. Make sure the grill is clean and generously sprayed with nonstick grilling spray. Preheat the barbecue to medium high (350°F [180°C] to 400°F [200°C]).

2. In a large bowl, combine the pork, green onions, 1 tablespoon (15 mL) of the soy sauce, peanuts, the cilantro, the basil, ginger, 2 teaspoons (10 mL) of the maple syrup, lemon zest, and the red pepper flakes and mix well. Shape the mixture into 4 patties. Place the patties on a plate, cover them, and refrigerate for 30 to 40 minutes.

3. In a small bowl, mix together the oil, the remaining soy sauce, and the remaining maple syrup.

4. Grill the patties for 4 to 5 minutes per side, or until cooked through. Generously brush the patties with the oil mixture during the last minute of cooking on each side.

5. Serve patties on the toasted rolls with the Sriracha or hoisin sauce and slices of tomato, cooked beets, or yellow onions.

CB's Biscuit Burgers

Yield: 5 main-course servings or 8–10 appetizer servings

You can serve these as appetizers for 8 to 10 people or as main-course sliders, with other barbecue/picnic side dishes.

1½ pounds (681 g) lean ground beef
1 cup (236 mL) diced onion
¼ cup (59 mL) finely diced green bell pepper
¼ cup (59 mL) finely diced red bell pepper
½ teaspoon (2.5 mL) freshly ground black pepper
¼ teaspoon (1.25 mL) seasoned salt
¼ teaspoon (1.25 mL) dried thyme
¼ teaspoon (1.25 mL) dried savory
½ (14.5-ounce [406-g]) can diced tomatoes
1 (6-ounce [168-g]) can tomato paste
3 tablespoons (45 mL) barbecue sauce
2 tablespoons (30 mL) red wine
2 (12-ounce [336-g]) cans refrigerated biscuits
2 tablespoons (30 mL) freshly grated Parmesan cheese
5 slices Swiss cheese (or your favorite cheese), cut into 2-inch (5-cm) squares

1. Preheat the barbecue to medium high (350°F [180°C] to 400°F [200°C]) for indirect cooking.

2. Spray 20 muffin cups liberally with nonstick grilling spray.

3. In a large nonstick skillet over medium heat, brown the ground beef for 5 minutes. Add the onion, peppers, pepper, salt, thyme, and savory and sauté until completely cooked through, about 10 minutes. Drain the fat in a colander and return the mixture to the skillet. Add the tomatoes, tomato paste, barbecue sauce, and wine, and continue cooking over medium-low heat for about 7 to 8 minutes, then set aside.

4. Open and separate the biscuits, then flatten each one to a circle about 5 inches (12.5 cm) in diameter and ⅛ inch (0.25 cm) thick.

5. Place the flattened biscuits in the muffin cups, forming a pocket up the sides of each cup. Add about 1½ tablespoons (22.5 mL) beef mixture to each biscuit pocket and sprinkle each with Parmesan cheese.

6. Bake in the barbecue for 10 minutes. Remove the pan from the barbecue and place a square of cheese on top of each muffin burger. Return the pan to barbecue and continue baking for about 6 to 8 minutes, until the biscuits are done and the edges are nicely browned.

7. Remove the biscuit burgers from the muffin pans and serve warm.

Onion, Chive, and Garlic Burgers

Yield: 4–6 servings

Before cooking any hamburger patties, make an indent using your thumb into the center of each patty. This reduces shrinkage and prevents the patties from puffing up when they are cooked.

2 pounds (908 g) ground beef
¼ cup (60 mL) finely chopped fresh chives
3 tablespoons (45 mL) Worcestershire sauce
3–4 cloves garlic, peeled and finely minced
1 small onion, peeled and finely minced
1½ teaspoons (7.5 mL) Montreal steak seasoning
½ teaspoon (2.5 mL) dried oregano
8–10 unsalted crackers, crushed into crumbs

1. Make sure the grill is clean and generously sprayed with nonstick spray. Preheat the barbecue to medium high (350°F [180°C] to 400°F [200°C]).

2. In a large bowl, mix together the beef, chives, Worcestershire sauce, garlic, onion, steak seasoning, and oregano. Add a small amount of the crushed cracker crumbs to hold the mixture together. Shape the mixture into 4 or 6 patties, place the finished patties on a large plate, and cover with plastic wrap.

3. To get the best flavor results, refrigerate the patties, covered, for 1 to 2 hours.

4. Grill or broil the patties 4 to 5 minutes per side, or until cooked to your desired doneness. Serve on grilled and buttered buns or Texas toast.

Green Onion and Brie Burgers

Yield: 4 servings

These take a little time, but they elevate the backyard burger to four-star restaurant status and will have your guests raving about your grilling skills. Leave out the jalapeño pepper for a less-spicy version.

4 green onions, thinly sliced, green and white parts
2 cloves garlic, peeled and finely minced
1 jalapeño pepper, seeded and finely minced
1 teaspoon (5 mL) dried oregano
½ teaspoon (2.5 mL) grated lemon zest
2 tablespoons (30 mL) extra-virgin olive oil
¼ teaspoon (1.25 mL) garlic salt
1½ pounds (681 g) ground beef
4 slices bacon, cooked, drained, and chopped
¼ teaspoon (1.25 mL) seasoned salt
⅛ teaspoon (0.6 mL) freshly ground black pepper
4 (1-ounce [28-g]) slices Brie cheese, rind removed
4 sesame-seed hamburger buns
¼ cup (59 mL) light mayonnaise
Tomato slices, for serving
Onion slices, for serving
Fresh lettuce, for serving

1. Make sure the grill is clean and generously sprayed with nonstick spray. Preheat the barbecue to medium high (350°F [180°C] to 400°F [200°C]).

2. In a small bowl, combine the green onions, garlic, jalapeño pepper, oregano, and lemon zest, mashing the mixture as you stir. Stir in the olive oil and garlic salt. Set aside.

3. In a large bowl, combine the ground beef, bacon, seasoned salt, and pepper. Form this mixture into 8 (4-inch [10-cm]) patties. Top 4 of the patties with a slice of Brie cheese and a scant tablespoon (15 mL) of the green onion paste. Cover with the 4 remaining patties, pinching the edges all around to seal the burgers.

4. Grill the burgers, turning once or twice, about 4 to 5 minutes per side for medium-rare. Near the end of the grilling time, lightly toast the bun halves on the grill.

5. In a small bowl, mix the mayonnaise with the remaining green onion paste. Spread this mixture on the bottoms of the toasted buns. To each bun, add a burger patty, condiments, tomato, onion, and lettuce and serve.

Sinful Foie Gras Burgers

Yield: 4 servings

The harvesting of goose livers, enlarged by feeding the birds corn, goes all the way back to Roman times. Now the subject of controversy, the plump livers are one of the most delicious and decadent foods known to man.

4 slices bacon, cooked and drained
2 pounds (908 g) ground beef (chuck)
Salt, to taste
Freshly ground black pepper, to taste
4 (⅓-inch (0.8-cm) slices foie gras, at room temperature
½ cup (118 mL) butter, melted
1 teaspoon (5 mL) garlic powder
4 hamburger buns

1. Make sure the grill is clean and generously sprayed with nonstick grilling spray. Preheat the barbecue to medium high (450°F [240°C] to 500°F [260°C]).

2. Cut each slice of cooked bacon in half lengthwise and set aside.

3. In a medium bowl, season the ground beef well with salt and pepper, then form the beef into 8 very thin, flat patties.

4. Place two half slices of bacon on one patty, add a slice of foie gras, and cover with another burger patty. Press and pinch the edges firmly together to completely enclose the bacon and foie gras. Repeat with the remaining patties. Sear the burgers over very high heat, then grill to your desire doneness, about 4 to 5 minutes per side for medium.

5. In a small bowl, combine the melted butter and garlic powder. Brush both halves of the buns with this mixture and toast the buns quickly on another part of the grill.

6. Remove the burgers from the grill and serve them on toasted buns with your favorite condiments and slices of tomato, onion, and lettuce.

Soupçon Duck Burgers

Yield: 4-6 servings

One very tasty condiment to use instead of ketchup on these burgers is hoisin sauce, commonly used with Peking Duck. It's tangy, fruity, and goes perfectly on these patties.

1 pound (454 g) ground duck
2 green onions, white and green parts, minced
1 tablespoon (15 mL) marmalade of your choice
1½ teaspoons (2.5 mL) minced garlic
1 teaspoon (5 mL) grated fresh ginger
1 teaspoon (5 mL) salt
¼ teaspoon (1.25 mL) freshly ground black pepper
2 tablespoons (30 mL) honey mustard
2 tablespoons (30 mL) crème fraîche or sour cream
2 tablespoons (30 mL) olive oil
2 cups (473 mL) sliced porcini mushrooms
½ cup (118 mL) chopped onion
1 tablespoon (15 mL) dried savory
½ teaspoon (2.5 mL) ground cumin
¼ teaspoon (1.25 mL) kosher salt
4 hamburger buns

1. In a large bowl, combine the duck, green onions, marmalade, garlic, ginger, salt, and pepper. Refrigerate this mixture 6 to 8 hours or overnight.

2. Make sure the grill is clean and generously sprayed with nonstick grilling spray. Preheat the barbecue to medium high (350°F [180°C] to 400°F [200°C]).

3. In a small bowl, whisk together the honey mustard and crème fraîche or sour cream and refrigerate until serving time.

4. In a nonstick skillet, heat the olive oil over medium-high heat. Add the mushrooms and sauté until tender. Add the onions and cook until translucent, then add the savory, cumin, and kosher salt. Stir well to combine, then simmer for 3 to 5 minutes, or until the sauce thickens.

5. Form the duck mixture into 4 to 6 patties. Grill the burgers for about 4 minutes on the first side and 2 on the back, or to taste.

6. While the burgers are cooking, toast the hamburger buns. After toasting, brush each bottom bun with a tablespoon (15 mL) of the honey-mustard dressing. At this point, you can brush each bun top with hoisin sauce.

7. Add the duck patties to the buns and serve.

Turkey Bird Burgers
Yield: 4 servings

The recipe can also be made with ground chicken or ground pork, or you can liven these up by serving jellied or whole-berry cranberry sauce as an additional condiment.

1½ pounds (681 g) ground turkey
4 tablespoons (60 mL) diced green bell pepper
4 tablespoons (60 mL) chopped fresh mushrooms
4 slices Swiss or cheddar cheese
4 tablespoons (60 mL) barbecue sauce
4 hamburger buns
4 thin slices sweet onion
Sliced tomatoes, for serving

1. Make sure the grill is clean and generously sprayed with nonstick grilling spray. Preheat the barbecue to medium high (350°F [180°C] to 400°F [200°C]).

2. Pat the ground turkey into 8 thin patties and place them on a sheet of foil or waxed paper.

3. Top 4 of the patties with equal parts peppers and mushrooms, and then add a slice of cheese, leaving a ½-inch (1-cm) border around the outer edge of each patty. Spread some barbecue sauce on each of the remaining patties, again leaving ½ inch (1 cm) around the outside edge.

4. Place the barbecue-sauced patties on top of the other patties, sauce side down. Pinch the patties together, pressing the edges with your fingers and a fork to seal.

5. Grill the turkey burgers until the meat is no longer pink in the center, or until a meat thermometer registers an internal temperature of 165°F (74°C), turning once. The meat is ready when it has just begun to brown on both sides.

6. Serve on buns with slices of onion and tomatoes and your favorite condiments, including more barbecue sauce.

Black Pepper–Crusted Cheddar Burgers
Yield: 6 servings

You can sauté some onions or mushrooms to put on the top of these burgers, or add a slice of a different cheese for really cheesy burgers.

2 pounds (908 g) ground beef (sirloin)
1 tablespoon (15 mL) dried marjoram
1 tablespoon (15 mL) Worcestershire sauce
1 teaspoon (5 mL) dry mustard
1 teaspoon (5 mL) kosher salt
6 (1-inch [2.5-cm]) cubes extra-sharp cheddar cheese
3 tablespoons (45 mL) olive oil
¼ cup (59 mL) coarsely ground black pepper
6 slices cheddar cheese
2 tablespoons (30 mL) butter, softened
6 hamburger buns

1. Make sure the grill is clean and generously sprayed with nonstick grilling spray. Preheat the barbecue to medium high (350°F [180°C] to 400°F [200°C]).

2. In a large bowl, mix together the sirloin, marjoram, Worcestershire sauce, mustard, and salt until combined.

3. Divide the meat mixture into 6 equal portions and gently shape each into a patty around a cube of cheese. Brush the patties all over with the olive oil and make an imprint in the center of each patty with your thumb to keep them from puffing up. Spread the pepper on a shallow plate and roll the edge of each burger in the pepper until well coated. Sprinkle some pepper on both sides of each patty as well.

4. Place the burger on the cooking grate, lower the lid, and grill for 4 minutes. Turn and continue grilling for 3 to 4 more minutes for medium-rare burgers.

5. Top each burger with a slice of cheddar cheese. Butter both sides of the buns and grill them over direct heat until lightly toasted, about 2 minutes.

6. Serve with your favorite condiments.

Savory Glazed Chicken Burgers

Yield: 6 servings

You can add ¼ pound (112 g) of bulk sausage to the mix to give it a little more texture and moistness.

1 pound (454 g) ground chicken
1 large egg
½ cup (118 mL) fresh white breadcrumbs
1 red onion, peeled and finely chopped
1 clove garlic, peeled and crushed
1 tablespoon (15 mL) olive or vegetable oil
1 tablespoon (15 mL) tomato sauce
3 tablespoons (45 mL) dark soy sauce
1 tablespoon (15 mL) honey
Juice of 1 lemon
4 ciabatta rolls

1. Make sure the grill is clean and generously sprayed with nonstick grilling spray. Preheat the barbecue to medium high (350°F [180°C] to 400°F [200°C]).

2. In a medium bowl, mix together the chicken, egg, breadcrumbs, onion, garlic, oil, and tomato sauce. Form this mixture into 6 burger patties.

3. Grill the burgers for about 3 to 4 minutes on each side, or until they are just beginning to brown and are cooked through.

4. While burgers are cooking, mix together the soy sauce, honey, and lemon juice in a small saucepan. Cook, stirring, over medium high heat for 3 to 4 minutes, or until the glaze thickens enough to coat the back of a spoon.

5. Remove the burgers from the grill, put the patties on the ciabatta rolls, and generously brush the meat with the savory glaze. Serve hot.

Chili-Size Burgers
Yield: 4 servings

This dish is said to take its name from the "hamburger size" ladle that legendary Los Angeles chili parlor proprietor Ptomaine Tommy used decades ago to spoon chili over the open-face burgers he served at his famed "Tommy's Joint."

1½ pounds (681 g) ground beef (round), divided
1 teaspoon (5 mL) dried thyme
½ teaspoon (2.5 mL) garlic powder
3 tablespoons (45 mL) vegetable oil
½ cup (118 mL) chopped green bell pepper
¼ cup (59 mL) chopped onion
1 clove garlic, peeled and finely chopped
½ pound (227 g) lean pork sausage
1 (16-ounce [454-g]) can whole chopped tomatoes
1 (16-ounce [454-g]) can red kidney beans
1 large canned green chili pepper, finely chopped
1 teaspoon (5 mL) salt
1 teaspoon (5 mL) paprika
½ teaspoon (2.5 mL) chili powder
1 pinch ground cinnamon
4 large hamburger buns
½ cup (118 mL) finely chopped sweet onion
½ cup (118 mL) grated sharp cheddar cheese

1. Make sure the grill is clean and generously sprayed with nonstick grilling spray. Preheat the barbecue to medium high (350°F [180°C] to 400°F [200°C]).

2. In a medium bowl, combine 1 pound (454 g) of the ground round, the thyme, and the garlic powder and form the mixture into 4 patties. In a heavy cast-iron skillet on the grill or a side burner, sear the burgers on both sides. Turn down the heat and cook for 5 to 8 more minutes, or until the juices run clear. Cover with aluminum foil and set aside.

3. In a cast-iron or oven-safe skillet, heat the oil. Add the bell pepper, onion, and garlic and sauté until the onions are transparent. Transfer to a bowl, cover, and set aside.

4. In the same skillet, brown the remaining ground round and the sausage. Drain off the fat and add the tomatoes, kidney beans, chopped chili pepper, salt, paprika, chili powder, and cinnamon. Simmer on the grill for 30 minutes.

5. Add the onion mixture and cook for 5 minutes more, stirring well.

6. Place the bottom half of a bun on a plate, add the beef patty, and smother with 2 to 3 large serving spoonfuls of the chili mixture. Sprinkle with chopped onion and shredded cheese and serve.

Fish Burgers with Spicy Sour Cream
Yield: 4 servings

You can substitute any firm-fleshed fish for the catfish especially shark, swordfish, or even crabmeat for a pricier but wonderful burger.

½ cup (118 mL) mayonnaise
½ cup (118 mL) sour cream
½ cup (118 mL) fresh basil leaves
¼ cup (59 mL) fresh parsley leaves
¼ cup (59 mL) coarsely chopped green onion
1 clove garlic, peeled and crushed
Kosher salt, to taste
1 pound (454 g) catfish filets, chopped into chunks
1 large egg
½ cup (118 mL) fresh breadcrumbs
Zest of 1 lime
2 tablespoons (30 mL) minced green onions
2 tablespoons (30 mL) chopped fresh parsley
1 tablespoon (15 mL) ground coriander
1 teaspoon (5 mL) grated fresh ginger
1 teaspoon (5 mL) chili powder
½ cup (118 mL) finely julienned carrots
Olive oil, for brushing

1. In a food processor, combine the mayonnaise, sour cream, basil, parsley leaves, chopped green onion, garlic, and salt to taste and process until all the herbs are tiny specks. Taste the mixture and add more salt if needed. Pour the sauce in a bowl, cover, and refrigerate for at least 1 hour to thicken.

2. Preheat the barbecue to medium high (350°F [180°C] to 400°F [200°C]). Cover the grill surface with a double layer of heavy-duty aluminum foil.

3. In a food processor, combine the fish, egg, breadcrumbs, lime zest, green onion, parsley, coriander, ginger, chili powder, and salt to taste and process to a very rough paste, being careful to not over process. Transfer this mixture to a bowl, mix in the carrots, cover, and refrigerate for 30 to 40 minutes so the mixture firms up.

4. Shape the fish mixture into 4 burgers and refrigerate again, this time for 15 to 20 minutes.

5. Spray the aluminum foil on the grill liberally with nonstick grilling spray, then brush the fish burgers lightly with olive oil and grill the patties a few minutes on each side, or until browned and done.

6. Serve the burgers on buns, with the sauce on the side.

Rasta Burgers

Yield: 4 servings

These spicy burgers were inspired by a trip to Ocho Rios, Jamaica, where they were served at a roadside jerk stand. They can be made even hotter by adding a small chopped habañero pepper to the mixture, but if you do so, wear rubber gloves when making the patties.

1 pound (454 g) lean ground beef
1 large egg, beaten
½ cup (118 g) soft breadcrumbs
1 small onion, peeled and chopped
2 tablespoons (30 mL) butter, softened
½ teaspoon (2.5 mL) coarse sea salt
½ teaspoon (2.5 mL) ground allspice
½ teaspoon (2.5 mL) curry powder
½ teaspoon (2.5 mL) dried thyme
½ teaspoon (2.5 mL) freshly ground black pepper
¼ teaspoon (1.25 mL) cayenne pepper

1. Make sure the grill is clean and generously sprayed with nonstick grilling spray. Preheat the barbecue to medium high (350°F [180°C] to 400°F [200°C]).

2. In a large bowl, mix together the ground beef, the egg, breadcrumbs, onion, butter, sea salt, allspice, curry powder, thyme, black pepper, and cayenne. With your hands, form this mixture into 4 large hamburger patties.

3. Grill or broil the patties for 4 to 5 minutes per side for medium, or to your desired doneness.

4. Serve on onion hamburger buns.

Burgers Santa Fe

Yield: 4 servings

Sargento's 4 Cheese Mexican blend includes Monterey Jack, mild cheddar, Queso Quesadilla, and Asadero cheeses. The combination adds a creamy, smooth flavor to these burgers.

1 pound (454 g) ground beef
½ pound (227 g) ground turkey
1 cup (236 mL) Sargento 4-Cheese Mexican blend, divided
½ cup (118 mL) salsa of your choice, divided
¼ cup (59 mL) crushed tortilla chips
¼ cup (59 mL) thinly sliced green onions, green and white parts
1 teaspoon (5 mL) chili powder
½ teaspoon (2.5 mL) ground cumin
½ teaspoon (2.5 mL) garlic salt
8 slices sourdough bread
2 tablespoons (30 mL) butter, softened
4 tomato slices
Lettuce, for serving

1. Make sure the grill is clean and generously sprayed with nonstick grilling spray. Preheat the barbecue to medium high (350°F [180°C] to 400°F [200°C]).

2. In medium bowl, combine the ground beef, ground turkey, ¾ cup (177 mL) of the cheese, ¼ cup (59 mL) of the salsa, the crushed tortilla chips, the green onion, the chili powder, the cumin, and the garlic salt and mix together lightly but thoroughly.

3. Shape this mixture into 4 (½-inch [1-cm] thick) patties. Grill the patties for 4 to 5 minutes per side, or until they reach your desired doneness.

4. Grill or lightly toast the sourdough bread on the grill. Butter both sides, then place the burgers on the bread. Top each patty with some of the remaining salsa and sprinkle with the remaining cheese. Serve with lettuce and tomato slices.

Italian Hamburgers
Yield: 6 servings

These burgers can also be served as smaller patties or as meatballs placed on top of spaghetti, drizzled with sauce, and sprinkled with more freshly grated Parmesan cheese, such as Parmigiano-Reggiano.

6 tablespoons (90 mL) dry breadcrumbs
⅓ cup (79 mL) finely minced onion
⅓ cup (79 mL) finely minced green or red bell peppers
1 clove garlic, peeled and minced
¾ teaspoon (3.75 mL) dried oregano
½ teaspoon (2.5 mL) dried savory
¼ teaspoon (1.25 mL) salt
¼ teaspoon (1.25 mL) freshly ground black pepper
1½ pounds (681 g) ground beef
6 tablespoons (90 mL) freshly grated Parmesan cheese, divided
1 (15-ounce [420-g]) can tomato sauce
¾ teaspoon (3.75 mL) Italian seasoning
4 large ciabatta buns

1. Make sure the grill is clean and generously sprayed with nonstick spray. Preheat the barbecue to medium high (350°F [180°C] to 400°F [200°C]).

2. In a large bowl, combine the breadcrumbs, onions, peppers, garlic oregano, savory, salt, and pepper and mix well. Add the beef and half of the Parmesan cheese and mix completely.

3. Shape this mixture into 6 patties. Grill for 4 to 5 minutes per side, or until they reach your desired doneness.

4. Meanwhile, in a small saucepan, heat the tomato sauce and Italian seasoning. Keep warm.

5. Place the patties open face on the ciabatta buns. Pour the sauce over the meat and buns and sprinkle each burger with some of the remaining Parmesan cheese.

Southern-Style Chicken-Fried Burgers
Yield: 4–6 servings

These patties make a great, hearty breakfast, especially covered in country gravy and served alongside that other Southern diet food: biscuits and gravy. Yup, calorie counters beware, but yum.

1½ pounds (681 g) ground beef
½ cup (118 mL) milk
½ cup (118 mL) all-purpose flour
1 teaspoon (5 mL) garlic powder
1 teaspoon (5 mL) dried oregano
Salt, to taste
Freshly ground black pepper, to taste
¼ cup (59 mL) bacon fat, melted

1. Make sure the grill is clean and generously sprayed with nonstick spray. Preheat the barbecue to medium high (350°F [180°C] to 400°F [200°C]).

2. Shape ground beef into 4 or 6 flat patties, cover, and refrigerate.

3. Pour the milk into a wide, flat pan and the flour into a similar pan. Add the garlic powder and oregano to the flour and stir well. Remove the chilled patties from the refrigerator and dip them into the milk, soaking both sides. Dredge the patties in the seasoned flour and shake off excess. Salt and pepper both sides of the burgers.

4. In a large cast-iron skillet placed directly on the grill or over a side burner, fry the patties in the bacon grease until they are browned on both sides and the outside is crispy.

5. Serve on buns or on a plate.

Kate's Open-Face Burgers
Yield: 4–6 servings

My wife, Kate, has a way of up-scaling burgers so they look like they'd be served in a four-star restaurant. By serving these burgers open face, she has elevated them to fancy-restaurant status.

1½ pounds (681 g) ground beef, divided
1 medium red onion, peeled and chopped
1 heaping tablespoon (22.5 mL) sour cream
1 heaping tablespoon (22.5 mL) mayonnaise
Salt, to taste
Freshly ground black pepper, to taste
¼ cup (59 mL) beef bouillon
1 tablespoon (15 mL) butter
1 teaspoon (5 mL) ground basil
1 teaspoon (5 mL) lemon juice

1. Make sure the grill is clean and generously sprayed with nonstick spray. Preheat the barbecue to medium high (350°F [180°C] to 400°F [200°C]).

2. In a large bowl, mix together 1¼ pounds (567 g) of the ground beef, the onion, the sour cream, the mayonnaise, the salt, and the pepper. Form the mixture into 4 to 6 patties.

3. Grill the patties until they reach your desired doneness. Transfer them to a platter and keep warm.

4. In a nonstick or cast-iron skillet, brown the remaining beef over high heat. Pour off the grease, add the beef bouillon, and cook, scraping up the browned bits from the bottom of pan for extra flavoring and character. Bring the mixture to a boil and add the butter, basil, and lemon juice.

5. Boil the liquid for 2 minutes to thicken it slightly, then pour the mixture over the hamburger patties, served either open-face on buns or thick slices of toasted Texas toast or on a plate, accompanied by barbecued beans or grilled vegetables.

Hamburger French Bread Loaf

Yield: 6 servings

You can substitute sourdough bread, either a round or a long loaf, or another unsliced artisan loaf for the French bread.

1 loaf unsliced French bread (not a baguette)
½ cup (118 mL) butter, softened
1 pound (454 g) ground beef
1 tablespoon (15 mL) Worcestershire sauce
Salt, to taste
Freshly ground black pepper, to taste
½ cup (118 mL) finely diced celery
1 cup (236 mL) finely diced carrots
1 large egg, beaten
1 (12-ounce [336-g]) can condensed cream of mushroom soup
½ green bell pepper, diced
5 slices Swiss cheese

1. Make sure the grill is clean and generously sprayed with nonstick spray. Preheat the barbecue to medium high (350°F [180°C] to 400°F [200°C]).

2. Slice a lid lengthwise off the top of the bread and hollow out inside, reserving 2 cups (473 mL) of the bread to make breadcrumbs. Butter the inside of the bread with the softened butter.

3. In a large bowl, mix together the fresh breadcrumbs, ground beef, Worcestershire sauce, salt, and pepper. In a large nonstick or cast-iron skillet, brown this mixture. Drain off the fat and transfer the mixture to a large bowl.

4. Cook the carrots and celery in ½ cup (118 mL) water in the microwave or on a stovetop burner until tender. Drain the cooked vegetables and add them, along with the egg, soup, and green pepper to the meat mixture. Stir well. Add the crumbs and stir, then fill the French bread shell with the mixture and top with the cheese slices. Butter the inside of the bread lid and replace it on the loaf of bread.

5. Wrap the loaf in foil, seal, and bake for 15 to 20 minutes in the barbecue. Remove the loaf from the grill and let it rest for 10 minutes, still wrapped.

6. With a very sharp knife cut the loaf into serving sections and lay the thick slices on plates.

Bacon-Wrapped Hamburger
Yield: 6 servings

Although I don't usually endorse brands, I find that the Whole Foods Black Forest bacon is perhaps the best I've ever eaten, and it will raise these burgers from special to extraordinary.

½ cup (118 mL) shredded cheddar cheese
1 tablespoon (15 mL) freshly grated Parmesan cheese
1 small onion, peeled and chopped
1 large egg
1 tablespoon (15 mL) ketchup
1 tablespoon (15 mL) Worcestershire sauce
1 teaspoon (5 mL) ground oregano
½ teaspoon (2.5 mL) salt
⅛ teaspoon (0.6 mL) freshly ground black pepper
1½ pounds (681 g) ground beef
12 slices hickory-smoked bacon
6 hamburger buns, split

1. Make sure the grill is clean and generously sprayed with nonstick grilling spray. Preheat the barbecue to medium high (350°F [180°C] to 400°F [200°C]).

2. In a large bowl, combine the cheddar cheese, Parmesan cheese, onion, egg, ketchup, Worcestershire sauce, oregano, salt, and pepper. Add the ground beef and mix thoroughly with your hands.

3. Shape the mixture into 6 large patties. Wrap 2 slices of bacon around the edge of each patty and secure with toothpicks. Refrigerate the patties for 20 minutes.

4. Grill the patties for 4 to 5 minutes on each side, or until done to your liking. Remove the toothpicks before putting the hamburgers onto the buns. If the bacon falls off, place it on top of the patties.

Hamburgers Parmigiano

Yield: 6 servings

To me, the only Parmesan cheese to use is freshly grated Parmigiano-Reggiano. It's a bit pricey, but it provides a huge flavor not found in other Parmesan cheeses.

2 tablespoons (30 mL) olive oil
⅓ cup (79 mL) finely minced red onion
1½ teaspoons (7.5 mL) minced garlic
2 pounds (908 g) fresh Italian plum tomatoes, coarsely chopped
2 tablespoons (30 mL) minced fresh basil
1 teaspoon (5 mL) freshly ground black pepper, divided
1 teaspoon (5 mL) sugar
½ teaspoon (2.5 mL) kosher salt
1 cup (236 mL) seasoned breadcrumbs, divided
¼ cup (59 mL) minced green onion, green and white parts
1½ tablespoons (22.5 mL) freshly grated Parmigiano-Reggiano cheese
1 tablespoon (15 mL) minced fresh Italian parsley
1 teaspoon (5 mL) dried basil
1 teaspoon (5 mL) dried oregano
2 large egg whites, divided
1½ pounds (681 g) ground beef
1 tablespoon (15 mL) cold water
6 thin slices mozzarella cheese

1. In a large skillet or saucepan over medium heat, heat the olive oil. Add the red onions and sauté, stirring constantly, until soft but not brown, about 4 minutes. Add the garlic and cook for an additional minute. Stir in the tomatoes, fresh basil, ½ teaspoon of the pepper, the sugar, and the salt, raise the heat to high, and bring the sauce to a boil. Reduce the heat to medium low and cook, stirring often, until the sauce is slightly thickened, about 25 minutes. Remove from the heat, cover the pan, and let the sauce rest for at least 1 hour before using.

2. Make sure the grill is clean and generously sprayed with nonstick grilling spray. Preheat the barbecue to medium high (350°F [180°C] to 400°F [200°C]). Lightly spray a shallow baking or roasting pan with nonstick cooking spray.

3. In a deep bowl, combine ½ cup of the breadcrumbs, the green onions, the cheese, the parsley, the dried basil, the oregano, and the remaining pepper. Fold in 1 of the egg whites, add the meat, and mix well. Shape this mixture into 6 patties and refrigerate for 15 minutes to firm up.

4. In a small bowl, beat the remaining egg white with the water. Place the remaining ½ cup (118 mL) breadcrumbs in a flat pan. Dip the patties in the egg white mixture and thoroughly dredge them in the breadcrumbs. Place the patties in the prepared pan and bake in the barbecue until the coating is crisp and lightly golden, about 15 minutes.

5. Remove the patties from the barbecue, spoon 2 tablespoons (30 mL) of the tomato sauce over each patty, and place a slice of cheese on top of each patty. Return the burgers to the barbecue for about 5 minutes, or until the sauce and cheese boil and bubble. Transfer the cooked patties to plates and serve.

Fabulous Feta Burgers
Yield: 4 servings

Imported feta cheese is usually made with goat's or sheep's milk, as is the original Greek feta cheese. Domestic feta is often made with cow's milk, which is a good choice for lactose-intolerant folks.

¼ cup (59 mL) plain yogurt
1 tablespoon (15 mL) crumbled feta cheese
½ teaspoon (2.5 mL) ground cumin
1 pound (454 g) ground beef
¼ cup (59 mL) minced green onions, green and white parts
¼ cup (59 mL) finely minced fresh cilantro leaves
1 large clove garlic, peeled, crushed, and minced
1 tablespoon (15 mL) minced fresh ginger
Lettuce, for serving
Peeled and sliced cucumber, for serving
4 onion rolls, split and toasted

1. In a small bowl, combine the yogurt, cheese, and cumin and blend with a fork until the cheese is finely crumbled and incorporated. Cover and refrigerate for an hour.

2. Make sure the grill is clean and generously sprayed with nonstick grilling spray. Preheat the barbecue to medium high (350°F [180°C] to 400°F [200°C]).

3. In a large bowl, combine the beef, green onions, cilantro, garlic, and ginger and stir to incorporate. Shape the meat mixture into 4 patties and grill for 4 to 5 minutes per side, or until the meat and juices are no longer pink and the burgers are done to your liking.

4. Place a lettuce leaf, a few slices of cucumber, and a beef patty on each onion roll half. Spoon 2 tablespoons (30 mL) of the yogurt mixture on top of each patty, cover with the top of the roll, and serve.

Les Onion Burgers Français
Yield: 4 servings

A favorite meal for campers, backpackers, and Boy Scouts, these burgers can easily be prepared in a skillet over an open fire and provide lots of protein and calories. We made a dish like this when I was a Boy Scout in Québec, Canada.

1 pound (454 g) ground beef
1 (10½-ounce [294-g]) can condensed French onion soup
4 slices cheddar or Swiss cheese
4 sesame-seed hamburger buns, split, buttered, and toasted

Un. Shape the beef into 4 (½-inch [1-cm] thick) burgers.

Deux. Make sure the grill is clean and generously sprayed with nonstick grilling spray. Preheat the barbecue to medium high (350°F [180°C] to 400°F [200°C]).

Trois. Grill the burgers until well browned on both sides and cooked to your liking, 4 to 5 minutes for medium.

Quatre. In a skillet set on a side burner or right on the grill, bring the soup to a boil. Add the burgers to the skillet, cover, and cook for 5 minutes, or until they reach your desired doneness. Open the lid and top the burgers with the cheese. Continue cooking until the cheese is melted, about 2 minutes more.

Cinq. Serve the burgers on the buns with the soup mixture poured into small bowls, for dipping.

Dorothy's Sloppy Joes
Yield: 4–6 servings

My mother, Dorothy, loved to cook these for us when we were in high school, and they became our favorite home-based "fast food." Here's to you Mom. We're still enjoying them and thinking of you.

1½ pounds lean ground beef
¼ cup (59 mL) finely minced onion
¼ cup (59 mL) finely minced green bell pepper
¾ cup (177 mL) ketchup
¼ cup (59 mL) hamburger chili sauce
1 tablespoon (15 mL) brown sugar
1 teaspoon (5 mL) prepared yellow mustard
½ teaspoon (2.5 mL) garlic powder
Salt, to taste
Freshly ground black pepper, to taste
4–6 hamburger buns, toasted, or pita bread pockets

1. Make sure the grill is clean and generously sprayed with nonstick grilling spray. Preheat the barbecue to medium high (350°F [180°C] to 400°F [200°C]).

2. In a heavy-duty nonstick or cast-iron skillet over medium heat, brown the ground beef with the onion and green pepper. Drain off the liquid.

3. Stir in the ketchup, chili sauce, brown sugar, mustard, and garlic powder and mix thoroughly. Season with salt and pepper.

4. Reduce the heat and simmer for 30 minutes, or until the mixture begins to look dry.

5. Serve on the toasted hamburger buns or in the pita bread pockets.

Onion Ring Burgers

Yield: 4 servings

I prefer sweet onions in this dish, and we are lucky to have a choice of Walla Walla, Vidalia, or Maui varieties, each of which adds a sweet tang to the burgers. If you like a stronger onion flavor, go for the white variety.

2 large eggs
1½ cups (354 mL) fresh breadcrumbs
1 pound (454 g) ground beef
2 teaspoons (10 mL) Worcestershire sauce
½ teaspoon (2.5 mL) granulated garlic
½ teaspoon (2.5 mL) ground thyme
½ teaspoon (2.5 mL) freshly ground black pepper, or to taste
¼ teaspoon (1.25 mL) salt, or to taste
1 large onion, peeled and sliced into 1½-inch (3.5-cm) thick rings
¼ cup (59 mL) white wine, or as needed

1. Make sure the grill is clean and generously sprayed with nonstick grilling spray. Preheat the barbecue to medium high (350°F [180°C] to 400°F [200°C]).

2. Spray a baking dish or casserole dish with nonstick cooking spray.

3. In a large, bowl whisk the eggs together and set aside. Pour the breadcrumbs into a shallow dish or a deep plate and set aside.

4. In a medium bowl, mix together the ground beef, Worcestershire sauce, garlic, thyme, pepper, and salt. Form this mixture into 4 patties. Dip a patty into the egg, then press it into the breadcrumbs to coat all sides. Repeat with the remaining patties.

5. Grill the breaded hamburgers on each side, about 2 minutes per side.

6. Place the onion rings in the bottom of the prepared baking or casserole dish. Salt and pepper the rings, then pour in ¼ cup (59 mL) white wine, or enough to barely cover the bottom of the pan, covering only ¼ inch (0.5 cm) or so of the onions. Carefully place the burgers on top of the onions in the baking dish without letting them touch the wine.

7. Bake in the barbecue for 15 to 20 minutes, or until the burgers are done to your liking.

8. Serve the burgers and onions as a main course, or put them on buns and add an onion ring to each burger.

Salsa-Onion Burgers

Yield: 6 servings

These tasty burgers are quick to make and have a lively and sharp flavor, thanks to the picante sauce and onion soup. They will please the most discriminating burger fanatic.

1½ pounds (681 g) ground beef
½ cup (118 mL) Picante sauce
1 (1-ounce [28-g]) envelope dry onion soup mix
6 onion or sesame-seed hamburger buns
Lettuce leaves, for serving
Tomato slices, for serving
Avocado slices, for serving

1. Make sure the grill is clean and generously sprayed with nonstick grilling spray. Preheat the barbecue to medium high (350°F [180°C] to 400°F [200°C]).

2. In a large bowl, mix together the beef, picante sauce, and soup. Shape this mixture firmly into 6 (½-inch [1-cm] thick) burgers. Cover and refrigerate for 30 minutes.

3. Grill the burgers for 8 to 10 minutes (4 to 5 minutes per side), or until they reach your desired doneness, turning only once halfway through the grilling time.

4. Serve on the buns with lettuce, tomato, avocado and additional picante sauce on the side.

Kobe Blue Burgers

Yield: 4 servings

If you prefer, use Waygu beef, the United States' own version of Kobe beef. It's a bit more expensive than ordinary hamburger, but the taste and moistness of these burgers makes it worth every penny.

1½ pounds (681 g) ground Kobe beef (chuck, round, or sirloin)
4 teaspoons (20 mL) smoky barbecue sauce of your choice
1 teaspoon (5 mL) balsamic vinegar
Salt, to taste
Freshly ground black pepper, to taste
4 tablespoons (60 mL) crumbled blue cheese
4 tablespoons (60 mL) minced sweet onion

1. Make sure the grill is clean and generously sprayed with nonstick grilling spray. Preheat the barbecue to medium high (350°F [180°C] to 400°F [200°C]).

2. In a large bowl, mix together the beef, barbecue sauce, vinegar, salt, and pepper. Form the mixture into 8 thin patties. Make a depression in the center of each of 4 of the patties and place 1 tablespoon (15 mL) blue cheese and 1 tablespoon (15 mL) of the minced onion in each depression. Top these with the four remaining patties, pressing on the edges with your fingers or a fork to seal the edges all around.

3. Cook the burgers on the grill until done to your taste (no more than medium, or, even better, medium-rare, 4 to 5 minutes per side). Serve on hamburger buns that have been buttered with garlic butter and grilled until light brown.

Cumin Burgers
Yield: 4 servings

Cumin is a key component of chili powder and curry powder. Here, it adds an interesting touch to our burgers. The corn is also a bit unusual, but we think it adds a pleasing crunch to the moist burgers.

1 pound (454 g) lean ground beef
½ pound (227 g) ground turkey
3 ounces (84 g) frozen corn kernels, thawed to room temperature
1 tablespoon (15 mL) ground cumin
2 teaspoons (10 mL) cumin seeds
¼ teaspoon (1.25 mL) seasoned salt
Freshly ground black pepper, to taste
4 slices Pepper Jack cheese

1. Make sure the grill is clean and generously sprayed with nonstick grilling spray. Preheat the barbecue to medium high (350°F [180°C] to 400°F [200°C]).

2. In a large bowl, combine the ground beef, turkey, corn, ground cumin, cumin seeds, salt, and pepper and stir until well blended.

3. Divide the mixture into 4 portions and, with your hands, form each into a burger patty about 1½ inches (3.5 cm) thick.

4. Cook the burgers for 4 to 5 minutes on each side, or until cooked to your preference.

5. Add a slice of cheese to each patty for the last minute on the grill, then serve the burgers on focaccia rolls or hamburger buns.

Beef and Pork Chili Burgers
Yield: 8 servings

Like a chili bowl in a sandwich, the only thing missing here is the beans, which we often serve alongside these tangy burgers. We prefer baked beans or beans with onion and bacon added to the pot.

1½ pounds (681 g) ground beef
½ pound (227 g) Italian pork sausage
⅓ cup (79 mL) tomato-based chili sauce
1 tablespoon (15 mL) chili powder
1 teaspoon (5 mL) ground thyme
½ teaspoon (2.5 mL) ground cumin
½ teaspoon (2.5 mL) garlic salt
Freshly ground black pepper, to taste

1. Make sure the grill is clean and generously sprayed with nonstick grilling spray. Preheat the barbecue to medium high (350°F [180°C] to 400°F [200°C]).

2. In a medium bowl, mix together the ground beef, Italian sausage, chili sauce, chili powder, thyme, cumin, garlic salt, and pepper. Divide this mixture into 8 portions and gently form each portion into a patty.

3. Grill the patties for 4 to 5 minutes per side, or until done to your preference. Serve the burgers on buns (grilled, if you like) accompanied by your favorite condiments and burger toppings.

Fire and Flame Burgers
Yield: 4 servings

If you are of a fiery persuasion and like an incendiary culinary experience, you can add even more flame to these by using ½ teaspoon (2.5 mL) of cayenne pepper in the mixture. But watch out—we've known people to burst into flame after trying the "fired-up" version.

1 pound (454 g) lean ground beef
¼ cup (59 mL) minced onion
2 cloves garlic, peeled and minced
1 small jalapeño pepper, finely minced
Salt, to taste
Freshly ground black pepper, to taste
3 tablespoons (45 mL) wasabi paste
¼ cup (60 mL) mayonnaise
8 slices toasted Texas toast
4 slices Pepper Jack cheese

1. Make sure the grill is clean and generously sprayed with nonstick grilling spray. Preheat the barbecue to medium high (350°F [180°C] to 400°F [200°C]).

2. In a large bowl, mix together the ground beef, onion, garlic, and jalapeño pepper. Season with salt and pepper, divide into 4 portions, and shape each portion into a patty.

3. Grill the patties for 5 minutes per side, or to your desired doneness.

4. In a small bowl, mix the wasabi paste with the mayonnaise.

5. Spread 1 tablespoon (15 mL) of mayo-wasabi mix on each slice of Texas toast. Put each burger on one slice of toast, add a slice of the cheese, and top with the second slice of toast.

Gyros (Heroes) Burgers

Yield: 4 servings

If you don't like pita bread, you can serve these on toast, hamburger buns, ciabatta rolls, focaccia bread, English muffins, or even toasted bagels.

½ pound (454 g) lean ground beef
½ pound (454 g) lean ground lamb
½ onion, peeled and finely grated
2 cloves garlic, peeled and pressed
1 slice bread, toasted and crumbled
½ teaspoon (2.5 mL) dried savory
½ teaspoon (2.5 mL) ground allspice
½ teaspoon (2.5 mL) ground coriander
½ teaspoon (2.5 mL) salt
½ teaspoon (2.5 mL) freshly ground black pepper
¼ teaspoon (1.25 mL) ground cumin

1. Make sure the grill is clean and generously sprayed with nonstick grilling spray. Preheat the barbecue to medium high (350°F [180°C] to 400°F [200°C]).

2. In a large bowl, combine the ground beef, lamb, onion, garlic and breadcrumbs. Season with the savory, allspice, coriander, salt, pepper, and cumin. Knead until the mixture is stiff; then shape it into 4 patties.

3. Cook the patties for 4 to 5 minutes on each side, or until done to your liking.

4. Serve in warm pita bread pockets with store-bought tzatziki sauce, finely minced onion, chopped tomato, and chopped lettuce.

Pinto's Pimento Burgers

Yield: 4 servings

Pimento is Spanish for "pepper." These peppers are sweeter and more aromatic than their bell pepper cousins, and they are best known as the small red stuffing in green olives. This recipe comes from "Pinto" Mendez from Santa Fe, N.M.

2 pounds (908 g) ground beef
4 (¼-inch [0.5 cm] thick) slices onion
Salt, to taste
Freshly ground black pepper, to taste
1 cup (236 mL) shredded extra-sharp Cheddar cheese
¼ cup (59 mL) mayonnaise
2 ounces (56 g) cream cheese
3 ounces (84 g) Goya bottled pimentos, drained and chopped
1 teaspoon (5 mL) cayenne pepper
12 strips bacon, cooked

1. Make sure the grill is clean and generously sprayed with nonstick spray. Preheat the barbecue to medium high (350°F [180°C] to 400°F [200°C]).

2. Divide the ground beef into 8 equal parts and form each into a thin patty. Place a slice of onion on 4 of the patties, then place the other patties on top and seal around the edges with a fork. Season with salt and pepper.

3. In a blender or food processor, combine the cheddar cheese, mayonnaise, cream cheese, pimentos, and cayenne pepper and blend or pulse until everything is well until combined. Transfer this mixture to a bowl and refrigerate until needed.

4. Grill the burger patties for about 4 to 5 minutes per side, watching them to avoid burning. When they are just about done top each patty with ¼ cup (59 mL) of the cheese-pimiento mixture, then close the lid and cook the burgers for about 2 more minutes, or until the cheese is melted.

5. Remove the patties from the grill. Place them on buns and top with bacon, lettuce, tomato, and whatever condiments you like.

Cajun Burgers
Yield: 4 servings

You can make your own Cajun seasoning by blending together 2 tablespoons (30 mL) salt with 1 tablespoon (15 mL) each of cayenne pepper, ground white pepper, freshly ground black pepper, and garlic powder.

1¼ pounds (567 g) ground beef
1 egg, beaten
3 tablespoons (45 mL) seasoned breadcrumbs
1 teaspoon (5 mL) paprika
3 green onions, white and green parts, chopped
1 tablespoon (15 mL) prepared mustard
2 tablespoons (30 mL) Cajun seasoning
¼ cup (59 mL) hot and spicy barbecue sauce
4 slices Cheddar or Swiss cheese

1. Make sure the grill is clean and generously sprayed with nonstick grilling spray. Preheat the barbecue to medium high (350°F [180°C] to 400°F [200°C]).

2. In a large bowl, mix together the ground beef, egg, breadcrumbs, paprika, green onions, mustard, and 1 tablespoon (15 mL) of the Cajun seasoning. Form this mixture into 4 thick patties.

3. In a small bowl, combine the remaining Cajun seasoning with the barbecue sauce and set aside.

4. Grill the patties for 4 to 5 minute per side, or to your desired doneness. Place the cheese slices on the patties and place the burgers on buns or rolls, topped with dollops of the seasoned barbecue sauce.

Garden Grown Herb Burgers
Yield: 4–6 servings

You can use any of your favorite herbs in this instead of those listed. Try sage, savory, oregano, marjoram, tarragon, chervil, or cilantro in any combination you like.

1½ pounds (681 g) lean ground beef
2 tablespoons (30 mL) chopped fresh basil
1 tablespoon (15 mL) chopped fresh thyme
1 tablespoon (15 mL) chopped fresh rosemary
1 tablespoon (15 mL) chopped fresh parsley
1 tablespoon (15 mL) minced chives
1 cup (236 mL) fresh breadcrumbs
1 large egg, lightly beaten
2 tablespoons (30 mL) lemon juice
½ teaspoon (2.5 mL) garlic salt
¼ teaspoon (1.25 mL) freshly ground black pepper

1. Make sure the grill is clean and generously sprayed with nonstick spray. Preheat the barbecue to medium high (350°F [180°C] to 400°F [200°C]).

2. In a large mixing bowl, combine the beef, basil, thyme, rosemary, parsley, chives, breadcrumbs, eggs, lemon juice, garlic salt, and pepper until well mixed.

3. Split the meat mixture into 4 to 6 equal portions. Shape each portion into a flat, oblong, sausage-like patty about 5 to 6 inches (12.5 to 15 cm) long.

4. Grill the patties for 4 to 5 minutes on each side, then remove the burgers from the heat and serve them on hoagie rolls, hot dog buns, or 6-inch (15-cm) long sections of baguette, sliced in half, with your favorite condiments.

Panther Burgers
Yield: 4–6 servings

These are a favorite at tailgate parties for the Carolina Panthers football team. The ingredients sound surprising, but the results are mouth-watering.

1½ pounds (681 g) ground beef
½ cup (118 mL) pecans, finely chopped
1 small onion, peeled and finely minced
1 teaspoon (5 mL) salt
¼ teaspoon (1.25 mL) freshly ground black pepper
¼ teaspoon (1.25 mL) ground ginger
¼ teaspoon (1.25 mL) ground clove
4 tablespoons (60 mL) peach jam, divided
1 tablespoon (14 mL) brown sugar
2 teaspoons (10 mL) apple cider vinegar

1. Make sure the grill is clean and generously sprayed with nonstick spray. Preheat the barbecue to medium high (350°F [180°C] to 400°F [200°C]).

2. In a large bowl, combine the ground beef, pecans, onion, salt, black pepper, ginger, cloves, and 2 tablespoons (30 mL) peach jam. Mix well and form into 4 to 6 patties.

3. In another bowl combine the remaining 2 tablespoons (30 mL) peach jam, brown sugar, and vinegar and mix well. Set aside.

4. Place the hamburger patties on the grill. After about 2 minutes, flip them. Baste the burgers with the jam mixture and continue grilling. After another 1 to 2 minutes, flip and baste again. Continue grilling until done, for a total of 4 to 5 minutes per side.

5. Place the burgers on buns, baste once more, then top with slices of tomato and onion and a few lettuce leaves, and serve.

A Dilly of a Burger
Yield: 4 servings

This recipe was inspired by a trip to Eastern Europe, where dill weed (the leaves and stems) and dill seed (the fruit of the plant) are used extensively in cooking.

1 pound (454 g) ground beef
3 tablespoons (45 mL) Dijon mustard
3 tablespoons (45 mL) sour cream
2 cloves garlic, peeled and minced
2 tablespoons (30 mL) minced fresh dill
⅛ teaspoon (0.6 mL) freshly ground black pepper
2 tablespoons (30 mL) butter, softened
4 hamburger buns
½ teaspoon (2.5 mL) garlic powder
1 teaspoon (5 mL) chopped fresh parsley

1. Make sure the grill is clean and generously sprayed with nonstick grilling spray. Preheat the barbecue to medium high (350°F [180°C] to 400°F [200°C]).

2. In a bowl, combine the beef, mustard, sour cream, garlic, dill, and black pepper and form the mixture into 4 equal-sized patties.

3. Place the burgers on the grill and cook for about 4 to 5 minutes per side.

4. Butter the buns and sprinkle them with the garlic powder and parsley. Quickly brown the buttered side on the grill, remove the buns from the grill, top with the burgers, and serve.

FOUR

Chicken

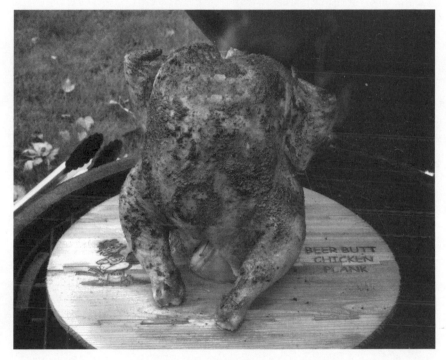

Rick Browne's Original Beer-Butt Chicken
Yield: 4–6 servings

This recipe uses a Chef Locke Beer-Butt Chicken plank to hold the beer can and flavor the chicken. This vertical cooking method helps drain off the fat as the chicken cooks vertically, and the beer steams the inside of the chicken while the outside is cooked by the barbecue heat and steam from the cedar plank, producing a very moist bird. Planks are available at your favorite barbecue or grocery store or by going online to www.tailgatingplanks.com/chef.

1 tablespoon (15 mL) hickory sea salt
1 teaspoon (5 mL) brown sugar
1 teaspoon (5 mL) garlic powder
1 teaspoon (5 mL) onion powder
1 teaspoon (5 mL) dried summer savory
1 teaspoon (5 mL) paprika
1 teaspoon (5 mL) dry yellow mustard
¼ teaspoon (1.25 mL) cayenne pepper
1 large chicken
1 (12-ounce [336-g]) can of your favorite beer
1 cup (236 mL) apple cider
2 tablespoons (30 mL) olive oil
2 tablespoons (30 mL) balsamic vinegar

1. Place an unopened can of beer in the hole of a Chef Locke Beer-Butt Chicken Plank and soak in water for 4–6 hours, weigh it down with other cans if necessary so that it is under water the entire time.

2. Preheat the barbecue to medium high (325°F [165°C] to 375°F [190°C]) for direct and indirect heating, putting a water pan under the unheated part of the grill.

3. In a small bowl, mix together the sea salt, brown sugar, garlic powder, onion powder, savory, paprika, mustard, and cayenne pepper until well incorporated. Wash and dry the chicken and season it generously inside and out with the rub. Work the mixture well into the skin and under the skin wherever possible. Place the chicken on a plate, cover, and set aside to dry marinate at room temperature for 20 to 30 minutes.

4. Remove the plank and can from the water and, leaving the can in the plank, open it and pour half the beer into a spray bottle. Add the cider, olive oil, and balsamic vinegar and set aside.

5. Place the plank directly over the flames or hot coals and cook the chicken for 10 minutes, then move the plank to the unheated side of the grill and cook for 80 to 90 minutes over indirect heat, spraying the chicken all around with the basting spray several times. The chicken is done when the internal temperature reaches 180°F (82°C). Remove the chicken and plank from the grill and place it on a heatproof countertop. After your guests have reacted appropriately, remove the chicken from the beer can with tongs while holding the hot plank with an oven mitt. (Careful! The can will be very hot.)

6. Give the chicken one more spritz of the basting spray, and then carve and serve. Or, if you're a showman, put on heatproof rubber gloves and literally pull the chicken apart at the table, separating out the meat and bones, continuing to work with your hands to make pulled chicken.

Captain Gallant Chicken

Yield: 6–8 servings

Captain Gallant of the French Foreign Legion, one of my favorite TV shows of the 1950s, inspired me so much as a kid that I'm dedicating this to him and to all members of le Légion Étrangère. Since this dish comes from North Africa, where he served, he gets the honors.

2 tablespoons (30 mL) olive oil or vegetable oil
1 medium onion, peeled, sliced, and separated into rings
2 cloves garlic, peeled
2½–3 pounds (1.1–1.3 kg) chicken breasts and thighs
3 tablespoons (45 mL) snipped fresh parsley
1 teaspoon (5 mL) ground cumin
1 teaspoon (5 mL) ground cardamom
1 teaspoon (5 mL) ground turmeric
1 teaspoon (5 mL) ground allspice
1 (16-ounce [454-g]) can chopped tomatoes, including juices
2 medium carrots, cut into 1-inch (2.5-cm) pieces
2 stalks celery, cut into 1-inch (2.5-cm) pieces
1 medium turnip, peeled and cubed
½ teaspoon (2.5 mL) salt
1 medium zucchini, cut into ½-inch (1-cm) pieces
½ cup (118 mL) raisins
2 tablespoons (30 mL) water
4 teaspoons (20 mL) cornstarch
3–4 cups (708 mL–.95 L) cooked rice or couscous

1. Preheat the barbecue to medium high (325°F [165°C] to 375°F [190°C]) for indirect heating.

2. In a large Dutch oven on a side burner over medium high heat, heat the oil. Add the onion and garlic and sauté until tender, but do not brown. Remove the onion and garlic and set aside. Add more oil to the Dutch oven if necessary and add the chicken. Cook until browned on all sides, approximately 15 minutes. Spoon off the chicken fat on the surface.

3. In a small bowl, mix together the parsley, cumin, cardamom, turmeric, and allspice. Stir this mixture into the Dutch oven, around the chicken. Return the onions and garlic to the pan. Add the tomatoes, carrots, celery, turnip, and salt, cover, and place the pan on the unheated side of the barbecue for indirect heating. Cook for 35 to 40 minutes.

4. Open the Dutch oven and stir in the zucchini and raisins. Replace the cover and simmer for about 15 to 20 more minutes, or until the chicken is tender and the vegetables are done.

5. Remove pan and let chicken rest, covered, for 10 minutes. Stir together the water and cornstarch and stir this mixture into the vegetables. Cook for 2 to 3 minutes, or until the mixture is bubbly and thickened.

6. Remove the chicken from the pan and place them on top of a platter of rice or couscous. Spoon the tomato and vegetable mixture over the chicken and serve.

40-Cloves-of-Garlic Barbecue Chicken
Yield: 4 servings

Slow cooking in liquid mellows out the garlic, and even folks who say they don't like garlic end up loving this dish and the "cloves become soft, nutlike things you can spread with a knife."

1 (4-pound [1.8-kg]) chicken
½ teaspoon (2.5 mL) salt
¼ teaspoon (1.25 mL) freshly ground black pepper
1 cup (236 mL) olive oil
2 tablespoons (30 mL) chopped fresh parsley
1 teaspoon (5 mL) chopped fresh rosemary
1 teaspoon (5 mL) chopped fresh thyme
1 teaspoon (5 mL) dried sage
1 bay leaf
1 celery rib
40 cloves garlic, peeled (from 3–4 heads garlic)

1. Preheat the barbecue to medium high (350°F [180°C] to 400°F [200°C]).

2. Wash the chicken and pat it dry. Sprinkle inside and out with the salt and pepper. Tie the legs together with kitchen string and fold the wings under the chicken.

3. Heat the oil in a 2- to 8-quart (1.9–7.6 L) Dutch oven over moderately high heat until hot but not smoking. Add the chicken and cook, turning carefully, until golden brown, about 10 minutes. Transfer the chicken to a plate.

4. Add the parsley, rosemary, thyme, sage, bay leaf, celery, and garlic to the pot. Put the chicken, breast side up, on top of the garlic and bake, covered tightly, in the barbecue, basting twice, until an instant-read thermometer inserted 2 inches (5 cm) into the fleshy part of a thigh registers 170°F (77°C), 30 to 40 minutes.

5. Transfer the chicken to a cutting board, reserving the pan juices, and let stand for 10 minutes. Cut the chicken into serving pieces and pour the herbed garlic over it. Spread the roasted garlic on toasted bread and arrange them around the chicken.

Molten Jerk Wings or Thighs
Yield: 4–6 servings

Do not let this marinade touch your skin. In fact, wear rubber or plastic gloves when mixing or handling it. The peppers can be hugely irritating, especially if you touch your face, nose, or mouth after you work with the marinade.

1 onion, peeled and chopped
⅔ cup (158 mL) green onions, green and white parts, chopped
6 tablespoons (90 mL) dried onion flakes
2 tablespoons (30 mL) ground allspice
2 tablespoons (30 mL) freshly ground black pepper
2 tablespoons (30 mL) cayenne pepper
2 tablespoons (30 mL) chili powder
2 tablespoons (30 mL) brown sugar
1½ tablespoons (22.5 mL) dried thyme
1½ tablespoons (22.5 mL) ground cinnamon
1½ tablespoons (22.5 mL) ground nutmeg
1 tablespoon (15 mL) soy sauce
1 teaspoon (5 mL) Louisiana hot sauce
¼ teaspoon (1.25 mL) minced habañero chile
¼ cup (59 mL) vegetable oil
12 chicken thighs, skin removed, or 24 chicken wings

1. In a food processor, combine all the ingredients except the chicken and blend until smooth.

2. Place chicken in a 1- to 2-gallon (3.8- to 7.6-L) resealable plastic bag. Pour in the marinade, seal the bag, and refrigerate for 2 days, turning the bag over occasionally.

3. Preheat the barbecue to medium high (350°F [180°C] to 400°F [200°C]).

4. Using tongs, remove the chicken from the marinade. Cook on the grill until the thighs or wings are cooked through and golden brown, approximately 10 to 15 minutes. Turn frequently to avoid charring.

5. Serve with creamy ranch dressing and crisp, cold carrot and celery sticks.

Peri Peri Chicken Wings
Yield: 8–10 servings

Peri peri is an African pepper that has wound its way around the world. In some places, such as Portugal, it is the favorite hot spice in homes and restaurants.

1 cup (236 mL) soy sauce
¼ cup (59 mL) teriyaki sauce
¼ cup (59 mL) orange marmalade
3 tablespoons (45 mL) brown sugar
2 tablespoons (30 mL) chopped peri peri peppers
1 tablespoon (15 mL) honey
2 cloves garlic, peeled and minced
½ teaspoon (2.5 mL) cayenne pepper
2½ pounds (1.1 kg) chicken wings

1. In a blender, combine all the ingredients except the chicken and process to a thick liquid. Place the chicken wings in a 1- to 2-gallon (3.8- to 7.6-L) resealable plastic bag and pour the marinade in over it.

2. Marinate the chicken in the refrigerator for 2 to 4 hours.

3. Drain the wings and boil the marinade for 12 minutes, after which point it is safe to use as a baste for the wings.

4. Preheat the barbecue to medium high (350°F [180°C] to 400°F [200°C]).

5. Place the wings on the hot grill, turning and basting often, and grill until the tips are just beginning to char, and the chicken is crisply browned all over, yet moist inside.

Spicy Peanut Butter Chicken Wings
Yield: 8–10 servings

Chunky or smooth? Your choice. You could also use cashew, almond, or any other nut butter in this recipe.

50 chicken wings
2 (12-ounce [355-mL]) bottles beer
1 cup (236 mL) molasses
½ cup (118 mL) smooth peanut butter
½ cup (118 mL) fresh lemon juice
½ cup (118 mL) Worcestershire sauce
¼ cup (59 mL) prepared mustard
2 tablespoons (30 mL) chili powder
1 teaspoon (5 mL) salt
¼ cup (59 mL) chopped fresh parsley, for garnish
1 to 2 lemons, sliced thin, for garnish

1. Preheat the barbecue to high (400°F [200°C] to 450°F [240°C]).

2. Remove and discard the tips from the wings and cut each wing in half at the joint. In a large saucepan, combine the beer, molasses, peanut butter, lemon juice, Worcestershire sauce, mustard, chili powder, and salt. Cook over low heat for about 15 minutes, or until the sauce is reduced and thickened to the consistency of thick gravy.

3. Place the wings in a large roasting pan and cover them with the sauce. Turn until each wing is well coated. Bake in the barbecue for 15 to 20 minutes.

4. Serve the wings on a large platter, garnish with parsley and lemon slices.

Tequila Grilled Hen
Yield: 4 servings

If you don't want to use tequila in this recipe, merely add ½ cup (118 mL) white wine or water to the bottle of margarita mix instead of the liquor.

2 lemons
2 limes
1 cup (236 mL) margarita mix
½ cup (118 mL) tequila
⅓ cup (79 mL) olive oil
2 teaspoons (10 mL) salt
1 clove garlic, peeled and minced
1 (4–5 pound [1.8–2.3 kg]) whole chicken
1–2 cups (236–473 mL) instant rice, soaked in warm water for 20 minutes
1 large onion, peeled and chopped
½ cup (118 mL) butter
Lemon wedges, for garnish
Lime wedges, for garnish

1. In a medium bowl, grate the zest from one of the lemons and one of the limes, then squeeze the juice from all 4 into the same bowl. Add the margarita mix, tequila, olive oil, salt, and garlic and stir. Put the chicken into a 1- to 2-gallon (3.8- to 7.6-L) resealable plastic bag. Pour the marinade in over the chicken and marinate overnight, or at least 6 hours.

2. Preheat the barbecue to medium high (350°F [180°C] to 400°F [200°C]) for direct and indirect heating.

3. Grease a Dutch oven.

4. Drain the chicken and transfer it to the prepared Dutch oven. Pour half of the marinade over the chicken. Cook over indirect heat for 1 to 1½ hours, generously basting the chicken with the marinade while it cooks.

5. Place the soaked instant rice and chopped onion around the chicken and dot with pats of the butter.

6. Pour the remaining marinade into a saucepan and boil for 10 minutes

7. Remove the Dutch oven from the barbecue and, with tongs, carefully remove the chicken. Cut it into quarters and place them on top of the rice-onion mixture. Garnish with the lemon and lime wedges and drizzle with the remaining marinade mixture. Return the Dutch oven to the barbecue for 10 to 15 minutes.

8. Remove the pot from the barbecue and serve the chicken right from the Dutch oven.

Barbecue Grilled Game Hen with Jalapeño–Cherry Sauce
Yield: 6–8 servings

2½ tablespoons (37.5 mL) light sesame oil
⅓ cup (79 mL) finely diced shallots
1½ tablespoons (22.5 mL) minced garlic
½ jalapeño pepper, seeds and ribs removed, chopped
1½ pounds (681 g) Bing cherries, pitted and diced
1½ teaspoons (7.5 mL) curry powder
½ teaspoon (2.5 mL) ground nutmeg
½ cup (118 mL) honey
¼ cup (59 mL) soy sauce
2 tablespoons (30 mL) balsamic vinegar
Juice of 2 lemons
Juice of 1 orange
4 Cornish game hens, split in half
¼ cup (59 mL) olive oil

1. Preheat the barbecue to medium high (350°F [180°C] to 400°F [200°C]) for direct and indirect heating.

2. In a heavy cast-iron skillet on a side burner, heat the sesame oil. Add the shallots, garlic and jalapeño pepper and sauté until tender. Add the cherries, then stir in the curry powder and nutmeg. Once the spices are dispersed, add the honey, soy sauce, vinegar, and fruit juices.

3. Brush both sides of the hens lightly with the olive oil and grill them, breast side down, until the skin starts to bubble and brown a little, about 10 minutes. Turn them breast side up and baste liberally with jalapeño–cherry sauce. Cook for another 10 minute.

4. Place the split hens in a Dutch oven and spoon the jalapeño–cherry sauce over the birds. Place the pot in the barbecue and cook for another 30 minutes, basting several times, until the birds are firm, have a nice glaze, and are nicely browned.

5. Serve one-half bird to each person. Pour the remaining sauce from the Dutch oven into individual bowls to serve on the side.

Que-Fried Chicken with Orange-Teriyaki Sauce
Yield: 6 servings

Any type of orange will do here, but if you want a real kick, use blood oranges. They're not quite as sweet as the other varieties, but the blood-red juice gives the chickens a reddish hue.

7 pounds chicken pieces
2 cups (473 mL) cornflake crumbs
⅓ cup (79 mL) grated orange zest (from about 3 oranges)
1 tablespoon (15 mL) onion powder
1 tablespoon (15 mL) dried oregano
½ teaspoon (2.5 mL) seasoned salt
½ teaspoon (2.5 mL) freshly ground black pepper
½ cup (118 mL) fresh-squeezed orange juice (from about 3 oranges)
2 tablespoons (30 mL) margarine or butter
⅓ cup (79 mL) sliced green onions, white and green parts
1–2 cloves garlic, peeled and minced
⅓ cup (79 mL) teriyaki sauce
¼ cup (59 mL) orange marmalade
3 tablespoons (45 mL) water

1. Preheat the barbecue to medium high (350°F [180°C] to 400°F [200°C]).

2. Using paper towels, pat the chicken dry, and set aside.

3. On a baking sheet or a wide, flat pan, combine the cornflake crumbs, orange zest, onion powder, oregano, salt, and pepper.

4. Pour the orange juice into wide, flat bowl. Dip the chicken pieces into the juice, then dredge them in the crumb mixture, coating each piece thoroughly. Arrange the coated chicken on a baking sheet and place it in the barbecue to cook for 10 to 15 minutes. Turn the pieces over and bake until the chicken is tender and coating is crisp, about 5 minutes longer.

5. While chicken is baking, heat the margarine or butter over medium heat in a small saucepan, until bubbly. Add the green onion and garlic and sauté until the onion is soft. Reduce the heat to low. Add the teriyaki sauce, orange marmalade, and water and cook until the sauce is bubbling hot and slightly thickened.

6. Place the cooked chicken on a serving platter, ladle the thick sauce over the chicken, and serve.

Bourbon Chicken Wings
Yield: 4–6 servings

If you are serving these wings to children, you can substitute cola, root beer or even ginger ale for the bourbon. Or, if your party isn't bourbon fans, you can use light or dark beer instead of the whiskey.

24 chicken wings
3 tablespoons (45 mL) bourbon
3 tablespoons (45 mL) olive oil
2 tablespoons (30 mL) yellow mustard barbecue sauce
1 tablespoon (15 mL) finely grated lemon zest
Juice of 1 lemon
1 cup (236 mL) fine, dry breadcrumbs
1 tablespoon (15 mL) sweet Hungarian paprika
Salt, to taste
Freshly ground black pepper, to taste

1. Cut chicken wings at the joints and discard the tips or reserve them for broth or stock. In a 2-gallon (7.6-L) resealable plastic bag, combine the wing joints, bourbon, olive oil, barbecue sauce, lemon zest, and lemon juice. Seal the bag, then turn it over several times to coat the wings. Refrigerate for 4 hours or overnight.

2. Preheat the barbecue to medium high (350°F [180°C] to 400°F [200°C]).

3. In a paper bag, mix together the breadcrumbs, paprika, salt, and pepper. Drain the wing joints and toss 4 or 5 at a time into the bag with the breadcrumb mixture, shaking the bag to coat the wings.

4. Place the wings on the grill and barbecue until crisp and golden, about 5 minutes on each side.

5. Serve with a dipping bowl of your favorite honey-mustard barbecue sauce.

Hakka Salt-Baked Chicken with Two Hakka Dipping Sauces
Yield: 4 servings

Hakka cuisine is the cooking style of the Hakka people, who are mainly found in the southeastern Chinese provinces of Guangdong and Fujian. Their cooking has been characterized as salty, fragrant, and fatty, and they pickle just about everything.

Chicken

1 (3½–4 pound [1.6–1.8 kg]) chicken, rinsed and patted dry
1 tablespoon (15 mL) Chinese rice wine
1 (2-inch [5-cm]) piece fresh ginger, roughly chopped
4 green onions, white and green parts, cut into 2-inch (5-cm) pieces
¼ cup (59 mL) fresh cilantro leaves
1 tablespoon (15 mL) Chinese five-spice powder
2 tablespoons (30 mL) dry vermouth
4½ pounds (2 kg) kosher salt

Garlic Sauce

2 tablespoons (30 mL) hot Japanese rice vinegar
1 tablespoon (15 mL) minced garlic
1 tablespoon (15 mL) sugar

Chili Sauce

1 tablespoon (15 mL) hot water
1 tablespoon (15 mL) Chinese chili sauce
1 teaspoon (5 mL) unseasoned Japanese rice vinegar
½ teaspoon (2.5 mL) sugar

1. Rub the cavity of the chicken with the rice wine and stuff it with the ginger, green onions, cilantro and five-spice powder. Place the chicken, breast up, on a rack and brush the outside with the vermouth. Let the chicken stand in a cool, airy place until the skin is dry to the touch, about 2 hours.

2. Preheat the barbecue to medium high (350°F [180°C] to 400°F [200°C]).

3. Wrap the chicken in a double layer of cheesecloth; bring the ends around and tie them together on top of the chicken breast. The chicken should be tightly wrapped in a neat ball.

4. Pour the salt onto a baking sheet with a lip, spread it out evenly, and put it into the hot barbecue for 10 minutes to heat and dry the salt.

5. Pour 1 inch (2.5 cm) of the hot salt into a large, heavy Dutch oven or roasting pan that will hold the chicken snugly. Place the wrapped chicken on the salt and completely cover it with the rest of the salt.

6. Either put a lid on the Dutch oven or cover the pan with 2 layers of heavy-duty aluminum foil. Place the chicken in the center of the barbecue and cook for 1½ hours. Check the temperature by shoving a meat thermometer into the thigh through the salt. When it's done, the chicken will register 160°F (71°C).

7. Make the garlic sauce by combining the vinegar, garlic, and sugar in a small bowl. Stir to dissolve the sugar. In another small bowl, make the chili sauce by combining the hot water with the chili sauce, vinegar, and sugar. Stir to dissolve the sugar. Let both sauces stand for 15 to 20 minutes. Stir before serving.

8. Remove the Dutch oven from the barbecue and carefully remove the chicken from the hot salt, lifting it out by the knot on top of the cheese-cloth. Try not to spill the juices that have gathered in the body cavity. Set the chicken on a large platter and cover it, still in the cheesecloth, with foil. Let it rest for 15 minutes. Discard the salt.

9. Remove the cheesecloth and carve the chicken or use a cleaver to chop it Chinese-style (bones and all) into bite-size pieces. Serve hot, accompanied by the two Hakka-style dipping sauces.

Barbecue Stuffing and Chicken One-Pot
Yield: 4 servings

Instead of this variety of stuffing, there are many others to choose from, or you can easily make your own from small cubes of stale bread, chopped onion, poultry seasoning, and your favorite dried herbs.

1 (3–4pound [1.3–1.8 kg]) chicken
1 (10¾-ounce [300-g]) can condensed cream of chicken soup
1 (10¾-ounce [300-g]) can condensed cream of celery soup
1 cup (236 mL) frozen peas
1 cup (236 mL) frozen carrots
1 (6-ounce [168-g]) package Stove Top Whole Wheat Chicken Stuffing
1 large egg, beaten
½ cup (118 mL) chopped onion
¼ cup (59 mL) butter, melted
¼–½ cup (59–118 mL) chicken broth

1. Place the cleaned chicken in a large pot, cover it with water, and boil it for 45 to 50 minutes.

2. Preheat the barbecue to medium high (350°F [180°C] to 400°F [200°C]).

3. Spray a Dutch oven or roasting pan with nonstick cooking or grilling spray.

4. When the chicken is very tender and ready to fall of the bones, remove the meat and tear it into small pieces. Put the pieces in the prepared Dutch oven or roasting pan.

5. Stir together the cream of chicken and cream of celery soups and pour the mixture over the chicken in the Dutch oven, then pour in the peas and carrots.

6. In a medium bowl, combine the stuffing mix, beaten egg, chopped onions, and melted butter and stir. If the mixture seems dry; add chicken broth to make the mixture very moist. Use the remaining broth to cover the chicken.

7. Put the pan in the barbecue and bake for 30 to 35 minutes. The chicken should be very tender.

8. Remove the chicken pieces from the Dutch oven and spoon the meat onto serving plates. Cover with 3 to 4 large serving spoons of the soup, stuffing, and vegetables from the pan.

Thai Beer-Can Chicken Satay

Yield: 4–6 servings

This is beer-butt chicken using Thai spices and marinades and a satay (peanut) dipping sauce. If you can't find Thai beer, substitute any American brand. The chicken won't know the difference.

Chicken

1 (4–5 pound [1.8–2.3 g]) chicken
2 (14-ounce [392-g]) cans unsweetened coconut milk
½ cup (118 mL) loosely packed chopped fresh cilantro
3½ tablespoons (52.5 mL) turbinado sugar
3 tablespoons (45 mL) yellow curry paste (or 1 tablespoon [15 mL] curry powder)
3 tablespoons (45 mL) Thai fish sauce
8 cloves garlic, peeled and roughly chopped
1½ teaspoons (7.5 mL) ground white pepper
1 (12-ounce [354-mL]) can Singha (or other Thai beer), to taste

Dipping Sauce

3 tablespoons (45 mL) vegetable oil
2 tablespoons (30 mL) red curry paste
½ cup (118 mL) finely diced shallots
2 teaspoons (10 mL) chili powder
½ cup (118 mL) finely ground roasted peanuts
¼ cup (60 mL) smooth peanut butter
¼ cup (60 mL) packed brown sugar
1 tablespoon (15 mL) tamarind juice
1½ teaspoons (7.5 mL) salt (or to taste)
4 cups (0.95 L) unsweetened coconut milk

1. With a sharp barbecue fork, poke the chicken multiple times in the breasts and thighs to help with the marinade process. Place the chicken in a 1- to 2-gallon (3.8- to 7.6-L) resealable plastic bag and set aside.

2. In a food processor combine the 2 cans coconut milk, cilantro, turbinado sugar, yellow curry paste, fish sauce, garlic, and white pepper and process until smooth. Pour the marinade over the chicken. Marinate the chicken in the refrigerator for at least 5 hours or overnight, turning occasionally.

3. Preheat the barbecue to medium high (350°F [180°C] to 400°F [200°C]) for indirect heating, putting a water pan under the unheated side of the grill.

4. Drain the chicken well and discard the marinade. Open the beer can and pour off half of the beer. Slide the chicken tail-side down over the can, using the legs to form a stabilizing tripod.

5. Place the vertical chicken on the unheated side of your grill and cook for 1½ to 2 hours, or until an instant-read thermometer reads 160°F (71°C)°. Carefully remove the chicken from the beer can and place it on a cutting board. Cut it into quarters or serving pieces.

6. In a small saucepan, heat oil over medium high heat until a drop of water sizzles when dropped into the pan. Add the shallots, red curry paste, and chili powder and heat until fragrant, approximately 2 to 3 minutes.

Add the peanuts, peanut butter, brown sugar, tamarind juice, salt, and the 4 cups (0.95 L) coconut milk. Reduce the heat to low and simmer gently until the oil rises to the surface. Remove the pan from the heat and spoon the satay sauce into small serving bowls, one per person. Keep warm.

7. Arrange the chicken on a heated platter and serve with the dipping sauce.

Perched Cornish Hens
Yield: 2–4 light servings

Rock Cornish or game hens are a hybrid of Cornish and White Rock chickens. In other words, they are just a breed of small chickens weighing up to 2½ pounds (1.1 kg) that are harvested when they are four to six weeks old.

2 Rock Cornish game hens
1 (24-ounce [710-mL]) can apple juice or cider
2 tablespoons (15 mL) brown sugar, divided
1 teaspoon (5 mL) minced garlic
1 teaspoon (5 mL) balsamic vinegar
½ teaspoon (2.5 mL) red pepper flakes
1 tablespoon (15 mL) granulated garlic
1 tablespoon (15 mL) paprika
1 tablespoon (15 mL) dried savory
1 teaspoon (5 mL) ground white pepper
1 teaspoon (5 mL) sea salt
1 teaspoon (5 mL) dried thyme
1 teaspoon (5 mL) ground cumin
2 (6-ounce [177-mL]) cans apple juice

1. Place the hens in a 1- to 2-gallon (3.8- to 7.6-L) resealable plastic bag. Pour in the 24-ounce (710-mL) can apple juice, 1 tablespoon (15 mL) of the brown sugar, the garlic, the vinegar, and the red pepper flakes. Shake until well mixed, place the sealed bag in a bowl, and refrigerate overnight.

2. Preheat the barbecue to medium high (350°F [180°C]) to 400°F [200°C]) for indirect heating, putting a water pan under the unheated side of the grill.

3. In a small bowl, mix together the remaining brown sugar, garlic, paprika, savory, pepper, salt, thyme, and cumin until well incorporated. Drain the chickens, discarding the marinade, and season them generously inside and out with the rub. Work the mixture well into the skin and under the skin wherever possible. Set aside, covered, at room temperature for 20 to 30 minutes.

4. Put the opened (6-ounce [177-mL]) apple juice cans on a counter and slide the game hens tail-side down over the cans, using the legs and the cans to form tripods to hold the hens upright. Place them on the unheated side of the grill and cook for 45 to 60 minutes. The birds are done when the internal temperature reaches 160°F (71°C).

5. Carefully remove the hens from the grill and let them rest for 10 minutes, covered. Remove the hens from the cans (the cans will be super hot, so use a potholder) and serve.

Maple Syrup-Barbecued Hens

Yield: 6–8 servings

As with all the recipes in this book that call for maple syrup, I highly suggest using pure maple syrup from the Eastern United States or Canada. The alternative, a sort of maple-flavored cane syrup, is not flavorful enough for these dishes.

2 (3–4 pound [1.3–1.8 kg]) broiling chickens
½ cup (118 mL) all-purpose flour
1 tablespoon (15 mL) dried oregano
Salt, to taste
Freshly ground black pepper, to taste
¼ cup (60 mL) butter
2 large onions, peeled and thinly sliced
1 teaspoon (5 mL) dried rosemary
1 teaspoon (5 mL) dried savory
¼ cup (118 mL) pure maple syrup, divided
½ cup (118 mL) apple cider

1. Preheat the barbecue to medium high (350°F [180°C] to 400°F [200°C]). Spray a roasting pan with nonstick cooking or grilling spray.

2. Cut the chickens into quarters. In a shallow bowl, combine the flour, oregano, salt, and pepper. Roll the chicken quarters in this mixture. In a large skillet, melt the butter. Add the chicken and cook until browned, then transfer it to the prepared roasting pan, leaving the drippings in the skillet.

3. Add the sliced onions to the drippings in the skillet, brown them quickly, and then pour them on top of the chicken. Sprinkle the onions and chicken with the rosemary and savory and pour 1 tablespoon (15 mL) of the maple syrup over each piece of chicken.

4. Deglaze the frying pan with the cider, stirring to pick up all the browned bits of chicken, flour, and onions, and pour over the chicken.

5. Bake in the barbecue for 40 minutes, uncovered.

Lemon-Lime and Garlic Hens

Yield: 2–4 servings

For a tropical feel, substitute pineapple juice and coconut milk for the lemon and lime juices.

2 (1¾–2 pound [785–908 g]) Cornish game hens
⅓ cup (79 mL) fresh lime juice
⅓ cup (79 mL) fresh lemon juice
¼ cup (59 mL) chopped fresh basil
¼ cup (59 mL) soy sauce
2 tablespoons (30 mL) minced garlic
2 teaspoons (10 mL) grated orange zest
¼ teaspoon (1.25 mL) crushed red pepper flakes
¼ cup (59 mL) orange marmalade
1 tablespoon (15 mL) butter

1. Halve and butterfly the hens by cutting along both sides of the backbone and spreading the birds out flat. Poke the breasts and thighs several times with a sharp fork.

2. In a small bowl, combine the lime and lemon juices, basil, soy sauce, garlic, orange zest, and red pepper flakes. Put the hens in a 1- to 2-gallon (3.8- to 7.6-L) resealable plastic bag and pour in the marinade. Seal the bag and shake it to distribute the marinade. Place the bag in a bowl and refrigerate for 4 hours or overnight.

3. Preheat the barbecue to medium high (350°F [180°C] to 400°F [200°C]).

4. Remove the hens from the bag, draining the marinade into a small saucepan. Meanwhile, cover the hens and let them come to room temperature.

5. Place the hens skin side down on the grill and brush them with marinade. Grill the hens until they are lightly browned on the bottom, about 10 minutes. Turn the hens over with tongs and continue grilling, basting occasionally and turning several times, until an instant-read thermometer registers 160°F (71°C).

6. To the remaining marinade in the small saucepan, whisk in the marmalade and bring to a boil. Stir in the butter and heat until melted, then pour the mixture in a sauce boat to place on the table.

7. Remove the hens from the grill and serve over wild rice.

Chicken Marengo
Yield: 4 servings

If you don't care for anchovies, either leave them out of this recipe or substitute 1 teaspoon (5 mL) anchovy paste. The olives are also optional, but they do add a nice flavor, even for folks like me who aren't olive fans.

1 (3–4 pound [1.3–1.8 kg]) chicken, cut into pieces
Kosher salt, to taste
Freshly ground black pepper, to taste
3 tablespoons (45 mL) olive oil
8 ounces (227 g) mushrooms, chopped
1 bay leaf
2 teaspoons (10 mL) minced garlic
1 teaspoon (5 mL) chopped onion
¼ teaspoon (1.25 mL) dried thyme
2 tablespoons (30 mL) all-purpose flour
1 cup (236 mL) diced tomatoes
½ cup (118 mL) dry white wine
6–8 anchovy fillets, chopped
¼ cup (59 mL) green olives, chopped
Chopped fresh parsley, for garnish

1. Preheat the barbecue to medium high (350°F [180°C] to 400°F [200°C]).

2. Sprinkle the chicken pieces with the salt and pepper. In a cast-iron skil·let on the grill, heat the oil until it just begins to smoke. Add the chicken pieces, skin side down, and cook for 3 to 5 minutes, or until golden brown. Turn and cook the other side.

3. Add the mushrooms, bay leaf, garlic, onion, and thyme. Shake the skillet so the mushrooms and spices are distributed evenly around the chickens, close the lid, and let the chicken cook for 15 minutes. Using tongs, transfer the chicken pieces to a platter and cover.

4. Sprinkle the ingredients left in the skillet with flour and stir to blend evenly. Add the tomatoes and wine and close the barbecue lid. Cook for 10 minutes, stirring occasionally.

5. Return the chicken to the skillet. Add the anchovies and more salt and pepper. Add the olives and continue to cook for 5 minutes. Sprinkle with chopped fresh parsley and serve.

Pollo En Vino Rojo (Chicken in Red Wine)

Yield: 4 servings

Do not use so-called cooking wines or wines you would not drink on their own for cooking. If you don't like the taste of a wine when you drink it, you won't like the taste of the dish you cook with it.

1 (2½–3 pound [1.1–1.3 kg]) fryer chicken, cut in pieces
½ cup (118 mL) distilled white vinegar
¼ cup (59 mL) olive oil
1 small onion, peeled and chopped
1 clove garlic, peeled
1 bay leaf
½ teaspoon (2.5 mL) dried oregano
½ teaspoon (2.5 mL) salt
⅛ teaspoon (0.6 mL) freshly ground black pepper
4 slices bacon
1 (8-ounce (227-g)) can diced tomatoes
1 carrot, chopped (about ½ cup [118 mL])
1 cup (236 mL) dry red wine

1. Place the chicken pieces in a 1- to 2-gallon (3.8- to 7.6-L) resealable plastic bag.

2. In a small bowl, combine the vinegar, oil, onion, garlic, bay leaf, oregano, salt and pepper. Pour this mixture over the chicken, close the bag, and refrigerate for 6 to 8 hours.

3. Preheat the barbecue to medium high (350°F [180°C] to 400°F [200°C]) for direct and indirect heating.

4. In a 12-inch (30-cm) cast-iron skillet, cook the bacon until crisp. Drain the bacon, reserving the drippings. Crumble the bacon and set it aside.

5. Drain the chicken pieces, pouring the marinade into a small bowl. Put the chicken in the skillet and turn to coat with the drippings, then place the skillet on the heated side of the grill and cook for 15 to 20 minutes, turning the pieces several times.

6. Spoon off most of the fat in the pan, then pour the marinade over the chicken. Add the tomatoes and their liquid, the carrot, and the red wine. Cover the skillet and return it to the unheated side of the grill. Cook for 35 to 40 minutes, or until the chicken is tender. Transfer the chicken pieces to a serving platter, cover, and let rest.

7. Add the crumbled bacon to skillet; stir well, and season with salt and pepper.

Harry's Asian-Style Drumsticks
Yield: 4 servings

You can make this dish using thighs or wings instead, or you can put all three together. The wings will cook in about half the time, and the thighs and drumsticks for about the same time. This recipe comes from Harry Kawahara from Pasadena, Calif.

¼ cup (59 mL) dark soy sauce
3 tablespoons (45 mL) dark brown sugar
2 tablespoons (30 mL) lemon juice
2 tablespoons (30 mL) sweet sherry
1 tablespoon (15 mL) vegetable oil
1 teaspoon (5 mL) ground ginger
⅓ cup (79 mL) chopped green onions, white and green parts
3–4 tablespoons (45–60 mL) chopped garlic
8–12 chicken drumsticks, each poked with a fork several times

1. In a 1- to 2-gallon (3.8- to 7.6-L) resealable plastic bag, combine the soy sauce, brown sugar, lemon juice, sherry, oil, ginger, green onions, and garlic.

2. Add the drumsticks and shake the bag several times to coat all sides of the chicken. Place the bag in the refrigerator for 4 to 6 hours or overnight, turning the bag over occasionally.

3. Preheat the barbecue to medium high (350°F [180°C] to 400°F [200°C]).

4. Drain the marinade into a saucepan and boil for 10 minutes to use as a basting liquid.

5. Place the drumsticks on the hot grill and cook for 20 to 25 minutes, turning often and basting several times, until the drumsticks are nicely browned and tender.

Smoke-Grilled Cornish Hens with Cherry Sauce

Yield: 2–4 servings

Change the flavor of these hens by using dried, chopped apricots, pineapple, raisins, dates, prunes, or peaches instead of the cherries.

1 (6-ounce [168-g]) package Stove Top stuffing mix with seasoning packet
½ cup (118 mL) white wine, microwaved for 1 minute
¼ cup (59 mL) butter
4 (2-pound [908-g]) Cornish game hens
1 tablespoon (15 mL) olive oil
¾ cup (177 mL) red currant jelly
¼ cup (59 mL) coarsely chopped dried red cherries
2 tablespoons (30 mL) garlic butter
2 teaspoons (10 mL) fresh lemon juice
½ teaspoon (2.5 mL) salt
¼ teaspoon (1.25 mL) ground allspice

1. Preheat the barbecue to low (200°F [100°C] to 250°F [120°C]) for indirect heating, putting a water pan under the unheated side of the grill.

2. In a medium bowl, combine the stuffing mix with its seasoning packet, the wine, and the butter. Stuff the hens with this mixture and place them on a the bbq grill rack. Brush the hens with the olive oil.

3. In a small saucepan, combine the jelly, cherries, garlic butter, lemon juice, salt, and allspice. Cook over low heat, stirring, until the jelly is melted, about 5 minutes. Measure out ⅔ cup (158 mL) of the sauce and set it aside.

4. Make a smoker package by putting a handful of soaked hickory or oak chips in a 12-inch (30-cm) square of heavy-duty aluminum foil, folding over the package, poking 3 to 4 holes in the top of the foil, and placing the package directly on the coals or open flame to add smoke to your grilling.

5. Use the remaining sauce to baste the hens while they cook for 3½ to 4 hours on the barbecue. Cover with foil after 1 hour.

6. Serve the hens whole or cut them in half with kitchen shears. Spoon the reserved sauce over the hens just before you serve them.

Jamaican Jerked Lemon Chicken
Yield: 4–6 servings

If you don't want to buy commercial jerk seasoning make your own by combining 2 teaspoons (10 mL) each onion powder, ground thyme, allspice, and black pepper and ½ teaspoon (2.5 mL) each ground cinnamon, cayenne pepper, and salt, mixing well, then storing in a sealed bottle until you need it.

1 (14.5-ounce [406-g]) can chicken broth
¾ cup (177 mL) frozen lemonade concentrate, thawed
2 tablespoons (30 mL) red wine vinegar
2 tablespoons (30 mL) Jamaican jerk seasoning
2 teaspoons (10 mL) grated lemon zest
2 garlic cloves, peeled and minced
½ teaspoon (2.5 mL) hot sauce
2 (4–5 pound [1.8–2.3 kg]) chickens, butterflied
4 teaspoons (20 mL) cornstarch
¼ cup (59 mL) sliced green onions, green and white parts, for serving

1. In a nonmetallic bowl, stir together the chicken broth, lemonade concentrate, vinegar, jerk seasoning, lemon zest, garlic, and hot sauce.

2. Rinse the chicken, pat it dry, and poke holes in the breasts and thighs with a barbecue fork. Place the chicken in a 1- to 2-gallon (3.8- to 7.6-L) resealable plastic bag set in a shallow dish and pour the marinade into the bag. Seal the bag, shake well, and refrigerate for 2 to 24 hours, turning the bag occasionally to distribute the marinade.

3. Preheat the barbecue to medium high (350°F [180°C] to 400°F [200°C]).

4. Remove the bag from the refrigerator and drain the marinade into a saucepan. Boil it for 10 minutes, reserve 1 cup (236 mL) for a basting sauce, and set the rest aside. Meanwhile, place the butterflied, marinated chickens directly on the grill and brush with some of the reserved marinade. Grill, turning several times and basting often, for 12 to 15 minutes, or until the chicken is tender and the juices, when the leg is pierced, run clear.

5. In a medium saucepan over medium heat, combine the reserved marinade with the cornstarch. Stir to incorporate and cook, stirring, until the sauce is bubbling and has thickened.

6. To serve, place the chicken on a warm platter over lettuce leaves, drizzle on the sauce, and sprinkle with the green onions.

Date-Stuffed Game Hens

Yield: 4 servings

Egypt produces more dates that any country on earth and has been cultivating them since 3200 B.C. However, you can find a nice selection of dates grown right in the United States, mostly from California, in your grocery store. Look for the Deglet Noor or Medjool varieties.

½ cup (118 mL) loosely packed chopped fresh cilantro leaves, divided
10 cloves garlic, peeled and minced
1 tablespoon (15 mL) ground cumin
1 tablespoon (15 mL) paprika
½ teaspoon (2.5 mL) dried marjoram
4 Cornish game hens
1 cup (236 mL) tawny port
½ cup (118 mL) olive oil
¼ cup (59 mL) balsamic vinegar or red wine vinegar
¼ cup (60 mL) honey
2 oranges, thinly sliced
2 lemons, thinly sliced
40 whole dates (approximately 1 pound [454 g]), pitted
3 tablespoons (45 mL) minced green olives
Salt, to taste
Freshly ground black pepper, to taste

1. In a small bowl, combine 6 tablespoons (90 mL) of the cilantro, the garlic, the cumin, the paprika, and the marjoram. Rub the mixture generously on both hens and transfer them to a 2-gallon (7.6-L) resealable plastic bag. In a separate small bowl, whisk together the port, oil, vinegar, and honey. Pour this mixture over the birds and into the cavities. Seal the bag and refrigerate for 8 to 10 hours.

2. Preheat the barbecue to medium high (350°F [180°C] to 400°F [200°C]) for indirect heating, putting a water pan under the unheated side of the grill.

3. When you are ready to cook, drain the hens and pour the marinade into a saucepan. Boil the marinade for 10 minutes and set aside. Arrange the orange and lemon slices in the bottom of a Dutch oven. Add the hens, breast side up, put 5 or 6 dates in each body cavity, sprinkle with the remaining dates and the olives, and season with the salt and pepper.

4. Place the Dutch oven on the grill rack over indirect heat. Lower the grill lid and cook, basting occasionally, until the hens are cooked through or until the internal temperature in the thickest part of the thigh reaches 160°F (71°C), about 40 minutes.

5. Transfer the hens to a warmed platter and cover with aluminum foil until ready to serve. Remove and discard the lemon and orange slices, place the pan back on the heated side of the barbecue and boil, whisking often, until the liquid has reduced to ½ cup (118 mL), about 5 minutes.

6. Garnish the hens with the remaining cilantro and serve with the sauce on the side.

Grill-Broiled Thai Chicken
Yield: 4 servings

You can replace the Sriricha with any of your favorite hot sauces, such as Tabasco, Louisiana Hot Sauce, or Frank's Red Hot, but the "Red Rooster" sauce is so traditionally Thai that the dish just doesn't taste the same without it.

1 bunch cilantro
1 cup (236 mL) plus 1 teaspoon (5 mL) sugar, divided
3 tablespoons (45 mL) oyster sauce
2 tablespoons dark soy sauce
2 tablespoons (30 mL) plus 1 teaspoon (5 mL) minced garlic, divided
1½ teaspoons (7.5 mL) Sriracha hot sauce, divided
4 large chicken breasts
½ cup (118 mL) water
½ cup (118 mL) distilled white vinegar
2 tablespoons (30 mL) Vietnamese fish sauce
2 tablespoons (30 mL) fresh lime juice
16–20 lettuce leaves
4 fresh mint springs, chopped
4 green onions, thinly sliced on the diagonal

1. In a food processor, combine the cilantro, 1 teaspoon (5 mL) of the sugar, the oyster sauce, the soy sauce, 1 teaspoon (5 mL) of the garlic, and ½ teaspoon (2.5 mL) of the Sriracha sauce. Process to a smooth paste, spread the paste on each chicken breast, and place the chicken breasts on a plate. Cover and refrigerate for 4 to 6 hours or overnight.

2. To make the sauce, combine the remaining sugar, remaining garlic, remaining Sriracha sauce, water, vinegar, fish sauce, and lime juice in a mixing bowl and whisk for 2 minutes to fully incorporate. Set aside.

3. Preheat the barbecue to medium high (350°F [180°C] to 400°F [200°C]) for direct and indirect heating, putting a water pan under the unheated side of the grill.

4. Without wiping off the marinade paste, place the chicken on the grill and cook, skin side down, for 5 to 7 minutes, or until the skin is crispy. Turn the breasts over and grill 4 minutes longer. Transfer the chicken to a cast-iron skillet or roasting pan and pour the sauce over the breasts. Cover the pan and place it on the unheated side of the barbecue grill. Cook for 20 to 25 minutes.

5. Remove chicken from the pan and pour the sauce into 4 small bowls. If you wish to eat Thai style, slice the breasts into ½-inch (1-cm) strips, place them on a platter alongside the lettuce leaves, and let guests take pieces of chicken, mint leaves, and green onions wrapped in lettuce and dip them into their own bowls of sauce.

Quick Chicken Kebabs
Yield: 4–6 servings

This dish makes a great last-minute barbecue meal when friends show up unexpectedly for dinner. Defrost some chicken breasts, mix them with the ingredients listed (most of which everyone keeps on hand) and you have a barbecue kebab feast in less than 30 minutes.

¼ cup (59 mL) olive oil
¼ cup (59 mL) fresh lemon juice
1 tablespoon (15 mL) minced garlic
1 teaspoon (5 mL) dried rosemary
½ teaspoon (2.5 mL) seasoned salt
⅛ teaspoon (0.6 mL) ground cinnamon
Freshly ground black pepper, to taste
1 pound (454 g) boneless, skinless chicken breasts
1 red bell pepper, cut into 1-inch (2.5-cm) square pieces
1 large onion, peeled and cut into 1-inch (2.5-cm) square pieces
Chopped fresh parsley, for garnish
2 tablespoons (30 mL) fresh lime juice
4–6 pita pockets
4–6 tablespoons (60–90 mL) ranch dressing

1. Preheat the barbecue to medium high (350°F [180°C] to 400°F [200°C]).

2. In a wide, flat baking pan, whisk together the oil, lemon juice, garlic, rosemary, salt, cinnamon, and pepper.

3. Cut the chicken into 1½-inch (3.5-cm) pieces and place them in the pan of marinade. Stir well and marinade, stirring every 5 minutes, for 20 minutes.

4. Remove the chicken from the pan and thread the pieces on skewers, alternating with the chunks of pepper and onion.

5. Place the kebabs on the hottest part of the grill and cook, turning often, for 8 to 10 minutes, or until the chicken has started to brown on the edges and is golden all over.

6. Remove the chicken and vegetables from the skewers and put them a large bowl. Sprinkle with parsley and drizzle with fresh lime juice. Serve with the pita bread and ranch dressing, putting 5 or 6 pieces of chicken and several pieces of pepper and onion in each pita pocket and then adding a tablespoon (15 mL) of the dressing.

Hula Hula Chicken

Yield: 4 servings

If you would prefer to use a fresh pineapple in this recipe, by all means do so. Cut it into slices, remove the core, and finely chop enough to make 1 cup (236 mL). Save the rest. Since there will be no syrup, increase the wine by ⅔ cup (158 mL).

1 (5–6 pound [2.3–2.7 kg]) chicken, cut in half, backbone removed
½ cup (118 mL) all-purpose flour
⅓ cup (79 mL) vegetable oil or vegetable shortening
1 teaspoon (5 mL) salt
¼ teaspoon (1.25 mL) freshly ground black pepper
½ cup (118 mL) packed brown sugar
2 tablespoons (30 mL) cornstarch
1 (20-ounce [560-g]) can pineapple pieces in syrup, finely chopped, divided
1 cup (236 mL) dry or sweet white wine
¾ cup (177 mL) cider vinegar
1 tablespoon (15 mL) soy sauce
1 tablespoon (15 mL) chicken soup base (or 2 bouillon cubes)
¼ teaspoon (1.25 mL) grated fresh ginger
1 medium green bell pepper, sliced
1 medium red bell pepper, sliced

1. Preheat the barbecue to medium high (350°F [180°C] to 400°F [200°C]) for direct and indirect heating, putting a water pan under the unheated side of the grill.

2. Spray an ovenproof or cast-iron skillet with nonstick cooking or grilling spray.

3. Wash the chicken, pat it dry, spray it with nonstick cooking or grilling spray, and coat it with the flour. In the prepared ovenproof or cast-iron skillet, heat the oil or shortening on the grill or a bbq side burner. Add the chicken and brown on all sides, turning several times.

4. Turn the chicken skin side up, season it with the salt and pepper and place it on the indirect side of the barbecue. Cook for 20 to 25 minutes.

5. In a large saucepan, combine the brown sugar and cornstarch. Stir in half the pineapple pieces with syrup, wine, vinegar, soy sauce, chicken soup base, and ginger. Bring to a boil, stirring constantly, and boil for 2 minutes.

6. Open the barbecue and pour the sauce over the chicken. Bake, uncovered, for 45 minutes, on the unheated side of the grill. Add the remaining pineapple and peppers and cook for an additional 15 minutes.

7. Cut each half chicken in half, place them on a platter, cover with the pineapple-pepper sauce from the skillet, and serve with a large bowl of steamed rice.

Grilled Jalapeño Chicken Poppers
Yield: 4–6 servings

Named after the city of Jalapa, the capital of Vera Cruz province in Mexico, these peppers can be hot or very hot, depending on where they are grown. We like the milder ones, which still have quite a kick.

½ cup (118 mL) fresh orange juice
¼ cup (59 mL) fresh lemon juice
1 teaspoon (5 mL) Dijon mustard
1 teaspoon (5 mL) Worcestershire sauce
¼ cup (59 mL) canola oil
2–3 cloves garlic, minced
¼ cup (59 mL) chopped fresh parsley
1 teaspoon (5 mL) dried oregano
Salt, to taste
Freshly ground black pepper o taste
2–3 whole chicken breasts
12–15 large jalapeño peppers
6 strips bacon, cut in half

1. Make sure the grill is clean and generously sprayed with nonstick grilling spray. Preheat the barbecue to medium high (350°F [180°C] to 400°F [200°C]).

2. In a small glass bowl, whisk together the orange juice, lemon juice, mustard, and Worcestershire sauce, then whisk in the oil a little at a time. Add the garlic, parsley, oregano, salt, and pepper.

3. Place the chicken breasts into a 1- to 2-gallon (3.8- to 7.6-L) resealable plastic bag. Pour in the marinade over the chicken. Refrigerate for several hours or overnight.

4. Grill the chicken breasts on the hot grill until cooked, about 8 minutes per side. Pour the marinade into a saucepan and boil it for 10 minutes.

5. Wearing rubber gloves, halve the peppers lengthwise and scrape out the seeds and membranes.

6. Cut the chicken breasts into pieces small enough to fit in the peppers. Wrap each stuffed pepper in a piece of bacon and secure with a toothpick. Grill until the peppers are soft and lightly charred on both sides.

7. Transfer the peppers to a platter and serve.

Barbecue-Baked Hot Wings
Yield: 4–6 servings

Some people like to cut the wings into three segments, throwing away the tips. But there is some good crunchy stuff on the wing tips, so if you must remove them, at least save the tips for a chicken soup base: Freeze them until you have 1 to 2 pounds (454 to 908 g) and cook in 1 cup (236 mL) water for 2 hours to make a very rich broth.

1 cup (236 mL) all-purpose flour
1 cup (236 mL) cornmeal
¼ cup (59 mL) seasoned salt
3 tablespoons (45 mL) garlic powder
2 tablespoons (30 mL) cayenne pepper
2 tablespoons (30 mL) dried oregano
1 large egg, beaten
2 cups (473 mL) milk
24 chicken wings
Butter-flavored cooking spray

1. Preheat the barbecue to medium high (400°F [200°C] to 425°F [220°C]).

2. Spray a large baking pan with nonstick grilling spray.

3. In a 2-gallon (7.6-L) resealable plastic bag, mix together the flour, corn-meal, salt, garlic powder, cayenne pepper, and oregano. Shake well to mix.

4. In a small bowl, whisk the egg into the milk. Dip each wing into the mixture and place 2 or 3 at a time into the bag of seasoned flour, shake to coat each wing, and arrange them on the prepared baking pan. Continue until you've dipped and floured all the wings.

5. Spray the wings with the butter spray so the coating is moist, slide the pan into the barbecue, and bake for 30 minutes. Turn the wings over, spray the second side to moisten, and cook for another 30 minutes, or until the wings are crisp and browned all over.

6. Serve the wings with bowls of your favorite hot and spicy barbecue sauce.

Cedar-Wrapped Stuffed Chicken Breasts
Yield: 4 servings

Cedar cooking papers (or wraps) are paper-thin sheets of wood that can be wrapped around a variety of food items and placed on the barbecue, in the oven, or in a stovetop steamer. You can buy cedar wraps from several websites, including tailgatingplanks. com and Amazon.com.

4 (10-inch [25-cm]) cedar papers
1 cup (236 mL) Chardonnay or other white wine, or more as needed
2 teaspoons (10 mL) olive oil plus more for brushing the chicken
2 shallots, peeled and minced
3 ounces (84 g) goat cheese
4 sun-dried tomato halves, chopped and rehydrated
¼ cup (59 mL) fresh basil leaves, chopped
Salt, to taste
Freshly ground black pepper, to taste
4 boneless, skinless chicken breasts

1. Place the papers in a shallow dish, add the wine, and soak for 10 minutes.

2. In a medium skillet, heat 2 teaspoons olive oil. Add the shallots and sauté over medium heat until softened, about 3 minutes. Transfer the shallots to a mixing bowl. Add the goat cheese, sun-dried tomatoes, and basil and stir together. Season with salt and pepper.

3. Preheat the barbecue to medium high (350°F [180°C] to 400°F [200°C]) for indirect heating, putting a water pan under the unheated side of the grill.

4. With your fist, pound the breasts until they flatten out a little bit, then make e a horizontal cut in the thicker side of each chicken breast, about 3 inches (7.5 cm) deep, to form a pocket. Stuff each pocket with 2 rounded tablespoons (45 mL) of the cheese-tomato-shallot mixture. Brush the breasts with olive oil and season them with salt and pepper.

5. Sear the chicken breasts on the grill for 2 minutes on each side. With a spatula or tongs, place 1 chicken breast in the middle of each paper and fold the edges toward each other. Secure the wrappers with cotton string, place the breasts on the grill, and cook for 7 minutes on each side or until the internal temperature reaches 165°F (74°C).

6. Remove chicken from the grill and serve wrapped, one per person. Provide scissors so they can cut the string themselves.

Backyard Grilled Tandoori Chicken

Yield: 4 servings

The traditional red-orange color of Indian tandoori chicken is mainly due to the use of a special paste. Since this is somewhat specialized and won't be used that often, we substitute red food coloring.

1 (4–5 pound [1.8–2.3 kg]) chicken
1 tablespoon (15 mL) lemon juice
1 tablespoon (15 mL) plus ½ teaspoon (2.5 mL) salt
6 cloves garlic, peeled
¼ ounce (7 g) fresh ginger
¼ cup (60 mL) plain yogurt
1 teaspoon (5 mL) coriander seed
1 teaspoon (5 mL) lemon juice
1 teaspoon (5 mL) vinegar
1 teaspoon (5 mL) corn oil
½ teaspoon (2.5 mL) cayenne pepper (optional)
½ teaspoon (2.5 mL) ground black cumin
1 teaspoon (5 mL) red food coloring
Melted butter, for brushing the chicken

1. Clean, wash, and dry the chicken. Make cuts over the breast and legs. Rub the chicken with lemon juice and 1 tablespoon (15 mL) of the salt and let it sit at room temperature for 30 minutes.

2. Make sure the grill is clean and generously sprayed with nonstick grilling spray. Preheat the barbecue to high (500°F [260°C] to 550°F [290°C]).

3. In a food processor, combine the garlic, ginger, yogurt, coriander, lemon juice, vinegar, oil, cayenne pepper, the remaining salt, and the cumin and process to a smooth liquid. Add the red food coloring and pulse until the coloring is fully incorporated.

4. In a deep bowl, cover the chicken with the marinade and cover the bowl with plastic wrap. Refrigerate for 12 hours or longer.

5. Remove and discard the excess marinade. Grill the chicken for 15 minutes, turning often.

6. Brush the chicken all over with melted butter and return it to the barbecue for 10 to 15 minutes. When it's done, the chicken should be golden brown all over and lightly charred in some spots.

Oven-Fried Cajun Chicken and Rice
Yield: 4 servings

Many people don't know the difference between Cajun and Creole cuisine, but here's an easy way to tell them apart. In most cases, a Creole cuisine dinner party includes many courses. Cajuns, however, love one-pot meals.

½ cup (118 mL) all-purpose flour
1½ teaspoons (7.5 mL) paprika
1 teaspoon (5 mL) poultry seasoning
½ teaspoon (2.5 mL) salt, plus more to taste
Freshly ground black pepper, to taste
1 (3½–4 pound [1.6–1.8 kg]) fryer, cut into pieces
¼ cup (59 mL) butter
2½ cup (591 mL) chicken stock
2 cups (473 mL) chopped tomatoes
1 cup (236 mL) uncooked rice
1 cup (236 mL) chopped celery
½ cup (118 mL) chopped onion
½ cup (118 mL) chopped green bell pepper
1 clove garlic, peeled and minced
3 tablespoons (45 mL) chopped fresh parsley, divided
1 thinly sliced lime, for garnish

1. Make sure the grill is clean and generously sprayed with nonstick grilling spray. Preheat the barbecue to medium high (400°F [200°C] to 450°F [240°C]).

2. In a medium bowl, mix together the flour, paprika, poultry seasoning, salt, and pepper and stir well.

3. Spray the chicken with nonstick grilling spray, then dredge the pieces well in the seasoned flour. Melt the butter in a cast-iron or nonstick skillet and place the chicken pieces, skin side down, in the butter.

4. Place the skillet in the barbecue and bake, uncovered, for 25 to 30 minutes, or until the chicken is lightly browned.

5. In a saucepan, mix together the stock, tomatoes, and salt and pepper to taste. Bring to a boil, stirring, and set aside.

6. Remove the chicken pieces from the skillet and place them on a plate. Do not pour off the drippings.

7. Pour the uncooked rice, celery, onion, green pepper, garlic and 2 tablespoons (30 mL) of the parsley into the chicken drippings and stir to mix. Place the chicken pieces on top of the rice, then pour the stock and tomatoes over the chicken and rice, making sure the rice is completely covered with liquid.

8. Return the skillet to the barbecue and bake, uncovered, for 40 to 45 minutes. If the rice starts to dry out, add more chicken stock. Spoon the rice mixture onto a deep serving tray, top with the chicken pieces, garnish with the lime slices, and serve.

Kebabs Del Pollo (Mexican-Style Kebabs)
Yield: 4 servings

We've separated the chicken, vegetables, and tomatoes onto different skewers because they all cook at different rates. The chicken needs to cook the longest, the veggies grill up more quickly, and the tomatoes should be put on the grill just long enough for them to start to blister and brown.

2 tablespoons (30 mL) olive oil
2 tablespoons (30 mL) chopped fresh cilantro
1 teaspoon (5 mL) ground cumin
Juice and zest from 1 lime
Salt, to taste
Freshly ground black pepper, to taste
3 skinless, boneless chicken breast halves, cut into 1-inch (2.5-cm) cubes
1 small zucchini, cut into ½-inch (1-cm) slices
1 onion, peeled, cut into wedges, and separated
1 red bell pepper, cut into 1-inch (2.5-cm) pieces
10 cherry tomatoes

1. In a shallow dish, mix together the olive oil, cilantro, cumin, and lime juice and zest. Season with salt and pepper. Add the chicken and mix well. Cover, and refrigerate for at least one hour. Return to room temperature to cook.

2. Preheat the barbecue to medium high (350°F [180°C] to 400°F [200°C]).

3. Thread the chicken onto 4 skewers. Alternate the zucchini, onion, and red bell pepper on 2 to 3 more skewers. Thread the tomatoes on 1 or 2 skewers.

4. Arrange the skewers directly on the grill and cook, turning each of them several times. Cook the chicken for approximately 10 minutes, or until cooked through and browned; cook the vegetables for about 8 minutes, or until they start to char on the edges; cook the tomatoes for 3 to 4 minutes, or until they just start to bubble and split.

5. Combine all the skewered food in a large serving bowl over a bed of white or stir-fried rice and serve.

Mexicali Chili-Chicken Burgers

Yield: 4 servings

If you want a hotter burger (in taste, not temperature) you could mince up a jalapeño pepper (2,500 to 5,000 Scoville units [SU]). If you want a cooler south-of-the-border taste, use a New Mexico (500 to 1,000 SU) or Santa Fe Grande (400 to 700 SU) pepper. Poblanos are in the middle (1,000 to 2,000 SU).

2 pounds (908 g) ground chicken
1 cup (236 mL) dry breadcrumbs
3 green onions, green and white parts, chopped
1 large egg, beaten
3 tablespoons (45 mL) chopped fresh cilantro, divided
1 small poblano pepper, minced
1 tablespoon (15 mL) ground cumin
1 teaspoon (5 mL) salt
1 teaspoon (5 mL) chili powder
1 teaspoon (5 mL) minced fresh garlic
½ teaspoon (2.5 mL) dried marjoram
1 cup (236 mL) tomatillo salsa
1 medium avocado, peeled, pitted, and cubed

1. Preheat the barbecue to medium high (350°F [180°C] to 400°F [200°C]).

2. In a medium bowl, combine the chicken, breadcrumbs, green onions, egg, 1 tablespoon (15 mL) of the cilantro, the poblano pepper, the cumin, the salt, the chili powder, garlic, and the marjoram and mix well. Shape the mixture into four 1-inch (2.5-cm) thick patties. Place the patties on a plate, cover, and refrigerate for 1 hour.

3. In a small bowl, mix together the salsa, avocado, and remaining cilantro and set aside.

4. Cook the burgers on the grill or on a well-oiled griddle for 5 to 6 minutes on each side, or until browned and cooked through. Place each patty on a toasted and buttered hamburger bun, topped with 1 to 2 tablespoons (15 to 30 mL) of the salsa mixture.

You Can't Beat Our Drumsticks

Yield: 2–4

In this recipe, we use ketchup, but some folks call it "catsup." Who is right? "Ketchup" is mentioned in books written in the early 1700s, while "catchup"—or the modified "catsup"—was used in 1690 in at least one book. So the folks at www.worldwide-words.org say both are right.

8 chicken legs (drumstick only)
3 tablespoons (45 mL) ketchup
2 teaspoons (10 mL) prepared mustard
2 teaspoons (10 mL) Worcestershire sauce
¼ cup (59 mL) finely diced onion
⅛ teaspoon (0.6 mL) garlic salt
¼ teaspoon (1.25 mL) hot sauce
⅛ teaspoon (0.6 mL) freshly ground black pepper

1. Preheat the barbecue to medium high (350°F [180°C] to 400°F [200°C]).

2. Rinse and dry the chicken legs. In a small bowl, combine the ketchup, mustard, Worcestershire sauce, onion, garlic salt, hot sauce, and black pepper. Brush this mixture on the chicken legs.

3. Grill for about 35 minutes, turning frequently, until the drumsticks are tender and a meat thermometer inserted into the leg registers 165°F (74°C).

Reed-san's Chicken Teriyaki

Yield: 4 servings

Reed-san is my son-in-law, husband to my daughter Tricia, father of our two newest grandchildren, and an aspiring barbecue chef, but his best feature is his enthusiastic enjoyment of my cooking. This recipe comes from Reed Kawahara from Walnut Creek, Calif.

4 boneless, skinless chicken breasts
6 tablespoons (90 mL) shoyu soy sauce
6 tablespoons (90 mL) sake
2 tablespoons (30 mL) sugar
2 cloves garlic, peeled and crushed
1 (1-inch [2.5 cm]) piece fresh ginger, peeled and finely minced
Salt, to taste
Freshly ground black pepper, to taste
2 tablespoons (30 mL) light sesame or vegetable oil

1. Cut the chicken breasts into bite-size pieces and place the pieces in a 1-gallon (3.8-L) resealable plastic bag.

2. In a small bowl, mix together the soy sauce, sake. sugar, garlic, ginger, salt, and pepper to taste. Pour this mixture over the chicken in the bag, seal, and refrigerate overnight. Turn the bag occasionally to distribute the marinade.

3. Preheat the barbecue to medium high (350°F [180°C] to 400°F [200°C]). Oil or spray metal kebab skewers.

4. Remove the chicken from the marinade, pour the marinade into a saucepan, and boil for 10 minutes. Let the chicken come to room temperature.

5. Thread the cubes of chicken onto the prepared metal kebab skewers. Brush the meat with the sesame or vegetable oil and place the kebabs directly on the hot grill for about 10 minutes, or until the chicken is tender. Baste the chicken with the marinade and turn the kebabs several times while they cook.

6. Remove the kebabs from the grill and present as full kebabs on a bed of rice or remove the chicken pieces from the skewers and place the meat on top of the rice. In either case, pour the remaining marinade/basting sauce over the chicken and rice, and serve.

Crispy Barbecue-Baked Bird

Yield: 4 servings

You could of course make your own crumbs by placing cornflakes in a paper or plastic bag and crushing them with a rolling pin or wine bottle.

3 cups (708 mL) cornflake crumbs
1 tablespoon (15 mL) salt
1 tablespoon (15 mL) freshly ground black pepper
1 pinch ground nutmeg
1 pinch ground cinnamon
1 cup (236 mL) melted butter
3 large eggs, beaten
1 (4–5 pound [1.8–2.3 kg]) chicken, cut into pieces

1. Preheat the barbecue to medium high (350°F [180°C] to 400°F [200°C]). Spray a nonstick baking dish with nonstick cooking spray.

2. In a wide, flat bowl mix together the cornflake crumbs, salt, pepper, nutmeg, and cinnamon, and stir to blend well.

3. In a medium bowl, whisk together the butter and eggs.

4. Dip the chicken pieces into the egg-butter mix, then dredge them in the seasoned cornflake crumbs.

5. Place the chicken in the prepared baking dish and put it into the barbecue to cook for 45 minutes, or until an instant-read thermometer inserted into a thigh or breast portion reads 165°F (74°C). The chicken should be white from skin to bone.

6. Remove the chicken from the barbecue and place it on a serving platter. Serve immediately with grilled corn and garlic mashed potatoes.

Double-Crusted Barbecue Chicken Pie

Yield: 4 servings

Instead of the pie crust, you could use puff pastry in this dish, placing one piece on the bottom, one on the top, and sealing together with water and a fork.

1 large frying chicken, cut into pieces
3 cups (708 mL) water
1 large onion, peeled and chopped
1 cup (236 mL) chopped celery
1 cup (236 mL) chopped carrots
Salt, to taste
Freshly ground black pepper, to taste
6 large eggs, hard-boiled
1 (12-ounce [336-g]) can condensed cream of mushroom soup
1 (2-ounce [56-g]) jar pimentos, drained and chopped
2 cups (473 mL) thinly sliced mushrooms
1 cup (236 mL) chopped green onions, green and white parts
2 ready-made, refrigerated deep-dish pie crusts
½ cup (118 mL) melted butter
2 tablespoons (30 mL) chopped fresh parsley

1. Put the chicken in a deep pot and add the water, onion, celery, carrots, salt, and pepper. Boil until the chicken is tender, about 1 hour.

2. Preheat the barbecue to medium high (350°F [180°C] to 400°F [200°C]). Grease well or spray with nonstick cooking spray a 9-inch (22.5-cm) glass pie plate. Line a baking sheet with aluminum foil.

3. Remove the chicken from the water, reserving the broth, and set it aside to cool. When the chicken is cool, tear the meat off the bones into bite-sized pieces and set aside.

4. Shell and slice the hard-boiled eggs and set them aside. In a bowl, whisk the cream of mushroom soup with the broth and vegetables from the stewing pot.

5. Place one of the pie crusts in the bottom of the prepared pie plate. Add a layer of the chicken, half the sliced eggs, half the pimentos, half the mushrooms, and half the green onions, and salt and pepper lightly. Pour 1½ cups (354 mL) of the broth mixture over the pie.

6. Repeat the layering of chicken, eggs, pimentos, mushrooms, and green onions on top of the first layers, salt and pepper lightly, and top with the second crust. Cut 3 small vents in the top crust so steam can escape, brush the edges with cold water, and press them together with your fingers, then with a fork. Cover pie with foil after brushing with butter

7. Brush the top of the pie with the melted butter and place the pan on the foil-lined baking sheet in the barbecue. Cook for about 1 hour, or until the crust is brown and the filling is bubbling. Remove the foil from the pie after 30 minutes to let the top crust brown.

8. Remove the pie from the barbecue, brush with any remaining butter, and sprinkle with the parsley. Cover with foil and let cool for 10 to 15 minutes.

9. With a large serving spoon, portion out the pie onto 4 plates and serve, making sure everyone gets some of the top crust.

Honeyed Bar-Bee-Que Breasts

Yield: 6 servings

For a slight variation on this recipe you can substitute maple syrup or cane syrup for the honey. I sometimes squeeze a lemon onto the breasts when they are first put in the foil.

¾ cup (177 mL) barbecue sauce
⅓ cup (90 mL) honey
½ teaspoon (2.5 mL) cayenne pepper
½ teaspoon (2.5 mL) freshly ground black pepper
½ teaspoon (2.5 mL) garlic powder
½ teaspoon (2.5 mL) minced chives
6 boneless, skinless chicken breasts

1. Preheat the barbecue to medium high (350°F [180°C] to 400°F [200°C]) for direct and indirect heating, putting a water pan under the unheated side of the grill.

2. In a small bowl, mix together the barbecue sauce, honey, cayenne pepper, black pepper, garlic powder, and chives and set aside.

3. Arrange the chicken breasts on the grill and cook for 3 minutes, then turn and grill for another 3 minutes. Turn again, brush with the honey-barbecue sauce, grill for 2 minutes, then turn one last time and generously baste again.

4. Place the breasts on a large piece of aluminum foil and brush with the remaining sauce. Fold the edges of the foil over the top of the chicken and seal the foil. Place the wrapped chicken on the unheated side of the grill for 20 minutes.

5. Carefully remove the chicken from the foil and serve immediately.

Twice-Marinated Spicy Jerk Chicken Wings
Yield: 8–10 servings

Michelle Rousseau and Suzanne Rousseau-Bernard are sisters who live, work, and thoroughly enjoy life in Montego Bay and Kingston, Jamaica. This is their recipe. They run one of the island's top catering businesses and are experts in authentic Jamaican and Caribbean food. Hope you like hot wings. Start preparing this recipe several days before you plan to serve it.

Chicken

5 pounds (2.3 kg) chicken drumsticks or wings
6 fresh limes, halved
1 (12-ounce) bottle Red Stripe beer

Jerk Marinade

3 pounds (1.4 kg) onions, peeled and chopped
1 pound (454 g) green onions, cleaned and chopped
½ pound (227 g) garlic, chopped
½ pound (227 g) ginger, peeled and chopped
½ pound (227 g) whole Scotch bonnet peppers
3 cups (708 mL) vegetable oil
3 cups (708 mL) soy sauce
1 cup (236 mL) white cane vinegar
¾ cup (177 mL) Kitchen Bouquet browning and seasoning sauce
3 ounces (84 g) whole allspice berries
2 ounces (56 g) fresh thyme leaves
3 tablespoons (45 mL) sea salt
3 tablespoons (45 mL) whole black peppercorns

Chicken Marinade

1 bunch green onions, green and white parts, cleaned and chopped
2 cloves garlic, peeled and chopped
2 tablespoons (30 mL) fresh thyme leaves
2 tablespoons (30 mL) dark rum
1 tablespoon (15 mL) pineapple juice
1 tablespoon (15 mL) chopped fresh ginger
1 tablespoon (15 mL) brown sugar
1 tablespoon (15 mL) chopped Scotch bonnet pepper
Salt, to taste
Freshly ground black pepper, to taste

1. Clean and wash the chicken. Rub it all over with the limes.

2. To make the jerk seasoning, blend together the onions, green onions, garlic, ginger, Scotch bonnet peppers, oil, soy sauce, vinegar, browning sauce, allspice, thyme, sea salt, and black peppercorns in a blender or food processor until finely ground. Store the mixture in an airtight container in the refrigerator, where it will keep for a while.

3. To prepare the chicken marinade, blend together the green onions, garlic, thyme, rum, pineapple juice, ginger, brown sugar, Scotch bonnet pepper, salt, and pepper in a food processor until the mixture becomes a paste.

4. Rub the chicken with salt and pepper. Rub the marinade paste all over the chicken, making sure it gets under the skin. Put the marinated chicken in an airtight bowl and refrigerate it overnight.

5. The next day, pour 2 cups (473 mL) of jerk seasoning over the marinated chicken thighs or wings. Wearing plastic gloves to protect your skin from the hot peppers, massage the seasoning into the chicken. Cover the chicken and refrigerate overnight once again, making sure that the meat is fully submerged in the marinade.

6. One hour before grilling, remove the chicken from the refrigerator and allow it to come to room temperature. Preheat the barbecue to medium high (350°F [180°C] to 400°F [200°C]).

7. Scrape the marinade off the chicken and put the chicken on the grill. If the grill flames up, douse the flames with a splash of Red Stripe beer. Cook with the grill top closed, turning often, for 45 minutes, or until the chicken is "charred" and well-caramelized on all sides.

8. Serve the chicken on a platter with a cool mango or papaya salsa, coleslaw, and roasted sweet potatoes.

Lightnin' Chicken Thi-Pye

Yield: 4 servings

This is a great recipe for kids. They love the crust, and the tender, juicy thighs are easy to eat. If you wish you can remove the skin and chop the thighs into smaller pieces before putting the chicken in the roasting pan.

2 pounds (908 g) boneless chicken thighs
¼ cup (59 mL) vegetable oil
1½ cups (354 mL) chicken broth
1 (10.75-ounce [28-g]) can condensed cream of chicken soup
½ cup (118 mL) cold margarine or butter
½ teaspoon (2.5 mL) dried basil
½ teaspoon (2.5 mL) dried rosemary
1½ cups (354 mL) milk
1½ cups (354 mL) Bisquick baking mix

1. Preheat the barbecue to medium high (350°F [180°C] to 400°F [200°C]). Grease a roasting pan.

2. Brush the chicken thighs with vegetable oil and grill until golden brown and firm, about 4 minutes per side.

3. Place the thighs in the bottom of the prepared roasting pan and pour the broth and cream of chicken soup over the thighs. Cut the margarine or butter into 8 pieces and distribute them over the soup. Sprinkle with the dried basil and rosemary.

4. In a medium bowl, mix together the milk and biscuit mix. Distribute the dough over the pan and bake in the barbecue until crust is browned, about 40 to 45 minutes.

Green Mountain Maple Barbecue Thighs

Yield: 4 servings

My favorite chili sauce for this is plain old Heinz Chili Sauce, but of course you can use a favorite brand instead.

3 tablespoons (45 mL) pure maple syrup
3 tablespoons (45 mL) bottled chili sauce
1 tablespoon (15 mL) cider vinegar
2 teaspoons (10 mL) Dijon mustard
4 boneless chicken thighs
1 tablespoon (15 mL) vegetable oil
Seasoned salt, to taste
Freshly ground black pepper, to taste

1. Preheat the barbecue to medium high (350°F [180°C] to 400°F [200°C]).

2. Pour the maple syrup into a small saucepan. Add the chili sauce, vinegar, and mustard and stir until well blended. Heat this mixture over high heat just until mixture starts to bubble. Set aside.

3. Brush the chicken with oil and season it with salt and pepper. Place the chicken skin side down on the barbecue grill and cook for 4 minutes. Turn and cook until the skin is browned and crunchy on the edges, turning occasionally, about 10 minutes. Brush both sides liberally with the barbecue sauce several times during the last 3 minutes of grilling. Serve immediately.

Grilled Tuscaloosa Chicken
Yield: 6–8 servings

This is a favorite with some tailgaters at University of Alabama football games, who spread the white sauce on everything. It's easy to make, needs no cooking, and the flavor really goes well with barbecued chicken. Only in Alabama do they use white barbecue sauce.

1½ cups (354 mL) mayonnaise
Grated zest of 1 lemon
Grated zest of 1 lime
½ cup (118 mL) fresh lemon juice
4 teaspoons (20 mL) chopped fresh rosemary
2 cloves garlic, crushed
2 (4-pound [1.8-kg]) chickens, cut into quarters
1 teaspoon (5 mL) kosher salt
½ teaspoon (2.5 mL) freshly ground black pepper

1. Preheat the barbecue to medium high (350°F [180°C] to 400°F [200°C]) for direct and indirect heating, putting a water pan under the unheated side of the grill.

2. To make the sauce, whisk together the mayonnaise, lemon zest, lime zest, lemon juice, rosemary, and garlic. (You can make this sauce 3 days ahead, if you cover and refrigerate it after making.)

3. Season the chicken with the salt and pepper, then place the chicken on the unheated area of the grill. Cover and grill for 20 minutes. Turn the chicken over, cover, and continue grilling until an instant-read thermometer inserted in the thickest part of the breast reads 165°F (74°C), about 20 minutes more.

4. Move the chicken over direct heat. Brush the chicken generously with the mayonnaise mixture and grill the chicken quarters, turning and basting occasionally until the mayonnaise on the chicken has been reduced to a mostly transparent glaze, 3 to 5 minutes.

5. Transfer to a platter and serve hot, with the remaining sauce in a small bowl on the side.

6. Roll Tide!

Iowa State Fair Chicken-on-a-Stick

Yield: 4 servings

At the Iowa State Fair, you can buy more than 50 foods on a stick, including chicken club, Buffalo chicken, pickles, pork chops, corn dogs, cheese, Cajun chicken, sesame chicken, German sausage, teriyaki beef, corn on the cob, turkey drumstick, hot bologna, shrimp, lamb, meatballs, chili dog, turkey tenders, deep-fried hot dogs, potatoes, chicken lips, and cornbread (bratwurst dipped in corndog batter).

1 tablespoon (15 mL) vegetable oil
1 medium sweet onion, peeled and chopped
1 cup (236 mL) chili sauce
¼ cup (59 mL) ketchup
2 tablespoons (30 mL) distilled white vinegar
2 tablespoons (30 mL) brown sugar
1 teaspoon (5 mL) paprika
1½ pounds (681 g) boneless, skinless chicken breast, cut into 6 × 1-inch (15 × 2.5-cm) strips

1. Preheat the barbecue to medium high (350°F [180°C] to 400°F [200°C]).

2. In a large skillet, heat the oil over medium high heat. Add the onion and sauté until soft and golden, about 4 minutes. Stir in the chili sauce, ketchup, vinegar, brown sugar, and paprika, reduce the heat, and simmer the sauce for 2 minutes. Pour the sauce into a 9 × 13-inch (22.5 × 32.5-cm) baking dish and set aside.

3. Thread the chicken strips onto metal skewers, place the skewers on the hot grill, and cook for 1 to 4 minutes on each side, until the chicken starts to brown.

4. Place the skewers of chicken in the baking dish with the sauce, turning them so the strips are well coated, and barbecue for 30 minutes.

Grilled Chicken Hearts

Yield: 4 servings

1 quart (0.95 L) cold water
¼ cup (59 mL) kosher salt
2 tablespoons (30 mL) sugar
1½ pounds (681 g) chicken hearts, trimmed
1 teaspoon (5 mL) plus a rounded ¼ teaspoon (2 mL) salt
1 clove garlic, peeled and grated
¾ cup (177 mL) olive oil
½ cup (118 mL) finely chopped fresh Italian parsley
2 tablespoons (30 mL) sherry vinegar
1 teaspoon (5 mL) sugar
¼ teaspoon (1.25 mL) dried oregano
⅛ teaspoon (0.6 mL) red pepper flakes
25 (1-inch [2.5-cm] thick) slices baguette
Vegetable oil, for brushing

1. In a large bowl, stir together the cold water, kosher salt, and the 2 tablespoons sugar until the salt and sugar have dissolved. Add the chicken hearts and refrigerate for 3 hours.

2. Preheat the barbecue to medium high (350°F [180°C] to 400°F [200°C]).

3. Bring ¼ cup (59 mL) water to a boil with 1 teaspoon (5 mL) of the salt, then stir in the garlic and remove the pan from the heat. Cool completely. Whisk in the olive oil, parsley, vinegar, the 1 teaspoon sugar, oregano, and red pepper flakes.

4. Drain the chicken hearts. Thread 2 hearts onto each skewer, leaving about ½ inch (1 cm) of space between them, and arrange the skewers on paper-towel-lined baking sheets to dry. Lightly grill the bread on both sides.

5. Brush the chicken hearts lightly with vegetable oil and season with the remaining salt. Oil the grill rack, then grill the skewers, covered only if using a gas grill, turning occasionally, about 3 minutes total for medium.

6. Serve the skewers on the bread.

Grilled Chicken and Roasted Pepper Salad

Yield: 4–6 servings

2 large red bell peppers
2 large green bell peppers
2 large yellow bell peppers
3 tablespoons (45 mL) chopped green onion, white and green parts
2 tablespoons (30 mL) olive oil
1 tablespoon (15 mL) lime juice
2 teaspoons (10 mL) Worcestershire sauce
1 teaspoon (5 mL) balsamic vinegar
¼ teaspoon (1.25 mL) freshly ground black pepper
¼ teaspoon (1.25 mL) dried oregano
¼ teaspoon (1.25 mL) dried basil
¼ teaspoon (1.25 mL) garlic powder
3 boneless, skinless chicken breasts
2 teaspoons (10 mL) seasoned or garlic salt
6 slices focaccia
2 tablespoons (30 mL) butter, softened
Minced fresh parsley, for garnish

1. Preheat the barbecue to medium high (350°F [180°C] to 400°F [200°C]) for direct and indirect heating. Put a water pan under the unheated side of the grill. Spray a baking or roasting pan with nonstick cooking spray.

2. Place the whole peppers directly on the grill and heat until they are blackened on all sides. Take the peppers off the grill, put them in brown paper bags, and fold the bags to seal. Let stand for 10 to 12 minutes.

3. Peel the peppers, cut them in half, remove the seeds and inner membrane, and cut them lengthwise into ¼-inch (0.5-cm) wide strips.

4. Place the strips in the prepared baking or roasting pan. In a bowl, mix together the green onion, olive oil, lime juice, Worcestershire sauce, balsamic vinegar, black pepper, oregano, basil, and garlic powder. Add this mixture to the peppers and stir to coat all the strips. Cover the pan and put it on the unheated side of the barbecue.

5. Brush the chicken breasts with the olive oil–balsamic vinegar mixture, then lightly sprinkle them with seasoned salt. Grill for 4 to 5 minutes per side, turning several times.

6. Transfer the chicken breasts to a cutting board and slice them into ¼-inch (0.5-cm) strips. Remove the pan of peppers from the barbecue and combine the chicken and peppers, stirring to mix them together.

7. Toast and butter the focaccia. Arrange 2 slices each on 4 plates, top with a generous helping of chicken and pepper strips, sprinkle with parsley, and serve

Spicy Braai Chicken
Yield: 4 servings

Loaded with spices, this dish was inspired by a filming trip to South Africa, a meal at Nyoni's Kraal, and an evening spent in the kitchen with chef/owner Colin Nyoni. I left out the mopane worms that they add to some dishes, probably because they're hard to get in the United States.

8 ounces (227 g) tomato sauce
½ cup (118 mL) dry red wine, divided
¼ cup (59 mL) paprika
1 tablespoon (15 mL) grated fresh ginger
¼ teaspoon (1.25 mL) cayenne pepper
½ teaspoon (2.5 mL) ground turmeric
¼ teaspoon (1.25 mL) ground cinnamon
¼ teaspoon (1.25 mL) ground allspice
⅛ teaspoon (0.6 mL) ground cardamom
⅛ teaspoon (0.6 mL) ground nutmeg
⅛ teaspoon (0.6 mL) ground cloves
2 tablespoons (30 mL) vegetable oil
2 medium onions, peeled and sliced
1 tablespoon (15 mL) minced garlic
1 teaspoon (5 mL) salt
1 (3½–4 pound [1.6–1.8 kg]) chicken, cut into pieces

1. In a small bowl, combine the tomato sauce, ¼ cup of the wine, the paprika, the grated ginger, the cayenne pepper, turmeric, cinnamon, allspice, cardamom, nutmeg, and cloves. Cover and set aside.

2. Preheat the barbecue to medium high (400°F [200°C] to 425°F [225°C]).

3. In a large skillet, heat the oil on the stovetop over high heat. Add the onion and garlic and sauté until the onion is tender but not brown. Stir in the tomato sauce and the salt, add the chicken pieces, stir, and spoon the onion mixture over the chicken pieces. Cover the skillet, place it in the center of the barbecue, and bake for 30 minutes.

4. Stir in the remaining red wine and cook, uncovered, for another 20 minutes, turning the chicken pieces often. Remove the pan from the barbecue and let it rest for 10 minutes, then transfer the chicken to a platter, pouring the sauce over it. Serve with pita or other flat bread.

Chicken Parmigiano-Reggiano
Yield: 4 servings

Often imitated by "Parmesan" cheeses, the real thing is a hard, granular cheese that is only produced in five regions of Italy and has a flavor and texture that is unrivalled. It costs a bit more, but it is well worth the extra money.

6 tablespoons (90 mL) freshly grated Parmigiano-Reggiano cheese, divided
¼ cup (59 mL) seasoned breadcrumbs
½ teaspoon (118 mL) dried thyme
¼ teaspoon (59 mL) dried oregano
¼ teaspoon (59 mL) garlic powder
Freshly ground black pepper, to taste
1 (3½–4 pound [1.6–1.8 kg]) chicken, quartered
2 large eggs, beaten
1 (10¾-ounce [301-g]) can condensed cream of celery soup
½ cup (118 mL) milk
Chopped fresh parsley, for garnish

1. Preheat the barbecue to medium high (400°F [200°C] to 425°F [225°C]). Spray a 2-quart (1.9-L) Dutch oven with nonstick cooking spray.

2. In a wide, flat pan, mix together 4 tablespoons (60 mL) of the cheese, the breadcrumbs, the thyme, the oregano, the garlic powder, and the pepper.

3. Dip the chicken in the egg, then press it into the crumb mixture.

4. Place the breaded pieces into the prepared Dutch oven. Bake in the barbecue for 20 minutes, turn the chicken, and bake for 20 minutes more.

5. In a small bowl, whisk together the soup and milk. Pour this mixture over the chicken. Sprinkle with the parsley and the remaining 2 tablespoons (30 mL) of cheese, and bake 20 minutes more, or until the chicken is tender. Remove the chicken and arrange it on platter. Stir the sauce and pour it over the chicken.

Grilled Chicken Liver and Bacon Skewers

Yield: 4 servings

Some folks (like me) love these livers but prefer them served with a generous helping of grilled onions. Just grill slices of onion you've brushed with butter over high heat in a skillet until they start to color and get very soft, drain them briefly on paper towels, then serve.

8 slices bacon, cooked for 1 minute, then cut into thirds
24 chicken livers, trimmed
24 mushrooms, stems removed
½ cup (118 mL) melted butter
Salt, to taste
Freshly ground black pepper, to taste

1. Preheat the barbecue to medium high (350°F [180°C] to 400°F [200°C]).

2. Wrap the cooked bacon pieces around the livers, then thread the livers onto 8 skewers, alternating with the mushrooms.

3. Pour the melted butter into a wide, flat baking dish. Roll the skewers in the melted butter, salt and pepper lightly, then place them directly on the hot grill and cook, turning and basting frequently with the melted butter, for 5 to 8 minutes.

4. Remove the cooked skewers and wrap them in aluminum foil until you have them all cooked. then serve 2 skewers per person accompanied by wild rice, garlic mashed potatoes, or cottage-fried potatoes and onions.

Grilled Chicken Marinated in Garlic

Yield: 4 servings

There are over 100 varieties of basil. The most popular in the United States are sweet, Thai, lemon, lime, clove, and Genovese. Any would work well in this recipe, but I use the astringent Thai variety. This recipe comes from Barbara Johnson from Salmon Creek, Wash.

¼ cup (59 mL) olive oil
½ cup (118 mL) coarsely chopped garlic
½ cup (118 mL) coarsely chopped fresh Thai basil leaves
2 tablespoons (30 mL) fresh lime juice
1 tablespoon (15 mL) sherry vinegar
1 tablespoon (15 mL) honey
2 teaspoons (10 mL) ancho chili powder
2 chickens, quartered

1. In a bowl, combine the olive oil, garlic, basil, lime juice, vinegar, honey, and chili powder and stir until thoroughly combined. Put the chicken in a 1- to 2-gallon (3.8- to 7.6-L) resealable plastic bag and pour the marinade in over it. Marinate for at least 2 to 3 hours, longer if possible.

2. Preheat the barbecue to medium high (400°F [200°C] to 450°F [240°C]).

3. Remove the chicken from the marinade. Place the chicken in the center of the barbecue and grill for 10 to 12 minutes on each side, turning several times and basting 4 to 5 times, until the chicken is browned with charred edges and a thermometer inserted into the thick part of the breast reads 165°F [74°C].

4. Pour any remaining marinade into a saucepan and boil for 10 minutes.

5. Place the chicken quarters on a heated platter, drizzle with the remaining basting sauce, and serve.

Grilled Chicken Thighs with Cumin Butter

Yield: 6 servings

This dish can also be made with chicken breasts. Cut a pocket in the side of the thickest part of the breast, fill it with 2 teaspoons (10 mL) cumin butter, tie it as you do here with the thighs, and cook in the skillet for 20 to 25 minutes in the skillet.

12 boneless chicken thighs, skin on
1 cup (236 mL) unsalted butter, softened
1 teaspoon (5 mL) finely diced red onion
1 teaspoon (5 mL) ground cumin
½ teaspoon (2.5 mL) garlic powder
¼ teaspoon (1.25 mL) ground cardamom
Salt, to taste
Freshly ground black pepper, to taste
¼ cup (59 mL) olive oil

1. Place the chicken thighs on a cutting board, skin side down, and pound them lightly with a tenderizing hammer or the bottom of a heavy-duty wine bottle to flatten them out more.

2. In a medium bowl, stir together the butter, onion, cumin, garlic powder, cardamom, salt, and pepper until well mixed. Spoon 1 tablespoon (15 mL) of the cumin butter into the cavity left in the thigh by the removal of the bone. Roll and tie each thigh in two places to keep the butter inside. Put all the stuffed and tied thighs into a very cold part of the refrigerator and chill for 1 hour. Cover the remaining butter and leave it at room temperature.

3. Preheat the barbecue to medium high (350°F [180°C] to 400°F [200°C]) for direct and indirect heating, putting a water pan under the unheated side of the grill.

4. Massage 1 teaspoon (5 mL) of the flavored butter all over the outside of each chicken thigh.

5. Place the thighs skin side down over the direct flames or charcoal and sear until the skin starts to brown and char at the edges. Turn over and cook for 1 minute, then transfer the thighs to a plate. Pour the olive oil in a cast-iron skillet. Add the thighs, skin side down, and place the skillet on the unheated side of the grill. Cook for 12 minutes, then spoon in the remaining cumin butter and cook another 3 minutes, or until the thighs are done and the butter is bubbly. Do not turn them.

6. Remove the chicken from the barbecue, snip off the string, and place two thighs on a large scoop of rice on each of 6 plates. Spoon the hot butter from the skillet over the chicken and rice and serve.

Herbed Chicken and Mushrooms

Yield: 4 servings

I like to use crimini mushrooms in this dish, but if you're feeling extravagant, buy some fresh morels and slice them in ¼-inch (0.5-cm) thick slices or strips. The flavor of freshly picked morels is incomparable.

1 (2½–3 pound [1.1–1.3 kg]) broiler-fryer chicken, cut up
⅓ cup (79 mL) lime juice
¼ cup (59 mL) vegetable oil
1 tablespoon (15 mL) dried chives
1 teaspoon (5 mL) dried tarragon
1 teaspoon (5 mL) dried basil
½ teaspoon (2.5 mL) hickory salt
⅛ teaspoon (0.6 mL) freshly ground black pepper
1 clove garlic, peeled and finely minced
1 cup (236 mL) butter
½ teaspoon (2.5 mL) garlic powder
2 cups (473 mL) sliced fresh mushrooms

1. Place the chicken pieces in a 1- to 2-gallon (3.8- to 7.6-L) resealable plastic bag and set aside. In a small bowl, combine the lime juice, oil, chives, tarragon, basil, salt, pepper, and garlic. Pour this mixture over the chicken and seal the bag. Marinate for about 1 hour at room temperature, turning the bag occasionally.

2. Preheat the barbecue to medium high (350°F [180°C] to 400°F [200°C]).

3. Drain the chicken, pouring the marinade into a saucepan. Place the chicken skin side down on the grill and cook for 20 minutes, or until lightly browned, brushing occasionally with the boiled marinade. Turn the chicken skin side up and cook for 15 to 20 minutes longer, or until tender, brushing frequently and generously with the remaining marinade.

4. While the chicken is cooking, melt the butter with the garlic powder in a heat-proof saucepan. Add the sliced mushrooms and place the pan alongside the chicken on the grill. Stir several times as they cook.

5. Pour any remaining marinade into a saucepan and boil for 10 minutes.

6. Remove the chicken and the pan of mushrooms from the barbecue. Place the chicken on a platter, pour the remaining marinade over the chicken, scatter the cooked mushrooms on top, and serve.

Barbecue Oven-Fried Chicken

Yield: 8 servings

This dish is perfect for folks on low-fat diets, as the chicken is baked, not fried. The only oil is a brief brushing with vegetable oil, and even that can be changed to sesame or canola oil, both of which are heart healthy.

2 stacks (72 crackers) Ritz Roasted Vegetable Crackers
8 chicken breasts
2 tablespoons (30 mL) vegetable oil
½ teaspoon (2.5 mL) garlic salt
¾ cup (177 mL) honey, at room temperature
½ cup (118 mL) lemon juice
2 tablespoons (30 mL) balsamic vinegar

1. Preheat the barbecue to medium high (250°F [120°C] to 275°F [140°C]). Spray a roasting pan with nonstick cooking or grilling spray.

2. Put the crackers, one stack at a time, in a 1-gallon (3.8-L) resealable plastic bag, seal, and use a rolling pin or wine bottle, to crush the crackers to fine crumbs. Go over the bag several times, until all the crackers have been crushed. Pour the crumbs into a wide, flat pan and set aside.

3. Wash and dry the chicken. Brush each breast with oil, sprinkle with a little garlic salt, and firmly press each breast into the crushed cracker crumbs. Make sure each piece of chicken is coated, front and back, with cracker crumbs.

4. Place the chicken, skin side up, in the prepared roasting pan.

5. Cook, uncovered, for 20 minutes, then turn the breasts and cook for another 20 minutes. Repeat this process twice more, so the chicken breasts are skin side up for the last 20 minutes.

6. While chicken is cooking, whisk together the honey, lemon juice, and balsamic vinegar in a small saucepan over low heat on a side burner or stovetop burner. Heat until the honey mixture is very thin. Set aside, and keep warm.

7. Transfer the breasts to a serving platter, drizzle the honey–lemon–balsamic sauce over them, and serve.

Grilled Cornish Hens with Habañero Glaze

Yield: 4 servings

If you want to be festive and creative, you could garnish these with mandarin orange segments or grilled fresh apricots, dried minced toasted onion flakes, or very thin slices of grilled habañero peppers.

4 Cornish hens, butterflied
3 tablespoons (45 mL) walnut oil
½ (16-ounce [454-g]) jar Rose's lime marmalade
Zest from 1 large lime, minced
1 habañero chile, seeded and minced
¼ cup (59 mL) extra virgin olive oil
¼ cup (59 mL) tequila
Paprika, for garnish

1. Preheat the barbecue to medium high (350°F [180°C] to 400°F [200°C]) for direct and indirect heating, putting a water pan under the unheated side of the grill and lining the top of the unheated side with aluminum foil.

2. Brush the butterflied hens with the walnut oil and place them on the heated side of the grill, skin side down, for 5 minutes. Turn and grill for another 5 minutes. Transfer the hens to the foil on the unheated side of the grill, skin side down, and cook for 10 minutes.

3. While the hens are first on the heated side of the grill, mix together the marmalade, lime zest, habañero, olive oil, and tequila in a small saucepan and heat over medium-high heat for 5 minutes, stirring constantly.

4. Liberally brush the marinade over the hens on the unheated side of the grill and cover them with the foil. After 10 minutes, remove the covering foil, turn the birds over, and baste the skin side. Cook 10 minutes more, baste again, and cook for a final 5 minutes. A quick-read thermometer inserted into the thickest part of the breasts should register 165°F (74°C).

5. Pour any remaining marinade into a saucepan and boil for 10 minutes. Remove the birds from the grill and place them skin side up on 4 large plates (or 8 plates, if you're splitting the birds in half). Pour the remaining marinade over the birds, sprinkle with paprika, and serve.

Coconut Curry Hens
Yield: 8 servings

Instead of using the mild curry we suggest, you can flame this dish up by using a hot variety. Curry is not a spice; rather, it's a mixture of cumin, red pepper, turmeric, ginger, white pepper, cinnamon, fenugreek, fennel, cardamom, cloves, Telicherry pepper, and, depending on the brand, assorted other spices and herbs.

1 (14-ounce [397-mL]) can unsweetened coconut milk
½ cup (118 mL) smooth peanut butter
2 tablespoons (30 mL) dark brown sugar
1 tablespoon (15 mL) mild curry powder
1 teaspoon (5 mL) ground coriander
1 teaspoon (5 mL) salt
½ teaspoon (2.5 mL) ground cumin
¼ teaspoon (1.25 mL) cayenne pepper
Juice of 1 lime
¼ cup (118 mL) olive oil
2 tablespoons (30 mL) freshly ground black pepper
3 pounds (1.3 kg) boneless, skinless chicken breasts
Toasted coconut flakes, for garnish
4 green onions, green and white parts, thinly sliced, for garnish

1. Preheat the barbecue to medium high (350°F [180°C] to 400°F [200°C]).

2. In a small saucepan, mix together the coconut milk, peanut butter, brown sugar, curry, coriander, salt, cumin, cayenne pepper, and lime juice. Place the pan over medium-high heat and bring to a boil, stirring. Lower the heat to a simmer and cook, stirring occasionally, until the sauce thickens, about 10 minutes.

3. In a small bowl, combine the olive oil and black pepper. Brush the chicken breasts with the peppered olive oil and place them on the grill, skin side down. Cook for 10 minutes, turn, and brush with more olive oil and pepper.

4. Remove the chickens from the barbecue and place them on a serving platter. Garnish with the toasted coconut flakes and green onions. Serve with the curry sauce in a sauce boat.

Chicken Under a Brick

Yield: 4 servings

I demonstrated this live on Live with Regis and Kelly. *Regis liked it so much that after the segment he asked if there was enough left for his lunch. Since I always double recipes when I do live TV, I had plenty left to serve to my friend.*

¼ cup (59 mL) plus 3 tablespoons (45 mL) olive oil, for frying
4 cloves garlic, peeled and minced
2 tablespoons (30 mL) finely chopped fresh basil (or 1 teaspoon [5 mL] dried)
1 tablespoon (15 mL) dried savory
1 tablespoon (15 mL) dried oregano
1 teaspoon (5 mL) sea salt
1 teaspoon (5 mL) freshly ground black pepper
½ teaspoon (2.5 mL) chili powder
1 (4–5 pound [1.8–2.3 kg]) whole chicken
½ cup (118 mL) fresh lime juice

1. In a small bowl, combine ¼ cup (59 mL) of the oil, the garlic, the basil, the savory, the oregano, the salt, the pepper, and the chili powder. Mix well and set aside.

2. Using kitchen scissors or a sharp knife, cut down each side of the backbone of the chicken and remove it. Turn the chicken breast side up and press firmly on the breastbone to flatten the chicken. You will hear a snap as the breastbone breaks off. Tuck the wings behind the back and put the chicken into a 1-gallon (3.8-L) resealable plastic bag. Pour the marinade in over it, seal the bag, shake to coat the chicken, and refrigerate for at least 4 hours or overnight, turning the bag over occasionally.

3. Preheat the barbecue to medium high (350°F [180°C] to 400°F [200°C]). Wrap a brick in two layers of heavy-duty aluminum foil and set it aside. Spray a cast-iron skillet with nonstick cooking spray.

4. Remove the chicken from the marinade, reserving the marinade, and let the chicken come to room temperature.

5. Place the flattened chicken, skin side down, on the prepared cast-iron skillet. Place the skillet directly on the hot grill. Immediately place the brick on top of the chicken, close the lid, and cook for 20 minutes. Using gloves or oven mitts, remove the brick. Using tongs, turn the chicken. Baste generously, replace the brick, and cook for another 20 minutes, or until the juices run clear and a thermometer inserted into the thick part of the breast reads 165°F (74°C).

6. Pour the marinade into a saucepan and boil it for 10 minutes so you can use it as a basting liquid.

7. Add the lime juice to the marinade, stir, and set aside. Transfer the whole chicken to a cutting board and cover it loosely with foil. Let stand for 10 minutes. Using a chef's knife, separate the chicken into breast, thigh, wing, and leg portions. Place the chicken on a serving platter, pour the lime marinade sauce over the pieces, and serve.

Fuzzy Navel Hens
Yield: 4 servings

This dish was inspired by my wife's love of the cocktail of the same name. If you prefer not to use alcohol, substitute ¼ cup (59 mL) peach nectar for the schnapps.

1 (3½–4 pound [1.6–1.8 kg]) broiler-fryer chicken, cut into pieces
¼ cup (59 mL) peach schnapps
¼ cup (59 mL) orange juice
¼ cup (59 mL) freshly squeezed lemon juice
3 tablespoons (45 mL) lime juice
1 clove garlic, peeled and minced
½ teaspoon freshly ground black pepper
1 teaspoon (5 mL) coarse salt, divided
1 lemon, thinly sliced

1. Place the chicken pieces in a 1- to 2-gallon (3.8- to 7.6-L) resealable plastic and set aside.

2. In a small bowl, mix together the schnapps, orange juice, lemon juice, lime juice, garlic, and black pepper. Pour this mixture into the bag over the chicken, seal the bag, shake to coat the chicken, and refrigerate overnight or for at least 3 hours.

3. Preheat the barbecue to medium high (350°F [180°C] to 400°F [200°C]).

4. Remove the chicken from the marinade.

5. Place the chicken on the grill, skin side down, sprinkle it with ½ teaspoon (2.5 mL) of the salt, and grill for 15 minutes. Turn the chicken, brush it with marinade; sprinkle it with the remaining salt, cover, and grill for 20 to 25 minutes longer, or until the juice of chicken runs clear or a thermometer inserted into the thick part of the breast reads 165°F (74°C).

6. Pour the marinade into a saucepan and boil for 10 minutes while the chicken comes to room temperature.

7. Place the chicken on a serving platter, drizzle with the remaining sauce, and garnish with sliced lemon.

Grilled Rum and Butter Chicken

Yield: 6 servings

If you don't want to use the liquor, substitute orange juice and add a teaspoon (5 mL) of bottled rum flavoring and a pinch of cinnamon.

⅔ cup (158 mL) plus 2 tablespoons (30 mL) dark rum
⅓ cup (79 mL) orange juice
⅓ cup (79 mL) plus ¼ cup (59 mL) melted butter
2 tablespoons (30 mL) honey
1 tablespoon (15 mL) minced garlic
1 teaspoon (5 mL) dried thyme
6 (4–5 ounce [112–140 g]) boneless, skinless chicken breast halves
Nutmeg, for garnish

1. In a small bowl, combine ⅔ cup (158 mL) of the rum, the orange juice, ⅓ cup (79 mL) of the butter, the honey, the garlic, and the thyme. Put the chicken in a large, resealable plastic bag with ⅔ cup (158 mL) of the marinade. Seal the bag tightly. Turn the bag several times to coat the chicken well. Refrigerate, turning occasionally, for at least 4 hours or overnight. Cover and chill the remaining marinade.

2. Preheat the barbecue to medium high (350°F [180°C] to 400°F [200°C]).

3. Remove chicken from the marinade. Place chicken on the grill, skin side up, and cook for 8 minutes, basting with the marinade. Turn the chicken and cook for another 10 to 12 minutes, or until a meat thermometer inserted into the thick part of the breast reads 165°F (74°C). Discard marinade.

4. Remove the cooked chicken breasts to a serving platter, add the remaining 2 tablespoons (30 mL) rum and of the remaining ¼ cup (59 mL) melted butter to the reserved marinade; drizzle some over the chicken; and pour the rest into a gravy dish or sauce boat. Sprinkle the chickens and sauce lightly with nutmeg and serve.

Buttery Buffalo Drumettes

Yield: 6–8 servings

Drumettes are the largest portion of the chicken wing, the part with the most meat. You can buy them frozen at most major grocery stores, or you can make your own.

24 chicken drumettes
2 cups (473 mL) buttermilk
⅔ cup (158 mL) all-purpose flour
⅔ cup (158 mL) cornmeal
1½ teaspoons (7.5 mL) Greek seasoning
1 teaspoon (5 mL) coarse salt
1 teaspoon (5 mL) freshly ground black pepper
1 teaspoon (5 mL) ground cumin
½ teaspoon (2.5 mL) cayenne pepper
½ teaspoon (2.5 mL) garlic powder, divided
¼ teaspoon (1.25 mL) onion powder
4 cups (0.95 L) peanut or safflower oil
1½ cups (354 mL) unsalted butter
1 cup (236 mL) hot pepper sauce

1. Preheat the barbecue to medium high (450°F [240°C] to 500°F [260°C]).

2. Place the chicken drumettes and buttermilk in a 1-gallon (3.8-L) resealable plastic bag. Marinate at room temperature for 30 minutes.

3. In a large paper bag, mix the together the flour and cornmeal. Add the Greek seasoning, salt, black pepper, cumin, cayenne pepper, garlic powder, and onion powder and shake to mix. Put 2 to 3 drumettes at a time into the bag of flour mixture and shake to coat them well, placing the coated drumettes on a plate until all the drumettes have been coated.

4. Pour the oil into a 4-quart (3.8-L) Dutch oven on a barbecue side burner and heat it to 350°F (180°C). Fry the drumettes 3 to 4 at a time, for 6 to 8 minutes, or until golden brown. Remove the drumettes from the oil and drain on paper towels.

5. Line a baking sheet with aluminum foil, place it in the barbecue, and close the lid to heat the pan.

6. In a deep saucepan, melt the butter over low heat. Pour in the hot pepper sauce and stir to blend. Remove the pan from the heat.

7. With tongs, dip each drumette into the butter, drain briefly, and place it on a platter. Repeat with the remaining drumsticks. Place the drumettes on the foil-lined baking sheet and cook for 2 minutes. Turn them over and cook for another 2 minutes.

8. Place the cooked drumettes on a platter and serve with the remaining butter on the side.

Bird Wings with Nectarine-Onion Relish
Yield: 4 servings

Instead of nectarines, you could use peaches, apricots, plums, dates, or even pears. This recipe comes from Terry Browne from Campbell River, British Columbia.

2 medium onions, peeled and finely chopped
2 tablespoons (30 mL) soy sauce
2 tablespoons (30 mL) cider vinegar
2 tablespoons (30 mL) honey
1 medium nectarine, pitted and chopped
1 teaspoon (5 mL) olive oil
Salt, to taste
Freshly ground black pepper, to taste
24 chicken wings

1. In a large bowl, mix together the onions, soy sauce, vinegar, honey, nectarine, olive oil, salt, and pepper. Pour the mixture into a resealable plastic bag, add the chicken wings, and make sure each wing is coated with relish (For more intense flavor, refrigerate up to 8 hours.)

2. Preheat the barbecue to medium high (350°F [180°C] to 400°F [200°C]).

3. Drain the wings and pour the marinade into a large nonstick skillet. Bring to a boil and cook over medium heat until the relish has thickened and reduced by half.

4. Transfer the thickened relish to a blender and blend to a smooth, thick sauce.

5. Cook the chicken wings on a wing rack or directly on the grill until they are almost done, about 15 to 20 minutes. Just before you remove them, brush each wing liberally with the relish, cook an additional 2 to 3 minutes, then serve as light lunch.

Chicken in Phyllo Dough
Yield: 8 servings

This recipe uses clarified butter, which is easy to make yourself. Slowly melt 1 stick of butter. Let it sit for a bit to separate. Skim off the foam that rises to the top, and gently pour the liquid butter off of the milk solids, which have settled to the bottom. One stick = 6 tablespoons (90 mL) clarified butter.

4 boneless, skinless chicken breasts, halved
Olive oil, for brushing
1 (10¾-ounce [301-g]) can condensed cream of celery soup
2 stalks celery, minced
1 onion, peeled and minced
6 sprigs fresh parsley, minced
2 tablespoons (30 mL) butter
Seasoned salt, to taste
Freshly ground black pepper, to taste
3 tablespoons (45 mL) clarified butter
2 teaspoons (10 mL) lime juice
8 sheets phyllo dough
5 chives, finely minced, for garnish

1. Preheat the barbecue to medium high (350°F [180°C] to 400°F [200°C]). Grease a baking sheet.

2. Place the chicken breasts on the barbecue and grill for 8 minutes per side, brushing with olive oil each time you turn the breasts. Remove the chicken breasts from the grill and set them aside to cool.

3. In a saucepan, combine the soup, celery, onion, and parsley. Bring to a boil, then reduce the temperature and simmer for 5 minutes. Whisk the 2 tablespoons (30 mL) butter into the thick soup. Season with salt and pepper. Set aside and keep warm.

4. In a small bowl, combine the clarified butter and lime juice. Stir and set aside.

5. Place a chicken breast at the short end of a phyllo sheet. Top the breast with 1 tablespoon (15 mL) soup mixture. Fold the long edges of the phyllo inward to partially cover the chicken. Roll the chicken in phyllo the entire length of the sheet. Repeat with the remaining chicken, soup, and phyllo sheets.

6. Brush the tops of the phyllo packages with the clarified butter mixture and place them on the prepared baking sheet. Bake until the phyllo is nicely browned, about 15 minutes; then brush with the clarified butter mixture and bake for additional 15 minutes. Reheat any remaining soup mixture to prevent contaminating the final dish.

7. Place the chicken on a serving platter, drizzle with the remaining soup sauce, sprinkle with finely minced chives, and serve.

Grenadine Limed Chicken
Yield: 4 servings

Use only Rose's grenadine syrup in this dish. Almost all other brands are made with modified corn syrup, but Rose's is made with real pomegranates.

¼ cup (59 mL) frozen limeade concentrate, thawed
2 tablespoons (30 mL) Rose's grenadine syrup
1 tablespoon (15 mL) vegetable oil
1 teaspoon (5 mL) onion salt
1 (2½-pound [1.1-kg]) broiler-fryer chicken, cut up
½ cup (118 mL) fresh lime juice
Salt, to taste
Freshly ground black pepper, to taste
1 tablespoon (15 mL) grated lime zest, for garnish

1. Preheat the barbecue to medium high (350°F [180°C] to 400°F [200°C]).

2. In a small bowl, mix together the limeade, grenadine, oil, and salt.

3. Brush the chicken pieces generously with the sauce. Place the chicken, skin side down, on the barbecue and grill for 10 to 15 minutes per side, turning and basting often.

4. Remove the chicken from the grill. Brush it with fresh lime juice, sprinkle with salt and pepper, and continue grilling, turning and basting 2 or 3 times, 20 to 30 minutes longer, or until the chicken is done.

5. Pour the remaining lime-grenadine basting sauce into a small sauce pitcher, microwave on high for 30 seconds, and serve it alongside the chicken for pouring over it. Garnish the chicken with the lime zest.

Greek Lemon Chicken

Yield: 4 servings

Limes, grapefruit, oranges, tangerine, tangelos, or mandarin oranges can all be easily substituted for the lemons in this dish, as all have acidic juice and tangy, acidic, aromatic skin. Of course, you'll have to change the name of the recipe.

¾ cup (177 mL) water
¼ cup (59 mL) fresh lemon juice
1 tablespoon (15 mL) dried lemon zest
2 teaspoons (10 mL) dried oregano
1 teaspoon (5 mL) dried savory
1 teaspoon (5 mL) salt
1 teaspoon (5 mL) garlic powder
¼ teaspoon (1.25 mL) lemon pepper
3 pounds (1.3 kg) chicken thighs and drumsticks
1 cup (236 mL) all-purpose flour
2 tablespoons (30 mL) vegetable oil
8 thin slices lemon
2 tablespoons (30 mL) minced fresh parsley

1. In a small bowl, whisk together the water, lemon juice, lemon zest, oregano, savory, salt, garlic powder, and lemon pepper. Prick the skin of the chicken pieces several times with a barbecue fork and place them in a 1-gallon (3.8-L) resealable plastic bag. Pour the marinade over the chicken; seal the bag, and shake to coat. Refrigerate overnight.

2. Remove the chicken from the marinade. Coat the chicken pieces with the flour, shaking off the excess.

3. Preheat the barbecue to medium high (350°F [180°C] to 400°F [200°C]). Spray a 12 × 8-inch (30 × 20-cm) baking pan with nonstick cooking or grilling spray.

4. In a large skillet, heat the oil until hot. Add half of the chicken and brown it well on all sides. Remove the chicken from the skillet with a slotted spoon. Repeat with the remaining chicken.

5. Place the chicken in the prepared baking pan and pour the marinade over the chicken. Bake, covered, basting occasionally, until the chicken is tender, about 50 minutes.

6. Serve the chicken pieces on a tray, topping each piece with a lemon slice and a sprinkle of parsley.

Seoul Chicken
Yield: 4 servings

Sesame seeds and sesame seed oil are often used in Korean and other Southeastern Asian cuisines. In this recipe, the sesame is a nice change from Italian or French dressing marinades.

1 (4½–5 pound [2–2.3 kg]) chicken
¼ cup (59 mL) dark sesame oil
1 (14-ounce [354 mL]) bottle sesame ginger salad dressing
1 cup (236 mL) sweet red wine
Grated fresh parsley, for garnish
Sesame seeds, for garnish

1. Cut the chicken into pieces and poke each piece several times with a sharp fork. Brush the chicken with sesame oil and place it in a 1- to 2-gallon (3.8- to 7.6-L) resealable plastic bag.

2. In a small bowl, combine the salad dressing and wine and stir to mix.

3. Pour the wine mixture into the plastic bag over the chicken, seal the bag, and refrigerate for 4 to 5 hours or overnight.

4. Preheat the barbecue to medium high (350°F [180°C] to 400°F [200°C]).

5. Remove the chicken from the marinade and pour the marinade into a small saucepan. Place the chicken pieces on the grill, cook for 35 to 40 minutes, basting during the last 20 minutes with the marinade.

6. Boil the marinade for 10 minutes after chicken finishes cooking so you can use it as a basting liquid. Transfer the chicken to a platter, brush it with any remaining marinade, and sprinkle it with parsley and sesame seeds.

Paper Bag Chicken
Yield: 4 servings

This is part of my "bagged barbecue" series. In the past, I've cooked turkeys, pork roasts, shrimp, and even apple pies in a bag. If you like the moistness of beer-butt chicken, you have to try this cooking method.

2½ tablespoons (37.5 mL) very soft butter
1 (3-pound [1.3-kg]) whole fryer chicken, cleaned and patted dry
1 teaspoon (5 mL) garlic salt
1 tablespoon (15 mL) chopped fresh rosemary
1 tablespoon (15 mL) paprika

1. Preheat the barbecue to medium high (425°F [220°C] to 450°F [240°C]) for direct and indirect heating, putting a water pan under the unheated side of the grill.

2. Rub butter over the outside and inside of the chicken, including under the skin where you can. Cross the chicken's legs and tie them together. Tie the wings to the body. Sprinkle the garlic salt, rosemary, and paprika all over the chicken. Do not stuff the chicken.

3. Lay a piece of waxed paper on the bottom (but not on the sides of a large brown paper grocery bag. Place the bag on a baking sheet or in a shallow roasting pan. Place the chicken, breast side up, on the waxed paper inside the bag. Balloon the bag, so the chicken doesn't touch the sides, and tie the bag at the very top or staple it after folding over the top inch (2.5 cm) of the bag.

4. Place the chicken on the tray on the heated part of the grill and bake for 1 hour. Reduce the heat by closing the vents and moving the tray to the unheated side of the grill and bake 45 minutes.

5. Transfer the bagged chicken to a serving platter and cut the bag open at the table. Carve the chicken and serve.

Honey-Ginger Chicken

Yield: 6 servings

If you want a more diet-sensitive dish, use skinless thighs. For even less fat, use skinless breasts, which have 1 percent fat per 100 grams. Thighs are 4 percent fat per 100 grams, so the difference isn't huge. Even so, many people prefer the thighs because they're juicier and have more taste.

3 tablespoons (45 mL) vegetable shortening
3 tablespoons (45 mL) butter or margarine
⅓ cup (79 mL) all-purpose flour
1 teaspoon (5 mL) ground ginger, divided
¼ teaspoon (1.25 mL) freshly ground black pepper
3 pounds (1.3 kg) chicken thighs
⅓ cup (79 mL) honey
⅓ cup (79 mL) chili sauce
⅓ cup (79 mL) soy sauce

1. Preheat the barbecue to medium high (350°F [180°C] to 400°F [200°C]).

2. In a 9 × 13-inch (22.5 × 32.5-cm) pan in the barbecue, melt the shortening and butter. In a small paper bag, mix together the flour, ½ teaspoon (2.5 mL) of the ginger, and the pepper. Spray the chicken thighs with nonstick cooking or grilling spray, drop them into the bag, and shake to coat with the flour mixture.

3. Place the chicken, skin side down, in the baking pan and cook, uncovered, for 30 minutes. Turn the thighs and bake for 15 more minutes. Remove the chicken from the barbecue.

4. Line a Dutch oven with foil and place the thighs on the foil. In a small bowl, stir together the honey, chili sauce, soy sauce, and the remaining ginger. Brush this mixture on the chicken and bake for 15 minutes, frequently basting with the honey-chili sauce.

5. Transfer the chicken to a serving platter and serve immediately.

Basil–Grilled Chicken
Yield: 4 servings

Julienne the basil leaves by rolling them in small cigar shapes and using a sharp knife to cut thin slices across the rolled leaves. Slice the basil just before using, as the leaves discolor quickly.

4 boneless chicken breasts, with skin
2 tablespoons (30 mL) softened butter
1 tablespoon (15 mL) cracked black pepper
¼ teaspoon (1.25 mL) garlic powder
⅓ cup (79 mL) melted butter
¼ cup (59 mL) finely chopped fresh basil
1 tablespoon (15 mL) freshly grated Parmigiano-Reggiano cheese
⅛ teaspoon (0.6 mL) salt
⅛ teaspoon (0.6 mL) freshly ground black pepper
¼ cup (59 mL) fresh basil cut in thin julienne strips

1. Preheat the barbecue to medium high (350°F [180°C] to 400°F [200°C]).

2. Massage the chicken breasts with the softened butter. In a flat dish, combine the cracked black pepper and the garlic powder. Press the breasts into the mixture, paying special attention to the thicker sides of the breast halves.

3. In a small bowl, combine the melted butter, chopped basil, Parmigiano-Reggiano, salt and pepper.

4. Place the chickens in the barbecue and cook skin side down for about 5 minutes. Baste with basil butter, turn, and cook for 8 minutes. Baste again and turn back over so the skin side is up. Baste with the rest of the butter and grill for 3 minutes.

5. Remove the chicken from the grill and place it on a warm platter. Sprinkle the julienned basil leaves over the breasts and garnish with halved cherry tomatoes.

Gai Yang Chicken
Yield: 4–6 servings

Although the fish sauce adds a distinctive flavor, some people can't abide the taste. For them, you can substitute 2 parts soy sauce and 1 part lime juice. This substitution is also good for vegetarians, as the fish sauce contains—you guessed it—fish, in this case fermented anchovies. This recipe comes from Stephen Ceideburg from Bangkok, Thailand.

3 tablespoons (45 mL) fresh cilantro leaves
3 tablespoons (45 mL) fish sauce
3 tablespoons (45 mL) light soy sauce
2 tablespoons (30 mL) fresh lime juice
1 tablespoon (15 mL) freshly ground black pepper
1 tablespoon (15 mL) minced garlic
3 pounds (1.3 kg) boneless, skinless chicken breasts, cut into long, 1-inch (2.5-cm) wide strips

1. In a blender or food processor, combine the cilantro, fish sauce, soy sauce, lime juice, pepper, and garlic. Blend until smooth. Place the chicken strips in a 1- to 2-gallon (3.8- to 7.6-L) resealable plastic bag and pour the marinade in over them. Shake and turn bag over several times to distribute the marinade. Refrigerate for 2 to 8 hours, turning occasionally.

2. Preheat the barbecue to medium high (350°F [180°C] to 400°F [200°C]).

3. Remove the chicken from the marinade. Pour the marinade into a saucepan and boil it for 10 minutes while the chicken comes to room temperature.

4. Grill the chicken for 8 to 10 minutes, turning frequently and brushing several times with the marinade. The strips should just be starting to brown.

5. Serve with steamed rice or cooked noodles.

Guitar Dan's Lemon-Pepper Chicken

Yield: 6 servings

It's fun to make your own lemon pepper—a bit time consuming, sure, but it's something you can do with your kids or grandkids on a slow day. For directions, go to www.ehow.com/how_17352_make-homemade-lemon. This recipe comes from Dan Brodsky from Scotts Valley, Calif.

1 cup (236 mL) pink lemonade
1 cup (236 mL) ginger ale
6 large chicken breast halves
10 tablespoons (150 mL) lemon pepper, divided
2 teaspoons (10 mL) dried thyme
1 teaspoon (5 mL) dried oregano
½ teaspoon (2.5 mL) onion powder
1 pinch ground clove
1 cup (236 mL) apple juice
1 cup (236 mL) vegetable oil
1 lemon, thinly sliced
4–5 sprigs fresh parsley

1. Preheat the barbecue to medium high (350°F [180°C] to 400°F [200°C]) for indirect heating, putting a water pan under the unheated side of the grill.

2. Mix together the pink lemonade and ginger ale. Add the chicken breasts and marinate, covered, for 30 minutes at room temperature. In a small bowl, combine 8 tablespoons (120 mL) of the lemon pepper, the thyme, oregano, onion powder, and clove, stir, and set aside. Remove the breasts from the marinade and rub them all over with the seasoning rub, including under the skin if you can. Refrigerate for 1 hour.

3. In a small bowl, combine the apple juice, oil, and the remaining lemon pepper.

4. Grill the chicken breasts over indirect heat for 20 minutes on each side, brushing lavishly and frequently with the sauce. The chicken is done when it's nicely browned and a thermometer inserted into the thick part of the breast reads 165°F (74°C).

5. Place the chicken on a serving tray, garnish with lemon slices and parsley, and serve.

Char-Baked Chicken and Dumplings
Yield: 4 servings

You could make this dish with just breasts or thighs, but I like getting forkfuls of dark and white meat. This is also a super dish for leftover turkey.

1 (3–3½ pound [1.3–1.6 kg]) chicken, cut in serving-size pieces
1½ cups (354 mL) frozen chopped carrots, thawed and drained
1½ cups (354 mL) frozen peas, thawed and drained
1 large onion, peeled and diced
1 tablespoon (15 mL) dried oregano
1 (10¾-ounce [301-g]) can condensed cheddar cheese soup
1 (10¾-ounce [301-g]) can condensed cream of mushroom with garlic soup
½ cup (118 mL) milk
½ teaspoon (2.5 mL) grated fresh ginger
1 cup (236 mL) biscuit mix
¼ cup (59 mL) yellow cornmeal
1 tablespoon (15 mL) finely crumbled bacon
3 tablespoons (45 mL) heavy cream

1. Boil the chicken in water for 1 hour, or until tender. Remove the chicken from the pot and cut it into small pieces, removing all bones, cartilage, and skin. Spray a 4-quart (3.8-L) Dutch oven with nonstick cooking or grilling spray and spread the chicken on the bottom of it. Cover the chicken with the carrots, peas, and diced onion. Sprinkle with oregano and stir to mix.

2. Preheat the barbecue to medium high (350°F [180°C] to 400°F [200°C]).

3. In a large bowl, combine the two soups. Add the milk and grated ginger and whisk everything together. Remove ½ cup (118 mL) of the mixture and reserve. Pour the remainder over the chicken pieces in the Dutch oven and cover the pan.

4. Bake in the barbecue for 30 minutes. Remove the cover, stir to mix the sauce and juices from chicken, replace the cover, and bake for 30 minutes more.

5. Open vents, add charcoal, or turn up the gas to increase the temperature to 450°F (240°C).

6. In a large bowl, stir together the biscuit mix, cornmeal, and bacon. Whisk in the cream and the reserved soup mixture to make a wet dough.

7. Remove the Dutch oven from the grill, drop spoonfuls of the dough on top of the chicken, return the oven to the barbecue, and bake for 20 to

25 minutes more, or until the biscuit dumplings are nicely browned on top and have puffed up.

8. Serve at the table, spooning the chicken mixture into wide soup bowls and topping each serving with 1 or 2 dumplings.

Charcoal-Grilled Chicken, Sinaloa-Style
Yield: 8 servings

Another way to cook this dish is over an open charcoal barbecue. Place the chicken in a wire fish holder, close, and lock. Place the basket 6 to 8 inches (15 to 20 cm) over grey coals. Cook, turning and basting often with the marinade, for 30 to 35 minutes.

2 (3½–4 pound [1.5–1.8 kg]) whole chickens
1 (12-ounce [341-mL]) bottle Pacifico or Tecate Mexican beer
1⅓ cups (315 mL) freshly squeezed orange juice
1 tablespoon (15 mL) epazote
2 teaspoons (10 mL) garlic salt
2 teaspoons (10 mL) chili powder
1 teaspoon (5 mL) dried thyme
1 teaspoon (5 mL) dried marjoram
1 teaspoon (5 mL) dried oregano
1 teaspoon (5 mL) freshly ground black pepper
4 bay leaves, broken into pieces
1 large onion, peeled and cut in ¼-inch (0.5-cm) slices
8 cloves garlic, peeled and chopped

1. Using kitchen shears, cut down both sides of the backbone of each chicken, through the joints where the legs attach, then on through the ribs. Remove the backbone.

2. In a food processor, combine the beer, orange juice, epazote, garlic salt, chili powder, thyme, marjoram, oregano, and black pepper and process. Place both chickens in a 2-gallon (7.6-L) resealable plastic bag, pour in the marinade, add the bay leaves, seal the bag, and shake to coat the chicken. Refrigerate for 4 to 6 hours or overnight, turning several times.

4. Preheat the barbecue to medium high (350°F [180°C] to 400°F [200°C]).

5. Remove the chicken from the marinade. Pour the marinade into a saucepan, add the onions and garlic, and boil it for 10 minutes while the chicken comes to room temperature.

6. Lay the chickens flat on the grill, skin side up, and grill for 35 to 45 minutes, turning and basting with the marinade every 10 minutes. They are ready when the meat is tender and a fork pricked deep into the thigh releases clear, not pink, juices. Discard the bay leaves.

7. Pour the remaining marinade into a saucepan and boil for 10 minutes. Cut the chickens into quarters and lay them on a warm platter. Drizzle with the remaining marinade/sauce and serve.

Mandarin Mandarin Chicken

Yield: 6 servings

Almost 100 percent of the canned mandarin oranges sold in the United States come from China, and almost all of those are the seedless Satsuma variety, which are grown in Japan.

1 (15-ounce [420-g]) can plus 1 (7-ounce [196-g]) can mandarin oranges
½ cup (118 mL) soy sauce
¼ cup (59 mL) vegetable oil
¼ cup (59 mL) chopped onion
1 tablespoon (15 mL) curry powder
1 tablespoon (15 mL) sesame seeds
2 teaspoons (10 mL) chili powder
¼ teaspoon (1.25 mL) garlic powder
2 (3–3½ pound [1.3–1.6 kg]) chickens, quartered

1. Drain the small can of mandarin oranges, reserving the juice.

2. In a food processor or blender, combine the soy sauce, the large can of mandarin oranges, the juice from the small can of mandarin oranges, the vegetable oil, the onion, the curry powder, the sesame seeds, the chili powder, and the garlic powder and process until smooth.

3. Place the chicken quarters in a 1- to 2-gallon (3.8- to 7.6-L) resealable plastic bag and pour the marinade into the bag over the chicken. Seal the bag and refrigerate for 3 to 4 hours, turning occasionally.

4. Preheat the barbecue to medium high (350°F [180°C] to 400°F [200°C]) for indirect heating, putting a water pan under the unheated side of the grill.

5. Remove chicken from the marinade. Pour the marinade into a saucepan and boil for 10 minutes while the chicken comes to room temperature.

6. Place the drained chicken quarters on the unheated side of the grill and cook, turning and basting frequently with the marinade, for about 40 minutes or until a thermometer inserted in the thick part of the breast registers 165°F (74°C).

7. Place cooked chicken on a platter, pour the orange sauce over it, garnish with the reserved mandarin orange segments, and serve.

Grilled Chikin Chili

Yield: 4 servings

Cumin is the second most popular spice in the world (after black pepper). It can be used whole or ground, and it adds an earthy and warming flavor to any foods in which it is used.

1 pound (454 g) boneless, skinless chicken thighs
1½ teaspoons (7.5 L) canola oil
1 large sweet onion, peeled and chopped
2 ribs celery, chopped
1 clove garlic, peeled and minced
1 (15-ounce [420-g]) can pinto beans, drained
1 (14-ounce [392-g]) can diced tomatoes
1 green bell pepper, diced
2 teaspoons (10 mL) chili powder
1 teaspoon (5 mL) ground cumin
¼ teaspoon (1.25 mL) celery salt
¼ teaspoon (1.25 mL) freshly ground black pepper
Shredded cheddar cheese, for serving
Chopped onions, for serving
Sour cream, for serving

1. Preheat the barbecue to medium high (350°F [180°C] to 400°F [200°C]). Spray a Dutch oven with nonstick cooking or grilling spray.

2. Brush the thighs with the oil and grill for 8 minutes per side, or until they are lightly browned, turning once. Remove any fat and cut the chicken into ½-inch (1-cm) pieces.

3. Place chicken in the prepared Dutch oven. Add the onion, celery, and garlic. Put the pot in the barbecue and cook until the vegetables are tender, about 10 minutes.

4. Open the Dutch oven and add the beans, tomatoes, green pepper, chili powder, cumin, celery salt, and black pepper. Cover simmer for 30 minutes, stirring several times.

5. Remove the cover and let the chili simmer for 15 to 20 minutes longer, or until the liquid has reduced by a third and the chili starts to thicken.

6. Serve in bowls with side bowls of shredded cheddar cheese, chopped onions, and sour cream.

Thai-d Up Chicken
Yield: 4 servings

Store fresh lemongrass in a tightly sealed plastic bag in the refrigerator for up to 3 weeks. You can also freeze it for about 6 months without any flavor loss.

¼ cup (59 mL) plus 3 tablespoons (45 mL) soy sauce, divided
2 tablespoons (30 mL) curry powder
1 tablespoon (15 mL) fish sauce
1 tablespoon (15 mL) grated fresh ginger
1 tablespoon (15 mL) honey
1 teaspoon (5 mL) five-spice powder
1 garlic clove, peeled and minced
1 stalk lemongrass, coarsely chopped
Freshly ground black pepper, to taste
1 pound (454 g) skinless, boneless chicken thighs
½ cup (118 mL) coconut milk
½ cup (118 mL) creamy or crunchy peanut butter
1 tablespoon (15 mL) Sriracha sauce
4 (½-inch [1-cm]) thick pineapple slices, cubed
1 medium onion, peeled and cubed
1 medium green bell pepper, cubed

1. In a food processor, combine the 3 tablespoons (45 mL) of the soy sauce, curry powder, fish sauce, ginger, the honey, five-spice powder, garlic, lemongrass, and the black pepper in a food processor and process until smooth. Chop the chicken into 1-inch (2.5-cm) cubes and put them in a 1-gallon (3.8-L) resealable plastic bag. Pour in the marinade, seal the bag, and shake to coat the chicken with the marinade. Refrigerate for 4 to 6 hours or overnight, turning several times.

2. Preheat the barbecue to medium high (350°F [180°C] to 400°F [200°C]).

3. Remove the chicken from the marinade and discard the liquid.

4. In a small saucepan, boil the coconut milk, peanut butter and Sriracha sauce together until the mixture begins to bubble, stirring often. Remove from the heat and keep warm.

5. Thread 4 or 5 cubes of chicken onto a skewer, interspersed with cubed pineapple, onion, and green pepper. Repeat with the remaining chicken and vegetables.

6. Cook skewers on the grill for 5 to 6 minutes on each side, brushing several times with the peanut sauce, or until the chicken is browned and vegetables are lightly charred on the edges.

7. Boil remaining peanut sauce for 10 minutes.

8. Place the skewers on a serving platter, drizzle with some of the remaining sauce, and serve.

Marti's Martini-Grilled Chicken
Yield: 4 servings

For a different taste, try adding pineapple juice and raspberry liquor (French martini), apple juice and schnapps (apple martini), mandarin orange vodka and cranberry juice (sunset martini), or any of a thousand other varieties of fruit juices mixed with gin. This recipe comes from Martha J. Browne from Indianapolis, Ind.

¼ cup (59 mL) fresh lemon juice
¼ cup (59 mL) dry gin
2 tablespoons (30 mL) vermouth
1 teaspoon (5 mL) grated lemon zest
1 teaspoon (5 mL) sugar
½ teaspoon (2.5 mL) dried oregano
Salt, to taste
Freshly ground black pepper, to taste
¼ cup (59 mL) vegetable oil
4 skinless chicken breasts

1. Preheat the barbecue to medium high (350°F [180°C] to 400°F [200°C]).

2. In a shallow dish, whisk together the lemon juice, gin, vermouth, lemon zest, sugar, oregano, salt, and pepper. Add the oil in a thin stream, whisking until it is emulsified.

3. Place the breasts in a 1-gallon (3.8-L) resealable plastic bag. Pour in the marinade, seal the bag, and shake to coat the chicken. Refrigerate for 4 to 6 hours or overnight, turning several times.

4. Remove chicken from the marinade. Pour the marinade into a saucepan and boil it for 10 minutes while the chicken comes to room temperature.

5. Grill the chicken for 10 to 12 minutes on each side, or until it is cooked through and a thermometer inserted into the thick part of the breast reads 165°F (74°C).

6. Place the breasts on a serving platter and drizzle with the remaining marinade.

Flying Jacob (Swedish Chicken Casserole)
Yield: 4–6 servings

The cook who devised this recipe, Ove Jacobsson, worked for an air-freight company. Hence the name for this very popular—in Sweden, anyway—dish. This recipe comes from Seija Nappe from Sundsval, Sweden.

8 slices smoked bacon
Oil for the skillet
4 boneless, skinless chicken breasts, cut into 1-inch (2.5-cm) pieces
Salt, to taste
Freshly ground black pepper to taste
½ cup (118 mL) chili sauce (or spicy ketchup)
1½ cups (354 mL) heavy cream
3 ripe bananas
1½ cups (354 mL) chopped peanuts
4 cups (0.95 L) cooked white rice

1. Preheat the barbecue to medium high (350°F [180°C] to 400°F [200°C]).

2. In a pan, fry the bacon slices over medium heat just until they start to crisp up. Remove the bacon from the pan and let it drain. Chop it into ½-inch (1-cm) pieces and set aside.

3. Oil a cast-iron skillet. Place half of the chicken pieces in the skillet and season with salt and pepper. Put the skillet in the barbecue and cook until the chicken is golden and completely cooked. Transfer the cooked chicken to a bowl. Repeat with the remaining chicken.

4. Whisk the chili sauce into the cream and mix thoroughly.

5. Put the rice in a Dutch oven or roasting dish. Top with the chicken and bacon. Cut 2 of the bananas into ½-inch (1-cm) thick slices and add it to the meat. Then pour on the cream-chili mixture and distribute it evenly. Slice and add the remaining banana. Add the chopped peanuts and place the Dutch oven in the barbecue to bake until the sauce gets a bit darker, about 15 to 25 minutes.

6. Serve with steamed rice.

Chicken Napolitano

Yield: 4–6 servings

You don't have to use Chianti; you can use any red or white wine in this dish, or even plain old water. But the wine must stand up to the lemons and the large amount of garlic, and Italian reds are among the hardiest wines.

¼ cup (59 mL) vegetable oil
1 (3–4 pound [1.3–1.8 kg]) chicken, split in half
8 cloves garlic, peeled and chopped
3 whole lemons, peel included, chopped
1 bunch fresh parsley, chopped
¼ cup (59 mL) chopped fresh oregano, chopped
2 teaspoons (10 mL) freshly ground black pepper
1 teaspoon (5 mL) kosher salt
 1 cup (236 mL) Chianti

1. Wash the chicken, drain, and pat dry.

2. Preheat the barbecue to medium high (350°F [180°C] to 400°F [200°C]).

3. Pour the oil in a shallow roasting pan and spread it over the bottom of the pan. Add the chicken pieces and cover with the garlic, lemons, parsley, oregano, pepper, and salt. Add the wine and put the pan in the barbecue. Cook for 40 minutes.

4. Remove the pan from the barbecue and transfer the chicken pieces to a flat pan. Let the chicken drain.

5. Pour the remaining contents of the pan into a food processor and process until almost smooth.

6. Place the drained chicken directly on the hot grill and cook for 4 minutes per side, basting once on each side, to crisp and brown the skin.

7. Place the cooked chicken on a platter and either spoon some of the sauce over each piece or pour it into a sauce boat for people to add at the table.

Spicy Grilled Punjab Chicken
Yield: 4 servings

If you can't find garam masala, you can make your own by combining ½ teaspoon (2.5 mL) each ground cumin and paprika with ¼ teaspoon (1.25 mL) each ground cinnamon, cayenne pepper, black pepper, and crumbled bay leaves and ⅛ teaspoon (0.6 mL) ground cloves.

1 (3-pound [1.3-kg]) chicken
3 tablespoons (45 mL) vegetable oil
2 tablespoons (30 mL) lemon juice
2 tablespoons (30 mL) plain yogurt
1 tablespoon (15 mL) freshly ground black pepper
1 tablespoon (15 mL) paprika
1 tablespoon (15 mL) garam masala
2 teaspoons (10 mL) ground cumin
2 teaspoons (10 mL) ground oregano
1 teaspoon (5 mL) salt
½ teaspoon (2.5 mL) hot chili powder
1 garlic clove, peeled and crushed
Cooked rice, for serving

1. Preheat the barbecue to medium high (350°F [180°C] to 400°F [200°C]).

2. Cut the chicken into wings, drumsticks, thighs, and 3 breast pieces.

3. In a medium bowl, combine all the remaining ingredients and mix well. Wearing rubber or plastic gloves, rub the paste well on every piece of chicken.

4. Place the chicken in the barbecue, skin side up, over direct heat and cook for 20 minutes, turning the pieces often so they all brown evenly.

5. Serve with steamed or boiled rice.

Chicken Tikka Kebabs

Yield: 4 servings

If you don't have saffron handy and don't want to have to take out a loan to buy some, you can use ¼ teaspoon (0.6 mL) of turmeric instead. It provides a rich yellow-orange color similar to what the unbelievably expensive saffron would produce.

1 cup (236 mL) plain yogurt
1 tablespoon (15 mL) curry powder
1 tablespoon (15 mL) olive oil, plus more for brushing
1 teaspoon (5 mL) grated garlic
1 (½-inch [1-cm]) piece fresh ginger, peeled and grated
½ teaspoon (2.5 mL) whole cumin seeds
¼ teaspoon (1.25 mL) ground white pepper
¼ teaspoon (1.25 mL) cayenne pepper
⅛ teaspoon (0.6 mL) saffron
Salt, to taste
Freshly ground black pepper, to taste
1 pinch ground nutmeg
3 large boneless, skinless chicken breasts, cut into 1½–2-inch (3.5–5-cm) pieces

1. In a large bowl, whisk together the yogurt, curry powder, olive oil, garlic, ginger, cumin, white pepper, cayenne pepper, saffron, salt, pepper, and nutmeg. Put the chicken in a 1- to 2-gallon (3.8- to 7.6-L) resealable plastic bag and pour the marinade in over them. Seal the bag and shake to coat the chicken. Refrigerate for 4 to 6 hours or overnight, turning several times.

2. Preheat the barbecue to medium high (350°F [180°C] to 400°F [200°C]).

3. Remove the chicken from the marinade and discard, let the chicken come to room temperature. Thread the chicken pieces onto metal or soaked bamboo skewers.

4. Place the skewers directly on the grill and cook for 4 to 5 minutes per side, turning several times so they do not burn and brushing several times with olive oil.

5. Serve the kebabs with pita bread and bowls of chopped tomatoes, chopped onions, and chopped parsley.

Pineapple-Chili Chicken Wings
Yield: 4–6 servings

I suggest using Anaheim or poblano chilies, which are two of the milder but are still quite hot. If you're a glutton for punishment, go ahead and use jalapeño or serrano peppers.

½ cup (118 mL) green chili peppers, peeled and seeded
1 cup (236 mL) pineapple juice
½ cup (118 mL) mashed pineapple chunks
¼ cup (60 mL) garlic powder
2½ tablespoons (30 mL) paprika
2 tablespoons (30 mL) salt
1 tablespoon (15 mL) lemon pepper
1 tablespoon (15 mL) soy sauce
¼ cup (59 mL) vegetable or olive oil
5 pounds (2.3 kg) chicken wings, separated, tips discarded

1. In a food processor, purée the chilies. Transfer the chilies to a bowl and add the pineapple juice and chunks, garlic powder, paprika, salt, lemon pepper, soy sauce, and oil and stir well.

2. Put the chicken wings in a wide, flat pan and cover them with the marinade. Refrigerate for 2 hours, turning the wings over often.

3. Preheat the barbecue to medium high (350°F [180°C] to 400°F [200°C]).

4. Remove the chicken from the marinade. Pour the marinade into a saucepan and boil it for 10 minutes while the chicken comes to room temperature. If you like your wings fiery, add a teaspoon (5 mL) of cayenne pepper to the marinade as it boils.

5. With tongs, place the wings on a baking sheet or a sheet of aluminum foil draped over the grilling surface, making sure the wings don't touch. Grill the wings, basting as needed with the saved marinade. The wings are done when they are browned and the edges are turning crispy.

Coca-Cola Barbecued Chicken
Yield: 4 servings

If you prefer another famous cola, use that instead. You could also use Dr. Pepper, RC Cola, or a local inexpensive cola.

3 pounds (1.3 kg) chicken, cut-up
⅓ cup (79 mL) all-purpose flour
2 teaspoons (10 mL) hickory salt
⅓ cup (79 mL) vegetable oil
1 cup (236 mL) ketchup
1 cup (236 mL) Coke
½ cup (118 mL) diced onion
½ cup (118 mL) diced celery
½ cup (118 mL) diced green bell pepper
2 tablespoons (30 mL) Worcestershire sauce
1 teaspoon (5 mL) chili powder

1. Preheat the barbecue to medium high (350°F [180°C] to 400°F [200°C]).

2. Rinse the chicken pieces and pat them dry. In a small brown paper bag, combine the flour and hickory salt. Add the chicken pieces to the bag and shake the bag to coat the chicken with the seasoned flour.

3. In a cast-iron skillet, heat the oil. Add the chicken and cook until browned. Transfer the chicken to paper towels to drain, then place the browned chicken in a 4-quart Dutch oven.

4. In medium bowl, combine the ketchup, Coke, onion, celery, bell pepper, Worcestershire sauce, and chili powder and mix well. Spoon the sauce over the chicken to cover. Place in the barbecue, cover, and bake about 1 to 1¼ hours, or until chicken is fork tender. Turn pieces over 1 to 2 times.

5. Transfer the chicken to a platter, cover it with foil, let it rest for 5 minutes, and serve.

Cranberry-Barbecued Wings

Yield: 4 servings

You could also use whole-berry canned cranberries. Just puree them first and add an extra ½ teaspoon (2.5 mL) sugar to the sauce.

1 (8-ounce [227-g]) can jellied cranberry sauce
1½ teaspoons (7.5 mL) dark brown sugar
1 teaspoon (5 mL) prepared mustard
1 teaspoon (5 mL) Worcestershire sauce
3½ pounds (1.6 kg) chicken wings (about 18)

1. In a medium saucepan, combine the cranberry sauce, brown sugar, mustard, and Worcestershire sauce and bring to a boil. Lower the heat and simmer for 20 minutes.

2. Preheat the barbecue to medium high (350°F [180°C] to 400°F [200°C]).

3. Using tongs, dip each wing into the sauce and shake off the excess. Thread the wings onto skewers (3 or 4 per skewer). Grill the skewered wings for 20 to 25 minutes, turning frequently and brushing with the sauce, until the wings are nicely browned all over, with a few charred edges.

4. Remove the wings from the barbecue and from the skewers and serve.

Afghan Chicken
Yield: 4 servings

Long, slow marinating in garlicky yogurt tenderizes, moistens, and adds deep flavor to the chicken, so you end up with a dish that's as delicious as it is nutritionally correct.

3 cups (708 mL) plain whole-milk yogurt
2 tablespoons (30 mL) lemon juice
2 large cloves garlic, peeled and chopped
1 large lemon, halved and seeded
1½ teaspoons (7.5 mL) salt
1 teaspoon (5 mL) ground cardamom
½ teaspoon (2.5 mL) cracked black pepper
2 large boneless, skinless chicken breasts
Soft pita or flatbread, for serving
Plain yogurt, for serving

1. In a blender, combine the yogurt, lemon juice, garlic, lemon halves, salt, cardamom, and pepper and blend until smooth.

2. Put the breasts in a flat pan, cut deep slashes into the meat side of the breasts, and spoon the yogurt mixture onto each breast, turning them and making sure all sides are covered with the marinade, ending up with the breasts bone-side down and the top of the chicken thickly covered with the yogurt. Cover the pan with plastic wrap and refrigerate overnight or as long as 36 hours. Don't bother to turn them over.

3. Preheat the barbecue to medium high (350°F [180°C] to 400°F [200°C]).

4. Remove the breasts from the marinade and wipe off all but a thin film. Grill for 6 to 8 minutes per side, or until thoroughly cooked. The meat will brown somewhat, but it should not char.

5. Serve with soft pita or Arab flatbread and fresh yogurt.

Lemon-Garlic Roasted Chicken with Garlic Sauce

Yield: 4 servings

Garlic Sauce

2 tablespoons (30 mL) olive oil
1 large head of garlic, cloves separated and peeled
2 teaspoons (10 mL) grated lemon zest
1 (14½-ounce [406-g]) can chicken broth
½ cup (118 mL) water
3 sprigs fresh parsley
2 tablespoons (30 mL) butter, softened, divided

Chicken

1 (3½–4 pound [1.6–1.8 kg]) chicken
Salt, to taste
Freshly ground black pepper, to taste
¼ cup (59 mL) plus 2 tablespoons (30 mL) butter, softened
2 lemons, quartered and seeded
1 small onion, peeled and quartered
4–6 cloves garlic, peeled
6 sprigs fresh rosemary
Fresh parsley sprigs, for garnish
Thin lemon slices, for garnish

1. Preheat the barbecue to medium high (350°F [180°C] to 400°F [200°C]) for indirect heating, putting a water pan under the unheated side of the grill.

2. In a small saucepan, heat the oil over medium-low heat. Add the garlic cloves and lemon zest and cook, stirring frequently, until the garlic just begins to brown. Stir in the broth, water, and parsley and heat until the mixture begins to bubble. Pour the sauce into a blender, process until smooth, and set aside.

3. Rinse chicken and pat it dry with paper towels. Season with salt and pepper, then massage the butter into the skin. Place the lemons, onion, garlic, and rosemary in the cavity.

4. Place the chicken, breast side up, on the grill directly above the drip pan. Close the barbecue and grill for about 1 hour, or until a meat thermometer inserted in the breast registers 165°F (74°C) and the juices run clear when the thigh is pierced.

5. When chicken is done, carefully transfer it from the grill to a cutting board. Let it sit, covered, for 10 minutes to recirculate the internal juices. Pour the garlic purée into a saucepan and whisk in the remaining butter over low heat until smooth.

6. Carve the chicken and serve it alongside a sauce boat of the warm garlic sauce. Garnish with the parsley and lemon slices.

Peruvian Grilled Chicken Thighs

Yield: 4 servings

This is my interpretation of a dish to served me at a Peruvian restaurant in Rio de Janiero. I passed on the grilled guinea pigs and chose this chicken dish instead, but even though I loved it, I always regretted not trying the local favorite: grilled pet.

2 ripe tomatoes, chopped
1 red onion, peeled and chopped
1 clove garlic, chopped
1 (7-ounce [196-g]) jar roasted red peppers, drained
¼ cup (59 mL) fresh cilantro leaves
¾ teaspoon (3.75 mL) salt, divided
⅛ teaspoon (0.6 mL) freshly ground black pepper
1 teaspoon (5 mL) ground coriander
¼ teaspoon (1.25 mL) cayenne pepper
8 chicken thighs

1. In a food processor, combine the tomatoes, onion, garlic, roasted peppers, cilantro, ¼ teaspoon (1.25 mL) of the salt, and the pepper and process until smooth. Set aside.

2. Make sure the grill is clean and generously sprayed with nonstick grilling spray. Preheat the barbecue to medium high (350°F [180°C] to 400°F [200°C]).

3. In small bowl, mix together the coriander, cayenne pepper, and the remaining salt. Rub this mixture into the thighs.

4. Grill the chicken, turning several times, for about 12 minutes or until a thermometer inserted into the thick part registers 165°F (74°C)°.

5. Remove the chicken from the barbecue and place it on a serving platter. Spoon the sauce generously on top of the chicken pieces.

Orange Grilled Chicken
Yield: 4–6 servings

Tang, the orange powdered breakfast drink developed for the first U.S. astronauts, adds a unique citrusy (excuse the expression) tang to rubs and sauces. You could also use other powdered drink mixes, such lemonade or limeade.

1 cup (236 mL) barbecue sauce
1 cup (236 mL) orange marmalade
¼ cup (59 mL) diced onion
1 tablespoon (15 mL) Tang powdered breakfast drink
1 teaspoon (5 mL) garlic salt
1 teaspoon (5 mL) citrus pepper
2 (3–3½ pound [1.3–1.6 kg]) chickens, cut-up

1. Make sure the grill is clean and generously sprayed with nonstick grilling spray. Preheat the barbecue to medium high (350°F [180°C] to 400°F [200°C]).

2. In a small bowl, combine the barbecue sauce, marmalade, onion, Tang, garlic salt, and citrus pepper. Mix well.

3. Place chicken, skin side down, on the grill and cook for 15 to 20 minutes, turning frequently and brushing with the sauce during the last 10 minutes, or until the chicken is tender and the juices run clear when the chicken is pierced with a knife.

4. In a small saucepan, heat the remaining sauce until it bubbles. Set aside.

5. Transfer the chicken pieces to a serving platter, drizzle with sauce, and serve.

Grilled Key Lime Chicken Pie
Yield: 4–6 servings

Unless you live in Florida, the "key limes" you buy in the supermarket aren't really key limes. Genuine key limes are only grown in Florida, and other varieties are grown in California, Texas, Mexico, and Central America.

1 cup (236 mL) key lime juice
¾ cup (177 mL) water
2 tablespoons (30 mL) vegetable oil
1 tablespoon (15 mL) grated fresh ginger
1 tablespoon (15 mL) honey
½ teaspoon (2.5 mL) freshly ground black pepper
½ teaspoon (2.5 mL) ground thyme
3 pounds boneless, skinless chicken breasts
1 package (9-inch [22.5-cm]) refrigerated deep-dish pie crust
1½ cups (354 mL) frozen corn, thawed and drained
1 cup (236 mL) small pearl onions, peeled

1. In a blender or food processor, combine the lime juice, water, oil, ginger, honey, pepper, and thyme and process until well combined.

2. Cut chicken breasts into 1-inch (2.5-cm) wide strips and place them in a 1- to 2-gallon (3.8- to 7.6-L) resealable plastic bag. Pour the marinade over the chicken, seal the bag, and refrigerate overnight.

3. Preheat the barbecue to medium high (350°F [180°C] to 400°F [200°C]) for direct and indirect heating, putting a water pan under the unheated side of the grill.

4. Wipe most of the marinade off the chicken and reserve the marinade left in the bag. Grill the strips for 5 minutes per side. Remove the chicken from the grill, cut it into ½-inch (1-cm) cubes. Line a pie tin with one of the piecrusts. Add the cubed chicken to the crust. Add the corn and pearl onions and stir gently. Pour the reserved marinade over the chicken and vegetables. Put the second crust on top; wet the edges with water, and press the crusts together with your fingers and a fork. Cut 3 small slits in the top crust to let steam escape.

5. Place the pie on the unheated side of the grill, and bake for 30 to 35 minutes, or until the pastry is golden brown and the filling is bubbly. Cool for 10 minutes before serving.

Grilled Sesame Chicken Breasts
Yield: 4 servings

Sesame seeds have a nutty, sweet aroma with a milky, buttery taste. When toasted, their flavor intensifies, yielding an almond- or peanut butter–like flavor. Sesame seeds are available in white, brown, black, and even red varieties.

¼ cup (59 mL) soy sauce
2 tablespoons (30 mL) white sesame seeds
1 tablespoon (15 mL) brown sugar
1 tablespoon (15 mL) minced garlic
1 tablespoon (15 mL) dark sesame oil
½ teaspoon (2.5 mL) freshly ground black pepper
¾ pound (340 g) skinless chicken breasts, cut into 1 × 3 × ½-inch (2.5 × 7.5 ×1-cm) strips
1 tablespoon (15 mL) black sesame seeds

1. In a small bowl, mix together the soy sauce, white sesame seeds, brown sugar, garlic, sesame oil, and pepper. Put the chicken in a 1-gallon (3.8-L) resealable plastic bag. Pour the marinade in over the chicken, seal the bag, and shake to mix well. Refrigerate for 2 to 4 hours.

2. Remove chicken from the marinade. Pour the marinade into a saucepan and boil for 10 minutes while the chicken comes to room temperature.

3. Preheat the barbecue for direct heating at 325F (165°C) to 350F (180°C). Make sure the grill has been well oiled or sprayed with a grilling spray.

4. Grill the chicken strips for 6 to 8 minutes, or until they have browned nicely, turning and basting often with the boiled marinade.

5. Place the strips on a serving platter, sprinkle with the black sesame seeds, and serve.

Hogan's Nuclear Chicken Wings

Yield: 4–6 servings

These are already ridiculously hot, but you can increase the temperature by adding chopped habañero peppers to the basting sauce.

¼ cup (59 mL) packed brown sugar
3 tablespoons (45 mL) habañero hot sauce
3 tablespoons (45 mL) Tabasco sauce
2 tablespoons (30 mL) olive oil
1 tablespoon (15 mL) distilled white vinegar
¼ teaspoon (1.25 mL) garlic powder
24 chicken wings, tips cut off and discarded
½ teaspoon (2.5 mL) cayenne pepper
Lettuce leaves, for serving
1 cup (236 mL) blue cheese salad dressing
Freshly cut celery stalks, for serving
Freshly cut carrot sticks, for serving

1. Preheat the barbecue to medium high (350°F [180°C] to 400°F [200°C]) for direct heating. Make sure the grill has been well oiled or sprayed with a grilling spray.

2. In a medium mixing bowl, combine the brown sugar, habañero sauce, Tabasco sauce, olive oil, vinegar, and garlic powder.

3. Place the wings on a baking sheet or a double layer of foil on the grill. Using a pastry brush, coat the wings with the sauce mixture, then sprinkle with the cayenne pepper. Bake the wings in the barbecue for 15 to 20 minutes, or until they are browned with some crispy, singed edges.

4. Arrange wings on the lettuce on a serving platter, and serve with bowls of the blue cheese dressing and sticks of celery and carrots to cool the effect of these fiery wings.

Jack Daniel's Tennessee Whiskey Chicken

Yield: 4–8 servings

Since the alcohol from the marinade and the sauce boils off, this could be served to children. Just don't tell them they're getting served Jack Daniel's without having to show ID.

2 (2–2½ pound [908 g–1.1 kg]) chickens, split in half
1½ cups (354 mL) Jack Daniel's bourbon whiskey, divided
Salt, to taste
Freshly ground black pepper, to taste
2 tablespoons (30 mL) butter
1 pound (454 g) white mushrooms, thinly sliced
6 green onions, white and green parts, chopped
2 cups (473 mL) Kitchen Bouquet browning and seasoning sauce

1. Split the two chickens down the backbone and remove the backbone. Place the chickens in a 2-gallon (7.6-L) resealable plastic bag. Pour in 1 cup (236 mL) of the whiskey, season with salt and pepper, seal the bag, and shake to mix. Refrigerate overnight or at least 4 hours.

2. Make sure the grill has been well oiled or sprayed with nonstick spray. Preheat the barbecue to medium high (350°F [180°C] to 400°F [200°C]).

3. Make a smoker package by putting a handful of soaked hickory or oak chips in a 12-inch (30-cm) square of heavy-duty aluminum foil, folding over the package, poking 3 or 4 holes in the top of the foil, and placing the package directly on the coals or open flame to add smoke to your grilling. Some suggest soaking the chips in the whiskey from the marinade instead of water, but you won't really notice any difference in the taste of the finished dish.

4. Remove the chickens from the marinade and grill them on the barbecue until browned all over, about 14 to 18 minutes, or until a thermometer inserted into the thick part of the breast reads 165°F (74°C).

5. While the chicken is grilling, heat the butter in a cast-iron or non-stick skillet. Add the mushrooms and green onion and sauté until tender. Add the remaining whiskey and the browning sauce and simmer for 10 minutes, or until the flavors have blended and the alcohol has evaporated. Keep the sauce warm.

6. Remove the chickens from the barbecue, cover them, and let them rest for 10 minutes. Separate the halves or quarter the chickens and serve.

Pico de Gallo Grilled Chicken
Yield: 6 servings

Pico de gallo, like most salsas, tastes much better served at room temperature, or even warmed slightly. Instead of the cherry tomatoes, you can use a regular tomato chopped into small pieces.

Pico de Gallo

12 small yellow cherry tomatoes, quartered
1 whole jalapeño pepper, seeded and minced
½ avocado, peeled, pitted, and chopped
¼ cup (59 mL) minced red onion
2 tablespoons (30 mL) teriyaki sauce
2 teaspoons (10 mL) fresh lime juice
Freshly grated zest from 1 lime
2 teaspoons (10 mL) minced fresh cilantro

Chicken

6 skinless, boneless chicken breast halves
½ cup (118 mL) teriyaki sauce
½ teaspoon (2.5 mL) grated lime zest
1 tablespoon (15 mL) lime juice
1 tablespoon (15 mL) minced garlic

1. In a medium bowl, combine the tomatoes, jalapeño pepper, and chopped avocado and stir gently to combine. Add the onion, teriyaki sauce, lime juice, lime zest, and cilantro and gently fold together. Cover the bowl with plastic wrap and set it aside so that the flavors can meld together.

2. Place the chicken breasts in a 1-gallon (3.8-L) resealable plastic bag. In a small bowl, combine the teriyaki sauce, lime zest, lime juice, and garlic and pour this marinade over the chicken. Seal the bag and shake to distribute the marinade. Marinate in the refrigerator for 1½ to 2 hours; turning the bag over occasionally.

3. Make sure the grill has been well oiled or sprayed with nonstick grilling spray. Preheat the barbecue to medium high (350°F [180°C] to 400°F [200°C]).

4. Remove the chicken from the marinade. Pour the marinade into a saucepan and boil for 10 minutes while the chicken comes to room temperature. Place the chicken breasts on the grill and cook, turning and basting occasionally, for 15 to 18 minutes, or until the chicken is tender and browned.

5. Place the chicken on a serving platter, spoon 1 tablespoon (15 mL) of pico de gallo over each breast, and serve.

Salt and Vinegar Grilled Chicken
Yield: 2–4 servings

If you wish, you can leave out the potato chip crumbs, but they really add a magic touch to this otherwise ordinary barbecued chicken recipe.

¼ cup (59 mL) olive oil
¼ cup (59 mL) red wine vinegar
2 tablespoons (30 mL) balsamic vinegar
2 teaspoons (10 mL) sugar
1 teaspoon (5 mL) dry mustard
1 teaspoon (5 mL) salt
½ teaspoon (2.5 mL) dried tarragon
½ teaspoon (2.5 mL) freshly ground black pepper
1 clove garlic, peeled and finely minced
¼ teaspoon (1.25 mL) dried rosemary
1 whole chicken, cut up
1 large egg
½ cup (118 mL) milk
½ cup crushed salt-and-vinegar potato chips

1. In a 2-gallon (7.6-L) resealable plastic bag, mix together the olive oil, vinegars, sugar, mustard, salt, tarragon, black pepper, garlic, and rosemary. Add the chicken pieces, seal the bag, and shake vigorously. Refrigerate overnight.

2. Preheat the barbecue to 350°F (180°C) to 375°F (190°C) for direct and indirect heating, putting a water pan under the unheated side of the grill.

3. Remove the chicken from the marinade and grill it, skin side up, turning every 10 minutes, for 30 minutes. In a small bowl, mix the egg with the milk. Remove the chicken from the barbecue and dip it in the egg mixture, then into the potato chip crumbs. Return the chicken to the barbecue and cook another 10 to 25 minutes, or until the coated chicken pieces are fork-tender and browned and a meat thermometer inserted into a piece registers 165°F (74°C).

Mustard–Garlic Chicken
Yield: 2 servings

This is a plain and simple way to barbecue. The wheat germ was something my mother always added. I never asked why, just ate my chicken like a good boy. I'm sure it's healthy, as the wheat germ is a concentrated source of protein, vitamins, and minerals.

2 tablespoons (30 mL) Dijon mustard
4 small cloves garlic, peeled
1 pinch cayenne pepper
Salt, to taste
Freshly ground black pepper, to taste
1 chicken breast, split
2 tablespoons (30 mL) wheat germ

1. Make sure the grill has been well oiled or sprayed with nonstick spray. Preheat the barbecue for direct heating at 350°F (180°C) to 400°F (200°C).

2. In a small food processor or a blender, process the mustard, garlic, cayenne pepper, salt, and pepper until smooth. Brush the mixture onto all surfaces of the chicken and lay the chicken in a shallow roasting pan. Sprinkle the wheat germ onto the chicken until evenly covered.

3. Grill until the chicken is nicely browned all over, about 12 to 15 minutes, turning often, or until a thermometer inserted in the breast shows an internal temperature of 165°F (74°C).

Pakistani Chicken Kebabs

Yield: 4–6 servings

You can substitute sour cream for the yogurt if you wish, but if you do, add 2 tablespoons (30 mL) of lime juice to the marinade,

1 pound (454 g) skinless, boneless chicken breasts, cut into 2-inch (5-cm) cubes
½ pound (227 g) chicken hearts
½ pound (227 g) chicken livers
2 cups (473 mL) plain yogurt
Freshly grated zest and juice of 1 lemon
1 tablespoon (15 mL) peanut oil
1 large onion, peeled and minced
2 teaspoons (10 mL) minced garlic
2 teaspoons (10 mL) grated fresh ginger
1 teaspoon (5 mL) sugar
⅛ teaspoon (0.6 mL) ground cinnamon
⅛ teaspoon (0.6 mL) ground nutmeg
⅛ teaspoon (0.6 mL) ground cumin
⅛ teaspoon (0.6 mL) kosher salt
⅛ teaspoon (0.6 mL) freshly ground black pepper
Paprika, for garnish

1. Place the chicken pieces, hearts, and livers in a 1-gallon (3.8-L) resealable plastic bag. In a small bowl, mix together the yogurt, lemon zest and juice, peanut oil, onion, garlic, ginger, sugar, cinnamon, nutmeg, cumin, salt, and black pepper. Pour this mixture into the bag over the chicken, shake to mix, and seal the bag. Marinate at room temperature for 2 hours, turning the bag several times.

2. Make sure the grill has been well oiled or sprayed with nonstick grilling spray. Preheat the barbecue for direct heating at 350°F (180°C) to 400°F (200°C).

3. Remove the chicken from the marinade. Pour the marinade into a saucepan and boil for 10 minutes. Alternate the breast meat, hearts, and livers on metal skewers. Place the skewers on the grill and cook for 10 to 12 minutes, turning often and basting with the cooked marinade.

4. When the chicken pieces have reached 160°F (71°C) and are nicely browned, the kebabs are ready. Sprinkle with paprika and serve on a platter of steamed rice.

Pan-Fried Parmigiano-Reggiano Chicken

Yield: 6 servings

Oven-baked chicken is healthier than deep-fried because less fat is used, but it tastes just as rich and sumptuous. If you are a fan of southern-fried chicken, you will love this oven-fried chicken recipe. The buttermilk adds a unique flavor and helps tenderize the chicken, and the cheese and flour turn into a golden-brown crust.

¼ cup (60 mL) butter
¾ cup (177 mL) buttermilk
1 cup (236 mL) all-purpose flour
½ cup (118 mL) freshly grated Parmigiano-Reggiano cheese
1 teaspoon (5 mL) dried oregano
1 teaspoon (5 mL) salt
1 teaspoon (5 mL) paprika
½ teaspoon (2.5 mL) dried thyme
½ teaspoon (2.5 mL) garlic powder
½ teaspoon (2.5 mL) black pepper
1 (3-pound [1.3-kg]) frying chicken, cut into pieces

1. Preheat the barbecue to medium high (400°F [200°C] to 425°F [220°C]) for direct and indirect heating, putting a water pan under the unheated side of the grill.

2. Line a shallow roasting pan with foil and put the pan in the barbecue. Put the butter in the pan and let it melt. Spread it around with a basting brush.

3. Pour the buttermilk into a bowl. In a separate bowl, combine the flour, cheese, oregano, salt, paprika, thyme, garlic powder, and pepper.

4. Dip the chicken pieces in the buttermilk, then into the seasoned flour. Place the chicken skin side down in the buttered pan and bake it in the barbecue for 30 minutes. Turn the pieces over, close the vents, place the pan on the unheated side of the grill, and bake for another 20 minutes.

5. Remove the fried chicken from the grill and serve with garlic mashed potatoes and grilled ears of corn.

Italian Stuffed Barbecued Chicken
Yield: 4 servings

½ cup (118 mL) soft breadcrumbs
⅓ cup (79 mL) freshly grated Parmigiano-Reggiano cheese
Salt, to taste
Freshly ground black pepper, to taste
5 sage leaves, roughly chopped
½ teaspoon (2.5 mL) sugar
¼ cup (59 mL) melted butter
½ cup (118 mL) hot water
1 (3-pound [1.3-kg]) chicken
2 large carrots
¾ cup (177 mL) dry or sweet white wine
¼ cup (59 mL) water
2 tablespoons (30 mL) extra virgin olive oil, plus more for brushing
4 sprigs rosemary

1. In a large bowl, combine the breadcrumbs, cheese, salt, pepper, sage leaves, sugar, and melted butter. Stir well to mix, then add the hot water and stir again.

2. Salt and pepper the inside of the chicken cavity, then stuff both ends of the chicken with the breadcrumb mix. Use poultry skewers to close the tail end so the stuffing won't fall out.

3. Preheat the barbecue to medium high (350°F [180°C] to 400°F [200°C]). Oil a roasting pan.

4. Peel the carrots, and cut them into quarters lengthwise. Arrange the carrots in the bottom of the prepared roasting pan. Pour the wine and water over the carrots, add the olive oil, and scatter with the rosemary sprigs.

5. Place the chicken on top of the carrots, brush the chicken with olive oil, and place the pan in the barbecue. Cook for 1¼ to 1½ hours, basting 3 to 4 times with the juices from the pan. If the chicken starts to get too brown on top, cover it loosely with foil, shiny side up.

6. Remove the chicken from the barbecue. With poultry shears, cut the chicken in half and spread the halves apart to let the stuffing get browned a bit. Baste one more time with the juices and transfer the chicken to a cutting board to rest for 10 minutes before carving.

7. Spoon the stuffing into a bowl and cover the bowl. Carve or quarter the chicken, placing the meat on a heated platter. Serve with the carrots and stuffing.

Sweet Chutney Chicken
Yield: 4 servings

Usually made fresh, chutney contains fruit and sugar to give it a sweet taste. Almost all chutney contains vinegar and aromatic spices such as clove, cinnamon, ginger, and onions, which give sour, hot and spicy flavors.

1 (8-ounce [227-g]) jar prepared chutney, spicy or sweet
½ cup (118 mL) orange marmalade
3 tablespoons (45 mL) fresh lemon juice
1 teaspoon (5 mL) salt
1 teaspoon (5 mL) curry powder
½ teaspoon (2.5 mL) ground cumin
1 pinch cinnamon
Freshly ground black pepper, to taste
1 tablespoon (15 mL) cornstarch
2 tablespoons (30 mL) hot water
1 (3½–4 pound [1.6–1.8 kg]) chicken, butterflied

1. Preheat the barbecue to high (450°F [240°C] to 500°F [260°C]) for direct heating.

2. In a 1-quart (0.95-L) saucepan, combine the chutney, marmalade, lemon juice, salt, curry powder, cumin, cinnamon, and pepper. Bring the mixture to a boil over medium high heat.

3. Meanwhile, stir the cornstarch into the hot water until smooth. Add the cornstarch mixture to the boiling chutney mixture. Boil for 1 minute, stirring. Remove the pan from the heat and set aside.

4. Arrange the chicken, skin side down, on a baking or roasting pan lined with foil (shiny side up). Bake for 20 minutes. Turn the chicken and bake for 20 minutes. Slather on the chutney sauce and bake for an additional 5 minutes, basting both sides.

5. Serve the chicken on a platter, cut into quarters, with the remaining sauce drizzled over the pieces.

Cedar Plank Chicken

Yield: 6–8 servings

You could also cook thick strips of chicken breast on the plank, but the leaner white meat can dry out too quickly. To cook chicken wings this way, remove the thin wing tip and cut the remaining wing in two sections. I get my planks from www.tailgatingplanks.com, and for this recipe I use their cedar plank.

2 tablespoons (30 mL) olive oil
1 clove garlic, minced
1 tablespoon (15 mL) chopped fresh basil
1 tablespoon (15 mL) chopped fresh oregano
1 tablespoon (15 mL) minced fresh parsley
½ teaspoon (2.5 mL) kosher salt
Freshly ground black pepper, to taste
½ cup (118 mL) grated Parmigiano-Reggiano cheese
2–3 pounds (908 g–1.3 kg) boneless chicken thighs, flattened

1. Soak a cedar plank in water for 4 to 6 hours or overnight.

2. Preheat the barbecue to medium high (350°F [180°C] to 400°F [200°C]) for indirect heating, placing a water pan under the grill.

3. In a food processor, combine the olive oil, garlic, basil, oregano, parsley, salt, and a few grinds of black pepper. Pulse for 10 to 15 seconds, then add the cheese and pulse for another 5 seconds.

4. Keep a spray bottle of water handy to extinguish any flames on the plank while the chicken is cooking. Place the chicken skin side up on the presoaked plank. Brush the chicken with the herb mixture, place the plank on an unheated portion of the grill, and cook for 35 to 40 minutes, or until the chicken is browned and a thermometer inserted into a thigh reads 165°F [74°C].

Chicken and Stuffing Bread

Yield: 4–6 servings

This recipe will work with most bread machines. It's best served warm and is fantastic for bacon, cheese and tomato sandwiches, which you can make even better by grilling.

1 cup (236 mL) chicken stock, at room temperature
1½ teaspoons (7.5 mL) active dry yeast
2⅛ cups (503 mL) bread flour
½ cup (118 mL) whole wheat flour
1⅞ tablespoons (28 mL) vital wheat gluten
1½ teaspoons sugar
1 tablespoon (15 mL) dried minced onion
1½ teaspoons (7.5 mL) hickory salt
1 tablespoon (15 mL) poultry seasoning
1 tablespoon (15 mL) olive oil
1 large egg, beaten
1 cup (236 mL) diced cooked (smoked) chicken
½ cup (118 mL) mushrooms, thinly sliced

1. Warm the stock. Bring all the ingredients to room temperature. Pour the yeast, bread flour, whole wheat flour, wheat gluten, sugar, onions, hickory salt, poultry dressing, olive oil, egg, and stock into the bread machine, in that order.

2. Set the baking control to medium.

3. Select "white bread" and push start.

4. Add the chicken and mushrooms 88 minutes into the cycle.

5. Serve warm for best results.

Baked Mushroom and Red Pepper Chicken
Yield: 4 servings

You can use breasts in this recipe if you wish; just cut them in half. We use thighs because they have more flavor and are moister and less expensive than the breasts.

3 red bell peppers
8 chicken thighs
1 cup (236 mL) all-purpose flour
2 tablespoons (30 mL) vegetable oil
1 red onion, peeled and chopped
1 white onion, peeled and chopped
3 green onions, white and green parts, chopped
1 tablespoon (15 mL) minced garlic
2 cups (473 mL) thinly sliced crimini mushrooms
1 tablespoon (15 mL) chopped fresh thyme
1 teaspoon (5 mL) chopped fresh rosemary
1 teaspoon (5 mL) chopped fresh oregano
¼ cup (59 mL) Greek yogurt
Salt, to taste
Freshly ground black pepper, to taste
1 cup (236 mL) chicken stock, or as needed
Paprika, for garnish

1. Grill the peppers over high heat until completely blackened. Wrap them in plastic wrap and let them rest for 20 minutes, then remove the plastic and pull off the skins. Remove the stems and seeds and slice the peppers into thin strips.

2. Preheat the barbecue to medium high (350°F [180°C] to 400°F [200°C]).

3. Roll the thighs in the flour. In a cast-iron Dutch oven or roasting pan, heat the oil. Add the thighs and sear until they are well browned. Remove the chicken from the pan and set aside. Add the onions and garlic to the pan and sauté over medium heat for about 15 to 20 minutes, or until the onions are translucent and just beginning to brown. Add the pepper strips, mushrooms, thyme, rosemary, oregano, and yogurt. Season with salt and pepper. Cook, stirring, for 5 minutes.

4. Return the chicken thighs to the pan and spoon the sauce over the thighs so they are covered. Cover the pan and cook for 50 minutes, or until the chicken is fork tender and falling off the bone, adding chicken stock as needed to keep the thighs covered.

5. Transfer the thighs to a warmed serving platter. Pour the yogurt-veggie sauce over the chicken, sprinkle with paprika, and serve.

Grilled Lemon and Artichoke Chicken
Yield: 4–8 servings

This is a favorite dish in the Mediterranean. This recipe was sent to me by a foodie friend who spent time on one of the Greek islands. This is my interpretation of the dish.

Sauce

1 large clove garlic, peeled and pressed
2 teaspoons (10 mL) kosher salt
6 tablespoons (90 mL) extra virgin olive oil
2 tablespoons (30 mL) fresh lemon juice

Marinade

¾ cup (177 mL) fresh lemon juice
Zest from 1 lemon
½ cup (118 mL) chopped fresh parsley
¼ cup (59 mL) light sesame oil
¼ cup (59 mL) olive oil
2 tablespoons (30 mL) minced garlic
1 teaspoon (5 mL) lemon salt
½ teaspoon (2.5 mL) freshly ground black pepper

Chicken

2 (3–4 pound [1.3–1.8 kg]) chickens, halved, backbones removed
12 baby artichokes, stems and outer leaves removed
4 lemons, halved lengthwise
¼ cup (59 mL) olive oil

1. To make the sauce, place the garlic and kosher salt in mortar and mash to a paste with a pestle. Transfer the paste to a small bowl. Add the oil and lemon juice, whisk to mix completely, and set aside.

2. Make the marinade. In a small bowl, combine the lemon juice, lemon zest, parsley, sesame and olive oils, garlic, lemon salt, and pepper and stir together. Place each chicken half in a 2-gallon (7.6-L) resealable plastic bag. Pour half the marinade into each bag, seal the bags, and shake to coat the chicken. Refrigerate for 4 to 12 hours, turning the bags occasionally.

3. Bring a large saucepan of salted water to a boil. Add the artichokes and cook until tender, about 8 minutes. Drain, cool, cut in half from top to bottom, and set aside.

4. Remove the chickens from the marinade; pour the marinade into a saucepan, and boil for 10 minutes while the chickens come to room temperature.

5. Preheat the barbecue to 350°F (180°C) to 400°F (200°C) for direct and indirect heating, putting a water pan under the unheated side of the grill.

6. Place the chickens, breast side down, on the unheated side of the grill. Cook for 45 minutes, then turn the chickens breast side up and grill for 20 to 25 minutes longer, or until a thermometer inserted into thickest part of thigh registers 165°F (74°C). Oil the lemon halves and place them on the grill halfway through this cooking time; they should be done at the same time as the chicken. Transfer the chickens to a cutting board, cover them with foil, and let rest for 10 minutes.

7. Place the chickens on a large serving platter and garnish with the artichokes and grilled lemons, which can also squeezed over the chickens and artichokes.

Tuscany Stuffed Chicken

Yield: 6 servings

---

6 boneless, skinless chicken breasts
6 ounces (168 g) chèvre
⅔ cup (158 mL) sun-dried tomatoes packed in olive oil
3 tablespoons (45 mL) chopped fresh basil
1 teaspoon (5 mL) kosher or coarse salt
½ cup (118 mL) all-purpose flour
3 large eggs, beaten
⅔ cup (158 mL) fresh sourdough breadcrumbs (or panko)
⅓ cup (79 mL) freshly grated Parmigiano Reggiano cheese
¼ cup (59 mL) melted butter

1. Preheat the barbecue to 350°F (180°C) to 400°F (200°C) for direct heating. Make sure the grill has been well oiled or sprayed with a grilling spray. Spray a roasting pan with nonstick cooking spray.

2. Place the chicken breasts in a heavy plastic bag and pound with a flat mallet or rolling pin until the chicken is about ⅓-inch (0.8-cm) thick.

3. In a food processor, combine the chèvre and sun-dried tomatoes and pulse until the mixture is combined but still has some chunks in it. Using a spatula, spread the mixture on the flattened chicken breasts and sprinkle with basil and salt. Roll up each breast, starting with smallest end, and tie in two places with butchers twine.

4. Put the flour in a shallow baking dish and put the beaten eggs in a second shallow dish. In a third shallow dish, combine the breadcrumbs and Parmigiano-Reggiano cheese. Dredge each chicken roll in the flour, then dip it in the egg wash, then press it into the crumbs to coat all sides.

5. Arrange the rolls in the prepared roasting pan so they are not touching each other. Bake for 40 to 50 minutes, or until the chicken is slightly browned and firm, brushing several times with the melted butter.

6. Remove the rolls from the barbecue and serve with grilled vegetables and your favorite pasta.

Guinness-Soused Chicken

Yield: 4 servings

The rich, full-bodied and slightly bitter taste of Guinness beer makes this dish sing. If you use an ordinary lager or pilsner beer, it just won't provide the same quality or punch that Guinness offers.

1 (3–4 pound [1.3–1.8 kg]) chicken, cut into serving pieces
2 tablespoons (30 mL) olive oil
1 tablespoon (15 mL) seasoned salt
1 (12-ounce [355-mL]) can Guinness Draught
1 tablespoon (15 mL) dark brown sugar
1 tablespoon (15 mL) lemon juice
1 tablespoon (15 mL) vegetable oil
1 tablespoon (15 mL) dark molasses
⅛ teaspoon (0.6 mL) hot sauce

1. Brush the chicken pieces with olive oil and rub the seasoned salt over each piece. Place the chicken pieces in a 2-gallon (7.6-kg) resealable plastic bag.

2. In a medium bowl, whisk together the beer, sugar, lemon juice, vegetable oil, and molasses. Pour this marinade into the bag over the chicken pieces, seal the bag, and shake to coat the chicken with the marinade. Refrigerate overnight.

3. Remove the chicken from the marinade. Add the hot sauce to the marinade.

4. Preheat the barbecue to 350°F (180°C) to 400°F (200°C) for indirect heating. Make sure the grill has been well oiled or sprayed with grilling spray.

5. Arrange the chicken, skin side up, on the unheated side of the grill and cook for 15 to 20 minutes, basting frequently. Turn the chicken over and continue cooking, brushing often with the marinade, until it is fork tender, 5 to 10 minutes longer. An instant-read thermometer inserted into the breast should read 165°F (74°C).

6. Put the chicken pieces on a platter and cover with foil. While the chicken cools, boil any remaining marinade for 10 minutes. Uncover the chicken, drizzle with marinade, and serve.

FIVE

Fish and Shellfish

Seafood Watch

All the recipes for fish or shellfish in this book follow the guidelines set out in the Seafood Watch program developed by the Monterey Bay Aquarium in Monterey, Calif. The following information is from its website (www.montereybayaquarium. org):

> The oceans supply us with food, help regulate our climate, and supply a livelihood for millions of people. Just as important, we depend on the oceans for recreation and renewal. But our seas are not the infinite bounty they appear to be. Today, no part of the oceans remains unaffected by human activities. And among the many factors influencing our ocean ecosystems, none has a greater impact than fishing.
>
> Humans have been fishing the oceans for thousands of years. But over the past five decades technology has allowed us to fish farther, deeper, and more efficiently than ever before. Scientists estimate that we have removed as much as 90 percent of the large predatory fish such as shark, swordfish, and cod from the world's oceans. In 2003, the Pew Oceans Commission warned that the world's oceans are in a state of "silent collapse," threatening our food supply, marine economies, recreation, and the natural legacy we leave our children.
>
> Ocean fish are wildlife—the last such creatures that we hunt on a large scale. And while the sheer size of the oceans is awesome, there are many signs that we have found their limits. Despite our best efforts, the global catch of wild fish leveled off over 20 years ago, and 70 percent of the world's fisheries are being harvested at capacity or are in decline.
>
> Yet there are fisheries being run in a sustainable way. We now need to improve the practices of the remaining fisheries and solve the most pressing issues, including overfishing, illegal and unregulated fishing, habitat damage, by-catch (accidentally catching unwanted species) and poor management.
>
> Aquaculture, or fish farming, sounds like a great solution to the ever-increasing pressures on our ocean resources. And it can be a useful alternative. Today, half of our seafood comes from farms. People are raising fish, shrimp, and oysters like farmers raise cattle and chickens. But the ecological impact of fish farming depends on the species chosen, where the farm is located, and how they are raised.
>
> As a society, we can create sustainable aquaculture that limits habitat damage; prevents the spread of disease and nonnative species; and minimizes the use of wild fish as feed.

Please dear readers, as you read this and peruse the following recipes, be aware of the fragility and value of our ocean and lake and river dwellers and, if the shrink wrapped packages of seafood you buy are not labeled, ask your butcher, grocer or seafood seller the origin of the fish or shellfish you are preparing to purchase.

You can easily download a copy or copies of the Monterey Bay Aquarium's regional Seafood Watch Pocket Guides at www.montereybayaquarium.org so that you can use them when your plan your fish and seafood barbecues.

Reprinted with permission of the Seafood Watch Program, Monterey Bay Aquarium.

French Crab Burgers
Yield: 4 servings

These burgers were inspired by French chef and cooking instructor Patrick Payette during a visit to Provence to film an episode of Barbecue America. *I loved them and wanted to share this treat.*

1 tablespoon (15 mL) celery seeds
6 bay leaves
1 teaspoon (5 mL) freshly ground black pepper
1 teaspoon (5 mL) sweet Hungarian paprika
½ teaspoon (2.5 mL) ground cardamom
½ teaspoon (2.5 mL) dry mustard
¼ teaspoon (1.25 mL) ground cloves
12 ounces (336 g) fresh crabmeat or 2 (6-ounce [168-g]) cans crabmeat, drained
3 cups (708 mL) fresh white breadcrumbs, divided
½ cup (118 mL) chopped green onions, green and white parts
4½ tablespoons (67.5 mL) mayonnaise, divided
1 pinch saffron
1 large egg, beaten
1½ tablespoons (22.5 mL) Dijon mustard
Juice of 1 lemon
4 hamburger buns, split

1. Make sure the grill is clean and generously sprayed with nonstick grilling spray. Preheat the barbecue to medium high (350°F [180°C] to 400°F [200°C]). Generously spray a fish basket or a double sheet of aluminum foil with nonstick spray.

2. In a spice grinder, grind the celery seeds and bay leaves to a powder. Transfer the mixture to a small bowl and add the pepper, paprika, cardamom, mustard, and cloves. Stir well and set aside.

3. In a separate small bowl, combine the crabmeat, 2½ cups (591 mL) of the breadcrumbs, the green onions, 2 tablespoons (30 mL) of the mayonnaise, the saffron, and 1½ teaspoons (7.5 mL) of the ground spice mixture. Stir in the beaten egg and, with your hands, shape the mixture into 4 (4½-inch [11-cm] diameter) patties.

4. Place the remaining breadcrumbs in a shallow bowl and dredge the patties in the crumbs, coating each one completely.

5. In a small bowl, combine the remaining mayonnaise with the mustard and lemon juice and stir until smooth. Set aside.

6. Put the crab patties in the prepared basket or on the prepared foil and place the basket or foil directly over the coals or flames. Cook the burgers until golden brown, 4 to 5 minutes per side. Place the buns on the grill to toast them when you turn the burgers.

7. Spread the mayonnaise mixture on one side of each bun, top each with a crab patty, and serve.

Willapa Bay Oyster Burgers
Yield: 4 servings

These are similar to the famed carpetbagger steak, only these are served on a bun. The oysters and bacon make these burgers a real treat for foodies and those who love these salty mollusks.

1 teaspoon (5 mL) olive oil
1 cup (236 mL) fresh oysters, drained and coarsely chopped
½ cup (118 mL) chopped mushrooms
4 strips of bacon, fried until crispy, crumbled, and drained
1 teaspoon (5 mL) dry white wine
1 teaspoon (5 mL) heavy cream
Freshly ground black pepper, to taste
1¼ pounds (568 g) lean ground beef
4 toasted hamburger buns, ciabatta rolls, or bagels
Garlic mayonnaise, for serving
Thinly-sliced onion, for serving
Lettuce, for serving
Sliced tomato, for serving

1. Make sure the grill is clean and generously sprayed with nonstick grilling spray. Preheat the barbecue to medium high (350°F [180°C] to 400°F [200°C]).

2. In a saucepan, heat the olive oil. Add the oysters and mushrooms and gently sauté until the mushrooms are tender. Drain the excess liquid and oil and add the bacon, wine, cream, and pepper. Stirring, bring the mixture to a boil. Immediately remove the pan from the heat and allow the mixture to cool completely. Pour it into a colander or bowl layered with paper towels to drain.

3. Form the ground beef into 8 thin hamburger patties. Spoon a tablespoon or so of filling onto the centers of 4 of the patties and spread it carefully, leaving the outer ½ inch (1 cm) clear. Reserve the remaining filling. Cover these patties with the remaining 4 and seal the edges by pressing down on the outer edges with your fingers or a fork (as you would with a pie crust).

4. Refrigerate the patties until they are cold. When ready to cook the burgers, warm the remaining filling in a saucepan and set aside to keep warm. Cook the patties as you would any burger, but take extra care when turning these stuffed burgers so that the mixture doesn't leak out and the patties don't break.

5. Split and toast the rolls just before the patties are done. Spread garlic mayonnaise on the bottom half of each roll and add a thin slice of onion, some lettuce, and a slice of tomato. Add a cooked patty and spoon the remaining filling over the patties. Top with the other half of the roll and serve on a heated platter.

Grilled Maine Lobster
Yield: 4 servings

Lobsters cooked on the grill have a wonderful smoky flavor, and they are easier to eat than traditional boiled whole lobsters.

2 shallots, peeled and minced
4 cloves garlic, peeled and mashed
1 pound (454 g) butter
⅔ cup (158 mL) fresh lemon juice
Juice of ½ medium orange
¼ cup (59 mL) chopped fresh parsley
2 tablespoons (30 mL) chopped fresh tarragon
Salt, to taste
Freshly ground black pepper, to taste
4 (2-pound [908-g]) live Maine lobsters
Fresh lemon wedges, for serving

1. In a saucepan, over moderate heat, sauté the shallots and garlic in 1 tablespoon of butter for 5 minutes or until soft. Add the the remaining butter, lemon juice, orange juice, parsley, tarragon, salt, and pepper and heat until the butter is melted. Set aside and keep warm, stirring occasionally.

2. Preheat the barbecue to medium high (400°F [200°C] to 450°F [240°C]).

3. Place a lobster on its back. Sever the spinal cord by inserting a sharp knife between tail and body; then split the lobster in half lengthwise. Remove the stomach and intestinal vein. Crack the claws and sprinkle the meat with salt and pepper. Repeat with the remaining lobsters. Paint the lobsters with the melted butter mixture and place them on the grill flesh side down. Cook until there is a light char on the meat, about 5 minutes. Turn, baste with butter, and grill until the meat is firm, about another 5 minutes.

4. Remove the lobsters from the grill and paint them with the melted butter mixture. Wrap the bodies in foil, remove the claws, and return the claws to the grill for 5 to 6 minutes more. Take the claws off the grill and serve the lobsters with lemon wedges.

Dungeness Crab Cakes with Basil Mayonnaise
Yield: 6 servings

Dungeness crabs inhabit the underwater eelgrass beds and waters of the Pacific West Coast, from Alaska's Aleutian Island to Point Conception, Calif.

1½ cups (354 mL) mayonnaise, divided
3 tablespoons basil leaves
2 teaspoons (10 mL) prepared yellow mustard
2 teaspoons (10 mL) fresh lemon juice
1 pinch cayenne pepper
2 tablespoons (30 mL) olive oil
2 stalks celery, finely minced
⅔ cup (158 mL) finely chopped sweet onion
1 pound (454 g) fresh Dungeness crabmeat
2⅔ cups (631 mL) fresh breadcrumbs, divided
¼ cup (59 mL) chopped fresh chives
2 tablespoons (30 mL) chopped fresh parsley
6 tablespoons (90 mL) all-purpose flour
3 large eggs
2 tablespoons (30 mL) vegetable oil
Paprika, for garnish

1. Finely chop the basil leaves and combine them with 1 cup (236 mL) of the mayonnaise. Add the mustard, lemon juice, and cayenne pepper. Cover and refrigerate.

2. Preheat the barbecue to medium high (350°F [180°C] to 400°F [200°C]).

3. In a large cast-iron skillet over the hot grill, heat the olive oil. Add the celery and onion and sauté until tender. Put the crabmeat in a large bowl and pour the sautéed mixture over it. Add ⅔ cup (158 mL) of the breadcrumbs, the chives, parsley, and the remaining mayonnaise. Season with salt and pepper. Using ⅓ cup (79 mL) crab mixture for each, form into 12 (2½-inch [6-cm] diameter) cakes.

4. Place the flour in a small bowl. In a separate small bowl, whisk the eggs. Place the remaining breadcrumbs in a third bowl. Dip each cake in the flour, then the eggs, then the breadcrumbs, patting the crumbs softly so they are well adhered. In a cast-iron or nonstick skillet placed directly on the grill, heat the vegetable oil. Add the crab cakes and cook until golden, turning once, about 10 minutes total.

5. Serve with the chilled basil-mayonnaise, sprinkled with paprika.

Lime-Broiled Sea Bass

Yield: 4 servings

Prized for its large size and good flavor, white sea bass is found off Southern California and both coasts of Mexico. Fished commercially and for sport since the early 1900s, populations were in decline from the 1960s to the 1980s, but today new management efforts have helped California's population recover.

1 pound (454 g) white sea bass fillets (about 4 fillets)
¼ cup (59 mL) melted butter
¼ teaspoon (1.25 mL) grated lime zest
¼ cup (59 mL) lime juice
⅛ teaspoon (0.6 mL) bottled hot pepper sauce
Salt, to taste
Freshly ground black pepper, to taste
¼ cup (59 mL) toasted sliced almonds
1 tablespoon (15 mL) snipped fresh parsley

1. Preheat the barbecue to medium high (350°F [180°C] to 400°F [200°C]).

2. Place the fillets on the unheated rack of a broiler pan. In a bowl, combine the melted butter, lime zest, lime juice, and hot pepper sauce. Brush this mixture on each fillet and sprinkle lightly with salt and pepper. Cook for 8 minutes. Brush with the lime mixture; turn, and brush again. Broil 8 to 10 minutes more, or until the fish flakes easily when tested with a fork.

3. Transfer the fish to a heated serving platter. Combine the remaining lime butter with the sliced almonds and snipped parsley. Spoon this mixture over each fish portion and serve.

Grilled Mussels with Spicy Fish Sauce

Yield: 4–6 servings

Ask for and buy farmed mussels whenever there is any doubt as to the source or reliability of these shellfish during September through December or during tidal changes.

2 pounds (908 g) fresh mussels
2 cloves garlic, peeled and finely minced
½ teaspoon (2.5 mL) red pepper flakes
3 tablespoons (45 mL) lemon juice
3 tablespoons (45 mL) Thai fish sauce
3 tablespoons (45 mL) water
2 teaspoons (10 mL) brown sugar
1 teaspoon (5 mL) dried lemon peel

1. Clean and scrub the mussels. Drain them very well.

2. Preheat the barbecue to medium high (500°F [260°C] to 600°F [315°C]).

3. While the mussels are draining, blend the garlic and red pepper flakes into a paste. Add the lemon juice, fish sauce, water, sugar, and dried lemon peel.

4. Place the clean, dry mussels in a single layer on the hot grill. Grill the mussels just until they are all open and aromatic.

5. Remove the mussels from the grill with long tongs. Spoon 1 teaspoon (5 mL) of sauce into each open mussel and serve with the remaining sauce in small bowls for dipping.

Santa Barbara Scallop Burgers
Yield: 4–6 servings

These are best made with fresh scallops; however, if you must, you can use frozen scallops, which have been thoroughly thawed and drained. You can also substitute shrimp or crab for the scallops.

½ cup (118 mL) light mayonnaise
3 tablespoons (45 mL) ketchup
½ teaspoon (2.5 mL) freshly ground pepper, plus more to taste
¼ teaspoon (1.25 mL) hot sauce
Salt, to taste
1½ cups (354 mL) frozen corn kernals, thawed and drained, divided
1½ pounds (681 g) sea scallops, coarsely chopped, divided
1½ teaspoons (7.5 mL) kosher salt
Extra virgin olive oil, for brushing
6 soft hamburger buns, split
6 lettuce leaves
6 thick tomato slices

1. In a small bowl, blend the mayonnaise with the ketchup and season with pepper, hot sauce, and salt. Cover and refrigerate.

2. In a food processor, process ¾ cup (177 mL) of the corn to a paste. Add ½ pound (227 g) of the scallops, the kosher salt, and ½ teaspoon (2.5 mL) of the pepper, and process to a paste. Add the remaining scallops and process until just blended, leaving small lumps in the mixture.

3. Spoon the scallop mixture into a large bowl and add the remaining corn kernels. Pat the mixture into burger shapes, cover, and refrigerate until you are ready to grill. (I recommend refrigerating for at least 2 to 4 hours.)

4. Make sure the grill is clean and generously sprayed with nonstick grilling spray. Preheat the barbecue to medium high (350°F [180°C] to 400°F [200°C]). Place a double sheet of thick aluminum foil on the grill surface, or use a flat griddle on the barbecue.

5. Brush the scallop burgers with olive oil and grill them until they are nicely charred on the outside and barely cooked in the center, about 3 to 4 minutes per side.

6. Spread a thin layer of the spicy sauce on both halves of the buns. Place the lettuce and tomato slices on the bottom halves and add the scallop burgers.

7. Serve immediately with the remaining spicy sauce on the side.

Jerry's Grilled Oysters with Butter Sauce
Yield: 6 servings

Farmed oysters account for 95 percent of the world's total oyster consumption, as aquaculture has made them available year round (no more "R months") and the farming of oysters and their filter-feeding action can actually benefit surrounding coastal waters.

6 shallots, peeled and minced
1 tablespoon (15 mL) finely chopped fresh chives
¾ cup (177 mL) dry white wine
1 pound (454 g) unsalted butter, cut into 1-inch (2.5-cm) thick pieces
Salt, to taste
Freshly ground black pepper, to taste
24 fresh Hood River oysters (or your favorite local variety)
Hungarian paprika, for garnish

1. Preheat the barbecue to medium high (450°F [240°C] to 500°F [260°C]).

2. In a saucepan, combine the shallots, chives and wine. Cook over medium heat until the wine is reduced by half. Remove from the heat and cool slightly. Whisk in the butter, 1 piece at a time, until the sauce is smooth. Season to taste with salt and pepper and keep warm over a double boiler of warm (not boiling) water.

3. Place the oysters on the grill and close the lid. Cook until the shells open, about 5 to 8 minutes. Transfer the oysters to a serving platter, being careful not to spill their natural juices. With an oyster knife, remove the top shells and spoon 1 teaspoon (5 mL) of the sauce over each oyster. Sprinkle lightly with paprika and serve.

Tilapia Creole
Yield: 4 servings

A mild white fish, tilapia is available year-round and comes frozen from China/ Taiwan or fresh from Central America. Please avoid the fish imported from Asian farms, as they suffer from pollution and weak management of the farms. Instead, buy from environmentally friendly U.S. farms.

1 pound (454 g) farmed tilapia fillets
1 tablespoon (15 mL) margarine or butter
⅓ cup (79 mL) chopped onion
¼ cup (59 mL) chopped celery
2 tablespoons (30 mL) finely chopped green bell pepper
1 (8-ounce [227-g)]) can stewed tomatoes, cut into pieces
1 tablespoon (15 mL) sugar
¼ teaspoon (1.25 mL) dried oregano
⅛ teaspoon (0.6 mL) pepper

1. Preheat the barbecue to medium high (350°F [180°C] to 400°F [200°C]).

2. Arrange the fish fillets in an 8-inch (20-cm) square 2-quart (1.9-L) baking dish. In a medium skillet, melt the margarine. Add the onion, celery, and green bell pepper and sauté until tender. Stir in the remaining ingredients and spoon this mixture over the fish.

3. Bake in the barbecue for 15 to 20 minutes or until the fish flakes easily with a fork.

Clams Casino Royale

Yield: 4–6 servings

Look for steamers or littlenecks, which are available worldwide and are cultured in many countries. Their popularity exceeds the supply harvested from the sea, so farmed clams today account for 89 percent of world clam consumption.

40 clams in shells
8 strips of bacon, chopped
½ pound (227 g) Monterey Jack cheese, sliced

1. Preheat the barbecue to medium high (350°F [180°C] to 400°F [200°C]).

2. In a large pot on the barbecue side burner, steam the clams until the shells open. Remove the clams from the shells. Save half of the shells, place the clams in a food processor, add water to cover, and process to a smooth liquid. Pour the puréed clams into a strainer. Repeat with the remaining clams. Let stand for several hours.

3. Spoon the puréed clams onto the half shells, place a piece of bacon and cheese on top of each, and grill for 5 to 10 minutes, or until the cheese melts.

Baked Feta Prawns

Yield: 6 servings

Imported feta cheese, made from sheep's or goat's milk, seem to be tangier and more flavorful than domestic cow's-milk feta.

2 pounds (908 g) shelled prawns (defrosted and drained if frozen)
⅓ cup (79 mL) olive oil
3 cloves garlic, peeled and minced
3 tablespoons (45 mL) lemon juice
1½ teaspoons (7.5 mL) chopped fresh thyme
6–7 medium plum tomatoes, seeded and finely chopped
10 ounces (280 g) feta cheese, crumbled
¾ teaspoon (3.75 mL) freshly ground black pepper
½ teaspoon (2.5 mL) kosher salt

1. Preheat the barbecue to medium high (350°F [180°C] to 400°F [200°C]).

2. Put the prawns in a shallow dish. In a small bowl, combine the olive oil, garlic, lemon juice, and thyme and pour this marinade over the prawns. Cover and refrigerate for 30 minutes or so.

3. Remove the pan from the refrigerator and stir in the tomatoes and feta cheese. Pour the shrimp and marinade into a flat roasting pan and sprinkle with pepper and kosher salt. Place the pan in the center of the barbecue and cook for 15 minutes, stirring occasionally.

4. Serve in flat bowls with lots of French bread to soak up the juices from the pan.

Grilled Tiger Prawns
Yield: 4–6 servings

Tiger shrimp have black and gray striped shells and, when cooked, turn a deep red color. The flesh of the tiger shrimp have a higher moisture content and shrink more than the white and brown shrimp.

1 medium avocado, peeled and pitted
3 medium tomatillos, husks removed
½ cup (118 mL) fresh cilantro leaves
2 cups (473 mL) cold water, divided
1 teaspoon (5 mL) salt, divided, plus more, to taste
3 medium plum tomatoes, roasted, peeled, and seeded
7 canned chipotle peppers, seeds removed
1½ pounds (681 g) tiger shrimp, peeled and deveined
1 medium fresh mango, peeled, pitted, and cut into thin wedges

1. Preheat the barbecue to medium high (350°F [180°C] to 400°F [200°C]).

2. In a blender or food processor, combine the avocado, tomatillos, cilantro, half the water, and half salt and blend to a smooth purée. Pour the purée into a bowl, cover, and set aside. Wash out the blender container.

3. In the same blender, combine the tomatoes, chipotles, the remaining water, and the remaining salt to a smooth purée. Pour the purée into a separate bowl and set aside.

4. Season the shrimp with salt and place them on the grill. Cook until tender, about 3 to 4 minutes, being careful not to overcook them.

5. Spoon the avocado sauce onto half of a medium plate and spoon the tomato-chipotle sauce on the other half. Garnish the plate with the mango slices and arrange the grilled shrimp between the two salsas.

Basil-Grilled Rainbow Trout

Yield: 3–6 servings

Farmed rainbows are the best under the Seafood Watch program. A good alternative, if you can find them, are Lake Superior trout, which are not on any endangered or cautionary list.

¾ cup (177 mL) peeled, seeded, and chopped tomato
2 tablespoons (30 mL) chopped fresh basil
2 teaspoons (10 mL) vinegar
2 teaspoons (10 mL) olive oil
¼ teaspoon (1.25 mL) salt
⅛ teaspoon (0.6 mL) freshly ground black pepper
⅛ teaspoon (0.6 mL) hot sauce
6 Lake trout fillets, skin left on (3 whole trout)

1. Preheat the barbecue to medium high (350°F [180°C] to 400°F [200°C]) for indirect heating, putting a water pan under the unheated side of the grill.

2. In a food processor, combine the tomato, basil, vinegar, olive oil, salt, pepper, and hot sauce and process until smooth. Place the fillets, skin side down, in a shallow dish, pour in half of the marinade, cover, and refrigerate for 1 hour.

3. Remove the trout from the marinade and place it on the grill flesh side down for 1 to 2 minutes. Turn, brush with the reserved marinade, and grill another 3 to 4 minutes, or until the fish flakes but is still translucent in the center.

Grilled Striped Bass with Lemon

Yield: 4–6 servings

Striped bass, either farmed or wild caught, are delicious fish and readily available from most supermarkets and fish counters.

2 (1½-pound [681-g] striped bass
½ cup butter, sliced
1 teaspoon (5 mL) garlic salt
1 teaspoon (5 mL) dried oregano
½ teaspoon (2.5 cm) dried thyme
1 lemon, zest grated and reserved, halved
3 tablespoons (45 mL) chopped fresh parsley

1. Preheat the barbecue to medium high (350°F [180°C] to 400°F [200°C]).

2. Rinse the fish thoroughly. Put each fish on a large piece of foil. Scatter chunks of the butter inside and on top of the fish. Sprinkle on the garlic salt, oregano, thyme, lemon zest, and parsley. Squeeze a lemon half over each fish, seal the foil, and place the fish on the grill for 12 to 13 minutes. Turn and grill the other side for 12 to 13 minutes.

3. Be careful when you open the foil packages, as the escaping steam can burn you. Serve with fried potatoes and steamed cauliflower.

Rainbow Trout with Mushroom-Rice Stuffing

Yield: 4 servings

We recommend using farmed rainbow trout in this recipe, but Lake Superior trout is a good alternative.

Stuffing

⅓ cup (79 mL) butter, divided
2 onions, peeled and chopped
¾ cup (177 mL) uncooked long-grain rice
1½ cups (354 mL) fish stock or chicken broth
1 pound (454 g) mushrooms, minced
3 tomatoes, peeled, seeded, and chopped
3 tablespoons (45 mL) chopped fresh parsley
2 tablespoons (30 mL) fresh lemon juice
Salt, to taste
Freshly ground black pepper, to taste

Fish

1 (4–5 pound [1.8–2.3 kg]) lake trout
2 tablespoons (30 mL) butter, plus more for dotting the trout
1 cup (236 mL) white wine, dry or sweet
3 tablespoons (45 mL) lemon juice
Salt, to taste
Freshly ground black pepper, to taste

1. In a Dutch oven or a deep roasting pan, melt half the butter. Add the onions and cook until translucent. Add the rice and stir until all the grains are well coated. Pour in the stock and bring to a boil. Cover, lower the heat, and simmer slowly for 20 minutes.

2. Preheat the barbecue to medium high (375°F [190°C] to 425°F [220°C]) for direct heating. Line a roasting pan with aluminum foil and butter or spray the foil with nonstick cooking spray.

3. In a skillet, melt the remaining butter. Add the mushrooms and sauté until all the liquid has evaporated. Mix in the chopped tomatoes, cook for 5 minutes, and pour this mixture into the pan of rice. Sprinkle with the chopped parsley and lemon juice; season with salt and pepper, and let cool.

4. Rub the inside of the trout with the 2 tablespoons (30 mL) butter, then season with salt and pepper. Stuff the fish with the cooled mushroom-rice stuffing. (The remaining stuffing can be cooked separately in a buttered, covered saucepan.) Close the body cavity opening with skewers or sew it closed with kitchen twine. Place the trout in the prepared roasting pan. Dot with butter, pour in white wine and lemon juice; season with salt and pepper, and bake in the preheated barbecue for 10 minutes per inch (2.5 cm) of the trout's thickest part, approximately 30 to 40 minutes.

Salmon with Citrus-Balsamic Vinaigrette

Yield: 4 servings

Your best bet here is to buy Alaskan wild-caught salmon. If it's not available, look for domestic farmed salmon. If you really want to splurge, the best salmon we've ever tasted is the Copper River line-caught variety.

¼ cup (59 mL) fresh-squeezed orange juice
2 tablespoons (30 mL) balsamic vinegar
Juice of 1 lemon
1 tablespoon (15 mL) olive oil
2 teaspoons (10 mL) finely chopped fresh parsley
2 teaspoons (10 mL) finely chopped fresh thyme
1 teaspoon (5 mL) finely chopped fresh basil
1 teaspoon (5 mL) finely minced shallot
1 teaspoon (5 mL) Dijon mustard
1 small clove garlic, peeled and pressed
⅛ teaspoon (0.6 mL) sea salt
Freshly ground black pepper, to taste
1¼ pounds (568 g) salmon fillet
1 lemon, thinly sliced, for garnish
Lettuce, for serving

1. Preheat the barbecue to medium high (425°F [220°C] to 475°F [250°C]). Line a pan with aluminum foil and spray the foil with nonstick cooking or grilling spray.

2. In a blender, combine the orange juice, vinegar, lemon juice, oil, parsley, thyme, basil, shallots, mustard, garlic, salt, and pepper. Pulse until thoroughly mixed. Set aside a portion for serving.

3. Place salmon in the prepared pan. Spoon a little of the vinaigrette over the fish and bake it in the barbecue for 12 minutes per inch (2.5 cm) of thickness, or until cooked through. The inside should be slightly medium-rare.

4. Remove the salmon from the pan and arrange it on a bed of lettuce on a serving platter. Spoon the remaining vinaigrette over each serving of fish, garnish with lemon slices, and serve.

King-Crab Stuffed Beefsteak Tomatoes

Yield: 6 servings

Alaskan King Crab is usually frozen, but it comes canned as well. If you can, choose the quick-frozen kind as it's much fresher and has a better, cleaner, fresher flavor.

6 medium beefsteak tomatoes
1 tablespoon (15 mL) butter
½ cup (118 mL) chopped celery
¼ cup (59 mL) chopped onion
¼ cup (59 mL) chopped green bell pepper
1½ cups (118 mL) coarse dry breadcrumbs
1 (6–8 ounce [168–224 g]) package frozen King Crab, thawed and drained, out of shells
1 teaspoon (5 mL) salt, plus more to taste
½ teaspoon (2.5 mL) dried basil
⅛ teaspoon (0.6 mL) freshly ground black pepper
¼ cup (59 mL) freshly grated Parmigiano-Reggiano cheese
Chopped fresh parsley, for garnish

1. Preheat the barbecue to medium high (350°F [180°C] to 400°F [200°C]). Spray a shallow roasting pan with nonstick cooking spray

2. Slice off the top ½-inch (1 cm) of each tomato, scoop out the pulp, strain out the seeds, and turn the tomato shells upside down to drain. Chop the pulp and set it aside.

3. In a skillet over medium heat, melt the butter. Add the celery, onion, and green bell pepper and sauté until tender. Add the reserved tomato pulp to the skillet and cook for 2 to 3 minutes. Remove the skillet from the heat and add the breadcrumbs, crab, salt, basil, and pepper.

4. Sprinkle the insides of the tomato shells with salt, and fill them with the crab-tomato mixture. Place the stuffed tomatoes in the prepared roasting pan, sprinkle with grated Parmigiano-Reggiano cheese, and bake in the barbecue for 20 to 25 minutes, or until the tomatoes are tender.

5. Sprinkle with freshly chopped parsley and serve.

Barbecue-Roasted Alaska Black Cod in Cider
Yield: 4 servings

Avoid Atlantic cod, which has been terribly overfished, and Northeast Arctic trawl-caught cod, because this method of harvesting does severe damage to seafloor habitats.

2 ounces (56 g) butter
3 medium leeks, trimmed and thinly sliced
2–3 shallots, peeled and thinly sliced
1 cup (236 mL) apple cider
4 (6–7 ounce [168–196 g]) Alaska black cod fillets
1 teaspoon (5 mL) chopped fresh thyme
Salt, to taste
Freshly ground black pepper, to taste
2 teaspoons (10 mL) olive oil
Chopped fresh parsley, for garnish

1. Preheat the barbecue to medium high (350°F [180°C] to 400°F [200°C]). Spray a large cast-iron skillet or roasting pan with nonstick spray.

2. In the prepared skillet or roasting pan, melt the butter over medium heat. Add the leeks and shallots and sauté for 2 minutes, or until the shallots and leeks are softened but not browned.

3. Add the cider. Arrange the fillets on top, season with the thyme, salt, and black pepper. Drizzle with olive oil and place the pan in the barbecue. Cook for about 10 to 12 minutes

4. When the fish is done, the outside should flake easily, but the inside should still be slightly medium-rare. Don't overcook, as this fish can become very dry if not cooked properly.

5. Place the fillets on a heated platter, spoon the sautéed onions and shallots over the top, sprinkle with fresh parsley, and serve.

Baked Catfish Parmesan
Yield: 6 servings

Due to the scavenging diet of these fish in the wild, we highly recommend that you only buy farmed catfish who are raised in tanks and fed a primarily vegetarian and grain-based diet.

6 (4–5 ounce [112–140 g]) catfish filets
⅓ cup (79 mL) melted butter
1 cup (236 mL) fresh dry breadcrumbs
¾ cup (177 mL) grated Parmigiano-Reggiano cheese
¼ cup (59 mL) chopped fresh parsley
2 teaspoons (10 mL) garlic salt
1 teaspoon (5 mL) paprika
½ teaspoon (2.5 mL) dried oregano
½ teaspoon freshly ground black pepper
¼ teaspoon (1.25 mL) dried rosemary
Lemon wedges, for garnish
Freshly chopped chives, for garnish

1. Preheat the barbecue to medium high (350°F [180°C] to 400°F [200°C]). Grease well a 9 × 13-inch [22.5 × 32.5-cm] baking dish.

2. Clean, wash, and pat dry the fish. Pour the butter into a wide, flat dish. In a similar dish, combine the breadcrumbs, Parmigiano-Reggiano cheese, parsley, garlic salt, paprika, oregano, pepper, and rosemary.

3. Dip the fillets in the melted butter and then press them into the crumb mixture, coating both sides.

4. Arrange the fish in the prepared baking dish and place the dish in the barbecue. Cook for about 30 minutes, or until the fish flakes easily when tested with a fork.

5. Garnish with lemon wedges and chopped chives and serve.

Herbed Grilled Halibut
Yield: 4–6 servings

Most Pacific halibut sold in the United States is line-caught, which has little deleterious affect on the environment. We prefer the thicker, less sweet Greek yogurt to most domestic brands for this recipe.

1 teaspoon (5 mL) ground coriander
¼ teaspoon (1.25 mL) ground cardamom
¼ teaspoon (1.25 mL) ground cumin
⅛ teaspoon (0.6 mL) freshly ground black pepper
1 cup (236 mL) Greek yogurt
½ cup (118 mL) melted butter
2 tablespoons (30 mL) lemon juice
1 (1½–2 pound [681–908 g]) Pacific halibut fillet
1 teaspoon (5 mL) salt
Fresh dill for smoking
Fresh thyme sprigs for smoking

1. Preheat the barbecue to medium high (350°F [180°C] to 400°F [200°C]) for direct heating. Line the grill with a sheet of aluminum foil sprayed with nonstick grilling spray.

2. In a small bowl, combine the coriander, cardamom, cumin, and pepper and mix well. In another bowl combine the yogurt, butter, and lemon juice.

3. Salt the halibut fillet. Brush one side with the melted butter mix. Generously sprinkle with the seasonings and repeat on the other side.

4. Place the fillet on the foil and cook until the fish browns on both sides and flakes, brushing often with the sauce, 25 to 30 minutes.

5. Make a smoker package by putting a handful of dill and thyme sprigs on a 12-inch (30-cm) square of heavy-duty aluminum foil, folding over the package, poking 3 or 4 holes in the top of the foil, and placing the package directly on the coals or open flame to add smoke to your grilling.

6. Halfway into the cooking time, place the foil package of herbs on the charcoal or gas flame and let it smoke until you remove the fish.

Baked Barramundi with Prune Filling

Yield: 8–10 servings

Avoid imported barramundi. First, they may be mislabeled Nile perch from Africa. Second, if they are farmed but not from the United States, they may be prone to disease. Barramundi is high in omega-3 fatty acids and is a great fish to serve your family.

3 cups (708 mL) pitted prunes, chopped fine
2½ cups (591 mL) fresh breadcrumbs
½ cup (118 mL) sweet sherry
Sea salt, to taste
Freshly ground black pepper, to taste
¼ cup (59 mL) freshly chopped fresh parsley
⅛ cup (28 mL) freshly chopped fresh dill
1 (10–12 pound [280–336 g]) whole barramundi, scaled and cleaned
5 lemons
Paprika, for garnish

1. Preheat the barbecue to medium high (350°F [180°C] to 400°F [200°C]). Spray a large sheet of aluminum foil with nonstick cooking or grilling spray.

2. In a medium bowl, mix together the prunes, breadcrumbs, and sherry. Season with the salt and pepper, add the parsley and dill, and stir to combine thoroughly.

3. Spoon the mixture into the cavity of the barramundi, quarter two lemons and insert into the cavity. Secure with satay skewers or sew the cavity shut with kitchen twine.

4. Lay the fish on the prepared aluminum foil. Squeeze 2 lemons over and around the fish, fold the foil to seal, and cook the whole fish for 10 to 12 minutes on each side.

5. Remove the foil, opening it carefully to avoid escaping steam. Remove the backbone from the fish and place the two fillets, skin side down, on a large serving platter. Squeeze 1 lemon over each fillet and garnish with fresh chopped parsley and sprinkles of paprika.

Pan-Roasted Flounder

Yield: 4–6 servings

Flounder is a Pacific flatfish that is much preferred over its Atlantic cousins, which have been highly overfished. Pacific sole and sanddabs are good substitutes.

3 tablespoons (45 mL) olive oil
1 large onion, peeled and chopped
2 tablespoons (30 mL) finely chopped shallots
½ cup (118 mL) Marsala wine
2 tablespoons (30 mL) butter
8 ounces (227 g) fresh chanterelles, sliced
¾ cup (177 mL) chicken (or vegetable) stock
Kosher salt, to taste
Lemon pepper, to taste
4 (½-pound [227-g]) flounder fillets, skin left on
2 tablespoons (30 mL) chopped fresh parsley
¼ cup (59 mL) grated mozzarella cheese
Sliced lemons or limes, for garnish

1. Preheat the barbecue to medium high (400°F [200°C] to 450°F [240°C]) for direct and indirect heating, putting a water pan under the unheated side of the grill. Line the grill with a large piece of aluminum foil and spray the foil with nonstick cooking or grilling spray.

2. In a nonstick skillet, heat the olive oil over high heat. Add the onions and sauté until translucent. Add the shallots and cook for another 30 seconds. Add the Marsala wine, reduce the heat to low, and cook until the liquid has reduced by half.

3. Add the butter and mushrooms and simmer for 2 to 3 minutes. Add the chicken stock, season with salt and lemon pepper, and let the sauce cook down until it thickens enough to lightly coat a spoon.

4. Lay the fillets on the prepared sheet of foil and cook for about 1 to 1½ minutes per side. Move the fillets to indirect heat, turn them skin side down, and cook for another 2 to 3 minutes on that side only.

5. Place 1 fillet on each plate and ladle mushroom mixture over the fillet. Garnish with the parsley, a sprinkle of the grated mozzarella cheese, and freshly sliced lemons or limes.

Stuffed Lake Whitefish

Yield: 4 servings

Once threatened by low population, this fish has recovered and is mostly harvested from the Great Lakes, where it is the dominant deep-water fish.

1 (3–4 pound [1.3–1.8 kg]) whitefish
1½ teaspoons (7.5 mL) lemon salt
¼ cup (59 mL) butter
½ cup (118 mL) chopped celery
½ cup (118 mL) chopped onion
1⅓ cups (318 mL) water
2 tablespoons (30 mL) grated lemon zest
1 teaspoon (5 mL) paprika
1 teaspoon (5 mL) poultry seasoning
½ teaspoon (2.5 mL) dried thyme
1½ cups (354 mL) uncooked instant rice
½ cup (118 mL) plain Greek yogurt
¼ cup (59 mL) chopped peeled lemon
¼ cup (59 mL) melted butter

1. Preheat the barbecue to medium high (350°F [180°C] to 400°F [200°C]). Butter a shallow roasting pan.

2. Sprinkle the fish inside and out with the lemon salt.

3. In a large skillet, melt the butter. Add the celery and onion and sauté until tender. Add the water, lemon zest, paprika, poultry seasoning, and thyme and bring to a boil. Add the rice and stir to moisten. Cover the pan, remove it from the heat, and let stand 5 to 10 minutes, or until all the liquid is absorbed. Add the yogurt and chopped lemon and mix lightly.

4. Stuff the cavity of the fish loosely with the stuffing. Sew the cavity shut with kitchen twine or use skewers to close the skin over the stuffing. Place the fish in the prepared roasting pan and brush generously with the melted butter. Place any extra stuffing in a small buttered baking dish alongside the fish and bake both for 40 to 50 minutes, basting the fish occasionally with the melted butter.

5. Remove the fish from the barbecue and place it on a warmed platter. Surround the fish with the rice stuffing.

Ye Olde Griddled Trout
Yield: 6 servings

Choose rainbow or other river or lake trout you catch yourself with a line, or substitute sanddabs, sole, or tilapia fillets.

6 fresh rainbow trout
6 sprigs fresh rosemary
6 sprigs fresh thyme
1 teaspoon (5 mL) dried sage
1 teaspoon (5 mL) garlic salt
Freshly ground black pepper, to taste
½ cup (118 mL) butter, softened
12–14 fresh butter lettuce leaves, washed and dried
¼ cup (60 mL) fresh breadcrumbs

1. Preheat the barbecue to medium high (350°F [180°C] to 400°F [200°C]). Oil or spray well a barbecue griddle or a sheet of aluminum foil placed on the grill.

2. Put 1 sprig of rosemary and 1 sprig of thyme inside the cavity of each fish.

3. In a small bowl, mash the sage, salt and pepper into the butter and stir to mix well. Brush this mixture on each side of each trout.

4. Cook the fillets for 4 to 5 minutes on each side, or until the skin is well browned and the flesh begins to flake off the bone. Baste frequently with the butter that melts off.

5. Transfer the trout to a heated platter lined with a bed of fresh lettuce. Sprinkle with the breadcrumbs and serve.

Grant's Grilled Ersters
Yield: 4 servings

Aquaculture has made oysters available year round and has reduced the cost of some of the more expensive varieties.

2–3 pounds (1.3–1.8 kg) fresh oysters, washed and lightly scrubbed
½ cup (118 mL) butter, melted
1 teaspoon (5 mL) lemon juice
½ teaspoon (2.5 mL) balsamic vinegar

1. Preheat the barbecue to medium high (350°F [180°C] to 400°F [200°C]).

2. Place the oysters directly on the hot grill, rounded side down. This helps keep in the juices when the shells pop open.

3. Cook until all the shells are open and steam is sizzling out of the open shells. Meanwhile, in a small bowl, mix together the butter, lemon juice, and vinegar.

4. Serve the oysters on a platter with the butter in a small bowl, or spoon ½ teaspoon (2.5 mL) butter onto each oyster.

Char-Grilled Sardines

Yield: 4 servings

Grilled fresh sardines are as popular in Portugal as hot dogs and hamburgers are in North America. People devour them by the dozen from street vendors, in informal seaside fish houses, at proper restaurants, and at backyard cookouts

2 teaspoons (10 mL) cornstarch
1¼ teaspoon (6.25 mL) cayenne pepper, divided
1 teaspoon (5 mL) garlic powder
1 teaspoon (5 mL) salt
¾ teaspoon (3.75 mL) ground turmeric
½ teaspoon (2.5 mL) ground white pepper
⅛ teaspoon (0.6 mL) freshly ground black pepper
8–10 whole large frozen sardines, thawed and drained
3 tablespoons (45 mL) olive oil, divided
¼ cup (59 mL) chopped fresh cilantro
3–4 tablespoons (60 mL) fresh lime juice
2 tablespoons (30 mL) fish sauce
1 tablespoon (15 mL) coconut milk
2 cloves garlic, peeled and minced
1 teaspoon (5 mL) brown sugar
Butter garlic toast, for serving

1. Preheat the barbecue to medium high (350°F [180°C] to 400°F [200°C]), making sure the grill is lightly sprayed with nonstick cooking or grilling spray.

2. In a small bowl, combine the cornstarch, ¾ teaspoon (3.75 mL) of the cayenne pepper, garlic powder, salt, turmeric, the white pepper, and the black pepper and mix together.

3. Place prepared sardines on a flat baking sheet. Drizzle them with about 1 tablespoon (15 mL) of the olive oil. Sprinkle with the seasoning mix and gently rub it onto both sides of each fish so they are nicely coated. Set aside to dry marinate for 10 to 15 minutes while the barbecue heats up.

4. In a small saucepan, combine the remaining olive oil, cilantro, lime juice, fish sauce, coconut milk, garlic, brown sugar, and the remaining cayenne pepper. Heat through over medium heat to bring out the flavors; do not boil.

5. Grill the fish for about 5 to 8 minutes per side. When done, the fish will appear golden and the skin will be crisp.

6. Serve with thick slices of buttered garlic toast, making an open-face sandwich with the fish and bread.

Flounder Stuffed with Shrimp

Yield: 4–6 servings

You can substitute sole or halibut for the flounder. For an alternative filling, use shrimp or crab.

1 pound (454 g) frozen cocktail bay shrimp, thawed, drained, and chopped
2 large eggs, lightly beaten
½ cup (118 mL) pimentos, drained and finely diced
¼ cup (59 mL) diced green onion
2 tablespoons (30 mL) milk
1 teaspoon (5 mL) mayonnaise
1 teaspoon (5 mL) dry mustard
¼ teaspoon (1.25 mL) Old Bay seasoning
⅛ teaspoon (0.6 mL) hot pepper sauce
1 (2-pound [908 g]) flounder fillet, preferably with skin on
2 tablespoons (30 mL) olive oil
Paprika, for garnish

1. Preheat the barbecue to medium high (375°F [190°C] to 425°F [220°C]). Spray or butter a roasting pan.

2. In a medium bowl, combine the shrimp, eggs, pimentos, green onions, milk, mayonnaise, dry mustard, Old Bay seasoning, and hot pepper sauce. Stir well and set aside.

3. Rinse and dry the flounder. Place the fillet skin side down on a flat baking pan. Spoon the crab mixture onto one side, roll the fillet jelly-roll style until it touches the other edge, forming a round cylinder. Tie in the center and near both ends with kitchen twine. Brush the entire flounder with oil and sprinkle all over with paprika.

4. Gently place the fillet into the prepared roasting pan and bake for 20 minutes, or until the flounder flakes easily with fork.

5. Cut the rolled flounder into 4 to 6 slices. Place each slice on a plate with a wide spatula. Sprinkle with paprika.

Barbecued Crab Casserole

Yield: 4 servings

Pacific cod is okay to buy; Atlantic or imported is not. We use Dungeness crab here, but you could also use stone or king crabs. Do not use fake crab (which is usually artificially colored hake) as it stays in chunks, unlike the crab, which separates nicely.

1 (1-pound [454-g]) package frozen cod fillets, thawed and drained
⅔ cup (158 mL) plus 2 tablespoons (30 mL) butter, melted, divided
1½ cups (354 mL) stuffing mix, crushed with a rolling pin, divided
1 cup (236 mL) fresh crabmeat
½ cup (118 mL) sliced mushrooms
1 large egg
2 tablespoons (30 mL) chopped fresh parsley
2 tablespoons (30 mL) lemon juice
¼ teaspoon (1.25 mL) salt
¼ teaspoon (1.25 mL) hot pepper sauce

1. Preheat the barbecue to medium high (350°F [180°C] to 400°F [200°C]).

2. In a medium bowl, mix together ⅔ cup (158 mL) of the melted butter, 1 cup (236 mL) of the stuffing, the crab, and the mushrooms. Set aside.

3. Place the cod fillets in an ungreased 8-inch (20-cm) square metal baking pan. Cover the fillets with the crab mixture.

4. In the same bowl you used for the crab mix, combine the remaining stuffing mix, egg, parsley, lemon juice, salt, hot sauce, and the remaining melted butter and stir to mix. Sprinkle over the crab mixture. Place the pan in the barbecue and bake for 30 to 35 minutes, or until the fish is heated through and flakes with fork.

Indian Candy (Smoked Salmon)
Yield: 12–16 servings

Use coho, chum, king, pin, red, silver, or sockeye salmon for this recipe, preferably wild caught from Alaska or the Northern Pacific coast.

3 pounds (1.3 kg) salmon fillets, skin and bones removed
5⅓ cups (1.3 L) hot water, divided
4 cups (0.95 L) packed dark brown sugar
1 cup (236 mL) pickling salt
1 cup (236 mL) maple syrup
1 cup (236 mL) warm honey

1. Cut the salmon into 1-inch (2.5-cm) cubes. In a large glass bowl, mix together 5 cups (1.2 L) of the water, the brown sugar, the picking salt, and the maple syrup. Stir until the salt and sugar are dissolved, then add the fish and gently fold to coat each piece. Cover the bowl and let the salmon brine in the fridge for 24 hours.

2. Remove the fish from the brine and discard the liquid. Insert a 4-inch (10-cm) bamboo skewer into each chunk of salmon and place the salmon on a cake rack set over a baking sheet.

3. Preheat the barbecue smoker to 180°F (85°C).

4. Let the fish drip dry for 20 to 25 minutes. (This air-drying step helps produce a glossy finish.) In a small bowl, mix together the honey and the remaining hot water.

5. Place the salmon on a rack in the smoker and smoke for 4 to 5 hours, brushing several times with the honey mixture until glossy.

6. If you like your salmon more moist, reduce the smoking time. For more leathery candy, smoke a full 8 hours. When the salmon is done, the skewer will be well secured into the fish, making a handy candy stick. Store, covered, in a wooden box in a cool place until ready to serve. Salmon can be stored in refrigerator for 3 to 4 days.

Sesame Sanddabs

Yield: 6 servings

Harvesting sanddabs with hook-and-line or Seine nets is the least harsh method of removing these fish from their soft seafloor habitats.

6 (5–6 ounce [140–168 g]) sanddab fillets
¼ cup (59 mL) olive oil
¼ cup (59 mL) sesame seeds
2 tablespoons (30 mL) lemon juice
½ teaspoon (2.5 mL) seasoned salt
Freshly ground black pepper, to taste

1. Preheat the barbecue to medium high (350°F [180°C] to 400°F [200°C]). Grease well a hinged wire fish basket.

2. Clean and wash the sanddab fillets and pat them dry with a paper towel. Place the fish in the prepared fish basket.

3. In a small bowl, whisk together the olive oil, sesame seeds, lemon juice, salt, and pepper. Baste the fish with the sauce.

4. Place the basket on the grill and cook for 6 minutes, basting with the sauce. Turn and cook for 7 to 8 minutes longer, or until the fish flakes easily when tested with a fork.

Grilled Lingcod

Yield: 4 servings

Only found off the West Coast of the United States, lingcod has rebounded from near obscurity to fairly healthy numbers due to wise management, but the bottom trawling used to harvest them is very damaging to the habitat.

2 tablespoons (30 mL) olive oil
½ cup (118 mL) all-purpose flour
1 teaspoon (5 mL) dried thyme
1 teaspoon (5 mL) dried savory
½ teaspoon (2.5 mL) garlic powder
Salt, to taste
Freshly ground black pepper, to taste
4 lingcod (or dolly varden) fillets
1 lemon, quartered
¼ cup (59 mL) slivered almonds
Paprika, for garnish

1. Preheat the barbecue to medium high (350°F [180°C] to 400°F [200°C]).

2. Brush a piece of aluminum foil with the olive oil. Place the foil on the grill.

3. In a shallow dish, combine the flour, thyme, savory, garlic powder, salt, and pepper. Roll the fillets in the flour mixture. If you've removed the skin, coat the flesh side only; otherwise, coat both sides.

4. Place the fish fillets on the foil and cook for 2 to 3 minutes per side, or until the fish flakes easily but is still moist inside.

5. Squeeze a lemon quarter over each fillet. Sprinkle with the almonds and paprika.

6. Serve on a warm plate with grilled potatoes, grilled tomatoes, and steamed rice.

Blackened Salmon Fillet with Papaya and Mango Salsa
Yield: 4 servings

There is a reason this recipe is in a grilling cookbook. Do not attempt this dish in your kitchen, unless you want to spend two days cleaning soot off the ceiling and walls.

1 teaspoon (5 mL) salt
1 teaspoon (5 mL) freshly ground black pepper
1 teaspoon (5 mL) cayenne pepper
1 teaspoon (5 mL) dried oregano
1 teaspoon (5 mL) granulated garlic
1 teaspoon (5 mL) dried thyme
1 teaspoon (5 mL) dried parsley
¼ cup (59 mL) diced mango
¼ cup (59 mL) diced papaya
¼ cup (30 mL) minced fresh cilantro
2 tablespoons (30 mL) diced onion
2 tablespoons (30 mL) sweet rice vinegar
4 (6-ounce [168 g]) salmon fillets
2 tablespoons (30 mL) olive oil

1. In a small bowl, combine the salt, black pepper, cayenne pepper, oregano, granulated garlic, thyme, and parsley and stir to blend.

2. Preheat the barbecue to medium high (350°F [180°C] to 400°F [200°C]).

3. In a medium bowl, combine the mango, papaya, cilantro, onion, and rice vinegar and mix together. Refrigerate until needed.

4. Dredge both sides of the salmon fillets in the Cajun seasoning and set aside. In a cast-iron skillet on the barbecue, heat the olive oil to smoking and then drain it from the pan. Add the salmon fillets and sear on both sides until cooked, approximately 4 minutes on each side, depending on thickness. Cooked salmon should be pale pink in the middle, and this can be determined by piercing the center with a sharp knife.

5. Serve with the fruit salsa on the side, accompanied by wild rice and grilled red and green bell peppers.

BC Halibut in Parmesan

Yield: 4 servings

Do not use packaged breadcrumbs in this recipe. In a food processor, pulse sourdough bread, dinner rolls, or another favorite bread into small chunks—but not as small as packaged crumbs. You may also use panko.

3 cups (708 mL) coarse sourdough breadcrumbs
1 cup (236 mL) grated fresh Parmigiano-Reggiano cheese
4 (⅓-pound [151-g]) halibut fillets
½ cup (118 mL) butter, melted
2 lemons, halved
1 teaspoon (5 mL) dried basil
1 teaspoon (5 mL) granulated garlic
1 teaspoon (5 mL) dried savory
1 teaspoon (5 mL) paprika
1 teaspoon (5 mL) kosher salt
1 teaspoon (5 mL) dried onion flakes
2 tablespoons (30 mL) chopped fresh parsley

1. In a shallow dish, combine the breadcrumbs and cheese and stir to incorporate. Set aside.

2. Preheat the barbecue to medium high (375°F [190°C] to 425°F [220°C]). Lightly grease a baking sheet.

3. Wash the fillets and gently pat them dry. Brush the fillets with melted butter, then squeeze half a lemon over each.

4. In a small bowl, mix together the basil, garlic, savory, paprika, salt, and onion flakes. Sprinkle the seasoning mixture on both sides of the fillets.

5. Roll the fillets in the breadcrumb-cheese mixture, coating all sides well. Pat down the fillets to make sure the mix stays on the fish and place breaded fillets on the prepared baking sheet and bake in the barbecue for 10 to 15 minutes without turning.

6. The fish is done when it flakes easily but is still a bit translucent in the center. Sprinkle with chopped parsley.

Grilled Swordfish Diablo

Yield: 6 servings

Look for broadbill, espanda, emperador, and shutome varieties of swordfish from Hawaii and North American waters.

½ cup (118 mL) dark soy sauce
½ cup (118 mL) fresh orange juice
¼ cup (59 mL) Sriracha sauce
¼ cup (59 mL) chopped fresh parsley
2 tablespoons (30 mL) fresh lemon juice
1 teaspoon (5 mL) freshly ground black pepper
¼ teaspoon (1.25 mL) cayenne pepper
2 cloves garlic, peeled and minced
6 (1½-inch [3.5-cm] thick) swordfish steaks

1. In a medium bowl, combine the soy sauce, orange juice, Sriricha, parsley, lemon juice, black pepper, cayenne pepper, and minced garlic and mix. Place the fish in a glass baking dish and pour the marinade over the fish. Refrigerate for 2 hours.

2. Make sure the grill is very well greased or sprayed with nonstick cooking or grilling spray. Preheat the barbecue to medium high (350°F [180°C] to 400°F [200°C]).

3. Remove the swordfish from the marinade and let it stand until it comes to room temperature, 15 to 20 minutes. Meanwhile, boil the reserved marinade for 10 minutes.

4. Grill the fish, basting frequently with the marinade, for 6 minutes on each side, or until the fish flakes easily when tested with a fork.

Sherry Rock Lobster Tails
Yield: 4 servings

Also called Caribbean spiny lobsters, these crustaceans are mainly grown in Florida, the Bahamas, California and Baja Mexico. Avoid the ones imported from Brazil and Central America, where they are overfished, caught illegally, and caught too early in their life cycles.

2 tablespoons (30 mL) plus 1 teaspoon (5 mL) salt
8 frozen rock lobster tails
½ cup (118 mL) butter
¼ cup (60 mL) all-purpose flour
1 teaspoon (5 mL) paprika
2 cups (473 mL) light cream
2 tablespoons (30 mL) lemon juice
2 tablespoons (30 mL) sherry, plus more for drizzling to taste
¼ cup (59 mL) fresh breadcrumbs
¼ cup (59 mL) freshly grated Parmigiano-Reggiano cheese
1 tablespoon (15 mL) butter, melted

1. In a large pot, bring 4 quarts (3.8 L) of water and 2 tablespoons (30 mL) of the salt to a boil. Add the lobster tails to the water and cook for 2 to 3 minutes. Drain, cut the meat from the shells, and dice the meat. Reserve the shells.

2. In a large skillet, melt the ½ cup (118 mL) butter. Add the lobster meat and sauté for 2 to 3 minutes. Remove the skillet from the heat. Blend in the flour, the remaining salt, and the paprika. Slowly pour in the cream. Return the skillet to the heat and cook, stirring constantly, until the mixture thickens. Let boil for 1 minute. Stir in the lemon juice and sherry.

3. Preheat the barbecue to medium high (350°F [180°C] to 400°F [200°C]).

4. In a small bowl, combine the breadcrumbs and cheese. Divide the lobster equally among the reserved shells and sprinkle lightly with the breadcrumb mixture. Arrange the shells side by side in a shallow pan and bake in the hot barbecue for 10 to 12 minutes, or until golden.

5. Remove the pan from the barbecue, drizzle the lobster with sherry, and serve with a bowl of lemon quarters.

Barbecued Salmon with Blueberry Salsa

Yield: 4 servings

For less tartness you can substitute mango or peaches for the grapefruit. For a different flavor and tartness, use pineapple chunks.

2 tablespoons (30 mL) finely chopped red onion
1 jalapeño pepper, chopped
1 tablespoon (15 mL) lime juice
1 teaspoon (5 mL) honey
½ large pink grapefruit, sectioned, membrane removed
1 cup (236 mL) blueberries, fresh or thawed
2 tablespoons (30 mL) chopped fresh cilantro
1 (1½-pound [681-g]) Pacific salmon fillet

1. Preheat the barbecue to medium high (350°F [180°C] to 400°F [200°C]), making sure the grill is sprayed or well oiled.

2. In a small bowl, mix together the onion, jalapeño pepper, lime juice, and honey; gently stir in grapefruit, blueberries, and cilantro.

3. Cut the salmon into 4 serving-size portions. Barbecue the pieces, skin side down, for about 10 minutes per inch (2.5 cm) of thickness.

4. Serve the salmon on individual plates. Spoon the salsa over the salmon or on the side.

Smoke-Grilled Sockeye

Yield: 4 servings

Any variety of salmon works well here, or you can substitute swordfish or mahi mahi (dorado) steaks.

1 teaspoon (5 mL) grated lime zest
¼ cup (59 mL) lime juice
1 tablespoon (15 mL) vegetable oil
1 teaspoon (5 mL) Dijon mustard
¼ teaspoon (1.25 mL) freshly ground black pepper
⅛ teaspoon (0.6 mL) ground cumin
4 (1½-pound [681-g]) salmon steaks, 1-inch (2.5-cm) thick
⅓ cup (79 mL) toasted sesame seeds
3 tablespoons (45 mL) chopped fresh dill

1. In a shallow dish, combine the lime zest and juice, oil, mustard, pepper, and cumin. Add the fish, turning to coat. Cover and marinate at room temperature for 30 minutes, turning occasionally.

2. Preheat the barbecue to medium high (350°F [180°C] to 400°F [200°C]), making sure the grill is oiled or sprayed with nonstick cooking or grilling spray.

3. Remove the fish from the marinade, sprinkle it with half the sesame seeds, and let it rest. Pour the marinade into a saucepan and boil it for 10 minutes.

4. Make a smoker package by putting a handful of soaked hickory or oak chips on a 12-inch (30-cm) square of heavy-duty aluminum foil, folding over the package, poking 3 or 4 holes in the top of the foil, and placing the package directly on the coals or open flame to add smoke to your grilling.

5. Place the salmon directly on the grill, cover, and cook for 8 minutes. Turn, baste with marinade, and sprinkle with the remaining sesame seeds. Cook for 8 to 10 minutes longer, or until the fish flakes easily when tested with fork.

6. Transfer the salmon to a heated platter and sprinkle with fresh dill.

Seared Mahi Mahi Steaks

Yield: 6 servings

If you can determine that the mahi mahi was long-line caught, run away. Look instead for hook-and-line caught mahi mahi from the southeastern U.S. shores.

6 (1-inch [2.5-cm] thick) mahi mahi steaks
3 tablespoons (45 mL) plus 2 teaspoons (10 mL) olive oil, divided
2 tablespoons (30 mL) garlic powder
2 teaspoons (10 mL) granulated sugar
2 teaspoons (10 mL) freshly ground black pepper
1 large, firm, slightly under ripe banana, peeled and diced
½ cup (118 mL) diced red bell pepper
½ cup (118 mL) diced yellow bell pepper
3 tablespoons (45 mL) chopped fresh cilantro
3 shallots, peeled and chopped
2 tablespoons (30 mL) fresh lime juice
1 tablespoon (15 mL) brown sugar
1 tablespoon (15 mL) rum
1 teaspoon (5 mL) grated fresh ginger
¼ teaspoon (1.25 mL) red pepper flakes
Kosher salt, to taste
Fresh spinach leaves, for serving

1. Brush the mahi mahi steaks with 3 tablespoons (45 mL) of the olive oil. In a small bowl, combine the garlic powder, granulated sugar, and pepper. Season the fish with this mixture and dry marinate for an hour.

2. In a medium bowl, combine the banana, red and yellow peppers, cilantro, shallots, lime juice, brown sugar, rum, and ginger and thoroughly fold them together. Cover and refrigerate for no longer than 1 hour.

3. Preheat the barbecue to medium high (350°F [180°C] to 400°F [200°C]).

4. Grill the mahi mahi steaks for 4 minutes per side. Mahi mahi can be dry when cooked even slightly too long, so check often to make sure the inside is slightly pink and the fish is very moist.

5. Place the steaks over fresh spinach leaves on a warmed platter. Serve the banana salsa on the side. Sprinkle lightly with red pepper flakes and a pinch or two of kosher salt.

Barbecued Blues

Yield: 6 servings

You can add more spices, such as cayenne pepper, garlic, and cumin, to the crumbs if you wish, but the subtle taste of the crab is hard to beat.

12 medium Florida soft-shell blue crabs
2 large eggs, beaten
¼ cup (59 mL) milk
2 teaspoons (10 mL) salt
¾ cup (177 mL) all-purpose flour
¾ cup (177 mL) dry breadcrumbs
Extra virgin olive oil, for frying
½ cup (118 mL) butter, melted
2 lemons, quartered

1. Remove the gills, eyes, mouth parts, and tail sections of the fresh crabs, or, if using frozen crabs, let them thaw. Rinse the crabs in cold water and drain.

2. In a wide, flat bowl, combine the eggs, milk, and salt. In another wide flat bowl, combine the flour and breadcrumbs.

3. Preheat the barbecue to medium high (350°F [180°C] to 400°F [200°C]).

4. Dip the crabs in the egg mixture and then press them in the flour-crumb mixture. For heavier breading, let the crabs sit for several minutes and repeat the procedure.

5. Place a cast-iron skillet on the hot grill and pour in enough oil to coat the bottom of the skillet by ¼ inch (0.5 cm). Add the crabs and cook until brown on one side. Turn carefully and brown the other side. The total cooking time should be approximately 8 to 10 minutes.

6. Place the crabs on paper towels to drain. Serve with the melted butter and lemon quarters.

Alaska Crab Legs with Butter Sauce

Yield: 4 servings

Alaska crab legs are already cooked, but they taste better if they're warmed up before serving.

½ cup (118 mL) unsalted butter, melted
3 tablespoons (45 mL) lemon juice
¾ teaspoon (3.75 mL) garlic salt
½ teaspoon (2.5 mL) dried savory
1 dash white pepper
1 dash hot sauce
1 tablespoon (15 mL) garlic powder
1 tablespoon (15 mL) chili powder
3–4 pounds (1.3–1.8 kg) Alaska king crab legs
2 tablespoons (30 mL) olive oil

1. Preheat the barbecue to medium high (350°F [180°C] to 400°F [200°C]),

2. Pour the melted butter into a medium saucepan. Add the lemon juice, garlic salt, savory, pepper, and hot sauce and stir. Keep warm.

3. In a small bowl, combine the garlic powder and chili powder. Brush both sides of the Alaska crab legs with olive oil, sprinkle with the garlic and chili mixture, and place them on the hot grill. Cook 4 to 5 minutes, turning once.

4. Transfer the crab to serving plates and serve with the butter dipping sauce.

John Davis' Oregon Cedar Salmon
Yield: 4–6 servings

Use only planks intended for cooking and bought at a grocery store or fish market. Do not use cedar planks from the lumberyard, as they are treated with harsh chemicals that can be poisonous.

1 pint fresh raspberries, 12–14 berries reserved
1 cup (236 mL) water
1 tablespoon (15 mL) plus 1 teaspoon (5 mL) balsamic vinegar, divided
1 teaspoon (5 mL) granulated sugar
1 (2½-pound [1.1-kg]) fresh salmon fillet, boned, skin on
¼ cup (60 mL) extra virgin olive oil
Coarse sea salt, to taste
Freshly ground black pepper, to taste
2 tablespoons (30 mL) packed brown sugar
2 tablespoons (30 mL) chopped green onions, green parts only
1 tablespoon (15 mL) ground ginger
1 tablespoon (15 mL) granulated garlic

1. Soak a cedar plank in warm water for 4 to 6 hours or overnight.

2. An hour before you're ready to cook the salmon, make the marinade: In a wide, flat baking pan, mix together the raspberries, water, 1 teaspoon (5 mL) of the vinegar, and the granulated sugar. Add the salmon to the marinade, flesh side down. After 30 minutes, turn the fillet skin side down.

3. Preheat the barbecue to medium high (550°F [290°C] to 600°F [315°C]).

4. Remove the salmon from marinade and drain. Discard the marinade. Remove the plank from the water and brush it with the olive oil. Place the salmon skin side down on the cedar plank, sprinkle it with salt and pepper, and place plank in the center of the grill.

5. Make the baste: In a small bowl, combine the remaining vinegar, brown sugar, green onions, ginger, and garlic.

6. Cover and grill for 20 to 30 minutes, or until the fish is cooked and the center is still just a little bit rare. (The white fat that appears on the surface is omega-3 oil and is not harmful.) Baste one or twice during the cooking time. Keep a spray bottle of water handy in case the edges of the board flame up.

7. Remove the whole plank from barbecue and place it on a serving tray over hot pads on the table. Sprinkle the reserved raspberries on top of the salmon and serve.

Rockport Lobster and Shrimp Burgers
Yield: 4 servings

In this recipe, you can easily substitute scallops for the shrimp. To be a bit more decadent, add 1 teaspoon (5 mL) fresh lemon juice to ½ cup (18 mL) melted butter, stir, and brush the lemon butter on the toasted buns before you add the tomato and the lobster patties.

4 (1-pound (454-g)) live lobsters
1 large tomato, cut into 4 slices
1 tablespoon (15 mL) granulated garlic
1 tablespoon (15 mL) sugar
Salt, to taste
Freshly ground black pepper, to taste
3 tablespoons (45 mL) extra virgin olive oil, divided
¼ pound (112 g) cooked cocktail shrimp
2 tablespoons (30 mL) heavy cream
4 teaspoons (20 mL) mayonnaise
2 teaspoons (10 mL) finely chopped chives
½ teaspoon (2.5 mL) grated fresh ginger
¼ teaspoon (1.25 mL) soy sauce
4 hoagie rolls or poppy seed hamburger buns

1. Preheat the barbecue to medium high (350°F [180°C] to 400°F [200°C]). On a side burner, stove, or gas burner, bring a large stockpot of water to a boil. Fill a large bowl with cold water.

2. Place the lobsters in the boiling water and cook for 5 minutes once the water returns to a boil. Using long tongs, transfer them to the bowl of cold water. When the lobsters are cool, remove the meat from the claws, legs, and tail. Cut the meat into large pieces. Place the pieces in a bowl, cover the bowl with plastic wrap, and refrigerate until needed.

3. Place a double sheet of heavy-duty aluminum foil on the grill and spray it generously with grilling spray. Arrange the tomato slices on the foil. Sprinkle them with garlic, sugar, salt, and pepper. Drizzle with 1 tablespoon (15 mL) of olive oil. Grill the tomatoes until they are softened and the edges are charred. With a spatula, remove them from the grill and let them cool.

4. In a food processor, puree the shrimp for a few seconds until smooth. Add the cream. Fold the shrimp mixture into the lobster meat and season with salt and pepper. Mold this mixture into 4 lightly packed patties, cover, and refrigerate.

5. In a bowl, combine the mayonnaise, chives, ginger, and soy sauce. Cover and set aside.

6. Place a new double sheet of heavy-duty aluminum foil on the grill and brush it well with the remaining 2 tablespoons (30 mL) olive oil. Add the patties and cook them until they are golden, about 5 minutes on each side.

7. Lightly toast the buns. To each bun, add a slice of tomato and a lobster patty. Serve the ginger-chive mayonnaise on the side.

Honeydew-Grilled Ahi

Yield: 6 servings

Don't buy long line-caught tuna. Instead, ask for tuna that's pole-and-line caught. Domestic fish, fish from the Canadian Pacific, or fish harvested worldwide by trolling are recommended.

¾ cup (177 mL) chopped honeydew melon
¼ cup (59 mL) minced sweet onion
2 tablespoons (30 mL) chopped green onions, green parts only
2 tablespoons (30 mL) extra virgin olive oil, plus more for brushing
2 tablespoons (30 mL) finely minced red and yellow bell peppers
1 tablespoon (15 mL) chopped fresh mint leaves
1 tablespoon (15 mL) lime juice
1 teaspoon (5 mL) finely chopped lemon zest
2 teaspoons (10 mL) freshly ground black pepper, plus more to taste
Salt, to taste
2 tablespoons (30 mL) garlic powder
2 teaspoons (10 mL) granulated sugar
6 (1-inch [2.5-cm] thick) tuna steaks

1. Preheat the barbecue to medium high (350°F [180°C] to 400°F [200°C]).

2. In a large bowl, combine the melon, onion, green onion, 2 tablespoons (30 mL) of the olive oil, the bell peppers, the mint, the lime juice, and the lemon zest and mix well. Add salt and pepper to taste. Transfer the mixture to a saucepan and warm gently over low heat. Cover and set aside.

3. In a small bowl, combine the garlic powder, sugar, and the 2 teaspoons (10 mL) black pepper. Brush the tuna steaks with olive oil, season them with the garlic-sugar-pepper mixture, cover with plastic wrap, and dry marinate for an hour.

4. Grill the steaks for 5 minutes per side. Red tuna turns very white when cooked; the inside should still be red/pink and should be very moist.

5. Serve the steaks on warmed plates. Spoon the relish on the steaks or serve it on the side.

Bluenose Seabass Fillets

Yield: 4–6 servings

Bluenose bass are fished in New Zealand. Most are caught with a hook and line, and the fillets are firm and are usually sold skinless.

1 tablespoon (15 mL) garlic powder
1 tablespoon (15 mL) onion powder
1 tablespoon (15 mL) celery salt
½ teaspoon (2.5 mL) ground mustard
½ teaspoon (2.5 mL) freshly ground black pepper
4¼ pounds (1.9 kg) bluenose fillets (or substitute halibut or tilapia)
¼ cup (60 mL) packed brown sugar
1 tablespoon (15 mL) lemon juice
1 teaspoon (5 mL) confectioners' sugar
1 dash soy sauce

1. In a small bowl, combine the garlic powder, onion powder, celery salt, mustard, and pepper. Rub the fillets with this mixture, gently working it into the flesh with your hands. Leave to dry marinate for 20 minutes.

2. Preheat the barbecue to medium high (350°F [180°C] to 400°F [200°C]).

3. In a separate small bowl, mix together the brown sugar, lemon juice, confectioners' sugar, and soy sauce and set aside.

4. Put a foil packet filled with a handful of alder or oak chips that have been soaked in water for an hour directly on the coals or gas flames. Put a piece of aluminum foil on the grill. Spray the foil with cooking spray. Place the salmon steaks on the foil and close the lid.

5. Smoke for about 7 to 9 minutes per side, brushing both sides heavily with the lemon sauce. When the fish flakes easily but is still a tiny bit pink in the center, remove the fillets from the heat and let them rest, covered with foil, for 2 to 3 minutes. Drizzle more sauce over each fillet and serve.

Red Snapper with Blue Zoo Caper-Anchovy Marinade
Yield: 4 servings

This marinade and sauce can be used on just about any fish. It's very flavorful and will bring up the taste profile of mild fish substantially. This recipe comes from Chef Chris Windus from Blue Zoo restaurant at the Dolphin Hotel in Walt Disney World, Fla.

2 tablespoons (30 mL) dried anchovy
2 tablespoons (30 mL) dried capers
2 tablespoons (30 mL) dried garlic
1 cup (236 mL) mayonnaise
2 tablespoons (30 mL) water
1 tablespoon (15 mL) olive oil
1 tablespoon (15 mL) chopped fresh parsley
½ teaspoon (2.5 mL) ground white pepper
4 red snapper fillets

1. Preheat the barbecue to medium high (350°F [180°C] to 400°F [200°C]).

2. In a nonstick skillet, combine the anchovies, capers, and garlic and cook over medium heat until dried and toasty.

3. Transfer the anchovy mixture to a medium bowl. Add the mayonnaise, water, olive oil, parsley and white pepper. Stir well.

4. Marinate the fish fillets in half of the thick paste for 20 to 30 minutes. Cook the fillets over a medium-hot grill for 1 to 2 minutes per side. Just before serving, spoon the remaining marinade over the fish.

Fiery Fish and Rice

Yield: 4 servings

Any white fish fillets can be used in this dish. If you wish, you can adjust the heat by either doubling the jalapeño pepper or leaving it out completely.

4 cups (0.95 L) cooked rice
¼ cup (59 mL) diced shallots
2 jalapeño peppers, finely minced
2 pounds (908 g) tilapia fillets (or substitute trout, sole, or flounder)
½ cup (118 mL) butter, melted
Salt, to taste
Freshly ground black pepper, to taste
Cayenne pepper, to taste
Lemon quarters, for serving

1. Preheat the barbecue to medium high (350°F [180°C] to 400°F [200°C]). Spray or butter a metal baking pan.

2. Place a layer of rice in the bottom of the prepared pan. Sprinkle with shallots and jalapeño pepper, then add a layer of fish fillets. Brush with butter and sprinkle with cayenne pepper. Repeat the layers, alternating fish and rice, buttering and seasoning each fish and rice layer, until you have two or three layers of each.

3. Bake in the barbecue until the top layer of fish flakes easily but is still moist inside.

4. Using a wide spatula, place 1 section of the dish (all layers) on each of the plates and serve with any remaining butter drizzled over the top fish layer. Provide lemon quarters to squeeze over the fish.

Braised Breaded Rainbow Trout

Yield: 4 servings

You can also fill the body cavity with cooked crab or shrimp and cook the same way.

1 (3-pound [1.3-kg]) rainbow trout or other local fresh trout
1 cup (236 mL) heavy cream
2 egg yolks
1 cup (236 mL) fresh breadcrumbs
1 cup (236 mL) cornmeal
1 teaspoon (5 mL) garlic powder
1 teaspoon (5 mL) dried summer savory
1 teaspoon (5 mL) ground basil
1 teaspoon (5 mL) ground marjoram
2 tablespoons (30 mL) butter, cut into 2 or 3 pieces
Sea salt, to taste
Lemon pepper, to taste
Melted butter, for serving
1 lemon, quartered

1. Preheat the barbecue to medium high (350°F [180°C] to 400°F [200°C]), making sure the grill has been oiled and sprayed with nonstick cooking or grilling spray.

2. Clean and pat dry the whole trout. In a wide, flat dish, mix together the cream and egg yolks. In a similar dish, combine the breadcrumbs, cornmeal, garlic powder, savory, basil, and marjoram.

3. Soak the fish in the egg mixture for 5 minutes. Drain the fish slightly and roll it in the breading mixture. Carefully put the breaded fish back in the egg mixture and repeat the soaking. Remove the fish and gently roll it in the dry ingredients again, pressing the mixture into the fish. Place the butter inside the cavity.

4. Place the fish directly on the grill. Sprinkle liberally with the salt and lemon pepper.

5. Cook for 3 to 4 minutes, or until the fish flakes easily. Using two spatulas (not tongs) gently turn the fish and grill for 3 to 4 minutes on the second side. If using a smoker, put the fish in the hottest part of smoker and cook for 5 to 6 minutes per side, or until the fish flakes easily.

6. With a very sharp knife, cut down the back of the fish and gently separate the halves, pulling the backbone and rib bones away from bottom layer. Divide each half into 2 pieces. Drizzle with melted butter and serve with fresh lemon quarters.

Grilled Flounder with Apple Salsa

Yield: 4–6 servings

In place of the Granny Smith apples, you can use pippin, honey crisp, or Arkansas Black apples. The key is to use tart apples, not the sweeter varieties.

4 Granny Smith apples, unpeeled, cored, and finely diced
1 (8-ounce [227-g]) can cranberry jelly
¼ cup (59 mL) pineapple rum
¼ cup (60 mL) chopped fresh cilantro
6 green onions, thinly sliced, green and white parts
2 teaspoons (10 mL) grated orange zest
1 teaspoon (5 mL) grated lemon zest
1 teaspoon (5 mL) grated lime zest
1 teaspoon (5 mL) finely minced jalapeño pepper
Salt, to taste
Freshly ground black pepper, to taste
¼ cup (59 mL) clarified butter
1 tablespoon (15 mL) lemon juice
2 (1-pound [454-g]) flounder fillets
½ cup (118 mL) barbecue rub of your choice
½ teaspoon (2.5 mL) cayenne pepper
Lemon wedges, for garnish
Fresh mint sprigs, for garnish

1. In a large bowl, combine the apple, cranberry jelly, rum, cilantro, green onion, citrus zests, and jalapeño pepper. Season well with salt and pepper, cover, and chill for at least 30 minutes.

2. Preheat the barbecue to medium high (350°F [180°C] to 400°F [200°C]). Place a large piece of aluminum foil on the grill and spray it with nonstick grilling spray.

3. In a small bowl, combine the clarified butter and lemon juice. Brush both sides of the flounder lightly with this mixture. Generously shake the barbecue rub on the both sides of the fillets, add a sprinkle of cayenne pepper, and let the fish rest for 5 minutes.

4. Place the fillets on the foil and cook for about 2 minutes. Turn and cook on the second side for another 1 to 2 minutes. The fish will cook very quickly, so be careful not to overcook it. When it's finished, the flesh will have just started to flake and the fish will be moist inside.

5. Serve the flounder with the apple salsa on the side, garnished with the lemon wedges and mint.

Teriyaki-Marinated Perch Fillets
Yield: 4–6 servings

Lake perch sold commercially are mainly harvested from Lake Erie or the other Great Lakes, even though they can be found in many lakes around the country.

2 pounds (908 g) fresh or frozen perch fillets
⅓ cup (79 mL) vegetable oil
2 tablespoons (30 mL) distilled white vinegar
2 tablespoons (30 mL) finely chopped green onion, white and green parts
3 tablespoons (45 mL) dark soy sauce
1 tablespoon (15 mL) grated fresh ginger
1 tablespoon (15 mL) brown sugar

1. Preheat the barbecue to medium high (350°F [180°C] to 400°F [200°C]). Butter a cast-iron skillet.

2. Thaw the fish, if using frozen. In a small bowl, mix together the oil, vinegar, green onion, soy sauce, ginger, and brown sugar. In a shallow dish, arrange the fish in a single layer. Pour the marinade over the fish, cover the dish with plastic wrap, and marinate for 30 to 60 minutes at room temperature, turning occasionally.

3. Remove the fish from the marinade. Transfer the marinade to a saucepan and boil it for 10 minutes. Place fish in the prepared cast-iron skillet and place the skillet on the grill. Cook for 8 to 9 minutes. Turn the fish and brush with the cooked marinade. Grill for 6 to 8 minutes, or until the fish flakes easily when tested with a fork.

Curried Au Gratin Oysters
Yield: 4–6 servings

You can substitute mussels for the oysters, but they are harder to find shucked, so you'll probably have to shuck 'em yourself. Aw, shucks!

1 large bunch fresh spinach, washed and dried
3 tablespoons (45 mL) butter, divided
6 large white or brown mushrooms, sliced
½ cup (118 mL) milk
40 small shucked oysters, drained, ½ cup (118 mL) oyster liquid reserved
2 tablespoons (30 mL) all-purpose flour
Kosher salt, to taste
½–1 teaspoon (5 mL) curry powder
½ teaspoon (2.5 mL) paprika
2 tablespoons (30 mL) dry sherry
1 teaspoon (5 mL) lemon juice
¼ cup (59 mL) fine dry breadcrumbs
Freshly grated Parmigiano-Reggiano cheese, to taste
Sourdough French rolls or toasted French bread, for serving

1. Bring a pot of water to a boil. Trim the spinach and cook it in the boiling water until just beginning to wilt. Drain, cool, and squeeze out the excess water. Coarsely chop the spinach and set it aside.

2. In a skillet, melt 1 tablespoon (15 mL) of the butter over medium heat. Add the mushrooms and sauté until they just begin to wilt. Transfer the mushrooms to a bowl and set aside.

3. Preheat the barbecue to medium high (350°F [180°C] to 400°F [200°C]). Lightly butter a medium casserole dish or Dutch oven.

4. In a small bowl, combine the milk with the reserved oyster liquid. In the same skillet you used for the mushrooms, melt another tablespoon (15 mL) of the butter. Add the flour and stir until blended. Slowly whisk in the milk mixture and mix well. Add the salt, curry powder, and paprika. When the sauce is smooth and hot, add the oysters and heat to a simmer. Cook until the oysters plump. Do not boil. Add the sherry and lemon juice and mix lightly.

5. Meanwhile, arrange a layer of spinach on the bottom of the prepared casserole or Dutch oven. Top with the mushrooms. Spoon the oysters and sauce over the mushrooms. Cover with the breadcrumbs and Parmesan cheese. Place the casserole in the barbecue and bake for 10 to 12 minutes.

6. Serve with sourdough French rolls or slices of toasted French bread to soak up the juices.

Grilled Caribbean Swordfish

Yield: 4 servings

This can also be prepared as swordfish kebabs. Cut the steaks into 1-inch (2.5-cm) cubes, marinate as directed, thread the fish onto metal skewers, and grill for about the same time.

¼ cup (59 mL) extra virgin olive oil, plus more for grilling the vegetables
Juice of 3 limes
¼ cup (59 mL) unsweetened coconut milk
¼ cup (60 mL) grated fresh ginger
¼ cup (59 mL) lightly-packed fresh cilantro leaves
1 tablespoon (15 mL) balsamic vinegar
2 cloves garlic, peeled and minced
1 jalapeño pepper, seeded and chopped
1 teaspoon (5 mL) cracked black pepper
4 (6–8 ounce [168–227 g]) swordfish steaks
Vidalia onions, sliced in ¼-inch (½-cm) slices
Red bell peppers, sliced in ¼-inch (½-cm) slices
Yellow bell peppers, sliced in ¼-inch (½-cm) slices
Shiitake mushroom caps for grilling, sliced ½-inch (1-cm) thick
Salt, to taste
Freshly ground black pepper, to taste

1. In a medium bowl, combine the ¼ cup (59 mL) olive oil, lime juice, coconut milk, ginger, cilantro, vinegar, garlic, jalapeño pepper, and pepper. Rub the swordfish steaks with this marinade, cover, and refrigerate overnight.

2. Preheat the barbecue to medium high (350°F [180°C] to 400°F [200°C]).

3. In a large bowl, mix the onions, peppers, and mushrooms with the remaining olive oil, salt, and pepper, stirring to coat all the vegetables with oil.

4. Remove the swordfish from the marinade. Pour the marinade into a saucepan and boil for 10 minutes while the fish comes to room temperature.

5. Grill the swordfish until it is well colored on both sides and the interior is medium, about 3 to 4 minutes per side.

6. Place the vegetables on the other side of the grill or into a grilling basket, and carefully cook them until they just begin to char on the edges.

7. Remove the fish from the grill and transfer it to warmed plates. Drizzle the marinade over the fish. Serve with generous servings of the grilled vegetables.

Tarragon Tails

Yield: 4 servings

You can enhance this recipe by pouring brandy over the tails just before you serve and flaming the dish at the table.

4 lobster tails, fresh or frozen
¼ cup (60 mL) lemon juice
Salt, to taste
Freshly ground black pepper, to taste
1 tablespoon (15 mL) chopped fresh tarragon, divided
½ cup (118 mL) olive oil
½ cup (118 mL) butter, melted
½ teaspoon (2.5 mL) celery salt

1. Preheat the barbecue to medium high (350°F [180°C] to 400°F [200°C]).

2. If using frozen lobster tails, let them thaw. Split the tails. Sprinkle them with lemon juice, salt, pepper, and half of the tarragon and let stand for 1 hour.

3. Brush the tails with the olive oil and cook, flesh side down, on the barbecue for 10 minutes. Turn shell side down and cook for 10 minutes longer.

4. Brush generously with the melted butter, sprinkle with the remaining tarragon and celery salt, and serve over rice or with buttered boiled potatoes.

Dirty Bag Shrimp

Yield: 4–6 servings

This seasoning is relatively mild, but you can fire it up by adding minced habañero or jalapeño pepper to the seasoning mix. If you have guests who don't want to get down and dirty with this dish, you can peel the shrimp before you cook them so they can eat with a fork.

2 pounds (908 g) shrimp, shell on
¼ cup (59 mL) butter, melted
3 tablespoons (45 mL) olive oil
1 tablespoon (15 mL) kosher salt
1 tablespoon (15 mL) celery salt
1 tablespoon (15 mL) paprika
1 teaspoon (5 mL) garlic powder
1 teaspoon (5 mL) onion powder
1 teaspoon (5 mL) salt
1 teaspoon (5 mL) freshly ground black pepper
1 teaspoon (5 mL) cayenne pepper
1 teaspoon (5 mL) dried thyme
4–6 brown paper lunch bags

1. Preheat the barbecue to medium high (350°F [180°C] to 400°F [200°C]).

2. Place the shrimp in a large bowl. In a small bowl, mix together the melted butter and oil. Pour this mixture over the shrimp, sprinkle with the kosher salt, and mix well to coat every piece. Place the shrimp directly on the grill and cook just until they are all pink on both sides. Do not over-cook, remove them from the grill the minute they change color.

3. In a small bowl, mix together the celery salt, paprika, garlic powder, onion powder, salt, black pepper, cayenne pepper, and thyme. Set aside.

4. Place 8 to 10 shrimp in each paper bag. Add 1 teaspoon (5 mL) of the spice mixture to each bag and shake the bags vigorously to coat all the shrimp with the seasonings.

5. Hand a bag to each person so they can tear open the bags and get their hands dirty! Supply lots of paper towels and hand wipes. Serve with plenty of lemon wedges and a sweet and smoky barbecue sauce for dipping.

Salmon and Mushroom Flounder

Yield: 4 servings

We use salmon because it has a widely different flavor profile from the flounder. It also has a different color, which pleases the eye as well as the taste buds.

⅓ cup (79 mL) butter
1 small onion, peeled and minced
¾ pound (336 g) mushrooms
4½ tablespoons (67.5 mL) all-purpose flour
1¾ cup (413 mL) milk
1½ teaspoons (2.5 mL) salt
⅛ teaspoon (0.6 mL) freshly ground black pepper
1 (14¾-ounce [436 mL]) can salmon
5 tablespoons (75 mL) chopped fresh parsley
¼ cup (59 mL) fresh chopped chives
2 tablespoons (30 mL) lemon juice
1 teaspoon (5 mL) dried tarragon
1 teaspoon (5 mL) paprika
½ teaspoon (2.5 mL) garlic powder
2 pounds (908 g) flounder or sole fillets
¼ cup (59 mL) butter, melted

1. In a medium saucepan, melt the ⅓ cup (79 mL) butter. Add the onion and mushrooms and cook until tender. In a small bowl, blend together the flour and milk. Add this mixture to the mushrooms and cook over low heat, stirring constantly, until the sauce has thickened. Season with the salt and pepper.

2. Preheat the barbecue to medium high (350°F [180°C] to 400°F [200°C]). Butter a baking dish.

3. In a medium bowl, combine the salmon, parsley, chives, lemon juice, tarragon, paprika, and garlic powder and mix well. Spread the salmon mixture on each of the flounder fillets. Roll the fillets and place them in the prepared baking dish, seam side down. Brush with the melted butter. Bake in the barbecue for 25 minutes, or until the fish flakes with fork.

4. Divide the fillets among serving plates, spoon the mushroom sauce over the fillets, and serve.

Salt and Pepper Calamari
Yield: 4 servings

This dish is superb when grilled on the barbecue, is easy to make, and takes only minutes to cook. And you won't have to worry about leftovers. Do not overcook the calamari, or it will be rubbery instead of tender.

1½–1¾ pounds (681–795 g) calamari steaks, pounded
1 tablespoon (15 mL) vegetable oil
2 teaspoons (10 mL) sea salt
1 teaspoon (5 mL) garlic powder
¾ teaspoon (3.75 mL) freshly ground black pepper
¼ teaspoon (1.75 mL) ground white pepper
½ lime, cut in wedges

1. Preheat the barbecue to medium high (350°F [180°C] to 400°F [200°C]), making sure the grill is well oiled and sprayed generously with nonstick cooking or grilling spray.

2. Rinse the calamari steaks and place them on a paper towel. Pat them very dry. Cut the calamari lengthwise into ½-inch (1-cm) wide strips and place them in a flat baking pan. Drizzle the oil over the calamari and stir to make sure they are all covered.

3. In a small bowl, mix together the salt, black pepper, garlic powder, and white pepper. Sprinkle this mixture over the oiled calamari. Mix until all the calamari strips are coated with the spices. Cover with plastic wrap and set aside to marinate.

4. Place the calamari on the hot grill and cook for 30 seconds to 2 minutes per side, depending on the heat of your grill.

5. Taste the calamari. If they are too salty, add lime juice. If they are not salty enough, add more salt.

Grilled Sea Scallops with Raspberry-Thyme Butter Sauce
Yield: 4 servings

Scallops should be cooked just until they are lightly browned on the outside. The inside should be moist, barely translucent, and medium-rare. Cook them any longer, and they become white hunks of rubber.

½ cup (118 mL) fresh raspberries, plus ¼ cup (59 mL) for garnish
2 tablespoons (30 mL) fresh thyme leaves, plus 3 sprigs for garnish
1 cup (236 mL) medium-dry white wine
2 tablespoons (30 mL) minced shallots
½ teaspoon (2.5 mL) sugar
2 pounds (908 g) large sea scallops
1 cup (236 mL) unsalted butter, chilled and cut into small pieces
¼ teaspoon (1.25 mL) salt
⅛ teaspoon (0.6 mL) freshly ground black pepper
2 tablespoons (30 mL) butter, melted

1. Preheat the barbecue to medium high (350°F [180°C] to 400°F [200°C]).

2. In a small bowl, use a spoon to crush ½ cup (118 mL) of the raspberries. Add 2 tablespoons (30 mL) of the thyme. Strain this mixture into a small, heavy, nonreactive saucepan. Add the wine, shallots, and sugar. Bring the mixture to a boil over medium heat. Lower the heat and simmer, uncovered, until the liquid is reduced to ⅓ cup (79 mL), 12 to 14 minutes. Strain the mixture, return it to the saucepan, and set aside

3. Rinse the scallops, pat them dry, and thread them onto 4 long, flat, metal skewers.

4. Warm the raspberry reduction over low heat. With a whisk, stir in the cold butter, 1 to 2 pieces at a time, whisking well. Stir in the salt and pepper. Cover the sauce and keep it warm.

5. Make a smoker package by putting a handful of soaked hickory or oak chips in a 12-inch (30-cm) square of heavy-duty aluminum foil, folding over the package, poking 3 or 4 holes in the top of the foil, and placing the package directly on the coals or open flame to add smoke to your grilling.

6. Place the scallops on the grill, brush them with the 2 tablespoons melted butter, and grill, turning once, until lightly golden and opaque, about 4 minutes on each side.

7. Pour the raspberry butter sauce onto a large serving tray and place the scallops on top of the sauce. Garnish the platter with the remaining raspberries and sprigs of thyme, and serve immediately.

Japanese Barbecued Swimming Fish
Yield: 4–6 servings

Dashi is available made with dried kelp, dried bonito fish flakes, dried sardines, or dried shiitake mushrooms. If you want to make your own, tons of recipes are available online.

⅓ cup (79 mL) dashi (Japanese fish sauce)
⅓ cup (79 mL) soy sauce
¼ cup (59 mL) lemon juice
⅓ cup (59 mL) rice vinegar, divided
1 hot red chili pepper, seeded and chopped
2 cups (473 mL) water
⅔ cup (158 mL) sugar
2 tablespoons (30 mL) plus 2 teaspoons (10 mL) salt, divided
1 (1½–2 pound [.68–1.1 kg]) mackerel
Lemon wedges, for garnish

1. Make the ponzu sauce: In a small bowl, whisk together the dashi, soy sauce, lemon juice, and 3 tablespoons of the rice vinegar. Set aside.

2. In a small skillet over medium heat, toast the chili pepper for a few seconds. Add 2 tablespoons of the remaining vinegar, and ⅓ cup (79 mL) of the ponzu sauce. Remove the skillet from the heat and refrigerate.

3. Make the dipping sauce: In a saucepan, bring the water and the remaining vinegar to a boil. Add the sugar and 2 teaspoons (10 mL) of the salt and stir until dissolved. Remove the sauce from the heat and set aside.

4. Preheat the barbecue to medium high (350°F [180°C] to 400°F [200°C]), making sure the grill has been well oiled or sprayed with a nonstick cooking or grilling spray

5. Clean and scale the fish and dry it with a paper towel. Make 2 deep crosswise cuts on each side. Put a skewer through the tail end of the fish, bending the skewer so that it comes out in the center, then reinsert and continue to the head, bending again so that the fish has an S-shape.

6. Sprinkle both sides of the fish lightly with the remaining salt. Press a liberal amount of salt onto the tail and fins. Grill the fish, turning it with the skewer to avoid damaging the skin, until it is golden on both sides and cooked through, about 10 to 12 minutes.

7. Remove the fish from the grill and place it on a large serving platter. Garnish the fish with lemon wedges. Serve with the remaining ponzu sauce and the dipping sauce on the side.

Stuffed Barbecued Clams

Yield: 4–6 servings

Great clams to use in this recipe include steamers, littlenecks, long-necked, jumbo, or horseneck clams.

2–3 dozen clams
Vegetable oil for cooking
1½ (8-ounce [118-mL]) bottle clam juice
1 cup (236 mL) fresh breadcrumbs
2 tablespoons (30 mL) butter, melted
2 tablespoons (30 mL) olive oil
1½ teaspoons (7.5 mL) dried thyme
1½ teaspoons (7.5 mL) dried parsley
1½ teaspoons (7.5 mL) granulated garlic
1½ teaspoons (7.5 mL) crushed red pepper

1. Preheat the barbecue to medium high (350°F [180°C] to 400°F [200°C]).

2. Wash the clams. Pour a little vegetable oil into a wide saucepan, add the clams, cover, and heat until all the clams are open. Remove the clams from the shells, reserving the juice. Pour the juice into a saucepan with the bottled clam juice and warm on the stovetop or on a side burner.

3. Chop the clams into small pieces. Place them in a bowl and add the breadcrumbs, butter, olive oil, thyme, parsley, garlic, and crushed red pepper and mix well. Spoon a little clam juice over the top of each clam.

4. Bake in the barbecue for 15 minutes. If the clams look too dry, spoon on more clam juice.

5. Remove the clams from the barbecue and serve with the heated clam juice on the side.

Grilled Fish Sinaloa Style

Yield: 6–8 servings

Chef Gilberto del Toro is not only a close friend, but also one of the best chefs in Mexico and, as far as I know, the only master Italian cuisine chef in the country. He cooked this dish for us over a small beach campfire, but you can do it just as well on your barbecue. This recipe comes from Chef Gilberto del Toro of Casa Bonita, Mazatlan, Mexico.

1 whole (8-pound [3.6-kg]) pargo, tilapia, Pacific flounder, or sole, cleaned and butterflied
1 cup (236 mL) canola oil
6 cloves garlic, peeled, divided
12 black peppercorns, divided
¼ cup (59 mL) dry white wine
2 bay leaves
1 tablespoon (15 mL) freshly squeezed lime juice
Salt, to taste
2 ancho peppers
½ yellow onion
3 Roma tomatoes
½ teaspoon (2.5 mL) coarse sea salt
⅛ teaspoon (0.6 mL) ground cumin
⅛ teaspoon (0.6 mL) dried oregano
Freshly ground black pepper, to taste
3 tablespoons (45 mL) olive oil
Juice of 2 limes
1 large red onion, peeled and thickly sliced
1 large tomato, sliced
1 green bell pepper, sliced
1 yellow bell pepper, sliced
1 red bell pepper, sliced
¼ cup (59 mL) butter, melted
1 (12-ounce [354-mL]) bottle Mexican beer

1. Rinse the fish thoroughly with cold running water and pat it dry with paper towels.

2. In a food processor, combine the canola oil, 3 cloves of the garlic, 6 of the peppercorns, the wine, the bay leaves, the tablespoon (15 mL) lime juice, and salt to taste. Process until well blended. Put the fish in a 2-gallon (7.6-L) resealable plastic bag and pour the marinade in over it. Refrigerate for at least 2 hours or as long as 8 hours.

3. Preheat the barbecue to medium high (300°F [150°C] to 350°F [180°C]).

4. Roast the ancho peppers on the grill over direct heat until they begin to char. Core and seed the anchos and soak them in cold water for 1 hour. Place the yellow onion, Roma tomatoes, and remaining garlic over indirect heat and cook until they become soft and fragrant, about 15 minutes.

5. Make the chili sauce: In a large mortar or a bowl, combine the remaining peppercorns, sea salt, cumin, and oregano. Grind with a pestle until pulverized. Gradually add the roasted peppers, roasted onion, roasted tomatoes, and roasted garlic, grinding to a smooth paste after each addition. Season with salt and pepper, add the olive oil, and set aside.

6. Line one side of a fish-grilling basket with aluminum foil. Remove the fish from the marinade and wipe off the excess. Place the fish, skin side down, on the foil. Season with salt, black pepper, and the lime juice. Brush the chili sauce onto the fish. Top with the sliced onion, tomato, and bell peppers. Brush on a little of the melted butter. Line the other side of the basket with foil and close the basket.

7. Transfer the fish basket to the grill, making sure the grill has an even, moderate flame, to avoid overcooking. Grill the fish, skin side down, until it flakes and the edges just start to brown, 8 to 10 minutes per side, opening the basket halfway through cooking to baste with the remaining butter and beer and to turn the basket over.

8. Remove the basket from the heat and let stand for a few minutes. Open the basket, transfer the fish to a serving tray, and serve immediately.

Grilled Oysters with Crabmeat Stuffing
Yield: 4–6 servings

You can substitute chopped shrimp, chopped thick slices of bacon, or cooked ham for the crabmeat.

14–20 oysters on the half shell
1 cup (236 mL) fresh crabmeat, or 1(7-ounce [196-g]) can
2 tablespoons (30 mL) chopped celery
1 tablespoon (15 mL) minced green bell pepper
1 teaspoon (5 mL) chopped chives
¼ cup (59 mL) mayonnaise
½ teaspoon (2.5 mL) salt
¼ teaspoon (1.25 mL) ground cumin
¼ teaspoon (1.25 mL) hot sauce
¼ teaspoon (1.25 mL) dry mustard
¼ cup (59 mL) fresh breadcrumbs
¼ cup (59 mL) grated cheddar cheese
Paprika, for garnish

1. Preheat the barbecue to medium high (400°F [200°C] to 450°F [240°C]).

2. Loosen the oysters from the bottoms of the shells and set the oysters aside.

3. In a small bowl, combine the crab, celery, bell pepper, and chives. Add the mayonnaise, salt, cumin, hot sauce, and mustard and stir. Add the breadcrumbs and stir again. Spoon a heaping tablespoon (22.5 mL) of this mixture on top of each oyster.

4. Place the oysters in a shallow baking dish or on a baking sheet and bake in the barbecue for about 12 to 15 minutes, or until the juices are bubbling and the stuffing is nicely browned.

5. Remove the oysters from the grill. Sprinkle the tops of the oysters with the cheddar cheese and paprika, and serve immediately.

Singapore Bacon-Wrapped Scallops with Soy Sauce Glaze
Yield: 4–6 servings

I cooked this recipe on Barbecue America, *and the crew devoured the scallops before the studio lights cooled down. Use high-quality bacon, and this becomes one of the best dishes you'll ever barbecue.*

3 tablespoons (45 mL) dark soy sauce
3 tablespoons (45 mL) brown sugar
1 tablespoon (15 mL) freshly squeezed lime juice
1 teaspoon (5 mL) butter
1 teaspoon (5 mL) lemon pepper
½ teaspoon (2.5 mL) garlic salt
2 tablespoons (30 mL) freshly squeezed lemon juice
2 tablespoons (30 mL) olive oil
1 pinch cayenne pepper
1 pound (454 g) scallops (about 16 large)
8 slices bacon, halved lengthwise
6 (12-inch [30-cm]) sprigs fresh rosemary, stick ends sharpened

1. In a small saucepan, combine the soy sauce, brown sugar, lime juice, butter, lemon pepper, and garlic salt. Bring to a boil over high heat. Decrease the heat to medium high and cook at a low boil for 4 minutes, or until the liquid is reduced by half. Cover and refrigerate.

2. In a 1- to 2-gallon (3.8–7.6 L) resealable plastic bag, combine the lemon juice, oil, and cayenne pepper. Add the scallops, turn the bag several times to coat, and marinate at room temperature for 1 to 2 hours.

3. Preheat the barbecue to medium high (350°F [180°C] to 400°F [200°C]), making sure the grill is well oiled or sprayed with a nonstick cooking or grilling spray.

4. Drain the scallops, discarding the marinade. Wrap 1 strip of bacon around each scallop. Transfer the wrapped scallops to a plate, seam side down. Thread the scallops crosswise (from edge to edge, and through the bacon, so the end of the bacon doesn't dangle) onto the rosemary skewers. Transfer to the grill and cook over direct heat for 4 minutes. Turn, brush with the glaze, and cook 3 to 4 minutes longer, or until the bacon is cooked through and crisp around the edges.

5. Transfer the skewers to a platter, brush with glaze, and serve immediately with steamed rice or buttered noodles.

Sizzlin' Salmon Burgers

Yield: 4 servings

If you have leftover salmon, this dish is a perfect way to use it up. You can also use canned salmon, but obviously the fresher salmon is preferable.

1½ cups (354 mL) cooked salmon, or 1 (12½-ounce [350-g]) can boneless, skinless pink salmon
2 tablespoons (30 mL) milk
1 large egg, beaten
½ cup (118 mL) panko
¼ cup (59 mL) shredded Swiss or Monterey Jack cheese
1 teaspoon (5 mL) minced chives
½ teaspoon (2.5 mL) dried thyme

1. Preheat the barbecue to medium high (350°F [180°C] to 400°F [200°C]). Place a sheet of aluminum foil on the grill and spray it with nonstick grilling spray or brush it with olive oil.

2. Put the cooked salmon into a medium bowl. Add the milk, egg, panko, cheese, chives, and thyme and stir to mix well. Let sit for 10 minutes.

3. Shape the salmon into 4 (½-inch [1-cm] thick) patties. Cook the patties on the sprayed foil for 2 to 3 minutes or until the bottoms are browned. Carefully turn with a spatula and cook 2 minutes more, or until the bottoms of the patties brown.

4. Serve each patty on a toasted onion hamburger bun, topped with lettuce, sliced tomato, and tartar sauce.

Grilled Octopus

Yield: 4–6 servings

The website italianfoodforever.com has a unique tip from contributor Deborah Mele on how to tenderize octopus: "I double bagged the octopus and ran it through the spin cycle in my washing machine. I must say this preparation created the most tender octopus we have ever made yet." I haven't tried this, but I imagine it works quite well on the hot water setting.

2 pounds (908 g) cleaned and trimmed octopus, legs only
½ cup (120 mL) extra virgin olive oil
¼ cup (59 mL) fresh lemon juice, squeezed lemon rinds reserved
¼ cup (118 mL) red wine vinegar
¼ cup (59 mL) finely chopped fresh parsley
1 tablespoon (15 mL) dried oregano
2 cloves garlic, peeled and mashed
 1 tablespoon (15 mL) coarse salt, plus more to taste
1 teaspoon (5 mL) cracked black pepper
2 lemons, quartered

1. Rub the red skin off the octopus. Rinse and dry the octopus on paper towels and chop it into bite-size pieces. Place the octopus in a pot of salted water and boil for 30 minutes, stirring often.

2. Remove the octopus from the pot, drain, and cool. Place the cooled octopus in a 2-gallon (7.6-L) resealable plastic bag.

3. In a small bowl, mix together olive oil, lemon juice, lemon rinds, vinegar, parsley, oregano, garlic, and salt and stir. Pour this mixture into the bag with the octopus. Shake the bag to coat all the pieces and marinate overnight in the refrigerator.

4. Preheat the barbecue to medium high (350°F [180°C] to 400°F [200°C]). Oil or spray the grill with a nonstick cooking or grilling spray.

5. Make a smoker package by putting a handful of soaked hickory or oak chips on a 12-inch (30-cm) square of heavy-duty aluminum foil, folding over the package, poking 3 or 4 holes in the top of the foil, and placing the package directly on the coals or open flame to add smoke to your grilling. Remove the octopus from marinade. Discard the marinade.

6. Place the octopus on the grill and cook, turning often, until the edges start to brown and crisp, about 4 to 5 minutes per side. Transfer to a serving bowl and squeeze lemon over the pieces. Season with salt and the pepper, stir, and serve.

Dr. Marsden's Barbecued Smelt

Yield: 6 servings

Smelt harvesting, called smelt dipping by locals, takes place in the early spring on tributaries of the Great Lakes. Thousands of the tiny fish head upriver to spawn, and locals bring nets and buckets to the river to scoop up these tasty critters. This recipe comes from Steve Marsden from Northville, Mich.

2½ tablespoons (30 mL) butter
¼ cup (59 mL) chopped onion
1 clove garlic, peeled and minced
2½ tablespoons (30 mL) chopped green bell pepper
1 tablespoon (15 mL) tomato sauce
1 tablespoon (15 mL) sugar
1 teaspoon (5 mL) freshly ground black pepper
2 pounds (908 g) dressed smelt

1. Preheat the barbecue to medium high (350°F [180°C] to 400°F [200°C]).

2. In a small saucepan, melt the butter. Add the onion and garlic and cook until soft, but not browned, add the bell pepper, tomato sauce, sugar, and black pepper and heat until the mixture just begins to bubble. Remove the pan from the heat and cool to room temperature.

3. Put the smelt in a 1-gallon (3.8-L) resealable plastic bag. Pour the cooled sauce in over it, turn the bag several times, and marinate for an hour.

4. Place the fish on the grill and cook for 5 to 8 minutes, turning several times with tongs. When the fish flake easily, remove them from the grill, place them on a warmed platter, and serve.

Shrimp and Scallop Burgers with Wasabi Mayonnaise
Yield: 4 servings

You can do this with all shrimp, or you could use crab, lobster, or another fish in place of the scallops. You can also sauté these burgers in a skillet in a little olive oil.

1 cup (236 mL) olive oil mayonnaise
2 tablespoons (30 mL) prepared wasabi paste
2 tablespoons (30 mL) light soy sauce
1 teaspoon (5 mL) grated fresh ginger
1 teaspoon (5 mL) sugar
1 pinch kosher salt
¾ pound (336 g) rock shrimp, divided
¼ pound (112 g) bay or sea scallops, divided
1 large egg
½ cup (118 mL) panko
¼ cup (59 mL) minced fresh parsley
¼ teaspoon (1.25 mL) garlic salt
⅛ teaspoon (0.6 mL) hot sauce
Freshly ground black pepper, to taste
4 hamburger buns
4 tomato slices

1. Make sure the grill is clean and generously sprayed with nonstick grilling spray. Preheat the barbecue to medium high (350°F [180°C] to 400°F [200°C]).

2. In a medium bowl, mix together the mayonnaise, wasabi paste, soy sauce, ginger, sugar, and salt. Taste, and add salt or pepper as you desire. Cover and refrigerate until ready to use.

3. In a food processor, pulse half the shrimp and half the scallops with the egg until the mixture is well blended.

4. With a sharp knife, chop the remaining shrimp and scallops. Put the chunks in a bowl. Add the processed shrimp and scallops, panko, parsley, garlic salt, hot sauce, and pepper to taste. Divide the mixture into 4 portions and form each into a 1½- to 2-inch (3.5–5 cm) patty.

5. Grill the patties until cooked through, about 3 to 4 minutes per side.

6. Place the patties on the hamburger buns. Top each with a slice of fresh tomato and a dollop of the wasabi mayonnaise.

SIX

Game Birds, Goose, and Duck

Barbecued Peking Duck with Cold Duck-Hoisin Sauce
Yield: 4 servings

You'll find either Mandarin pancakes at an Asian grocery store or at a major grocery outlet, or you can make them yourself. Several websites offer video demonstrations showing how to make them. To make green onion brushes, use a sharp knife to cut green onions (after trimming away the root) into 2-inch (5-cm) long pieces. Cut vertically into the onion about 1 inch (2.5 cm), then rotate the onion 90 degrees and make another cut so that onion is quartered into a four-segmented "brush."

1 (5–6 pound [2.3–2.7 kg]) duck
1 cup (236 mL) Cold Duck sparkling wine
1 cup (236 mL) honey
½ cup (118 mL) hoisin sauce
1 tablespoon (15 mL) ground ginger
1 teaspoon (5 mL) garlic powder
¼ teaspoon (1.25 mL) salt
1 (16-ounce [473 mL]) can apple juice or white grape juice

1. Wash and dry the duck and place it in a 1- to 2-gallon (3.8- to 7.6-L) resealable plastic bag. In a medium bowl, combine the wine, honey, hoisin sauce, ginger, garlic powder, and salt. Pour the marinade in over the duck, seal the bag, and shake to coat. Refrigerate for 4 to 6 hours or overnight, turning 2 or 3 times.

2. Remove the duck from the marinade. Pour the marinade into a saucepan and boil for 10 minutes. Cool, cover, and refrigerate the marinade. Using twine or butcher string, make a loop through both wings and hang the duck from a cabinet, ceiling fixture, or pot rack with a pan under it. Let the duck dry for 1 day.

3. Preheat the barbecue to medium high (350°F [180°C] to 400°F [200°C]) for indirect heating, putting a water pan under the unheated side of the grill.

4. Place the duck on the upright, opened can of apple juice. Cook the bird for 2 to 3 hours, basting with the marinade once an hour.

5. When duck breast reaches an internal temperature of 160°F (71°C), remove the duck from the barbecue. Remove the duck from the can and baste once more with thick coat of marinade. Boil remaining marinade for 10 minutes.

6. Cut the duck skin and meat into bite-size pieces. Serve with hoisin sauce, green onion brushes, and mandarin pancakes. To eat, use the brush to spread hoisin sauce on the pancakes, add a piece of duck skin and a piece of duck meat, and wrap or fold up the pancake.

Grilled Rhubarb-Cherry Glazed Duck
Yield: 4–6 servings

This delicious grilled duck is prepared in two stages. First, the duck is parboiled in a tasty orange broth. Then the pieces are grilled and basted with a fruity glaze.

1 (4–5 pound [1.8–2.2 kg]) duck
5 cups (1.2 L) water
2 cups (473 mL) orange juice
¼ cup (59 mL) balsamic vinegar
3 tablespoons (45 mL) dark soy sauce
2 tablespoons (30 mL) honey
1 (½-inch [1-cm]) piece fresh ginger
½ cup (118 mL) chopped rhubarb
¼ cup (59 mL) orange marmalade
¼ cup (59 mL) pitted and chopped cherries
1 large cinnamon stick, broken into small pieces
2 whole cloves

1. Rinse and dry the duck. Discard the giblets and neck and cut the duck into quarters. Cut off the legs and wings. Pull off the excess fat. Poke the duck pieces all over with a fork and set them aside.

2. In a large Dutch oven or saucepan, combine the water, orange juice, vinegar, soy sauce, honey, and ginger over medium-high heat and bring to a boil. Add the duck pieces and return to a simmer, making sure duck is covered with liquid. Simmer, covered, for 15 to 20 minutes. Remove the duck pieces from the pan and drain well, discarding the liquid. Pat the duck pieces dry with paper towels.

3. While the duck is boiling, combine the rhubarb, marmalade, cherries, cinnamon stick, and cloves in a small saucepan over medium-low heat. Cook, stirring frequently, for 15 to 20 minutes or until reduced by half. Set the glaze aside.

4. Preheat the barbecue to medium high (350°F [180°C] to 400°F [200°C]) for direct heating. Make a smoker package by putting a handful of soaked hickory or oak chips on a 12-inch (30-cm) square of heavy-duty aluminum foil, folding over the package, poking 3 or 4 holes in the top of the foil, and placing the package directly on the coals to add smoke to your grilling.

5. Poke the duck pieces all over with a fork again. Brush the duck pieces with glaze, place them on the grill with the wings on the outside, and grill, covered, for 15 to 20 minutes. Turn the pieces over, poke them with a fork yet again, and brush them with glaze. Continue turning, poking, and brushing with glaze every 15 to 20 minutes, or until the pieces are done (when poked with a fork, the juices will run clear and the duck will be a beautiful reddish-brown), 35 to 45 minutes total.

6. Remove the duck pieces from the barbecue, cover with foil, and let rest for 20 minutes. Remove the foil and present on a serving platter.

Barbecued Pineapple-Orange Duck
Yield: 4–6 servings

You can change the liquid in the sauce to apricot, lemon-lime, tangerine, pink grape-fruit, or another juice of your choice. Just use zest from the same fruit, or, for apricot, finely diced dried apricots.

2 (4-pound [1.8-kg]) ducklings
Salt, to taste
Freshly ground black pepper, to taste
½ cup (118 mL) sherry
½ cup (118 mL) soy sauce
½ cup (120 mL) pineapple-orange juice
1 tablespoon (15 mL) grated orange zest
1 teaspoon (5 mL) ground ginger
2 tablespoons (30 mL) butter

1. Preheat the barbecue to medium high (350°F [180°C] to 400°F [200°C]) for direct or indirect heating, putting a water pan under the unheated side of the grill.

2. Season the ducklings with salt and pepper. Place them on a roasting rack in a Dutch oven or roasting pan. Fill the bottom of the pan with 1 inch (2.5 cm) of beer or water and cook over direct heat for 15 minutes. Move the pan to the indirect side of grill and cook for about 2 hours in the barbecue or 3 to 4 hours in a smoker.

3. In a small saucepan, combine the sherry, soy sauce, pineapple-orange juice, orange zest, ginger, and salt and pepper, to taste. Cook, stirring, over medium heat until the sauce just begins to bubble. Turn off the heat and swirl in the butter. Set aside. Reserve and keep half of the sauce warm to use on the cooked duck. Use the remaining sauce to baste the birds during the last 30 minutes of cooking.

4. When the internal temperature reaches 135°F (60°C), the ducks are done. Remove them from the roaster, cover them with foil, and let sit for 15 minutes.

5. Remove the foil and carve the ducks. Pour the sauce into a gravy boat and serve it with the duck.

Braised Duck in Barbecue Sauce
Yield: 4–6 servings

Like all game birds, ducks should be allowed to hang at a temperature just above freezing for at least 48 hours before they are cooked. The length of time and temperature at which they are allowed to hang beyond that period will control how "high" or gamey they become.

2 wild ducks
1 cup (236 mL) red wine vinegar
¼ cup (60 mL) olive oil
1 large onion, minced
1 clove garlic, peeled and minced
2 cups (473 mL) chicken stock
1 bay leaf
1 cup (236 mL) bottled chili sauce
2 teaspoons (10 mL) Worcestershire sauce
½ cup (118 mL) all-purpose flour
Salt, to taste
Freshly ground black pepper, to taste
½ cup (118 mL) bacon fat

1. Skin the ducks and cut them into serving-size pieces. Cover the pieces with water and the vinegar. Let stand for several hours or overnight.

2. Preheat the barbecue to medium high (350°F [180°C] to 400°F [200°C]). Spray a roasting pan or baking dish with nonstick cooking spray.

3. In a large saucepan, heat the olive oil. Add the onion and garlic and cook until tender but not brown. Add the chicken stock, bay leaf, chili sauce, and Worcestershire and simmer for 30 minutes.

4. Drain the duck pieces and dry them. Put the flour, salt, and pepper in a small brown paper bag. Drop in the duck pieces one at a time and shake to flour each piece. In a skillet, sauté the duck pieces in the bacon fat until nicely browned, then arrange them on the bottom of the prepared dish.

5. Pour the barbecue sauce over the duck pieces and bake for 2½ to 3 hours, or until the duck is tender.

6. Cover the duck with foil and let it rest for 10 minutes before serving.

30-Minute Roast Duck
Yield: 4 servings

This recipe will only work with small ducks in a very hot barbecue with lots of basting and attention.

2 oranges, quartered
2 (1¾–2½ pound [795g–1.1 kg]) wild ducks
½ cup (118 mL) port
1 cup (236 mL) butter, melted
Salt, to taste
Freshly ground black pepper, to taste

1. Preheat the barbecue to medium high (450F [240°C] to 475F [250°C]).

2. Place 4 orange quarters in the cavity of each duck. Place the ducks on a rack in a roasting pan.

3. Stir the port into the melted butter. Brush the ducks with the mixture and salt and pepper them generously.

4. Roast the ducks for 30 minutes, brushing generously with the butter every 5 minutes. Reheat the remaining butter.

5. Remove the ducks from the pan, cover them with foil, and let rest for 10 minutes. Carve and serve with the pan juices and any remaining butter in a sauce boat.

Honey-Mango Roasted Duck
Yield: 4–6 servings

Sliced fresh mango makes a perfect garnish for this dish. If you can't get them fresh, use canned or bottled mango slices.

1½ cups (354 mL) mango juice, divided
½ cup (118 mL) apple juice
1 (4–5 pound [1.8–2.2 kg]) domestic duck
1 cup (236 mL) honey
2 tablespoons (30 mL) granulated garlic
½ teaspoon (2.5 mL) lemon salt
½ teaspoon (2.5 mL) freshly ground black pepper
½ teaspoon (2.5 mL) dried rosemary
½ teaspoon (2.5 mL) dried thyme
½ teaspoon (2.5 mL) dried savory

1. Preheat the barbecue to medium high (450°F [240°C] to 500°F [260°C]). Spray a roasting pan or Dutch oven with nonstick cooking spray.

2. In a small bowl, mix together ½ cup (118 mL) of the mango juice and the apple juice. Using a kitchen injector, inject the liquid into the breasts and thighs of the duck. Place the duck in a baking dish and pour the remaining mango juice, then the honey, over the duck.

3. In a separate small bowl, combine the granulated garlic, lemon salt, black pepper, rosemary, thyme, and savory and stir to mix. Sprinkle the herbs and spices all over the duck, including the inside cavity.

4. Place the duck in the prepared roasting pan or Dutch oven. Put the pan in the barbecue and roast until done, about 1¼ hours, or until a knife inserted into the thigh produces clear juice. The duck is done when a thermometer inserted into the thick part of the breast reads 135°F (60°C).

5. Remove the duck from the pan, reserving the pan juices. Boil the juice for 5 minutes to serve alongside the duck.

6. Carve the duck into quarters or pieces. Place the duck on a platter and garnish with slices of fresh mango and a sprinkling of chopped parsley.

Curried Honey Duck

Yield: 4 servings

When cooking duck in the barbecue, either use a roasting pan or you turn the pieces often, watching for flare-ups from the easily-ignited duck fat.

1 (2½–3 pound [1.1–1.3 kg]) fresh duck or thawed frozen duck
Salt, to taste
Freshly ground black pepper, to taste
1 yellow onion, peeled
2 whole cloves
¼ cup (59 mL) honey
1½ tablespoons (22.5 mL) curry powder

1. Preheat the barbecue to medium high (350°F [180°C] to 400°F [200°C]).

2. Rinse the duck and pat it dry. Salt and pepper the duck inside and out. Stick the cloves in the yellow onion and place it in the cavity. In a small bowl, combine the honey and curry powder.

3. Place the duck in the barbecue and cook for 1 hour, basting every ten minutes with the honey-curry mixture.

4. The duck should cook for a total of 1½ hours, or until a leg joint moves easily, the skin is nicely browned, and a meat thermometer inserted in the thigh reads 140°F (60°C).

5. Remove duck from the barbecue and let it rest, covered, for 10 minutes. Carve and serve.

Irish Whiskey Duck

Yield: 4 servings

You could also use rum, Grand Marnier, scotch, brandy, or any other flammable potable.

1 (4½-pound [2-kg]) duck
Salt, to taste
Freshly ground black pepper, to taste
Giblets from the duck, neck included, chopped
1 onion, peeled and sliced
2 cups (473 mL) chicken stock
½ teaspoon (2.5 mL) dried thyme
½ teaspoon (2.5 mL) dried oregano
1 bay leaf
1 cup (236 mL) orange marmalade
½ cup (118 mL) Irish whiskey
Orange slices, twisted, for garnish
Chopped fresh parsley, for garnish

1. Make sure the grill is clean and generously sprayed with nonstick grilling spray. Preheat the barbecue to medium high (350°F [180°C] to 400°F [200°C]). Spray a roasting pan with nonstick grilling spray.

2. Rinse the duck, remove all the excess fat from the cavity, and dry. Season with salt and pepper. Place the duck on a rack in the prepared roasting pan. Put the pan in the barbecue and cook for 1½ hours.

3. Put the chopped giblets in a saucepan. Add the onion, chicken stock, thyme, oregano and bay leaf and simmer until the stock is reduced to 1 cup (236 mL). Add the marmalade and stir. Brush this mixture on the duck several times during the last hour of roasting.

4. Transfer the duck to a heated platter. Warm the Irish whiskey, ignite it with a long charcoal lighter, and pour the blazing liquid over the duck at the table. Garnish with orange twists and parsley and serve.

Wild Duck in Foil

Yield: 4 servings

This dish is meant to be prepared with wild ducks. The fattier domestic ducks will produce too much fat for this recipe to work well. Wild ducks are leaner and have a totally different taste.

2 (2–2½ pound [908 g–1.1 kg]) wild ducks
Salt, to taste
Freshly ground black pepper, to taste
2 stalks celery, chopped
2 small onions, peeled and chopped
2 carrots, chopped
1 sprig parsley, chopped
½ cup (118 mL) butter, melted
½ teaspoon (2.5 mL) dried tarragon
½ teaspoon (2.5 mL) dried oregano
½ teaspoon (2.5 mL) dried thyme
1 (10½-ounce [311-mL]) can chicken or turkey broth
¼ cup (60 mL) red currant jelly

1. Preheat the barbecue to medium high (400°F [200°C] to 450°F [240°C]).

2. Clean the ducks. Salt and pepper the inside cavity of each duck. In a large bowl, mix together the celery, onions, carrots, and parsley. Place half of this mixture in the cavity of each duck.

3. Place each duck on a 12-inch (30-cm) square piece of heavy-duty aluminum foil. Brush the ducks with the butter, then season them with salt and pepper. In a small bowl, combine the tarragon, oregano, and thyme. Sprinkle half of this mixture over each duck. Tie each duck's legs together and bring the foil up over the ducks. Seal the edges with double, tight folds to make airtight packages.

4. Place the packages in a shallow baking pan and roast in the barbecue for 1¾ hours. Remove the ducks from barbecue and place them on a cutting board. Open the packages carefully so as not to burn yourself with the escaping steam, but also so that you don't spill any of the juices.

5. Remove the vegetables from the cavities. Pour the juices from the ducks and foil packages into a small saucepan. Heat over medium high, stirring, and add the chicken stock and jelly. When the mixture is bubbling and well mixed, pour it into a sauce boat to serve at the table.

6. Split ducks in half through the backbone. Put them on a serving platter, drizzle with some of the sauce, and serve.

Fruit-Stuffed Duck

Yield: 6 servings

You can use just about any of your favorite fruits in this recipe: nectarines, peaches, plums, dates, raisins, pears, apricots, and so on.

2 young, plump wild ducks, cleaned
1½ teaspoons (7.5 mL) salt, divided
1 cup (236 mL) chopped unpeeled apple
½ cup (118 mL) chopped celery
7 fresh figs, chopped
2 small onions, peeled and chopped
6 tablespoons (90 mL) bacon drippings
1⅓ cups (315 mL) water
⅔ cup (158 mL) orange juice
Parsley, for garnish
Grapes, for garnish
Apple wedges, for garnish

1. Preheat the barbecue to medium high (300°F [150°C] to 325°F [165°C]).

2. Rub the cavity of each duck with 1 teaspoon (5 mL) of the salt. In a bowl, combine the apple, celery, figs, and onion. Stuff half of this mixture into the cavity of each duck and close the cavities with skewers.

3. In a heavy roasting pan or Dutch oven, brown the ducks in the bacon drippings. Add the water, orange juice, and the remaining salt. Cover tightly the pan and place it in the barbecue. Cook, basting 2 or 3 times, for 45 to 60 minutes, or until tender. When the duck is finished, a thermometer inserted into the thick part of the breast will read 135°F (60°C).

4. Remove the ducks from the barbecue, place them on a serving platter, cover, and let rest 5 minutes. Garnish with the parsley, grapes, and apple wedges.

Tanzanian-Style Duckling

Yield: 4 servings

Duckling is a great delicacy in Tanzania. It is usually served to special guests, accompanied by cooked bananas, rice, potatoes, and cassava.

¼ cup (60 mL) olive oil
1 cup (236 mL) diced onions
1 cup (236 mL) diced tomatoes
1 teaspoon (5 mL) salt
1 teaspoon (5 mL) curry powder
½ teaspoon (2.5 mL) crushed red pepper flakes
1 (6-pound [2.7 kg]) duckling, cut into 12 pieces
2 quarts (1.9 L) water
4 large bananas, peeled

1. Preheat the barbecue to medium high (350°F [180°C] to 400°F [200°C]).

2. In a 6-quart (5.7-L) Dutch oven or roasting pan, heat the olive oil. Add the onions, tomatoes, salt, curry powder, and red pepper flakes and sauté until the onions are soft and just beginning to brown. Add the duck pieces and sauté for 5 minutes, turning the duck once.

3. Move the Dutch oven to the unheated side of the grill, add the water and peeled bananas, and cook for 30 minutes.

4. Serve the duck arranged on a heated platter, accompanied by the cooked bananas.

Charcoal Teal in Orange Sauce

Yield: 4 servings

The ducks are called charcoal teal, but in this case we're cooking them on charcoal, too. It's important to soak the ducks in salt water, as they can be a bit harsh otherwise.

1 cup (236 mL) butter
1 (14-ounce [41-mL]) jar apricot-pineapple preserves
4 teal ducks
2 gallons (7.6 L) water
¼ cup (60 mL) salt, plus more to taste
Freshly ground black pepper, to taste

1. Make sure the grill is clean and generously sprayed with nonstick grilling spray. Preheat the barbecue to medium high (350°F [180°C] to 400°F [200°C]).

2. In a saucepan, melt the butter. Stir in the apricot-pineapple preserves to make a sauce.

3. Split each duck in half. In a large pot, combine the water with the 4 tablespoons (60 mL) salt. Add the ducks to the water and soak for 2 hours. Rinse the ducks and sprinkle them generously with salt and pepper. Sear the ducks on the hot grill, skin side down, until they are golden brown.

4. Turn the ducks over and cook for an additional 15 to 20 minutes, basting frequently with the butter-preserve sauce. Warm any remaining sauce.

5. Place the ducks on a heated platter, drizzle with the remaining sauce, and serve.

Wild Duck with Pecan Stuffing
Yield: 4 servings

Instead of pecans, you can use the same amount of unsalted walnuts, hazelnuts, cashews, Brazil nuts, or pistachios. You can also substitute currants or black raisins for the golden raisins we use here.

4 (1-pound [454-g]) wild ducks, cleaned
4 cups (0.95 L) panko
1½ cups (354 mL) chopped pecans
1 cup (236 mL) diced onion
1 cup (236 mL) chopped celery
1 cup (236 mL) golden seedless raisins
¼ cup (59 mL) chopped, cooked carrots
2 large eggs, beaten
¼ cup (59 mL) buttermilk
12 slices hickory-smoked bacon
½ cup (118 mL) bottled chili sauce
¼ cup (59 mL) Worcestershire sauce
¼ cup (59 mL) steak sauce
Chopped fresh parsley, for garnish
Orange slices, for garnish
Cranberries, for garnish

1. Preheat the barbecue to medium high (350°F [180°C] to 400°F [200°C]).

2. Rinse the ducks thoroughly with water and pat dry.

3. In a large bowl, combine the panko, pecans, onion, celery, raisins, carrots, eggs, and buttermilk and mix well. Spoon this stuffing into the duck cavities and sew the cavities closed with butcher's twine or seal with skewers.

4. Place the ducks, breast side up, on a rack in a roasting pan. Wrap 3 slices of bacon around each duck. Bake, uncovered, in the barbecue for 1 hour.

5. In a small bowl, whisk together the chili sauce, Worcestershire sauce, and steak sauce. Pour this mixture over the ducks and bake for an additional 20 to 30 minutes, or to your desired degree of doneness.

6. Transfer the ducks to a cutting board and cut them in half with a knife or kitchen shears. Place the duck halves on a serving platter. Skim off the fat from the pan drippings and pour the sauce into a sauce boat to serve alongside the ducks.

7. Sprinkle the ducks with the chopped parsley and garnish with orange slices and cranberries, if desired.

Five-Spice and Honey Roasted Pheasant
Yield: 2–4 servings

If you received the pheasant from a hunter or bagged it yourself, be careful to look for shot in the meat. While lead shot has been banned and is no longer a problem, breaking a tooth on a piece of shot is still not a good thing.

1 teaspoon (5 mL) kosher salt
1 teaspoon (5 mL) garlic powder
1 teaspoon (5 mL) dried thyme
½ teaspoon (2.5 mL) five-spice powder
Freshly ground black pepper, to taste
2 (2½–3 pound [1.1–1.3 kg]) pheasants
¼ cup (59 mL) fresh lemon juice
1 cup (236 mL) honey

1. Preheat the barbecue to medium high (425°F [220°C] to 450°F [240°C]). Spray a baking dish or roasting pan with nonstick cooking spray.

2. In a small bowl, combine the salt, garlic powder, thyme, five-spice powder, and pepper and mix well. Season the cavities of the pheasant generously with one-third of this seasoning mix.

3. Place the pheasant into the prepared baking dish or roasting pan. Pour the lemon juice, then the honey, over the pheasant. Season with the remaining two-thirds of the seasoning mix.

4. Place the pan in the barbecue and roast for 25 to 30 minutes, or until a knife inserted in a thigh produces clear juices or a thermometer inserted into the thick part of the thigh reads 165°F (74°C). Be careful not to overcook the pheasant, as it is a very dry bird with very little fat.

Fred's Pineapple and Cherry-Stuffed Pheasant
Yield: 2–4 servings

I like to use Barry Farm cherry jelly, but Smuckers makes a very nice jelly that works fine, too. This recipe comes from Fred and Dottie Anderson from Battle Creek, Mich.

1 small pineapple, peeled, cored, and chopped
½ cup (118 mL) dried cherries, soaked in hot water for 20 minutes
1 small onion, peeled and quartered
1 stalk celery, sliced
1 teaspoon (5 mL) dried rosemary
1 teaspoon (5 mL) poultry seasoning
½ teaspoon (2.5 mL) dried sage
2 tablespoons (30 mL) olive oil
1 tablespoon (15 mL) butter, melted
1 (4-pound [1.8-kg]) pheasant, cleaned and checked for shot
Salt, to taste
Freshly ground black pepper, to taste
6 strips bacon
⅓ cup (79 mL) cherry or sour cherry jelly, warmed on stove or microwave

1. Preheat the barbecue to medium high (350°F [180°C] to 400°F [200°C]) for indirect heating, putting a water pan under the unheated side of the grill.

2. Make the stuffing: In a small bowl, mix together the pineapple, cherries, onion, celery, rosemary, poultry seasoning, and sage and set aside.

3. In a separate small bowl, mix together the olive oil and butter. Massage about half of this mixture well into the bird. Season the inside and outside well with salt and pepper, then fill the cavity with the stuffing mixture.

4. Put the bird on the unheated side of the grill, cover it with bacon strips, and cook for 1 to 1½ hours, turning often. After about 30 minutes, remove the bacon and brush the pheasant with the remaining oil-butter mixture. Brush with half the cherry jelly, cover with foil, and cook for the remaining time.

5. Remove bird from the barbecue and brush the top with the remaining jelly. Cover with foil and let rest for 10 minutes. Carve and serve.

Baked Pheasant with Apples

Yield: 2–4 servings

Try this with fresh apricots, fresh peaches, or sliced plums—all pitted, of course, but leave the skins on and add ½ teaspoon (2.5 mL) of lemon juice to the pan when you sauté these fruits.

¼ cup (60 mL) butter
1 pheasant, quartered
4 medium apples, chopped
1 teaspoon (5 mL) sugar
¼ teaspoon (1.25 mL) nutmeg
3 tablespoons half-and-half
¼ teaspoon (1.25 mL) salt
¼ teaspoon (1.25 mL) freshly ground black pepper

1. Preheat the barbecue to medium high (350°F [180°C] to 400°F [200°C]). Spray with nonstick cooking spray or butter a casserole dish or Dutch oven.

2. In a skillet, melt the butter. Add the pheasant and brown it on all sides. Remove the pheasant from the pan.

3. Add the apples to pan and sauté. Add the sugar. When the apples are softened, place them in the bottom of the prepared casserole dish or Dutch oven.

4. Place the pheasant pieces on top of the apples along with the juices from pan. Sprinkle with the nutmeg, pour the half-and-half over the top, and sprinkle with the salt and pepper.

5. Cover the casserole and bake for 1 to 1½ hours in the barbecue. Remove the lid for the last 15 minutes to brown the pheasant.

Pheasant à L'Orange

Yield: 4 servings

Adding olive oil to the butter helps keep the butter from browning and burning.

2 tablespoons (30 mL) all-purpose flour
1 teaspoon (5 mL) chicken bouillon powder or granules
½ teaspoon (2.5 mL) salt
¼ teaspoon (1.25 mL) freshly ground black pepper
4 pieces skinless pheasant breasts and legs
2 tablespoons (30 mL) butter
1 teaspoon (5 mL) olive oil
2 oranges, peeled and finely diced
Grated zest of 1 orange
½ cup (118 mL) water
2 tablespoons (30 mL) orange marmalade
2 tablespoons (30 mL) Triple Sec

1. Preheat the barbecue to medium high (300°F [150°C] to 325°F [165°C]).

2. Put the flour, bouillon, salt, and pepper in a paper bag. Add the pheasant pieces and shake to coat each piece.

3. In a cast-iron skillet or shallow baking pan, heat the butter and olive oil. Add the pheasant pieces and cook until brown.

4. In a bowl, combine the chopped oranges with their juice, orange zest, water, marmalade, and Triple Sec and mix. Pour this mixture over the pheasant, cover with foil, and bake for 30 to 40 minutes, or until the pheasant is cooked through and a thermometer inserted into the thick part of the thigh reads 165°F (74°C).

5. Remove the pheasant from the barbecue, cover it with foil, and let it rest for 10 minutes. Transfer the pheasant to a serving platter over white rice and pour the pan sauce over everything.

Bread-Pan Pheasant

Yield: 2–4 servings

The enclosed small pan really concentrates the heat, while the wine and stock keep the bird very moist, the bacon prevents the top of the very lean bird from burning, and the glaze creates a beautifully browned pheasant to present to your guests.

1 (3½–4 pound [1.5–1.8 kg]) pheasant
Salt, to taste
Freshly ground black pepper, to taste
½ teaspoon (2.5 mL) poultry seasoning
Olive oil, for brushing
1 medium onion, peeled and quartered
1 apple, cored and quartered
½ cup (118 mL) red currant jelly
1 teaspoon (5 mL) butter
1 pinch ground cloves
3 slices bacon
2 cups (473 mL) chicken stock
2 cups (473 mL) Gewürztraminer (or other sweet white wine)

1. Preheat the barbecue to medium high (350°F [180°C] to 400°F [200°C]).

2. Clean the pheasant and sprinkle the salt, pepper, and poultry seasoning inside the cavity. Brush the skin with olive oil and liberally salt and pepper the skin. Stuff the cavity with the onion and apple.

3. In a small saucepan, heat the jelly, stirring, until it melts. Add the butter and cloves and stir until well mixed.

4. Fit the bird, breast side down, into a bread loaf pan. The pan should be tight around the sides of the bird with no room to spare. Brush the bird with half of the jelly glaze and lay the bacon slices on the bird. Add equal amounts of stock and wine to come halfway up the sides of pan.

5. Roast, uncovered, in the barbecue for 30 minutes. Open the barbecue lid, remove the bacon from the bird, and brush with the remaining jelly glaze. Bake for 10 more minutes, or until the top of the bird is browned and the glaze is bubbling.

6. Transfer the bird to a heated dish. Serve with wild rice and steamed or grilled Brussels sprouts.

Baked Pheasant in Foil

Yield: 4 servings

You can buy Spice Parisienne in some fancy food stores or upscale markets, but you can easily make your own, as we do here. Store it in a spice container or a bottle with a tight lid, and sprinkle a small amount on vegetables, meats, fish, or poultry when you cook.

Spice Parisienne

3 medium bay leaves
2 tablespoons (30 mL) ground white pepper
1 tablespoon (15 mL) ground nutmeg
1 tablespoon (15 mL) ground cinnamon
1 tablespoon (15 mL) dried thyme
1½ teaspoons (2.5 mL) ground mace
1½ teaspoons (2.5 mL) ground cloves
1½ teaspoons (2.5 mL) ground ginger

Pheasant

1 (3½–4 pound [1.5–1.8 kg]) pheasant
¼ cup (59 mL) butter, melted
Salt, to taste
1 orange, quartered
1 lemon, quartered
½ cup (118 mL) dry white wine

1. Preheat the barbecue to medium high (350°F [180°C] to 400°F [200°C]).

2. In a small bowl, combine the ingredients for the Spice Parisienne and mix well.

3. Brush the entire surface of the bird with the melted butter. Sprinkle the cavity and surface with salt. Sprinkle a very small amount of the Spice Parisienne on the outside of the pheasant. Stuff the orange and lemon quarters into the cavity.

4. Place bird on a large sheet of heavy-duty aluminum foil, bring edges of the foil together, and seal tightly. Place the foil-wrapped bird in a shallow roasting pan and bake in the barbecue for 1¼ hours.

5. Open the foil and allow pheasant to cook for another 15 minutes. Remove the pheasant and foil from pan. Pour the drippings into a small saucepan, add the wine, and bring to a boil.

6. Cut the pheasant into quarters and serve with the clear wine gravy.

Brine-Marinated Barbecued Pheasant

Yield: 2 servings

Brining really is the way to go with pheasant. This process keeps the bird moist, and it also cuts some of that rich gaminess. Brine overnight, then roast the bird with plenty of butter under the breast skin and baste often.

7 cups (1.7 L) water
½ cup (118 mL) kosher salt
1 cup (236 mL) packed brown sugar
¼ cup (59 mL) pure maple syrup
1 medium onion, peeled and chopped
2 cloves garlic, peeled and smashed
3 tablespoons (45 mL) fresh lemon juice
⅛ teaspoon (0.6 mL) ground allspice
1 dash hot pepper sauce
1 (2–2½ pound [908 g–1.1 kg]) pheasant
3 tablespoons (45 mL) butter, divided
4 slices hickory-smoked bacon

1. In a large pot, bring the water and salt to a boil. Let the water cool for 30 minutes and add 1 full tray (about 2 cups [473 mL]) of ice cubes at the end of that time.

2. In a medium bowl, combine the brown sugar, maple syrup, onions, garlic, lemon juice, allspice, and hot sauce. Pour this mixture into a 2-gallon (7.6-L) resealable plastic bag. Add the pheasant and refrigerate overnight, turning the bag several times.

3. Remove the pheasant from the brine-marinade and discard the liquid. Let the pheasant come to room temperature, about 15 minutes.

4. Preheat the barbecue to medium high (350°F [180°C] to 400°F [200°C]).

5. Place the brined pheasant breast up in a roasting pan. With your fingers, work 1 tablespoon (15 mL) of the butter under the breast skin.

6. Rub the rest of the butter all over the pheasant. Cover the bird with the bacon slices and roast, uncovered, for about 1½ hours, checking for doneness after an hour. The juices should run clear when a thigh is poked with a knife.

Pheasant in a Bag

Yield: 2 servings

You can adapt most chicken recipes to pheasant, and vice versa. Pheasant can be stuffed, braised, barbecued or baked. But they do have a stronger—though not unpleasant—flavor than chicken.

1 (2-pound [908-g]) pheasant, cleaned
⅓ cup (79 mL) butter, melted
4 cloves garlic, peeled and minced
1 medium onion, peeled and chopped
Salt, to taste
Freshly ground black pepper, to taste
3 tablespoons (45 mL) honey

1. Preheat the barbecue to medium high (325°F [165°C] to 375°F [190°C]).

2. Rub the outside of the pheasant with the butter. Place the garlic, onion, and a little more butter in the cavity of the bird. Salt and pepper the pheasant inside and out.

3. Put the bird in a brown paper bag and tie the end. Set the bag on a baking sheet and bake for 1½ hours in the barbecue. If the pheasant isn't nicely browned when you open the bag, being careful of the steam, place the pheasant back in the barbecue, brush with more butter, and let it brown up for 10 to 12 minutes.

4. Remove the pheasant and either cut it into quarters or halve it along the breastbone. Brush the skin with the honey and serve.

Pheasant Baked in Cream

Yield: 4 servings

Yes, I know it's cream, but whole milk or reduced fat milk just doesn't cut it in this recipe—the resulting gravy will be thin and bland, and won't enhance the flavor of the pheasant. Remember, cream contains fat, which is sorely needed for cooking very, very lean wild game birds.

2 pheasants
1½ cups (354 mL) Bisquick baking mix
1 teaspoon (5 mL) garlic salt
1 teaspoon (5 mL) freshly ground black pepper
½ teaspoon (2.5 mL) paprika
½ teaspoon (2.5 mL) poultry seasoning
1 cup (236 mL) buttermilk
¼ cup (59 mL) butter
1 (14½-ounce [428-mL]) can chicken broth
1 pint (473 mL) heavy cream
Paprika, for garnish

1. Preheat the barbecue to medium high (350°F [180°C] to 400°F [200°C]).

2. Cut the pheasants into breast, drumstick, and thigh portions, discarding the wings and back or saving them for stock.

3. In a brown paper bag, mix together the Bisquick, garlic salt, pepper, paprika, and poultry seasoning. Dip the pheasant pieces in the buttermilk, drop them into the bag, and shake to thoroughly coat.

4. In a Dutch oven or large roasting pan, melt the butter. Add the coated pheasant pieces and cook until browned. When all the pieces have browned, add the chicken broth and transfer the pan to the barbecue. Bake for 1½ hours. Check periodically for liquid; if it gets dry, add more chicken broth.

5. After 1½ hours of baking, pour the cream over the pheasant. Cover and bake for another 45 to 60 minutes, checking occasionally to make sure the cream doesn't dry up. Add more if necessary so that you have enough liquid to make a nice gravy.

6. Remove the pan from the barbecue. Transfer the pheasant and gravy to a deep platter, sprinkle with paprika, and serve with wild or steamed white rice, with cranberry sauce on the side.

Soused Grouse

Yield: 4 servings

There are about twenty-five kinds of grouse, most of which are quite edible and, in fact, are quite delicious. The grouse I used for this recipe was a ruffed grouse brought back from a hunt in New Brunswick.

¼ cup (60 mL) butter
3 tablespoons (45 mL) olive oil
8 grouse breasts, cleaned
8 ounces (227 g) sliced fresh mushrooms
2 cloves garlic, peeled and smashed
1 cup (236 mL) dry sherry
1 cup (236 mL) chicken broth
2 lemons, thinly sliced
2 tablespoons (30 mL) chopped fresh parsley, divided
½ cup (118 mL) brandy

1. Preheat the barbecue to medium high (300°F [150°C] to 325°F [165°C]). Butter or spray with nonstick cooking spray a roasting pan or Dutch oven.

2. In a large cast-iron or nonstick skillet, heat the butter and olive oil. Add the grouse and cook until browned. Transfer the grouse to the prepared roasting pan or Dutch oven, reserving the drippings.

3. Sauté the mushrooms and garlic in the pan drippings. Deglaze the pan with the sherry and chicken broth, stirring to pick up any browned bits. Pour this mixture over the grouse breasts. Cover with the lemon slices and half of the parsley.

4. Cover the roasting pan or Dutch oven and bake in the barbecue for 3 hours, adding more broth or sherry if necessary.

5. Remove the cover for the last 15 minutes of cooking to brown the grouse. Stir the brandy into the sauce. When the grouse is browned, place the breasts on a heated serving platter and drizzle with the pan drippings. Sprinkle with the remaining parsley and serve.

Smothered Grouse

Yield: 4–6 servings

Instead of the sour cream, you could use crème fraîche or plain yogurt into which you've stirred in 2 teaspoons (10 mL) of fresh lime juice.

2 tablespoons (30 mL) all-purpose flour
1 teaspoon (5 mL) dried thyme
½ teaspoon (2.5 mL) salt
½ teaspoon (2.5 mL) dried rosemary
¼ teaspoon (1.25 mL) freshly ground black pepper
⅛ teaspoon (0.6 mL) cayenne pepper
2 ruffed grouse, halved
½ cup (118 mL) chicken broth
1 (1-ounce [28-g]) envelope dry onion soup mix
2 cups (473 mL) sour cream, at room temperature
1 tablespoon (15 mL) plum jelly
½ cup (118 mL) butter, divided
8 ounces (227 g) mushrooms, sliced
4 large shallots, peeled and minced

1. Preheat the barbecue to medium high (350°F [180°C] to 400°F [200°C]) for direct and indirect heating, putting a water pan under the unheated side of the grill.

2. Put the flour, thyme, salt, rosemary, pepper, and cayenne pepper in a small brown paper bag and shake to mix. Add 1 or 2 pieces of the grouse at a time, shake to coat with the flour, and set aside on a plate.

3. In a small saucepan, heat the chicken broth. Add the soup mix, sour cream, and jelly and stir until warm and well mixed.

4. In a large cast-iron skillet, melt 6 tablespoons (90 mL) of the butter over high heat. Add the bird pieces and sauté until golden brown, about 6 to 8 minutes. Remove the grouse pieces. Add the remaining butter to the skillet. Add the mushrooms and shallots and sauté until softened. Spoon over the bird, add the sour cream–jelly sauce, cover, and bake in the barbecue over indirect heat for about 1 hour.

5. Transfer the grouse from the skillet to a serving platter. Quarter the grouse, pour the pan drippings and sauce over the pieces, and serve.

Grouse with Cherry Sauce

Yield: 4 servings

You can make your own stuffing for this as well. In a skillet, sauté 1 medium minced onion and 2 minced celery stalks in 3 tablespoons (45 mL) butter until the celery is soft. Tear 6 slices of raisin bread into small pieces and add them to the skillet. Add 1 teaspoon (5 mL) salt, ½ teaspoon (2.5 mL) freshly ground black pepper, and ½ teaspoon (2.5 mL) poultry seasoning and mix well. Use this mixture to stuff the birds.

1 (6-ounce [168-g]) package Stove Top cornbread stuffing with seasoning packet
1½ cups (354 mL) hot water
¼ cup (59 mL) butter
2 grouse
¾ cup (177 mL) cherry jelly
¼ cup (59 mL) chopped dried red cherries
1 tablespoon (15 mL) garlic butter
2 teaspoons (10 mL) fresh lemon juice
½ teaspoon (2.5 mL) garlic salt
¼ teaspoon (1.25 mL) ground allspice

1. Preheat the barbecue to medium high (200°F [95°C] to 220°F [105°C]) for indirect slow cooking, putting a water pan under the unheated side of the grill. Spray a roasting pan with nonstick cooking spray.

2. In a medium bowl, combine the stuffing mix with seasoning packet, water, and butter. Stuff this mixture into the grouse and place them in the prepared roasting pan. Put the pan on the unheated side of the barbecue.

3. In a small saucepan, combine the jelly, cherries, garlic butter, lemon juice, garlic salt, and allspice. Cook over low heat, stirring, until the jelly is melted. Reserve ⅔ cup (158 mL) of the sauce. Use the remaining sauce to brush on the grouse several times as it cooks for 4 to 5 hours.

4. Remove the grouse from the barbecue and quarter them or cut them in half with a sharp knife or kitchen shears. Place the birds on a serving platter, drizzle with the remaining sauce, and serve.

Maui-Style Quail
Yield: 4 servings

On a hunting trip to Maui a few years back, I had the pleasure of going on a quail shoot, and this is how our guide prepared what we brought home. Fresh pineapple juice was used, but since that's hard to get outside of Hawaii, we use canned here.

1 (20-ounce [591-mL]) can pineapple juice
8 ounces (236 mL) mango or passion fruit juice
2 teaspoons (10 mL) Worcestershire sauce
2 teaspoons (10 mL) Dijon mustard
1 teaspoon (5 mL) dried rosemary
1 teaspoon (5 mL) ground cumin
Salt, to taste
Freshly ground black pepper, to taste
8 whole quail (skin on), split at backbone
1 tablespoon (15 mL) cornstarch
1 medium pineapple, cut into 1-inch (2.5-cm) thick slices
2 small lemons, thinly sliced

1. In a large bowl, mix together the pineapple juice, mango juice, Worcestershire sauce, mustard, rosemary, cumin, salt, and pepper and stir well. Place the birds in a 2-gallon (7.6-L) resealable plastic bag and pour in the marinade. Refrigerate for 1 hour.

2. Remove the quail from the marinade and drain briefly. Pour the remaining marinade into a saucepan and boil for 10 minutes. Add the cornstarch and stir until sauce thickens. Remove the pan from the heat.

3. Preheat the barbecue to medium high (375°F [190°C] to 400°F [200°C]) for indirect heating. Make sure the grill is clean and generously sprayed with nonstick grilling spray.

4. Place the birds skin side down on the unheated side of grill for 10 to 12 minutes. Turn the birds and grill the second side for 5 to 6 minutes. Baste the birds with the boiled marinade.

5. Serve the grilled quail on a bed of pineapple and lemon slices, accompanied by the remaining marinade.

Buttered Barbecued Quail
Yield: 4 servings

Simple and delicious, the quail and butter provide all the flavor, and the light seasoning enhances it. Use real butter here—margarine or butter substitutes will not work.

4 quail
1 tablespoon (15 mL) light canola oil or olive oil
½ teaspoon (2.5 mL) salt
½ teaspoon (2.5 mL) freshly ground black pepper
¼ cup (59 mL) butter
Paprika, to taste
Kosher salt, to taste

1. Preheat the barbecue to medium high (350°F [180°C] to 400°F [200°C]) for direct heating, placing a water pan under the unheated side of the grill. Make sure the grill is clean and generously sprayed with nonstick grilling spray.

2. Lightly brush the quail with the vegetable oil and season with salt and pepper. Place the quail on the grill over direct heat and cook for 5 to 6 minutes per side.

3. Transfer the birds to a warmed platter, cover with foil, and let rest for 5 minutes.

4. In a small saucepan, melt the butter. Split the quail along the breastbone and brush generously with the melted butter.

5. Sprinkle with paprika and a pinch of kosher salt and serve.

Quail with Red Grape and Green Onion Salsa

Yield: 4 servings

You can substitute any fruit-based salsa (pineapple, mango, apricot, peach, etc.) here, but the grapes go very well with the subtle flavor of the quail.

1 tablespoon (15 mL) butter
3 tablespoons (45 mL) olive oil, divided
2 cups (473 mL) red seedless grapes, halved lengthwise
½ cup (118 mL) chopped white onion
1 clove garlic, peeled and smashed
¼ cup (59 mL) dry white wine
Salt, to taste
Freshly ground black pepper, to taste
3 tablespoons (45 mL) chopped green onions, white and green parts
8 boneless quail, butterflied

1. Preheat the barbecue to medium high (350°F [180°C] to 400°F [200°C]) for direct grilling. Make sure the grill is clean and generously sprayed with nonstick grilling spray.

2. In a medium saucepan, heat the butter and 1 tablespoon (15 mL) of the olive oil. Add the grapes, onion, and garlic and sauté until softened. Add the wine and heat until the liquid is reduced by half. Add salt and pepper, to taste. Stir in the green onions, remove from the heat, and let cool.

3. Brush the quail on both sides with the remaining olive oil. Cook directly on the grill for about 5 to 6 minutes per side. Serve the quail with the red grape–green onion salsa.

Sage-Smoked Champagne Quail

Yield: 6 servings

I wouldn't suggest going out and buying a fancy and expensive French champagne for this dish. Instead, use a domestic brand such as Korbel or Martini & Rossi.

12 quail
1 (7.5-mL) bottle champagne
4 apples, cored and diced
1 (3/8-ounce [10.5-g]) jar dried sage; divided
½ teaspoon (2.5 mL) salt
12–24 slices pepper-cured bacon
½ cup hickory chips, soaked for 3 hours

1. In a large bowl, combine quail and champagne. Cover and refrigerate for 1 hour. Drain the quail, discarding the marinade.

2. In a medium bowl, combine the apples, 1 teaspoon (5 mL) of the sage, and salt. Stuff the quail with this mixture and wrap 1 or 2 bacon slices around each quail, securing ends with a wooden toothpick. Refrigerate. Place the remaining sage in ¼ cup (59 mL) water and soak for 10 minutes. Squeeze out the excess water and keep the herb wet.

3. Preheat the barbecue to low (230°F [110°C] to 250°F [120°C]) for indirect heating. Make sure the grill is clean and generously sprayed with non-stick grilling spray. Place a water pan under the unheated side of the grill.

4. Make a smoker package by placing the soaked hickory chips on a 12-inch (30-cm) sheet of aluminum foil, topping the chips with the soaked sage, folding the foil to make a package, and poking holes in the top of the foil.

5. Place the quail, breast side up, on the indirect side of the grill. Put the smoker package on the hot coals or gas flame. Close the lid and cook for 30 minutes, or until a thermometer inserted in the breast reads 165°F (74°C).

6. Remove the quail from the grill and serve.

Barbecue Grilled Quail with Jalapeño-Cherry Sauce
Yield: 4–6 servings

This sauce, while somewhat complicated, is a delightful mix of sweet, tart, and salty. It can be made ahead and frozen to be used later.

2½ tablespoons (37.5 mL) light sesame oil
⅓ cup (79 mL) diced shallots
1½ tablespoons (22.5 mL) minced garlic
½ jalapeño pepper, seeds and ribs removed, chopped
1½ pounds (681 g) Bing cherries, pitted and diced small
1½ teaspoons (7.5 mL) curry powder
½ teaspoon (2.5 mL) ground nutmeg
½ cup (118 mL) honey
¼ cup (59 mL) soy sauce
2 tablespoons (30 mL) balsamic vinegar
Juice of 2 lemons
Juice of 1 orange
8 semi-boneless quail
¼ cup (59 mL) olive oil

1. In a heavy pot, heat the sesame oil over medium low heat. Add the shallots, garlic, and jalapeño pepper and sauté until tender. Add the cherries, curry powder, and nutmeg and stir. Once the spices are dispersed, add the honey, soy sauce, vinegar, and fruit juices. Cook, uncovered, for 30 to 40 minutes, stirring often. The consistency should be like that of a chunky tomato sauce. Remove the pan from the heat and allow the sauce to cool to room temperature. Set aside and keep warm.

2. Preheat the barbecue to medium high (350°F [180°C] to 400°F [200°C]) for direct and indirect heating, putting a water pan under the unheated side of the grill.

3. Brush both sides of the quail lightly with the olive oil and grill them, breast side down, until the skin starts to bubble and brown a little. Turn them breast side up and baste liberally with the jalapeño–cherry sauce. Continue to turn and baste the quail every couple of minutes or so until the birds are firm and have a nice glaze on them, about 10 minutes, depending on your grill.

4. Serve them hot off the grill with a bowl of extra sauce on the side.

Five-Spice Grilled Quail

Yield: 4 servings

Quail are now commonly pen raised and available online and from many specialty meat dealers. Even your local butcher can order them if you ask for them ahead of time. Because of their small size, they cook quickly and are perfect for grilling.

⅓ cup (79 mL) port
¼ cup (59 mL) vegetable oil
2 tablespoons (30 mL) dark soy sauce
2½ teaspoons (12.5 mL) five-spice powder, divided
1½ teaspoons (7.5 mL) dark brown sugar
1 teaspoon (5 mL) fish sauce
8 (5-ounce [140-g]) quail
1 teaspoon (5 mL) dried rosemary
½ teaspoon (2.5 mL) sea salt
½ teaspoon (2.5 mL) freshly ground black pepper
½ teaspoon (2.5 mL) dried savory
3 tablespoons (45 mL) olive oil

1. In a small bowl, mix together the port, vegetable oil, soy sauce, 1½ teaspoons (7.5 mL) of the five-spice powder, brown sugar, and fish sauce and and stir well.

2. Put the quail in a 1- to 2-gallon (3.8- to 7.6-L) resealable plastic bag. Pour in the marinade, seal, and shake the bag to coat the quail. Refrigerate for 4 to 6 hours or overnight, turning several times.

3. Preheat the barbecue to medium high (350°F [180°C] to 400°F [200°C]) for indirect heating, putting a water pan under the unheated side of the grill.

4. In a small bowl, combine the remaining five-spice powder, the rosemary, the sea salt, the black pepper, and the savory and mix well. Set aside.

5. Remove the quail from the bag and discard the marinade. Pat the quail dry with paper towels, then lightly brush them with olive oil. Sprinkle the quail generously with the seasonings.

6. Grill the quail, breast side down, on the indirect side of the grill for 15 to 20 minutes, or until the juices are slightly pink, turning once after 7 to 8 minutes.

7. Remove the quail from the grill, cover with foil, let sit for 10 minutes, and serve.

Partridge in Flames

Yield: 4–6 servings

The tender meat of this game bird is perfect for roasting, grilling, broiling, or brais-ing. Serve it as the main meal or as a flavorful addition to stir-fry's, soups, or stews.

1 tablespoon (15 mL) butter
1 tablespoon (15 mL) olive oil
8–10 partridge breasts
1 (16-ounce [454-g]) can mandarin orange slices, drained
¼ cup (59 mL) Grand Marnier

1. In a large cast-iron skillet on the gas grill or a side burner, melt butter and oil over high heat. Add the breasts and quickly sauté until they are nicely browned, about 1 minute per side.

2. Add the mandarin orange segments, then add the liquor and flame. When the flames die out, the dish is ready to serve.

3. Serve the breasts with mandarin orange sauce on a 50/50 mixture of wild rice and white rice with fresh chopped chives and grilled whole baby carrots, leaving some of the green stem on the carrots for effect.

Partridge with Onion Gravy

Yield: 4–6 servings

Typical of small wild game birds, partridges are so lean they are best prepared with moist heat or by wrapping fat or bacon around the meat to prevent it from drying out when it is cooked.

½ cup (118 mL) all-purpose flour, divided
½ teaspoon (2.5 mL) ground cumin
Salt, to taste
Freshly ground black pepper, to taste
6–8 partridge breasts
8 slices bacon
3 tablespoons (45 mL) peanut oil
1 cup (236 mL) dry white wine
½ cup (118 mL) thinly sliced onion
1 teaspoon (5 mL) grated lemon zest
½ teaspoon (2.5 mL) lemon salt
¼ teaspoon citrus pepper

1. Preheat the barbecue to medium high (350°F [180°C] to 400°F [200°C]).

2. Put ¼ cup (59 mL) of the flour, the cumin, salt, and pepper in a brown paper bag and shake to mix. Add 1 to 2 breasts at a time, shake to coat them with the seasoned flour, and set aside.

3. In a large cast-iron skillet, fry the bacon. Remove the bacon and set it aside. Add the peanut oil to the bacon drippings. Add the breasts, place the skillet on the hot grill, and cook for 10 to 12 minutes on each side or until done and a thermometer inserted into a breast reads 170°F (77°C).

Remove the partridge from pan and place the breasts on paper towels to drain. Cover with foil. Reserve ¼ cup (59 mL) of the pan drippings.

4. Add the remaining flour to the drippings and, whisking continuously until smooth, cook 1 minute. Gradually add the wine and stir well. Add the onion slices and cook over medium heat, stirring constantly, until thickened and bubbly. Stir in the grated lemon zest, lemon salt, and citrus pepper.

5. Arrange the breasts on a bed of spinach leaves. Drizzle with half the gravy and onions and pour the remaining gravy into a sauce boat to serve at the table.

Partridge Rice Bake
Yield: 6 servings

You can use wild rice in this recipe, but first boil it in water for 15 minutes, then use as the recipe here directs.

1 partridge, cut up
3 cups (708 mL) water
3 tablespoons (45 mL) lemon juice
1 (1-ounce [28-g]) envelope dry onion soup mix
1 cup (236 mL) uncooked long-grain rice
1 (10¾-ounce [301-g]) can condensed cream of mushroom soup
1 cup (236 mL) milk
1 (6-ounce [170-g]) can French fried onion rings

1. In a large saucepan, simmer the partridge in the water and lemon juice for 20 minutes.

2. Preheat the barbecue to medium high (350°F [180°C] to 400°F [200°C]) for indirect heating, putting a water pan under the unheated side of the grill. Butter a casserole dish well.

3. In a small bowl, mix together the soup mix and rice and stir. Pour this mixture into the prepared casserole dish. Top with the cooked partridge pieces. Mix together the mushroom soup and milk and pour this mixture over the pheasant.

4. Cover and bake in the barbecue for 1 hour, Uncover the partridge, sprinkle with the onion rings, and cook for another 15 minutes.

5. Remove the onion rings, pour the mixture onto a deep serving platter, place the rings on top again, and serve.

Breast of Wild Goose with Lingonberry Sauce

Yield: 4–6 servings

Goose needs to be pricked thoroughly before cooking to release excess fat, then roasted on a rack and drained of fat regularly. A quick way to ensure crisp skin is to turn the heat up at the end of roasting and sprinkle a little water over the bird. The water will evaporate and leave the skin crisp.

½ cup (118 mL) olive oil
½ cup (118 mL) water
¼ cup (59 mL) apple cider vinegar
3 tablespoons (45 mL) Worcestershire sauce
1 teaspoon (5 mL) garlic powder
1 teaspoon (5 mL) onion powder
1 (3-pound [1.3-kg]) full breast of wild (or domestic) goose
1 (12-ounce [336-g]) jar lingonberry preserves
½ cup (118 mL) gin

1. In a 2-gallon (7.6-L) resealable plastic bag, mix together the olive oil, water, vinegar, Worcestershire sauce, garlic powder, and onion powder. Add the goose breast and marinate for 2 to 4 hours in the refrigerator.

2. Remove the goose breast from the marinade. Pour the marinade into a saucepan and boil for 10 minutes while the goose comes to room temperature.

3. Preheat the barbecue to medium high (350°F [180°C] to 400°F [200°C]) for indirect heating, putting a water pan under the unheated side of the grill.

4. In a saucepan, combine the preserves and gin and cook over medium heat, stirring often, until the mixture thickens.

5. Place the goose breast on the grill and cook, turning occasionally and basting 2 to 3 times, until the goose breast reaches an internal temperature of 160°F (71°C) degrees. Remove the goose from the barbecue, cover it with foil, and allow it to rest for 15 minutes before slicing.

6. Serve the warm lingonberry-gin sauce on the side.

Goose with Mushrooms and Sour Cream

Yield: 4–6 servings

Goose can be wild or domestic. Young geese, less than 8 months old and weighing 8 to 10 pounds (3.6–4.5 kg) are more tender than older geese. Like most foods, goose should only be thawed in the refrigerator. A whole goose needs 24 to 36 hours to thaw completely.

1 (5–8 pound [2.3–3.6 kg]) goose
¼ teaspoon (1.25 mL) garlic salt
¼ teaspoon (1.25 mL) paprika
Goose fat as needed for browning (or use bacon fat)
1½ stalks celery, chopped
1 carrot, chopped
1 medium onion, peeled and chopped
4 tablespoons (60 mL) all-purpose flour, divided
1¼ teaspoon (1.25 mL) salt
½ teaspoon (2.5 mL) dried rosemary
¼ teaspoon (1.25 mL) dried thyme
1 cup (236 mL) sour cream
8 ounces (227 g) sliced crimini mushrooms

1. Preheat the barbecue to medium high (300°F [150°C] to 325°F [165°C]).

2. Wash and dry the goose inside and out. Remove any fat deposits you can find and put them in a skillet. Cut off the neck and wing tips and set aside. Season the inside and outside of the goose with the garlic salt and paprika.

3. Place the goose on a rack in a shallow baking pan and bake, uncovered, in the barbecue for 1 hour, or until the goose is browned and the fat drippings in the pan have cooked away. While the goose is baking, simmer the giblets, neck and wing tips in enough water to cover them for 20 minutes.

4. Heat up the skillet of goose fat and cook until most of the fat has melted. Add the celery, carrot, and onion and sauté until the vegetables are soft and beginning to brown. Stir in 2 tablespoons (30 mL) of the flour, 1 cup (236 mL) of the liquid from the giblets (or chicken stock), the salt, rosemary, and thyme.

5. Stir the remaining 2 tablespoons (30 mL) of flour into the sour cream. Slowly add this mixture to the gravy, stirring. Transfer the goose from the shallow pan to a roasting pan, sprinkle on the mushrooms and pour the gravy over the bird and mushrooms.

6. Cover and roast for 2 hours, or until tender and a thermometer inserted into the thick part of the breast reads 160°F (71°C). Remove the pan from the barbecue, remove the bird from the mushroom gravy, cover, and let rest for 15 to 20 minutes to let the juices reabsorb. Pour the gravy into a sauce boat and serve at the table alongside the carved roast goose.

Goose à L'Orange

Yield: 4–6 servings

Goose is an incredibly fatty bird and will shrink considerably during roasting. For that reason, it is a good idea to periodically check the level of rendered fat in the roasting pan. If it is getting too high, use a basting bulb to remove some of the excess.

1 (6–8 pound [2.7–3.6 kg]) goose
2 tablespoons (30 mL) butter or margarine
1 medium onion, peeled and minced
¼ teaspoon (1.25 mL) dried tarragon
½ cup (118 mL) orange juice
¼ cup (59 mL) currant jelly
2 tablespoons (30 mL) grated orange zest
⅛ teaspoon (0.6 mL) salt
⅛ teaspoon (0.6 mL) dry mustard
2 tablespoons (30 mL) port
1 orange, peeled and sectioned
1½ teaspoons (7.5 mL) cornstarch

1. Preheat the barbecue to medium high (350°F [180°C] to 400°F [200°C]).

2. Wash the goose and pat it dry. Skewer the neck skin to the back. Cross the wing tips over the back and tie them together. Place the goose breast side up on a rack in a shallow roasting pan and place it in the barbecue.

3. In a cast-iron skillet, melt the butter or margarine over medium heat. Add the onion and tarragon and cook until the onion is tender. Add the orange juice, jelly, zest, salt, and mustard and cook, stirring constantly, until the jelly melts. Reduce the heat and stir in the port and orange sections.

4. Pour half the sauce into a saucepan and set it aside. Baste the goose with the remaining sauce 2 to 3 times an hour while it cooks. If the goose starts to get too brown, cover it with aluminum foil (shiny side up). The goose is ready when it's nicely browned all over and a meat thermometer inserted into the breast reads 160°F (71°C), about 1½ hours. Remove the goose from the barbecue, cover it with foil, and let it rest for 15 to 20 minutes before carving.

5. Place the saucepan of reserved sauce over medium heat and slowly whisk in the cornstarch until the mixture thickens and boils for 1 minute. Pour the sauce into a sauce boat and serve it with the goose.

Breast of Wild Goose with Apple-Whiskey Sauce

Yield: 6 servings

If you want to try wild goose but don't know a hunter who will give you some goose breasts, several websites can ship goose to you at a very reasonable cost.

½ cup (118 mL) olive oil
½ cup (118 mL) water
¼ cup (59 mL) apple cider vinegar
3 tablespoons (45 mL) Worcestershire sauce
1 teaspoon (5 mL) garlic powder
1 teaspoon (5 mL) onion powder
1 (3-pound [1.3-kg]) full breast of wild (or domestic) goose
1 (12-ounce [336-g]) jar apple jelly or lingonberry preserves
½ cup (118 mL) Canadian Club whisky
1 tablespoon (15 mL) brown sugar

1. In a 1-gallon (3.8-L) resealable plastic bag, combine the olive oil, water, vinegar, Worcestershire sauce, garlic powder, and onion powder. Add the goose breast and shake the bag to coat the meat well. Marinate for 2 hours in the refrigerator.

2. Preheat the barbecue to medium high (350°F [180°C] to 400°F [200°C]) for indirect heating, putting a water pan under the unheated side of the grill.

3. Remove the goose breast from the marinade. Pour the marinade into a saucepan and boil for 10 minutes while the goose comes to room temperature. Pat the meat dry and place the goose on the grill.

4. While goose is cooking, heat the apple jelly and whisky in a saucepan over medium heat, stirring often, until the mixture thickens. Add the brown sugar, set aside, and keep warm.

5. Use the boiled marinade to baste the meat, cooking until the goose breast reaches an internal temperature of 160°F (71°C), about 11 to 12 minutes a side. Don't overcook the goose. Remove the goose from the grill, cover it with foil, and allow it to rest for 5 to 10 minutes before slicing.

6. Reheat the warm apple-whisky sauce and serve on the side.

Fiery Goose Balls

Yield: 4–6 appetizer servings

For a bit more fire, add 1 teaspoon (5 mL) of your favorite hot sauce to the marinade.

1 cup (236 mL) beer
1 cup (236 mL) Italian dressing
1–2 goose breasts, cut into 3–inch (7.5-cm) cubes
1 large onion, peeled and cut into 2–inch (5-cm) pieces
3–4 jalapeño peppers, halved vertically and horizontally
12–20 slices of bacon

1. In a 1-gallon (3.8-L) resealable plastic bag, combine the beer and Italian dressing. Add the goose cubes, seal the bag, and refrigerate overnight.

2. Remove the meat from the marinade and drain, discarding the marinade.

3. Preheat the barbecue to medium high (320°F [160°C] to 340°F [170°C]), making sure the grill is well sprayed or oiled.

4. Place a piece of onion on one side of each meat cube and a slice of jalapeño pepper on the other side. Wrap with bacon and secure with toothpicks. Repeat until all the cubes are prepared. Place directly on the hot grill and cook until the bacon is crisp and browned, turning several times.

5. Place cooked cubes on a platter and serve. You can remove the jalapeño pepper before eating if you like; otherwise, provide lots of chilled adult beverages to quench the fire.

Hanoi-Style Grilled Squab
Yield: 4 servings

Slightly sweet, slightly salty, this Asian marinade caramelizes on the grill. Two Cornish game hens may be substituted for the squab. This recipe comes from Stephen Ceideburg from Hi-Chi Minh City, Vietnam.

4 (1-pound [454-g]) squab, washed, dried, and trimmed of fat
¼ cup (59 mL) fish sauce
2 tablespoons (30 mL) minced shallots
2 cloves garlic, peeled and minced
2 teaspoons (10 mL) sugar
2 teaspoons (10 mL) olive oil
1 teaspoon (5 mL) toasted sesame oil
½ teaspoon (2.5 mL) freshly ground black pepper

1. Place each squab on its back on a cutting board. With a sharp knife or poultry shears, split each bird in half through the breast bone and remove the backbone.

2. In a 1-gallon (3.8-L) resealable plastic bag, mix together the fish sauce, shallots, garlic, sugar, olive oil, sesame oil, and black pepper. Add the squab, turn the bag to coat evenly, seal the bag, and marinate in the refrigerator for 4 hours or overnight.

3. Remove the squab from the marinade. Pour the marinade into a saucepan and boil for 10 minutes while the squabs come to room temperature.

4. Preheat the barbecue to medium high (350°F [180°C] to 400°F [200°C]) for direct grilling.

5. Place the birds on the grill and cook for about 6 minutes. Baste once or twice. Turn the squab, baste once or twice more, and cook for about 6 minutes longer, or until the juices run clear when the squab is pierced with a fork. Boil the remaining sauce for 10 minutes.

6. Serve with steamed rice and barely grilled sweet peppers and onion slices which have been drizzled with the remaining marinade while grilling.

Pan-Roasted Squab

Yield: 4 servings

Yes, Virginia, squab—as in pigeons. But these haven't spent their days parading and "decorating" statues in your local park. These are farm-raised birds, whose diet is controlled, and they are incredibly delicious.

4 (1-pound [454-g]) squab
2 quarts (1.9 L) vegetable stock, divided
¼ teaspoon (1.25 mL) dried thyme
3 tablespoons (45 mL) unsalted butter, divided
3 large shallots, peeled and diced
¼ pound (112 g) Bing cherries, pitted
1 cup (236 mL) sweet red wine
Salt, to taste
Freshly ground black pepper, to taste
1 tablespoon (15 mL) vegetable oil
1 large bunch fresh spinach, washed, dried, and trimmed

1. Preheat the barbecue to medium high (400°F [200°C] to 425°F [220°C]).

2. Cut the legs and breast meat (with wings attached, but tips cut off) from the carcass of each squab. Cover and refrigerate the legs and breasts. Place the wing tips and carcasses in a roasting pan and cook in the barbecue until well browned, about 30 minutes.

3. Reserve ¾ cup (177 mL) of the vegetable stock and pour the remainder over the squab pieces in the pan. Add the thyme. Close the barbecue and simmer the stock for 2 to 3 hours. Strain the stock through a fine sieve to remove the bones and skin. You should end up with about 4 cups (0.95 L) of strained stock. If there is more, pour the stock into a saucepan and boil to reduce it to that amount.

4. In a saucepan, melt 1 tablespoon (15 mL) of the butter. Add the shallots and sauté until softened. Add the cherries and cover with the red wine. Raise the heat and boil until the wine is almost completely evaporated. Add the strained stock and cook at a brisk simmer until reduced to 2 cups (473 mL) of thick sauce, about 1 hour. Season with salt and pepper.

5. In a roasting pan or Dutch oven large enough to hold the squab pieces in a single layer, heat the remaining butter and the oil. Add the breast pieces and lightly brown on all sides, then remove them from the pan. Return the pan to the barbecue and cook the legs for 5 minutes. Add the breast meat and cook for 3 to 5 minutes, or until medium-rare. Remove the pan from oven and let the meat rest, loosely covered, for about 5 minutes.

6. Make a bed of spinach on a large platter. Arrange the squab pieces on top, pour the cherry sauce over the squab, and serve immediately.

Wild Turkey Steaks with Tomato-Orange Salsa

Yield: 6 servings

Of course, you can use any kind of salsa you wish in this dish, but we love the interplay of the sweet oranges, fiery chilies, and sweet tomato.

1 (1½-pound [681-g]) wild turkey breast, cut into 3 thick slices
½ cup (118 mL) all-purpose flour
½ cup (118 mL) diced, seeded tomato
½ cup (118 mL) peeled, diced orange
1 (4-ounce [112-g]) can diced green chili peppers, drained
½ cup (118 mL) thinly sliced green onions
3 tablespoons (45 mL) chopped fresh cilantro
1 tablespoon (15 mL) minced fresh ginger
¼ teaspoon (1.25 mL) salt
3 tablespoons (45 mL) butter
Cilantro sprigs, for garnish

1. Preheat the barbecue to medium high (220°F [105°C] to 230°F [110°C]) for indirect heating, putting a water pan under the unheated side of the grill.

2. Cut each turkey slice into 2 pieces. Dredge each piece in the flour, cover, and set aside.

3. In a medium bowl, combine the tomato, orange, chili peppers, green onions, chopped cilantro, ginger, and salt. Set aside at room temperature.

4. In a large cast-iron skillet, melt the butter over medium high heat. Add the turkey steaks and bake in the barbecue for 10 to 12 minutes on each side, or until lightly browned.

5. Remove the pan from the barbecue and transfer the steaks to a warmed serving platter. Spoon salsa on top, garnish with the cilantro sprigs, and serve.

Blackened Wild Turkey Alfredo

Yield: 4 servings

You can spend quite a bit of money buying blackened seasoning with someone's name on it—but why? This simple recipe will match the best brands on the market at a quarter of the price. Plus, it's fun and easy to make yourself.

Blackened Seasoning

2 tablespoons (30 mL) paprika
1 tablespoon (15 mL) ground oregano
1 tablespoon (15 mL) ground thyme
1 tablespoon (15 mL) cayenne pepper
1 teaspoon (5 mL) freshly ground black pepper
1 teaspoon (5 mL) finely ground white pepper
1 teaspoon (5 mL) garlic powder

Turkey

1 (12–16 ounce [336–454 g]) skinless, boned wild turkey breast
2 tablespoons (30 mL) olive oil
2½ teaspoons (12.5 mL) Blackened Seasoning, divided
8 ounces (227 g) uncooked ziti or penne pasta
1 cup (236 mL) chopped asparagus tips
1 cup (236 mL) peeled baby carrots, halved
1 (15-ounce [420-g]) bottle Bertollini Garlic Alfredo pasta sauce (or your favorite brand)

1. Mix together the ingredients for the blackened seasoning and transfer to a jar. Covered, the mixture will last for months.

2. Place the turkey in a 1-gallon (3.8-L) resealable plastic bag. Add the oil, and 2 teaspoons (10 mL) of the blackened seasoning. Turn the bag to coat the turkey and marinate for 2 hours.

3. Preheat the barbecue to medium high (350°F [180°C] to 400°F [200°C]) for direct grilling, making sure the grill has been well-oiled or sprayed with nonstick cooking or grilling spray.

4. Sear the turkey on the hot grill, turn once, and cook until the inside is no longer pink, about 3 minutes per side. Transfer the turkey from the grill to a cutting board and cut it into ½-inch (1-cm) cubes. Set aside.

5. Cook the pasta according to the package directions, adding the asparagus and carrots for the last 8 minutes of cooking. Drain and return the pasta and vegetables to the pan. Stir in the grilled turkey, Alfredo sauce, and ½ teaspoon (2.5 mL) blackened seasoning. Heat just until the sauce barely begins to bubble, stir, and serve.

Stuffed Roasted Wild Turkey

Yield: 8–10 servings

Wild turkeys are smaller than domestic turkeys, and their meat is darker, richer, more intense in flavor, and firmer in texture. The breast tends to cook faster than the legs or thighs, so barding the breast with bacon or covering it with foil and basting the whole bird with butter or oil and pan drippings is recommended.

1 cup (236 mL) fresh cranberries
1 cup (236 mL) apricot jam
¼ cup (59 mL) fresh orange juice
3 tablespoons (45 mL) Wild Turkey (80 proof) bourbon
1 (10–12 pound [4.5–5.4 kg]) wild turkey
1 medium onion, peeled and cut into large chunks
1 orange, quartered
Freshly ground black pepper, to taste
½ pound (227 g) thickly sliced bacon

1. In a small saucepan, combine the cranberries, jam, orange juice, and bourbon. Bring to a boil over high heat. Reduce the heat to medium and cook, stirring occasionally, for 2 minutes.

2. Preheat the barbecue to medium high (475°F [250°C] to 525°F [275°C]) for direct and indirect heating, putting a water pan under the unheated side of the grill. Grease a roasting pan or shallow Dutch oven.

3. Place the onion and orange in the cavity of the turkey and season the outside with black pepper. Cover the turkey breast and legs with the bacon, truss the turkey, and place it on a V-shaped rack in the prepared roasting pan or Dutch oven.

4. Cook for 15 minutes over direct heat, then move the pan to the unheated side of the grill and close the vents to lower the temperature. Cover the turkey with aluminum foil and cook, basting occasionally with the pan drippings, 15 to 20 minutes per pound (454 g), or until a turkey leg feels very loose when wiggled and a thermometer inserted into the thick part of the breast reads 165°F (71°C).

5. Remove the bacon and brush the bird frequently with glaze during the last hour of cooking.

6. Remove the turkey from the barbecue, cover it with foil, and let it stand for 20 minutes before carving.

Marinated Grilled Breasts of Dove

Yield: 4 servings

Depending on how large they are, we usually figure 3 to 4 double breasts of dove for each person.

1¼ (295 mL) cups Italian dressing
1 cup (236 mL) sweet red wine
1 teaspoon (5 mL) ground thyme
½ teaspoon (2.5 mL) seasoned salt
¼ teaspoon (1.25 mL) cayenne pepper
Freshly ground black pepper, to taste
12–20 fresh double breasts of dove

1. In a bowl large enough to hold all of the doves you are going to cook, combine the Italian dressing and wine. Add the ground thyme, seasoned salt, cayenne pepper, and pepper. Add the dove breasts, cover, and refrigerate for 4 to 5 hours.

2. Remove the doves from the marinade. Pour the marinade into a large skillet or a roasting pan and boil for 10 minutes while the doves are cooking.

3. Preheat the barbecue to 350°F (180°C) to 400°F (200°C) for direct and indirect heating, making sure the grill has been well oiled or sprayed with a grilling spray. Place a water pan under the unheated side of the grill.

4. Grill the doves until golden brown, about 3 minutes per side.

5. Add the doves to the pan of boiled marinade. Place the pan on the unheated side of the grill and simmer for 15 minutes.

6. Remove the doves from the pot and arrange them on a serving platter. Pour the sauce into a gravy boat and serve alongside the birds.

SEVEN

Hot Dogs
and Sausages

Hoisin-Glazed Dogs

Yield: 4 entrée servings or 8–10 appetizer servings

½ cup (118 mL) hoisin sauce
2 tablespoons (30 mL) honey
1 tablespoon (15 mL) minced fresh ginger
½ teaspoon (2.5 mL) minced garlic
8 hot dogs
8 hot dog buns, split
½ cup (118 mL) chopped green onions

1. Preheat a gas or charcoal grill to medium (350°F [180°C] to 400°F [200°C]) for direct grilling.

2. In a small saucepan, heat the hoisin, honey, ginger, and garlic over medium heat. Simmer for 2 to 3 minutes, then remove the pan from the heat. Reserve ¼ cup (59 mL) of the sauce.

3. Lightly score diagonal cuts across the hot dogs. Liberally brush hot dogs with the sauce.

4. Place the hot dogs on the grill and cook, basting often with the sauce, for 10 to 12 minutes, or until they are done to your liking.

5. During the last 3 to 4 minutes, open the hot dog buns and lightly toast them over indirect heat. Brush the buns with the reserved hoisin sauce. Place the hot dogs in the heated buns. Sprinkle the chopped green onions on the hot dogs.

Wrappin' Cheese Dogs

Yield: 5–10 servings

1 pound (454 g) bacon
20 hot dogs
1 (12-ounce [340-g]) package American processed cheese slices
20 hot dog buns

1. Fry the bacon until barely beginning to crisp. Drain on paper towels and set aside.

2. Preheat a gas or charcoal grill to medium (350°F [180°C] to 400°F [200°C]) for direct grilling. Cover the grill with aluminum foil or place a baking sheet on the grill.

3. Split the hot dogs down the middle. Cut the cheese slices into ¼-inch (0.5-cm) wide strips and place the strips in the middle of the hot dogs. Wrap the bacon around the hot dogs and cheese slices.

4. Place the hot dogs on the foil or baking sheet and bake until the cheese is melted and bacon is crisp, about 10 minutes.

5. Place the hot dogs in the buns and serve.

Q-Doggies
Yield: 8–16 servings

3 tablespoons (45 mL) olive oil
½ cup (118 mL) chopped onion
2 cups (473 mL) ketchup
1 cup (236 mL) finely chopped red bell pepper
½ cup (118 mL) water
⅓ cup (79 mL) lime or lemon juice
3 tablespoons (45 mL) dark brown sugar
3 tablespoons (45 mL) cider vinegar
1 tablespoon (15 mL) Worcestershire sauce
1 tablespoon (15 mL) steak sauce (such as A1)
2 teaspoons (10 mL) prepared yellow mustard
2 teaspoons (10 mL) Dijon mustard
20 hot dogs
20 hot dog buns

1. Preheat the barbecue to medium high (350°F [180°C] to 400°F [200°C]).

2. In a saucepan over medium heat on a barbecue side burner, heat the olive oil. Add the onion and cook until tender and slightly brown, 10 to 12 minutes. Add the ketchup, red pepper, water, lime juice, brown sugar, vinegar, Worcestershire sauce, steak sauce, and mustards and bring to a boil. Reduce the heat, cover, and simmer for 20 minutes.

3. Cut ¼-inch (0.5-cm) deep slits on 4 sides of each hot dog and place the hot dogs in a cast-iron skillet or Dutch oven. Pour the sauce over the hot dogs.

4. Place the skillet over direct heat, close the lid, and bake 30 to 35 minutes, or until the hot dogs are nicely browned and the sauce is bubbling.

Hotter 'n' Hades Dogs
Yield: 4–8 servings

8 jumbo hot dogs (the thicker the better)
4 jalapeño peppers, roughly chopped
1 (8-ounce [227-g]) package Mexican 4-cheese blend
8 strips pepper bacon
8 hot dog buns, toasted
2 tablespoons (30 mL) garlic butter, melted

1. Preheat a gas or charcoal grill to medium (350°F [180°C] to 400°F [200°C]) for direct grilling.

2. Slit and stuff each hot dog with chopped jalapeño pepper and shredded cheese. Wrap each hot dog in a slice of pepper bacon to hold it together.

3. Grill the hot dogs until the bacon is nicely browned on the bottom and both sides, gently rolling them to cook both sides without letting the filling spill out, 8 to 10 minutes.

4. Brush the insides of the buns with the garlic butter and grill them until just beginning to brown, about 1 minute.

5. Serve the hot dogs on the buns with or without the bacon, or remove the bacon, chop it, and add it to the cheese and pepper filling.

Pan-Fried Barbecued Franks

Yield: 4–8 servings

8 all-beef hot dogs
¼ cup (59 mL) mayonnaise
¼ cup (59 mL) prepared yellow mustard
8 hamburger buns
Tomato slices, for serving
Onion slices, for serving
Lettuce leaves, for serving

1. Preheat a gas or charcoal grill to medium (350°F [180°C] to 400°F [200°C]) for direct grilling.

2. Cut the dogs down the center and butterfly them so they lay flat. Arrange them cut side down on the grill and cook until the bottom is just starting to blacken, about 10 minutes. With tongs, turn the hot dogs and cook until the other side is well browned.

3. Place the top and bottom halves of the hamburger buns on the barbecue and grill until well toasted. In a small bowl, mix together the mayonnaise and mustard and stir to blend.

4. Remove the buns from the grill and, while they are still warm, generously spread mayonnaise- mustard mixture on the bottom of each bun.

5. Cut the cooked hot dogs in half lengthwise (hence the wide hamburger buns) and place a hot dog on each bun. Add tomato, onion, and lettuce, cover with top of the bun, and enjoy.

Corn Dogs

Yield: 4–8 servings

1 cup (236 mL) cornmeal
1 cup (236 mL) all-purpose flour
2 tablespoons (30 mL) sugar
2 teaspoons (10 mL) baking powder
½ teaspoon (2.5 mL) salt
1 large egg, lightly beaten
1 cup (236 mL) milk
2 tablespoons (30 mL) vegetable shortening, melted
10 hot dogs
Wooden skewers
Vegetable oil, for frying

1. In a medium bowl, mix together the corn meal, flour, sugar, baking powder, and salt. Add the egg and milk. Blend in the melted shortening and mix well.

2. Half-fill a deep pot with vegetable oil and heat in on a barbecue side burner to 350°F (180°C). Skewer the hot dogs lengthwise and dip them in the batter. Stand them skewer-side up in the pot and fry them until the batter is golden brown, about 2 to 3 minutes. Drain on paper towels and serve hot.

Tacoed Hot Dogs
Yield: 4–8 servings

⅓ cup (79 mL) chili sauce
1 teaspoon (5 mL) minced hot chili pepper (or ¼ teaspoon [1.25 mL] red pepper sauce)
8 hot dogs
8 hot dog buns, buttered
⅔ cup (158 mL) shredded lettuce
⅓ cup (79 mL) shredded cheddar cheese
⅓ cup (79 mL) diced onions

1. Preheat the barbecue to medium high (350°F [180°C] to 400°F [200°C]).

2. In a small saucepan, mix together the chili sauce and chili pepper. Place the pan on the grill and heat for 5 to 8 minutes while the hot dogs are being grilled.

3. Toast the buns for 2 to 3 minutes, until they begin to brown. Put the hot dogs in the buns and spoon the chili sauce mixture over the hot dogs. Top with shredded lettuce, cheese, and diced onions and serve.

Baked Beans 'n' Dogs
Yield: 4–8 servings

½ cup (118 mL) chopped onion
½ cup (118 mL) ketchup
¼ cup (59 mL) molasses
2 tablespoons (30 mL) brown sugar
1 tablespoon (15 mL) prepared mustard
½ teaspoon (2.5 mL) Worcestershire sauce
1 (28-ounce [784-g]) can and 1 (16-ounce [454-g]) can pork and beans in tomato sauce
10 hot dogs

1. Preheat a gas or charcoal grill to medium (300°F [150°C] to 325°F [165°C]) for direct grilling.

2. In a 2-quart (1.9-L) Dutch oven, combine the onion, ketchup, molasses, brown sugar, mustard, and Worcestershire sauce. Add the beans and mix well. Place the pot in the barbecue and bake for 30 minutes. Lay the whole hot dogs on top of the beans and bake 30 minutes longer, or cut the dogs into 1-inch (2.5-cm) pieces and mix them into the beans.

Crescent Dogs
Yield: 4–8 servings

8 hot dogs
8 slices cheddar cheese, cut into ¼-inch (0.5-cm) strips
1 (8-ounce [227-g]) can refrigerated crescent roll dough

1. Preheat a gas or charcoal grill to medium (350°F [180°C] to 400°F [200°C]) for direct grilling. Line a baking sheet with aluminum foil.

2. Split each hot dog down the middle lengthwise, almost all the way through. Place 2 strips of the cheese down the middle of each dog.

3. Separate the crescent dough into triangles. Wrap each dog, starting with the side opposite the point, stretching the dough a little as you wrap to completely cover the hot dog.

4. Place the dogs on the foil-lined baking sheet and bake in the barbecue for 10 to 12 minutes, or until the crescent rolls are golden brown. Serve hot with mustard, ketchup, and other favorite condiments.

Whiskeyed Up Dogs
Yield: 4–8 servings

¼ cup (59 mL) ketchup
¼ cup (59 mL) brown sugar
¼ cup (59 mL) whiskey
1 teaspoon (5 mL) ground cumin
½ teaspoon (2.5 mL) freshly ground black pepper
1 dash hot sauce
10 hot dogs

1. Preheat a gas or charcoal grill to medium (350°F [180°C] to 400°F [200°C]) for direct grilling.

2. In a cast-iron skillet, combine the ketchup, brown sugar, whiskey, cumin, pepper, and hot sauce.

3. Cut the hot dogs diagonally in pieces. Add the pieces to the skillet, and place the skillet on the grill.

4. Cook, stirring several times, for 12 to 15 minutes, or until the sauce is boiling and the dogs are cooked through.

5. Serve with toothpicks.

Mashed Tater Dogs

Yield: 4–8 servings

10 hot dogs
5–7 medium russet potatoes, boiled, cooled, and cut into bite-size pieces
1 tablespoon (15 mL) butter
1 tablespoon (15 mL) all-purpose flour
2 cups (473 mL) milk
1½ cups (354 mL) grated cheddar cheese
2 tablespoons (30 mL) minced onion
1 teaspoon (5 mL) dried basil
Salt, to taste
Freshly ground black pepper, to taste
Chopped fresh parsley, for garnish

1. Preheat a gas or charcoal grill to medium (350°F [180°C] to 400°F [200°C]) for direct grilling. Lightly butter a 9 ×13-inch (22.5 × 32.5-cm) casserole dish.

2. Cut the hot dogs into bite-size pieces. and put the hot dog pieces and potatoes in the prepared casserole dish.

3. In a saucepan over medium heat, melt the butter. Whisk in the flour, forming a paste. Continue to whisk as you add the milk and cook until the mixture just starts to brown. Whisk in the cheese, minced onion, basil, salt, and pepper.

4. Pour this mixture over the hot dogs and potatoes, cover the casserole, and bake for 30 minutes in the barbecue. Uncover and cook for another 10 minutes.

5. Sprinkle with the parsley and serve.

Coney Island Dogs

Yield: 4–8 servings

1 pound (454 g) ground beef
1 large onion, peeled and minced
1 (16-ounce [454-g]) can thick tomato sauce
2 teaspoons (10 mL) chili powder
1 teaspoon (5 mL) salt
1 teaspoon (5 mL) ground cumin
10 hot dogs
10 hot dog buns

1. Preheat a gas or charcoal grill to medium (350°F [180°C] to 400°F [200°C]) for direct grilling.

2. In a skillet, brown the beef. Halfway through the browning, add the onion. Heat until the beef is browned and onions are soft. Drain. Add the tomato sauce, chili powder, salt, and cumin, and simmer for at least 30 minutes.

3. Grill the hot dogs, turning several times, for 8–10 minutes, or until they are puffed up, browned, and starting to char in some spots.

4. Open the buns and toast them on the grill for 2 to 3 minutes.

5. Place the hot dogs in the buns and cover each dog with 1–2 tablespoons (15–30 mL) of the meat mixture. Serve with additional chopped onions and grated cheese.

Mexican Chihuahua Dog Casserole
Yield: 4 servings

8 hot dogs
1 small onion, peeled and chopped
1½ cups (354 mL) grated cheddar cheese
1 teaspoon (5 mL) chili powder
1 teaspoon (5 mL) ground cumin
1 (11.5-ounce [326-g]) package flour tortillas, 8 tortillas
1 (16-ounce [454-g]) can chili (with or without beans)

1. Preheat a gas or charcoal grill to medium (350°F [180°C] to 400°F [200°C]) for direct grilling. Grease well a 2-quart (1.9-L) Dutch oven or casserole.

2. Split each hot dog. Fill the dogs with some of the onion and cheese and sprinkle each with a little of the chili powder and cumin.

3. Place the tortillas on the hot grill just long enough to warm and soften them, about 1 minute.

4. Wrap a tortilla around each hot dog; place the wrapped hot dogs in the bottom of the prepared Dutch oven or casserole. Pour the chili over the dogs, sprinkle with the remaining onion and cheese, and season lightly with the remaining chili powder and cumin.

5. Bake in the barbecue for 20 to 25 minutes, or until the cheese is melted and the mixture is bubbling.

Big Bad Dogs
Yield: 4–8 servings

10 foot-long hot dogs
2 tablespoons (29 mL) Dijon-style honey mustard
Celery salt, to taste
Freshly ground black pepper, to taste
8 strips bacon
8 slices extra-sharp cheddar cheese
10 tablespoons (150 mL) red chili hot dog relish
10 foot-long hot dog buns, buttered and toasted

1. Preheat a gas or charcoal grill to medium (350°F [180°C] to 400°F [200°C]) for direct grilling.

2. Slice each hot dog almost in half along its entire length. Spread the dogs apart and brush the inside of each with mustard. Sprinkle with the celery salt and pepper.

3. Grill the bacon in a skillet until just firm, drain, and halve each slice lengthwise. Cut each cheese slice in thirds. Place 2 strips of bacon and three strips of cheese in each split hot dog. Tie each hot dog partially closed in two places with butchers twine.

4. Place the dogs on the grill, cut side up, and cook over high heat until browned on the bottom and both sides, about 8 minutes. Roll carefully to cook the sides so you don't spill the melted cheese.

5. Remove the twine from the dogs, add a generous tablespoon (15 mL) of the relish on top, and serve them on the buns.

Creamy Seattle Dogs
Yield: 4–8 servings

---

6 tablespoons (90 mL) olive oil
1 cup (236 mL) thinly sliced Walla Walla, Maui, or Vidalia onion
10 hot dogs
1 (8-ounce [227-g]) package cream cheese
10 hot dog buns, toasted
Prepared yellow or spicy brown mustard, for serving
Vidalia Onion Sauce, for serving (optional; recipe follows)

1. Preheat a gas or charcoal grill to medium (350°F [180°C] to 400°F [200°C]) for direct grilling.

2. In a skillet, heat the olive oil over medium heat. Add the onions and cook slowly, stirring frequently, until they are softened and well browned, 10 to 15 minutes.

3. Place the hot dogs on the grill and cook for 10 to 12 minutes, or until they are done to your liking.

4. While the dogs are cooking, put the cream cheese in a heat-proof bowl on the unheated side of the grill, or on top of the barbecue if it gets hot, to soften it. Spread open the buns and toast them on the grill.

5. To serve, spread the softened and warmed cream cheese on the buns. Add a cooked hot dog to each bun, then add the mustard and onions or the optional Vidalia Onion Sauce.

Vidalia Onion Sauce

Yield: 1–1½ cups (236–354 mL)

1 tablespoon (15 mL) olive oil
1 large Vidalia onion, peeled and finely diced
¼ red bell pepper, finely diced
¼ green bell pepper, finely diced
2 tablespoons (30 mL) chopped fresh parsley
1 tablespoon (15 mL) lemon juice
1 teaspoon (5 mL) brown sugar
¼ teaspoon (1.25 mL) salt
¼ teaspoon (1.25 mL) cayenne pepper

1. In a skillet on the barbecue side burner, heat the oil over medium high. Add the onions and peppers and sauté until the onions are translucent and the peppers have wilted slightly. Stir in the parsley, lemon juice, brown sugar, salt, and cayenne pepper. Serve warm.

Au Gratin Doggies and Spuds

Yield: 6–8 servings

2 cups (473 mL) peeled, cubed, and cooked russet potatoes
2 tablespoons (30 mL) butter or margarine
¼ cup (59 mL) all-purpose flour
1 cup (236 mL) milk
½ pound (227 g) Velveeta cheese, cubed
1 teaspoon (5 mL) garlic salt
⅛ teaspoon (0.6 mL) freshly ground black pepper
10 hot dogs, cut into 2-inch (5-cm) long pieces
1 (10-ounce [280-g]) package frozen peas and pearl onions, thawed and drained

1. Preheat a gas or charcoal grill to medium (350°F [180°C] to 400°F [200°C]) for direct grilling. Butter a 2-quart (1.9-L) roasting or baking pan.

2. Cook the potatoes in boiling water until just tender, drain, and set aside to cool.

3. In a small saucepan, melt the butter over medium heat. Whisk in the flour, add the milk, and stir until it thickens. Add the cheese, garlic salt, and pepper and stir until the cheese melts. Add the hot dogs and peas and onions, mix well. Pour the mixture into the prepared pan.

4. Top with the cooled potatoes and mix gently. Bake, uncovered, in the barbecue for 25 minutes, or until heated through.

Holy Guacamole Dogs

Yield: 5–10 servings

---

2 medium ripe avocados, halved, pitted, and peeled
1–2 tablespoons (15–30 mL) fresh lemon juice
½ cup (118 mL) chunky medium salsa
⅛ teaspoon (0.6 mL) sea salt
10 hot dogs
10 hot dog buns
½ cup (118 mL) minced onion
Paprika, for garnish

1. Make the guacamole: Put the avocado in a bowl. Sprinkle with lemon juice, mash with a fork, and fold in the salsa and sea salt. Stir lightly to mix. Refrigerate until ready to use.

2. Preheat a gas or charcoal grill to medium (350°F [180°C] to 400°F [200°C]) for direct grilling.

3. Grill the hot dogs for 10 to 12 minutes, turning frequently.

4. Place the hot dogs in the buns and top each with a generous amount of guacamole, minced onion, and a sprinkle of paprika.

Sonora Hot Dogs

Yield: 5–10 servings

---

10 slices bacon
10 hot dogs
10 small yellow chili peppers
10 teaspoons (50 mL) salsa verde
10 teaspoons (50 mL) guacamole
10 bolillos (Mexican hot dog buns) or regular buns
1 (15-ounce [420-g]) can pinto beans, heated
4 Roma tomatoes, chopped
1 medium white onion, peeled and diced
Mustard, for serving
Mayonnaise, for serving
Lime quarters, for squeezing

1. Preheat a gas or charcoal grill to medium (350°F [180°C] to 400°F [200°C]) for direct grilling.

2. Wrap 1 slice of bacon around each hot dog and secure with toothpicks. Place the hot dogs and chili peppers on the grill and cook, turning the hot dogs only once to ensure strong sear marks, until the bacon is just beginning to crisp, about 7 to 8 minutes.

3. Remove the hot dogs and peppers from the grill. Set the peppers aside. Place each dog inside a bolillo. (Bolillos are hollowed out in the middle with closed ends. If you can't find them at a Mexican bakery, use regular buns.)

4. Put 1 teaspoon (5 mL) each of salsa verde and guacamole in the groove of each bolillo. Divide the pinto beans, tomatoes, and onion among the dogs, then spoon mustard and mayonnaise on top of each. Squeeze fresh lime juice over the whole mess and dig in. Serve the grilled chili peppers on the plate beside the hot dogs.

World's Best Chili Dogs

Yield: 8 servings

¾ pound (336 g) ground beef
1 cup (236 mL) chopped onion
1 (8-ounce [227-g]) can tomato sauce
1 teaspoon (5 mL) brown sugar
½ teaspoon (2.5 mL) salt
½ teaspoon (2.5 mL) chili powder
½ teaspoon (2.5 mL) Worcestershire sauce
¼ teaspoon (1.25 mL) freshly ground black pepper
¼ teaspoon (1.25 mL) hot pepper sauce
10 hot dogs
10 hot dog buns, split and lightly toasted
1 cup (236 mL) shredded cheddar cheese (optional)
Minced onion, for serving (optional)

1. In a cast-iron skillet over medium heat, brown the beef and onions, breaking up the beef into small pieces as it cooks. Drain the fat and reduce the heat to low. Stir in the tomato sauce, brown sugar, salt, chili powder, Worcestershire sauce, pepper, and hot pepper sauce. Simmer for 10–12 minutes, stirring occasionally.

2. Preheat a gas or charcoal grill to medium (350°F [180°C] to 400°F [200°C]) for direct grilling.

3. Grill the hot dogs for 8 to 10 minutes, turning often, until they puff up, begin to char on the edges, and sizzle on the grill.

4. Place the cooked hot dogs inside the toasted buns and ladle ¼ cup (59 mL) chili sauce over each hot dog. Add the cheese and onion if you wish.

Little Italy Pizza Doggies

Yield: 5–10 servings

1½ cups (354 mL) shredded mozzarella cheese
1 cup (236 mL) shredded provolone cheese
1 (16-ounce [454-g]) can pizza sauce
1 cup (236 mL) minced onion
1 cup (236 mL) minced mushrooms
1 teaspoon (5 mL) dried oregano
1 teaspoon (5 mL) dried thyme
1 teaspoon (5 mL) garlic powder
10 hot dogs
1 tablespoon (15 mL) olive oil
¼ cup (59 mL) butter, melted
10 hot dog buns, opened and flattened
Chopped fresh parsley, for garnish

1. Preheat a gas or charcoal grill to medium (350°F [180°C] to 400°F [200°C]) for direct grilling.

2. In a small bowl, mix together the cheeses and set aside. In a medium bowl, combine the pizza sauce, onion, mushrooms, oregano, thyme, and garlic powder and set aside.

3. Slit the hot dogs lengthwise and brush the insides with olive oil. Grill, cut side down, for 5 minutes. Turn and cook the other side for 3 minutes. Transfer the dogs to a plate. Brush the melted butter on the inside portion of the flattened buns, grill for 2 minutes, and turn.

4. Place one split hot dog, skin side down, on each bun. Spoon on 2–3 tablespoons (30–45 mL) of spiced tomato sauce over each dog and sprinkle each with 2–3 tablespoons (30–45 mL) of the mixed cheese. Close the barbecue lid and cook the pizza dogs until the cheese is melted.

5. With a spatula, transfer the hot dogs to a serving platter. Sprinkle with the chopped parsley and serve.

Cuban-Style Hot Dogs with Black-Eyed Peas

Yield: 5–10 servings

This recipe comes from Three Guys from Miami, *who host a website featuring Cuban food and eclectic cooking books.*

2 cups (473 mL) plus 2 teaspoons (10 mL) extra virgin olive oil, divided
1 tablespoon fresh rosemary, finely chopped
3 cloves garlic, peeled and sliced
3 cups (708 mL) cooked black-eyed peas
2 tablespoons (30 mL) roasted garlic
2 tablespoons (30 mL) Dijon mustard
½ teaspoon (2.5 mL) salt
½ teaspoon (2.5 mL) freshly ground black pepper
10 hot dogs
10 hot dog buns
2 cups (473 mL) sweet pickle relish

1. Preheat a gas or charcoal grill to medium (350°F [180°C] to 400°F [200°C]) for direct grilling.

2. In a deep pot, heat 2 teaspoons (10 mL) of the olive oil on the grill. Add the rosemary and sliced garlic and heat for about 1 minute. Stir in the black-eyed peas and add just enough water to cover. Cook for 5 minutes. Transfer the mixture to a blender and purée, adding the roasted garlic and remaining olive oil in a steady stream. When the mixture is smooth, add the Dijon mustard, salt, and pepper.

3. Place hot dogs on the grill and cook until crispy and warmed through, about 8 to 10 minutes. Slit the buns down the middle and toast them on the grill for 1 minute.

4. Remove the buns and hot dogs from the grill. Spread pea purée on one side of each bun and brush mustard on the other. Place a hot dog in each roll, slit each hot dog down the middle, and fill the dogs with the sweet relish.

Southern Belle's Slaw Dogs

Yield: 10 servings

This recipe comes from Robert Krumbine from Charlotte, NcC.

¼ cup (59 mL) white wine vinegar
3 tablespoons (45 mL) sugar
¾ teaspoon (3.75 mL) freshly ground black pepper
½ teaspoon (2.5 mL) kosher salt
½ teaspoon (2.5 mL) Gulden's spicy brown mustard
⅛ teaspoon (0.6 mL) celery seed
1 (12-ounce [336-g]) package prepared coleslaw
10 hot dogs
10 hot dog or bratwurst buns
¼ cup (59 mL) barbecue sauce

1. Preheat a gas or charcoal grill to medium (350°F [180°C] to 400°F [200°C]) for direct grilling.

2. In a medium bowl, combine the vinegar, sugar, pepper, salt, mustard, and celery seed. Add the coleslaw and toss to combine. Cover and set aside.

3. Grill the hot dogs, turning frequently, for 5 to 10 minutes. or until they are browned and heated through. Toast the inside of the buns golden brown.

4. Place the hot dogs in the buns and brush each dog with 1 tablespoon (15 mL) of the barbecue sauce. Spoon ⅓ cup (79 mL) of the enhanced coleslaw over each dog. Serve immediately.

Garlic Mojo Hot Dogs
Yield: 5–10 servings

Mojo is a Cuban sauce is usually made from the juice of sour oranges that you can use on pork, sausages, poultry, and seafood. If you can find sour orange juice, please use it; otherwise, use regular O.J.

¼ cup (59 mL) olive oil
6 cloves garlic, peeled and chopped
1 tomato, halved, seeded, and chopped
⅓ cup (79 mL) fresh lime juice
⅓ cup (79 mL) fresh orange juice
½ teaspoon (2.5 mL) ground cumin
½ teaspoon (2.5 mL) kosher salt, plus more to taste
¼ teaspoon (1.25 mL) freshly ground black pepper, plus more to taste
10 hot dogs
10 hot dog buns, toasted
1½ cups (354 mL) finely shredded romaine lettuce
2 avocados, halved, pitted, and diced
⅔ cup (158 mL) finely chopped pineapple

1. Preheat a gas or charcoal grill to medium (350°F [180°C] to 400°F [200°C]) for direct grilling.

2. In a cast-iron skillet on the grill, heat the oil. Add the garlic and stir for 30 seconds. Add the tomato, lime juice, orange juice, cumin, salt, and pepper and bring to a simmer. Remove the skillet from the heat. Season the mojo sauce to taste with more salt and pepper and set aside.

3. Grill the hot dogs for 8 to 10 minutes, turning frequently. Remove them from the barbecue and place them in the toasted hot dog buns. Add the lettuce and avocado, a generous tablespoon (15 mL) or more of the mojo sauce per dog, and chopped pineapple.

Sausage Wellington
Yield: 8–10 servings

You can make this a bit hotter by adding ½ teaspoon (2.5 mL) cayenne pepper, or even hotter by adding 1 small diced jalapeño pepper to the mix.

2 large eggs, divided
2 cups (473 mL) fresh breadcrumbs (or panko)
1 cup (236 mL) finely chopped onion
1 cup (236 mL) white button mushrooms, stems removed, chopped
1 teaspoon (5 mL) dried sage
1 teaspoon (5 mL) dried thyme
½ teaspoon (2.5 mL) freshly ground black pepper
1 pound (454 g) reduced-fat or low-fat ground pork sausage
1 sheet frozen puff pastry (½ [17-ounce (476-g)] package), thawed in the refrigerator
1 tablespoon (15 mL) cold milk

1. Preheat the barbecue to medium high (350°F [180°C] to 400°F [200°C]). Line an 11 x 17-inch (27.5 × 42.5-cm) baking sheet with aluminum foil. Lightly spray the foil with nonstick cooking or grilling spray.

2. In a large bowl, beat 1 of the eggs. Add the breadcrumbs, onion, mushrooms, sage, thyme, and pepper and stir to mix. Add the sausage and mix with your hands until thoroughly blended.

3. Unfold the puff pastry and stretch it slightly to a 10 × 12-inch (25 × 30-cm) rectangle. Spread the sausage mixture on one side of the pastry, leaving a 1-inch (2.5-cm) edge along that side. With your hands, form the sausage mixture into a rectangle about 4 inches (10 cm) wide and 10 inches (25 cm) long. Brush the 1-inch (2.5 cm) of pastry with cold water.

4. Carefully fold the pastry from the side opposite the meat to cover the sausage, stretching slightly to seal. Seal the edges with a fork, pressing into the dough. Tuck the ends under.

5. Cut three slits 1½ inches (3.5 cm) apart on the top of the pastry with the tip of a sharp knife to allow steam to escape. Beat the remaining egg with the milk and brush this mixture over the pastry.

6. Place the pastry on the prepared baking sheet and bake in the barbecue for 30 minutes, or until the pastry is golden brown.

Smoked Sweet 'n' Sassy Sausage
Yield: 4 servings, 8–10 as appetizers

These can be served as an appetizer in a bowl with toothpicks, or as a main course, either ladled over mashed potatoes or spooned into a hoagie or onion roll that has been toasted and slathered with garlic butter.

1 (20-ounce [560-g]) can pineapple chunks with natural juices
⅓ cup (79 mL) prepared sweet and sour sauce
1 tablespoon (15 mL) light brown sugar
1 red or green bell pepper, seeded and sliced into long strips
1 tablespoon (15 mL) olive oil
1 teaspoon (5 mL) canola oil
1 pound (454 g) smoked sausage, cut into 1-inch (2.5-cm) thick slices
1 tablespoon (15 mL) minced fresh ginger
¼ teaspoon (1.25 mL) cayenne pepper

1. Preheat the barbecue to medium high (350°F [180°C] to 400°F [200°C]).

2. Drain the pineapple and reserve 2 tablespoons (30 mL) of the juice. In a small bowl, blend the reserved juice with the sweet and sour sauce and brown sugar. Set aside.

3. Place the pepper strips in a bowl, add the olive oil, and stir to coat each strip with oil. Lay the pepper strips crosswise on the surface of the grill and cook for 2 minutes per side, or until they are softened with small char on some pieces.

4. In a cast-iron skillet, heat the canola oil. Place the sausage in the skillet and set the skillet in the barbecue. Cook, stirring, for 10 minutes.

5. Add the pepper strips, ginger, and cayenne pepper and stir. Add the sweet and sour sauce mixture and the pineapple chunks and heat until it begins to bubble. Stir once or twice and transfer to a serving bowl.

Savory Sausage Biscuits
Yield: 20–24 biscuits

For a bit more flavor, you could add ¼ cup (118 mL) of minced onion, chopped cooked bacon, or chopped chives to the batter. This recipe comes from Margaret Hillard from Salisbury, N.C.

½ pound (227 g) bulk pork breakfast sausage
1½ cups (354 g) biscuit mix
1 cup (236 mL) grated cheddar cheese
1 large egg, beaten
2 tablespoons (30 mL) milk
1 teaspoon (5 mL) dried savory
¼ teaspoon (1.25 mL) salt
⅛ teaspoon (0.6 mL) dried thyme
⅛ teaspoon (0.6 mL) freshly ground black pepper

1. Preheat the barbecue to medium high (350°F [180°C] to 400°F [200°C]).

2. In a well-oiled cast-iron skillet over medium heat, cook the sausage, stirring, for 6 to 8 minutes, or until the meat is no longer pink. Thoroughly drain the grease. In a large bowl, combine the biscuit mix, cheese, egg, milk, and sausage with a fork.

3. Sprinkle the sausage mixture with the savory, salt, thyme, and black pepper and blend with your hands. Shape the mixture into 20 to 24 balls, each about 1 tablespoon (15 mL). Place the balls 2 inches (5 cm) apart on an ungreased baking sheet and flatten each slightly.

4. Bake in the barbecue for 20 minutes or until lightly browned.

Huntsman Sausage Tarts
Yield: 12–14 tarts

Huntsman cheese is made up of layers of double Gloucester and Stilton. If you can't find it, just use Stilton.

1 pound (454 g) fresh bulk sausage
1 cup (236 mL) chopped sweet onions
8 ounces (227 g) button mushrooms, cleaned and chopped
1½ cups (354 mL) fresh breadcrumbs
6 ounces (168 g) crumbled Huntsman cheese
⅓ cup (79 mL) oil-packed sun-dried tomatoes, drained and chopped
2 teaspoons (10 mL) dried thyme
¼ teaspoon (1.25 mL) garlic salt
¼ teaspoon (1.25 mL) freshly ground black pepper
1 (12-ounce [336-g]) package wonton wrappers

1. Preheat the barbecue to medium high (350°F [180°C] to 400°F [200°C]).

2. Lightly spray a muffin pan with nonstick cooking spray.

3. In a cast-iron skillet on a barbecue side burner, cook the sausage until browned, breaking the meat into small pieces with a fork. Drain the sausage, reserving 1 tablespoon (15 mL) drippings in the skillet.

4. Sauté the onions in the drippings until soft. Add the mushrooms and cook, stirring, until all the liquid evaporates. Transfer to a bowl and cool for 5 minutes.

5. Stir in the drained sausage, breadcrumbs, scheese, sun-dried tomatoes, thyme, salt, and pepper, and gently fold together.

6. Press a wonton wrapper into each cup, fluting the edges with a fork. Bake in the barbecue for 5 minutes. Remove the pan from the barbecue, fill each shell with sausage mixture, and continue to bake for 7 to 9 minutes, or until the tops of the tarts are browned.

Kansas City Reuben Brats

Yield: 4 servings

You could use just about any sausage in this recipe, including Polish, knackwurst, or kielbasa.

1 pound (454 g) bratwurst (4 sausages)
1 (15-ounce [443-mL]) jar or can sauerkraut
½ pound (227 g) shredded Swiss cheese
4 bratwurst buns
Hot mustard and honey mustard, for serving

1. Preheat a gas or charcoal grill for direct grilling over medium heat (350°F [180°C] to 400°F [200°C]).

2. Grill the bratwursts, turning often, for 10 to 12 minutes, or until the brats are nicely browned and some of the edges are charred.

3. Place the bratwursts in the buns and generously spoon 2–3 tablespoons (30–45 mL) of sauerkraut over each brat. Cover each brat with 2–3 table-spoons (30–45 mL) of Swiss cheese and place the buns and brats back in the barbecue for 2 to 3 minutes, or until the cheese has melted.

4. Remove the brats from the barbecue and serve with hot and honey mustards.

Apple-Sausage Deep-Dish Pie

Yield: 4 servings

8 link sausages or ½–1 pound (227–454 g) bulk sausage
1 medium onion, peeled and chopped
1 (21-ounce [621-mL]) can apple pie filling
1 (9-inch [22.5-cm]) deep-dish pie shell
1½ cups (354 mL) shredded cheddar cheese
1 teaspoon (5 mL) ground sage
½ teaspoon (2.5 mL) dried marjoram
½ cup (118 mL) margarine
1½ cups (118 mL) all-purpose flour
1 cup (236 mL) packed brown sugar

1. Preheat the barbecue to medium high (350°F [180°C] to 400°F [200°C]).

2. Lightly brown sausage links or brown and crumble the sausage; remove sausage and cook onion in the grease, remove onion and drain. Pour the apple pie filling into the pie shell. Spoon the sausage and onions on top of the filling. Top with the shredded cheese, sage, and marjoram.

3. In a large bowl, cut the margarine into the flour and brown sugar. Sprinkle this mixture over the top of the cheese. Bake in the barbecue for 35 minutes, or until the edges of the pastry begin to brown and the mixture bubbles.

Hot Italian Sausage in Sour Cream

Yield: 6 servings

Italian sausages are flavored with anise and fennel. They can be very hot, with added chili peppers and paprika, or sweet, with added sugar and garlic.

2 tablespoons (30 mL) butter
2½ pounds (1.1 kg) hot (or sweet) Italian sausage
2 medium onions, peeled and sliced thin
2 tablespoons (30 mL) all-purpose flour
1½ cups (354 mL) apple cider
½ teaspoon (2.5 mL) salt
1 cup (236 mL) sour cream

1. Preheat the barbecue to medium high (300°F [150°C] to 325°F [165°C]).

2. In a cast-iron or nonstick skillet, melt the butter. Add the sausages and brown well on all sides. Remove sausages, leaving 2 tablespoons (30 mL) drippings in the skillet. Add the onions and sauté until soft and just beginning to brown. Stir in the flour. Add the apple cider and salt and cook until bubbly.

3. Return sausages to the skillet, cover, and place in the barbecue for 20 minutes. Blend in the sour cream and stir well. Keep stirring until sauce is hot, but do not allow it to boil.

4. Serve over mashed potatoes or hot buttered noodles.

Curried Sausage Burgers

Yield: 8 servings

3½ pounds (1.6 kg) coarsely ground pork
1½ pounds (681 g) lean ground beef
1 tablespoon (15 mL) curry powder
1 tablespoon (15 mL) freshly ground black pepper
1½ ounces (42 mL) salt
1½ teaspoons (22.5 mL) ground coriander
1 teaspoon (5 mL) ground sage
1 teaspoon (5 mL) dry mustard
½ teaspoon (2.5 mL) ground cumin
½ teaspoon (2.5 mL) grated fresh ginger
Olive oil, for brushing or grilling spray
8 focaccia rolls or onion rolls

1. Preheat a gas or charcoal grill for direct grilling over medium heat (350°F [180°C] to 400°F [200°C]).

2. In a large bowl, mix together the ground pork, ground beef, curry powder, pepper, salt, coriander, sage, dry mustard, cumin, and ginger, kneading until the meat becomes sticky. Form the mixture into 8 thick patties.

3. Brush the patties with olive oil or spray with grilling spray. Grill for 6 to 8 minutes, or until they start to get brown and the edges char slightly.

4. Remove the burgers from the grill and serve them on the focaccia buns or onion rolls.

Kielbasa Braised in Beer

Yield: 6 servings

For a little more zest, you could use andouille, linguica, or a combination of both instead of the kielbasa.

2 teaspoons (10 mL) olive oil or butter, divided
6 kielbasa sausages
1 large sweet onion, peeled and sliced into ¼-inch (0.50cm) rings
¾ cup (177 mL) beer

1. Preheat the barbecue to medium high (350°F [180°C] to 400°F [200°C]).

2. In a large Dutch oven, heat 1 teaspoon (5 mL) of the olive oil or butter. Place the pot in the barbecue. Add the kielbasa sausages and bake, turning several times with tongs, until deep golden brown on all sides, about 15 minutes. Transfer the sausages to a platter.

3. Add the remaining olive oil or butter and the sweet onion rings to the drippings. Toss the onions to coat with the oil. Cook, stirring often, until the onions are limp and golden but not brown.

4. Return the kielbasa to the pot with the onions. Add the beer and cook, turning halfway through, until the beer has cooked down to a syrup, about 12 to 15 minutes.

5. Serve the kielbasa on toasted hot dog buns or hoagie rolls.

Swiss Sausage Bake

Yield: 4–6 servings

6 slices sandwich bread
2 pounds (908 g) bulk sausage
1 teaspoon (5 mL) prepared mustard
1 (6-ounce [168-g]) package Swiss cheese, sliced
3 large eggs, beaten
1½ cups (354 mL) milk
¾ cup (177 mL) half-and-half
1 teaspoon (5 mL) Worcestershire sauce
¼ teaspoon (1.25 mL) salt
¼ teaspoon (1.25 mL) freshly ground black pepper
¼ teaspoon (1.25 mL) ground nutmeg

1. Lightly grease a 9 × 13-inch (22.5 × 32.5-cm) baking pan.

2. Arrange the bread in the prepared pan. Set aside.

3. In a cast-iron skillet, sauté the sausage until nicely browned. Drain thoroughly and transfer to a medium bowl.

4. Add the mustard to the sausage. Sprinkle this mixture over the bread. Cover with the cheese slices.

5. In a separate bowl, combine the eggs, milk, half-and-half, Worcestershire sauce, salt, pepper, and nutmeg and whip until well mixed. Pour this mixture over the sausage, cover with plastic wrap, refrigerate overnight.

6. Preheat the barbecue to medium high (350°F [180°C] to 400°F [200°C]).

7. Remove the casserole from the refrigerator and bring it to room temperature.

8. Bake the casserole for 30 to 40 minutes, or until the top is browned and bubbly. Let it rest for 10 minutes, then serve.

Bockwurst and Applekraut
Yield: 6 servings

We use the lighter, sweeter pork bockwurst here, but if you prefer you can use bratwurst or Italian sausage.

3 cups (708 mL) pippin apples, peeled, cored, and sliced
1 (27-ounce [756-g]) can sauerkraut, drained
1 pound (454 g) bockwurst links, halved crosswise
1 cup (236 mL) raisins, dark or golden
¼ cup (59 mL) packed brown sugar
1 teaspoon (5 mL) caraway seeds
½ teaspoon (2.5 mL) freshly ground black pepper
¼ cup (59 mL) dry white wine

1. Preheat the barbecue to low (230°F [110°C] to 250°F [120°C]). Butter or spray well a Dutch oven or roasting pan.

2. Place the sliced apples in the bottom of the prepared pan. Add the sauerkraut, bockwurst, raisins, brown sugar, caraway seeds, and pepper. Stir in the wine.

3. Place the Dutch oven in the barbecue, cover, and cook for 3 to 4 hours.

Susan's Sausage Stuffing
Yield: 12–14 cups (2.8–3.3 L)

This recipe makes enough delicious rice-sausage-fruit stuffing to stuff a 12- to 14-pound (5.4- to 6.4-kg) turkey. Stuff the bird just before you put it in the oven. If you make the stuffing in advance, refrigerate it and return it to room temperature before using. This recipe comes from Susan Biddle from Washington, D.C.

1 cup (236 mL) chopped pecans
1 pound (454 g) bulk pork sausage
2 tablespoons (30 mL) butter or margarine
1 large onion, peeled and diced
4 large celery ribs, diced
8 ounces (227 g) fresh button mushrooms, cleaned and sliced
¼ teaspoon (1.25 mL) seasoned salt
Freshly ground black pepper, to taste
2 sprigs fresh thyme
1 teaspoon (5 mL) minced fresh basil
1¼ cups (295 mL) uncooked wild rice, cooked according to pkg. directions
1¼ cups (295 mL) uncooked long-grain white rice, cooked according to pkg. directions
½ cup (118 mL) dried cranberries
½ cup (118 mL) minced dried apricots

1. Preheat the barbecue to medium high (350°F [180°C] to 400°F [200°C]).

2. Place the pecans on a baking sheet and bake in the barbecue until the nuts are golden brown, about 20 to 25 minutes. Let cool.

3. In a cast-iron or nonstick skillet over high heat, brown the sausage, stirring often to break it up. With a slotted spoon, transfer the sausage to a large bowl.

4. In the same skillet, melt the butter with the sausage drippings. Add the onion, celery, mushrooms, salt, and pepper and sauté until tender. Remove from the heat and stir in the thyme and basil.

5. Add the toasted pecans, wild and white rice, cranberries, and apricots. Toss well to mix. Either stuff your bird immediately or refrigerate the stuffing until needed.

Pecan–Cornbread Stuffing

Yield: 8 cups (1.9 L)

Use about ¾ cup (177 mL) of stuffing per pound (454 g) of turkey, and stuff the turkey just before roasting.

4 cups (0.95 L) dry bread cubes
4 cups (0.95 L) crumbled cornbread
½ cup (118 mL) golden raisins
¼ cup (59 mL) butter or margarine
2 cups (473 mL) finely chopped onions
1 cup (236 mL) finely chopped celery
1 cup (236 mL) chopped pecans
1 pound (454 g) bulk sweet or hot Italian sausage
1 cup (236 mL) chicken stock
1 tablespoon (15 mL) poultry seasoning
½ teaspoon (2.5 mL) freshly ground black pepper

1. In a large bowl, combine the bread cubes and the crumbled cornbread. Pour ½ cup (118 mL) boiling water over raisins and allow them to soak until plump.

2. In large nonstick skillet, melt the butter. Add the onions, celery, and pecans and sauté until the onions are wilted, about 7 minutes. Pour this mixture into the bread mixture and stir well.

3. On a flat griddle plate or grill, cook the sausage until cooked through and it starts to brown, about 5 to 7 minutes.

4. Using a slotted spoon, lift the sausage from the skillet and set aside. Discard the drippings.

5. Drain the raisins. Add them to the cornbread mixture, along with the sausage, stock, poultry seasoning, and pepper, and mix well.

6. Use to stuff a turkey (within 20 minutes) or, if cooking separately, spoon the stuffing into a greased 2½-quart (2.4-L) casserole and bake, uncovered, at 325°F (165°C) for 1 hour.

South Wales Sausage Rolls

Yield: 4–8 servings

Making bread into crumbs is easier if you first put the bread in the freezer for an hour or let it dry out for an hour before processing.

4 slices soft white bread
2 slices whole-wheat bread
½ cup (118 mL) heavy cream
1 pound (454 g) ground beef sausage
1 pound (454 g) ground pork sausage
1 medium carrot, peeled and finely diced
½ medium onion, peeled and finely diced
1 tablespoon (15 mL) kosher salt
½ teaspoon (2.5 mL) dried basil
¼ teaspoon (1.25 mL) dried thyme
¼ teaspoon (1.25 mL) garlic powder
½ teaspoon (2.5 mL) ground cumin
½ teaspoon (2.5 mL) dried marjoram
½ teaspoon (2.5 mL) ground white pepper
1 (17.3–ounce [484-g]) box puff pastry, thawed
1 egg white
1 tablespoon (15 mL) milk

1. Preheat the barbecue to medium high (350°F [180°C] to 400°F [200°C]). Line two baking sheets with aluminum foil.

2. Tear the white and whole-wheat bread into small pieces and place the pieces in a food processor. Pulse into crumbs. Transfer the breadcrumbs to a bowl and cover with the cream. Set aside.

3. Place ground beef and pork sausages in the food processor and pulse until the meat is almost puréed. (Pulse; do not process continuously, as the heat of the blade can begin cooking the meat.) Transfer the meats to a large mixing bowl and stir to blend. Add the carrot, onion, salt, basil, thyme, garlic powder, cumin, marjoram, pepper, and the now-soaked breadcrumbs. Mix thoroughly with your hands, but do not overdo it, or the resulting meat mixture will be tough and too firm.

4. Roll out one sheet of puff pastry into a rectangle about 10 × 14 inches (25 × 35 cm). Cut the sheet in half lengthwise so you have 2 long strips. Divide the sausage mixture in half and set half aside. Divide the remaining half into 2 portions. Form each sausage portion into a log and place it down the center of a puff pastry strip. Gently pull up the pastry sides to meet, forming an encased sausage roll. Wet your fingers lightly with water and moisten along the seam to seal the dough. Repeat with the remaining sausage and dough.

5. Cut each sausage roll into 4 pieces. Place the pieces seam side down on the prepared baking sheet. In a small bowl, combine the egg white and milk. Brush each sausage roll with the egg-milk glaze. Place the pan in the barbecue and cook for 35 to 40 minutes, or until the top of pastry is golden. Let cool 5 minutes before serving.

Big Chef Kevin's Jambalaya
Yield: 4–6 servings

---

1 pound (454 g) bulk pork sausage, crumbled
1 pound (454 g) chorizo smoked sausage, sliced
1 pound (454 g) smoked hot andouille sausage, sliced
2 cups (473 mL) minced onions
1 red bell pepper, chopped
1 green bell pepper, chopped
3 cloves garlic, peeled and chopped
1 (16-ounce [454-g]) can stewed tomatoes
3 bay leaves
6 green onions, minced, green and white parts
½ cup (118 mL) chopped fresh parsley
1 teaspoon (5 mL) hot Creole seasoning
½ teaspoon (2.5 mL) ground thyme
3 cups (708 mL) Uncle Ben's converted rice, uncooked
2 cups (473 mL) water
Salt, to taste
Freshly ground black pepper, to taste

1. Preheat the barbecue to medium high (350°F [180°C] to 400°F [200°C]) for direct and indirect heating, putting a water pan under the unheated side of the grill.

2. In a Dutch oven, heat and brown the sausages in the barbecue, stirring several times, about 12 to 15 minutes. Drain, reserving the drippings. Transfer the sausages to a bowl with a slotted spoon and set aside.

3. In the same pot, sauté the onions, red and green bell peppers, and garlic in the drippings until the vegetables are just limp. Add the stewed tomatoes, stir, and add the bay leaves, green onions and parsley. Stir. Add the Creole seasoning, thyme, and sausage, and stir well. Add the uncooked rice and water, and the salt and pepper; stir well, and cover.

4. Return the Dutch oven to the barbecue and bring to a boil. Uncover the pot and move it to the unheated side of the grill. Cook until most of water is absorbed, about 15 to 20 minutes, occasionally scraping the bottom to keep the rice from sticking.

5. Bake until the rice is tender, stirring and fluffing often with a large fork. Remove from the heat and serve.

Barbecued Garlic Sausages and 'Shrooms
Yield: 4 servings

This recipe works best with very garlicky sausages, such as linguica, knackwurst, chorizo, or kielbasa.

6 plump garlic sausages, mild or hot
2 tablespoons (30 mL) butter
8 ounces (227 g) crimini mushrooms, diced
1 medium yellow onion, peeled and diced
¼ cup (59 mL) heavy cream
1 tablespoon (15 mL) Dijon mustard
3–4 medium Roma tomatoes, sliced
1–1½ cups (236–354 mL) shredded Swiss or Monterey Jack cheese

1. Preheat the barbecue to medium high (350°F [180°C] to 400°F [200°C]). Grease a Dutch oven or roasting pan.

2. With a sharp knife, split the sausages in half lengthwise. Arrange them in the bottom of the prepared pan in a single layer.

3. In a cast-iron skillet, melt the butter over medium heat. Add the mushrooms and onion and sauté until lightly browned. Fold in the heavy cream and mustard; bring to a boil, and cook until the liquid is reduced by a third and thickened.

4. Spoon the mushroom-onion mixture over the sausages. Top with the sliced tomatoes and sprinkle with the cheese. Bake, uncovered, in the barbecue until the sausages and cheese brown lightly, 15 to 20 minutes.

5. Serve with heaping spoonfuls of steamed or boiled white rice.

Sausage and Kraut Gumbo
Yield: 6–8 servings

Throw in cooked okra and 1 teaspoon (5 mL) filé powder in step 4 for an even more authentic gumbo.

2 (14-ounce [392-g]) cans sauerkraut, drained
1 pound (454 g) hot or sweet bulk Italian sausage
1½ pounds (681 g) smoked Polish sausage, cut into 1-inch (2.5-cm) thick slices
3 tablespoons (45 mL) margarine
1½ cups (354 mL) chopped white onion
1½ cups (354 mL) chopped unpeeled apple
2 cups (473 mL) chicken broth
½ teaspoon (2.5 mL) caraway seeds
1 cup (236 mL) cooked okra (optional)
1 teaspoon (5 mL) filé powder (optional)

1. Preheat the barbecue to medium high (350°F [180°C] to 400°F [200°C]).

2. Rinse the sauerkraut well with cold water, drain, and set aside.

3. Roll the Italian sausage into 1½-inch (3.5-cm) balls. Place the balls and the Polish sausage slices in a Dutch oven. Put the Dutch oven in the barbecue and cook until the sausage is well browned, about 15 to 20 minutes. With a slotted spoon, remove the sausage from the pot and set it aside, reserving the drippings.

4. Add the margarine to the drippings, then add the onion and apples and cook, stirring occasionally, until the onion is translucent. Stir in the chicken broth, caraway seeds, sauerkraut and sausage, and mix until well combined. Add the okra and file powder, if using.

5. Cover the Dutch oven and bake for about 35 minutes, or until the flavors are blended and the sausage balls are cooked through.

6. Scoop the gumbo into large bowls over thick slices of buttered garlic bread, sprinkle with parsley, and serve.

Buttermilk Sausage Corn Muffins
Yield: 18 muffins

When I'm feeling daring, I add ½ teaspoon (2.5 mL) of ground cumin and ¼ teaspoon (1.25 mL) of cayenne pepper to the mix to increase the flavor and heat of these muffins.

2 cups (473 mL) all-purpose flour
¾ cup (177 mL) cornmeal
2 teaspoons (10 mL) baking powder
2 tablespoons (30 mL) sugar
1 tablespoon (15 mL) finely minced onion
1 teaspoon (5 mL) dried oregano
½ teaspoon (2.5 mL) garlic salt
1¾ cups (413 mL) buttermilk
1 large egg, beaten
½ pound (227 g) bulk hot Italian sausage

1. Preheat the barbecue to medium high (350°F [180°C] to 400°F [200°C]). Grease an 18-cup muffin pan.

2. In a large mixing bowl, combine the flour, cornmeal, baking powder, sugar, onion, oregano, and garlic salt. Add the buttermilk, egg, and sausage and mix very well.

3. Spoon the meat batter into the prepared muffin pan, filling each cup about two-thirds full.

4. Bake in the barbecue for 25 to 30 minutes, or until the muffins are golden brown on top and a toothpick inserted into the center of one comes out clean.

Kentucky Round Steak

Yield: 6–8 servings

If you like bologna, you'll love this upscale barbecued version that looks like a round ham when cooked.

½ cup (118 mL) packed brown sugar
¼ cup (59 mL) prepared yellow mustard
2 tablespoons (30 mL) soy sauce
1 tablespoon (15 mL) Dijon mustard
1 (3–6 pound [1.3–2.7 kg]) whole beef bologna roll
25–30 whole cloves
1 (12-ounce [355-mL]) bottle dark beer

1. Preheat the barbecue to medium high (200°F [95°C] to 240°F [115°C]) for direct and indirect heating, putting a water pan under the unheated side of the grill.

2. In a small bowl, whisk together the brown sugar, yellow mustard, soy sauce, and Dijon mustard.

3. Remove the plastic wrap from the bologna. Cut ¼-inch (0.5-cm) deep cross-hatched slits all around the bologna (like a baked ham). Insert a clove into each square on the bologna, then coat the bologna with the mustard mixture, being careful not to disturb the cloves.

4. Place the bologna roll in a roasting pan on the indirect side of the grill. Pour enough of the beer into the pan to barely cover the bottom.

5. Cook, occasionally adding more beer as needed to keep liquid in the pan, for 2 to 3 hours, or until the top is nicely browned.

6. Remove the cloves, slice, and serve, or grill individual slices quickly on the hot grill.

Amber's Sausage and Egg Crescent Pie

Yield: 4–6 servings

For a bit of color, you may add 3 tablespoons (45 mL) each of finely diced red, green, and yellow bell peppers to this dish. This recipe comes from Amber Lynch from Southington, Conn.

1 pound (454 g) loose breakfast sausage
2 (8-ounce [227-g]) cans refrigerated crescent roll dough
1 teaspoon (5 mL) dried oregano
½ teaspoon (2.5 mL) ground cumin
4 ounces (112 g) Swiss cheese, thinly sliced
4 ounces (112 g) Velveeta cheese, thinly sliced
12 large eggs
3 tablespoons (45 mL) milk
Salt, to taste
Freshly ground black pepper, to taste

1. Preheat the barbecue to medium high (350°F [180°C] to 400°F [200°C]).

2. In a cast-iron or nonstick skillet, brown the sausage, stirring to avoid clumping. Drain the fat and set aside.

3. Spread one package of the crescent rolls in the bottom of a 9 × 13-inch (25 × 32.5-cm) pan, pressing with your fingers to cover the entire bottom of the pan. Place the drained, crumbled sausage meat on top of the dough. Sprinkle with the oregano and cumin.

4. Cover the sausage with alternating slices of Swiss and Velveeta cheese. Beat the eggs with the milk, add salt and pepper, and pour this mixture over the sausage and cheese.

5. On a floured cutting board, roll out the remaining crescent roll dough with a rolling pin to a size large enough to cover the egg and sausage mixture. Lay the dough over the pan and press dough to side of pan to seal. Bake in the barbecue for 35 to 40 minutes, or until the dough is browned on top and the eggs are firm.

6. Remove the pan from the barbecue, cool for 10 minutes, cut into slices. and serve.

Grilled Italian Sausage Buns
Yield: 4 servings

---

4 (4-ounce [112-g]) links hot Italian sausage
1 red bell pepper, halved and seeded
1 green bell pepper, halved and seeded
1 Anaheim pepper, halved and seeded
1 small onion, peeled and cut into thick slices
1 tablespoon (15 mL) olive oil, plus more for brushing the vegetables
1 teaspoon (5 mL) balsamic vinegar
Salt, to taste
Freshly ground black pepper, to taste
4 (6-inch [15-cm]) hoagie rolls, split and toasted

1. Preheat the barbecue to medium high (350°F [180°C] to 400°F [200°C]).

2. Pierce the sausages in a few places with a fork and set them aside. Place the split bell peppers and Anaheim pepper on the grill and brush both sides with olive oil. Brush the onion slices with olive oil and place them on the grill.

3. Place the sausages on the grill. Cook the sausages, turning often, until they are well browned and the juices run clear. Cook the vegetables, turning often, until they are all tender and the onions are beginning to char. Transfer the onions to a bowl. Remove the sausages from the grill, cover them with foil, and set aside. Continue cooking the peppers until they are pretty much blackened all over.

4. Place the peppers in a paper bag, close the bag, and let the peppers cool slightly. Remove them from the bag and peel off the charred skin. Cut the peppers into thin strips. Add them to the bowl with the onions and sprinkle with the 1 tablespoon (15 mL) olive oil and the balsamic vinegar. Sprinkle with the salt and pepper.

5. Place the sausages on the toasted hoagie rolls and top each with a generous helping of the pepper and onion mixture.

Polish and Veg Kebabs
Yield: 4 servings

8 small boiling onions
2 medium yellow summer squash, cut into 2-inch (5-cm) thick rounds
½ cup (118 mL) vegetable oil
¼ cup (59 mL) white wine vinegar
1 clove garlic, peeled and minced
½ teaspoon (2.5 mL) salt
½ teaspoon (2.5 mL) dried oregano
½ teaspoon (2.5 mL) dried thyme
Freshly ground black pepper, to taste
1 red bell pepper, cut into 1½-inch (3.5-cm) squares
1 green bell pepper, cut into 1½-inch (3.5-cm) squares
1 pound (454 g) Polish sausages (about 4), cut into 2-inch (5-cm) thick slices

1. In a large saucepan, cook the onions in boiling salted water for 10 minutes. Add the squash and cook for 2 minutes. Drain the vegetables and transfer them to a 1- to 2-gallon (3.8- to 7.6-L) resealable plastic bag.

2. In a medium bowl, whisk together the oil, vinegar, garlic, salt, oregano, thyme, and pepper. Pour this mixture in over the vegetables. Cover and refrigerate 8 hours or overnight, turning bag occasionally.

3. Preheat the barbecue to medium high (350°F [180°C] to 400°F [200°C]).

4. Drain the vegetables. Pour the marinade into a saucepan and boil for 10 minutes.

5. Alternately thread the onions, squash, bell pepper pieces, and sausage onto metal or soaked bamboo skewers. Cook on the grill for 12 to 15 minutes, turning and brushing frequently with the marinade.

Sausage-Stuffed Onions
Yield: 4

The Braunschweiger almost melts into the filling and adds a distinctive liverwurst flavor to this dish.

4 large yellow or Spanish onions
½ pound (227 g) lean pork sausage
½ teaspoon (2.5 mL) dried rosemary
½ teaspoon (2.5 mL) seasoned salt
Freshly ground black pepper, to taste
¼ pound (112 g) Braunschweiger sausage

1. Preheat the barbecue to medium high (350°F [180°C] to 400°F [200°C]). Butter or spray with nonstick cooking spray a casserole or roasting pan.

2. Peel the onions and parboil them in boiling salted water for 20 minutes. Drain well and allow to cool slightly. With a spoon, core the onions, and mince the onion you remove. Place the minced onion in a bowl and set the onion shells aside. To the minced onion, add the pork sausage, rosemary, salt, and pepper and stir to mix.

3. Spoon a quarter of the Braunschweiger into the bottom of each onion shell, then add the cooked sausage mixture. Place the stuffed onions in the prepared pan and bake for 25 to 35 minutes, or until the sausage is well done and the onions are browned on the outside.

4. Drain the onions on paper towels and serve hot.

Lindy's Sausage-Noodle Casserole

Yield: 4 servings

This recipe comes from Lindy Hart from Santa Cruz, Calif.

1 pound (454 g) lean pork sausage
½ cup (118 mL) chopped celery
¼ cup (59 mL) chopped onion
8 ounces (227 g) egg noodles
1 (10-ounce [280-g]) can condensed cream of mushroom soup
⅔ cup (158 mL) milk
½ cup (118 mL) extra-sharp cheddar cheese
¼ cup (59 mL) seasoned breadcrumbs

1. Preheat the barbecue to medium high (350°F [180°C] to 400°F [200°C]). Butter or spray with nonstick cooking spray a casserole dish.

2. In a cast-iron or nonstick skillet, fry the sausage, breaking it into small pieces. Add the celery and onion and cook until tender.

3. Cook the egg noodles according to the package directions.

4. In a small bowl, mix together the soup and milk. Add this mixture to the sausage. In the prepared casserole, layer half of the noodles, half of the sausage, and half of the cheese. Repeat the layers.

5. Cover and bake in the barbecue for 30 minutes.

Italian Sausage–Stuffed Meatloaf

Yield: 4–6 servings

This meatloaf has a surprise inside—whole Italian sausages in the middle of the beef and pork mixture.

4 sweet Italian sausages
2 pounds (908 g) ground beef
1 pound (454 g) ground pork
1 cup (236 mL) cooked and drained red kidney beans (or use canned)
½ cup (118 mL) grated onion
½ cup (118 mL) bottled chili sauce
3 green onions, chopped, white and green parts
2 large eggs, beaten
3 tablespoons (45 mL) chili powder
1 tablespoon (15 mL) grated garlic
1 tablespoon (15 mL) Dijon mustard
2 teaspoons (10 mL) garlic salt
1½ teaspoons (7.5 mL) freshly ground black pepper
1½ teaspoons (7.5 mL) ground cumin
1 teaspoon (5 mL) dried basil
1 teaspoon (5 mL) dried oregano
1 cup (236 mL) diced red bell pepper
1 cup (236 mL) diced green (or yellow) bell pepper
2 cups (473 mL) coarsely grated sharp cheddar cheese
1 cup (236 mL) coarsely chopped fresh parsley

1. Preheat the barbecue to medium high (350°F [180°C] to 400°F [200°C]). Grease or spray with nonstick cooking spray a shallow baking pan.

2. In a cast-iron or nonstick skillet, cook the sausages for 20 minutes, or until nicely browned. Transfer the sausages to paper towels to drain.

3. In a large bowl, combine the ground beef and pork, kidney beans, onion, chili sauce, green onions, eggs, chili powder, garlic, mustard, garlic salt, pepper, cumin, basil, and oregano. Mix gently with your hands, being careful not to over mix.

4. On a flat surface, place a 24-inch (60-cm) long piece of waxed paper. Spread the meat loaf mixture with a spatula to form a 11 × 14-inch (27.5 × 35-cm) rectangle about ½-inch (1-cm) thick. Spoon the diced peppers evenly over the surface, patting them lightly into the meat. Sprinkle with the cheddar cheese and parsley and pat them into the meat.

5. Place the reserved sausages in a line along a 14-inch (35-cm) side of the meat rectangle. Using the waxed paper, carefully roll the meat and stuffing into a jelly roll shape and place it in the prepared baking pan, seam side down.

6. Bake in the barbecue for 60 to 70 minutes, or until the top of the meat-loaf is browned. With two spatulas, carefully transfer the meatloaf to a warmed serving platter. Cover and let rest for 15 minutes before slicing.

Barbecued Southern Sausage Bread

Yield: 4 servings

You cold also use chopped bratwurst or andouille in this recipe for two different flavor profiles.

1 pound (454 g) hot Italian sausage
1 refrigerated bread dough
1 cup (236 mL) shredded mozzarella cheese
1 tablespoon (15 mL) dried oregano
½ teaspoon (2.5 mL) minced garlic

1. Preheat the barbecue to medium high (350°F [180°C] to 400°F [200°C]). Spray a baking sheet with nonstick cooking or grilling spray.

2. Fry the sausage until brown, stirring to break up lumps. Strain and set aside.

3. Lightly flour a sheet of aluminum foil. Unwrap the bread dough and place it on the foil. Spread the cooked sausage over the entire dough. Sprinkle the shredded mozzarella cheese on top of the sausage and sprinkle with oregano and garlic. Roll the dough into a loaf again, making sure the slits are on top.

4. Transfer the loaf to the prepared baking sheet and cook for 28 to 32 minutes, or until golden brown.

5. Let cool for about 5 to 8 minutes before slicing.

Skillet Sausage Meatball Surprise

Yield: 4–6 servings

If you're adventurous, you could use Limburger, Stilton, Roquefort, livarno, or another strong-flavored cheese as the "surprise," instead of the blue cheese.

1 pound (454 g) bulk sausage
1 large egg, lightly beaten
½ cup (118 mL) fine dry breadcrumbs
½ teaspoon (2.5 mL) dried sage
4 ounces (112 g) blue cheese, cut or rolled into ½-inch (1-cm) cubes or balls
½ cup (118 mL) ketchup
¼ cup (59 mL) chopped green onion, green and white parts
3 tablespoons (45 mL) balsamic vinegar
2 tablespoons (30 mL) brown sugar
1 tablespoon (15 mL) soy sauce

1. Preheat the barbecue to medium high (350°F [180°C] to 400°F [200°C]). Lightly spray a cast-iron skillet with nonstick cooking spray.

2. In a large mixing bowl, combine the sausage, egg, breadcrumbs and sage.

3. Take a cube or ball of the blue cheese and form 2 tablespoons (30 mL) of the sausage mixture around the cheese. Shape into a 1½-inch (3.5-cm) ball. Repeat with the remaining cheese and sausage.

4. In a small mixing bowl, whisk together the ketchup, green onion, vinegar, sugar, and soy sauce and set aside.

5. Place the sausage balls in the prepared skillet. Place the skillet in the barbecue, pour the sauce over the meatballs, and cook for 25 to 30 minutes, turning occasionally.

6. Pour the meatballs and sauce into a serving bowl and serve.

EIGHT

Lamb

Grilled Lamb with Four Sauces

Yield: 4–6 servings

Darina Allen is a true celebrity in Ireland. Her cooking shows have been televised, and her books are a staple in most Irish homes. She is the founder of Ballymaloe, a successful cooking school in East Cork, Ireland, that is one of the best, and most friendly, in Europe. She generously shared this recipe with us.

4 racks (1 pound [454 g] or 6 chops each) of spring lamb
Salt, to taste
Freshly ground black pepper, to taste
Fresh mint sprigs, for garnish
Fresh Mint Chutney (recipe follows)
Onion Sauce (recipe follows)
Red Currant Sauce (recipe follows)
Irish Mint Sauce (recipe follows)

1. Score the fat on the lamb with several shallow cuts. Refrigerate until ready to use.

2. Preheat a charcoal or gas grill for direct cooking to 425°F (220°C). Make sure the grill rack is clean, and oil it thoroughly with nonstick spray.

3. Sprinkle the lamb generously with the salt and pepper. Transfer the lamb to the prepared grill rack over direct heat, fat side up, lower the grill lid, and cook for 15 to 20 minutes, or until the remaining thin layer of fat is nicely crisped and browned, and a meat thermometer inserted into the meaty section of the chop reads 130°F (54°C), for medium-rare.

4. Transfer the lamb to a warm serving dish and let rest for 5 to 10 minutes.

5. Carve lamb and serve 2 to 3 cutlets per person, depending on size (of both the guest and the chop). Serve with the four sauces on the side.

Fresh Mint Chutney

1 handful fresh mint
¼ cup (60 mL) minced onions
2–3 tablespoons (30–45 mL) sugar
1 large cooking apple, such as Jonathan, Gravenstein, or Jonagold, peeled, cored, and coarsely chopped
1 pinch salt
1 pinch cayenne pepper

1. In a food processor, process all the mint, onions, and sugar to a paste. Add the apples, pulse once or twice, and season with the salt and cayenne pepper. It will look like a thick, chunky jam.

Onion Sauce

¼ cup (60 mL) unsalted butter
3 pounds (1.3 kg) yellow onions (3–4 large), finely chopped
1 teaspoon (5 mL) salt
1 teaspoon (5 mL) freshly ground black pepper
1 tablespoon (15 mL) all-purpose flour
1½ cups (354 mL) milk

1. In a saucepan, melt the butter over low heat. Add the onions and cook, covered, until very soft but not browned, about 10 to 15 minutes. Season with salt and pepper. Stir in the flour and add the milk. Bring to a simmer and simmer gently, stirring, 5 minutes longer, or until the sauce looks like a thick salsa.

Red Currant Sauce

⅔ cup (158 mL) sugar
½ cup (118 mL) water
¾ cup (177 mL) fresh or frozen red currants

1. In a saucepan over medium heat, combine the sugar and water and stir until the sugar dissolves. Bring to a boil and add the currants. Boil, uncovered, for 4 to 5 minutes, or until the currants burst. Serve hot or cold.

Irish Mint Sauce

½ cup (118 mL) water
2–3 tablespoons (30–45 mL) sugar
1 cup (236 mL) malt vinegar
½ cup (118 mL) firmly packed, finely chopped fresh mint leaves

1. In a saucepan over medium heat, bring the water and 2 tablespoons (30 mL) of the sugar to a boil and cook until the sugar dissolves. Remove the pan from the heat and add the vinegar and mint, stirring well. Taste and season with up to 1 additional tablespoon (15 mL) of sugar if you must, but no more!

2. Cover and let stand for at least 3 hours before serving. Store in an airtight container in the refrigerator for up to 3 weeks.

Beer-Braised Lamb Shanks with Pearl Onions and Raisins
Yield: 6 servings

The easiest way to peel pearl onions is to place them in a basket, lower the basket into boiling water for 1 minute, lift it out, and lower it into cold water to cool them. Cut off the root ends and slip the skins off.

4 (1 pound [454 g]) lamb shanks
Salt, to taste
Freshly ground black pepper, to taste
¼ cup (59 mL) olive oil
12 pearl onions
2 large carrots, peeled and cut into ½-inch (1-cm) thick slices
1 large tomato, cored and roughly chopped
1 cup (236 mL) golden raisins
¼ cup (59 mL) minced garlic
¼ cup (59 mL) chopped fresh mint, divided
2 tablespoons (30 mL) chopped fresh basil
2 (12-ounce [355 mL]) bottles Guinness beer
6 cups (1.4 L) beef or vegetable stock
¼ cup (56 mL) whiskey

1. Preheat the barbecue to medium high (350°F [180°C] to 400°F [200°C]).

2. Sprinkle the lamb shanks with salt and pepper. In a large cast-iron or roasting pan, heat the oil over high heat until hot but not smoking. Add the shanks and sear on all sides, 3 to 5 minutes per side. Remove the shanks from the pan and set aside.

3. Leave 2 tablespoons (30 mL) of the oil in the pan. Reduce the heat to medium high, add the onions and carrots, and sauté, stirring occasionally and scraping up the browned bits, until the onions are lightly browned, 5 to 6 minutes. Add the tomato, raisins, garlic, half the mint, and the basil. Sauté, stirring often, for 2 minutes. Add the beer, bring to a boil, reduce the heat to low, and simmer for 7 minutes.

4. Add the stock, turn the heat back up to medium and bring to a boil. Add the lamb shanks, cover the pan, and move the pan to the barbecue. Cook the meat until the shanks are very tender, 60 to 80 minutes.

5. Remove the shanks from the pan and skim off the grease. If the sauce is not thick enough, place the pan back on the burner over high heat and reduce to the desired consistency. Stir in the remaining mint and the whiskey and season with salt and pepper. Return the shanks to the sauce, ladling the sauce over the meat, and serve.

Danny Boy's Lamb Ribs

Yield: 2–4 servings

Lamb, most unfortunately, is the forgotten meat in America. A recent survey tells us that 35 percent of Americans have never tasted lamb. In fact, the per capita annual consumption is less than a pound (454 g) a person. Compare that to New Zealand where they consume 57 pounds (25.9 kg) per person each year; Australia, at 30 pounds (13.6 kg) per person; Saudi Arabia, at 27 pounds (12.3 kg); and Ireland, at 20 pounds (9.1 kg) (according to the U.S. Lamb Board). This recipe comes from Dan Brodsky from Scotts Valley, Calif.

1 tablespoon (15 mL) olive oil
½ cup (118 mL) minced onion
1 clove garlic, peeled and minced
¼ cup (59 mL) ketchup
2 tablespoons (30 mL) dry red wine
1 tablespoon (15 mL) balsamic vinegar
1½ teaspoons (7.5 mL) brown sugar
½ teaspoon (2.5 mL) dried rosemary
¼ teaspoon (1.25 mL) dried oregano
¼ teaspoon (1.25 mL) ground cinnamon
⅛ teaspoon (0.6 mL) ground nutmeg
2 (½-pound [227-g]) lamb sparerib racks, trimmed of fat

1. In a 1- to 1½-quart (0.95- to 1.4-L) pan over medium heat, heat the oil. Add the onion and garlic and cook, stirring often, until the onions are soft but not brown, 6 to 8 minutes. Mix in the ketchup, wine, vinegar, brown sugar, rosemary, oregano, cinnamon, and nutmeg. Turn the heat to high and bring to a boil, stirring. Cook for 1 minute. Let cool slightly. If you're making the sauce ahead, cover and refrigerate for up to 2 days. Place the lamb ribs in a 1- to 2-gallon (3.8- to 7.6-L) resealable plastic bag and and add the marinade. Marinate overnight.

2. Preheat the barbecue to medium high (350°F [180°C] to 400°F [200°C]) for direct and indirect heating, putting a water pan under the unheated side of the grill.

3. Remove the lamb from the marinade and wipe off the excess, reserving marinade. Place the ribs on the grill and cook, turning once, for 4 minutes. Watch carefully, since the meat is fatty. Move the ribs to the unheated side of the grill and cook, turning, until they are browned on all sides, 15 to 17 minutes total for medium-rare. While ribs are grilling, boil the marinade for 10 minutes. Serve the warmed sauce on the side.

Lamb Chops and Grilled Peppers

Yield: 4 servings

Spring lambs are between 3 and 5 months of age. If you can find lamb that has only been pastured, the taste will be much finer, more delicate, and more delicious than feed-lot raised lamb.

3 tablespoons (45 mL) olive oil
2 large red bell peppers, sliced
2 large yellow bell peppers, sliced
2 pounds (908 g) red onions, peeled and sliced into ¼-inch (0.5-cm) rings
2 large cloves garlic, peeled and minced
1 tablespoon (15 mL) chopped fresh rosemary
Freshly ground black pepper, to taste
1 teaspoon (5 mL) ground sage
3 tablespoons (45 mL) red wine vinegar
1 tablespoon (15 mL) balsamic vinegar, divided
4 (2-inch [5-cm] thick) lamb rib or loin chops
2 teaspoons (10 mL) balsamic vinegar

1. Preheat the barbecue to medium high (350°F-400°F).

2. In a cast-iron skillet, heat the oil over medium heat. Add the peppers, onions, garlic, and rosemary and sauté until the peppers and onions are very soft, about 10 minutes. Season with the black pepper and sage. Add the red wine vinegar and 1 teaspoon (5 mL) of the balsamic vinegar, cover, reduce the heat to low, and cook for 10 minutes.

3. Place the chops on the grill and cook for 11 to 15 minutes, depending on the thickness of the chops.

4. Brush each chop with the remaining balsamic vinegar and arrange the grilled chops on a platter over the cooked onions and peppers.

Assyrian Grilled Leg of Lamb with Pomegranate Sauce
Yield: 8–10 servings

This is a recipe I copied off a radio show hosted by San Francisco chef and restaurateur Narsai David a bunch of years ago. To this day, it produces the best leg of lamb I have ever eaten. But you must marinate it for 2 to 3 days!

1 (4-pound [1.8-kg]) boneless leg of lamb
1 (32-ounce [946-mL]) bottle pomegranate juice
1 cup (236 mL) olive oil
Juice of 2 lemons
3 whole Spanish onions, peeled and sliced
4 cloves garlic, peeled and chopped
2 teaspoons (10 mL) chopped fresh rosemary
2 teaspoons (10 mL) salt
1 teaspoon (5 mL) dried marjoram
1 teaspoon (5 mL) dried oregano
1 teaspoon (5 mL) dried summer savory
1 teaspoon (5 mL) coarsely ground black pepper
2 tablespoons (30 mL) butter
1 tablespoon (15 mL) brown sugar
1 tablespoon (15 mL) chopped fresh rosemary, or 1½ teaspoons (7.5 mL) dried
Seeds of one medium pomegranate

1. Have the butcher butterfly the leg of lamb, or do it yourself.

2. In a glass, enamel, stainless steel, or plastic bowl, whisk together the pomegranate juice, olive oil, lemon juice, onions, garlic, the 2 teaspoons fresh rosemary, salt, marjoram, oregano, savory, and pepper. Pour this marinade into a 1- to 2-gallon (3.8- to 7.6-L) resealable plastic bag, seal the bag, turn once or twice to coat the meat, and marinate for 2 to 3 days in the refrigerator. (No kidding, 2 to 3 days! It's well worth the wait.) Turn the bag over 2 to 3 times each day.

3. Preheat the barbecue to medium high (350°F [180°C] to 400°F [200°C]).

4. Remove lamb from the marinade and let it come to room temperature. Pour the marinade into a saucepan. Add the butter, brown sugar, and remaining fresh or dried rosemary, heat, and stir until the sauce is well mixed and the sugar dissolves. Measure out ½ cup (118 mL) of the marinade and reserve it for basting. Add the pomegranate seeds to the remaining marinade, stir quickly, remove the pan from the heat, and pour the warm sauce into a serving dish to pass at the table.

5. Place the lamb on hot grill and cook for 12 to 15 minutes on each side, brushing occasionally with the reserved marinade.

6. Serve the lamb thinly sliced, with the warm pomegranate sauce.

Yucatan Leg of Lamb

Yield: 6–8 servings

Chipotle chilies are merely dried and smoked jalapeño peppers. They have a brown, wrinkled appearance and a sweet, smoky, chocolate flavor.

1 (6–7 pound [2.7–3.2 kg]) whole leg of lamb
3 tablespoons (45 mL) black peppercorns
3 tablespoons (45 mL) dried oregano
3 tablespoons (45 mL) dried thyme
2 tablespoons (30 mL) cumin seeds
3–4 dried chipotle peppers, broken
4 teaspoons (20 mL) sea salt
3 tablespoons (45 mL) olive oil
6 cups (1.4 L) beef stock
Salt, to taste
Freshly ground black pepper, to taste

1. Preheat the barbecue to medium high (325°F[165°C] to 350°F [180°C]) for direct and indirect heating, putting a water pan under the unheated side of the grill.

2. Debone the lamb, removing excess fat. Form the boned lamb into a roast shape, and tie it tightly with kitchen string. (Use the bones and trimmings to make lamb stock.)

3. In a cast-iron skillet, toast the peppercorns, oregano, thyme, and cumin seeds over medium heat, stirring frequently, to release their flavors. Remove them from the heat when they turn brown and just begin to smoke and transfer them to a spice grinder or mortar. Add the 1 broken chipotle pepper and the salt and grind the mixture into a fine powder.

4. Rub the lamb with the olive oil, massaging it into every nook and cranny. Sprinkle the lamb generously with the spice mixture.

5. Place the lamb on a rack in a roasting pan and cook for 1 to 1½ hours on the unheated side of the grill, or until a meat thermometer registers an internal temperature of 120°F (49°C).

6. Turn up the gas or add charcoal to raise the temperature to around 450°F (240°C) and move the leg of lamb to the heated side of the grill. Cook for 5 to 10 minutes, or until brown. The internal temperature should rise to 130°F (54°C). Remove the lamb from the barbecue, cover, and let rest for 15 minutes to allow the meat juices to recirculate.

7. Skim the fat from the roasting pan. Add the beef stock and the remaining broken chipotles and cook over high heat, stirring occasionally, until the liquid has reduced by two-thirds. Season with the salt and pepper.

8. Carve the lamb and serve it on a warm platter, with the sauce spooned over the meat.

Grilled Lamb Patties

Yield: 4 servings

For a juicier patty, mix in ¼ pound (112 g) of ground pork or sausage meat or chopped uncooked bacon slices.

1½ pounds (681 g) ground lamb
4 ounces (112 g) feta cheese, crumbled
2 tablespoons (30 mL) chopped fresh mint
1 teaspoon (5 mL) salt
½ teaspoon (2.5 mL) pepper

1. Preheat the barbecue to medium high (350°F [180°C] to 400°F [200°C]).

2. In a bowl, gently mix together the lamb, cheese, mint, salt, and pepper. Form this mixture into 8 patties.

3. Cook the patties on the grill for 4 minutes per side for medium doneness.

Greek Lamb and Pasta

Yield: 4 servings

If you cannot find Greek kefalotiri cheese, you can substitute either Romano or Parmesan cheese.

1 (16-ounce [454-g]) package ziti

Cream Sauce

1¼ cups heavy cream, more as needed
20 cloves garlic, peeled
1 shallot, peeled and quartered

Lamb

6 tablespoons (90 mL) olive oil
1 large onion, peeled and chopped
1½ pounds (681 g) ground lamb

Sauce

6 ripe Roma tomatoes, seeded and chopped
1 (8-ounce [227-g]) can tomato purée
3 cloves garlic, peeled and minced
1 teaspoon (5 mL) dried oregano
¼ teaspoon (1.25 mL) ground cinnamon
½ teaspoon (2.5 mL) salt, plus more to taste
Freshly ground black pepper, to taste
½ cup (118 mL) fresh breadcrumbs, divided
1 large egg, beaten
½ cup (118 mL) all-purpose flour
4 ounces (112 g) freshly grated kefalotiri cheese

1. Preheat the barbecue to medium high (350°F [180°C] to 400°F [200°C]).

2. Place cream, garlic, and shallot in a small saucepan. Bring to barely a simmer, cover and cook until garlic and shallot are very soft, 1 to 2 hours. Transfer to a blender and puree, adding more cream as needed. Set aside

3. Spray a Dutch oven or roasting pan with nonstick cooking or grilling spray. Grease a deep 9 ×13-inch (22.5 × 32.5-cm) baking dish or roasting pan.

4. Cook the ziti according to package directions. Drain and set aside.

5. In the Dutch oven, heat the olive oil. Add the onion and sauté for 5 minutes, then add the lamb. Cook until the meat is completely browned, stirring to break it up as it cooks. Add the tomatoes, tomato puree, garlic, oregano, and cinnamon, stir well, and bring to a boil. Cover, reduce the heat, and simmer for 12 to 15 minutes. Remove the pan from the heat and season with salt and pepper to taste. Add ¼ cup (59 mL) of the bread-crumbs and quickly stir in the beaten egg.

6. Cover the bottom of the prepared baking dish with the remaining bread-crumbs, half of the cooked pasta, the cooked meat, half of the sauce, and half of the cheese, in that order. Add another layer of pasta, the remaining cream sauce, and the remaining cheese. Bake for 45 minutes in the barbecue.

7. Remove the pan from the grill, let the dish cool for 10 minutes, and serve.

Asian Barbecued Leg of Lamb

Yield: 8–10 servings

There are several basic types of Chinese rice vinegar, including sweet varieties that contain sugar, ginger, orange peel or cloves.

⅔ cup (158 mL) hoisin sauce
6 tablespoons (90 mL) sweet rice vinegar
½ cup (118 mL) minced green onions
¼ cup (59 mL) mushroom soy sauce
¼ cup (60 mL) minced garlic
2 tablespoons (30 mL) honey
1 tablespoon (15 mL) toasted sesame seeds
½ teaspoon (2.5 mL) sesame oil
½ teaspoon (2.5 mL) ground white pepper
½ teaspoon (2.5 mL) freshly ground black pepper
1 (5–6 pound [2.3–2.7 kg]) boneless butterflied leg of lamb

1. In a 1- to 2-gallon (3.8- to 7.6-L) resealable plastic bag, mix together the hoisin sauce, rice vinegar, green onions, mushroom soy sauce, garlic, honey, sesame seeds, sesame oil, white pepper, and black pepper. Place the lamb in the bag, seal, and turn over several times to coat. Refrigerate for 8 hours or overnight.

2. Preheat the barbecue to medium high (350°F [180°C] to 400°F [200°C]) for direct grilling. Make sure the grill is well oiled or sprayed before starting the fire.

3. Remove the lamb from the marinade. Pour the marinade into a saucepan and boil for 10 minutes while the lamb comes to room temperature.

4. Place the leg of lamb on the grill and cook for 13 to 15 minutes on each side, basting frequently with the marinade. Cook to a minimum internal temperature of 145°F (63°C) or to your desired doneness.

5. Transfer the meat to a serving platter, cover with foil, and allow it to rest for 10 minutes before slicing and serving. Reboil the remaining marinade for 10 minutes. Drizzle the slices with the remaining marinade and serve.

Spicy-Sweet Lamb Cutlets

Yield: 4 servings

In place of the plum jam, you could use fig jam or blood orange marmalade. For a sweet-hot flavor, add a minced habañero or jalapeño pepper.

3 tablespoons (45 mL) plum jam
2 tablespoons (30 mL) tomato sauce
2 tablespoons (30 mL) brown sugar
2 tablespoons (30 mL) dark soy sauce
1 tablespoon (15 mL) dry mustard
2 teaspoons (10 mL) Worcestershire sauce
1 teaspoon (5 mL) five-spice powder
8 lamb cutlets, trimmed
1 tablespoon (15 mL) toasted sesame seeds
Parsley sprigs, for garnish

1. In a small bowl, whisk together the jam, tomato sauce, brown sugar, soy sauce, mustard, Worcestershire, and five-spice powder.

2. Place the cutlets in a 1- to 2-gallon (3.8- to 7.6-L) resealable plastic bag, pour in the marinade, seal the bag, and shake to coat. Refrigerate for 4 to 6 hours or overnight, turning several times.

3. Preheat the barbecue to medium high (350°F [180°C] to 400°F [200°C]), making sure the grill has been well oiled or sprayed with nonstick cooking or grilling spray.

4. Remove the cutlets from the marinade. Pour the marinade into a saucepan and boil for 10 minutes while the lamb comes to room temperature.

5. Cook the cutlets directly on the hot grill for 2 to 3 minutes on each side, turning once. Brush both sides with the marinade while grilling. When the meat is still pink inside but browned outside, it's ready to serve.

6. Place the cutlets on a warmed platter, garnish with the toasted sesame seeds and parsley, and serve.

Crown Roast of Lamb

Yield: 8 servings

Your butcher will wire or tie together two racks of lamb loin chops for you, usually resulting in a 16-bone roast with the ends of the bones Frenched (meat and fat cut off the ends of the ribs to expose the bare bones).

½ cup (118 mL) olive oil
½ pound (227 g) mild Italian sausage
1 pound (454 g) crimini mushrooms, chopped
1½ cups (354 mL) chopped onion
1 cup (236 mL) diced celery
1 clove garlic, peeled and minced
½ cup (118 mL) water
1 (7-ounce [196-g]) package seasoned stuffing mix
1 cup (236 mL) slivered almonds, toasted
1 (4–5 pound [1.8–2.3 kg]) crown roast of lamb
2 cloves garlic, peeled and slivered
2 tablespoons (30 mL) fresh lemon juice
2 tablespoons (30 mL) kosher salt
1 teaspoon (5 mL) cracked black peppercorns
Cherry tomatoes or pearl onions, slit, for garnish

1. In a large saucepan, heat the oil. Crumble the sausage in the pan and cook until brown. Add the mushrooms, onions, celery, and minced garlic and cook for 5 minutes, or until tender. Stir in the water and bring to a boil. Add the stuffing mix and toss well. Stir in the almonds.

2. Preheat the barbecue to medium high (350°F [180°C] to 400°F [200°C]) for direct grilling. Line a shallow roasting pan with heavy-duty aluminum foil.

3. With a sharp knife, make slits in several places in the meaty part of the roast. Insert a sliver of garlic into each slit. Brush the roast with the lemon juice, and rub it with the salt and cracked pepper.

4. Place the roast, bone ends up, in the prepared roasting pan. Insert a meat thermometer in the thickest part of the roast, making sure it does not touch fat or bone. Fill the cavity with the stuffing mix and cover the stuffing and the bone ends of the ribs with aluminum foil.

5. Bake for 1 hour and 15 minutes. Remove the foil from the stuffing and bake an additional 15 minutes, or until the meat thermometer registers 160°F (71°C). Transfer the roast to a warmed platter, cover the entire roast with foil, and let rest for 10 minutes so the juices can be reabsorbed. Remove the foil, place the cherry tomatoes or slit pearl onions on the ends of the bones, and serve.

Shepherd's Pie on the Grill
Yield: 6–8 servings

The Oxford Companion to Food *proposes that shepherd's pie, a dish of minced lamb topped with mashed potatoes, was probably invented sometime in the eighteenth century by housewives looking for ways to serve leftover meat to their families. Things haven't changed much in 300 years!*

3 tablespoons (45 mL) vegetable oil
1½ pounds (681 g) ground lamb
2 medium onions, peeled and coarsely chopped
2 medium carrots, cut into ¼-inch (0.5-cm) slices
2 tablespoons (30 mL) all-purpose flour
1 tablespoon (15 mL) tomato paste
2 cups (473 mL) chicken stock
½ cup (118 mL) dry red wine
1 teaspoon (5 mL) Worcestershire sauce
1 teaspoon (5 mL) dried oregano
1 teaspoon (5 mL) dried rosemary
1½ teaspoons (7.5 mL) garlic salt
2 pounds (905 g) russet potatoes, peeled and quartered
1 large clove garlic, peeled and minced
1 teaspoon (5 mL) salt, divided
1 teaspoon (5 mL) freshly ground black pepper, plus more to taste
6 tablespoons (90 mL) butter, softened
¾ cup (177 mL) whole milk, warmed in the microwave for 20 seconds
2 large egg yolks

1. Preheat the barbecue to medium high (350°F [180°C] to 400°F [200°C]). Spray or grease a 9 × 13-inch baking or roasting pan.

2. In a 6-quart (5.7-L) Dutch oven, heat the oil over medium-high heat until a drop of water sizzles when dropped in. Add the lamb and cook, stirring, to brown all the meat, 5 to 6 minutes. Using a slotted spoon, transfer the lamb to a large bowl.

3. In the fat remaining in the pan, sauté the onions and carrots for 4 minutes, or until softened. Add the garlic, flour, and tomato paste, stir, and cook for 2 minutes. Pour in the chicken stock, wine, and Worcestershire sauce. Add the oregano, rosemary, and browned lamb. Bring to a boil, then move the Dutch oven to the barbecue, cover, and simmer 25 to 30 minutes.

4. While the lamb is cooking, put the potatoes in a large saucepan. Add water to cover and ½ teaspoon (2.5 mL) of the salt. Bring to a boil, reduce the heat to medium, and cook until the potatoes are tender when pierced with a knife, 15 to 20 minutes. Drain the potatoes well in a colander, transfer them to a bowl, and mash while they are still warm, adding the butter, garlic salt, the remaining salt, and pepper as you mash. Stir in the warm milk and egg yolks.

5. Pour the lamb mixture into the prepared baking dish or roasting pan. Spoon mashed potatoes over the entire filling, spreading the potatoes with a spatula to seal all the edges. Bake until the top is golden brown, 20 to 25 minutes. Let rest for 5 to 10 minutes and serve.

Grilled Whole Spring Lamb

Yield: 8–10 servings

Lamb is flavorful enough on its own that it doesn't need much seasoning. At the same time, lamb's flavor is robust enough that it goes well with any number of bold seasonings.

5 pounds (2.3 kg) kalamata olives, pitted
1 head garlic, peeled
6 sprigs fresh rosemary, trimmed
Juice from 2 large lemons
Grated zest from 1 large lemon
5 pounds (2.3 kg) Yukon gold potatoes, peeled and quartered
5 pounds (2.3 kg) ground lamb
2 tablespoons (30 mL) minced fresh parsley
2 tablespoons (30 mL) dried oregano
1 tablespoon (15 mL) ground sage
2 teaspoons (10 mL) salt
2 teaspoons (10 mL) dried rosemary leaves
1 teaspoon (5 mL) pepper
1 (25-pound [11.4 kg]) spring lamb, skinned

1. Preheat the barbecue to medium high (350°F [180°C] to 400°F [200°C]) for indirect heating, putting 2 to 3 water pans end to end under the center of the grill. Bank coals along both sides of the long part of the grill.

2. In batches in a blender, combine the olives, garlic, fresh rosemary, lemon juice, and zest and pulse to a chunky paste consistency. Set aside.

3. In a large bowl, combine the potatoes, ground lamb, parsley, oregano, sage, salt, dried rosemary, and pepper. Pack this mixture loosely into the lamb. Sew tightly closed with kitchen twine.

4. Lay the lamb on several large sheets of aluminum foil. Smear liberally with the olive paste, ensuring that the thicker parts of meat, such as the leg, receive more paste. Wrap the lamb tightly with foil and wrap it again with another layer of foil.

5. Place the lamb on the grill and cook, turning frequently to prevent burning. Because the lamb is skinned and thus more likely to burn, monitor the cooking process closely.

6. The lamb is done when it's nicely browned and an instant-read thermometer inserted into the thick part of the leg registers 145°F (63°C) for medium-rare or 160°F (71°C) for medium. Lamb is best at medium-rare, when it is still pink and juicy inside.

Roast Leg of Lamb with Mandarin Oranges
Yield: 6–8 servings

Make your own citrus salt by stirring together 1 tablespoon (15 mL) each of finely grated lemon, lime, and orange zest with ½ cup (118 mL) sea salt, cooking in a 200°F (95°C) oven for 2 hours, pouring into a clean coffee grinder, and processing until finely ground.

1 (5½-pound [2.5-kg]) boneless leg of lamb, tied
3 large cloves garlic, peeled and cut into thin slivers
¼ cup (59 mL) olive oil
2 (11-ounce [308-g]) cans mandarin oranges, drained, juice reserved
2 tablespoons (30 mL) grated mandarin orange zest
1 tablespoon (15 mL) citrus salt
2 teaspoons (10 mL) dried oregano
1 teaspoon (5 mL) dried rosemary
1 teaspoon (5 mL) lemon pepper

1. Preheat the barbecue to medium high (350°F [180°C] to 400°F [200°C]). Spray a roasting pan or Dutch oven with nonstick cooking spray.

2. With a sharp paring knife, cut small slits in the lamb. Insert garlic slivers in the slits. Place lamb, rounded side up, in the prepared roasting pan or Dutch oven. Set aside.

3. In small bowl, combine the olive oil, 1 can of mandarin oranges, half of the reserved juice from the cans, the grated mandarin orange zest, the citrus salt, the oregano, the rosemary, and the pepper. Brush this mixture over the lamb. If using a meat thermometer, insert it into the thickest part of the lamb without touching bone.

4. Place the lamb in the barbecue and roast for 1½ to 2 hours, or until a meat thermometer registers 135°F (57°C) for rare or 150°F (65°C) for medium, basting the lamb frequently with the pan juices. Remember that the meat will rise 10°F (3°C) in temperature when covered with foil and allowed to rest for 15 minutes after cooking.

5. Transfer the lamb to a large serving platter, reserving the pan drippings. Arrange the remaining can of mandarin oranges around the lamb. Cover loosely with foil and let stand for 15 minutes before carving.

6. Pour all the drippings from the roasting pan into a fat separator cup. Let stand so that fat separates from the juices at the bottom. Pour off the fat and discard. Pour the pan juices back into the roasting pan and add the remaining mandarin orange liquid. Place the roasting pan over low heat and heat to serving temperature, stirring constantly. Pour the sauce into a sauce boat.

Grilled Lamb Neck Fillets

Yield: 4 servings

Ask your butcher to cut these fillets from the middle neck or best-end-neck of lamb. This is a sweet, well-marbled, inexpensive meat, and it is delicious, tender, and juicy when grilled.

¼ cup (59 mL) fresh lime juice
1 tablespoon (15 mL) honey
1 tablespoon (15 mL) vegetable oil
2 (1 pound [454 g]) lamb neck fillets
¼ cup (59 mL) olive oil, divided
3 cloves garlic, peeled and minced
½ teaspoon (2.5 mL) dried oregano
½ teaspoon (2.5 mL) dried rosemary
½ teaspoon (2.5 mL) dried sage
½ teaspoon (2.5 mL) dried thyme
¼ teaspoon (1.25 mL) salt
Freshly ground black pepper, to taste

1. In a small bowl, combine the lime juice, honey, and vegetable oil.

2. Preheat the barbecue to medium high (350°F [180°C] to 400°F [200°C]).

3. Butterfly the lamb necks lengthwise, but don't cut all the way through. Open them out and flatten them with your hand.

4. In a separate small bowl, combine half the oil, the garlic, oregano, rosemary, sage, thyme, and the salt, and plenty of freshly ground black pepper. Massage this mixture into the lamb and set aside.

5. Place the lamb on the grill and cook for 2 to 3 minutes on each side, basting with the honey-lime sauce if desired, until they are browned and still slightly pink inside. Transfer to a warmed platter and drizzle with the sauce.

6. Serve with boiled new potatoes slathered in butter and sprinkled with freshly ground parsley.

Stuffed Lamb Roast, Saudi Style

Yield: 4 servings

Stuffed baby lamb or kid goat is so typical of Saudi Arabian food that no feast, whether a royal affair or a family gathering, is complete without it. The meat, surrounded by masses of rice and garnished with hard-boiled eggs, is presented to the gathering on a huge tray.

4 cups (0.95 L) cooked rice
2 cups (473 mL) sliced onions
2 cups (473 mL) chopped pistachios
1½ cups (354 mL) sultana raisins
1 cup (236 mL) butter, melted
½ cup (118 mL) chopped almonds
3½ teaspoons (17.5 mL) salt, plus more to taste
2 tablespoons (30 mL) ground coriander
1 teaspoon (5 mL) ground candied ginger
½ teaspoon (2.5 mL) coarsely ground black pepper, plus more to taste
1 (15-pound [6.8-kg]) baby lamb, prepared for roasting
½ cup (118 mL) olive oil, divided
4 (4–5 inch [10–12.5 cm]) rosemary branches

1. Preheat the barbecue to medium high (350°F [180°C] to 400°F [200°C]) for direct and indirect heating, putting a water pan under the unheated side of the grill.

2. In large bowl, combine the rice, onions, pistachios, raisins, melted butter, almonds, salt, coriander, ginger, and black pepper and mix well.

3. Rinse the lamb inside and out, wipe dry, and brush the outside and inside of the lamb with 2 tablespoons (30 mL) of the olive oil, seasoning both areas generously with salt and pepper. Place 2 rosemary branches inside the cavity, fill with the stuffing, top with the remaining 2 rosemary branches, and sew the cavity shut using a large needle and butcher's twine.

4. Put the stuffed lamb in a large roasting or baking pan, or form 4 sheets of heavy-duty aluminum foil into a pan around the lamb. Pour the remaining olive oil over it and place it in the barbecue over direct heat. Cook until the lamb just begins to brown. Cover the lamb with parchment paper or two large grocery bags cut so they lie flat.

5. Move the pan to the unheated side of the barbecue, shut the vents, and cook for 3 to 3½ hours, or until a meat thermometer registers 135°F (57°C) for medium rare. Baste frequently with the pan drippings.

6. Remove the lamb from the barbecue. Spoon the stuffing into a large bowl and cover. Cover the lamb with foil for 20 minutes to let the juices recirculate, carve, and serve with the stuffing.

Fruit-Nut Stuffed Lamb Breasts

Yield: 4–6 servings

You can of course use different fruit and nut combinations, for example, apricots and plums with pecans and cashews, figs and prunes with candied walnuts and salted peanuts, or peaches and pears with pine nuts.

2 (1½-pound [681-g]) breasts of lamb
½ teaspoon (2.5 mL) salt, plus more to taste
Freshly ground black pepper, to taste
1 tablespoon (15 mL) butter
2 tablespoons (30 mL) chopped onion
2 tablespoons (30 mL) chopped celery
1 cup (236 mL) soft breadcrumbs
½ cup (118 mL) diced unpeeled apple
½ cup (118 mL) seedless raisins
½ cup (118 mL) chopped pistachios and walnuts
½ teaspoon (2.5 mL) poultry seasoning
¼ cup 59 mL) olive oil
2 tablespoons (30 mL) lemon juice
Minced fresh parsley, for garnish

1. Preheat the barbecue to medium high (350°F [180°C] to 400°F [200°C]).

2. Place 1 lamb breast skin side down in shallow baking dish and season with salt and pepper.

3. In a medium skillet, melt the butter. Add the onion and celery and sauté. Turn off the burner, add ½ teaspoon (2.5 mL) salt, the breadcrumbs, the apple, the raisins, the mixed nuts, and the poultry seasoning and stir until well combined.

4. Spoon the stuffing over the first lamb breast. Cover with second breast and sprinkle the breast with salt and pepper. Tie the lamb breasts together with several pieces of butchers twine so the stuffing won't leak out.

5. In a small bowl, mix together the olive oil and lemon juice. Place the baking dish in the barbecue and cook the lamb for about 2 hours, or until tender, basting 4 or 5 times with the olive oil and lemon mixture.

6. Remove the lamb from the barbecue, cover with foil, and let rest for 5 minutes. Cut the string, transfer the stuffing to a serving dish, and carve the lamb breasts. Garnish with minced fresh parsley.

Lamb Loin Chops with Dijon Crust
Yield: 4 servings

For a slight variation, coat the chops with honey-Dijon, mango mustard, herb-and-balsamic mustard, or curry mustard, or choose from about a thousand other flavored mustards available online or in grocery stores.

3 tablespoons (45 mL) fresh French breadcrumbs
2 teaspoons (10 mL) minced fresh rosemary
2 teaspoons (10 mL) minced garlic
4 tablespoons (60 mL) olive oil, divided
2 teaspoons (10 mL) kosher salt, divided
1 teaspoon (5 mL) coarsely ground black pepper, divided
8 large lamb loin chops
4 teaspoons (20 mL) Dijon mustard

1. Preheat the barbecue to medium high (350°F [180°C] to 400°F [200°C]). Spray with nonstick cooking spray or grease baking sheet.

2. In a small bowl, combine the breadcrumbs, rosemary, and garlic. Drizzle with 2 tablespoons (30 mL) of the olive oil and season with ½ teaspoon (2.5 mL) of the salt and ½ teaspoon (2.5 mL) of the pepper.

3. Season the lamb with the remaining salt and pepper, then drizzle with the remaining olive oil. Place the lamb on the grill and cook for about 3 minutes on each side, turning once. Remove from the grill.

4. Liberally cover one side of each lamb chop with the mustard; then pack the breadcrumb mixture on top. Place the lamb on the prepared baking sheet on the unheated side of the barbecue and cook just until the crumbs brown on top.

5. Using a spatula, transfer the chops to a warmed platter and serve.

Honey-Baked Lamb Ribs
Yield: 8 servings

For sweetener, you can substitute orange or lime marmalade, pure maple syrup, or molasses for the honey.

4¾ pounds (2.2 kg) lamb ribs
3 red onions, peeled and chopped
1⅓ cups (315 mL) Zinfandel
⅓ cup (79 mL) fresh lemon juice
⅓ cup (79 mL) dark soy sauce
¼ cup (59 mL) fresh cilantro leaves
1½ tablespoons (22.5 mL) honey
1 tablespoon (15 mL) minced garlic
1 tablespoon (15 mL) extra virgin olive oil
1¼ teaspoons (6.25 mL) salt
1 teaspoon (5 mL) freshly ground black pepper
¼ teaspoon (1.25 mL) ground allspice
¼ teaspoon (1.25 mL) favorite hot sauce

1. Place the lamb in a 1- to 2-gallon (3.8- to 7.6-L) resealable plastic bag. In a small bowl, combine the onions, wine, lemon juice, soy sauce, cilantro, honey, garlic, oil, salt, pepper, allspice, and hot sauce and mix well. Pour this mixture all over the lamb. Cover and refrigerate for 2 hours.

2. While the ribs are marinating, preheat the barbecue to medium high (375°F [190°C] to 425°F [220°C]) for indirect grilling, putting a water pan under the unheated side of the grill. Spray with nonstick cooking spray and grease a roasting or baking pan.

3. Remove the ribs from the marinade. Pour the marinade into a saucepan and boil for 10 minutes while the lamb ribs come to room temperature.

4. Grill the ribs directly on the heated grill for 2 minutes per side, then place them in the prepared pan and bake for 30 minutes, or until the ribs are cooked through, turning and basting often with the marinade.

Mustard-Barbecued Lamb Chops
Yield: 4–6 servings

It's shocking how few Americans eat, or have ever tried, lamb. Around the world, lamb is an important and popular meat, but somehow we don't appreciate it. In Ireland, Scotland, England, France, Portugal, Spain, the entire Middle East, Asia, and Africa, lamb is an important met. This recipe comes from Patrick Clark, former chef of Tavern on the Green in New York City.

7 cloves garlic, peeled and crushed, divided
2 sprigs fresh rosemary
2 sprigs fresh thyme
20 black peppercorns
1 tablespoon (15 mL) dried oregano
½ cup (118 mL) olive oil
12 lamb rib chops
1 tablespoon (15 mL) canola oil
1 small red onion, peeled and diced
½ carrot, peeled and diced
½ serrano pepper, seeded and chopped
¼ cup (59 mL) red wine vinegar
½ cup (118 mL) ketchup
1½ tablespoons (22.5 mL) Dijon mustard
1 tablespoon (15 mL) honey

1. In a small bowl, mix together 5 of the crushed garlic cloves, the rosemary, the thyme, the peppercorns, the oregano, and the olive oil to make a marinade. Place the lamb chops, trimmed of fat, in a shallow baking dish or 1-gallon (3.8-L) resealable plastic bag. Pour the marinade over the lamb and refrigerate overnight.

2. Preheat the barbecue to medium high (350°F [180°C] to 400°F [200°C]).

3. In a medium saucepan over medium high heat, heat the canola oil. Add the onion, the carrot, and the remaining garlic, and sauté for 3 minutes. Add the serrano and red wine vinegar and stir. Add the ketchup, Dijon mustard, and honey, turn the heat to low, and simmer for 25 minutes.

4. Let the sauce cool and purée it in a blender. Strain and thin with a little water if needed.

5. Wipe the marinade off the lamb chops and place the chops on the grill. Grill the meat until medium-rare, about 4 to 5 minutes on each side. About a minute before the lamb is done, brush the chops lavishly on both sides with the mustard sauce.

6. When you serve the lamb chops, spread the additional sauce on both sides.

Moroccan Lamb Shanks Braised with Dried Fruits
Yield: 4 servings

I was treated to this dish on a trip to Marrakesh, Morocco, to film an episode for Barbecue America. *Instead of the Dutch oven suggested here, this was put together in a clay tagine pot and baked in a community barbecue oven. It was the best lamb I have ever eaten.*

Marinade

2 tablespoons (30 mL) olive oil
1 small onion, peeled and grated
1 tablespoon (15 mL) minced garlic
1 teaspoon (5 mL) ground cinnamon
½ teaspoon (2.5 mL) ground coriander
½ teaspoon (2.5 mL) ground ginger
½ teaspoon (2.5 mL) salt
¼ teaspoon (1.25 mL) freshly ground black pepper

Lamb

4 (¾–1 pound [336–454 g]) lamb shanks
2 tablespoons (30 mL) olive oil
2 cups (473 mL) sliced onions
2 cups (473 mL) sliced carrots
¾ cup (177 mL) Madeira wine
1¾ cups (413 mL) beef or chicken broth
Zest of 1 lemon, chopped
¾ cup (177 mL) dried pitted prunes
¾ cup (177 mL) dried figs, halved
½ cup (118 mL) dried apricots
Juice of 1 lemon
2 tablespoons (30 mL) dark brown sugar
2 tablespoons (30 mL) chopped crystallized ginger

1. Make the marinade: In a 1- to 2-gallon (3.8- to 7.6-L) resealable plastic bag, combine the oil, onion, garlic, cinnamon, coriander, ginger, salt, and pepper. Add the lamb shanks, seal, and shake the bag. Refrigerate for 4 to 6 hours or overnight, turning several times.

2. Remove the meat from the marinade. Pour the marinade into a saucepan and boil for 10 minutes while the meat comes to room temperature.

3. Preheat the barbecue to medium high (350°F [180°C] to 400°F [200°C]).

4. In a 4- to 6-quart (3.8- to 5.7-L) Dutch oven, heat the olive oil over medium heat. Add the lamb shanks 2 at a time, and cook for about 8 minutes. Transfer the lamb to a platter, cover, and keep warm.

5. Add the onions and carrots to the pot and cook over medium heat, stirring often, until the onions are nicely browned, about 10 minutes. Add the wine, scraping up any browned bits in the pot, then add the beef broth and lemon zest. Bring to a simmer, put the lamb shanks back in the pot in one layer, and spoon the sauce and vegetables over them.

6. Place the pot in the barbecue and cook for 1½ hours, turning the lamb several times and basting it with the pan juices. Add the prunes, figs, apricots, lemon juice, sugar, and ginger, and bake for another 30 minutes. Remove the Dutch oven from the barbecue and transfer the lamb to a deep serving dish, spooning the fruit mixture around the lamb shanks.

7. Heat the sauce over high heat for about 5 minutes, or until it reduces by a third and turns a rich, glossy brown. Pour the sauce over the lamb and serve.

Lamb Pita Patties

Yield: 4 servings

You could also serve these on toasted ciabatta bread, grilled slices of sourdough bread, or toasted and buttered sesame seed buns.

1½ pounds (681 g) ground lamb
1 medium yellow onion, peeled
1 large egg, lightly beaten
½ cup (118 mL) soft, plain breadcrumbs
1 small red chili pepper, seeded and minced
1½ teaspoons (7.5 mL) ground cumin
1 teaspoon (5 mL) ground allspice
½ teaspoon (2.5 mL) ground cinnamon
Salt, to taste
Freshly ground black pepper, to taste
1 cup (236 mL) Greek yogurt
1 large clove garlic, peeled
¼ cup (59 mL) minced fresh mint
4 large, soft fresh pitas
1 tablespoon (15 mL) diced, peeled cucumber
½ red onion, peeled and sliced thinly, for garnish
½ small red cabbage, shredded, for garnish

1. Preheat the barbecue to medium high (350°F [180°C] to 400°F [200°C]), making sure the grill has been well oiled or sprayed with grilling spray.

2. Place the ground lamb in a bowl and grate the yellow onion directly onto it. Add the egg, breadcrumbs, chili pepper, cumin, allspice, cinnamon, salt, and pepper. Mix thoroughly to completely combine the flavors. With your hands, form the mixture into patties.

3. Put the yogurt in a small bowl. Grate the garlic with a zester and add it to the yogurt. Sprinkle in the mint, stir, and set aside.

4. Place the patties on the grill and cook for about 5 minutes. Turn the patties over and cook for another 4 to 5 minutes. Cook the pitas during the last 2 to 3 minutes that the lamb is cooking, turning several times, until they are soft brown.

5. Remove the pitas from the grill, spread them open, and place a patty inside each. Add a dollop of the mint-garlic yogurt and a sprinkle of the cucumber, garnish with the red onion and cabbage, and serve.

Double Grilled Persian Lamb Kebabs

Yield: 6–8 servings

Lamb leg and shoulder cuts are best for kebabs. Remove the excess fat and cut the meat into 1- to 1½-inch (2.5- to 3.5-cm) cubes. Double-grilling these kebabs makes for perfectly cooked meat without overcooking the vegetables.

2 cups (473 mL) plain yogurt
1 cup (236 mL) finely diced onion
2 tablespoons (30 mL) chopped fresh thyme leaves
1 tablespoon (15 mL) lemon juice
Freshly ground black pepper, to taste
3 pounds (1.1 kg) leg of lamb, cut into 1½-inch (3.5 cm) cubes
2 large onions, peeled and cut into 8 wedges each
2 large green bell peppers, each cut into 8 wedges
12 mushrooms, stems removed
2 large tomatoes, each cut into 8 wedges

1. In a 2-gallon (7.6-L) resealable plastic bag, combine the yogurt, diced onion, thyme, lemon juice, and pepper. Add the lamb cubes and marinate overnight in the refrigerator, turning the bag several times.

2. Preheat the barbecue to medium high (350°F [180°C] to 400°F [200°C])

3. Remove the lamb from the marinade. Pour the marinade into a saucepan and boil for 10 minutes while the lamb cubes come to room temperature. Thread the lamb onto metal skewers. Thread the onion, green peppers, and mushrooms onto 3 separate metal skewers. Brush the vegetables with the marinade.

4. Place the meat and vegetable skewers directly on the grill. Cook the onions for 12 minutes, the lamb for 10 minutes, the green pepper for 7 minutes, and the mushrooms for 3 minutes. Brush several times with the marinade while they are cooking.

5. Let the skewers cool for 2 to 3 minutes. Remove the meat and vegetables from the skewers.

6. On clean skewers, alternate lamb, grilled vegetables, and tomato. Place these skewers on the grill and brush again with the marinade. Grill to finish cooking, turning and basting frequently, until the lamb is medium-rare and the vegetables begin to blacken in spots, 5 to 7 minutes.

Grilled Marinated Brochettes of Lamb

Yield: 4 servings

Metaxa, a strong yet sweet and mellow Greek liquor (actually a blend of brandy and two kinds of wine), has been around since 1888. Like brandy, it comes in several versions: 3-star, 5-star, and (hard to find) 7-star. We use the less expensive variety in this recipe.

1½ pounds (681 g) boneless lamb loin or leg of lamb
16 pearl onions
1 cup (236 mL) diced onions
½ cup (118 mL) Greek 3-Star Metaxa
2 tablespoons (30 mL) red wine vinegar
2 cloves garlic, peeled and crushed
2 teaspoons (10 mL) grated lemon zest
2 teaspoons (10 mL) ground cumin
2 teaspoons (10 mL) dried thyme
2 teaspoons (10 mL) honey
1 teaspoon (5 mL) dried rosemary
Salt, to taste
Freshly ground black pepper
2 tablespoons (30 mL) olive oil
Freshly chopped parsley, for garnish

1. Preheat the barbecue to medium high (350°F [180°C] to 400°F [200°C]).

2. Cut the lamb into 16 (1½-inch [3.5-cm]) cubes.

3. Peel the pearl onions, then steam or parboil them until nearly cooked but still firm. Drain and set aside.

4. In a large bowl, combine the diced onions, Metaxa, vinegar, garlic, lemon zest, cumin, thyme, honey, rosemary, salt, and pepper and blend well. Add the lamb and stir well. Cover the bowl with plastic wrap and marinate for 30 minutes or longer at room temperature.

5. Remove the lamb cubes from the marinade. Pour the marinade into a saucepan and boil for 10 minutes. Thread the meat and pearl onions onto 4 skewers, alternating lamb cubes and onions, starting and ending with the lamb. Brush the skewers with the oil and some of the marinade.

6. Grill the kebabs for 3 minutes on each side for rare, brushing often with the marinade. Cook longer if desired, but lamb should be cooked no longer than 5 minutes a side, or to medium. Any longer, and the meat will be too tough and dry to enjoy.

7. Either place a kebab in front of each person or transfer the meat and onions to a serving bowl and let your guests help themselves. Either way, sprinkle the kebabs or bowl with parsley.

Barbecue-Roasted Lamb Shoulder

Yield: 4–6 servings

Have your butcher debone and flatten out the shoulder to make it easier for you to stuff.

1 (3–4 pounds [1.3–2.2 kg]) boneless lamb shoulder roast
1 clove garlic, peeled and cut into slivers
2 cups (473 mL) fresh breadcrumbs
2 shallots, peeled and minced
2 slices bacon, chopped
Grated zest of 1 orange
1 large egg, beaten
1 tablespoon (15 mL) finely chopped fresh parsley
1 teaspoon (5 mL) dried basil
½ teaspoon (2.5 mL) dried tarragon
Juice of 1 orange
¼ cup (59 mL) butter, melted
1 tablespoon (15 mL) honey
¼ teaspoon (1.25 mL) ground cinnamon

1. Preheat the barbecue to medium high (350°F [180°C] to 400°F [200°C]). Spray with nonstick cooking spray or oil a roasting pan or Dutch oven.

2. Open the lamb shoulder and spread it flat, fatty side down. Make small slits in the meat and insert garlic slivers into the slits.

3. In a large bowl, combine the breadcrumbs, shallots, bacon, orange zest, egg, parsley, basil, and tarragon. Spread the stuffing over the lamb. Roll up the meat, tucking in any loose ends. Tie securely in several places with string.

4. In a small bowl, combine the orange juice, butter, honey, and cinnamon.

5. Place the rolled lamb roast in the prepared roasting pan or Dutch oven and bake in the barbecue for about 1 hour, or until the meat is just pink (with an internal temperature of 130°F [54°C]). During the last 15 minutes of roasting, brush the lamb with the orange juice–honey basting liquid.

6. Remove the lamb from the barbecue, cover and let rest for 10 to 15 minutes. With a very sharp knife, cut the lamb into 1-inch (2.5-cm) thick slices. Drizzle the slices with the remaining basting liquid, and serve.

Jamaican Jerk Lamb

Yield: 4–6 servings

The paste recipe makes about 1½ cups (354 mL), enough for about 2 pounds (908 g) of lamb, chicken, beef, pork or whatever you want to jerk. Refrigerated in a glass jar with a nonreactive lid, it should last for up to two weeks. I would not recommend using 12 peppers unless you have an asbestos throat or want to immolate your friends from the inside.

2 pounds (908 g) lamb loin, cut into 1-inch (2.5-cm) slices
4 cloves garlic, peeled and coarsely chopped
4 shallots, peeled
2–12 Scotch bonnet peppers (depending how much heat you want), stemmed and seeded
2 bunches green onions, chopped, green and white parts
1 medium onion, peeled and coarsely chopped
1 cup (236 mL) coarsely chopped fresh parsley
¼ cup (59 mL) fresh lime juice
3 tablespoons (45 mL) soy sauce
3 tablespoons (45 mL) salt
2 tablespoons (30 mL) vegetable oil
2 tablespoons (30 mL) water
1 tablespoon (15 mL) brown sugar
1 tablespoon (15 mL) finely chopped fresh ginger
2 teaspoons (10 mL) fresh or dried thyme
2 teaspoons (10 mL) ground allspice
1 teaspoon (5 mL) freshly ground black pepper
½ teaspoon (2.5 mL) grated nutmeg
¼ teaspoon (1.25 mL) ground cinnamon
⅛ teaspoon (0.6 mL) ground cloves
Steamed rice, for serving
Baked sweet potatoes, for serving

1. In a food processor, combine everything except the lamb and blend to a watery paste.

2. With a brush, (not your hands) brush the marinade on both sides of the loin slices. Place the lamb in a glass baking dish, cover, and marinate for 3 to 4 hours or overnight.

3. Preheat the barbecue to medium high (350°F [180°C] to 400°F [200°C]).

4. Brush off some of the marinade (again, do not use your hands), and grill the chops until they are brown on the outside but still pink inside, about 3 to 4 minutes per side.

5. Remove the chops from the grill and serve with steamed rice or baked and buttered sweet potatoes.

Barbecued Moussaka

Yield: 4–6 servings

It's important to use Greek-style yogurt in this recipe. It's very thick and creamy (the same texture as sour cream), and two popular brands, Fage and Chobani, are readily available at major grocery stores in the United States.

2 medium or large eggplants
½ teaspoon (2.5 mL) salt, plus more to taste
2 tablespoons (30 mL) olive oil, divided
1¼ pounds (566 g) lean ground lamb
2 medium onions, peeled and finely chopped
2 cloves garlic, peeled and chopped
3 ounces (89 mL) sweet red wine
2 tablespoons (30 mL) tomato purée
1½ tablespoons (22.5 mL) chopped fresh parsley
1 teaspoon (5 mL) ground cinnamon
Freshly ground black pepper, to taste
¼ cup (59 mL) feta cheese
2 tablespoons (30 mL) freshly grated Parmigiano-Reggiano
¾ cup (168 g) Greek yogurt
1 large egg, beaten

1. Preheat the barbecue to medium high (350°F [180°C] to 400°F [200°C]). Spray a casserole or roasting pan with nonstick cooking spray.

2. Slice the eggplants into approximately ⅓-inch (0.8-cm) thick slices; leaving the skin on. Put the slices into a colander and sprinkle them with about ½ teaspoon (2.5 mL) of the salt. Place a heavy bowl directly on top of the eggplant slices to weigh them down. After an hour, squeeze the excess juice from the slices, dry them well with paper towels, and spread them out on a baking sheet. Drizzle with 1 tablespoon (15 mL) of the olive oil and roast them in the barbecue for 30 minutes, or until the edges are lightly browned. Remove them from the baking sheet and set aside.

3. Lightly spray a nonstick skillet with nonstick cooking spray. Put the ground lamb in the skillet and cook until nicely browned. Drain the meat and discard the drippings.

4. Wipe out the skillet and add the remaining olive oil. Add the onions and garlic and sauté for 10 minutes. Return the lamb to the pan, add the wine, tomato puree, parsley, and cinnamon and stir to combine. Season with salt and pepper and cook for 20 minutes, stirring several times.

5. In a small bowl, combine the feta and Parmigiano-Reggiano. In a separate bowl, mix together the yogurt, half of the cheese mixture, and the egg and season with black pepper.

6. Line the bottom of the prepared casserole dish or roasting pan with slices of eggplant and top with a layer of meat. Repeat the layers, alternating eggplant and meat, until you run out. Spoon on the yogurt mixture and use a rubber spatula to spread it to all 4 edges of the pan. Sprinkle with the remaining cheese and bake for 1 hour, until golden and bubbling. Let stand for about 20 minutes before serving.

Lamb and Chipotle Mayo Sliders

Yield: 4–5 servings

These sliders can also be made with pork, beef, chicken, turkey, or even venison. Serve with coleslaw and baked beans.

1–1½ pounds (454–681 g) ground lamb
Salt, to taste
Freshly ground black pepper, to taste
1 ounce (28 g) shredded sharp cheddar cheese
4 slices bacon, cooked and halved lengthwise
2 tablespoons (30 mL) mayonnaise
1 tablespoon (15 mL) chopped chipotle pepper
1 teaspoon (5 mL) fresh lime juice
8–10 small slider rolls

1. Preheat the barbecue to medium high (350°F [180°C] to 400°F [200°C]).

2. Season the lamb with salt and pepper. Form the meat into 8 to 10 slider-sized patties.

3. Cook the patties on a grill pan or cast-iron skillet on the hot grill for 4 to 5 minutes. Flip them, add the shredded cheese and bacon, and cook for another 4 to 5 minutes.

4. In a small bowl, whisk together thoroughly the mayonnaise, chipotle, and lime juice.

5. Toast the rolls slightly, spread them with the chipotle mayo, add the patties and bun tops, and serve.

Lemon-Oregano Lamb Chops

Yield: 4 servings

Marinade variations include lime and basil, orange and cumin, and grapefruit and rosemary.

2 tablespoons (30 mL) fresh lemon juice
2 teaspoons (10 mL) chopped fresh oregano
1 teaspoon (5 mL) extra virgin olive oil
1 clove garlic, peeled and minced
8 (4 ounce [112 g]) lamb loin chops, trimmed
½ teaspoon (2.5 mL) celery salt
¼ teaspoon (1.25 mL) freshly ground black pepper

1. In a large, resealable plastic bag, combine the lemon juice, oregano, olive oil, and garlic. Add the lamb to the bag and turn to coat. Seal and marinate at room temperature for 15 minutes, turning the bag occasionally.

2. Preheat the barbecue to medium high (350°F [180°C] to 400°F [200°C]), making sure grill is well sprayed with nonstick cooking or grilling spray.

3. Remove the lamb from the bag and discard the marinade. Sprinkle the lamb lightly with the celery salt and pepper. Grill for 3 minutes on each side, or until the meat reaches your desired degree of doneness.

4. Serve with grilled vegetables and couscous.

Grilled Lamb Liver with Honey and Figs
Yield: 4 servings

Before cooking the liver, make ⅛-inch (0.25 cm) cuts at 1-inch (2.5-cm) intervals around the outside of the liver. Liver tends to shrink and curl when it is cooked, and these cuts will help to prevent that.

4 tablespoons (60 mL) butter, divided
1 tablespoon (15 mL) honey
8 large figs, 4 quartered and 4 halved
¾ cup (177 mL) balsamic vinegar
4 cups (0.95 L) concentrated veal stock
1 cup (236 mL) Pinot Noir
1 bay leaf
1 tablespoon (15 mL) finely chopped fresh rosemary
2 (1 pound [454 g]) fresh lamb livers, trimmed of membranes and sinews
Salt, to taste
Freshly ground black pepper, to taste
2 tablespoons (30 mL) olive oil
Chopped fresh parsley, for garnish
Smashed garlic potatoes, buttered, for serving

1. Preheat the barbecue to high (450°F [240°C] to 500°F [260°C]).

2. In a small saucepan, combine 3 tablespoons (45 mL) of the butter and the honey over medium heat and cook to a light caramel color. Add the quartered figs and cook for 2 to 3 minutes. Add the balsamic vinegar and reduce the heat to low heat. Simmer until the liquid is reduced by half. Add the veal stock, wine, bay leaf, and rosemary and simmer for 4 to 5 minutes. The figs should be mushy. Pass the sauce through a fine sieve. Whisk the remaining 1 tablespoon (15 mL) of butter into the sauce, sprinkle with salt and pepper, and set aside to keep warm.

3. Season the livers with salt and pepper and coat them with olive oil. Grill the livers until there are light grill marks on each side, about 1 to 1½ minutes per side for medium-rare. Place the halved figs on the grill and cook for 1 to 2 minutes, or until they pick up grill marks as well.

4. Transfer the cooked livers to a serving platter, garnish with the grilled fig halves, pour the fragrant sauce over everything, and garnish with the fresh parsley.

5. Serve with smashed, buttery, garlic new potatoes.

NINE

Marinades

North Carolina–Style Marinade
Yield: 7½ cups (1.8 L)

1 quart (0.95 L) cider vinegar, or to taste
1 (14-ounce [392-g]) bottle ketchup
1¾ cups (414 mL) water
½ cup (112 g) brown sugar
¼ cup (56 g) white sugar
¼ cup (56 g) salt
1½ teaspoons (7 g) crushed red pepper
1½ teaspoons (7.5 mL) freshly ground black pepper

1. Combine all the ingredients and mix well. Less vinegar may be used depending on your taste.

Tri-Tip Marinade
Yield: 2¾ cups (649 mL)

1 large onion, peeled and chopped
1 cup (236 mL) teriyaki sauce
1 cup (236 mL) Chianti
¼ cup (59 mL) clarified butter
¼ cup (59 mL) olive oil
¼ cup (59 mL) A1 steak sauce
3 tablespoons (45 mL) minced garlic
1 teaspoon (5 mL) hot sauce

1. Combine all the ingredients and mix well. Use several long rosemary branches tied together at one end as a basting brush for this marinade.

Lemon-Honey Marinade
Yield: 1 cup (236 mL)

½ cup (118 mL) butter, melted
Juice of 1 lemon
2 tablespoons (30 mL) honey
2 teaspoons (10 mL) olive oil
¾ teaspoon (3.75 mL) freshly ground black pepper
1 pinch sea salt

1. In a small bowl, whisk together the butter, lemon juice, honey, oil, pepper, and salt.

Assyrian Pomegranate Marinade

Yield: 6–7 cups(1.4–1.7 L)

3 whole Spanish onions, peeled and sliced
4 cups (946 mL) pomegranate juice
4 cloves garlic, peeled and chopped
1 cup (236 mL) olive oil
Juice of 2 lemons
2 teaspoons (10 mL) fresh rosemary (or 1 tablespoon [15 mL] dried)
2 teaspoons (10 mL) salt
1 teaspoon (5 mL) dried marjoram
1 teaspoon (5 mL) dried oregano
1 teaspoon (5 mL) dried summer savory
1 teaspoon (5 mL) freshly ground black pepper

1. In a glass, enamel, stainless steel, or plastic bowl, whisk together all the ingredients until completely mixed.

Beef Brisket Marinade

Yield: 4½ cups (1 L)

2 (12-ounce [355-mL]) cans Coke
1½ cups (354 mL) barbecue sauce of your choice
2 beef bouillon cubes dissolved in 4 ounces (118 mL) water
4 cloves garlic, peeled and minced
2 tablespoons (30 mL) lime or lemon juice
1 tablespoon (15 mL) Worcestershire sauce
Seasoned salt, to taste
Freshly ground black pepper, to taste

1. Combine all the ingredients and mix well. This marinade also works very well with pork or beef ribs.

Poultry Marinade

Yield: 1½ cups (354 mL)

½ cup (118 mL) soy sauce
¼ cup (59 mL) lime juice
¼ cup (59 mL) orange juice
¼ cup (59 mL) chopped green onion, green and white parts
2 tablespoon (30 mL) rice wine vinegar
1 tablespoon (15 mL) brown sugar
1 tablespoon (15 mL) honey
1 tablespoon (15 mL) poultry seasoning
1 teaspoon (5 mL) minced garlic
1 teaspoon (5 mL) olive oil
½ teaspoon (2.5 mL) ground ginger
1 pinch nutmeg
Kosher salt, to taste
Freshly ground black pepper, to taste

1. In a large bowl, whisk together all the ingredients. Use this marinade on any poultry, including red meat poultry such as ostrich and emu.

Salmon Marinade

Yield: 2 cups (473 mL)

½ cup (118 mL) soy sauce
½ cup (118 mL) packed brown sugar
¼ cup (59 mL) balsamic vinegar
¼ cup (59 mL) ground ginger
¼ cup (59 mL) granulated garlic
¼ cup (59 mL) chopped green onions (green parts only)

1. In a large bowl whisk together all the ingredients. This marinade is great on fish or chicken.

Teriyaki Marinade

Yield: 2¼ cups (532 mL)

1 cup (236 mL) soy sauce
1 cup (236 mL) water
¾ cup (177 mL) dry sherry
½ cup (118 mL) packed brown sugar
¼ cup (59 mL) minced green onion
1 teaspoon (5 mL) minced garlic
1 pinch ground ginger

1. In a bowl, combine the soy sauce, water, sherry, brown sugar, green onion, garlic, and ginger and stir well until the sugar dissolves. Use this to marinate eggplant, meat, poultry, or grilled vegetables.

Duck Marinade
Yield: 2½ cups (591 mL)

1 cup (236 mL) Cold Duck sparkling wine
1 cup (236 mL) honey
½ cup (118 mL) hoisin sauce
1 tablespoon (15 mL) ground ginger
1 teaspoon (5 mL) garlic powder
¼ teaspoon (1.25 mL) salt

1. In a large bowl, whisk together all the ingredients. This marinade is great on duck, goose, or chicken.

Grilled Vegetable Marinade
Yield: ¾ cup (177 mL)

½ cup (118 mL) balsamic vinegar
2 cloves garlic, peeled and minced
1 tablespoon (15 mL) brown sugar
2 teaspoons (10 mL) olive oil
2 teaspoons (10 mL) dried oregano
1 teaspoon (5 mL) dried thyme
½ teaspoon (2.5 mL) freshly ground black pepper
½ teaspoon (2.5 mL) sea salt

1. In a large bowl, whisk together all the ingredients. This marinade is great on grilled vegetables, shrimp, scallops, and fish.

Beef Rib Marinade
Yield: 3¾ cups (885 mL)

2 cups (473 mL) orange juice
½ cup (118 mL) extra virgin olive oil
½ cup (118 mL) balsamic vinegar
½ cup (118 mL) Worcestershire sauce
1 tablespoon (15 mL) garlic salt
1 tablespoon (15 mL) dry mustard
1 tablespoon (15 mL) brown sugar
1 teaspoon (5 mL) paprika
1 teaspoon (5 mL) chili powder
1 teaspoon (5 mL) Louisiana hot sauce

1. In a large bowl, whisk together all the ingredients. This marinade is great on steaks, roasts, and ribs (both beef and pork).

Chicken or Turkey Marinade
Yield: 1–1¼ cups (236–295 mL)

1 onion, peeled and chopped
⅔ cup (158 mL) chopped green onion, green and white parts
½ cup (118 mL) soy sauce
6 tablespoons (90 mL) dried onion flakes
¼ cup (59 mL) vegetable oil
2 tablespoons (30 mL) ground allspice
2 tablespoons (30 mL) freshly ground black pepper
2 tablespoons (30 mL) cayenne pepper
2 tablespoons (30 mL) Mexene Chili Powder
2 tablespoons (30 mL) sugar
4½ teaspoons (22.5 mL) dried thyme
4½ teaspoons (22.5 mL) ground cinnamon
1½ teaspoons (7.5 mL) ground nutmeg
1 teaspoon (5 mL) hot sauce
¼ teaspoon (1.25 mL) dried ground habañero chile

1. In a food processor, combine all the ingredients and blend until smooth. Pour the marinade into a sealable container and use it as a marinade or baste.

Peri Peri Chicken Wing Marinade
Yield: 2 cups (473 mL)

1 cup (236 mL) soy sauce
¼ cup (59 mL) teriyaki sauce
¼ cup (59 mL) orange marmalade
3 tablespoons (45 mL) brown sugar
2 tablespoons (30 mL) minced peri peri peppers
1 tablespoon (15 mL) honey
2 cloves garlic, peeled and minced
½ teaspoon (2.5 mL) cayenne pepper

1. In a large bowl, whisk together all the ingredients. This very spicy marinade is super on chicken wings and any other poultry.

Satay Chicken Wing Marinade
Yield: 5¾ cups (1.4 L)

2 (12-ounce [355-mL]) bottles beer
1 cup (236 mL) molasses
½ cup (118 mL) smooth peanut butter
½ cup (118 mL) fresh lemon juice
½ cup (118 mL) Worcestershire sauce
¼ cup (59 mL) prepared mustard
2 tablespoons (30 mL) chili powder
1 teaspoon (5 mL) salt

1. In a saucepan, combine all the ingredients. Cook over low heat for about 15 minutes, or until the marinade is reduced and thickened to the consistency of thick gravy. Let cool before using.

Venison Marinade

Yield: 2 cups (473 mL)

1 cup (236 mL) soy sauce
½ cup (118 mL) dry red wine
¼ cup (59 mL) olive oil
¼ cup (59 mL) butter, melted
2 tablespoons (30 mL) balsamic vinegar

1. In a bowl, combine all the ingredients. This marinade works well with any game—venison, buffalo, elk, moose, and so on.

Tilapia Marinade

Yield: 1¾ cups (413 mL)

1 cup (236 mL) extra virgin olive oil
1 small onion, peeled and chopped
1 red bell pepper, chopped
Juice of 1 lemon
Juice of 1 lime
1 tablespoon (15 mL) apple cider vinegar
1 teaspoon (5 mL) dried savory
1 teaspoon (5 mL) red pepper flakes
1 teaspoon (5 mL) sea salt

1. In a bowl, combine all of the ingredients. Mix well until the salt dissolves. This marinade is wonderful on fish, especially tuna, swordfish, and tilapia.

Tequila Marinade

Yield: 2½ cups (591 mL)

2 lemons
2 limes
1 cup (236 mL) margarita mix
½ cup (118 mL) tequila
⅓ cup (79 mL) olive oil
2 teaspoons (10 mL) salt
1 clove garlic, peeled and minced

1. Grate the zest from the lemon and lime into a bowl. Squeeze the lemon and lime juice into the same bowl. Add the margarita mix, tequila, olive oil, salt, and garlic and stir. This is perfect for chicken, fish, shrimp, scallops, oysters, crab, and just about anything else you cook on a barbecue.

Ribeye Marinade
Yield: 2 cups (473 mL)

1 cup (236 mL) prepared yellow mustard
¼ cup (60 mL) honey
3 tablespoons (45 mL) cider vinegar
3 tablespoons (45 mL) water
2 tablespoons (30 mL) chopped fresh parsley
2 tablespoons (30 mL) dried rosemary
2 tablespoons (30 mL) dried thyme
1 tablespoon (15 mL) Worcestershire sauce
½ teaspoon (2.5 mL) Louisiana hot sauce
¼ teaspoon (1.25 mL) freshly ground black pepper

1. In a large bowl, mix together all the ingredients. This marinade is perfect for any steaks, but especially ribeyes, T-bones, and porterhouse.

Thai Chicken Marinade
Yield: 4 cups (0.95 L)

2 (14-ounce [414-mL] cans unsweetened coconut milk
½ cup (118 mL) loosely packed chopped fresh cilantro
8 cloves garlic, peeled and roughly chopped
3½ tablespoons (30 mL) light brown sugar
3 tablespoons (45 mL) yellow curry paste (or 1 tablespoon [15 mL] curry powder)
3 tablespoons (45 mL) Thai fish sauce
1½ teaspoons (7.5 mL) ground white pepper
½ teaspoon (2.5 mL) cayenne pepper

1. In a blender, combine the coconut milk, cilantro, garlic, sugar, curry paste, fish sauce, white pepper, and cayenne pepper and blend until smooth. This marinade is delightful with chicken, fish, shrimp, or scallops. It's a bit fiery, but you can always leave out the cayenne pepper—or add more!

Jamaican Jerk Marinade
Yield: 2¼ cups (531 mL)

1 (14½-ounce [428-mL]) can chicken broth
¾ cup (177 mL) frozen orange juice concentrate, thawed
2 tablespoons (30 mL) red wine vinegar
1 tablespoon (15 mL) Jamaican jerk seasoning
1 small habañero chile, seeded and finely minced
2 teaspoons (10 mL) finely shredded orange peel
2 cloves garlic, peeled and minced
½ teaspoon (2.5 mL) hot sauce

1. In a nonmetallic bowl, stir together the chicken broth, orange juice concentrate, vinegar, jerk seasoning, habañero, orange peel, garlic, and hot sauce.

Texas Beef Marinade
Yield: 3½ cups (826 mL)

1½ cups (354 mL) water
1 (12-ounce [355-mL]) bottle pale ale
¼ cup (59 mL) light molasses
5 sprigs fresh thyme
1 tablespoon (15 mL) sugar
1 tablespoon (15 mL) salt
1 bay leaf
½ teaspoon (2.5 mL) ground white pepper

1. In a heavy saucepan, combine all the ingredients and bring to a boil. Cool the marinade completely before using.

Gilberto's Fish Marinade
Yield: 1½ cups (354 mL)

1 cup (236 mL) canola oil
3 cloves garlic, peeled
6 black peppercorns
¼ cup (59 mL) sweet white wine
2 bay leaves
1 tablespoon (15 mL) freshly squeezed lime juice
Salt, to taste

1. In a food processor, combine the oil, garlic, peppercorns, wine, bay leaves, lime juice, and salt and process until well blended. This marinade is great on fish or poultry.

Game Hen Marinade
Yield: 2 cups (473 mL)

1 cup (236 mL) tawny port
½ cup (118 mL) olive oil
¼ cup (59 mL) balsamic vinegar or red wine vinegar
¼ cup (60 mL) honey

1. In a small bowl, whisk together the port, oil, vinegar, and honey. This is a super marinade for chicken, duck, or game hens.

Peri Peri Pork Rib Marinade

Yield: 2 cups (473 mL)

---

1 cup (236 mL) soy sauce
¼ cup (59 mL) peri peri or Scotch bonnet peppers, stemmed, seeded, and chopped
¼ cup (59 mL) teriyaki sauce
¼ cup (59 mL) orange marmalade
3 cloves garlic, peeled and minced
3 tablespoons (45 mL) brown sugar
2 tablespoons (30 mL) honey
½ teaspoon (2.5 mL) cayenne pepper

1. In a food processor, combine the soy sauce, peppers, teriyaki sauce, orange marmalade, garlic, brown sugar, honey, and cayenne pepper, and process until smooth. Transfer to a container, cover, and set aside. This is a wonderful marinade for spicy pork ribs.

Montevideo Pork Marinade

Yield: 2 cups (473 mL)

This recipe comes from the owner of Mercado del Puerta, a barbecue restaurant in Montevideo, Uruguay.

1 cup (236 mL) water
½ cup (118 mL) sugar
2 tablespoons (30 mL) salt
6 juniper berries, lightly crushed
2 fresh habañero chilies, chopped
1 teaspoon (5 mL) freshly ground white pepper
1 teaspoon (5 mL) freshly ground black pepper
1 teaspoon (5 mL) freshly ground coriander
3 bay leaves, crushed
4 whole cloves
1 teaspoon (5 mL) dried thyme

1. In a mixing bowl, combine the water, sugar, and salt, stirring until dissolved. Add the juniper berries, habañeros, white and black pepper, coriander, bay leaves, cloves, and thyme and mix well.

TEN

Pork

Barbecued Crown Roast of Pork

Yield: 6–8 servings

This is a classic dish for special occasions. Have your butcher tie the crown roast for you. He or she will tie two racks of pork together in a circle. The center of the crown roast is often filled with stuffing, vegetables, or mashed potatoes.

1 (7–8 pound [3.2–3.6 kg]) crown roast of pork
10 cloves garlic, peeled and thinly sliced
2 tablespoons (30 mL) chopped fresh rosemary
1 tablespoon (15 mL) chopped fresh sage
1 tablespoon (15 mL) kosher salt
½ teaspoon (2.5 mL) freshly ground black pepper

1. With a sharp knife cut small slits around the roast. Insert the slices of garlic into these slits. In a small bowl, combine the rosemary, sage, salt, and pepper and stir to mix well. Spread the rub all over the roast and in the crevices. Let stand at room temperature for 1 hour.

2. Preheat the barbecue to medium high (400°F [200°C] to 450°F [240°C]) for direct and indirect heating, putting a water pan under the unheated side of the grill.

3. Make a smoke package by putting a handful of soaked wood chips (hickory, pecan, or cherry) on a large sheet of aluminum foil. Fold over the foil to form an envelope and puncture the top (do not go through the whole package) of the foil with a pencil 2 or 3 times. Place the packet directly on the hot coals or gas flame.

4. Grill the roast over direct heat for 30 minutes, turning several times. Move the roast over indirect heat and cook until the internal temperature reaches 145°F (63°C), about 2½ to 3 hours longer.

5. Remove the roast from the grill, lightly cover it with foil, and let it rest 20 minutes before carving. Cut and remove the string from the roast and slice the roast between the rib bones.

Backyard Roast Barbecued Suckling Pig

Yield: 12–14 servings

The best place to buy a suckling pig is from a local farmer. The odds are that the pig will have been organically raised. Tell them you're planning a barbecue so they'll leave the head on and tie the feet in a crouching position when they prepare the animal. When making the sauce, you can add wine, orange juice, Coke, or any other flavored liquid. If you wish to thicken the sauce, whisk in 2 tablespoons (30 mL) of flour that has been blended with 2 tablespoons (30 mL) of butter and boil for 2 minutes, stirring often.

1 (20–25 pound [9.1–11.4 kg]) young suckling pig
1 gallon (3.8 L) distilled white vinegar
2 cups (473 mL) apple cider
1 cup (236 mL) honey
1 cup (236 mL) dark soy sauce
1 cup (236 mL) orange juice

4 limes, sliced
4 lemons, sliced
1 tablespoon (15 mL) seasoned salt
6 cups (1.4 L) fresh breadcrumbs
3 cups (708 mL) chopped onions
3 cups (708 mL) chopped celery
3 cups (708 mL) chopped apples
2 cups (473 mL) chopped apricots
1 cup (236 mL) butter, melted
Olive oil for rubbing
1 cup (236 mL) chicken stock
1 cup (236 mL) dry white wine

1. Wash the pig inside and out and soak it in very cold water with the vinegar for 8 hours. This freshens and whitens the meat.

2. In a large bowl, combine the apple cider, honey, soy sauce, orange juice, sliced limes, sliced lemons, and seasoned salt.

3. In a separate large bowl, combine the breadcrumbs, onions, celery, apples, and apricots and mix well. Fill the cavity of the pig with this mixture and pour the melted butter over the stuffing. To close the opening, use an ice pick or upholstery needle to punch rows of holes about an inch (2.5 cm) apart on both sides of the stomach flaps. Then lace it up with thick string just as you would a shoe. Rub olive oil all over the skin and cut several small slits in the skin, making sure they don't go all the way through to the meat.

4. Form 3 large sheets of heavy-duty aluminum foil in a pan slightly larger than the pig, and place this pan in the bottom of the barbecue. Surround the pan with briquettes. Light the briquettes and replace the cooking grates over the charcoal and drip pan. It will take about 25 to 30 minutes for the briquettes to be ready for cooking.

5. Place the pig on its back on the grill. Fit aluminum foil caps over the ears and tail to avoid burning. (Remove the foil about ½ hour before the cooking time is completed.) Place a wooden block or baseball in the pig's mouth, so that a red apple can be inserted when the pig is done cooking. Place a meat thermometer in the pig.

6. Add approximately 12 briquettes to each side every 1½ hours to maintain the heat. Baste often and generously with the honey-cider basting sauce. The pig will cook for approximately 10 minutes per pound (454 g). The thermometer will read 160°F (71°C) when the suckling pig is done.

7. Remove the pig from the grill and wrap it in foil. Let it sit for 20 minutes so the juices are reabsorbed back into meat.

8. Skim the fat off the juices in the roasting pan. Ladle the remaining liquid into a large saucepan and place it on the side burner. Add the stock and wine and bring to a simmer. Stir to dissolve all the roasting juices coagulated on the bottom and cook for about 10 minutes.

9. To serve the barbecued pig, slice the skin from the base of the tail to the back of the neck and peel the skin down the sides. Carve the small hams first, slice the rib sections next, and carve the front shoulders and jowl last.

Brown(e) Sugared Ribs

Yield: 4–6 servings

This complicated dish was developed for Bon Appétit magazine. Their verdict was "the best ribs we've ever had."

2 racks pork ribs

Brine

2 cups (473 mL) warm water
2 cups (473 mL) light beer (such as Corona)
½ cup (118 mL) packed brown sugar
3 tablespoons (45 mL) coarse salt
3 tablespoons (45 mL) olive oil
Juice of 1 lemon
Juice of 1 lime

First Rub

1 cup (236 mL) prepared yellow mustard
½ cup (118 mL) packed brown sugar
2 tablespoons (30 mL) dried summer savory
2 tablespoons (30 mL) granulated garlic
2 tablespoons (30 mL) paprika
¼ teaspoon (1.25 mL) ground cloves

Second Rub

¼ cup (59 mL) packed brown sugar
1 teaspoon (5 mL) cayenne pepper
1 teaspoon (5 mL) dry yellow mustard

1. The night before you plan to serve, place the ribs in a 2-gallon (7.6-L) resealable plastic bag. In a large bowl, combine the brine ingredients and stir well. Pour the brine into the bag. Refrigerate overnight, turning the bag occasionally.

2. Drain the ribs, discarding the brine liquid. Pat the ribs dry, and then slather them with the prepared yellow mustard, rubbing it into the flesh on both sides. Set aside.

3. In a medium bowl, mix together the first rub ingredients and sprinkle the ribs generously with half of this mixture, reserving the other half. Dry marinate the coated ribs for 1 hour.

4. Soak a handful of wood chips (hickory, pecan, apple, cherry, or alder) in water for 1 hour.

5. When you are ready to begin cooking the ribs, place a drip pan in the center of the bottom of the grill, heat the charcoal in a chimney until the coals are ready, and pour half of the hot briquettes on each side of the drip pan. Pour 1 inch (2.5 cm) of water into the drip pan. If you are using a 3-burner gas grill, place the drip pan over the middle burner, and turn the burners on both sides to medium. Fill the pan with 1 inch (2.5 cm) of water. If you are using a 2-burner grill, only ignite one burner, and rotate the ribs once after about 1½ hours.

6. Drain the soaked woodchips and put them on a 12–inch (30-cm) square of heavy duty aluminum foil. Fold the foil over the chips to make a small package and punch 3 or 4 holes in the top (do not go through the bottom layer of foil). Place the package on one of the heated gas jets or directly on the coals on one side of the bottom of the barbecue.

7. Oil the grill with a paper towel dipped in olive oil and place the ribs in the center of the grill, over the drip pan, membrane side down. Cover and grill the ribs for 2 to 3 hours, turning two or three times.

8. In a small bowl, mix together the ingredients for the second rub.

9. When the ribs are tender and the meat has shrunken back from the bones by ¼ inch (0.5 cm) or so, transfer the ribs to a double-layer of heavy-duty aluminum foil. Sprinkle the meat side only with the second rub. Seal the ribs in the foil and return them to the grill for 20 minutes.

10. Remove the ribs from the grill, cut them apart, and serve them on a heated platter with a tangy barbecue sauce on the side, accompanied by coleslaw, baked beans, and cornbread or corn muffins.

Country Style Ribs

Yield: 4–6 servings

These ribs are cut from the blade end of the pork loin and contain a lot of fat. They may also contain a bone and are usually eaten with a fork instead of being picked up like racks of pork ribs.

4–5 pounds (1.8–2.3 kg) country-style pork ribs
1 tablespoon (15 mL) extra virgin olive oil
½ cup (118 mL) dark soy sauce
⅓ cup (79 mL) ketchup
¼ cup (59 mL) lemon juice
2 tablespoons (30 mL) brown sugar
1 tablespoon (15 mL) minced garlic
1 teaspoon (5 mL) dry mustard
1 teaspoon (5 mL) chili powder
¼ teaspoon (1.25 mL) freshly ground black pepper
⅛ teaspoon (0.6 mL) cayenne pepper
2 oranges, thinly sliced
2 lemons, thinly sliced
3 tablespoons (45 mL) chopped fresh parsley

1. Preheat the barbecue to medium high (350°F [180°C] to 400°F [200°C]).

2. Cut the excess fat from ribs. In a Dutch oven or roasting pan, heat the oil. Add the ribs and cook until browned.

3. Add the soy sauce, ketchup, lemon juice, brown sugar, garlic, mustard, chili powder, pepper, and cayenne pepper, turning to coat evenly. Cover the pan with a lid or foil and bake in the barbecue for 45 to 50 minutes.

4. Uncover the pan and spoon the sauce over the ribs. Leave the pan uncovered and bake for 45 to 50 minutes longer, or until the ribs are tender and a rich brown. To serve, place the ribs on a warmed serving tray, spoon the extra sauce over the ribs, garnish with orange and lemon slices; sprinkle with parsley, and serve.

Drunken Ribs
Yield: 4 servings

If you don't care for bourbon, you can substitute just about any alcohol, including gin, rum, vodka, whiskey, brandy, wine, or beer.

4 pounds (1.8 kg) pork spareribs
½ cup (118 mL) bourbon
¼ cup (59 mL) dark beer
¼ cup (59 mL) dark soy sauce
¼ cup (59 mL) packed brown sugar
 3 tablespoons (45 mL) molasses
2 tablespoons (30 mL) Dijon or yellow mustard

1. Place the ribs in a 2-gallon (7.6-L) resealable plastic bag. In a large bowl, whisk together the bourbon, beer, soy sauce, brown sugar, molasses, and mustard. Pour this mixture into the bag over the ribs, shake to coat the ribs, and refrigerate for 2 to 3 hours.

2. Preheat the barbecue to 350°F (180°C) to 400°F (200°C) for direct and indirect heating. Place a water pan under the unheated side of the grill.

3. Remove the ribs from the marinade. Pour the marinade into a saucepan and boil for 10 minutes while the ribs come to room temperature.

4. Place ribs on a rack in a roasting pan. Roast in the barbecue until brown and crisp, 1¼ to 1½ hours, turning several times and basting frequently with sauce.

Bulgogi Baby Back Ribs
Yield: 4 servings

These ribs are marinated and cooked in a Korean style bulgogi sauce, but remember to baste them only when they are on the unheated side of the grill.

2 slabs pork baby back ribs
2 cups (473 mL) soy sauce
1 cup (236 mL) sweet sherry
½ cup (118 mL) sugar
½ cup (118 mL) chopped green onions
¼ cup (59 mL) toasted sesame oil
¼ cup (59 mL) grated fresh ginger
2 tablespoons (30 mL) chopped garlic
2 tablespoons (30 mL) crushed red pepper

1. Place the ribs in a 2-gallon (7.6-L) resealable plastic bag. In a medium bowl, combine the soy sauce, sherry, sugar, green onions, sesame oil, ginger, garlic, and crushed red pepper. Pour this marinade over the ribs, cover, and refrigerate for 4 to 5 hours.

2. Preheat the barbecue to 350°F (180°C) to 400°F (200°C), for direct and indirect grilling, making sure the grill has been well oiled or sprayed with a grilling spray. Place a water pan under the unheated side of the grill.

3. Remove the ribs from the marinade, wipe off the excess, and let the meat come to room temperature. Pour the remaining marinade into a saucepan and boil for 10 minutes.

4. Grill the ribs on all sides over the hot side of the grill until they are nicely browned, then move them to the unheated side. Cook, basting frequently with the boiled marinade, for approximately 1½ to 2 hours. The ribs are done when the meat pulls away from the bone at the bottom.

5. Boil the remaining marinade for 10 minutes. Cut the ribs apart, place them on a serving tray, drizzle with the remaining marinade, and serve.

Greek Pork Ribs
Yield: 6–8 servings

These ribs are wonderful served with a Greek salad that includes lots of crumbled feta cheese, sliced olives, and sliced red onions.

3 slabs (10–20 pounds [4.5–9 kg]) pork ribs
2–3 tablespoons (30–45 mL) olive oil
Salt, to taste
Freshly ground black pepper, to taste
½ cup (118 mL) butter
1 onion, peeled and chopped
2 cloves garlic, minced
2 lemons, juiced and chopped into chunks
1 cup (236 mL) apple cider vinegar
½ cup (118 mL) Worcestershire sauce
1 tablespoon (15 mL) kosher salt
1 teaspoon (5 mL) chopped fresh rosemary
1 teaspoon (5 mL) cracked black pepper
1 teaspoon (5 mL) red pepper flakes
¼ teaspoon (1.25 mL) Penzeys Greek Seasoning
10–12 large lettuce leaves
1 red onion, peeled and thinly sliced, for garnish

1. Generously brush the ribs with olive oil, then sprinkle with salt and pepper and set the ribs aside.

2. In a cast-iron skillet, melt the butter. Add the onion and garlic and sauté until tender. Add lemon juice and chunks, vinegar, Worcestershire sauce, salt, rosemary, black pepper, red pepper flakes, and Greek seasoning, bring to a simmer, and simmer for 10 minutes.

3. Preheat the barbecue to 350°F (180°C) to 400°F (200°C) for direct and indirect heating, putting a water pan under the unheated side of the grill and making sure the grill has been well oiled or sprayed with a grilling spray.

4. Place the ribs on the heated side of the grill. Cook, turning frequently, for approximately 1 hour, depending on the thickness of the ribs. Transfer the ribs to 2 large sheets of heavy-duty aluminum foil. Generously brush the sauce on both sides of each of the slabs and seal the foil package. Put the package on the unheated side of the grill and cook for approximately 25 to 35 minutes.

5. Remove the foil package from the grill, open it carefully to avoid the escaping steam, and place the ribs on a serving platter over lettuce and red onion slices.

Coriander Spareribs
Yield: 8 servings

Coriander was probably one of the first spices used. It was known as early as 5000 B.C., and it is a common ingredient in Middle Eastern, Mediterranean, Indian, Asian, Latin American, Chinese, African, and Mexican cuisines.

5 pounds (2.3 kg) pork ribs
⅓ cup (79 mL) gin
¼ cup (59 mL) packed brown sugar
¼ cup (59 mL) lemon juice
3 tablespoons (45 mL) minced garlic
3 tablespoons (45 mL) ground coriander
2 tablespoons (30 mL) grated lemon zest
1 tablespoon (15 mL) ground sage
1 teaspoon (5 mL) ground cumin
1 teaspoon (5 mL) red pepper flakes
1 teaspoon (5 mL) kosher salt
1 teaspoon (5 mL) cracked black pepper

1. Preheat the barbecue to 375°F (190°C) to 425°F (220°C) for direct heating.

2. Cut the ribs into 2-bone sections. In a medium bowl, stir together the gin, brown sugar, lemon juice, garlic, coriander, lemon zest, sage, cumin, red pepper flakes, salt, and pepper. Add the ribs, stirring gently to coat with the seasoning paste. Place the coated ribs in a 1- to 2-gallon (3.8- to 7.6-L) resealable plastic bag and refrigerate for at least 4 hours or overnight.

3. Place the ribs in a Dutch oven or roasting pan and bake, covered, in the barbecue until the ribs are almost tender when pierced, about 1 hour. Uncover the pan and continue baking, stirring occasionally, until well browned, about 30 minutes.

4. Place the ribs on a serving platter and serve.

Maple-Barbecued Oven Spareribs
Yield: 4 servings

Use pure maple syrup instead of the imitations made with corn syrup. The real stuff is more expensive, but it's worth it.

1½ cups (354 mL) pure maple syrup
2 tablespoons (30 mL) bottled chili sauce
2 tablespoons (30 mL) cider vinegar
1½ tablespoons (22.5 mL) chopped onion
1 tablespoon (15 mL) Worcestershire sauce
1 tablespoon (15 mL) butter
1 teaspoon (5 mL) salt
½ teaspoon (2.5 mL) dry mustard
⅛ teaspoon (0.6 mL) freshly ground black pepper
2 pounds (908 g) pork spareribs
Chopped chives, for garnish

1. Preheat the barbecue to 350°F (180°C) to 400°F (200°C) for direct heating.

2. In a large saucepan, combine the maple syrup, chili sauce, vinegar, onion, Worcestershire sauce, butter, salt, mustard, and black pepper and bring to a boil.

3. Wipe the spareribs with damp paper towels. Brush sauce on both sides of the ribs and place them in a Dutch oven or roasting pan. Bake for 1½ hours, turning and basting frequently with the remaining sauce.

4. Transfer the ribs to a serving platter, sprinkle with chives, and serve.

Memphis Dry Ribs
Yield: 2–4 servings

Practiced by many Memphis restaurants but perfected by Charlie Vergo's Rendezvous, these ribs are extremely flavorful and less messy than the wet kind.

½ cup (118 mL) paprika
½ cup (118 mL) garlic salt
½ cup (118 mL) packed brown sugar
¼ cup (59 mL) freshly ground black pepper
2 tablespoons (30 mL) chili powder
1 tablespoon (15 mL) dried oregano
1 (2½–4 pound [1.1–1.8 kg]) slab pork ribs
½ cup (118 mL) olive oil
½ cup (118 mL) beer
¼ cup (59 mL) lemon juice
1 tablespoon (15 mL) A1 steak sauce

1. Preheat a smoker to 190°F (90°C) to 220°F (105°C).

2. In a medium bowl, combine the paprika, garlic salt, brown sugar, pepper, chili powder, and oregano. Put a generous amount of this rub on the ribs, massaging it into the meaty side of the rib, and put them on an oiled grill rack in the smoker for 4 hours.

3. In a small bowl, combine the olive oil, beef, lemon juice, and A1. Moisten or mop the ribs once or twice an hour with this baste. When the meat has pulled away from the bones by about ½ inch (1 cm), the ribs are ready.

4. Remove the ribs from the smoker, sprinkle on more rub, and serve.

Memphis Wet Ribs
Yield: 2–4 servings

Half of the barbecue restaurants in Memphis use a dry rub like this recipe, and the other half slather them with a sweet and smoky rib sauce. Some do both!

1 tablespoon (15 mL) paprika
1 tablespoon (15 mL) onion salt
1 tablespoon (15 mL) garlic powder
1 tablespoon (15 mL) brown sugar
1 teaspoon (5 mL) ground cumin
1 teaspoon (5 mL) freshly ground black pepper
½ teaspoon (2.5 mL) cayenne pepper
1 (2½–4 pound [1.1–1.8 kg]) slab pork ribs
1 cup (236 mL) apple cider vinegar
1 cup (236 mL) dry white wine
¼ cup (59 mL) balsamic vinegar

1. Preheat a smoker to 190°F (90°C) to 220°F (105°C).

2. In a small bowl, combine the paprika, onion salt, garlic powder, brown sugar, cumin, black pepper, and cayenne pepper. Put a generous amount of this rub on ribs, massaging it into the meaty side of the rib, and put them on an oiled grill rack in the smoker for 4 hours.

3. In a separate bowl, mix together the apple cider vinegar, wine, and balsamic vinegar. Baste the ribs once or twice an hour with this basting sauce. When the meat has pulled away from the bones by about ½ inch (1 cm), the ribs are ready.

4. Remove the ribs from the smoker, generously coat them with your favorite barbecue sauce, and serve.

Coca-Cola Barbecued Ribs

Yield: 4 servings

It goes without saying that you can use another brand of cola if you wish, but as long as you're experimenting, try a good quality root beer, cream soda, or Big Red or Big Blue sodas.

1 cup (236 mL) packed brown sugar
1 (12-ounce [355-mL]) can Coke
½ cup (118 mL) smoky Texas-style barbecue sauce
2 medium onions, peeled and chopped
2 cloves garlic, peeled and minced
2 tablespoons (30 mL) soy sauce
Salt, to taste
Freshly ground black pepper, to taste
3–4 pounds (1.3–1.8 mL) pork ribs, cut in half across the bones

1. In a large casserole, combine the brown sugar, Coke, barbecue sauce, onions, garlic, soy sauce, salt, and pepper and stir until mixed.

2. Place the ribs in the sauce mixture and marinate for 2 hours. Drain the ribs and pour the marinade into a saucepan. Boil the marinade for 10 minutes. Reserve half the sauce to serve at the table.

3. Preheat the barbecue to 350°F (180°C) to 400°F (200°C) for direct and indirect heating, putting a water pan under the unheated side of the grill. Make sure the grill has been well oiled or sprayed with grilling spray.

4. Grill the ribs over direct heat for 1 minute per side, then move them to the indirect side of the grill and cook for 30 minutes, turning often and basting with the remaining sauce. When the meat pulls away from the bone ends, the ribs are done.

Spareribs with Onion Sauce

Yield: 4 servings

If you love onions, you'll love these ribs. To deliver a culinary coupe de grace, serve with fried onion rings.

4 pounds (1.8 kg) pork spareribs
2 tablespoons (30 mL) vegetable oil
3 cups (708 mL) sliced white onions
4 cloves garlic, peeled and minced
2 green onions, chopped, green parts only
½ cup (118 mL) rice wine vinegar
½ cup (118 mL) bottled chili sauce
¼ cup (59 mL) molasses
2 teaspoons (10 mL) dried marjoram
2 teaspoons (10 mL) ground allspice
2 teaspoons (10 mL) dry mustard
2 teaspoons (10 mL) Worcestershire sauce

1. Preheat the barbecue to 375°F (190°C) to 425°F (220°C) for direct and indirect heating, putting a water pan under the unheated side of the grill.

2. Cut the ribs into 3-rib pieces, place them on the heated side of the grill, and cook for 20 minutes. Remove the ribs from the grill and arrange them in a 9 × 13-inch (22.5 × 32.5-cm) pan.

3. In a cast-iron skillet, heat the oil over medium heat. Add the white onions, garlic, and green onions and sauté for 2 to 3 minutes, or until the onions are limp. Add the vinegar, chili sauce, molasses, marjoram, allspice, mustard, and Worcestershire sauce and bring to a simmer. Simmer for 10 minutes, then pour the onion sauce over ribs.

4. Bake in the barbecue for 1 to 1½ hours, or until the ribs are very tender and juicy. If the ribs look like they are browning too quickly, cover them with foil.

5. Remove the ribs from the grill, let them cool slightly, and serve with mashed potatoes.

Hot 'n' Spicy Ribs

Yield: 4 servings

You can make these hot ribs even hotter by adding 1 or 2 minced habañero or jalapeño peppers to the sauce, but have a fire extinguisher handy.

3 pounds (1.3 kg) pork spareribs or back ribs
¼ cup (59 mL) melted bacon grease
1 tablespoon (15 mL) ground cumin
1 cup (236 mL) spicy barbecue sauce
¼ cup (59 mL) orange juice
3 tablespoons (45 mL) hot sauce
1–1½ teaspoons (5–7.5 mL) red pepper flakes

1. Brush the ribs with the melted bacon fat, sprinkle them with the cumin, and refrigerate for 25 minutes.

2. Preheat the barbecue to medium high (350°F [180°C] to 400°F [200°C]) for direct and indirect heating, putting a water pan under the unheated side of the grill.

3. Grill the ribs over direct heat for 15 to 20 minutes, turning once, to brown them nicely.

4. Meanwhile, in a small bowl, combine the barbecue sauce, orange juice, hot sauce, and red pepper flakes.

5. Place the ribs, bone side down, in a double thickness of heavy-duty foil, pour the sauce over the ribs, seal the foil, and place them over the unheated side of the grill for 1 hour.

Plum-Glazed Pork Ribs

Yield: 5–6 servings

Substitute peach, nectarine, pear, or pineapple jelly and purée for a different fruity rib recipe.

4–4½ pounds (1.8–2 kg) pork spareribs
1 (12-ounce [336-g]) bottle chili sauce
1 (10-ounce [280-g]) jar plum jelly
½ cup (118 mL) plums, puréed
1 tablespoon (15 mL) hot sauce
Freshly ground black pepper, to taste
Kosher salt, to taste

1. Preheat the barbecue to 350°F (180°C) to 400°F (200°C) for direct and indirect heating, putting a water pan under the unheated side of the grill. Spray a shallow roasting pan or Dutch oven with nonstick cooking spray.

2. Place the pork ribs, bone side up, on a rack in the prepared pan or Dutch oven. Bake, uncovered, in the barbecue for 45 minutes.

3. in a large saucepan, combine the chili sauce, jelly, puréed plums, hot sauce, pepper, and salt and bring to a boil, stirring constantly.

4. Turn the pork ribs meat side up, brush liberally with about ½ cup (59 mL) of the sauce; and bake until tender, 45 to 60 minutes, brushing generously and frequently during the last 25 minutes of cooking.

5. Boil the remaining sauce for 10 minutes. Serve the ribs with the remaining sauce in a sauce boat to serve at the table.

Ribs in a Bag

Yield: 4 servings

This is an old-fashioned method for preparing very moist ribs. Make sure the bag is completely over a baking pan or a double layer of heavy-duty aluminum foil so it doesn't catch on fire.

1 cup (236 mL) barbecue sauce
1 cup (236 mL) beer
2 teaspoons (10 mL) garlic powder
2 teaspoons (10 mL) Worcestershire sauce
1 teaspoon (5 mL) hot sauce
¼ teaspoon (1.25 mL) bitters
¼ teaspoon (1.25 mL) hickory smoke powder
2½–3 pounds (1.1–1.3 kg) pork ribs
Kosher salt, to taste
Cayenne pepper, to taste
2 tablespoons (30 mL) all-purpose flour
2 cups (473 mL) chopped onions
2 tablespoons (30 mL) chopped fresh parsley
2 tablespoons (30 mL) chopped fresh mint

1. Preheat the barbecue for direct heating at 350°F (180°C) to 400°F (200°C).

2. In medium bowl, whisk together the barbecue sauce, beer, garlic powder, Worcestershire sauce, hot sauce, bitters, and hickory smoke powder and mix well.

3. Season the ribs with salt and cayenne pepper and place them in a large turkey-size plastic baking bag. Sprinkle in the flour, add the ribs, and set the bag in a large, shallow roasting or baking pan.

4. Pour the barbecue sauce over the ribs. Sprinkle the ribs with the onion, parsley, and mint.

5. Tie the bag tightly and punch several holes in the top of the bag. Place the pan in the barbecue and cook for 3 to 4 hours.

6. Carefully remove the ribs from the bag, being careful to avoid the escaping steam, and place the ribs on a serving platter. Brush the ribs with the bag drippings and sauce from the roasting pan.

Sugar-Free Pork Ribs
Yield: 4 servings

These ribs were designed for those who have diabetes. They're cooked with no sugar whatsoever. In fact, you can leave out the Splenda and still have a very delicious sauce.

¼ cup (59 mL) chili powder
1 tablespoon (15 mL) garlic powder
1 tablespoon (15 mL) Splenda
2 teaspoons (10 mL) ground cumin
1½ teaspoons (7.5 mL) ground oregano
1 teaspoon (5 mL) dried thyme
¾ teaspoon (3.75 mL) dry mustard
¾ teaspoon (3.75 mL) kosher salt
¼ teaspoon (1.25 mL) freshly ground black pepper
2 cloves garlic, peeled and minced
3–4 pounds (1.3–1.8 kg) pork ribs
2 limes, thinly sliced
1 large lemon, thinly sliced

1. In a small bowl, combine the chili powder, garlic powder, Splenda, cumin, oregano, thyme, mustard, salt, pepper, and garlic.

2. Wash and dry the ribs, Massage the spice mixture into the meaty side of the ribs, wrap with plastic wrap, and refrigerate 8 hours or overnight.

3. Remove the ribs from the plastic wrap.

4. Preheat the barbecue to 350°F (180°C) to 400°F (200°C) for direct and indirect heating, putting a water pan under the unheated side of the grill.

5. Arrange the ribs on the heated side of the grill and shut the lid. Grill for 15 minutes total, turning once.

6. Remove the ribs from the grill, wrap them with aluminum foil and place them on the unheated side of the grill. Cook for 1½ hours, or until the meat is tender and has pulled away from the bones.

7. Transfer the ribs to a serving platter and garnish with the sliced limes and lemon.

Southern Style Pork Ribs
Yield: 4–6 servings

We use a custom North Carolina–style vinegar and pepper sauce, with a few additions, to cook up these ribs. If you wish, you can leave out the cane syrup and mustard for a tangier, more rustic sauce.

4 pounds (1.8 kg) country-style pork ribs
1½ cups (354 mL) water, divided
1 cup (236 mL) finely chopped onion
½ cup (118 mL) vinegar
¼ cup (59 mL) Steen's cane syrup
2 tablespoons (30 mL) red pepper flakes
2 teaspoons (10 mL) dry mustard
1 teaspoon (5 mL) salt
1 teaspoon (5 mL) paprika
¼ teaspoon (1.25 mL) hot sauce

1. Preheat the barbecue to 350°F (180°C) to 400°F (200°C) for direct heating.

2. Place the ribs in a roasting pan, add ½ cup (118 mL) of the water, cover, and bake for 1 hour.

3. While the ribs are baking, mix together the remaining water, onion, salt, vinegar, cane syrup, red pepper flakes, mustard, paprika, and hot sauce in a small saucepan and simmer gently for 10 minutes. Remove the pan from the heat, cover, and keep warm.

4. Remove the ribs from the barbecue and drain off the liquid. Brush the barbecue sauce over the ribs and return the pan to the barbecue. Bake uncovered on the unheated side of the grill for another 1½ hours, or until the meat pulls away from the bone, basting frequently with the sauce and drippings from the roasting pan.

5. Remove the ribs and cover them with foil. Let them rest for 10 minutes, then cut into individual ribs and serve.

Red Dragon Ribs

Yield: 6–8 servings

These are very red, very hot, and quite delicious served with a cold beer or cocktails.

6 pounds (2.7 kg) pork spareribs, cut into 3-rib sections
Salt, to taste
Freshly ground black pepper, to taste
1 (16-ounce [454-g]) can apricot halves, including syrup
¼ cup (59 mL) honey
¼ cup (59 mL) red wine vinegar
¼ cup (59 mL) soy sauce
1 red bell pepper, chopped
1 small onion, peeled and quartered
2 cloves garlic, peeled and chopped
1 tablespoon (15 mL) red pepper flakes
1 tablespoon (15 mL) paprika
½ teaspoon (2.5 mL) cayenne pepper
½ teaspoon (2.5 mL) red food coloring

1. Preheat the barbecue to 350°F (180°C) to 400°F (200°C) for direct heating.

2. Place the ribs bone side up in a single layer in 2 baking pans. Season well with the salt and pepper and cook, uncovered, for 20 minutes, turning once.

3. In a blender, combine the apricots and syrup, honey, vinegar, soy sauce, bell pepper, onion, garlic, red pepper flakes, paprika, cayenne pepper, and food coloring and blend to a smooth purée.

4. Brush the ribs with some of this mixture, cover, and bake, bone side up, for 20 minutes. Turn the ribs, brush with more sauce, and bake, uncovered, for 40 minutes longer or until crispy and brown.

Dottie's Sweet and Sour Riblettes

Yield: 4 servings

With St. Louis–style ribs such as these, the brisket bones and hanging meat are removed from the bottom of the rib rack, making a cleaner rack that will cook evenly. This recipe comes from Dottie Anderson from Battle Creek, Mich.

1 cup (236 mL) packed dark brown sugar
¼ cup (59 mL) all-purpose flour
1 teaspoon (5 mL) salt
1 teaspoon (5 mL) dry mustard
½ teaspoon (2.5 mL) freshly ground black pepper
2 cups (473 mL) apple juice
¾ cup (177 mL) distilled white vinegar
½ cup (118 mL) soy sauce
¼ cup (59 mL) balsamic vinegar
2½–3 pounds (1.1–1.3 kg) St. Louis–cut pork spareribs, cut in half across the bones and into 2-rib pieces
2 tablespoons (30 mL) peanut oil
2 cloves garlic, peeled and chopped
3 tablespoons (45 mL) chopped fresh parsley

1. Preheat the barbecue to 350°F (180°C) to 400°F (200°C) for direct and indirect heating, making sure the grill has been well oiled or sprayed with grilling spray. Spray a large roasting pan with nonstick cooking spray.

2. In a large bowl, combine the brown sugar, flour, salt, dry mustard, and black pepper; stir in the apple juice, white vinegar, soy sauce, and balsamic vinegar and set aside.

3. Place the ribs on the grill and cook for 10 to 12 minutes, turning several times, until they are nicely browned.

4. Place the prepared roasting pan on the heated side of the grill or on a side burner. Add the oil and heat until it begins to smoke. Add the browned ribs, pour in the sauce mixture, and bring to a boil. Boil for 5 minutes and add the garlic.

5. Move the pan to the unheated side of the grill, close the vents to lower the temperature, and simmer for 1½ hours.

6. Transfer the contents to a deep serving dish, garnish with parsley, and serve with steamed or fried rice.

Smoked Pork Spareribs

Yield: 4 servings

I use a wonderful new product to provide smoke when I'm cooking on the bbq, they're called Smoke Bombs" and their available at most grocery or barbecue stores, or online at www.tailgatingplanks.com/smoke. Simply soak them in water for 10 minutes then place on hot coals.

2 tablespoons (30 mL) paprika
2 tablespoons (30 mL) chili powder
1 tablespoon (15 mL) brown sugar
1 tablespoon (15 mL) seasoned salt
1 tablespoon (15 mL) granulated garlic
1 tablespoon (15 mL) dried oregano
1 teaspoon (5 mL) ground cumin
½ teaspoon (2.5 mL) ground allspice
¼ teaspoon (1.25 mL) ground cloves
1 (2–2½ pounds [908 g–1.1 kg]) slab pork spareribs
2 cups (473 mL) apple juice
½ cup (118 mL) balsamic vinegar
¼ cup (59 mL) olive oil

1. In a small bowl, combine the paprika, chili powder, brown sugar, seasoned salt, garlic, oregano, cumin, allspice, and cloves and mix well. Set aside.

2. Trim the thin end meat from the ribs and reserve it for another use. Massage 2 to 3 tablespoons (30 to 45 mL) of the rub into the meat, using enough to cover all of the meat and rubbing most of it on the meaty side. Wrap the ribs in plastic wrap and refrigerate for 24 hours.

3. Preheat the barbecue to 220°F (105°C) to 240°F (115°C) for indirect heating, making sure the grill is sprayed or oiled well. Put a water pan under the unheated side of the grill. If cooking with charcoal place one mesquite and one cherry "Smoke Bomb" on the coals, or if using gas, place the bombs on a 12-inch (30-cm) square of heavy-duty aluminum foil, folding over the package, poking 3 or 4 holes in the top of the foil, and placing the package on open flame to add smoke to your grilling.

4. In a spray bottle, combine the apple juice, balsamic vinegar, and olive oil.

5. Place the ribs directly on the unheated portion of the grill, meaty side up. Make sure the ribs are not over or near flame or direct heat, otherwise they will burn. Smoke the ribs for 3 hours, spraying the ribs with the basting spray after the first hour of cooking and then every 30 minutes.

6. Turn the ribs and cook for 1 hour. Turn the ribs meaty side up again and cook for 70 to 80 minutes, spraying every 15 minutes. Check the ribs for doneness by lifting the meat at the center of the slab. It should bend and begin to split, and at least ½ inch (1 cm) of bones should be visible on the ends. If not, cook for 20 to 30 minutes more and check again. Wrap the ribs in foil, let them rest for 10 minutes, and serve.

Lemon-Herb Pork Loin

Yield: 6–8 servings

If you prefer orange to lemon, try using Tang breakfast drink in the herbal rub and grated orange zest instead of the lemon zest; squeeze half an orange over the meat.

1 (5–6 pound [2.3–2.7 kg]) boneless pork loin roast
1 lemon, quartered
¼ cup (59 mL) plus 3 tablespoons (45 mL) olive oil, divided
½ cup (118 mL) chopped fresh parsley, plus more for garnish
¼ cup (59 mL) minced onion
¼ cup (59 mL) grated lemon zest
1 tablespoon (15 mL) chopped fresh basil
2 teaspoons (10 mL) lemon salt
3 medium cloves garlic, peeled and mashed
¾ cup (177 mL) dry sherry
Lemon slices, for garnish

1. Using a sharp knife, score the fat on the loin well. Squeeze the lemon quarters over the meat and rub ¼ cup (59 mL) of the olive oil into the roast.

2. In a small bowl, combine the parsley, minced onion, lemon zest, basil, lemon salt, and garlic.

3. Put the pork on a 12-inch (30-cm) piece of aluminum foil and rub the herb mixture all over it. Seal the foil and refrigerate overnight.

4. Preheat the barbecue to 350°F (180°C) to 400°F (200°C) for direct heating, making sure the grill has been well oiled or sprayed with grilling spray.

5. Remove the pork from the refrigerator and let it stand at room temperature for 1 hour. Remove the foil. Brush the pork with remaining olive oil and grill over direct heat for 15 minutes, turning to braise all sides.

6. Once the meat is browned, place in a roasting pan or Dutch oven and cook for about 2½ hours, or until a meat thermometer inserted in thickest part of the roast registers 160°F (71°C). Remove the roast from the pan, cover it with foil, and let it rest for 15 minutes.

7. Pour the sherry into the roasting pan and stir to deglaze. Cook for 2 to 3 minutes, pour into a sauce boat, and serve at the table.

8. Carve the roast into ¼-inch (0.5-cm) slices, place them on a serving tray, garnish with fresh parsley and lemon slices, and serve.

Smoked Baby-Backs

Yield: 6–8 servings

You can use full pork ribs in this recipe; just double the time in the smoker.

5 pounds (2.3 kg) baby-back pork ribs
½ gallon (1.9 L) apple juice
1 tablespoon (15 mL) kosher salt
1 head garlic, separated into cloves, peeled, and mashed
2 cups (473 mL) smoky barbecue sauce
1 tablespoon (15 mL) granulated garlic
1 teaspoon (5 mL) cracked black pepper

1. Preheat a barbecue smoker to 225°F (110°C).

2. Cut the ribs into 3- to 4-rib portions and place them in a large pot. Pour in enough apple juice to cover, add the salt and mashed garlic cloves, cover the pot, and bring to a boil. Remove the pot from the heat and let it stand for 15 minutes. Transfer the ribs to a flat pan and reserve 2 cups (473 mL) of the apple juice.

3. Place the ribs in the smoker and smoke for 1⅓ to 2 hours, maintaining a temperature of about 220°F (105°C).

4. In a saucepan, whisk together the barbecue sauce and the reserved apple juice from the pot. Add the granulated garlic and cracked black pepper and stir to mix well. Heat over medium-high heat for 15 minutes. Baste the ribs with this sauce during their last 30 minutes in the smoker.

Pulled Pork with Root Beer Barbecue Sauce
Yield: 8–10 servings

You could substitute an alcoholic beer, or another soft drink for the root beer if you wish. The method of cooking is exactly the same.

1 (2½–3 pound [1.1–1.3 kg]) pork sirloin roast
1 tablespoon (15 mL) olive oil
½ teaspoon (2.5 mL) salt
½ teaspoon (2.5 mL) freshly ground black pepper
2 medium onions, peeled and thinly sliced, divided
4 cups (0.95 L) root beer, divided
2 tablespoons (30 mL) minced garlic
1 cup (236 mL) bottled chili sauce
½ teaspoon (2.5 mL) hot pepper sauce
Lettuce leaves, for serving
Tomato slices, for serving
10 hamburger buns, toasted

1. Preheat the barbecue to 375°F (190°C) to 425°F (220°C) for direct heating. Spray a Dutch oven or roasting pan with nonstick cooking or grilling spray.

2. Place the roast in the prepared Dutch oven or roasting pan. Brush the meat with the olive oil, season generously with salt and pepper, put the pan on the grill, and cook until all sides of the roast are browned, about 12 to 15 minutes.

3. Remove the pan from the heat and add half the onions, 1 cup (236 mL) of the root beer, and the garlic. Cover and cook on the grill for 2 to 3 hours.

4. While roast is cooking, combine the remaining root beer and the chili sauce in a deep saucepan. Bring to a boil; reduce the heat, and simmer, uncovered, stirring occasionally, for about 30 minutes, or until the sauce is reduced to 2 cups (473 mL). Add the hot pepper sauce and stir.

5. When a thermometer inserted into the thick part of the roast reads 160°F (71°C), transfer the meat to a deep pan and use two serving forks (or plastic bear claws) to pull the meat apart into shreds. Stir half of the sauce into the meat.

6. To serve, add lettuce leaves and tomato slices to the toasted buns and put a generous spoonful of pulled pork onto each bun. Top with the remaining onion slices. Serve the remaining sauce at the table.

Sugarcane Pork Loin

Yield: 4–8 servings

If you can't find sour oranges, you can substitute 2 parts sweet orange juice with 1 part fresh lemon juice and 1 part fresh lime juice. Likewise, soaked bamboo or metal skewers can be used if you can't find sugarcane—but try hard as the the the effect is worth it. Ask your grocery store produce manager, and I'll bet he or she can order whole sugar cane.

4 pounds (1.8 kg) pork loin, cut into 1½-inch (3.5-cm) cubes
2 large red onions, peeled and cut into 1-inch (2.5-cm) cubes
8 (8–10 inch [20–25 cm] long) sugarcane stalks, sharpened
1½ cups (354 mL) sour orange juice (Bergamot or Seville varieties)
½ cup (118 mL) olive oil
6 cloves garlic, peeled and minced
½ cup (118 mL) chopped fresh cilantro
1 jalapeño pepper, seeded
Salt, to taste
Freshly ground black pepper, to taste
1 small fresh pineapple, cut into ¼-inch (0.5-cm) slices
Fresh mint leaves, for garnish

1. Alternately skewer the pork and red onion cubes onto the sharpened sugarcane stalks. Place the skewers in a shallow glass dish and set aside.

2. In a medium bowl, whisk together the orange juice, olive oil, garlic, cilantro, and jalapeño pepper. Reserve ½ cup (118 mL) of this mixture for basting, and pour the remainder over the pork and onion skewers. Cover the skewers with plastic wrap and refrigerate for at least 1 hour, turning frequently.

3. Preheat the barbecue to 350°F (180°C) to 400°F (200°C) for direct heating, making sure the grill has been well oiled or sprayed with a grilling spray.

4. Pat the pork skewers dry, season well with salt and pepper, and place them on the grill over direct heat. Grill for approximately 4 minutes per side, turning once, until browned all over, brushing at the end with the reserved marinade.

5. Place skewers on a bed of sliced pineapple and garnish with the fresh mint leaves.

Rosemary–Garlic Grilled Pork Loin

Yield: 4–6 servings

For a smoky rosemary taste, soak an additional 3 to 4 sprigs of fresh rosemary in water for 30 minutes, put them on a double sheet of aluminum foil, and place on the hot coals to smoke while you're grilling the pork.

4 medium cloves garlic, peeled and minced
3 tablespoons (45 mL) chopped fresh rosemary
1 tablespoon (15 mL) garlic oil
1 teaspoon (5 mL) dried rosemary
1 teaspoon (5 mL) freshly ground black pepper
½ teaspoon (2.5 mL) kosher salt
1 (4–5 pound [1.8–2.3 kg]) boneless pork loin roast

1. In a small bowl, mix together the garlic, oil, fresh and dried rosemary, pepper, and salt, crushing the rosemary slightly with the spoon as you mix. Spread this mixture over the pork, covering the entire surface. Wrap the loin tightly in plastic wrap and refrigerate for 6 to 8 hours.

2. Remove the plastic wrap and let the pork rest for 20 to 25 minutes to come to room temperature.

3. Preheat the barbecue to 400°F (200°C) to 450°F (240°C) for direct and indirect heating, putting a water pan under the unheated side of the grill. Make sure the grill has been well oiled or sprayed with grilling spray.

4. Place the pork loin on the grill and cook until done. Pork loin can be pink and juicy inside and still be fully cooked, but it is important that the temperature reach 155°F (68°C).

5. Remove the pork from the grill, cover it with foil, and let it rest for 10 minutes before slicing. Serve the sliced loin on a bed of garlic mashed potatoes or cheese-onion grits.

Brazilian Roasted Pork Loin with Chili–Lime Sauce

Yield: 6–8 servings

This recipe also works well with pork shoulder, a rack of pork loin rib chops, or the newest barbecue sensation, pork neck meat roast.

5 jalapeño peppers, stemmed, seeded, and chopped
1 white onion, peeled and chopped
4 cloves garlic, peeled and chopped
¼ cup (59 mL) fresh parsley sprigs, stems removed
1 tablespoon (15 mL) plus 1 teaspoon (5 mL) kosher salt, divided
½ teaspoon (2.5 mL) ground cloves, divided
1 (4½–5 pound [2–2.3 kg]) bone-in pork loin roast (10 chops)
1 cup (236 mL) orange juice
½ cup (118 mL) freshly squeezed lime juice (from about 4 limes)
½ cup (118 mL) packed light brown sugar
1 tablespoon (15 mL) minced fresh ginger
½ teaspoon (2.5 mL) freshly ground black pepper

1. In a blender or food processor, combine the jalapeño peppers, the onions, the garlic, the parsley, 1 teaspoon (5 mL) of the salt, and ¼ teaspoon (1.25 mL) of the ground cloves and process until a paste forms. You'll end up with about ½ cup (118 mL) sauce. Refrigerate until ready to use.

2. In a saucepan over medium heat, combine the orange juice, lime juice, brown sugar, and ginger and stir and heat for 10 minutes to combine flavors.

3. Preheat the barbecue to 350°F (180°C) to 400°F (200°C) for direct heating, making sure the grill has been well oiled or sprayed with grilling spray. Grease a Dutch oven.

4. Place the roast, fat side up, on a cutting board and massage it with salt and pepper. Place it on the grill and brown well on all sides.

5. Remove the roast from the grill and put it in the refrigerator to cool for 20 minutes. Cover it with the paste and put it into the prepared Dutch oven. Return it to the grill and roast for 1½ to 2 hours, or until a thermometer inserted into the thickest part of the roast reads 160°F (71°C). Brush often with the orange-lime-sugar-ginger sauce.

6. Remove the roast from the barbecue, cover it with foil, and let it rest for 10 to 15 minutes. Slice and serve.

Bamberger Apricot Pork Loin Roast
Yield: 4–6

This dish was inspired by a barbecue cook in Bamberg, Germany, whom I met when we went there to film an episode for my Barbecue America: The World Tour *public TV series. It's probably one of the best pork dishes I've ever eaten.*

2 cups (473 mL) dried apricots
3 cups (708 mL) boiling water
1 tablespoon (15 mL) olive oil
1 (4–5 pound [1.8–2.3 kg]) pork loin roast
½ cup (118 mL) apricot nectar
2 medium potatoes, peeled and sliced
2 medium onions, peeled and sliced
1 tablespoon (15 mL) chopped fresh rosemary
½ teaspoon (2.5 mL) ground allspice
½ teaspoon (2.5 mL) kosher salt
¼ teaspoon (1.25 mL) freshly ground black pepper
⅛ teaspoon (0.6 mL) ground cloves
1½ teaspoons (7.5 mL) all-purpose flour
2 tablespoons (30 mL) dry sherry

1. Place the apricots in a bowl and cover them with the boiling water. Cover and let sit for 30 minutes. Drain and set aside.

2. Preheat the barbecue to 350°F (180°C) to 400°F (200°C) for direct heating. Oil or spray a Dutch oven or deep roasting pan.

3. In a cast-iron skillet, heat the oil. Add the pork and cook, turning to brown all sides. In a large bowl, mix together the soaked apricots, apricot nectar, potatoes, onions, rosemary, allspice, salt, pepper, and cloves and stir to mix.

4. Transfer the pork roast to the prepared Dutch oven or roasting pan and pour the apricot mixture around the meat. Cover and bake in the barbecue for 45 minutes, or until the pork is cooked and the vegetables are tender. Transfer the meat, vegetables, and apricots to a serving dish and cover.

5. Skim off as much fat as possible from the pan drippings. In a small bowl, combine the flour and sherry. Stir this mixture into the gravy and cook, scraping the browned bits from the bottom of the pan, until slightly thickened, about 5 minutes.

6. Carve the roast at the table and serve it with the potato-onion-apricot mixture and the gravy on the side.

Herbed Pork and Apples
Yield: 10–12 servings

You can substitute peaches, pears, nectarines, or large (seeded) plums for the apples in this recipe.

1 teaspoon (5 mL) dried sage
1 teaspoon (5 mL) dried thyme
1 teaspoon (5 mL) dried rosemary
1 teaspoon (5 mL) dried marjoram
1 teaspoon (5 mL) salt
1 teaspoon (5 mL) freshly ground black pepper
1 (6-pound [2.7 kg]) pork loin roast
4 medium pippin apples; cored and cut in chunks
1 large red onion, peeled and cut in chunks
3 tablespoons (45 mL) brown sugar
½ teaspoon (2.5 mL) ground cinnamon
½ teaspoon (2.5 mL) ground nutmeg
1 cup (236 mL) apple juice
⅔ cup (158 mL) pure maple syrup

1. In a small bowl, combine the sage, thyme, rosemary, marjoram, salt, and pepper. Massage this rub into the roast. Cover and refrigerate for several hours or overnight.

2. Preheat the barbecue to 350°F (180°C) to 400°F (200°C) for direct heating. Oil well or spray with nonstick cooking spray a roasting pan.

3. Place the meat in the prepared pan and bake, uncovered, for 1½ hours.

4. In a medium bowl, mix together the apples, onion, brown sugar, cinnamon, and nutmeg and pour this mixture around the roast. Cook for 1 hour, or until the internal temperature of the meat reaches 160°F (71°C).

5. Transfer the roast to a cutting board, cover it with foil, and keep it warm. Pour the apple and onion chunks onto a serving platter and cover with foil.

6. Skim the excess fat from the meat juices in the pan. Add the apple juice and maple syrup. Cook over the hot grill or on a side burner, stirring constantly, until the liquid has reduced to 1 cup (236 mL).

7. Uncover and slice the roast. Place it on a platter with the apples and onions and serve with the gravy.

Honey-Sesame Tenderloin
Yield: 4 servings

Sesame seeds may be the oldest condiment known to man, dating back to 1600 B.C. They add a nutty taste and a light crunch to foods and are reported to contain chemicals that help lower cholesterol.

1 (1½–2 pound [681–908 g]) pork tenderloin, split lengthwise
½ cup (118 mL) soy sauce
2 cloves garlic, peeled and minced
2 tablespoons (30 mL) dark sesame oil
1 tablespoon (15 mL) grated fresh ginger
1 teaspoon (5 mL) ground ginger
¼ cup (59 mL) honey
1 tablespoon (15 mL) brown sugar
¼ cup (59 mL) sesame seeds

1. Place the tenderloin in a 1- to 2-gallon (3.8- to 7.6-L) resealable plastic bag. Add the soy sauce, sesame oil, fresh ginger, and ground ginger, shake to combine all the ingredients and coat the tenderloin, seal the bag, and refrigerate overnight.

2. Remove the pork from the marinade. Pour the marinade into a saucepan and boil for 10 minutes while the pork comes to room temperature. Drain the meat and pat it dry with paper towels.

3. Preheat the barbecue to medium high (350°F [180°C] to 400°F [200°C]). Oil well or spray with nonstick cooking spray a roasting pan or Dutch oven.

4. In a wide, flat baking pan, mix together the honey and brown sugar. Place the sesame seeds in a similar dish. Roll the pork loin in the honey mixture, coating well, then roll it in the sesame seed, including both ends.

5. Place the pork loin in the prepared roasting pan or Dutch oven and roast for 20 to 30 minutes, or until a meat thermometer inserted into the center of the roast registers 160°F (71°C).

6. Transfer the meat to a serving platter, cover it, and let it rest for 15 minutes. Uncover and slice thinly to serve.

Balsamic Roast Pork Tenderloin with Cherry Salsa
Yield:10 servings

Seventy percent of all cherries produced in the United States come from Washington, Oregon, Idaho, and Utah. If you can't get fresh cherries, you can always find dried cherries in the dried fruit or produce section of your grocery store.

½ cup (118 mL) chopped onion
½ cup (118 mL) chopped red or yellow bell pepper
½ cup (118 mL) chopped green chili peppers
½ cup (118 mL) fresh Bing or Lambert cherries, pitted and chopped
½ cup (118 mL) barbecue sauce
½ cup (118 mL) cherry jam
1½ tablespoons distilled white vinegar
1½ tablespoons chopped fresh cilantro
1 (4–5 pound [1.8–2.3 kg]) pork loin roast
¼ cup (60 mL) balsamic vinegar
4 tablespoons (60 mL) extra virgin olive oil
8 cloves garlic, peeled and thinly sliced
1 tablespoon (15 mL) cracked black pepper
1 tablespoon (15 mL) granulated garlic
1 teaspoon (5 mL) kosher salt
Leaves of 4 sprigs fresh rosemary, finely chopped
Leaves of 4 sprigs fresh thyme, finely chopped

1. In a small bowl combine the onion, bell pepper, chili peppers, cherries, barbecue sauce, jam, white vinegar, and cilantro and mix well. Cover and refrigerate for several hours or overnight.

2. Coat the loin with the balsamic vinegar, rubbing the vinegar into the meat, then brush it with the extra virgin olive oil. Cut small slits in the roast and insert the slices of garlic into the slits.

3. Just before cooking, combine the black pepper, granulated garlic, salt, rosemary, and thyme and rub this mixture into the meat.

4. Preheat the barbecue to 350°F (180°C) to 400°F (200°C) for direct heating, making sure the grill has been well oiled or sprayed with grilling spray.

5. Place the roast on the grill and cook, turning every 15 to 20 minutes, for 20 minutes per pound (454 g), or until the internal temperature reaches 160°F (71°C).

6. Remove the roast from grill, cover it with aluminum foil, and let it rest for at least 10 minutes. Transfer it to a carving board, slice, and serve with the cherry salsa.

Cilantro and Brown Sugar–Seared Medallions

Yield: 6 servings

Do not handle the chilies with your bare hands. Instead, use plastic gloves or tongs. If you do touch the chilies, wash your hands immediately.

¼ cup (59 mL) loosely packed chopped fresh cilantro
¼ cup (59 mL) packed dark brown sugar
¼ cup (59 mL) extra virgin olive oil
4 cloves garlic, peeled and coarsely chopped
1 teaspoon (5 mL) salt
½ teaspoon (2.5 mL) paprika
½ cup (118 mL) butter, softened
2 tablespoons (30 mL) minced fresh cilantro
2 teaspoons (10 mL) minced, seeded serrano chile
3 pounds (1.3 mL) pork tenderloin medallions

1. In a food processor, combine the ¼ cup cilantro, brown sugar, oil, garlic, salt, and paprika and process for 1 minute, or until you get a thick, paste-like rub.

2. In a small bowl, mix together the butter, minced cilantro, and chile until well combined. Transfer the butter mixture to a piece of plastic wrap and use the wrap form a 3-inch (7.5-cm) long log. Freeze the log for 15 minutes or until firm enough to slice.

3. Preheat the barbecue to 350°F (180°C) to 400°F (200°C) for direct heating, making sure the grill has been well oiled or sprayed with grilling spray.

4. With your hands, rub ½ teaspoon (2.5 mL) of the cilantro-brown sugar mixture onto each side of each pork medallion. Grill the medallions, uncovered, on the hot grill for 4 to 6 minutes, turning halfway through the cooking time, until the internal temperature reaches 160°F (71°C).

5. Cut the serrano butter into ¼-inch (0.5-cm) thick slices. Place one butter pat on each pork medallion and continue heating just until the butter begins to melt.

6. Remove the pork medallions from the grill and serve immediately.

Bourbon and Honey Loin Kebabs

Yield: 4 servings

You can substitute gin, rum, Marsala wine, or your favorite liquor, wine, or beer for the bourbon.

½ cup (118 mL) bourbon
½ cup (118 mL) honey
½ cup (118 mL) dry mustard
1 teaspoon (5 mL) dried tarragon
3–4 sweet potatoes, cut into 24 (1-inch [2.5-cm]) cubes
4 medium ripe unpeeled peaches, pitted and quartered
1 (1–1½ pound [454–681 g]) boneless pork loin roast, cut into 24 (1-inch [2.5-cm]) cubes
4 green bell peppers, each cut into 8 pieces
1 medium Spanish onion, cut into 8 pieces
Olive oil for grilling

1. In a small bowl, mix together the bourbon, honey, mustard, and tarragon. Stir well and set aside.

2. Boil the sweet potatoes in 3 cups (708 mL) of water until crisp-tender.

3. Preheat the barbecue to 350°F (180°C) to 400°F (200°C) for direct heating, making sure the grill has been well oiled or sprayed with grilling spray.

4. Thread the sweet potato, alternating with the peach cubes, on 2 skewers, the pork on 4 skewers, and the bell peppers, alternating with the onions, on 2 skewers. Brush the pork and sweet potato kebabs with the honey glaze and grill all of the skewers for 5 minutes on each side or until thoroughly heated, basting both sides occasionally with glaze. They should all be ready at about the same time.

5. Remove the potatoes, peaches, pork, peppers and onions from the skewers. Put them in a warmed bowl and stir gently to mix. Place the bowl in the center of the table and serve with skewers so guests can skewer what they want out of the bowl.

Pork Piccata
Yield: 4 servings

Instead of the mayonnaise, you could use a creamy lemon salad dressing.

1 (1 pound [454 g]) pork tenderloin
¼ cup (59 mL) fresh breadcrumbs or panko
2 tablespoons (30 mL) freshly grated Parmigiano-Reggiano cheese
1 tablespoon (15 mL) butter
1 clove garlic, peeled and finely minced
½ cup (118 mL) light mayonnaise
2 tablespoons (30 mL) capers, drained
1 tablespoon (15 mL) heavy cream or milk
1 tablespoon (15 mL) lemon juice

1. Slice pork into ¾-inch (1.5-cm) thick slices. Put a sheet of plastic wrap over each slice and use a tenderizing mallet or other culinary weapon to pound them to ¼ inch (0.5 cm) thickness.

2. Preheat the barbecue to 350°F (180°C) to 400°F (200°C) for direct heating. Put a sheet of aluminum foil on the grill.

3. In a shallow baking dish, combine the breadcrumbs and cheese and stir to mix. Melt the butter, add the garlic, and pour this mixture into a shallow bowl or baking dish.

4. Brush the flattened tenderloins generously with mayonnaise, reserving the remaining mayonnaise. Press the tenderloins into the crumb and cheese mixture. Place the pork on the heated foil, drizzle with the garlic butter, and cook for 3 minutes. Turn, drizzle the second side with the garlic butter and cook for an additional 2 to 3 minutes, or until the pork is browned with a few crispy edges. Place the pork on a warmed serving tray and cover with foil.

5. In a small bowl, combine the remaining mayonnaise, capers, cream or milk, and lemon juice. Mix well and pour into a sauce boat. Ladle some of the sauce over the pork slices and serve, bringing the remaining sauce to the table for your guests to add.

6. Serve the piccata with rice and seasonal steamed or grilled vegetables.

Satay Stuffed Pork Loin

Yield: 6 servings

Given a pork loin and 15 minutes of lead time, I was called on to make up a pork dish at a culinary event several years ago. Since I was traveling in a mobile home, I found only peanut butter, peanuts, garlic, and some spices in the cupboard, and came up with this recipe. To this day, it's one of my favorite pork loin recipes.

1 (5–6 pound [2.3–2.8 kg]) boneless loin of pork
1 cup (236 mL) chunky peanut butter
½ cup (118 mL) packed dark brown sugar
¼ cup (59 mL) finely chopped unsalted peanuts
¼ cup 59 mL) dark sesame oil
3 tablespoons (45 mL) soy sauce
2 teaspoons (10 mL) minced garlic
¼ teaspoon (1.25 mL) dried thyme
⅛ teaspoon (0.6 mL) ground cloves
Salt, to taste
Freshly ground black pepper, to taste

1. Preheat the barbecue to 350°F (180°C) to 400°F (200°C) for direct heating. Spray with nonstick cooking spray or oil a roasting pan.

2. In a food processor, combine the peanut butter, brown sugar, peanuts, sesame oil, soy sauce, garlic, thyme, and cloves and pulse to a thick paste. Cut ½ inch (1 cm) into the length of the meat, then cut parallel to the outside surface all the way to the middle, unrolling the meat as you cut, until you have a ½-inch (1-cm) thick roast.

3. Spread the peanut mixture on the surface of the meat, covering it to within 1 inch (2.5 cm) of the edges. Roll up the roast lengthwise very tightly and tie it in 3 or 4 places with butcher string.

4. Salt and pepper the outside of the meat and place it in the prepared roasting pan. Cook for 1 to 1½ hours, or until the internal temperature reaches 160°F (71°C).

5. Transfer the meat to a large platter or cutting board, cover it with foil, and let it rest for 15 minutes. Remove the string, slice the roll into ½-inch (1-cm) thick slices, and serve.

Apricot Barbecued Pork Loin

Yield: 6 servings

To French your loin roast bones, cut and scrape the meat off 3 to 4 inches (7.5 to 10 cm) of the bone ends with a sharp knife, so the bones are completely exposed. You can put some fancy paper "panties" on the ends of the bones—we don't.

1 cup (236 mL) dried apricots, minced or finely diced
½ cup (118 mL) water
1 lemon, halved and seeded, ½ juiced, ½ quartered
1 teaspoon (5 mL) ground cinnamon
1 cup (236 mL) apricot nectar
3 tablespoons (45 mL) honey
2 tablespoons (30 mL) orange juice
1 (6-pound [2.8-kg]) bone-in pork loin roast, bone tips Frenched

1. In a medium saucepan, combine the dried apricots, water, lemon juice, and cinnamon and bring to a boil. Reduce the heat and simmer for 12 to 15 minutes, or until the apricots are tender. Add the apricot nectar, honey, and orange juice and simmer for 3 to 4 minutes.

2. Preheat the barbecue 350°F (180°C) to 400°F (200°C) for direct heating. Spray a roasting pan or Dutch oven with nonstick cooking spray.

3. Spread the glaze over the pork loin and cook, uncovered, in the prepared roasting pan or Dutch oven for 2 hours or 20 minutes per pound (454 g), or until a meat thermometer inserted in the thickest part of the meat registers 155°F (68°C). Baste the meat frequently with pan drippings.

4. Remove the roast from the pan, cover it in foil, and allow it to stand for 15 minutes. Pour the pan juices into a saucepan and bring to a boil, then reduce the heat and simmer for 4 to 5 minutes. Pour the sauce into a sauce boat to serve at the table.

Smoked Pork Loin in Pastry

Yield: 4–6 servings

Frozen puff pastry is nothing like frozen pie dough. It tastes terrific and has a beautiful texture. Working with frozen puff pastry dough is as easy as opening a can of refrigerated biscuits or cinnamon rolls.

1 (2½-pound [1.5-kg]) pork loin
Salt, to taste
Freshly ground black pepper, to taste
½ teaspoon (2.5 mL) paprika
½ teaspoon (2.5 mL) dried oregano
½ teaspoon (2.5 mL) garlic powder
¼ teaspoon (1.25 mL) five-spice powder
1 (2-sheet) package Pepperidge Farm puff pastry
½ cup (118 mL) butter, melted
1 egg white
2 tablespoons (30 mL) cold water

1. Preheat the barbecue to 400°F (200°C) to 450°F (220°C) for direct heating.

2. Season the tenderloin with salt and pepper. Grill for 15 to 20 minutes, or until the meat is browned all over. Remove it from the grill and let it cool. In a small bowl, mix together the paprika, oregano, garlic powder, and five-spice powder.

3. Place 1 sheet of puff pastry on a floured cutting board and place the tenderloin on the pastry. Brush the meat with the butter, and sprinkle it with the seasoning mix. Mix together the egg white and water and brush the edges of the pastry with this mixture. Fold the pastry over and seal it by pressing the edges together. Brush the top with the egg white mixture.

4. Place the pastry on a nonstick or well-sprayed baking sheet. Cook in the barbecue for about 40 minutes, or until the pastry is crisp and golden brown. Sprinkle cold water into the barbecue occasionally or place a metal cup or cleaned tin can filled with water in the barbecue to keep the moisture level up.

5. Remove the pan from the barbecue, place the pastry on a cutting board, cover with foil, and let rest for 5 minutes.

6. Serve with a favorite barbecue sauce on the side.

Maple-Mustard Glazed Pork Roast
Yield: 6 servings

Very little preparation and a relatively short cooking time make this a perfect last-minute dish for drop-in family, friends, or old school buddies.

⅔ cup (158 mL) pure maple syrup
3 tablespoons (45 mL) Dijon mustard
2 tablespoons (30 mL) apple cider vinegar
2 tablespoons (30 mL) dark soy sauce
Salt, to taste
Freshly ground black pepper, to taste
1 (2-pound [908-g]) boneless pork loin roast

1. Preheat the barbecue to 350°F (180°C) to 400°F (200°C) for direct heating.

2. In a small bowl, stir together the maple syrup, mustard, vinegar, soy sauce, salt, and pepper. Spread this mixture evenly over the pork roast and place the roast in a shallow pan. Roast until a meat thermometer inserted in the thickest part reads 160°F (71°C), about 45 minutes to 1¼ hours.

3. Remove the roast from the barbecue, cover it, and let it rest for 10 minutes before slicing and serving.

Pork Medallions with Raspberry Sauce
Yield: 10–12 servings

You could also prepare this recipe with apple slices, cherries, gooseberries, blackberries, or chopped apricots.

1 (8-pound [3.6-kg]) pork loin, cut into ½-inch (1-cm) medallions
1 teaspoon (5 mL) salt
1 teaspoon (5 mL) freshly ground black pepper
¼ cup (59 mL) peanut oil
2 cups (473 mL) raspberry jelly
1 cup (236 mL) raspberry vinegar
¾ cup (177 mL) pineapple juice
1 teaspoon (5 mL) dried tarragon
4 cups (0.95 L) fresh raspberries

1. Preheat the barbecue to 350°F (180°C) to 400°F (200°C) for direct heating.

2. Season the medallions with salt and pepper. In a large cast-iron skillet on the barbecue grill or on a side burner, heat the oil. Add the medallions and brown well on both sides. Drain and set aside.

3. Combine the jelly, vinegar, pineapple juice, and tarragon. Pour this mixture over the medallions in the skillet and simmer for 10 minutes. Turn the meat, cover the skillet, and simmer for 10 minutes, or until tender.

4. Using tongs, transfer the medallions to a heated serving platter. Add the raspberries to the sauce in the pan, stir once, pour the sauce over the meat on the platter, and serve immediately.

Pineapple and Prune-Stuffed Pork
Yield: 6–8 servings

You could also use apples, apricots, peaches, plums, raisins, nectarines, pears, or any combination of these fruits to stuff the pork.

1 (5–6 pound [2.3–2.8 kg]) boneless pork loin roast
1 cup (236 mL) chopped, drained pineapple
1 cup (236 mL) dried prunes, chopped
½ cup (118 mL) fresh breadcrumbs
¼ cup (59 mL) sesame oil
½ cup (118 mL) packed dark brown sugar
2 teaspoons (10 mL) minced fresh garlic
⅛ teaspoon (0.6 mL) ground cloves
½ cup (118 mL) pineapple juice
¼ cup (59 mL) prune juice
Salt, to taste
Freshly ground black pepper, to taste

1. Preheat the barbecue to 350°F (180°C) to 400°F (200°C) for direct heating. Oil or spray with nonstick cooking spray a roasting pan.

2. Cut ½ inch (1 cm) into the length of the meat, then cut parallel to the outside surface all the way to the middle, unrolling the meat as you cut, until you have a ½-inch (1-cm) thick roast.

3. Spread the pineapple, prunes, and breadcrumbs on the meat, leaving 1 inch (2.5 cm) at both sides uncovered. Drizzle with the sesame oil and sprinkle with the brown sugar, garlic, and cloves. Roll up lengthwise very tightly and tie in 3 or 4 places with butcher's string.

4. Mix together the pineapple and prune juices and set aside.

5. Place the roast in the prepared roasting pan and pour the fruit juices over the roast, salt and pepper the roast generously and cook in the barbecue for 1 to 1½ hours, or until the internal temperature reaches 160°F (71°C), basting often with the juice and meat drippings.

6. Transfer the meat to a large platter or cutting board, cover it with foil, and let it rest for 15 minutes. Remove the string and slice the roast into ½-inch (1-cm) slices.

Pork Wellington

Yield: 4 servings

Garam masala is a basic blend of ground spices common in Indian and South Asian cuisines. It is used alone or with other seasonings. Garam (meaning "hot") refers to the spice intensity, not the heat. Garam masala is pungent, but it is not "hot" like chili peppers. It is available at most grocery stores.

½ cup (118 mL) olive oil
2 tablespoons (30 mL) garam masala
1 tablespoon (15 mL) minced garlic
1 (5-pound [2.3-kg], 2-piece) pork tenderloin, each piece cut in half (not split) so thin end is alongside thicker end
½ cup (118 mL) plus 2 tablespoons (30 mL) butter, divided
1 cup (236 mL) diced Granny Smith apples, peeled or unpeeled
½ cup (118 mL) chopped dried apricots
½ cup (118 mL) dried cranberries
½ cup (118 mL) diced onion
¼ cup (59 mL) water
1 tablespoon (15 mL) sugar
2 teaspoons (10 mL) curry powder
20 (9 × 14–inch [22.5 × 35-cm]) sheets phyllo dough

1. In a small bowl, combine the oil, garam masala, and garlic and mix well. Marinate the pork in this mixture for 1 hour. Sear the pork and refrigerate it for 15 minutes.

2. In a large skillet, melt 2 tablespoons (30 mL) of the butter. Add the apples, apricots, cranberries, and onion and sauté for 2 to 3 minutes. Add the water, sugar, and curry powder and simmer until all the water has evaporated. Cool this mixture in the refrigerator for 1 hour.

3. Preheat the barbecue to 350°F (180°C) to 400°F (200°C).

4. Melt the remaining butter. On a baking sheet, layer 5 sheets of phyllo, brushing each with melted butter. Spread ¼ cup (59 mL) of the fruit mixture along the edge of the pastry, place 1 piece of tenderloin on top of the fruit, and roll up as a strudel. Place the roll seam side down on another baking sheet, score the top, and brush with melted butter. Repeat with the remaining pork loin and phyllo.

5. Bake in the barbecue for 30 to 40 minutes, or until the pastry is golden brown. Let rest, covered, for 5 minutes, and serve.

Dr. Tom's Cedar-Plank Pork Tenderloins
Yield: 4–6 servings

Dr. Thomas Kovaric of Vancouver, Wash., is a cardiologist and interventional cardiologist, a foodie, and, unfortunately for people like me, skinny as a rail. He is my cardiologist and is responsible for my being alive today. He loves to cook and shared this recipe with me one day, just before my cardiology rehab class.

½ cup (118 mL) hoisin sauce
¼ cup (59 mL) rice wine vinegar
¼ cup (59 mL) packed brown sugar
1 tablespoon (15 mL) sesame oil
1 tablespoon (15 mL) soy sauce
2 large cloves garlic, peeled and crushed
1½ teaspoons (7.5 mL) grated fresh ginger
½ teaspoon (2.5 mL) cracked black peppercorns
2 (¾–1 pound [336–454 g]) pork tenderloins

1. Soak a Chef Locke cedar plank in water for 8 hours.

2. In a medium saucepan, combine the hoisin sauce, vinegar, brown sugar, sesame oil, soy sauce, garlic, ginger, and peppercorns and cook over medium heat for 4 to 5 minutes. Remove from the heat and cool slightly. Reserve ½ cup (118 mL) of the sauce for serving.

3. Place the tenderloins in a 1- to 2-gallon (3.8- to 7.6-L) resealable plastic bag and pour in the remaining sauce. Shake to coat the meat, seal the bag, and refrigerate for 2 to 3 hours. Remove the meat from the marinade and let it rest for 10 minutes.

4. Preheat the barbecue to 350°F (180°C) to 400°F (200°C) for direct heating. Place the soaked plank on the grill for 3 minutes. Have a spray bottle of water handy to douse any flare-ups once the meat is cooking.

5. Flip the plank over with tongs and place the tenderloins side by side on the hot plank. Close the lid and grill for 15 to 20 minutes, or until the pork reaches an internal temperature of 150°F (65°C).

6. Remove the tenderloins from the plank, cover them with foil, and let them rest for 5 to 8 minutes. Slice and serve with the reserved sauce.

Hawaiian Pork Loin

Yield: 6–8 servings

If you have a juicer and can make fresh pineapple juice from a whole pineapple, this recipe soars into the heavens. Concentrated juices are okay, but the taste of really fresh pineapple makes this recipe resonate.

1 (4–5 pound [1.8–2.3 kg]) bone-in pork loin roast
1 large yellow onion, peeled, thinly sliced, slices cut in half
1 (6-ounce [168-g]) can frozen pineapple-orange juice concentrate, thawed
⅓ cup (79 mL) soy sauce
⅓ cup (79 mL) chopped green onion, green and white parts
1 teaspoon (5 mL) lemon salt
Freshly ground black pepper, to taste
1 (12-ounce [336-g]) can mandarin oranges, drained

1. Preheat the barbecue to 350°F (180°C) to 400°F (200°C) for direct heating.

2. Place the roast, fat side up, on a rack in a roasting pan. With a sharp knife, make several 2- to 3-inch (5- to 7.5-cm) deep cuts into the meat between each chop. Put a half-slice of onion into each slit.

3. In a small bowl, combine the pineapple-orange juice concentrate, soy sauce, green onions, lemon salt, and pepper. Spoon half of the liquid over the pork. Roast in the barbecue for 1 hour and 30 minutes, brushing often with the remaining sauce, until a meat thermometer registers 155°F (68°C) and the pork is richly glazed and browned.

4. Remove the roast from the barbecue, cover with foil, and let rest for 15 minutes. Place the roast on a serving platter to slice at the table, garnished with the mandarin orange segments.

Annie's Pork Tenderloin

Yield: 4–6 servings

Annie Browne Goodwin of Indianapolis, Ind., is a veterinarian, mother of twins, wife of the second-best grilled-cheese-sandwich cook on earth, and, most importantly, my niece. She loves food, loves to cook, and is one of the bright spots on the earth today. Her smile brightens any room and her laugh cheers everyone who hears it.

1 cup (236 mL) dry red wine
½ cup (118 mL) cognac
½ cup (118 mL) Madeira
1 bay leaf
½ teaspoon (2.5 mL) dried rosemary
½ teaspoon (2.5 mL) dried thyme
Salt, to taste
Freshly ground black pepper, to taste
1 (3½-pound [1.5-kg]) pork loin roast
1 (10-ounce [280-g]) jar orange marmalade
1 cup (236 mL) Dijon mustard
½ cup (118 mL) butter, melted
Ground white pepper, to taste
1 large onion, peeled and sliced
2 tablespoons (30 mL) all-purpose flour

1. In a 1- to 2-gallon (3.8- to 7.6-L) resealable plastic bag, mix together the red wine, cognac, Madeira, bay leaf, rosemary, thyme, salt, and pepper. Add the pork loin, and marinate in the refrigerator for at least 24 hours.

2. Remove pork from the marinade. Pour the marinade into a saucepan and boil for 10 minutes while the pork roast comes to room temperature. In a small bowl, combine the marmalade, mustard, butter, salt, to taste, and white pepper and set aside.

3. Preheat the barbecue to 400°F (200°C) to 450°F (220°C) for direct heating. Oil or spray with nonstick spray a Dutch oven.

4. Cover both sides of the meat with the mustard glaze. Place the meat in the prepared Dutch oven with the onion slices and add ½ cup (118 mL) water. Place the pot in the barbecue and cook for 1 hour. Remove the pork, add the flour and half of the reserved marinade, and stir to combine. Return the pork to the pan and cook for another 30 minutes, basting often with the sauce/drippings.

5. Transfer the meat to a platter, cover it with foil, and let it rest for 20 minutes. Slice the pork and serve it with the remaining marinade.

Pecan and Walnut Crusted Pork

Yield: 6–8 servings

If you prefer, you could substitute any other nuts, such as chopped hazelnuts and peanuts, for the pecans and walnuts, or use coarsely chopped breadcrumbs instead of any nuts. This recipe comes from Milan Chuckovich from Boise, Idaho.

1 cup (236 mL) chopped fresh mango
¼ cup (59 mL) finely chopped red bell pepper
1 green onion, green and white parts, thinly sliced
2 tablespoons (30 mL) lime juice
½ jalapeño pepper, seeded and minced
1 tablespoon (15 mL) chopped fresh cilantro
3 tablespoons (45 mL) packed dark brown sugar
2 teaspoons (10 mL) chopped fresh rosemary leaves
2 teaspoons (10 mL) minced garlic
¼ teaspoon (1.25 mL) dried thyme
⅛ teaspoon (0.6 mL) ground cloves
Salt, to taste
Freshly ground black pepper, to taste
¼ cup (59 mL) olive oil, divided
1 (5–6 pound [2.3–2.8 kg]) boneless pork loin roast
¼ pound (112 g) pecan halves, finely chopped
¼ cup (59 mL) walnut halves, finely chopped

1. In a small bowl, combine the mango, bell pepper, green onion, lime juice, jalapeño pepper, and cilantro and mix well. Cover this salsa and store it at room temperature.

2. In a food processor, combine brown sugar, rosemary, garlic, thyme, cloves, salt, pepper, and 1 tablespoon (15 mL) of the olive oil and pulse until you have a thick paste. Massage this paste onto the pork loin, covering it completely. Wrap the pork in plastic and refrigerate overnight.

3. Pour the remaining olive oil into a spray bottle. Mist the pork loin with it, taking care not to disturb the marinating paste. In a shallow bowl, combine the pecans and walnuts. Roll the loin in the nut mixture.

4. Prepare a water smoker or barbecue for smoke cooking. Place the meat, fat side up, on the grill, cover, and smoke-cook at a temperature between 200°F (100°C) to 250°F (120°C). Cook for 3 to 6 hours, adding briquettes, wood, and water as needed. The meat is done when its internal temperature reaches 150°F (65°C) to 155°F (68°C).

5. Transfer the meat to a large platter or cutting board, cover it with foil, and let it rest for 15 minutes before slicing. Serve the salsa on the side.

Mexican Seville-Orange Pork
Yield: 6 servings

To substitute for 1½ cup (354 mL) Seville orange juice, combine 1 teaspoon (5 mL) finely grated grapefruit zest, 3 tablespoons (45 mL) sweet orange juice, 3 tablespoons (45 mL) grapefruit juice, and 2 tablespoons (30 mL) lemon juice.

3½–4½ pounds (1.6–2 kg]) bone-in pork loin roast, untrimmed
1 tablespoon (15 mL) plus ½ teaspoon (5 mL) salt, divided
1 cup (236 mL) plus 4 tablespoons (60 mL) Seville orange juice, divided
½ cup (118 mL) minced onion
3 habañero chilies, minced
¼ cup (59 mL) chopped cilantro
½ teaspoon (2.5 mL) sugar
1 tablespoon (15 mL) achiote seeds
¼ teaspoon (1.25 mL) cumin seeds
¼ teaspoon (1.25 mL) dried oregano
12 black peppercorns
¼ teaspoon (1.25 mL) ground allspice
4 cloves garlic, peeled
⅛ teaspoon (0.6 mL) hot paprika
12–20 flour or corn tortillas, warmed

1. Rub the pork with 2 teaspoons (10 mL) of the salt and ⅔ cup (158) of the orange juice and set it aside.

2. In a small bowl, combine the onion, habañero, cilantro, sugar, ½ teaspoon (2.5 mL) of the remaining salt, and ⅓ cup (79 mL) of the remaining orange juice and stir well. Set aside.

3. In a spice grinder or a clean coffee grinder, grind together the achiote seeds, cumin, oregano, black peppercorns, and allspice to a fine powder. In a mortar or sturdy metal bowl, mash the garlic with the paprika and remaining salt. Pour this mixture into a small bowl, add the remaining orange juice and the powdered spices, and stir to a thick paste. Coat the pork with the paste, wrap it carefully in plastic wrap, and refrigerate for 6 to 8 hours or overnight.

4. Preheat the barbecue to 300°F (150°C) to 350°F (180°C) for direct heating. Place the roast on a rack at the bottom of a Dutch oven or roasting pan and cover with a tight fitting lid. Cook for 2½ hours. Turn the meat over and baste it with the juices at the bottom of the pot. Cook for another 2½ hours, basting frequently, until the meat is soft and falling off the bone.

5. With 2 serving forks or barbecue bear claws, shred the meat and place it in a serving bowl. Pour the fat and juices from the pan over the meat. Serve hot with the tortillas and the salsa, so that each person can make his or her own fajitas.

Port Pork Loin

Yield: 4–6 servings

Do not use a 30-year-old port wine in this recipe. Get a good, inexpensive port from the supermarket and use that for the roast. Spending a lot of money for a premium wine and then diluting its subtle flavors and nuances with onions and seasonings makes no economic or culinary sense.

2 teaspoons (10 mL) granulated garlic
1 (2½–3 pound [1.1–1.3 kg]) pork loin, boned, rolled, and tied
Kosher salt, to taste
Freshly ground black pepper, to taste
¼ cup (60 mL) unsalted butter
4 medium onions, peeled and quartered
1 cup (236 mL) ruby port
¾ cup (177 mL) beef stock
1 teaspoon (5 mL) cornstarch
Paprika, for garnish
Chopped fresh parsley, for garnish

1. Preheat the barbecue to 350°F (180°C) to 400°F (200°C) for direct and indirect heating, putting a water pan under the unheated side of the grill.

2. With your hands, rub the granulated garlic all over the pork loin. Sprinkle with salt and pepper. Place a Dutch oven on the heated part of the grill, add the butter, and heat until it melts. Add the pork loin and brown on all sides. Add the onions, pour the port and beef stock over the meat and onions, and bake for 30 minutes, basting frequently with the liquid in the pan.

3. Move the Dutch oven to the unheated side of the barbecue and bake for 1 hour. When a meat thermometer registers an internal temperature of 155°F (68°C), the meat is done.

4. Transfer the pork to a cutting board, cover it with foil, and let it rest for 10 to 15 minutes. Remove the onion halves with a slotted spoon and keep them warm. Meanwhile, boil the pan juices over low heat, until the gravy has reduced by half, add the cornstarch, and stir to blend and thicken.

5. Slice the pork, arrange it on a heated platter, and surround the meat with the onions. Sprinkle with the paprika and parsley and serve with the gravy in a sauce boat.

Jamaican Jerk Tenderloin
Yield: 4 servings

To make your own toasted coconut, spread flaked or shredded coconut on a baking sheet and toast it at 300°F (150°C) in the barbecue or oven for 5 to 10 minutes, or until lightly golden. Let cool and set aside.

1 (1½–2 pound [681–908 g]) pork tenderloin, cut in 4 pieces
6 tablespoons (90 mL) butter, melted, divided
½ teaspoon (2.5 mL) garlic salt
¼ teaspoon (1.25 mL) freshly ground black pepper
1 large onion, peeled and thinly sliced
2 cloves garlic, peeled
2 large tomatoes, quartered
1 small habañero chile, seeded and finely minced
¼ teaspoon (1.25 mL) ground allspice
⅛ teaspoon (0.6 mL) ground cinnamon
1 bay leaf
4 slightly green bananas
2 tablespoons (30 mL) all-purpose flour
1 tablespoon (15 mL) lemon juice
4 tablespoons (60 mL) shredded or flaked coconut, toasted

1. Preheat the barbecue to 350°F (180°C) to 400°F (200°C) for direct heating, making sure the grill has been well oiled or sprayed with grilling spray. Spray a roasting pan with nonstick cooking spray.

2. Brush the pork tenderloin pieces with 3 tablespoons (45 mL) of the melted butter and season with the garlic salt and pepper. Place the pork on the hot grill and sear all sides, 2 minutes per side.

3. With tongs, transfer the browned tenderloins to the prepared roasting pan. Add onion and garlic cook on the grill, stirring, until the onion is browned. With tongs, transfer the browned tenderloins to the prepared roasting pan. Add the tomatoes, habanero pepper, allspice, cinnamon, and bay leaf. Cover and bake for 25 minutes, or until the sauce is bubbling and a meat thermometer inserted into the meat registers 150°F (65°C).

4. Remove the meat from the pan, cover it with foil, and let it rest for 5 minutes. Pour the onion-tomato mixture onto a serving tray and keep it warm.

5. Slice the bananas in half lengthwise. In a large, nonstick skillet, heat the remaining butter. Roll the bananas in the flour, add them to the skillet, and cook until brown, sprinkling them with the lemon juice as they cook.

6. To serve, place the pork tenderloins on top of the vegetables in the platter, arrange the bananas around the sides of the platter, and sprinkle with toasted coconut.

Pork Reuben Burgers

Yield: 8 servings

This makes a delightful party burger served with German potato salad, grilled corn, and lots of very cold beer.

2 pounds (908 g) ground pork
1 teaspoon (5 mL) salt
Freshly ground black pepper, to taste
1 clove garlic, peeled and minced
½ cup (118 mL) chopped sauerkraut, drained
8 slices Swiss cheese
8 rye hamburger buns, split and toasted
1½ cups (354 mL) Thousand Island dressing

1. Preheat the barbecue to 350°F (180°C) to 400°F (200°C) for direct heating, making sure the grill has been well oiled or sprayed with grilling spray.

2. In a large bowl, combine the pork, salt, pepper, and garlic and mix well but gently with a fork. Shape this mixture into 16 thin patties. Spoon 1 tablespoon (15 mL) of sauerkraut into the center of 8 of the patties, top each with a second patty, and press the edges together to seal.

3. Grill the burgers for 5 to 6 minutes on each side, or until the pork is thoroughly cooked but not dry. Top each patty with a slice of cheese. Spread the buns with Thousand Island dressing, add a burger to each, and serve immediately.

Barbecued Pork Kebabs

Yield: 8 servings

Cut cantaloupe and honeydew melon into 1½-inch (3.5-cm) cubes and alternate on two skewers. Grill for 2 to 3 minutes, basting with the marinade, and serve alongside the pork.

¾ cup (177 mL) sugar
¾ cup (177 mL) dark soy sauce
¾ cup (177 mL) diced onion
2 teaspoons (10 mL) minced garlic
1 teaspoon (5 mL) grated fresh ginger
2 green onions, minced, green and white parts
¾ teaspoon (3.75 mL) freshly ground black pepper
3¼ pounds (1.5 kg) boneless pork loin, cut into 1½-inch (3.5-cm) cubes

1. In a large bowl, whisk together the sugar, soy sauce, onion, garlic, ginger, green onions, and black pepper. Add the pork and toss to coat. Pour the pork and marinade into a 1- to 2-gallon (3.8- to 7.6-L) resealable plastic bag, seal, and refrigerate for at least 2 hours or overnight.

2. Preheat the barbecue to 350°F (180°C) to 400°F (200°C) for direct heating, making sure the grill has been well oiled or sprayed with grilling spray.

3. Remove the pork from the marinade. Pour the marinade into a sauce-pan and boil for 10 minutes while the meat comes to room temperature.

4. Thread the pork onto 8 metal skewers and place the skewers on the grill. Cook, brushing several times with the marinade, until the pork is no longer pink in the center, 3 to 5 minutes per side.

Grilled Miso Pork Strips
Yield: 4 servings

Mirin is a sweet Japanese rice wine. Miso is a paste, with a peanut butter–like con-sistency, made from fermented soybeans. Both are indispensible to Japanese cooks.

2 tablespoons (30 mL) miso
1 tablespoon (15 mL) sake
2 teaspoons (10 mL) soy sauce
2 teaspoons (10 mL) sugar
2 teaspoons (10 mL) mirin
1 teaspoon (5 mL) dark sesame oil
1 pound (454 g) boneless pork loin, cut into 4 × 1 × ½-inch (10 × 2.5 × 1-cm) strips

1. In a 1- to 2-gallon (3.8- to 7.6-L) resealable plastic bag, combine the miso, sake, soy, sugar, mirin, and sesame oil. Add the pork strips, shake to coat the meat with the marinade, and refrigerate overnight.

2. Preheat the barbecue to 400°F (200°C) to 450°F (220°C) for direct heating, making sure the grill has been well oiled or sprayed with grilling spray.

3. Remove the meat from the marinade and let it come to room tempera-ture, about 20 minutes. Place the strips on the hot grill and cook for about 2 to 3 minutes per side. Transfer the pork to a heated platter and serve with steamed rice and grilled green beans.

French Canadian Pork Pie
Yield: 4 servings

This pie is a French Canadian Christmas eve tradition I remember from the time I lived in Montreal, Québec. They make their pie crust with lard, which gives you the best, flakiest, tastiest crust ever, but we're opting for refrigerated pie crusts here.

1 pound (454 g) lean ground pork
1 pound (454 g) lean ground beef
½ cup (118 mL) water
1 medium onion, peeled and chopped
1 clove garlic, peeled and minced
¾ teaspoon (3.75 mL) salt
½ teaspoon (2.5 mL) dried savory
½ teaspoon (2.5 mL) dried thyme
¼ teaspoon (1.25 mL) freshly ground black pepper
⅛ teaspoon (0.6 mL) ground cloves
Refrigerated dough for double-crust 9-inch (22.5-cm) pie
1 tablespoon (15 mL) milk
1 egg yolk

1. Preheat the barbecue to 400°F (200°C) to 450°F (220°C) for direct heating.

2. In a saucepan, combine the pork, beef, water, onion, garlic, salt, savory, thyme, pepper, and cloves. Cook over medium heat, stirring occasionally, until the mixture comes to a boil. Reduce the heat and simmer until the meat is cooked, about 5 minutes.

3. Roll and fit the pastry into an aluminum foil pie pan and with a slotted spoon, spoon the meat mixture into the pie crust. Add the top crust and pinch the edges to seal. Cut slits in top crust so steam can escape. Cover the edges of the pie with strips of aluminum foil to prevent the edges from burning. In a small bowl, combine the milk and egg yolk. Brush the crust with this mixture.

4. Bake for 20 minutes, remove the foil, and bake for an additional 15 to 20 minutes, or until the entire crust is golden brown.

5. Let cool for 10 minutes before slicing and serving.

Four-Times Pork Meatloaf

Yield: 8–10 servings

If you like pork and/or bacon, this is the perfect meatloaf for you. Loaded with four kinds of pork, this is not a diet dish, but it sure is delicious. You can also refrigerate it, slice it, and layer the slices with mayonnaise, tomatoes, and a slice or two of Swiss cheese for sandwiches.

2 green bell peppers, finely chopped
2 medium onions, peeled and finely chopped
¼ cup (59 mL) diced celery
¼ cup (59 mL) diced carrots
2 large eggs, lightly beaten
1 pound (454 g) ground pork
1 pound (454 g) bulk sausage meat
½ pound (227 g) Canadian bacon, chopped
¼ pound (112 g) hickory smoked bacon, cooked and crumbled
1 cup (236 mL) rolled oats
½ teaspoon (2.5 mL) salt
½ teaspoon (2.5 mL) black pepper
½ teaspoon (2.5 mL) garlic powder
¼ teaspoon (1.25 mL) onion powder
1 cup (236 mL) ketchup
½ cup (118 mL) bottled chili sauce
1 tablespoon (15 mL) dark brown sugar
1 pinch ground cloves

1. Preheat the barbecue to 350°F (180°C) to 400°F (200°C) for direct heating. Spray 2 loaf pans with nonstick cooking spray.

2. In a large bowl, combine the peppers, onions, celery, carrots, eggs, ground pork, sausage, Canadian bacon, crumbled bacon, rolled oats, salt, pepper, garlic powder, and onion powder. Mix gently but thoroughly and divide the mixture among the prepared loaf pans.

3. In a small bowl, combine the ketchup, chili sauce, brown sugar, and cloves and stir to mix. Spoon this mixture over the meatloaves, place the pans in the barbecue, and bake for 90 minutes, or until they are cooked all the way through. The topping should be bubbling.

4. Remove the meatloaves from the barbecue, cover, and let cool for 10 minutes before serving.

Pork Meatballs with Cranberry Barbecue Glaze
Yield: 6–8 servings

Cranberries? On pork? You bet. The tart-sweet flavor of the cranberries works well with the herbed pork meatballs and offers a flavor profile that will surprise you.

2 tablespoons (30 mL) butter
½ cup (118 mL) minced onion
1 cup (236 mL) ketchup
1 cup (236 mL) fresh cranberries, chopped
2 tablespoons (30 mL) brown sugar
2 tablespoons (30 mL) distilled white vinegar
1 tablespoon (15 mL) Worcestershire sauce
1 tablespoon (15 mL) prepared mustard
1½ pounds (681 g) ground pork
¼ cup (59 mL) onion
¼ cup (59 mL) celery
¼ cup (59 mL) fresh breadcrumbs
1 large egg, well beaten
¼ cup (59 mL) whole cranberry sauce
½ teaspoon (2.5 mL) dried thyme
½ teaspoon (2.5 mL) ground cumin

1. In a skillet, melt the butter. Add the ½ cup minced onion and sauté until tender. Add the ketchup, cranberries, brown sugar, vinegar, Worcestershire sauce, and mustard and simmer for 20 minutes. Cover and set aside.

2. Preheat the barbecue to 350°F (180°C) to 400°F (200°C) for direct heating. Spray a roasting pan with nonstick cooking spray.

3. In a large bowl, combine the pork, celery, onion, breadcrumbs, egg, cranberry sauce, thyme, and cumin. Mix well with your hands. Roll the mixture into 1½-inch (3.5-cm) balls.

4. Place the meatballs in the prepared roasting and bake for 20 minutes. Drain off the fat, pour the cranberry barbecue sauce over the meat, and bake for an additional 25 minutes, or until the meat is cooked through and the sauce is bubbling nicely.

Ham and Coke

Yield: 6–8 servings

If you know you're dealing with a salty ham, put in a pan and cover with cold water, bring to a boil, then pour off the liquid. Rinse the ham in hot water and place it in a colander to drain. You can, if you wish, use a different cola in this recipe.

1 (4–5 pound [1.8–2.3 kg]) bone-in ham
2 medium onions, peeled and quartered
1 (2-L) bottle Coke
1 handful cloves
½ cup (118 mL) mustard-based barbecue sauce of your choice
2 tablespoons (30 mL) brown sugar
2 tablespoons (30 mL) molasses
2 teaspoons (10 mL) dry mustard
¼ teaspoon (1.25 mL) ground cloves

1. Put the ham in a deep stock pot or roasting pan over a side burner or stovetop burner, flat side down. Add the onion, then pour the cola over the ham. The ham should be at least three-quarters covered; if not, add more cola. Bring to a boil, reduce the heat, and simmer, loosely covered, for 2½ hours. If ham is too tall for the lid, cover the pot with aluminum foil.

2. Preheat the barbecue to 475°F (230°C) to 525°F (275°C) for direct heating. Line a shallow roasting pan with aluminum foil.

3. Remove the ham from the pot, reserving the braising liquid, and place it in the foil-lined pan. Let it cool for 15 minutes, then use a sharp knife to cut off the tough skin, leaving a thin layer of fat. Score the fat with a sharp knife to make fairly large diamond shapes, and stud each diamond with a whole clove.

4. In a small bowl, mix together the barbecue sauce, brown sugar, molasses, mustard, and ground cloves and stir well. Spread the barbecue sauce mixture over the ham, taking care not to dislodge the cloves. Cook for approximately 20 to 25 minutes, or until the glaze is browned and bubbly.

5. While ham is baking, pour the braising liquid into a large saucepan, removing and reserving the onions. Boil liquid until it reduces by two-thirds.

6. Remove ham from the pan, cover it loosely with foil, and let it rest for 20 minutes. Slice the ham, put the slices on a serving platter, drizzle with the reduced braising liquid, and garnish with the cooked onions.

Bavarian Roasted Picnic Ham

Yield: 10–12 servings

Picnic hams are often treated like hams. ut it you treat and cook them like pork roasts, you'll end up with a delightful, moist roast with a pork loin-like texture and color. This recipe comes from Chef Lothar Stiller from Munich, Germany.

1 (8–10 pound [3.6–4.5 kg]) fresh picnic ham, rind removed
Kosher salt, to taste
⅛ teaspoon (0.6 mL) freshly ground black pepper, plus more, to taste
12 whole cloves
2 cloves garlic, peeled and minced
1 cup (236 mL) apple brandy, divided
1½ cups (354 mL) apple cider, divided
½ cup (118 mL) honey
½ cup (118 mL) packed brown sugar
2 teaspoons (10 mL) cider vinegar
1 teaspoon (5 mL) dry mustard
3½ cups (614 g) gingersnap crumbs, divided
⅔ cup (158 mL) heavy cream
1 teaspoon (5 mL) grated fresh ginger
½ teaspoon (2.5 mL) salt
⅛ teaspoon (0.6 mL) ground cinnamon
⅛ teaspoon (0.6 mL) ground nutmeg

1. Preheat the barbecue to 425°F (220°C) to 475°F (250°C) for direct and indirect heating, putting a water pan under the unheated side of the grill.

2. Place the picnic ham fat side up on a rack in large shallow roasting pan. Sprinkle with the kosher salt and pepper. Score the fat in diamonds and stud each diamond with a whole clove. Put the pan in the barbecue and cook for 20 minutes. Move the pan to the indirect side and close the barbecue vents.

3. Spread the minced garlic over the ham. In a small bowl, mix together ½ cup (118 mL) of the brandy and ½ cup (118 mL) of the cider. Baste the ham with the cider mixture every 15 minutes for 2 hours. In a medium bowl, mix together the honey, brown sugar, vinegar, and mustard, and spread this mixture over the top of the ham. Roast for 20 minutes. Press 1½ cups (177 mL) of the gingersnap crumbs into the top of the ham. Roast, basting with the pan juices, for 20 minutes. Press 1½ cups (354 mL) of the remaining gingersnap crumbs into the top of the ham.

4. Continue to roast the ham, basting frequently with pan juices, until a thermometer inserted into it reads 155°F (68°C), about 45 minutes. Cover the ham with aluminum foil if the topping gets too brown.

5. Transfer the ham to a serving platter; cover it, and keep it warm. Deglaze the pan with the remaining brandy and cider. Strain the pan juices into a small saucepan and add the remaining gingersnap crumbs, the fresh ginger, salt, 1/8 teaspoon (0.6 mL) of the pepper, the cinnamon, and the nutmeg. Cook over low heat, stirring constantly, until thickened, about 10 minutes. Slice the ham and serve it with the sauce on the side.

Smoked Ham Steak

Yield: 4 servings

This is a very simple dish that anyone can make. If it's raining or snowing or too hot outside, you can cook it in the oven.

1 (1-pound [454-g], 1-inch [2.5-cm] thick) smoked ham steak
10–15 whole cloves, or more if you love cloves
2 tablespoons (30 mL) brown sugar
2 tablespoons (30 mL) fine dry breadcrumbs
1 tablespoon (15 mL) butter, melted
1 teaspoon (5 mL) grated orange zest
½ teaspoon (2.5 mL) dry mustard
1 orange
¾ cup (177 mL) orange juice

1. Preheat the barbecue to 275°F (140°C) to 300°F (150°C) for direct heating. Spray a 7 × 11-inch (17.5 × 27.5 cm) baking dish with nonstick cooking spray.

2. Place the ham slice in the prepared baking dish. Insert the cloves at 1-inch (2.5-cm) intervals. In a small bowl, mix together the brown sugar, breadcrumbs, butter, orange zest, and dry mustard and sprinkle this mixture over the ham.

3. Cut the orange into ¼-inch (1.25-cm) thick slices. Arrange the slices on top of the sugar-breadcrumb mixture. Carefully pour the orange juice over and around the ham.

4. Bake for about 40 minutes, covering with foil the last 15 minutes or so if the oranges or the breadcrumbs are getting too brown.

5. Transfer the ham to a serving platter, cut it into 4 pieces, making sure everyone gets a slice of orange, and serve.

Apple, Ham, and Cheddar Pie

Yield: 4–8 servings

You can also make this pie with fresh apples but the canned filling is quicker and works fine for this fairly easy-to-make entrée.

Refrigerated dough for double-crust 9-inch (22.5-cm) pie
1 (4-pound [1.8-kg]) fully-cooked, bone-in ham, cut into ½-inch (1-cm) cubes
1 (20-ounce [560-g]) can apple pie filling
2 tablespoons (30 mL) barbecue sauce
2 tablespoons (30 mL) honey
1 tablespoon (15 mL) prepared yellow mustard
½ cup (118 mL) shredded cheddar cheese
1 egg white, whipped until foamy

1. Preheat the barbecue to 350°F (180°C) to 400°F (200°C) for indirect heating.

2. Put 1 pie crust in the bottom of a metal pie pan and set aside. Remove all the fat from the ham and sauté the cubes in a large nonstick skillet over high heat until the meat starts to brown on all sides, about 12 to 15 minutes. Remove the meat from the skillet and drain thoroughly on paper towels.

3. Spoon the ham into the pie shell. Stir together the pie filling, barbecue sauce, honey, and mustard, and spread this over the ham. Sprinkle the cheddar cheese on top. Cover with the top crust and press the edges to seal. Make 3 small slices in the top crust to let steam escape. Brush the crust with the whipped egg white. Cover the edges with aluminum foil strips to prevent overbrowning.

4. Place the pie on the unheated side of the grill and cook for 35 minutes, or until crust is nicely and evenly browned, removing the foil strips 10 minutes before the end of the cooking time.

5. Let the pie cool for 15 to 20 minutes, then slice and serve it as a main luncheon or dinner course.

Black-Eyed Peas and Ham
Yield: 6–8 servings

Once a staple of Southern cooking, this dish was developed by slaves who were given the ham hocks and other unwanted pig parts to cook. They cleverly combined them with boiled peas to make a tasty, very economical, and hearty dish.

1 pound (454 g) dry black-eyed peas
2 ham hocks
1 medium red bell pepper, chopped
2 tablespoons (30 mL) whole black peppercorns
1 tablespoon (14 mL) sugar
1 teaspoon (5 mL) salt
½ teaspoon (2.5 mL) red pepper flakes
2 medium onions, peeled and chopped
1 cup (236 mL) diced celery
1 cup (236 mL) diced carrots

1. Wash the peas thoroughly and pick them over. Place the peas in a saucepan, add 2 quarts (1.9 L) water, and soak overnight.

2. Preheat the barbecue to medium-high heat (350°F [180°C] to 400°F [200°C]).

3. Place the ham hocks in a Dutch oven with enough water to cover them. Add the red bell pepper, peppercorns, sugar, salt, and red pepper flakes. Bring to a boil on the grill, reduce the heat, and simmer for 1½ to 2 hours, or until the ham hocks are very tender.

4. Pour the soaked peas into the ham-hock pot. Add the onions, celery, carrots, and enough water to cover everything. Cover the pot and bring to a boil. Reduce the heat to a simmer and cook for 2 hours, or until the peas and vegetables are tender.

5. Spoon into bowls and serve with hot cornbread and dirty rice.

Ham in Beer

Yield: 6–8 servings

You could use a sweet red wine, such as Marsala; a sweet white, such as Riesling; or, if you're feeling celebratory, a domestic champagne to pour over the ham.

1 (5–6 pound [1.8–2.3 kg]) smoked ham
1 cup (236 mL) packed brown sugar
¼ cup (60 mL) water
½ teaspoon (2.5 mL) dry mustard
20 whole cloves
10 bay leaves
36 ounces (1.1 L) dark or light beer

1. Preheat the barbecue to 400°F (200°C) to 450°F (220°C) for direct heating.

2. Remove all but a thin layer of fat from the ham, Score the ham all the way around in a cross-hatch pattern and place it in a deep roasting pan.

3. In a small bowl, combine the brown sugar, water, and dry mustard and mix to a thick liquid. Brush this mixture on the ham to completely cover it. Stick the cloves in the cross-hatch squares, stick the bay leaves into the ham with toothpicks, and place the ham in the barbecue to cook for 2½ to 3 hours.

4. After 1½ hours, gently pour the beer over and around the ham, being careful not to wash away the brown sugar glaze.

5. When a thermometer inserted into the ham reads 145°F (63°C), transfer the ham to a platter, cover it with foil, and let it rest for 15 to 20 minutes.

6. Pour the liquid in the pan into a sauce boat to use as a sauce for the ham.

7. Remove the foil and slice the ham. Discard the bay leaves. Serve immediately.

Grape-Glazed Smoked Ham

Yield: 6–8 servings

The Welch's drink empire began in 1869, when a dentist, Dr. Tomas Welch, began extracting juice from Concord grapes to supply churches with grape juice for communion.

1 (6-ounce [177-mL]) can pineapple juice
¼ cup (59 mL) honey
¼ cup (59 mL) Concord grape wine (such as Manischewitz or Kesser)
3 tablespoons (45 mL) butter
3 tablespoons (45 mL) brown sugar
1½ tablespoons (22.5 mL) grape jam
1 (5–6 pound [2.3–2.7 kg]) smoked ham, bone in
25–30 whole cloves

1. Preheat the barbecue to 350°F (180°C) to 400°F (200°C) for direct heating.

2. In a small saucepan, combine the pineapple juice, honey, wine, butter, brown sugar, and grape jam and heat until the glaze is warmed through.

3. Place 2 crisscrossed sheets of aluminum foil, long enough to fold over and enclose the ham, in a Dutch oven or roasting pan and add the ham, flat end down. Make several horizontal slashes around the ham through the tough skin.

4. Pour half of the glaze over the ham, fold up and seal the foil, and place the pan in the barbecue. Cook for 2½ to 3 hours (30 minutes per pound [454 g]).

5. Fold down the foil and use a sharp knife to cut off the tough skin, leaving a thin layer of fat around the ham. Score the meat in a diamond pattern. Insert a whole clove into the center of each diamond.

6. Pour the remaining glaze over the ham and continue baking, uncovered. Baste often with the pan drippings and glaze. Cook until a meat thermometer inserted into the ham reads 155°F (68°C) and the ham is nicely browned all over.

7. Remove the pan from the barbecue and bring the foil up to loosely cover the ham. Let the meat rest for 20 minutes, then transfer it to a cutting board, pouring the pan drippings into a sauce boat.

8. Slice and serve the ham with the sauce on the side.

Canadian Maple-Smoked Ham

Yield: 8–10 servings

If you have an unsmoked ham and wish to add a smoky flavor, make a smoker package by putting a handful of soaked hickory or oak chips on a 12-inch (30-cm) square of heavy-duty aluminum foil, folding over the package, poking 3 or 4 holes in the top of the foil, and placing the package directly on the coals or open flame.

1 (7–10 pound [3–4.5 kg]) smoked butt portion ham
1 cup (236 mL) maple syrup
1 cup (236 mL) prepared yellow mustard
2 tablespoons (30 mL) brown sugar
¼ teaspoon (1.25 mL) ground nutmeg
⅛ teaspoon (0.6 mL) ground cloves
⅛ teaspoon (0.6 mL) ground cinnamon

1. Preheat the barbecue to 350°F (180°C) to 400°F (200°C) for direct and indirect heating, putting a water pan under the unheated side of the grill and making sure the grill has been well oiled or sprayed with grilling spray. Spray a roasting pan with nonstick cooking spray.

2. Trim all fat and skin from ham. In a small bowl, mix together the maple syrup, mustard, brown sugar, nutmeg, cloves, and cinnamon.

3. Place the ham over the direct heat and sear all sides, about 5 minutes. Remove the ham from the grill and place it in the prepared roasting pan. Baste the ham with the sauce and place the roasting pan on the unheated side of the grill. Cook, basting frequently with the remaining sauce and the pan drippings, for 1 to 1½ hours, or until a thermometer inserted into the ham reads 155°F (68°C).

4. Transfer the ham to a cutting board, cover it with foil, and let it rest for 20 minutes. Pour the drippings into a sauce boat to serve at the table.

Man-Sized Grilled Ham and Cheese Sandwiches
Yield: 4 servings

To make these sandwiches even better—and bigger—add strips of cooked bacon and an additional layer of Swiss cheese before you grill them. You may need to grill them for another minute or so, but turn often.

1 cup (236 mL) thinly sliced red onion
1 cup (236 mL) thinly sliced white onion
2 tablespoons (30 mL) honey
1 tablespoon (15 mL) Dijon mustard
1 teaspoon (5 mL) apple cider vinegar
2–3 tablespoons (30–45 mL) butter, softened
8 (¼-inch [0.5-cm] thick) slices sourdough bread
4 (¼-inch [5-cm] thick) slices country smoked ham
4 (¼-inch [0.5-cm] thick) slices extra-sharp cheddar cheese
⅛ teaspoon (0.6 mL) paprika, for garnish

1. Preheat the barbecue to 350°F (180°C) to 400°F (200°C) for direct heating, making sure the grill has been very generously oiled or sprayed with grilling spray.

2. In a wide skillet, cook the red and white onions, honey, mustard, and vinegar until the onions have wilted and much of the liquid has cooked off, about 2 to 3 minutes. Set aside.

3. Generously butter all 8 slices of bread on one side. Place 4 slices butter side down on a plate, divide the onion mixture among the 4 slices, top with the ham slices and the cheddar cheese slices, and cover with the top bread slices butter side up.

4. Grill for 1 to 2 minutes per side until bread is nicely browned and cheese is beginning to bubble out the sides of the sandwiches.

5. Remove the sandwiches from the grill, sprinkle them lightly with the paprika, cut them in half, and serve.

Blackberry Pork Chops

Yield: 4 servings

If you're not a blackberry fan, use blueberries, raspberries, strawberries, or another berry. This sauce will be tangy.

3 cups (708 mL) fresh blackberries
¼ cup (60 mL) good Cabernet or Pinot Noir
1 cup (236 mL) plus ½ teaspoon (2.5 mL) sugar, divided
2 tablespoons (30 mL) rice wine vinegar
2 tablespoons (30 mL) butter
1 tablespoon (15 mL) garlic powder
1 teaspoon (5 mL) dried sage
½ teaspoon (2.5 mL) salt
¼ teaspoon (1.25 mL) paprika
¼ cup (59 mL) honey mustard
4 (16-ounce [454-g]) porterhouse pork chops
3–4 sprigs fresh rosemary or sage

1. In a small saucepan, combine the berries and wine. Poach for 10 minutes. Remove the pan from the heat, strain the berries, and mash them in the strainer. In a separate saucepan, combine 1 cup (236 mL) of the sugar and the vinegar and simmer for 2 to 3 minutes. Stir in the berry juice and reduce until syrupy. Swirl in the butter. Set aside.

2. In a small bowl, combine the remaining sugar, the garlic powder, sage, salt, and paprika. Massage the mustard into the chops and then sprinkle the rub over them, coating them evenly. Put the chops on a plate, cover them with plastic wrap, and refrigerate for 4 to 24 hours.

3. Preheat the barbecue to 350°F (180°C) to 400°F (200°C) for direct and indirect heating, putting a water pan under the unheated side of the grill. Make sure the grill has been well oiled or sprayed with grilling spray.

4. Grill the chops for 5 to 6 minutes on each side. Seal the chops in heavy duty foil and place them on the unheated side of the grill for 10 minutes per side, or until a meat thermometer horizontally inserted into the center registers 155°F (63°C). Remove the chops from the heat and let them rest still wrapped in the aluminum foil for 5 minutes before serving.

5. Serve with the blackberry sauce, garnished with sprigs of fresh rosemary or sage.

Pork Chops Stuffed with Prunes and Apricots

Yield: 8 servings

I've seen similar recipes that use ground pork or sausage in the stuffing. I'd rather use this much lighter stuffing, where fruit is the accent.

8 pitted prunes
12 dried apricots
⅔ cup (158 mL) dry red wine
1 cup (236 mL) panko
½ cup (118 mL) minced onion
1 large egg, beaten
1 teaspoon (5 mL) minced fresh parsley
¼ teaspoon (1.25 mL) seasoned salt
⅛ teaspoon (0.6 mL) freshly ground black pepper
8 (1-inch [2.5-cm] thick) pork chops
2 tablespoons (30 mL) vegetable oil
2 tablespoons (30 mL) dried rosemary
1 tablespoon (15 mL) dried thyme
1 cup (236 mL) apple juice
¾ cup (177 mL) dry white wine
1 tablespoon (15 mL) cornstarch
1 teaspoon (5 mL) all-purpose flour
¼ cup (59 mL) water

1. Preheat the barbecue to 350°F (180°C) to 400°F (200°C) for direct heating, making sure the grill has been well oiled or sprayed with grilling spray. Spray a large roasting pan or baking dish with nonstick cooking spray.

2. In a small saucepan, combine the prunes, apricots, and red wine and simmer over low heat for 5 to 8 minutes. Drain, chop coarsely, and set aside.

3. In a medium bowl, combine the panko, onion, egg, parsley, seasoned salt, and pepper and mix well. Mix in the chopped fruit and set aside.

4. Make pockets in the pork chops and stuff the pockets with the fruit mixture. In a large skillet, heat the oil over medium heat. Add the pork chops and brown them on both sides.

5. Transfer the chops to the prepared roasting pan or baking dish, reserving the drippings in the skillet. Sprinkle the chops with the rosemary and thyme, cover, and bake for 35 to 40 minutes, or until a thermometer inserted into the pork chops reads 155°F (68°C).

6. To the skillet drippings, add the apple juice and white wine. Bring to a boil and cook for 2 minutes. In a small bowl, combine the cornstarch, flour, and water. Stir this mixture into the apple juice mixture and cook, stirring constantly, until thickened, about 3 to 5 minutes.

7. Remove the chops from the grill, cover them with foil, and let them rest for 5 minutes. Serve the sauce with the pork chops.

Plum and Prune Chops

Yield: 8–10 servings

Prunes have a bad name, it seems, and that's why some companies are now calling them California dried plums. Either way, they are the same fruit; the wrinkled variety just has an association with old folks like me and a certain digestive affect. But they are delicious with pork and ham.

1 (15-ounce [420-g]) can pitted purple plums
1 (18-ounce [504-g]) package dried prunes
1 cup (236 mL) Japanese plum wine (Takara or Kinsen brand)
10 (¾-inch [1.5-cm] thick) porterhouse pork chops
2 (5.5-ounce [155 g]) envelopes Shake 'n' Bake coating mix for pork

1. Preheat the barbecue to 350°F (180°C) to 400°F (200°C) for direct heating. Spray a roasting pan or Dutch oven with nonstick cooking spray.

2. Drain the plums, discarding the syrup, and place them in a large bowl. Put the dried prunes in a saucepan, barely cover them with water, and bring to a boil. Let them sit for 5 minutes. Drain the prunes, discarding the water, and mix them with the plums.

3. Spoon the prune-plum mixture into the bottom of the prepared roasting pan or Dutch oven, drizzle it with the plum wine, and stir. Let sit so the fruit absorbs the wine.

4. Coat the chops as directed on the coating mix package. Sprinkle any remaining mix over the fruit. Place the chops on top of the prune-plum mixture, place the pan in the barbecue, and bake for about 30 minutes.

5. When the chops reach an internal temperature of 160°F (71°C), they are done. Remove the pan from the barbecue, cover with it aluminum foil or a lid, and let it rest for 10 minutes.

6. Remove the chops from the fruit, ladle the fruit onto a warmed serving platter, and place the chops back on top of the fruit. Spoon some of the juice from the cooking pan over each chop.

Pork Chops and Baked Beans

Yield: 6 servings

I like to take the salt pork out of the beans at the end, chop it into very small pieces, and then stir it back into the beans.

1 pound (454 g) dry navy beans
1 pound (454 g) salt pork
2 cloves garlic, peeled and minced
1 large onion, peeled and chopped
¼ cup (59 mL) ketchup
1 teaspoon (5 mL) ground cumin
1 teaspoon (5 mL) dried thyme
1 teaspoon (5 mL) dried oregano
1 teaspoon (5 mL) hot sauce

½ teaspoon (2.5 mL) dry mustard
2 tablespoons (30 mL) molasses
1 tablespoon (15 mL) bacon grease
6 large pork loin chops, bone-in
Kosher salt, to taste
Freshly ground black pepper, to taste
2 tablespoons (30 mL) chopped fresh parsley

1. Cover the beans with water and soak overnight.

2. Preheat barbecue to 325°F (165°C) to 375°F (190°C) for direct and indirect heating.

3. Rinse the salt pork and place it in a Dutch oven or deep cast-iron roasting pan on the heated side of the grill. Add the beans and water to cover and bring to a boil. Reduce the heat, cover the pot, and simmer, stirring often, until the beans are barely cooked, 2 to 3 hours.

4. Add the garlic, onion, ketchup, molasses, cumin, thyme, oregano, hot sauce, and dry mustard and stir well.

5. In a cast-iron skillet, heat the bacon grease. Add the pork chops and cook until browned. Season the chops with salt and pepper.

6. Place the browned chops on top of the beans and bake on the unheated side of the barbecue, covered, for 1½ hours, or until the pork chops are tender.

7. Transfer the chops to a warmed platter. Ladle beans into wide, shallow bowls, place the pork chops on top of the beans in the bowls, sprinkle with parsley and serve.

Smothered Pork Chops

Yield: 4 servings

You can use other soups in this dish, such as tomato, celery, cream of asparagus or broccoli, or even French onion.

4 (1½-inch [3.5-cm] thick) pork chops, about 10 ounces (280 g) each
Olive oil, for brushing
Sea salt, to taste
Freshly ground black pepper, to taste
½ cup (118 mL) uncooked rice
1 large onion, peeled and thickly sliced
1 (10.5-ounce [304-g]) can condensed golden mushroom soup
½ teaspoon (2.5 mL) brown sugar
Paprika, for garnish

1. Preheat the barbecue to 350°F (180°C) to 400°F (200°C) for direct heating, making sure the grill has been well oiled or sprayed with grilling spray. Butter a 2-quart (1.9-L) Dutch oven.

2. Trim the fat from the pork chops, brush them with olive oil, season them with salt and pepper, and place them directly on the grill. Cook until the chops are brown on both sides, about 5 to 8 minutes.

3. Pour the rice into the prepared Dutch oven. Place the pork chops on top of the rice and put 1 thick slice of onion on each chop. Sprinkle the chops with salt and pepper. Pour the soup over the chops, sprinkle them with brown sugar, and cover. Bake in the barbecue for 1 hour.

4. Remove the pot from the barbecue, sprinkle the chops with paprika, and serve.

Pork Chops Parmesan
Yield: 6 servings

You could use domestic Parmesan cheese, but why not use the best? Surely you're worth it. There is no packaged, grated Parmesan cheese that comes anywhere near the flavor of this imported variety.

6 (6–8 ounce (168–227 g]) center-cut pork chops
3 large eggs, beaten
1 cup (236 mL) milk
1½ cups (354 mL) fresh breadcrumbs, divided
1¾ cup (413 mL) freshly grated Parmigiano-Reggiano cheese
3 tablespoons (45 mL) finely chopped fresh parsley
½ teaspoon (2.5 mL) granulated garlic
Kosher salt, to taste
Freshly ground black pepper, to taste
1 tablespoon (15 mL) garlic oil

1. Preheat the barbecue to 325°F (165°C) to 375°F (190°C) for direct heating, making sure the grill has been well oiled or sprayed with grilling spray.

2. Put chops directly on the grill and brown them for 2 to 3 minutes per side. Remove the chops from the grill and let them cool.

3. In a small bowl, beat together the eggs and milk. In a separate small bowl, mix together the breadcrumbs, 1¼ cups (295 mL) of the Parmigiano-Reggiano cheese, the parsley, and the granulated garlic. Season with salt and pepper.

4. Dip each pork chop into the egg mixture, then into the breadcrumb mixture, coating evenly.

5. Place a large cast-iron skillet on the grill. Add the garlic oil and heat until a drop of water sizzles when added. Place the coated and browned pork chops in the skillet and cook for 25 minutes, or until the internal temperature reaches 155°F (68°C).

6. Remove the chops from the skillet, cover them with foil, and let them rest for 5 minutes. Transfer them to a serving platter, sprinkle with the remaining Parmigiano-Reggiano cheese, and serve.

Brown Sugar–Crusted Pork Loin Chops

Yield: 4 servings

These chops are awesome, and the caramelized brown-sugar coating adds a wonderful flavor and complexity to the seasoned pork.

Marinade

1 gallon (3.8 L) plus 1 cup (236 mL) warm water, divided
1 cup sugar
1 cup (236 mL) kosher salt
1 cup (236 mL) packed brown sugar
2 tablespoons (30 mL) dried rosemary
2 tablespoons (30 mL) dried thyme
1 tablespoon (15 mL) ground coriander
1 tablespoon (15 mL) whole black peppercorns
1 tablespoon (15 mL) minced garlic
1 teaspoon (5 mL) ground cumin
2 oranges, quartered
2 lemons, quartered
4 bay leaves
1 medium white onion, peeled and chopped
6 (12-ounce [336-g]) bone-in porterhouse pork loin chops

Sugar Seasoning

½ cup (118 mL) packed brown sugar
1 tablespoon (15 mL) freshly ground black pepper
2 teaspoons (10 mL) kosher salt
¼ teaspoon (1.25 mL) ground allspice
2 tablespoons (30 mL) olive oil

1. For the marinade, heat 1 cup (236 mL) of the water to boiling in the microwave. Add the sugar and salt and stir until they're dissolved. Pour this mixture into the remaining warm water. Add the brown sugar, rosemary, thyme, coriander, peppercorns, garlic, cumin, oranges, lemons, bay leaves, and onion and stir to mix. Pour the marinade into a 2-gallon (7.6-L) resealable plastic bag, add pork chops, and shake the bag to mix well. Refrigerate overnight.

2. Remove chops from the marinade, discarding the marinade. Pat the chops dry and let them come to room temperature.

3. Preheat the barbecue to 400°F (200°C) to 450°F (220°C) for direct heating, making sure the grill has been well oiled or sprayed with grilling spray.

4. For the seasoning, in a shallow baking pan, mix together the brown sugar, pepper, salt, and allspice. Brush both sides of the chops with olive oil and press each chop into the sugar mixture to coat both sides.

5. Place the meat on the hot grill and cook for 3 to 4 minutes per side, or until the sugar is browned and caramelized and the internal temperature of the chops reaches 155°F (68°C).

6. Transfer the chops to a warmed platter, cover them with foil, and let them rest for 5 minutes before serving.

Scarlet Ginger Pork Chops

Yield: 4 servings

Cochineal is a natural red food coloring that is derived from bugs—the tiny cochineal bug, to be specific. It is produced by drying and pulverizing the whole bugs, boiling them, and drying them again. It's frequently used in jams, jellies, preserves, gelatin cheese, cookies, desserts, juices, and beverages.

½ cup (118 mL) sugar
½ cup (118 mL) soy sauce
¼ cup (59 mL) sake
2 tablespoons (30 mL) minced fresh garlic
2 tablespoons (30 mL) grated fresh ginger
¼ teaspoon (1.25 mL) cochineal powder
⅛ teaspoon (0.6 mL) cayenne pepper
8 (1½-inch [3.5-cm] thick) bone-in pork loin chops

1. In a 1-gallon (3.8-L) resealable plastic bag, mix together the sugar, soy sauce, sake, garlic, ginger, cochineal, and cayenne pepper. Add the pork chops, seal the bag, and refrigerate overnight.

2. Preheat the barbecue to 350°F (180°C) to 400°F (200°C) for direct heating, making sure the grill has been well oiled or sprayed with grilling spray.

3. Remove the chops from the bag and wipe off the excess marinade. Place the chops on the grill and cook for 5 to 6 minutes per side, or until a thermometer inserted into the thick part of the chop reads 160°F (71°CO). Remove the chops from the grill and serve.

Lime Pork Chops

Yield: 4 servings

You can cook these with lemon, orange, grapefruit, or tangerine juices instead, but we feel the lime has the best interplay with the grilled pork.

⅓ cup (79 mL) fresh lime juice
2 tablespoons (30 mL) cider vinegar
1 tablespoon (15 mL) honey
1 teaspoon (5 mL) grated lime zest
Salt, to taste
Freshly ground black pepper, to taste
4 (4–6 ounce [112–168 g]) boneless center-cut pork chops
Fresh lime slices, for garnish

1. In a 1- to 2-gallon (3.8- to 7.6-kg) resealable plastic bag, combine the lime juice, vinegar, honey, lime zest, salt, and pepper. Add the pork chops to the marinade, shake to coat the chops, and refrigerate for 1 hour.

2. Preheat the barbecue to 350°F (180°C) to 400°F (200°C) for direct heating, making sure the grill has been well oiled or sprayed with grilling spray.

3. Remove the chops from the marinade. Pour the marinade into a saucepan and boil for 10 minutes while the pork chops come to room temperature.

4. Cook the chops on the heated side of the grill for 3 minutes per side, basting on each side with the marinade. Move them to the unheated side and cook for another 6 to 7 minutes per side, again basting several times, until the inside is barely pink and a thermometer inserted into the chop reads 155°F (68°C).

5. Boil the remaining marinade for 10 minutes. Place the chops on a warm platter, drizzle them with the marinade, and garnish with the lime slices.

Turbinado Porterhouse Pork Chops
Yield: 4 servings

If you can find it, it's best to use turbinado sugar, which is made from refined sugar cane extract, instead of brown sugar, which is made by adding molasses to refined sugar. Turbinado sugar is often labeled as "raw natural cane sugar" or "sugar in the raw" and is available online and most likely at your local grocery store as well.

3 tablespoons (45 mL) turbinado sugar
2 tablespoons (30 mL) chili powder
1 tablespoon (15 mL) paprika
2 teaspoons (10 mL) dried thyme
1½ teaspoons (7.5 mL) salt
1 teaspoon (5 mL) freshly ground black pepper
1 teaspoon (5 mL) red pepper flakes
1 teaspoon (5 mL) ground cumin
4 (8–10 ounce [224–280 g]) porterhouse pork chops
2 teaspoons (10 mL) olive oil
1 teaspoon (5 mL) dark brown sugar
¼ cup (59 mL) bourbon
¼ cup (56 g) cold butter

1. In a small bowl, combine the turbinado sugar, chili powder, paprika, thyme, salt, pepper, red pepper flakes, and cumin. Pour this mixture into a shallow baking pan.

2. Brush the chops lightly with olive oil. With your hands, press the chops into the rub, coating both sides very well. Place the chops in a pan, cover them with foil, and refrigerate overnight.

3. Preheat the barbecue to 350°F (180°C) to 400°F (200°C) for direct heating and indirect heating, making sure the grill has been well oiled or sprayed with grilling spray.

4. Remove chops from the refrigerator and let them sit, covered, until they come to room temperature, about 20 to 25 minutes.

5. Grill the chops for 3 minutes per side, turning only once. Transfer them to a cast-iron skillet on the unheated side of the grill and bake for 15 to 20 minutes, turning after 7 minutes and sprinkling the chops with the brown sugar. Do not turn them again.

6. Transfer the chops to a platter, cover them with foil, and let them rest for 10 minutes. Meanwhile, pour the bourbon in the skillet, add the butter, and cook, stirring to loosen the brown bits from the bottom of the skillet.

7. Serve 1 chop per person with 1 to 2 tablespoons (30 to 45 mL) skillet bourbon sauce drizzled over each chop.

Corn-Stuffed Pork Chops
Yield: 4 servings

You can use any stuffing mix brand you like, or you can make your own stuffing. I've used two brands—Uncle Ben's Classic and Stove Top—with great success, but if you have the time, homemade stuffing is the best.

1 (15-ounce [420-g]) can creamed corn
1½ cups (354 mL) cornbread stuffing mix
½ cup (118 mL) minced onion
¼ cup (59 mL) minced celery
1 teaspoon (5 mL) paprika
½ teaspoon (2.5 mL) ground sage
4 (¾-inch [1.5-cm] thick) boneless pork chops
1 tablespoon (15 mL) brown sugar
1 teaspoon (5 mL) Dijon mustard

1. Preheat the barbecue to 375°F (190°C) to 425°F (220°C) for direct heating. Butter or spray with nonstick cooking spray a large, deep cast-iron skillet.

2. In the prepared skillet, combine the creamed corn, stuffing mix, onion, celery, paprika, and sage. Arrange the pork chops on top, pressing them partially into the stuffing mixture.

3. In a small bowl, combine the brown sugar and mustard and stir to blend. Spread this mixture evenly over the pork chops.

4. Bake for 30 minutes, or until chops are no longer pink inside, the mustard-sugar topping is browned and bubbling, and the stuffing is lightly browned.

5. Remove the chops, cover them, and let them rest for 5 minutes.

6. Serve the chops with the stuffing on individual plates.

Pesto-Stuffed Pork Chops

Yield: 4 servings

There are many kinds of pesto. We use a traditional basil pesto here, but you could also use a mint or cilantro pesto with great results.

½ cup (118 mL) bottled or homemade pesto, divided
2 tablespoons (30 mL) pine nuts
2 tablespoons (30 mL) black currants
1 teaspoon (5 mL) dried rosemary
½ teaspoon (2.5 mL) ground cumin
½ teaspoon (2.5 mL) paprika
½ teaspoon (2.5 mL) salt
4 (6–8 ounce [168–227 g]) bone-in thick-cut pork chops
2 tablespoons (30 mL) olive oil
1 cup (236 mL) thinly sliced onion
2 tablespoons (30 mL) freshly grated Parmigiano-Reggiano cheese

1. Preheat the barbecue to 350°F (180°C) to 400°F (200°C) for direct heating, making sure the grill has been well oiled or sprayed with grilling spray.

2. In a bowl, combine the pesto, pine nuts, and currants and stir to combine. Reserve ½ cup of the pesto mixture to serve with chops. In a separate bowl, combine the rosemary, cumin, paprika, and salt and stir.

3. With a sharp knife, cut a wide pocket horizontally three-quarters of the way into each chop, being careful to not cut all the way through on any side. Rub the pork chops with the cumin mixture, then fill each pork chop with 1 tablespoon (15 mL) of the remaining pesto mixture. Close the pockets with wooden toothpicks.

4. In a large cast-iron skillet or roasting pan, heat the oil. Add the onion and cook, stirring constantly, until the onion is just beginning to turn brown, about 5 minutes. Transfer the onion to a plate. Add the pork chops to the skillet and cook for 1 to 2 minutes per side, or until browned. Cover the pork chops with the reserved onions, cover the skillet, and bake in the barbecue for 20 to 25 minutes, or until the pork is cooked through.

5. Remove the toothpicks. Top with the reserved pesto and the Parmigiano-Reggiano cheese and serve.

Coffee-Marinated Grilled Chops

Yield: 4 servings

If you don't have an espresso maker at home, buy a cup of espresso to go at your local coffee shop and bring it home.

1 cup (236 mL) espresso
½ cup (118 mL) dark molasses
2 tablespoons (30 mL) apple cider vinegar
1 teaspoon (5 mL) brown sugar
1 teaspoon (5 mL) finely minced garlic
1 teaspoon (5 mL) kosher salt
1 teaspoon (5 mL) dried oregano
4 (6–8 ounce [168–227 g], 1½-inch [1.5-cm] thick) bone-in pork chops

1. In a 2-gallon (7.8-L) resealable plastic bag, combine the espresso, molasses, cider vingar, sugar, garlic, salt, and oregano. Add the pork chops and turn the bag over several times. Put the first bag into a second bag, in case the exposed bones pierce the bag, and refrigerate for 3 to 4 hours or overnight.

2. Preheat the barbecue to 350°F (180°C) to 400°F (200°C) for direct and indirect heating, putting a water pan under the unheated side of the grill.

3. Remove the chops from the marinade. Pour the marinade into a saucepan and boil for 10 minutes while the pork comes to room temperature.

4. Put the pork chops on the heated side of the grill and cook for about 3 minutes per side, until browned on both sides, brushing generously with the marinade. Move the chops to the unheated side of the grill and cook for an additional 4 to 5 minutes per side, until the chops are cooked all the way through and their internal temperature reaches 155°F (68°C).

5. Remove the pork from the grill, cover it with foil, and allow it to rest for 5 to 6 minutes before serving.

Char Siu Chinese Pork

Yield: 4 servings

Maltose is a powder that can be made from wheat, rice, barley, or other grains. You can find it in the baking aisle of any grocery store or supermarket, at homebrew shops, or online. I always add the food coloring for the dramatic effect, but it's optional.

1 (1 pound [454 g]) pork butt, cut into 4 pieces
¼ cup (59 mL) maltose
2 tablespoons (30 mL) honey
2 tablespoons (30 mL) hoisin sauce
2 tablespoons (30 mL) soy sauce
1½ tablespoons (22.5 mL) dry sherry
1 teaspoon (5 mL) five-spice powder
1 teaspoon (5 mL) dark sesame oil
½ teaspoon (2.5 mL) ground white pepper
4 drops red food coloring (optional)
3 cloves garlic, peeled and minced

1. Put the pork in a wide, flat baking pan. In a saucepan, combine the maltose, honey, hoisin sauce, soy sauce, sherry, five-spice powder, sesame oil, white pepper, and food coloring and stir to mix. Cook over medium heat until the sauce becomes slightly thickened and sticky. Remove the pan from the heat and pour the sauce over the pork. Add the garlic, stir, cover, and refrigerate overnight.

2. Preheat the barbecue to 400°F (200°C) to 450°F (220°C) for direct and indirect heating, putting a water pan under the unheated side of the grill. Make sure the grill has been well oiled or sprayed with a grilling spray.

3. Remove the pork from the marinade. Pour the marinade into a saucepan and boil for 10 minutes while the meat comes to room temperature.

4. Place the pork on the heated side of the barbecue and grill for 7 minutes per side, brushing generously with the boiled char siu sauce. Move the meat to the unheated side of the grill and cook for 15 to 20 minute, turning several times and basting often.

5. Remove the meat from the barbecue and slice it into thin slices or bite-size pieces. Pour the sauce into a saucepan and boil for 10 minutes. Drizzle with the remaining sauce and serve immediately over steamed white rice.

Phuong's Vietnamese Barbecued Pork

Yield: 2–4 servings

Bun thit nuong is a simple and popular meal in Vietnam, consisting of cold rice vermicelli mixed with fresh vegetables and topped with this hot barbecued pork. This recipe comes from Phuong Tran from Salmon Creek, WA.

1 pound (454 g) pork butt or neck, partially frozen, thinly sliced
3 green onions, green and white parts, diced
1–2 small Thai chilies, minced
2 tablespoons (30 mL) Vietnamese fish sauce
2 teaspoons (10 mL) sugar
1 teaspoon (5 mL) minced garlic
Juice of 1 lime
Sea salt, to taste
Freshly ground black pepper, to taste
3 carrots, julienned
1 (8-ounce [227-g]) package rice vermicelli
2 tablespoons (30 mL) peanut oil
2 cups (473 mL) Mung bean sprouts, washed and dried
½ head romaine lettuce, shredded
1 small cucumber, peeled, seeded, and thinly sliced
1 bunch fresh cilantro, washed
½ bunch fresh mint, washed
¼ cup (59 mL) chopped roasted peanuts
1 cup (236 mL) nuoc cham sauce

1. Preheat the barbecue to 350°F (180°C) to 400°F (200°C).

2. In a large bowl, mix together the pork, green onions, peppers, fish sauce, sugar, garlic, lime juice, salt, and pepper. Marinate at room temperature for 15 to 30 minutes.

3. Bring a large saucepan of water to a boil on the side burner. Add the carrots and blanch for 30 seconds. With a slotted spoon, transfer the carrots to a bowl of ice water to stop cooking. Place the rice vermicelli in a heatproof bowl and pour the boiling carrot water over them. Let them sit for 5 to 8 minutes, or until softened. Drain the noodles, rinse them in cold water, drain them again, and set aside.

4. In a large cast-iron skillet or on a barbecue griddle, heat the oil. Remove the pork from its marinade, drain it briefly, and cook it in the skillet or on the griddle until just cooked through, about 2 minutes. Remove the pork from the heat and keep it warm.

5. Divide the carrots, sprouts, and lettuce equally among 2 to 4 deep serving bowls. Divide the rice noodles equally on top of the vegetables. Place 4 or 5 slices of pork on top of each bowl of noodles, covering a third of them. Place the sliced cucumber neatly over another third of the noodles. Finally, lay sprigs of cilantro and mint over the remaining third.

6. Sprinkle peanuts over each bowl and serve with nuoc cham in a sauce boat to pour over the noodles.

Mojo Pork Butt in a Bag
Yield: 6–8 servings

This is a great way to present dinner at the table. The bag may be singed but not burnt, and you'll get an amazed look from your guests. Don't tell them what's in the bag; let them guess. Then rip open the bag to reveal the perfectly cooked roast.

1 (5–6 pound [2.3–2.8 kg]) pork butt
4 canned chipotle peppers in adobo sauce, rinsed
½ cup (118 mL) orange juice
¼ cup (59 mL) roughly chopped onion
2 tablespoons (30 mL) lime juice
1 tablespoon (15 mL) honey
1 tablespoon (15 mL) olive oil
2 teaspoons (10 mL) dried oregano, crushed
3 cloves garlic, peeled and minced
½ teaspoon (2.5 mL) salt

1. Place the pork butt in a 1- to 2-gallon (3.8- to 7.6-L) resealable plastic bag set in a shallow dish.

2. In a food processor, combine the chipotle peppers, orange juice, onion, lime juice, honey, olive oil, oregano, garlic, and salt and pulse until the mixture is almost smooth. Pour this mixture over the meat in the plastic bag, seal, and refrigerate for 1½ to 2 hours. Drain the meat and discard the marinade.

3. Preheat the barbecue to 450°F (240°C) to 500°F (260°C) for direct heating.

4. Place the roast in the barbecue and grill for 4 to 5 minutes per side to brown the meat all over. Place the meat in a brown paper grocery bag, fold over the top, staple the bag closed, and place it on a baking sheet on the grill. Make sure no part of the bag is directly over the charcoal or gas flames. Close the grill cover and cook for 1½ to 2 hours, or until a meat thermometer inserted into the roast (right through the side of the bag) registers 160°F (71°C) to 170°F (77°C).

5. Remove the baking sheet and pork from the grill. Let the meat rest in the sealed bag for 10 minutes. Place the bag of meat on a heated platter and rip it open at the table, being careful to avoid the steam that will be released. Slice and serve.

Hong Shao Rou (Red Cooked Pork)

Yield: 4–6 servings

This is a popular barbecue dish around Shanghai, China. The red comes from the effect the soy sauce has on the meat over the long cooking time. In China, the remaining sauce is saved and used again and again, with some families using sauces that go back for generations.

1 (2–3 pound [908 g–1.3 kg]) boneless pork butt, cut into 4 × 1 × ¼-inch (10 × 2.5 × 0.5-cm) strips
1 cup (236 mL) beef stock
¾ cup (177 mL) dark soy sauce
2 tablespoons (30 mL) rice wine
2 teaspoons (10 mL) sugar
1 teaspoon (5 mL) grated fresh ginger
2 whole pods star anise
Salt, to taste
Freshly ground black pepper, to taste
Steamed rice or garlic mashed potatoes, for serving

1. Preheat the barbecue to 350°F (180°C) to 400°F (200°C) for direct heating, making sure the grill has been well oiled or sprayed with grilling spray.

2. Grill the meat strips on the hot grill for 2 minutes per side, then place them in a deep roasting pan. Add the stock, soy sauce, rice wine, sugar, ginger, and anise. Season with salt and pepper. Bring to a boil over medium-high heat. Reduce the heat to low, cover, and simmer for 45 to 60 minutes, or until the meat is very tender.

3. Serve over steamed rice or garlic mashed potatoes.

Honey-Molasses Pork Tenderloin with Sweet Potatoes

Yield: 4 servings

To make the pork a little more fiery, add 1 finely minced habañero pepper to the marinade and increase the allspice to 1 teaspoon (5 mL).

1 (1½-pounds [681-g]) pork tenderloin
½ teaspoon (2.5 mL) garlic salt
½ teaspoon (2.5 mL) freshly ground black pepper
2 tablespoons (30 mL) molasses
1 tablespoon (15 mL) balsamic vinegar
1 tablespoon (15 mL) honey
2 teaspoons (10 mL) olive oil
1 teaspoon (5 mL) dried rosemary
½ teaspoon (2.5 mL) ground allspice
4 large sweet potatoes, peeled and cut into 2-inch (5-cm) chunks
¼ cup (59 mL) butter, melted
2 tablespoons (30 mL) brown sugar
⅛ teaspoon (0.6 mL) ground cloves

1. Preheat the barbecue to 350°F (180°C) to 400°F (200°C) for direct heating. Oil or spray with nonstick cooking spray a roasting pan.

2. Place the pork tenderloin in a shallow pan and season it with the garlic salt and black pepper. In a medium bowl, whisk together the molasses, balsamic vinegar, honey, olive oil, rosemary, and allspice. Pour this mixture over the pork tenderloin, turn the tenderloin several times to coat all sides, and marinate for about 15 to 20 minutes.

3. Place the sweet potatoes in the prepared roasting pan, drizzle them with the melted butter, and sprinkle them with the brown sugar and cloves. Roast for 15 minutes. Place the pork tenderloin in the center of the pan, surrounded by the sweet potatoes. Roast for 20 to 25 minutes, turning the tenderloin and stirring the vegetables several times, until the potatoes are tender and the internal temperature of the pork registers 155°F (68°C).

4. Remove the meat from the pan, cover it with foil, and let it rest for 10 minutes before slicing. Pour the sweet potatoes onto a large serving tray and top with the sliced tenderloin.

Mustard and Maple Glazed Pork
Yield: 4 servings

Maple butter is an incredible product for cooking and is available at the websites for the Vermont Trade Winds Farm, Maple Syrup World, Shady Maple Farms, and Maple Community.

1 (2½–3 pound [1.1–1.3 kg]) boneless pork loin, tied
2 cloves garlic, peeled and thinly sliced
3 tablespoons (45 mL) maple sugar
1½ teaspoons (7.5 mL) grated fresh ginger
1 teaspoon (5 mL) freshly cracked black peppercorns
½ teaspoon (2.5 mL) kosher salt
¼ cup (59 mL) maple butter
Maple sugar candies, for garnish (optional)

1. Using a small, sharp knife, make thin slits all over the pork loin roast. Insert a garlic slice into each slit. In a small bowl, mix together the maple sugar, ginger, pepper, and salt. Reserve half of this maple paste and rub the rest all over the pork. Place the roast in a shallow pan, cover it with plastic wrap, and refrigerate overnight.

2. Remove the roast from the refrigerator and let it rest for 30 to 40 minutes to return to room temperature.

3. Preheat the barbecue to 425°F (220°C) to 475°F (250°C) for direct and indirect heating, putting a water pan under the unheated side of the grill and making sure the grill has been well oiled or sprayed with grilling spray. Spray a roasting pan with nonstick cooking spray.

4. Place the pork on the grill and roast over indirect heat for 15 minutes, or until it begins to brown. Place the roast into the prepared roasting pan, spread it with the maple butter, and sprinkle it with the reserved maple sugar mixture. Place the pan in the barbecue and cook for about 35 minutes, or until an instant-read thermometer inserted in the roast registers 155°F (68°C). Baste several times with the pan liquid.

5. Transfer the roast to a cutting board and let rest for 15 minutes before slicing. Pour the pan liquid into a small serving pitcher to serve at the table. Carve the pork into thin slices and arrange it on a platter. Garnish with the maple sugar candies, if using, and serve.

Puerto Rican Lechón Asado (Roast Pork)

Yield: 6–8 servings

This is my version of a very popular pork dish I tasted in Puerto Rico. The meat should be so tender you barely have to chew it, and it is fully flavored by the pungent sour orange, garlic, and oregano.

½ cup (118 mL) olive oil
Juice of 1 large orange
Juice of 2 limes (or 2 sour oranges)
10 cloves garlic, peeled
1 tablespoon (15 mL) dried oregano
1 tablespoon (15 mL) minced fresh cilantro
2 teaspoons (10 mL) salt
2 teaspoons (10 mL) freshly ground black pepper
1 (5–6 pound [2.3–2.8 kg]) pork shoulder
3 tablespoons (45 mL) butter
3 tablespoons (45 mL) all-purpose flour
1 cup (236 mL) dark beer (or less, as needed)

1. In a blender or food processor, combine the oil, orange juice, lime juice, garlic, oregano, cilantro, salt, and pepper and process until smooth.

2. Score the fat on the roast and rub the pork all over with the marinade. Put the roast in a 2-gallon (7.6-L) resealable plastic bag and refrigerate overnight, turning occasionally.

3. Remove the meat from the bag and let it come to room temperature.

4. Preheat the barbecue to 325°F (165°C) to 375°F (190°C) for direct and indirect heating, putting a water pan under the unheated side of the grill. Oil or spray with nonstick cooking spray a Dutch oven.

5. Place the roast, fat side down, in the prepared Dutch oven. Place the pot in the barbecue over indirect heat and roast for 1 hour, covered. Remove the lid, turn the roast fat side up and cook, uncovered, basting with the pan juices occasionally, for 2½ to 3 hours, until the roast is very tender and well browned on the outside and the internal temperature has risen to 155°F (68°C).

6. Place the roast on a cutting board, reserving the pan juices. Cover the roast with foil and let it rest for 15 to 20 minutes.

7. In a saucepan, melt the butter. Sprinkle in the flour, stirring constantly until the mixture turns light brown. Skim the fat from the pan juices and pour the juices into pour the juices into a meauring cup and add enough beer to make 2 cups (454 mL). Pour this mixture into the saucepan, and bring the gravy to a simmer, and cook, stirring, until it thickens.

8. Cut the roast into thin slices. Present the meat on a warmed serving platter, drizzled with some of the gravy. Serve the rest of the gravy in a sauce pitcher.

Griots (Haitian Glazed Pork)

Yield: 6–8 servings

This rich, flavorful dish is very popular at parties and family gatherings in Haiti. Cubes of pork are soaked in a sour orange marinade, roasted until tender, and caramelized in oil.

1 (4–4½ pounds [1.8–2 kg]) pork shoulder, cubed
Juice from 3 sour oranges (or 2 large oranges and 3 limes)
1 large onion, peeled and thinly sliced
1 medium green or red bell pepper, thinly sliced
1 small Scotch bonnet pepper, minced
3 shallots, peeled and sliced
4 cloves garlic, peeled and minced
2 teaspoons (10 mL) salt
2 teaspoons (10 mL) dried thyme
1 teaspoon (5 mL) allspice
1 teaspoon (5 mL) freshly ground black pepper
½ teaspoon (2.5 mL) cinnamon
¼ cup (59 mL) peanut oil

1. In a large, nonreactive bowl, combine the pork, sour orange juice, onion, bell pepper, Scotch bonnet pepper, shallots, garlic, salt, thyme, allspice, pepper, and cinnamon and stir to mix together well. Pour into a 2-gallon (7.8-L) resealable plastic bag and refrigerate for 6 to 24 hours.

2. Preheat the barbecue to 350°F (180°C) to 400°F (200°C).

3. Pour the pork and marinade into a large Dutch oven or roasting pan and place it in the barbecue. Cook for 1½ to 2 hours, or until the pork is very tender.

4. Remove the roasting pan from the barbecue and, with a slotted spoon, transfer the meat to a colander and let it drain briefly. Pour the pan liquid into a large saucepan. With a paper towel, wipe out the roasting pan. Return the pan to the barbecue, add the oil, and let it heat for 2 minutes. Spoon in the meat and cook for 20 to 30 minutes more, stirring occasionally. Any liquid will evaporate away and the meat will begin to fry in the oil and brown.

5. While the meat is baking, place the saucepan with the reserved liquid on a side burner. With a slotted spoon, remove the solids. Bring the liquid to a boil and cook until it is reduced by two-thirds.

6. Remove the roasting pan from the barbecue, ladle the meat onto a serving platter, and drizzle with the reduced sauce mix.

Pork and Chili Burritos

Yield: 10–12 servings

If you wish, you may cook pinto or refried beans separately and spoon them on the burritos as you are making them.

1 (3-pound [1.3-kg]) boneless pork shoulder, cut into ½-inch (1-cm) cubes
1½ pounds (681 g) onions, diced
1 pound (454 g) tomatillos, husked, cooked, and mashed
½ pound (227 g) green bell peppers, diced
2 medium tomatoes, chopped
¼ cup (59 mL) chopped fresh cilantro
1 jalapeño pepper, minced
1 tablespoon (15 mL) salt
1 teaspoon (5 mL) garlic powder
½ teaspoon (2.5 mL) ground cumin
¼ teaspoon (1.25 mL) ground cloves
¼ teaspoon (1.25 mL) black pepper
2 bay leaves
Juice of ½ lemon
1½ teaspoons (7.5 mL) cornstarch
¾ cup (177 mL) Corona beer
12 (12-inch [30-cm]) flour tortillas
Shredded Monterey Jack, for serving
Shredded cheddar cheese, for serving

1. Preheat the barbecue to 350°F (180°C) to 400°F (200°C). Spray a Dutch oven with nonstick cooking spray and grease a 9 × 13-inch (22.5 × 32.5-cm) baking pan.

2. Place the roast in the prepared Dutch oven. Add 1 gallon (3.8 L) water and bring to boil. Reduce the heat and simmer, covered, for 35 minutes. Drain off and discard the water.

3. Add the onions, tomatillos, bell peppers, tomatoes, cilantro, jalapeño pepper, salt, garlic powder, cumin, cloves, pepper, and bay leaves to the meat and simmer for 15 minutes. Add the lemon juice. In a small bowl, mix together the cornstarch and beer. Stir this into the meat mixture and simmer for 15 minutes longer, stirring constantly.

4. Wrap the tortillas in foil and place them in the barbecue for a few minutes to soften. Place a heaping ½ cup (177 mL) of meat mixture on each tortilla. Fold the sides in and roll the burritos up from one end. Place the burritos in the prepared baking pan. Sprinkle generously with cheese and place the pan in the barbecue until the cheese melts. Remove the burritos from the pan with a wide spatula and serve.

Cider and Apple Barbecued Pork Neck

Yield: 4 servings

The pork neck is a well muscled and very flavorful cut of meat with a lot more fat than the pork shoulder but still a lot less than the pork belly. The fat is present throughout the cut, and, as it melts, it will baste and flavor the meat deliciously. You don't have to eat the fat, but the meat will be heavenly.

1 small onion, peeled and sliced
2 bay leaves, crumbled
6 whole cloves
2 cloves garlic, peeled and crushed
⅓ cup (79 mL) packed brown sugar
2 tablespoons (30 mL) fennel seeds
1 teaspoon (5 mL) olive oil
½ teaspoon (2.5 mL) salt
Freshly ground black pepper, to taste
1 (2¾–3pound [1.1–1.3 kg]) pork neck
8½ cups (2 L) apple cider
6 small red apples, cored and quartered

1. In a blender, combine the onion, bay leaves, cloves, garlic, brown sugar, fennel seeds, olive oil, salt, and pepper and process to a smooth paste.

2. Place the pork in a baking pan and smear it all over with the paste. Cover the pan with plastic wrap and refrigerate for at least 2 to 3 hours or overnight.

3. Preheat the barbecue to 325°F (165°C) to 350°F (180°C) for direct heating. Oil or spray with nonstick cooking spray a roasting pan or Dutch oven.

4. Place the pork and any leftover paste into the prepared roasting pan or Dutch oven and pour in the cider. Cover and cook for 2 to 2½ hours, or until the meat is fork tender. Add more apple cider or water to the pan if the liquid gets too low.

5. Uncover the pork and add the apples to the pan. Cook for 25 minutes, or until the apples are tender.

6. Remove the meat, cover it with foil, and let it rest for 20 minutes. Slice the meat and place it on a serving platter, surrounded by the apples. Pour 2 cups (473 mL) of the pan liquid over the meat and serve.

Creole Butterfly Chops

Yield: 4 servings

A certain TV chef took an age-old Southern recipe for spices and called it his "essence," when really it's been around forever as plain old Creole or Cajun seasoning. The amount we make here should keep for 3 to 4 months if it is stored properly.

2 tablespoons (30 mL) paprika
2 tablespoons (30 mL) cayenne pepper
2 tablespoons (30 mL) garlic powder
1 tablespoon (15 mL) onion powder
1 tablespoon (15 mL) dried oregano
1 tablespoon (15 mL) dried thyme
1 teaspoon (5 mL) black pepper
4 butterfly pork chops
2 tablespoons (30 mL) clover honey
1 tablespoon (15 mL) freshly cracked black peppercorns

1. In a small bowl, combine the paprika, cayenne pepper, garlic powder, onion powder, oregano, thyme, and black pepper. Pour the seasoning mixture into a jar with a lid and set aside.

2. Place 1 chop in a large plastic freezer bag and tenderize it with a mallet. Repeat with the other 3 chops. Brush both sides of each chop with honey and sprinkle both sides with the Creole seasoning. Lay the chops in a shallow baking pan, cover with plastic wrap, and refrigerate overnight.

3. Preheat the barbecue to 350°F (180°C) to 400°F (200°C) for direct and indirect heating, putting a water pan under the unheated side of the grill. Make sure the grill has been well oiled or sprayed with a grilling spray.

4. Remove the chops from refrigerator, remove the plastic wrap, and let the meat sit for 20 minutes to come to room temperature.

5. Place the chops on the heated side of the grill and cook for 5 minutes per side. Transfer them to the unheated side and cook for an additional 10 to 15 minutes.

6. Remove the chops from the barbecue. Season with the fresh cracked black pepper and serve hot.

Barbecued BLT Burgers with Cheese
Yield: 4 servings

They do call them hamburgers, don't they? Well, these are made not with ham but with two other cuts of the pig. You can use a different cheese if you wish, or leave it out altogether.

1½ pounds (681 g) ground pork
1 tablespoon (15 mL) minced chives
½ teaspoon (2.5 mL) dried oregano
½ teaspoon (2.5 mL) garlic powder
Salt, to taste
Freshly ground black pepper, to taste
8 slices Swiss cheese
4 thick slices beefsteak tomato
4 thick slices hickory-smoked bacon, cooked and halved
Fresh lettuce leaves, for serving
4 hamburger buns, toasted and buttered

1. Preheat the barbecue to 350°F (180°C) to 400°F (200°C) for direct and indirect heating, putting a water pan under the unheated side of the grill. Line the unheated side of the grill with a sheet of aluminum foil, shiny side down. Make sure the grill has been well oiled or sprayed with a grilling spray.

2. In a large bowl, combine the pork, chives, oregano, garlic powder, salt, and pepper. Mix with your hands until all the herbs are incorporated into the meat. Form the mixture into 8 thin hamburger patties.

3. Place 4 of the patties on a cutting board or other flat surface and top each with 1 slice of cheese, 1 slice of tomato, 2 pieces of bacon, and 1 more slice of cheese. Top each with another patty and, with your fingers and a fork, crimp the edges together to seal in the filling.

4. Place the burgers on the grill and cook over direct heat for 2 minutes per side to brown the meat. Carefully transfer the patties to the foil on the unheated side of the grill and cook for 3 to 4 minutes per side, or until the burgers are nicely browned and cooked through.

5. Transfer the burgers to a platter and let them rest for 3 to 4 minutes. Serve them with fresh lettuce on the toasted buns.

Puerco Asado (Cuban Pork Roast)

Yield: 6–8 servings

Thick slices of this cooked roast, covered in the onion-orange sauce, will satisfy the hungriest of your guests. Serve with black beans, flour or corn tortillas, and Spanish rice.

1 (5–6 pound [2.3–2.8 kg]) pork shoulder roast
6–8 cloves garlic, peeled and thinly sliced
1 teaspoon (5 mL) freshly ground black pepper
½ teaspoon (2.5 mL) kosher salt
2 large white onions, peeled and thinly sliced
¾ cup (177 mL) orange juice
¼ cup (59 mL) lime juice
1 teaspoon (5 mL) dried oregano
1 teaspoon (5 mL) ground cumin

1. With a sharp knife, cut 20 or so tiny slices in the roast and insert a slice of garlic into each cut. Season the roast with pepper and salt. Place the meat in a 2-gallon (7.8-L) resealable plastic bag. Add the onions, orange juice, lime juice, oregano, and cumin, seal the bag, and refrigerate for 1 to 2 days, turning the bag occasionally to distribute the marinade.

2. Preheat the barbecue to 300°F (150°C) to 325°F (165°C) for direct and indirect heating, putting a water pan under the unheated side of the grill. Make sure the grill has been well oiled or sprayed with grilling spray. Oil a roasting pan.

3. Remove the roast from the marinade.

4. Place the roast on the grill and cook until well-browned on all sides, 15 to 20 minutes. Remove the roast from the grill and place it in the prepared roasting pan. Pour the marinade over the meat, cover, and bake on the un-heated side of the grill for 5 to 6 hours. Close the barbecue vents to lower the heat and cook until a thermometer inserted into the thick part of the roast reads 155°F (68°C).

5. Remove the roast from the barbecue, cover it, and let it stand for 20 minutes before carving. Pour the onion-orange juice into a sauce boat and serve it at the table with the meat.

Mexican Pork Chili

Yield: 6–8 servings

You can add beans to the chili or, better yet, cook the beans separately so people can add them to their own bowls, or not, as they desire.

8 strips bacon, diced
½ cup (118 mL) all-purpose flour
1 (2-pound [908-g]) pork shoulder, cut into ½-inch (1-cm) cubes
1 medium onion, peeled and chopped
3 cloves garlic, peeled and chopped
2 cups (473 mL) chicken broth
3 tablespoons (45 mL) chili powder
1–3 pickled jalapeño peppers, chopped
¼ teaspoon (1.25 mL) salt

1. Preheat the barbecue to medium high (350°F [180°C] to 400°F [200°C]).

2. In a deep roasting pan or Dutch oven set directly on the grill, cook the bacon until crisp. Remove it from the pan with a slotted spoon and drain, leaving the drippings in the pot. Set the bacon aside.

3. Put the flour in a brown paper bag and add the pork a handful at a time. Shake to coat the meat in the flour.

4. Spoon the meat into the Dutch oven and cook it in the bacon drippings until it is well browned on all sides. Add the bacon, onion, and garlic and cook until the onion is soft. Add the broth, chili powder, jalapeño peppers, and salt and bring to boil. Lower the heat and simmer, uncovered, for 2 hours.

5. Provide bowls of sour cream, shredded cheddar cheese, and chopped green onions on the side.

Orange-Braised Pork with Fruit

Yield: 6–8 servings

You can also cut the shoulder into strips or steaks for this recipe and treat it about the same. But if you use steaks, grill them directly on the grill for 2 to 3 minutes per side to brown for the first step, then add them to the pan with the other ingredients and follow the recipe.

2 tablespoons (30 mL) olive oil
1 (3½-pound [1.5-kg]) pork shoulder, cut into 2-inch (5-cm) cubes
2 teaspoons (10 mL) dried marjoram
½ cup (118 mL) Marsala wine
½ cup (118 mL) orange juice
½ cup (118 mL) water
¼ cup (59 mL) lemon juice
1 tablespoon (15 mL) grated orange zest
1 teaspoon (5 mL) grated fresh ginger
2 bay leaves
1 cup (236 mL) fresh figs, stems removed, halved
2 Golden Delicious apples, cored and sliced
1 orange, peeled, sectioned, and diced

1. Preheat the barbecue to 350°F [180°C] to 400°F [200°C] for direct heating. Oil or spray with cooking spray a roasting pan or Dutch oven.

2. In the prepared roasting pan or Dutch oven, heat the oil. Add the pork and sauté until browned on all sides. Sprinkle with the marjoram and add the wine, orange juice, water, lemon juice, orange zest, ginger, and bay leaves. Cover and simmer until the pork is very tender, about 2 hours. Transfer the meat to a serving dish and cover, reserving the pan juices in the pan.

3. To the reserved pan juices, add the figs, apples and orange pieces and bring to a boil on the grill or a side burner. Cover the pan, reduce the heat, and simmer for about 10 minutes, just until the apples are soft. Spoon the fruit and juices over the pork and serve.

Betty Sue's Brunswick Stew
Yield: 12–14 servings

Brunswick stew is a traditional dish from the South, but the exact origin is uncertain. The stew must be thick; otherwise, it would be vegetable soup with meat added. Most variations have more meat and vegetables than liquid. It is very similar to another southern favorite, burgoo. This recipe comes from Betty-Sue Barnswood from Tuscaloosa, Ala.

2 pounds (908 g) pork shoulder
2 pounds (908 g) chicken breasts, skinned
2 pounds (908 g) beef roast
4 (16-ounce [454-g]) cans chopped tomatoes
1 (32-ounce [908-g]) bottle ketchup
1 (18-ounce [504-g]) bottle barbecue sauce
1 (18-ounce [504-g]) bottle mustard-based barbecue sauce
2 medium onions, peeled and chopped
1 tablespoon (15 mL) Worcestershire sauce
2 teaspoons (10 mL) chili powder
4 (17-ounce [482-g]) cans creamed corn
4 (17-ounce [482-g]) cans whole kernel corn, with juice
3 (10-ounce [280-g]) packages frozen lima beans

1. Preheat the barbecue to 350°F [180°C] to 400°F [200°C] for direct heating.

2. In a 20- to 30-quart (19- to 28-L) stewpot or turkey frying pot set right on the grill or on a side burner, cook the pork, chicken, and beef in 3 quarts (2.9 L) of water, boiling until the meat is very tender, about 20 to 25 minutes. Drain the meat, reserving 3 cups (708 mL) of the cooking water, and set it aside.

3. Add the tomatoes to the same pot and bring to a boil. Add the ketchup, barbecue sauces, onion, Worcestershire sauce, and chili powder. Cook for 1 hour. Tear the beef and pork into bite-size pieces, add them the stew, and stir to mix. Add the creamed and whole kernel corn. Tear the chicken into bite-size pieces and add it to the pot, along with the lima beans, and simmer for an additional 30 to 45 minutes.

4. Serve with thick slices of garlic bread to sop up the juices.

Grilled Pork Steaks

Yield: 4 servings

You can also use pork chops for this recipe, but the steaks tend to have a bit more marbling and therefore are more tender and juicy than most pork chops.

⅓ cup (79 mL) butter, melted
1 tablespoon (15 mL) lemon juice
2 cloves garlic, peeled and minced
1 pinch kosher salt
4 pork shoulder steaks, cut ½-inch (1-cm) thick

1. Preheat the barbecue to 350°F [180°C] to 400°F [200°C] for direct and indirect heating, putting a water pan under the unheated side of the grill. Make sure the grill has been well oiled or sprayed with grilling spray.

2. Pour the melted butter into a small saucepan. Stir in the lemon juice, garlic, and salt and heat over medium heat (do not boil) until the garlic is tender, about 5 minutes. Remove the pan from the heat.

3. Arrange the steaks on a plate and brush the butter sauce on the top of each.

4. Place the chops over direct heat and sear for 1 minute, coating the top side of the steaks with the butter mixture while the other side is grilling. Flip the steaks and sear the other side for 1 minute.

5. Move the steaks to the unheated side of the grill and cook for 4 to 5 minutes per side, brushing several times with the lemon-butter sauce. The steaks are done when their internal temperature reaches 160°F (71°C).

Cider-Brined Pork Shoulder

Yield: 4 servings

Not a conventional brine containing sugar, salt, and water, this brining liquid this brining liquid adds mild sweetness while tenderizing the meat.

1 quart (0.95 L) apple juice
1 cup (227 g) molasses
1 (6–7 pound [2.7–3.2 kg] boneless pork shoulder
1 teaspoon (5 mL) garlic salt
1 teaspoon (5 mL) citrus pepper
⅓ cup (79 mL) all-purpose flour
2 teaspoons (10 mL) dried rosemary
1 teaspoon (5 mL) minced garlic
2 teaspoons (10 mL) chopped fresh parsley

1. In a large resealable plastic bag, combine the apple juice and molasses. Add the pork shoulder and marinate for in the refrigerator for 36 hours, turning bag occasionally.

2. Preheat the barbecue to 325°F (165°C) to 350°F (180°C) for direct and indirect heating, putting a water pan under the unheated side of the grill. Make sure the grill has been well oiled or sprayed with grilling spray.

3. Remove the pork from the marinade and drain briefly, reserving the marinade. Season the pork with the garlic salt and citrus pepper, place it on the heated side of the grill, and cook until all sides of the shoulder are browned, about 20 minutes. Pour 2 cups (236 mL) of the reserved marinade into a saucepan and boil for 10 minutes.

4. Transfer the pork to a roasting pan on the unheated side of the grill and bake for 2 hours, or until a thermometer inserted into the thick part of the roast reads 155°F (68°C). Remove the meat from the barbecue, cover it with foil, and let it rest for 20 minutes.

5. Sprinkle the flour into the roasting pan, add the remaining apple juice-molasses marinade, and cook over medium-high heat, stirring. Add the rosemary and minced garlic and simmer for 10 minutes, stirring frequently. Pour into a sauce boat to serve with the meat.

6. Slice the roast and serve on a warmed platter, sprinkled with the parsley.

Cinnamon and Cranberry Tenderloins
Yield: 4 servings

You could also use fresh or frozen cranberries in this recipe, but you'd need to add sugar or honey. We took the easy route and used our favorite whole-berry cranberry sauce instead.

3 tablespoons (45 mL) olive oil, divided
2 teaspoons (10 mL) ground cinnamon
2 (1½–2 pounds [681–908 g]) pork tenderloins
Salt, to taste
Freshly ground black pepper, to taste
1 onion, sliced
2 cloves garlic, peeled and minced
2 cups (473 mL) whole-berry cranberry sauce
½ cup (118 mL) chicken stock

1. Preheat the barbecue to 350°F [180°C] to 400°F [200°C] for direct heating, making sure the grill has been well oiled or sprayed with grilling spray. Oil a roasting pan with 2 tablespoons (30 mL) of the olive oil.

2. In a bowl, stir the cinnamon into the remaining olive oil. Brush this mixture on the tenderloins and season with salt and pepper.

3. Place the tenderloins on the grill and brown for 2 to 3 minutes per side. With tongs, transfer the pork to the prepared roasting pan. Surround the pork with the sliced onions and sprinkle the onions with the garlic.

4. Place the roasting pan in the barbecue and cook for 15 minutes, occasionally stirring the onions and turning the tenderloins. Pour the cranberry sauce and chicken stock around the meat, cover the roasting pan, and cook for another 10 minutes.

5. Transfer the tenderloins to a cutting board, cover them with foil, and let the meat rest for 10 minutes. Heat the pan sauce, stirring to reduce it slightly.

6. Slice the tenderloins at an angle across the grain, and place the slices on a warmed serving platter. Pour the cranberry-onion gravy over the meat and serve.

Grilled Pork Liver Italiano

Yield: 4 servings

Caul fat is the white lacy membrane that surrounds an animal's stomach. Specialty butchers and Italian and Chinese grocery stores often stock caul fat or can order it for you. It virtually melts off while the meat cooks, and it keeps the liver from drying out.

½ pound (227 g) caul fat
1 pound (454 g) fresh pork liver
Sea salt, to taste
Freshly ground black pepper, to taste
6–8 bay leaves, cut in half

1. Soak the caul fat in warm water for 10 minutes to make it more pliable.

2. Cut the liver into 1 x 2 inch (2.5 x 5 cm) pieces, discarding any sections with veins. Sprinkle each piece lightly with salt and pepper.

3. Preheat the barbecue to 350°F [180°C] to 400°F [200°C] for direct heating, making sure the grill has been well oiled or sprayed with grilling spray.

4. Drain and carefully unfold the caul fat. Cut it into pieces large enough to wrap around each piece of liver in one layer. Place half a bay leaf on a piece of liver and wrap it with the fat. Sprinkle with more salt and pepper and set aside. Repeat with each of the liver pieces, the bay leaves, and the caul fat.

5. Place the wrapped liver pieces on the hot grill and cook until they liver is browned on one side, about 3 to 4 minutes. Carefully turn the liver pieces with a spatula and cook on the other side for about the same time. Be careful not to overcook. Ideally, the liver will be nicely browned on the outside and still a little pink in the middle. The caul fat will have mostly melted off by the time you're finished grilling.

6. Transfer the liver to a heated platter and serve immediately with a loaf of soft Italian bread to soak up the juices.

Rothenberg-Style Spicy Pork Shanks

Yield: 6 servings

Pork shanks are the lower portion of the rear and front legs of the pig. This flavorful cut can be braised whole, or the shanks be be cut into cross sections for a less-expensive alternative to veal osso buco. The meat becomes silky and delicious when cooked slowly at low heat.

6 (1½-pound [681-g]) pork shanks
⅓ cup (79 mL) all-purpose flour
2 tablespoons (30 mL) chili powder
1 tablespoon (15 mL) kosher salt, plus more to taste
1 tablespoon (15 mL) freshly ground black pepper, plus more to taste
¼ cup (59 mL) olive oil plus 2 tablespoons, divided
1 large onion, peeled and diced
2 medium carrots, diced
2 medium celery stalks, diced
2 tablespoons (30 mL) minced garlic
1 cup (236 mL) dry red wine
6 cups (1.4 L) chicken or vegetable stock
1 tablespoon (15 mL) chopped fresh rosemary
3 bay leaves
1 tablespoon (15 mL) chopped fresh thyme

1. Put 2 of the pork shanks in a 2-gallon (7.8-L) resealable plastic bag. Pour in the flour, chili powder, salt, and pepper, shake to coat the shanks, and remove the meat from the bag. Repeat with the remaining shanks.

2. In a large skillet, heat half of the olive oil until very hot. Add half of the pork shanks and cook for about 10 minutes, turning often, until the shanks are nicely browned. Remove the shanks, setting them on a plate. Wipe out the skillet, add the remaining oil, and brown the remaining meat.

3. Spray an 8-quart (7.6-L) Dutch oven with nonstick cooking spray. Place the shanks in the Dutch oven and set aside.

4. Preheat the barbecue to 320°F (165°C) to 350°F (180°C) for indirect heating, putting a water pan under the unheated side of the grill.

5. In a large skillet over medium heat, cook the onion, carrots, celery, and garlic in 2 tablespoons olive oil for 6 to 8 minutes, or until the vegetables are softened. Add the wine and bring to a boil. Reduce the heat and simmer for 3 to 4 minutes to slightly reduce the liquid.

6. Pour the vegetables and wine into the Dutch oven. Add the stock, rosemary, bay leaves, and thyme and season with salt and pepper. Bring to a boil. The shanks should be mostly covered; if not, add water as needed. Cover the Dutch oven and place it on the indirect side of the grill. Cook, turning the shanks every 30 minutes, for 2½ hours, or until the meat is very tender.

7. Transfer the braised shanks to a large, deep platter, cover, and keep warm.

8. Strain the gravy, discarding the vegetables and herbs, and pour it back into the Dutch oven. Bring to a boil and cook until the gravy is reduced to 4 cups (0.95 L), about 15 to 20 minutes. Skim off the fat, pour the gravy over the braised shanks, and serve.

Barbecue Caramelized Bacon

Yield: 2–4 servings (probably 2, once you taste it)

You can go out and buy fancy bacon that's been sugared, slow baked, and is the best bacon you've ever tasted (like the Black Forest bacon at Whole Foods), or you can make your own.

12 slices thick bacon
½ cup (118 mL) packed dark brown sugar
¼ teaspoon (1.25 mL) cayenne pepper
1 pinch hickory smoke powder
2 tablespoons (30 mL) water

1. Preheat a gas or charcoal grill to 350°F [180°C] to 400°F [200°C] for direct grilling. Line a baking sheet with heavy-duty aluminum foil. Spray a wire rack with nonstick cooking spray and place the rack on the baking sheet.

2. Cut the bacon slices in half and arrange them in a single layer on the wire rack. In a small bowl, combine the brown sugar, cayenne pepper, smoke powder, and water and mix well. Brush this mixture generously over both sides of the bacon. Bake in the barbecue for 30 minutes, or until the bacon is beginning to crisp on the edges as the sugar caramelizes.

3. Remove the bacon from the barbecue, drain it quickly on paper towels, and serve.

The Ultimate Grilled Ham and Chee$e $andwiche$

Yield: 4 sandwiches

A little whimsical adventure in expensive eating takes us to Sweden, London (twice), Spain, and the hills of Vermont.

¼ pound (112 g) Moose House moose milk cheese ($500)
8 slices Harrod's Roquefort and Almond sourdough bread ($24.50 per loaf)
8 slices Jamón Ibérico pata negra ham ($2,803.95)
Organic butter from Vermont ($60)

Cost of 4 sandwiches: $3,388.45 (and that doesn't include shipping).

The cheese is from moose cows (or cow moose) milked on a 59-acre dairy farm in Bjursholm, Sweden, and costs $500 a pound. They won't ship less than a pound (454 g) to the United States.

The ham slices are from a ham cured by Manuel Maldonado in Extremadura, Spain, and, sold at Selfridges in London, the whole leg costs $2,803.95.

Since you can't just buy slices, that's our price.

The bread comes from London as well. Baked by Harrods' master baker Paul Hollywood, the Roquefort and Almond sourdough bread loaf sells for $24.50. Since they only sell full loaves, we can't just buy 8 slices, so we figure that's the price of the bread. But don't worry; we won't throw the rest away.

The butter comes from the Animal Farm in Orwell, Vermont, and costs $60 per pound. They don't sell it in quantities smaller than a full pound (454 g).

Grilled Spam and Pineapple

Yield: 4–6 servings

Spam, introduced in 1937 as "the Miracle Meat," is most popular in Alaska and Hawaii. Smokejumpers carry cans of it in their backpacks so they have a high-fat and high-calorie food that they can eat right out of the can, if necessary, when they're stuck on a mountainside fighting a forest fire.

3 tablespoons (45 mL) brown sugar
1 tablespoon (15 mL) prepared yellow mustard
1 pinch nutmeg
3 tablespoons (45 mL) honey
1 tablespoon (15 mL) melted butter
1 pinch cinnamon
1 (12-ounce [336-g]) can Spam, cut into 6 slices
6 slices fresh pineapple (same thickness as the Spam slices)
6 sesame seed hamburger buns (optional)

1. Preheat the barbecue to 350°F [180°C] to 400°F [200°C] for direct heating, making sure the grill has been well oiled or sprayed with grilling spray.

2. In a small bowl, mix together the brown sugar, mustard, and nutmeg. In a separate small bowl, mix together the honey, butter, and cinnamon.

3. Place the Spam and pineapple slices side by side on the grill. Brush the Spam with the mustard glaze and the pineapples with the honey glaze. Cook for 3 minutes, turn the ham and pineapple slices, and brush the second side with the glazes. Cook for an additional 3 minutes.

4. Remove the Spam and pineapple from the grill and either place them on toasted sesame hamburger buns or serve them on plates with potato salad and coleslaw.

Barbecued Pig's Feet
Yield: 6–8 servings

Some people love them; others wouldn't even eat them on a bet. We're offering them up here, just in case you want to try these "delicacies" . . . or you lose that bet.

8 fresh pig's feet, halved lengthwise
2 quarts (1.9 L) water
2 quarts (1.9 L) vinegar
2 large onions, peeled and chopped
2 green bell peppers, cored, seeded, and chopped
¼ cup (59 mL) red pepper flakes
3 tablespoons (45 mL) salt
1 tablespoon (15 mL) freshly ground black pepper
2–3 cups (473–708 mL) barbecue sauce of your choice

1. Wash the pig's feet well. Place them in a large pot on the gas grill and pour in the water and vinegar. Add the onions, green bell peppers, red pepper flakes, salt, and black pepper and bring to a boil. Reduce the heat and simmer until the pig is tender, about 2½ hours. Skim off the surface scum and stir the meat several times.

2. Preheat the barbecue to 350°F [180°C] to 400°F [200°C] for direct heating, making sure the grill has been well oiled or sprayed with grilling spray.

3. With tongs or a slotted spoon, remove the pigs' feet from the broth tongs and arrange them in a single layer in 2 roasting pans. Spoon the barbecue sauce over the pig's feet and cook them in the barbecue for 35 to 40 minutes, basting a couple of times.

4. When they are tender, crispy at the edges, and browned all over, they are ready to serve.

Grilled Pork Belly

Yield: 4–6 servings

Bacon comes from the pork belly, and this cut of meat is very popular in Asia, especially China and Korea. Grilling the uncured fatty piece of pork produces a heavenly, if somewhat caloric, tasty delight.

2 pounds (908 g) pork belly, skinned
2 shallots, peeled and diced
1 medium yellow onion, peeled and diced
1 green onion, sliced, green and white parts
1 red chili pepper, finely diced
2 tablespoons (30 mL) sugar
2 tablespoons (30 mL) grated garlic
2 tablespoons (30 mL) dark soy sauce
2 tablespoons (30 mL) olive oil
1 tablespoon (15 mL) grated lime zest
1 tablespoon (15 mL) Thai fish sauce
1 tablespoon (15 mL) dark sesame oil
1 tablespoon (15 mL) rice wine vinegar
Salt, to taste
Freshly ground black pepper, to taste

1. Cut the pork belly into 6 to 8 pieces and place them in a 1- to 2-gallon (3.8- to 7.6-L) resealable plastic bag.

2. In a large bowl, combine the shallots, yellow and green onion, chili pepper, sugar, garlic, soy sauce, olive oil, lime zest, fish sauce, sesame oil, vinegar, salt, and pepper and stir to dissolve most of the sugar. Pour this marinade into the bag over the pork belly, seal, and shake the bag to coat all the meat. Refrigerate overnight.

3. Remove the pork from the marinade. Pour the marinade into a saucepan and boil for 10 minutes while the pork belly comes to room temperature.

4. Preheat the barbecue to 350°F [180°C] to 400°F [200°C] for direct heating, making sure the grill has been well oiled or sprayed with grilling spray.

5. Place the pork belly on the grill and cook, brushing with marinade, for about 5 minutes per side, or until the pork belly is browned and crispy. Dripping fat may cause the fire to flare up, so close the lid when not basting the pork.

6. Transfer the pork to a heated platter and serve with barbecue-baked potatoes and grilled red, green, and yellow bell peppers.

ELEVEN

Rubs and
Seasonings

The ingredients in the following rubs should be mixed together well, rubbed gently into meat, fish, poultry, or game, and left to dry marinate for at least 2 to 4 hours, but in most cases I prefer to let the rub do its job for 6 to 8 hours, or, better yet, overnight.

Beer-Butt Chicken Rub

1 tablespoon (15 mL) paprika
1 tablespoon (15 mL) sea salt (ground fine)
1 teaspoon (5 mL) brown sugar
1 teaspoon (5 mL) garlic powder
1 teaspoon (5 mL) onion powder
1 teaspoon (5 mL) dried summer savory
1 teaspoon (5 mL) dry yellow mustard
¼ teaspoon (1.25 mL) cayenne pepper

White Barbecue Rub

¼ cup (59 mL) onion powder
¼ cup (59 mL) ground white pepper
2 tablespoons (30 mL) garlic powder
2 tablespoons (30 mL) granulated sugar
1 tablespoon (15 mL) salt

Greek Lamb Rub

10 cloves garlic, peeled and minced
1 tablespoon (15 mL) dried mint
2 teaspoons (10 mL) (or less) salt
1½ teaspoons (7.5 mL) ground allspice
1½ teaspoons (7.5 mL) ground nutmeg
1 teaspoon (5 mL) freshly ground black pepper
½ teaspoon (2.5 mL) ground cinnamon

Curried Rub

¼ cup (59 mL) chili powder
2 teaspoons (10 mL) celery salt
1 teaspoon (5 mL) onion powder
1 teaspoon (5 mL) curry powder
1 teaspoon (5 mL) ground cumin
1 teaspoon (5 mL) garlic powder
1 teaspoon (5 mL) dry mustard
1 teaspoon (5 mL) ground white pepper
1 teaspoon (5 mL) dried oregano
1 teaspoon (5 mL) parsley flakes

Tangy Rub

1 tablespoon (15 mL) honey granules
1 tablespoon (15 mL) lemon granules
1 tablespoon (15 mL) Worcestershire Powder (Page 540)
1 teaspoon (5 mL) granulated sugar
1 teaspoon (5 mL) garlic powder
½ teaspoon (2.5 mL) ground thyme

Pig Man Rub

3 tablespoons (45 mL) paprika
2 teaspoons (10 mL) seasoned salt
2 teaspoons (10 mL) freshly ground black pepper
2 teaspoons (10 mL) garlic powder
2 teaspoons (10 mL) ground green peppercorns
1 teaspoon (5 mL) cayenne pepper
1 teaspoon (5 mL) dried summer savory
1 teaspoon (5 mL) dry mustard
1 teaspoon (5 mL) dried thyme
1 teaspoon (5 mL) ground coriander
1 teaspoon (5 mL) ground allspice
½ teaspoon (2.5 mL) chili powder

HiBrow Rub

1 clove garlic, peeled and crushed
10 allspice berries, crushed
2 tablespoons (30 mL) olive oil
½ teaspoon (2.5 mL) finely chopped fresh rosemary

Marrakesh Rub

2 tablespoons (30 mL) paprika
1 teaspoon (5 mL) salt
1 teaspoon (5 mL) sugar
½ teaspoon (2.5 mL) coarsely ground black pepper
½ teaspoon (2.5 mL) ground ginger
½ teaspoon (2.5 mL) ground cardamom
½ teaspoon (2.5 mL) ground cumin
½ teaspoon (2.5 mL) ground fenugreek
½ teaspoon (2.5 mL) ground cloves
¼ teaspoon (1.25 mL) ground cinnamon
¼ teaspoon (1.25 mL) ground allspice
¼ teaspoon (1.25 mL) cayenne pepper

Cowboy Rub

1 tablespoon (15 mL) chili powder
1 tablespoon (15 mL) paprika
1 teaspoon (5 mL) cayenne pepper
1 teaspoon (5 mL) curry powder
1 teaspoon (5 mL) ground turmeric
1 teaspoon (5 mL) ground ginger
1 teaspoon (5 mL) ground cumin
1 dash ground nutmeg

Memphis "Dry" Rib Rub

½ cup (118 mL) paprika
½ cup (118 mL) garlic salt
½ cup (118 mL) packed brown sugar
¼ cup (59 mL) freshly ground black pepper
2 tablespoons (30 mL) chili powder
1 tablespoon (15 mL) dried oregano

Memphis "Wet" Rib Rub

1 tablespoon (15 mL) paprika
1 tablespoon (15 mL) onion salt
1 tablespoon (15 mL) garlic powder
1 tablespoon (15 mL) brown sugar
1 teaspoon (5 mL) ground cumin
1 teaspoon (5 mL) freshly ground black pepper
½ teaspoon (2.5 mL) cayenne pepper

HiLonesome Rub

2 tablespoons (30 mL) coarsely ground black pepper
4 teaspoons (20 mL) garlic powder
4 teaspoons (20 mL) onion powder
1 tablespoon (15 mL) Worcestershire powder*
2 teaspoons (10 mL) cornstarch
2 teaspoons (10 mL) ground cumin
2 teaspoons (10 mL) salt
1 teaspoon (5 mL) paprika
1 teaspoon (5 mL) beef bouillon granules
½ teaspoon (2.5 mL) lemon pepper
¼ teaspoon (1.25 mL) ground rosemary
* available online from Oregon Spice Company (www.oregonspice.com)

Chinese Five-Spice Rub

1 teaspoon (5 mL) ground cinnamon
1 pod star anise, ground
¼ teaspoon (1.25 mL) crushed fennel seed
¼ teaspoon (1.25 mL) freshly ground black pepper
¼ teaspoon (1.25 mL) ground Szechuan peppercorns
⅛ teaspoon (0.6 mL) ground cloves

Veggie Rub

2 tablespoons (30 mL) ground sage
2 tablespoons (30 mL) granulated garlic
2 tablespoons (30 mL) dried parsley
2 tablespoons (30 mL) salt
2 tablespoons (30 mL) coarsely ground black pepper
2 tablespoons (30 mL) granulated sugar
2 tablespoons (30 mL) paprika

Onion Prime Rib Rub

1½ teaspoons (7.5 mL) kosher salt
1½ teaspoons (7.5 mL) onion powder
1 teaspoon (5 mL) freshly ground black pepper
1 teaspoon (5 mL) smoked paprika
1 teaspoon (5 mL) celery seeds

Savory Rub

⅓ cup (79 mL) paprika
3 tablespoons (45 mL) dry mustard
3 tablespoons (45 mL) onion powder
3 tablespoons (45 mL) garlic powder
2 tablespoons (30 mL) ground basil
2 tablespoons (30 mL) dried savory
1 tablespoon (15 mL) cayenne pepper
1 tablespoon (15 mL) freshly ground black pepper
1 tablespoon (15 mL) salt

Volcanic Rub

1 cup (236 mL) hot chili powder
¼ cup (59 mL) garlic salt
2 tablespoons (30 mL) cayenne pepper
2 tablespoons (30 mL) freshly ground black pepper
1 teaspoon (5 mL) hot paprika

Beef Rib Rub

¼ cup (59 mL) paprika
¼ cup (59 mL) mild or hot chili powder
¼ cup (59 mL) packed brown sugar
¼ cup (59 mL) freshly ground black pepper
1 tablespoon (15 mL) cayenne pepper
1 tablespoon (15 mL) garlic powder
1 tablespoon (15 mL) salt

Scandinavian Rub

3 tablespoons (45 mL) sugar
2 teaspoons (10 mL) salt
1 teaspoon (5 mL) whole cumin seeds
¼ teaspoon (1.25 mL) ground cardamom

Thai Duck Rub

2 teaspoons (10 mL) salt
2 teaspoons (10 mL) ground Szechuan peppercorns
1 teaspoon (5 mL) ground ginger
1 teaspoon (5 mL) five-spice powder

Mojo Pork Rub

2 teaspoons (10 mL) dried oregano
2 teaspoons (10 mL) ground cumin
2 teaspoons (10 mL) sweet paprika
2 teaspoons (10 mL) granulated garlic
1 teaspoon (5 mL) sea salt
¼ teaspoon (1.25 mL) cayenne pepper

Chocolate Cumin Spice Rub

2 tablespoons (30 mL) unsweetened cocoa
2 tablespoons (30 mL) ground cumin
2 tablespoons (30 mL) freshly ground black pepper
1 tablespoon (15 mL) ground allspice
1 tablespoons (15 mL) sea salt

Blackened Beef Rub

1 tablespoon (22.5 mL) paprika
2 teaspoons (10 mL) salt
2 teaspoons (10 mL) freshly ground black pepper
1 teaspoon (7.5 mL) garlic powder
1 teaspoon (7.5 mL) onion powder
½ teaspoon (2.5 mL) cayenne pepper
½ teaspoon (2.5 mL) dried thyme
½ teaspoon (2.5 mL) dried oregano

Pacific NW Salmon Rub

1 cup (236 mL) packed light brown sugar
1 cup (236 mL) non-iodized table salt
3 tablespoons (45 mL) granulated garlic
3 tablespoons (45 mL) granulated onion
1 tablespoon (15 mL) dried dill weed
1 tablespoon (15 mL) dried savory
2 teaspoons (10 mL) dried tarragon

North of the Border Chile Rub

Dave DeWitt of Albuquerque, N.M., shared his spin on a Southwestern rub that would work on goat, as in cabrito (pit-roasted goat). Use this rub for grilling or smoking beef, pork, or lamb.

3 tablespoons (45 mL) ground ancho chile
2 teaspoons (10 mL) ground chile de arbol
2 teaspoons (10 mL) ground chipotle chile
2 teaspoons (10 mL) dried oregano, Mexican preferred
2 teaspoons (10 mL) onion salt
1 teaspoon (5 mL) ground cumin
1 teaspoon (5 mL) garlic powder

TWELVE

Sauces

Barbecue Sauces

There are as many varieties and recipes for barbecue sauces as there are barbecues, but here is a primer of the most popular sauces found in the United States.

Carolina Sauces. East of Raleigh: vinegar, black pepper, ground cayenne pepper, and sugar. This is a sauce as simple as it is thin. In the Western part of the state, vinegar, black pepper, and cayenne pepper are cooked in a pot, to which is then added ketchup, Worcestershire sauce, or molasses, plus a bit of sugar to sweeten the pot, resulting in a thin red sauce.

Georgia Sauce. The folks here think mustard and pork (ham) go pretty well together, so they use ketchup, vinegar, brown sugar, and mustard to make a thicker yellow sauce.

Alabama Sauce. This vinegary white sauce is thickened with eggs or mayonnaise. This creamy yellow sauce is not heavy, and it is chilled and put on food right before serving. Heating it would break down the eggs.

Kentucky Sauce. Kentucky's "black" sauce, which is indeed black, peppery, and very thin, is actually a clear vinegar sauce to which they add molasses and sometimes a dash or two of Worcestershire sauce.

Memphis Sauce. Like Kentucky sauce, this one includes vinegar; like the Carolinas, it includes Tabasco from the Bayou. These ingredients are mixed with lots of tomato sauce and maybe a squirt or two of ketchup.

Texas Sauce. Very full of smoky tomato flavor, this is the thickest of all the regional sauces, mainly because it also contains chopped onions. Sugar is left out—no sissy sweeteners for Texas.

Kansas City Sauce. KC folks stir tomato sauce, vinegar, salt, molasses, mustard, chilies or cayenne pepper, and sugar (brown or white) into a thick sauce (but, not as thick as the Texans' sauce). Most commercially bottled sauces are basically Kansas City–style sauces.

California Sauce. Californians combine ingredients from Asian and Pacific cuisines, including soy, teriyaki, oyster, fish, and hoisin sauces; flavored vinegars; honey or turbinado sugar; and fruit juices such as apple, apricot, pineapple, and mango to make light and flavorful basting, marinating, and serving sauces.

New Mexico Sauce. Cayenne pepper, ancho chili powder, and pasilla chili powder are used to fire up the culinary senses. Many New Mexican sauces start out like Texas-, Kansas City–, or Memphis-style sauces, but then the chili powder, raw chilies and red peppers are added.

Hawaii Sauce. These sauces are similar to California's, but they are more of a sweet-and-sour sauce. Hawaiian sauces use pineapple, mango, and papaya juice as both a tenderizer and a sauce base. Soy sauce, fresh and ground ginger, five-spice powder, lemon juice, rice vinegar, and molasses are added for delicious, fresh, fruity sauces.

Pacific Northwest Sauce. Two things influence sauces in the Pacific Northwest: the abundance of really, really fresh salmon and the abundance of really, really fresh berries—primarily blueberries, raspberries, and marionberries. Hence this region produces fruity, light sauces that are good on fish as well as other barbecued foods.

Dr. Pepper Barbecue Sauce

Yield: 3–4 cups (708 mL–.95 L)

If you can find it, use the original Dr. Pepper made with pure sugar, not corn syrup or other sweeteners. This recipe comes from Greg Gilbert from La Center, Wash.

½ cup (118 mL) unsalted butter
1 large yellow onion, peeled and chopped
4 cloves garlic, peeled and finely minced
1 (12-ounce [340-mL]) can Dr. Pepper
1 cup (236 mL) ketchup
½ cup (118 mL) cider vinegar
½ cup (118 mL) packed dark brown sugar
⅓ cup (79 mL) Worcestershire sauce
3 tablespoons (45 mL) tomato paste
1 tablespoon (15 mL) balsamic vinegar
2 teaspoons (10 mL) chili powder
1 teaspoon (5 mL) kosher salt
1 teaspoon (5 mL) freshly ground black pepper
¼ teaspoon (1.25 mL) cayenne pepper

1. In a heavy saucepan, melt the butter. Add the onion and garlic and sauté until translucent, about 10 minutes.

2. Add the remaining ingredients to the saucepan, bring to a simmer, and simmer for about 15 minutes. Reduce the heat and cook at a low simmer for 20 to 30 minutes to thicken the sauce.

3. Transfer the sauce to a blender and purée, or use an immersion blender.

4. Transfer the sauce to a tightly covered container and store in the refrigerator for up to 2 weeks.

Balsamic Barbecue Sauce

Yield: 2–3 cups (473–708 mL)

If you don't like the fire of the Sriracha sauce, use your favorite hot sauce, or just leave the hot sauce out for a milder balsamic flavor.

1 cup (236 mL) beer
1 cup (236 mL) ketchup
½ cup (118 mL) packed brown sugar,
⅓ cup (79 mL) balsamic vinegar
1 tablespoon (15 mL) minced garlic
2 teaspoons (10 mL) ground cumin
2 teaspoons (10 mL) Sriracha sauce
1 teaspoon (5 mL) chili powder
1 teaspoon (5 mL) freshly ground black pepper

1. In a saucepan, combine all the ingredients. Bring to a boil, reduce the heat, and simmer, stirring frequently, for 25 minutes, or until reduced to about 2 or 3 cups (473-708 mL).

2. Transfer the sauce to a covered container and chill for up to 2 weeks.

Jamaican Mango and Scotch Bonnet Sauce
Yield: 3 cups (708 mL)

Scotch bonnets are one of the hottest peppers you can buy in a regular grocery store. Please wear gloves when handling and be very careful, as touching your nose, lips, or eyes with pepper on your hands or gloves can be extremely painful.

2 tablespoons (30 mL) peanut oil
4 ripe mangoes, peeled, pitted, and roughly chopped
1 large white onion, peeled and diced
1 carrot, peeled and diced
1 Scotch bonnet pepper, seeded and finely minced
½ cup (118 mL) apple cider vinegar
½ cup (118 mL) ketchup
¼ cup (59 mL) packed brown sugar
½ teaspoon (2.5 mL) garlic salt

1. In a saucepan, heat the peanut oil over medium heat. Add the mangoes, onion, carrot, and pepper and sauté for 10 minutes or until the onion is soft and translucent.

2. Deglaze the saucepan with the vinegar, scraping up any bits left on the surface, and add the ketchup and brown sugar. Bring to a slow boil, reduce the heat, and simmer for 30 minutes.

3. Remove the pan from the heat and add the garlic salt.

4. Transfer the mixture to a food processor or blender and pulse or process until smooth.

5. Strain through a medium sieve.

Any-Porter-in-a-Storm Barbecue Sauce
Yield: 3 cups (708 mL)

If you aren't a fan of dark beers, you can use regular lighter beer, but the strongly flavored varieties really give this sauce richness.

1 cup (236 mL) porter of your choice
1 cup (236 mL) ketchup
¼ cup (59 mL) distilled white vinegar
¼ cup (59 mL) Worcestershire sauce
¼ cup (59 mL) packed brown sugar
1 tablespoon (15 mL) onion powder
1 teaspoon (5 mL) dry mustard
½ cup (118 mL) finely chopped onion
Zest of 1 lemon

1. In a large saucepan, mix together the beer, ketchup, vinegar, Worcestershire sauce, brown sugar, onion powder, and mustard. Bring to a boil, reduce the heat, and simmer for 12 minutes.

2. Add the onion and lemon zest and stir well. Simmer for another 6 minutes.

3. If you don't like the minced onion chunks, purée the sauce in a blender.

Tucumcari Barbecue Sauce

Yield: 3–4 cups (708 mL–.95 L)

The coriander is essential to the unique Southwestern flavor of this sauce, and the peppers reinforce the fiery nature of the region.

1 cup (236 mL) rice vinegar
1 cup (236 mL) cider vinegar
2 tablespoons (30 mL) ground coriander
1 teaspoon (5 mL) chili powder
⅛ teaspoon (0.6 mL) ground cloves
¼ cup (59 mL) olive oil
1 medium onion, peeled and diced
2 tablespoons (30 mL) minced garlic
1 cup (236 mL) packed brown sugar
¼ cup (59 mL) dark molasses
1½ cups (354 mL) ketchup
1 cup (236 mL) puréed chipotle peppers in adobo
1 tablespoon (15 mL) Worcestershire sauce
Salt, to taste
Freshly ground black pepper, to taste

1. In a saucepan, combine the vinegars, coriander, chili powder, and cloves. Bring to a boil over medium heat, then reduce the heat and simmer until the liquid is reduced in half. Set aside.

2. In a large saucepan, heat the olive oil. Add the onion and sauté lightly until the onions are just translucent. Add the garlic.

3. Add the brown sugar and molasses and cook for 10 minutes.

4. Add the reserved vinegar mixture, the ketchup, the peppers, and the Worcestershire sauce and cook over low heat for 45 to 50 minutes.

5. Season to taste with salt and pepper. Transfer the sauce to a food processor and process until smooth.

Plum Good Barbecue Sauce

Yield: 3 cups (708 mL)

This sauce is wonderful on pork tenderloin, pork ribs, or pork chops. You can also add chopped plums to make it a chunky sauce.

2 cups (473 mL) bottled chili sauce
½ cup (118 mL) plum jam
⅓ cup (79 mL) lime juice
¼ cup (60 mL) honey
1 teaspoon (5 mL) garlic salt
1 teaspoon (5 mL) favorite hot sauce

1. In a large saucepan, combine all the ingredients and heat over medium heat until blended.

2. Cool and store in a covered container in the refrigerator for up to 3 weeks.

Hong Kong Grilling Sauce
Yield: 2 cups (473 mL)

This is a pseudo-satay sauce. You can leave out the sesame seeds if you prefer, but they do add a nice crunch. Do not use low-fat peanut butter—it's too sweet. This recipe comes from Stephen Petersen from Battle Ground, Wash.

½ cup (118 mL) dark soy sauce
⅓ cup (79 mL) olive oil
⅓ cup (79 mL) cooking sherry
¼ cup (60 mL) toasted sesame seeds
¼ cup (60 mL) packed brown sugar
2 tablespoons (30 mL) smooth peanut butter
2 tablespoons (30 mL) medium-hot curry powder
1 teaspoon (5 mL) grated fresh ginger
1 tablespoon (15 mL) minced garlic
4 green onions, finely diced, white and green parts

1. In a blender or food processor, combine the soy sauce, olive oil, sherry, sesame seeds, brown sugar, peanut butter, and curry powder and blend until relatively smooth.

2. Pour this mixture into a saucepan and heat over medium heat for 5 to 6 minutes. Add the ginger, garlic, and green onions, stirring well.

3. Remove the sauce from heat and serve warm, or transfer it to a sealed container and refrigerate for up to 2 weeks. Use as a dip for kebabs of pork, chicken, lamb, or beef, or brush it on during the last 5 minutes of cooking.

North Carolina Barbecue Sauce
Yield: 3½–4 cups (826 mL–.95 L)

This is one of perhaps 3 million adaptations of North Carolina sauce. Some purists would cry if they knew we added ketchup and steak sauce, but it sure tastes great.

1½ cups (354 mL) packed brown sugar
½ cup (118 mL) salted butter
½ cup (118 mL) distilled white vinegar
1 cup (236 mL) ketchup
1 cup (227 g) Heinz 57 sauce
1 cup (236 mL) finely minced onion
2–3 tablespoons (30–45 mL) red pepper flakes
1 tablespoon (15 mL) celery seeds
1 tablespoon (15 mL) dry mustard

1. In a large saucepan, combine the sugar and butter. Cook over medium high heat, stirring often, until it begins to boil and bubble.

2. Add the vinegar and whisk or stir until smooth. Add the ketchup, steak sauce, onion, red pepper flakes, celery seeds, and mustard and cook over low heat for 10 minutes, stirring often.

3. Brush the sauce on ribs or pork shoulder, butt, or chops during the last 5 minutes of cooking, or use with pulled pork to make sandwiches.

Cranberry Grillin' Glaze

Yield: 1½ cups (354 mL)

This glaze is perfect for roast chicken or turkey. Just brush it on the bird during the last 5 minutes of cooking, and serve extra in a small bowl to add at tableside. This recipe comes from Kate Browne from Ridgefield, Wash.

1 (8-ounce [227-g] can cranberry sauce
3 tablespoons (45 mL) honey
3 tablespoons (45 mL) apple cider vinegar
1 teaspoon (5 mL) olive oil
1 teaspoon (5 mL) kosher salt
½ teaspoon (2.5 mL) ground cinnamon

1. In a large bowl, combine all the ingredients and mix well. Put the sauce in a sealed container and refrigerate for 2 to 3 hours before using.

Dutch Oven Barbecue Sauce

Yield: 2 cups (473 mL)

This hearty sauce was first made for a camping trip, where we used it to slather over beef short ribs that fell off the bone after cooking. Pout the sauce over meat in a large pan, cook until the meat is tender, and serve the meat with the remaining sauce on the side.

1 green bell pepper, chopped
1 small white onion, peeled and chopped
½ cup (118 mL) ketchup
¼ cup (59 mL) packed brown sugar
¼ cup (59 mL) dark molasses
¼ cup (59 mL) soy sauce
1 tablespoon (15 mL) balsamic vinegar
1 teaspoon (5 mL) dry mustard
1 teaspoon (5 mL) lemon juice

1. In a large saucepan, mix together the pepper, onion, ketchup, brown sugar, molasses, soy sauce, vinegar, mustard, and lemon juice and bring to a boil over high heat.

Terry's Yaki Marinade/Sauce

Yield: 3 cups (708 mL)

For a bit more flavor, substitute a dry white wine for the water. This recipe comes from Terry Callon from Victoria, British Columbia.

1 cup (236 mL) dark soy sauce
1 cup (236 mL) water
¾ cup (177 mL) dry sherry
½ cup (118 mL) packed brown sugar
¼ cup (59 mL) minced green onion, white and green parts
1 teaspoon (5 mL) minced fresh ginger
1 teaspoon (5 mL) minced garlic

1. In a large saucepan, combine the soy sauce, sherry, brown sugar, green onion, ginger, and garlic and heat over medium-high heat, stirring often to dissolve the sugar. Use the sauce to marinate pork, chicken, beef, lamb, or wild game meats such as venison, elk, or moose, or as a dipping sauce for fish, shrimp, or shellfish.

Suckling Pig Basting Sauce

Yield: 3 cups (708 mL)

A suckling pig is defined as one that's approximately 2 to 6 weeks old and weighs 12 to 16 pounds (5.4 to 7.3 kg). It is truly a delicacy with incredibly tender meat. You can use this as a basting sauce or pour some of the sauce in the body cavity of a suckling pig you're cooking upside down on the grill.

1 cup (236 mL) honey
1 cup (236 mL) soy sauce
1 cup (236 mL) orange juice
¼ cup (59 mL) lime juice
4 limes, sliced
4 lemons, sliced
2 tangerines, sliced
1 tablespoon (15 mL) salt

1. In a large bowl, mix together the honey, soy sauce, orange and lime juices, lime, lemon, and tangerine slices, and salt. Cover until ready to use.

Spicy Fish Sauce

Yield: 1 cup (236 mL)

If you love swordfish, shark, or other firm-fleshed fish, this sauce is the answer to a perfect barbecue. Just brush it on during the last few minutes of cooking; otherwise, the sugar will burn. You can also serve it on the side. Or try it as a dipping sauce for grilled shrimp or oysters. This recipe comes from Kevin Lynch from Southington, Conn.

2 cloves garlic, peeled and finely minced
½ teaspoon (2.5 mL) red pepper flakes
½ cup (118 mL) dry white wine
¼ cup (59 mL) lemon juice
¼ cup (59 mL) Thai fish sauce
2 tablespoons (30 mL) brown sugar
1 tablespoon (15 mL) grated lemon zest
Salt, to taste
Freshly ground black pepper, to taste

1. In a medium bowl, mash the garlic and pepper flakes into a paste. Add the wine, lemon juice, fish sauce, brown sugar, lemon zest, salt, and pepper.

Pomegranate Marinade/Sauce

Yield: 5–6 cups (1.2–1.4 L)

This marinade is wonderful for a leg of lamb, lamb chops, or lamb ribs. Place meat in resealable plastic bag, add the marinade, and refrigerate for 24 to 48 hrs. Remove the meat and boil the marinade for 10 minutes, then use it as a serving sauce.

3 whole Spanish onions, peeled and thinly sliced
4 cups (906 mL) pomegranate juice
1 cup (236 mL) olive oil
6 cloves garlic, peeled and roughly chopped
Juice of 2 large lemons (about ¼ cup [59 mL])
2 teaspoons (10 mL) chopped fresh rosemary or ¾ teaspoon (3¾ mL) dried
2 teaspoons (10 mL) salt
1 teaspoon (5 mL) dried marjoram
1 teaspoon (5 mL) dried oregano
1 teaspoon (5 mL) dried summer savory
1 teaspoon (5 mL) freshly ground black pepper
Seeds of 1 large pomegranate

1. In a large glass or plastic container, combine all the ingredients and stir until thoroughly mixed.

2. Cover and refrigerate until ready to use.

Tuscaloosa Barbecue Sauce

Yield: 2–3 cups (473–708 mL)

While I'm not a big fan of liquid smoke, the small amount used here does add a mild smoky flavor to the sauce. But you can leave it out without too much loss of taste.

1 (6-ounce [168-g]) can tomato paste
¾ cup (177 mL) distilled white vinegar
½ cup (118 mL) dark molasses
¼ cup (59 mL) A1 steak sauce
¼ cup (59 mL) beer
2 tablespoons (30 mL) orange marmalade
1½ teaspoon (2.5 mL) sea salt
1 teaspoon (5 mL) crushed garlic
½ teaspoon (2.5 mL) freshly ground black pepper
½ teaspoon (2.5 mL) ground ginger
¼ teaspoon (1.25 mL) ground nutmeg
¼ teaspoon (1.25 mL) celery seed
¼ teaspoon (1.25 mL) dried oregano
⅛ teaspoon (0.6 mL) cayenne pepper
¼ teaspoon (1.25 mL) liquid smoke

1. In a medium saucepan, combine all the ingredients except the liquid smoke and bring to a boil over medium-high heat.

2. Reduce the heat to low and simmer gently, uncovered, for 15 to 20 minutes, stirring occasionally.

3. Remove the sauce from the heat and add the liquid smoke, stirring well.

4. Use to baste meat during the last few minutes of cooking.

Peppered Blue Que Sauce

Yield: 1½–2 cups (354–473 mL)

This sauce is wonderful on steaks or seafood and gives chicken breasts a sophisticated flavor. With the cream, it won't keep, so use it up, slathering on a bunch at the table.

2 tablespoons (30 mL) butter
2 tablespoons (30 mL) all-purpose flour
1¼ cups (295 mL) heavy cream
⅔ cup (158 mL) crumbled blue cheese
½ teaspoon (2.5 mL) salt
½ teaspoon (2.5 mL) freshly ground black pepper
1 pinch dried thyme

1. In a saucepan, melt the butter over medium heat. Stir in the flour until blended. Gradually stir in the cream and cook until thickened. Remove the pan from the heat and stir in the cheese, salt, pepper and thyme. Serve warm.

2. If the sauce is too thin, you can add more flour, ½ teaspoon (2.5 mL) at a time, or the same amount of cornstarch.

Bourbon Salmon Marinade/Sauce
Yield: 1 cup (236 mL)

I love this on salmon, but you can also use it on other firm-fleshed fish, such as swordfish, tuna, or halibut. Place the fish filets or steaks in a plastic bag, pour in the marinade, and refrigerate for several hours.

½ cup (118 mL) extra virgin olive oil
½ cup (118 mL) good-quality bourbon
1 teaspoon (5 mL) onion (or garlic) powder
1 teaspoon (5 mL) finely chopped fresh dill
1 teaspoon (5 mL) dark brown sugar
1 pinch kosher salt
1 pinch ground white pepper

1. In a small bowl, mix together all the ingredients.

2. If you wish to use this as a basting or serving sauce, boil the liquid in a saucepan for 10 minutes and let it cool before using.

Catfish Basting Sauce
Yield: 1 cup (236 mL)

If you don't like the taste of cilantro on fish (some folks say it overpowers delicate fish, such as catfish or trout), substitute parsley. Pour the marinade over catfish in a plastic sealable bag and marinate for 30 minutes to 1 hour. Remove the fish from the bag and grill it. Boil the marinade for 10 minutes, then use it to baste the fish on the grill.

½ cup (118 mL) dry red wine
¼ cup (59 mL) chopped fresh cilantro
1 tablespoon (15 mL) dry mustard
1 tablespoon (15 mL) chili powder
1 tablespoon (15 mL) olive oil
1 tablespoon (15 mL) lime or lemon juice
1 teaspoon (5 mL) paprika
1 teaspoon (5 mL) pepper
¼ teaspoon (1.25 mL) salt
1 dash hot pepper sauce

1. In a medium bowl, mix together all the ingredients.

Chardonnay Marinade/Sauce

Yield: 2 cups (473 mL)

We use Chardonnay here, but you can substitute Sauvignon Blanc or Chenin Blanc quite nicely. Place meat (beef, pork or lamb) in a large sealable plastic bag, add the marinade, seal the bag, and refrigerate overnight. Remove the meat from the marinade and wipe off the excess. Pour the remaining marinade in a saucepan and boil for 10 minutes, then cool and use as baste for the meat while cooking. This recipe comes from Tricia Kawahara from Walnut Creek, Calif.

½ cup (118 mL) soy sauce
½ cup (118 mL) Chardonnay
½ cup (118 mL) water
1 bunch green onions, coarsely chopped, green and white parts
5 cloves garlic, peeled and crushed and coarsely chopped
3 tablespoons (45 mL) packed brown sugar
1 tablespoon (15 mL) minced fresh ginger
1 tablespoon (15 mL) minced fresh basil (or 1 teaspoon [5 mL] dried)
1 teaspoon (5 mL) sesame oil
Freshly ground black pepper, to taste
1 pinch kosher salt

1. In a large mixing bowl, combine all the ingredients and stir well.

Tart Cranberry-Citrus Barbecue Glaze

Yield: 1¾ cups (413 mL)

This glaze is great for roast turkey, goose, or chicken, but it can also be very tasty on pork ribs or roasts.

1 (8-ounce [227-g]) can cranberry sauce
¼ cup (59 mL) dried cranberries, finely chopped
¼ cup (59 mL) cranberry juice
3 tablespoons (45 mL) orange juice
1 teaspoon (5 mL) minced orange zest
⅛ teaspoon (0.6 mL) dried rosemary crushed

1. In a saucepan, combine all the ingredients and bring to a boil. Cook until the liquid is reduced by a third.

2. Remove the sauce from the heat and let it cool. Cover and refrigerate until needed.

3. Use as a baste only during the last 5 minutes of cooking.

Albuquerque Ancho Chili Sauce

Yield: 6 cups (1.4 mL)

You can make this fiery sauce even fiery-er (my word) by adding a Scotch bonnet or habañero pepper.

6 ancho chilies
1 cup (236 mL) cranberry-apple juice
½ cup (118 mL) lemon juice
¼ cup (59 mL) red wine vinegar
1 tablespoon (15 mL) Worcestershire sauce
2 tablespoons (30 mL) olive oil
3 shallots, peeled and minced
3 cloves garlic, peeled and minced
3 cups (708 mL) ketchup
¼ cup (59 mL) packed brown sugar
¼ cup (59 mL) honey
2 tablespoons (30 mL) butter
1 tablespoon (15 mL) paprika
1 tablespoon (15 mL) chili powder
1 tablespoon (15 mL) dry mustard

1. Wash, seed, de-stem, and loosely chop the chilies. Add them to a saucepan and pour in the cranberry-apple juice, lemon juice, vinegar, and Worcestershire sauce, and cook over medium-high heat for 5 minutes.

2. Pour the mixture into a blender or food processor and blend until smooth.

3. In a large saucepan, heat the olive oil. Add the shallots and garlic and sauté until tender, about 4 to 5 minutes. Add the chile mixture, ketchup, brown sugar, honey, butter, paprika, chili powder, and dry mustard and bring to a boil.

4. Reduce the heat and simmer the sauce for 30 to 40 minutes.

5. Cool the sauce and store it in a covered container until needed.

Barbecue Ham Steak Sauce

Yield: 2 cups (473 mL)

This sauce is wonderful for making pulled pork sandwiches. Mix it with the cooked meat and serve on hamburger buns. You can also use it to baste ham steaks during the last 5 minutes of grilling. This recipe comes from Kara Petersen from Battle Ground, Wash.

¾ cup (177 mL) ketchup
¼ cup (59 mL) cider vinegar
¼ cup (59 mL) packed dark brown sugar
2 tablespoons (30 mL) prepared yellow mustard
2 teaspoons (10 mL) Worcestershire sauce
½ teaspoon (2.5 mL) garlic salt
½ teaspoon (2.5 mL) hot sauce

1. In a small saucepan, mix together all of the ingredients and heat over medium-high heat for 15 minutes.

2. Cool before using.

Curried Lemon-Guava Barbecue Sauce
Yield: 2 cups (473 mL)

You can use orange marmalade or apricot-pineapple jam instead of the guava jelly. Apply this sauce to pork ribs, chops, or roasts during the last 5 minutes of cooking, or serve at the table for guests to add extra themselves.

1 (10-ounce [280-g]) jar guava jelly
¼ cup (59 mL) lemon juice
¼ cup (59 mL) apple cider vinegar
¼ cup (59 mL) dry white wine
2 shallots, peeled and minced
2 green onions, minced, green and white parts
3 tablespoons (45 mL) brown sugar
3 tablespoons (45 mL) tomato paste
1 tablespoon (15 mL) chopped fresh rosemary
2 teaspoons (10 mL) dry mustard
1 teaspoon (5 mL) ground cumin
½ teaspoon (2.5 mL) mild or hot curry powder

1. In a large saucepan, combine the jelly, lemon juice, vinegar, wine, shallots, green onions, brown sugar, tomato paste, rosemary, mustard, cumin, and curry powder and bring to a boil over medium heat.

2. Reduce the heat to low and simmer for 30 minutes. Remove the pan from the heat and let the sauce cool to room temperature.

Love-Dem-Onions Barbecue Sauce
Yield: 2–3 cups (473–708 mL)

Using several members of the onion family makes this unique barbecue sauce very sweet, so you can add a teaspoon (5 mL) of cayenne pepper to fire it up a bit if you wish.

¼ cup (59 mL) finely chopped dried apricots
2 tablespoons (30 mL) olive oil
1 large onion, peeled and finely chopped
2 tablespoons (30 mL) chopped shallots
1 cup (236 mL) tomato sauce
¼ cup (59 mL) cider vinegar
¼ cup (59 mL) packed brown sugar
¼ cup (59 mL) tomato paste
2 tablespoons (30 mL) chopped fresh chives
2 tablespoons (30 mL) A1 steak sauce
1 tablespoon (15 mL) minced garlic
1 teaspoon (5 mL) dry mustard
Salt, to taste
Freshly ground black pepper, to taste

1. Place the apricots in a bowl and add very hot water to cover. Soak for 30 minutes, drain, and set aside.

2. In a large saucepan or skillet, heat the oil over medium high heat. Add the onion and shallots and cook until translucent.

3. Add the drained apricots, tomato sauce, vinegar, brown sugar, tomato paste, chives, steak sauce, garlic, mustard, salt, and pepper and simmer, covered, for 25 to 30 minutes.

4. Pour the mixture into a blender or food processor and process until smooth.

5. Transfer the sauce to a covered container and store in the refrigerator until ready to use.

Maui Citrus Marinade/Sauce
Yield: 8 cups (1.9 L)

This marinade does wonders for less tender cuts of pork, such as pork steaks or ham. Marinate in a resealable plastic bag for at least 2 to 3 hours for best results. If you use papaya juice, do not marinate longer than 6 hours, or the enzymes in the juice can make the meat mushy.

3 cups (708 mL) dark, low-sodium soy sauce
3 cups (708 mL) cider vinegar
1 cup (236 mL) coconut milk
½ cup (118 mL) papaya juice (or fresh orange juice)
½ cup (118 mL) packed brown sugar
3 lemons, thinly sliced
3 limes, thinly sliced
1 large orange, thinly sliced
2 tablespoons (30 mL) minced fresh ginger
1 teaspoon (5 mL) kosher salt

1. In a large bowl, mix together all the ingredients.

Harry's Horseradish Sauce
Yield: 1 cup (236 mL)

Horseradish dates back 3,000 years. It has been used as an aphrodisiac, a treatment for tuberculosis, a rub for lower-back pain, a bitter herb for Passover, and an accompaniment with food. This recipe comes from Chris "C. B." Browne from Culver City, Calif.

1 cup (236 mL) low-fat or olive oil mayonnaise
¼ cup (60 mL) prepared horseradish
2 tablespoons (30 mL) Louisiana hot sauce
2 tablespoons (30 mL) sugar
1 tablespoon (15 mL) spicy brown mustard
½ teaspoon (2.5 mL) kosher salt
Freshly ground black pepper, to taste

1. In a large bowl, mix together all of the ingredients. Refrigerate for 30 minutes to 1 hour to blend the flavors and stabilize the sauce.

2. Serve on the side with brisket, roast beef, or roast pork tenderloin.

Jack's Whiskey Barbecue Sauce
Yield: 2 cups (473 mL)

Of course, you can use a favorite brand of Scotch or whiskey, but the amber liquid distilled in Lynchburg, Ky., seems to add a special touch to this sauce. Try this on lamb or pork chops.

1 (10¾-ounce [301-g]) can condensed tomato soup
1 cup (236 mL) Jack Daniel's whiskey
2 tablespoons (30 mL) packed brown sugar
1 tablespoon (15 mL) Worcestershire sauce
1 teaspoon (5 mL) ground white pepper
1 teaspoon (5 mL) olive oil
¼ teaspoon (1.25 mL) garlic powder
1 dash Tabasco

1. In a saucepan, mix together all the ingredients and cook over medium heat, stirring constantly, for 5 minutes.

2. Cool the sauce and transfer it to a sealable glass or plastic container. Store the sauce in the refrigerator until ready to use.

Montego Bay Jerk Sauce
Yield: 1 cup (236 mL)

The name "allspice" comes from the fact that the flavor suggests a combination of nutmeg, cinnamon, and cloves. It is by far the most important ingredient in Jamaican jerk recipes. Use this sauce on chicken, lamb, pork, beef, chicken, venison, rabbit, or, you guessed it—anything you cook that in any way resembles meat or poultry. It's a bit overwhelming for most fish dishes though. Please be very careful when handling Scotch bonnet peppers, one of the hottest peppers on the planet. Use rubber or plastic gloves, and if these are not available, wash your hands thoroughly after handling. One mistaken rubbing of an eye, and you will never, ever forget the experience!

½ cup (118 mL) allspice berries
½ cup (118 mL) packed brown sugar
6–8 cloves garlic
4–6 Scotch bonnet peppers
2 tablespoons (30 mL) dark soy sauce
1 tablespoon (15 mL) ground thyme
1–2 bunches green onions
1 teaspoon (5 mL) ground cinnamon
½ teaspoon (2.5 mL) ground nutmeg
Salt, to taste
Freshly ground black pepper, to taste

1. In a food processor or blender, combine all the ingredients and process until smooth. Pour the sauce into a covered glass jar or plastic container and refrigerate. The sauce will keep for weeks if refrigerated.

Kiwi Suds Marinade/Sauce

Yield: 3½ cups (827 mL)

The name of this recipe doesn't refer to the fuzzy brown fruit with green insides. Rather, the recipe was given to me by a Kiwi (aka New Zealander) on a trip to Christchurch a few years ago. You can use American beer, but it won't be as authentic a recipe. To use, place meat or poultry in a sealable plastic bag, pour in the marinade, seal the bag, and refrigerate overnight. Drain off the marinade and reserve it. While grilling the food, pour the marinade into a saucepan and boil for 10 minutes. Use it as a basting sauce or serve at the table.

1 (16-ounce [455-mL]) can Steinlager (or favorite) beer
1 (10¾-ounce [301-g]) can condensed tomato soup
2 tablespoons (30 mL) soy sauce
1 tablespoon (15 mL) Worcestershire sauce
1 tablespoon (15 mL) sweet chili sauce
1 tablespoon (15 mL) olive oil
3 cloves garlic, crushed
1 teaspoon (5 mL) brown sugar
½ teaspoon (2.5 mL) dried savory
½ teaspoon (2.5 mL) dried oregano
½ teaspoon (2.5 mL) dried basil
¼ teaspoon (1.25 mL) kosher salt
¼ teaspoon (1.25 mL) lemon pepper

1. In a large glass or metal bowl, mix together all the ingredients.

2. Transfer the sauce to a sealable container and refrigerate until ready to use.

Cheju Do Bulgogi Sauce

Yield: 2 cups (473 mL)

The best meat to use with this Korean barbecue sauce is flanken-style short ribs, which are cut across the sixth, seventh, and eighth rib bones into ⅓ to ½-inch (0.75–1 cm) thick slices, which is thinner than other cuts. I prefer the ⅜-inch (0.75-cm) cut; if the meat is too thick, it will burn on the outside before it's cooked on the inside. Marinate the meat overnight in a resealable plastic bag. Drain the meat and boil the marinade for 10 minutes. Baste only during the last 5 minutes of grilling.

1 cup (236 mL) soy sauce
1 cup (236 mL) packed brown sugar
3–4 cloves garlic, peeled and minced
1 (1-inch [2.5-cm]) piece ginger, minced
2 tablespoons (30 mL) sesame oil
1 bunch green onions, finely chopped, green and white parts

1. In a saucepan, combine the soy sauce, brown sugar, garlic, ginger, and sesame oil and stir over low heat until the sugar is dissolved.

2. Remove from the heat and add the green onions.

Gaucho-Style Barbecue Sauce
Yield: 1¾–2 cups (413–473 mL)

In South America, they usually don't slather on barbecue sauce when they cook meat. Rather, they lightly salt the meat, cook it medium-rare, and serve a sauce like this on the side. In Argentina, the average person consumes 2 pounds (908 g) of meat per day!

1 cup (236 mL) chopped fresh Italian parsley
½ cup (118 mL) olive oil
¼ cup (59 mL) red wine vinegar
1 tablespoon (15 mL) finely minced garlic
1 tablespoon (15 mL) dried oregano
1 teaspoon (5 mL) red pepper flakes
½ teaspoon (2.5 mL) dried thyme
½ teaspoon (2.5 mL) dried rosemary
1 pinch kosher salt

1. In a large bowl, mix together all of the ingredients. Pour the sauce into a sealed container and refrigerate for at least 24 hours.

2. After marinating meat or poultry, boil the marinade for 10 minutes, then serve in at the table to drizzle over medium-rare steaks or beef roasts. The marinade seems to lose flavor when used as a baste.

Lexington Barbecue Mustard Sauce
Yield: 1¾ cups (413 mL)

This is the only kind of sauce served in some parts of North and South Carolina, Georgia, and Alabama. It is heaven-sent served with barbecued or smoked ham or mixed with pulled pork and served on a bun. Add some coleslaw and soar heaven-ward yourself.

¾ cup (177 mL) yellow mustard
¾ cup (177 mL) red wine vinegar
¼ cup (59 mL) sugar
1½ tablespoons (22.5 mL) butter
2 teaspoons (10 mL) salt
1¼ teaspoons (6.25 mL) freshly ground black pepper
½ teaspoon (2.5 mL) Worcestershire sauce
½ teaspoon (2.5 mL) hot sauce

1. In a medium saucepan, combine all of the ingredients, stirring to blend.

2. Simmer the sauce over low heat for 30 minutes. Let stand at room temperature for 1 hour before using.

A-Cuppa-Espresso Grilling Sauce
Yield: 6 cups (1.4 mL)

The term espresso refers to the method of brewing the ground coffee beans. Normally, espresso employs beans that are roasted darker than regular coffee beans and then finely ground.

¼ cup (60 mL) extra virgin olive oil
¼ cup (60 mL) mashed garlic
2 cups (473 mL) ketchup
2 cups (473 mL) honey
1 cup (236 mL) cider vinegar
½ cup (118 mL) dark soy sauce
¼ teaspoon (1.25 mL) kosher salt
Freshly ground black pepper, to taste
½ cup (118 mL) espresso (or very strong coffee)

1. Preheat a skillet over medium high heat and add the olive oil. Add the garlic and cook until it barely begins to turn light brown, about 1 minute.

2. Add the ketchup, honey, cider vinegar, and soy sauce and stir well. Add the salt and pepper and briskly stir in the espresso.

3. Cook just until the sauce begins to bubble. Reduce the heat and simmer for 15 to 20 minutes.

4. Let the sauce cool and store it in a covered container in the refrigerator, where it will last up to 2 to 3 weeks.

Stagecoach Barbecue Sauce
Yield: 8 cups (1.9 L)

Served alongside a brisket or with fiery hotlinks, this sauce is the essence of Texas barbecue. Smoky, not very sweet, and mouthwateringly tangy, it should be served alongside the meat, not slathered on it at the barbecue.

1 medium onion, peeled and minced
2 tablespoons (30 mL) bacon drippings
3 cups (708 mL) canned crushed tomatoes
1½ cups (354 mL) ketchup
1 cup (236 mL) freshly squeezed orange juice
½ cup (118 mL) water
4 cloves garlic, peeled and chopped
6 tablespoons (90 mL) freshly squeezed lemon juice
6 tablespoons (90 mL) red wine vinegar
2 tablespoons (30 mL) chili powder
2 tablespoons (30 mL) dark molasses
1 tablespoon (15 mL) ground coriander
1 tablespoon (15 mL) dry mustard
1 tablespoon (15 mL) A1 steak sauce (or other steak sauce)
½ teaspoon (2.5 mL) kosher salt
¼ teaspoon (1.25 mL) Tabasco

1. In a deep skillet or saucepan, sauté the onion in the bacon drippings until the onions are golden brown, about 10 to 12 minutes.

2. Add the remaining ingredients to the pan, increase the heat to high, and bring to a boil.

3. Reduce the heat to low and simmer for 1 hour, stirring frequently.

4. Cool the sauce, pour it into a sealable container, and refrigerate it for up to 3 weeks.

Carolyn's Kansas City–Style Sauce
Yield: 5–6 cups (1.1–1.2 L)

I've named this sauce after my favorite barbecue person in the world, Carolyn Wells, cofounder of the famous Kansas City Barbecue Society, a great barbecue chef, and a dear friend.

1 cup (236 mL) apple juice
1 cup (236 mL) tomato sauce
1 (6-ounce [168-g]) can tomato paste
½ cup (118 mL) Worcestershire sauce
½ cup (118 mL) packed brown sugar
½ cup (118 mL) molasses
½ cup (118 mL) cider vinegar
¼ cup (59 mL) butter
1 tablespoon (15 mL) maple sugar pepper or citrus pepper
1 tablespoon (15 mL) prepared yellow mustard
1 tablespoon (15 mL) chili powder
2½ teaspoons (12.5 mL) balsamic vinegar
1 teaspoon (5 mL) dried summer savory
1 teaspoon (5 mL) onion powder
1 teaspoon (5 mL) garlic salt
2–3 generous dashes hot sauce

1. In a large saucepan, combine the ingredients and cook over low heat, partially covered, until the sauce is thick and covers the back of a spoon, about 30 to 40 minutes.

2. Cool the sauce, transfer it to a bottle, and refrigerate for up to 3 weeks.

Carolina-Style Sauce
Yield: 4 cups (0.95 L)

This simple-to-make Carolina-style barbecue sauce is perfect with pulled pork. Mix some in with the meat and serve the rest at the table for folks to add at their own discretion.

4 cups (0.95 L) cider vinegar
¼ cup (59 mL) packed brown sugar
4 teaspoons (20 mL) sea salt
4 teaspoons (20 mL) crushed red pepper flakes
2 teaspoons (10 mL) coarsely ground black pepper

1. In a saucepan, combine all the ingredients and cook over low heat for 15 to 20 minutes, stirring constantly.

2. Cool the sauce, transfer it to a bottle, and refrigerate for up to 3 weeks.

Low-Fat Italian Barbecue Sauce
Yield: 2 cups (473 mL)

This sauce is perfect on grilled sausages or veal steaks. It can also be used as a pasta sauce—just add a couple of tablespoons (30 mL) of diced fresh basil when you serve.

½ teaspoon (2.5 mL) olive oil
2 tablespoons (30 mL) finely chopped yellow onion
2 cloves garlic, peeled and finely minced
1 pound (454 g) Roma tomatoes, cored and seeded
3 tablespoons (45 mL) molasses
2 tablespoons (30 mL) tomato paste
2 tablespoons (30 mL) red wine vinegar
1 tablespoon (15 mL) Worcestershire sauce
1 teaspoon (5 mL) dry mustard
1 teaspoon (5 mL) chili powder
1 teaspoon (5 mL) dried basil
1 teaspoon (5 mL) dried oregano
½ teaspoon (2.5 mL) minced fresh thyme (or ¼ teaspoon [1.25 mL] dried)

1. In a large saucepan, heat the oil. Add the onion and garlic and sauté for 3 to 4 minutes, just until the garlic starts to brown.

2. Put the tomatoes into a food processor and blend until smooth. Add the remaining ingredients and pulse several times to mix well.

3. Pour this mixture into the saucepan with the garlic and onion and simmer, uncovered, over very low heat for 15 to 20 minutes, stirring often.

4. Let the sauce cool, pour it into a glass or plastic container, and refrigerate for up to 3 weeks.

Georgia Bacon and Tomato Barbecue Sauce
Yield: 2 cups (473 mL)

This is tailor-made for hamburgers, meatloaf, meatballs, or grilled sausages. But it can also be used quite successfully on pork, beef, or lamb ribs. Brush the sauce on the ribs only during the last 5 minutes of cooking.

6 slices smoked bacon
½ cup (118 mL) finely minced onion
½ cup (118 mL) finely minced green bell pepper
1 (10¾-ounce [301-g]) can condensed tomato soup
½ cup (118 mL) water
¼ cup (59 mL) A1 steak sauce
2 tablespoons (30 mL) Worcestershire sauce
1 tablespoon (15 mL) cider vinegar
1 tablespoon (15 mL) minced fresh parsley (or 1 teaspoon [5 mL] dried)
2 teaspoons (10 mL) brown sugar
½ teaspoon (2.5 mL) salt

1. In a large saucepan or deep skillet, fry the bacon until crisp. Drain the bacon and set it aside, reserving 3 tablespoons (45 mL) of the fat in the pan.

2. Add the onion and green pepper to the pan and sauté over medium heat until the onions and peppers are tender and the onions are just beginning to brown.

3. Stir in the soup, water, steak sauce, Worcestershire sauce, vinegar, parsley, brown sugar, and salt. Cover, and simmer for 15 to 20 minutes, stirring occasionally.

4. Crumble the bacon and stir it into the sauce. Serve the sauce warm at the table, or use it as a baste.

Dude Ranch Sauce
Yield: 7 cups (1.7 L)

Brisket is an inexpensive cut of beef that you must cook long and slow to break down the muscle tissues. Your best bet is the point cut, which has a thick deckle or fat layer. This recipe makes enough for a 15- to 20-pound (6.8- to 9.1-kg) brisket.

3 cups (708 mL) ketchup
1¼ cups (295 mL) Worcestershire sauce
1 cup (236 mL) apple sauce
1 cup (236 mL) butter
½ cup (118 mL) distilled white vinegar
½ cup (118 mL) bacon grease
3 onions, peeled and chopped
1 tablespoon (15 mL) celery salt
1 tablespoon (15 mL) garlic salt
1 tablespoon (15 mL) cayenne pepper
1 tablespoon (15 mL) freshly ground black pepper
½ teaspoon (2.5 mL) ground cinnamon

1. In a saucepan, combine all the ingredients and simmer over very low heat for 1 hour.

2. Cool the sauce, pour it into a glass or plastic container, and refrigerate until needed. Bring it to room temperature to serve.

Lime Chutney Marinade/Sauce
Yield: 2 cups (473 mL)

Chutneys are very popular in India, where they are served with just about every meal. They are usually composed of pears, apples, or mangoes cooked with onions, raisins, and spices. This chutney sauce is amazing on thick slices of barbecued pork loin.

2 limes
1½ cups (354 mL) mango chutney
2 tablespoons (30 mL) lime juice
Zest of 1 lime, finely minced
1 teaspoon (5 mL) packed brown sugar
¼ cup (59 mL) light corn syrup
½ teaspoon (2.5 mL) ground cumin
⅛ teaspoon (0.6 mL) cayenne pepper
Several grinds black pepper
1 pinch dried marjoram

1. Peel and seed the limes. Place the lime pulp in a blender and pulse until finely chopped.

2. Add the lime juice, zest, chutney, and brown sugar, and pulse until the mixture is a thick and chunky liquid.

3. Pour the mixture into a large mixing bowl and, while stirring, add the corn syrup, cumin, cayenne pepper, black pepper, and marjoram, then mix well.

Sunday Barbecue Rhubarb Sauce
Yield: 2 cups (473 mL)

Rhubarb is actually a vegetable, but it is commonly thought of as a fruit. If it wasn't, a strawberry-rhubarb pie probably wouldn't attract anyone.

2–3 teaspoons (10–15 mL) olive oil
½ cup (118 mL) finely diced onion
2¼ cups (532 mL) thinly sliced rhubarb
⅓ cup (79 mL) packed dark brown sugar
2 tablespoons (30 mL) beer
½ cup (118 mL) ketchup
2 tablespoons (30 mL) apple cider vinegar
1 tablespoon (15 mL) honey
2 teaspoons (10 mL) Dijon mustard
½ teaspoon (2.5 mL) kosher salt
Freshly ground black pepper, to taste

1. In a large frying pan, heat the olive oil over medium-high heat. Add the onion and sauté until translucent. Add the rhubarb, brown sugar, and beer, bring to a boil, and cook for approximately 8 to 10 minutes, or until the rhubarb can be mashed with a spoon or fork. Remove the pan from the heat and pour the rhubarb mixture into a bowl to cool.

2. Pour the cooled rhubarb-onion mixture into a blender and pulse while adding the ketchup, vinegar, honey, mustard, salt, and pepper. Purée until relatively smooth.

3. If the sauce is too thick, thin it out by adding beer, 1 tablespoon (15 mL) at a time.

Morning's Mustard Marinade/Sauce
Yield: 2 cups (473 mL)

Marinades should always be stored in a refrigerator, and after you remove the meat, fish or poultry you must boil the marinade for at least 10 minutes to kill any bacteria left over from the meat, fish, or poultry juices.

6 sprigs fresh rosemary
1 cup (236 mL) tarragon vinegar
6 tablespoons (90 mL) Dijon mustard
¼ cup (59 mL) lemon juice
2 tablespoons (30 mL) minced garlic
2 tablespoons (30 mL) olive oil
¼ teaspoon (1.25 mL) seasoned salt
Freshly ground black pepper, to taste

1. In a bowl, combine all of the ingredients and stir well. Refrigerate until ready to use.

Momma's Margarita Sauce
Yield: 2 cups (473 mL)

My mom loved margaritas, so one day when I was home from college I whipped this up for her to pour over grilled shrimp. There wasn't a drop left!

½ cup (118 mL) triple sec
½ cup (118 mL) lime juice
½ cup (118 mL) tequila
½ cup (118 mL) honey
1 pinch kosher salt

1. In a saucepan, combine the triple sec, lime juice, tequila, honey, and kosher salt and cook over low heat for 10 minutes, stirring constantly.

2. Let the sauce cool, transfer it to a bottle, and store it in the refrigerator for up to 3 weeks. Brush it on grilled oysters, muscles, shrimp, or clams, or slather it on chicken wings during the last few minutes of cooking for a festive and tangy sauce. Accompany it with margaritas, of course.

Raspberry Butter Sauce

Yield: 2½–3 cups (591–708 mL)

One of the best meals I've ever had in a restaurant was at the Old Yacht Club Inn in Santa Barbara, Calif., one summer evening. I had this sauce over a luscious salmon fillet. I almost licked the plate clean, the sauce was so phenomenal. This recipe comes from the Old Yacht Club Inn.

2 shallots, peeled and finely diced
1 cup (236 mL) sweet white wine
2 sprigs fresh dill or tarragon
1 cup (236 mL) crème fraîche or heavy cream
2 tablespoons (30 mL) seedless red raspberry jam
1 cup (236 mL) cold butter
1 pint (473 mL) red raspberries, divided
2 tablespoons (30 mL) finely chopped fresh dill or tarragon leaves

1. In a heavy saucepan, combine the shallots, wine, and herb sprigs. Bring to a boil over medium heat and cook until the liquid is reduced to 1 tablespoon (15 mL) or less. Be careful to avoid boiling dry.

2. Add the crème fraîche or whipping cream and boil to reduce by half. Remove the herbs. Whisk in the raspberry jam.

3. Reduce the heat to very low. Cut the butter into 1-tablespoon (15-mL) slices and whisk it into the cream one slice at a time, allowing each slice to melt into the sauce. Continue until all butter is incorporated into sauce.

4. Whisk in half the raspberries. Whisk in the chopped herbs. Keep the sauce warm over very low heat until ready to serve. (If the sauce gets too hot, the butter will start to melt out. If this happens, whisk in 1 tablespoon (15 mL) of cold butter to rebind the sauce.)

5. Just before serving, gently stir in the remaining raspberries. Serve over salmon, swordfish, or any firm white fish.

Remus's Kansas City Classic Sauce

Yield: 2 cups (473 mL)

Remus Powers, the barbecue persona of Ardie Davis of Kansas City, Mo., swears in the judges at many of the biggest barbecue contests in America and has been a dear friend for years.

½ teaspoon (2.5 mL) curry powder (Oriental preferred)
½ teaspoon (2.5 mL) chili powder
½ teaspoon (2.5 mL) paprika
¼ teaspoon (1.25 mL) ground allspice
¼ teaspoon (1.25 mL) ground cinnamon
¼ teaspoon (1.25 mL) ground mace
¼ teaspoon (1.25 mL) freshly ground black pepper
¼ cup (59 mL) distilled white vinegar
1 cup (236 mL) ketchup
⅓ cup (79 mL) dark molasses
½ teaspoon (2.5 mL) hot pepper sauce

1. In a bowl, combine the curry powder, chili powder, paprika, allspice, cinnamon, mace, and pepper. Add the vinegar and stir.

2. Add the remaining ingredients and stir until mixture is thoroughly blended. This sauce may be served room temperature or heated.

Piedmont Pig Pickin' Mustard Sauce

Yield: 2½ cups (591 mL)

The Piedmont area of North Carolina is famous for its pig pickin' parties, where a whole pig, usually a female, is cooked over a charcoal fire then literally picked apart by the hungry hoards who have smelled the pig cooking for up to 8 hours.

1¼ cups (295 mL) prepared yellow mustard
½ cup (118 mL) balsamic vinegar
⅓ cup (79 mL) packed brown sugar
2 tablespoons (30 mL) butter
1 tablespoon (15 mL) Worcestershire sauce
1 tablespoon (15 mL) lemon juice
1 teaspoon (5 mL) cayenne pepper
1 dash hot sauce

1. In a large saucepan, combine all the ingredients and simmer over a low heat for 30 minutes.

2. Let the sauce cool, transfer it to a covered container, and store it in the refrigerator, where it will keep for several weeks.

Sweet Ass Onion Sauce
Yield: 5 cups (1.2 L)

We are lucky to have three varieties of "sweet" onions available: Maui, Vidalia, and Walla Walla. All three are so sweet they can be eaten raw like apples. Georgians plant an average of 15,000 acres of these tasty onions near Vidalia, Georgia. This sauce works especially well with beef, but can be used for just about any barbecue meat.

1 large Vidalia onion, finely chopped
3 cups (708 mL) ketchup
1 cup (236 mL) apple cider vinegar
½ cup (118 mL) butter
6 tablespoons (90 mL) honey
¼ cup (59 mL) distilled white vinegar
¼ cup (59 mL) prepared yellow mustard
1 tablespoon (15 mL) Worcestershire sauce
Juice of 1 lemon
1 teaspoon (5 mL) mesquite seasoned salt*
1 teaspoon (5 mL) freshly ground black pepper

1. In a large saucepan, mix together all the ingredients and simmer for 10 to 15 minutes over medium heat.

*Available online from Oregon Spice Company (www.oregonspice.com)

Pineapple-Coconut Barbecue Sauce
Yield: 4 cups (0.95 L)

This sauce is great on grilled chicken, fish steaks, or grilled shrimp.

2 cups (473 mL) sweet soy sauce
2 cups (473 mL) dark soy sauce
2 cups (473 mL) pineapple juice
1 (8-ounce [227-mL]) can coconut milk
¼ cup (59 mL) five-spice powder
2 tablespoons (30 mL) lime juice

1. In a large saucepan, combine the soy sauces, pineapple juice, coconut milk, five-spice powder, and lime juice and simmer, stirring frequently, over low heat for 60 to 70 minutes, or until the liquid is reduced by one-quarter.

2. Cool the sauce to room temperature before using.

Maple Syrup and Apple Glaze
Yield: 1½ (354 mL)

This sauce works wonderfully on thick slices of barbecued ham, whole roast ham, or pork tenderloins. Buy the best maple syrup you can afford (such as Grade A dark). The taste is worth it. This recipe comes from Tyler and Betsy Smith from Southington, Conn.

⅔ cup (158 mL) salt-free chicken stock
½ cup (118 mL) applesauce
3 tablespoons (45 mL) pure maple syrup
2 tablespoons (30 mL) balsamic vinegar
1 tablespoon (15 mL) cornstarch
2 teaspoons (10 mL) soy sauce
¼ teaspoon (1.25 mL) ground ginger

1. In a small saucepan, combine the stock, applesauce, maple syrup, vinegar, cornstarch, soy sauce, and ginger. Bring to a boil, stirring, and cook for 10 minutes.

2. Keep warm until ready to serve. If not using the same day, let the sauce cool and store it in a tightly covered glass or plastic container.

Sturgeon Marinade/Sauce
Yield: 2 cups (473 mL)

This marinade/sauce is best served with firm-fleshed fish, such as shark, halibut, salmon steaks, or swordfish. Use it to marinate fish, then drain the marinade and boil it for 10 minutes to use it as a baste or sauce.

2 cups (473 mL) Chablis
2 tablespoons (30 mL) lemon juice
2 tablespoons (30 mL) Dijon mustard
1 tablespoon (15 mL) butter
1 tablespoon (15 mL) dried parsley
1 teaspoon (5 mL) salt
½ teaspoon (2.5 mL) granulated sugar
½ teaspoon (2.5 mL) cayenne pepper

1. In a saucepan, mix together all the ingredients and cook over medium heat for 5 minutes, stirring well.

THIRTEEN

Side Dishes

Grilled Peppers and Rice
Yield: 4–6 servings

You can use long-grain white or brown rice in this dish, but the wild rice makes it a special side dish, worthy of the best steaks, chops, or wild game dishes.

1 green bell pepper
1 red bell pepper
2 tablespoons (30 mL) olive oil, plus more for brushing
4 onions, sliced
2 cups (473 mL) cooked wild rice, warm
¼ cup (59 mL) chopped fresh basil
1½ tablespoons (22.5 mL) fresh lemon juice
1 tablespoon (15 mL) minced fresh parsley
½ teaspoon (2.5 mL) salt
Freshly ground black pepper, to taste

1. Make sure the grill is clean and generously sprayed with nonstick grilling spray. Preheat the barbecue to medium high (350°F [180°C] to 400°F [200°C]).

2. Cut the bell peppers in 2-inch (5-cm) wide strips. Put them in a 1- to 2-gallon (3.8- to 7.6-L) resealable plastic bag, pour in the 2 tablespoons olive oil, seal the bag, and shake to coat all the pepper strips.

3. Slice onions in ½-inch (1-cm) thick slices and brush each slice with olive oil.

4. Grill the peppers and onions directly on the grill for 3 to 4 minutes per side, or until the vegetables are soft and charred in some places. Transfer them to a cutting board and dice them into small pieces.

5. In a large bowl combine the rice, peppers, onions, basil, lemon juice, parsley, salt, and pepper and toss to thoroughly mix. Serve with roasts, poultry, or grilled fish.

Craisin-Apricot-Cheddar Rice
Yield: 4–6 servings

Instead of the dried cranberries, you can use raisins, golden raisins, currants, or minced dried apricots, apples, or even dates.

¼ cup (59 mL) dried cranberries
1 cup (236 mL) uncooked instant rice
½ teaspoon (2.5 mL) salt
¼ teaspoon (1.25 mL) ground white pepper
2 tablespoons (30 mL) butter
¼ cup (59 mL) finely shredded aged white cheddar cheese
¼ cup (59 mL) thinly sliced green onions, green and white parts
2 tablespoons (30 mL) finely diced apricots
¼ cup (59 mL) sour cream

1. Make sure the grill is clean and generously sprayed with nonstick grilling spray. Preheat the barbecue to medium high (350°F [180°C] to 400°F [200°C]).

2. Soak the dried cranberries in a bowl of hot water for 20 minutes.

3. In a Dutch oven or roasting pan, prepare the rice according to the package instructions, adding the salt and white pepper to the cooking water. Place the pan directly on the barbecue, cooking the rice as you grill the meat, fish, or poultry for the main dish.

4. When the rice is soft, gently stir in the butter, cheddar cheese, green onions, dried cranberries, apricots, and sour cream. Serve immediately.

Southern Dirty Rice

Yield: 6–8 servings

The cooked chicken and some of the spices make this dish look "dirty." Don't overcook the rice as you want some resistance, or "tooth," as you bite into each grain.

1½ pounds (681 g) chicken livers, gizzards, necks, wings, and backs
1 quart (0.95 L) water
1 tablespoon (15 mL) Creole Seasoning (recipe follows)
½ cup (118 mL) butter
2 cups (473 mL) uncooked converted rice
2 cups (473 mL) chopped onions
1 cup (236 mL) chopped celery
1 cup (236 mL) chopped red bell pepper
¼ cup (60 mL) chopped parsley
2 tablespoons (30 mL) minced garlic

1. Preheat the barbecue to medium high (350°F [180°C] to 400°F [200°C]).

2. Place the chicken in a Dutch oven or roasting pan. Add the water and Creole Seasoning and place the pan in the barbecue to boil for about 30 minutes. Remove the pan from the barbecue, remove the chicken from the pan, and skim any fat off the surface of the water. Let the chicken cool. Debone and chop the chicken into small pieces and return it to the liquid in the pot.

3. In a heavy pot or saucepan on a side burner or stovetop burner, melt the butter. Add the rice and sauté until brown.

4. Add the onions, garlic, celery, bell pepper, parsley, and garlic and sauté until onions are transparent.

5. Return the Dutch oven to the barbecue and reheat the original cooking water with the deboned chicken pieces. Add the rice mixture. The water should cover the chicken and rice by 1 inch (2.5 cm); add more water if necessary. Bring to a boil and cook until the water has almost evaporated.

Creole Seasoning

5 tablespoons (75 mL) paprika
3 tablespoons (45 mL) salt
2 tablespoons (30 mL) onion powder
2 tablespoons (30 mL) garlic powder
2 tablespoons (30 mL) dried oregano
2 tablespoons (30 mL) dried basil
1 tablespoon (15 mL) dried thyme
1 tablespoon (15 mL) black pepper
1 tablespoon (15 mL) cayenne pepper

1. In a small bowl, combine all the ingredients. Store in a tightly sealed container.

Smoked Tomato and Basil Rice

Yield: 4 servings

In Italy, basil has always been a token of love. In Romania, when a man accepts a sprig of basil from a woman, they become engaged. So beware to whom you serve this. The apple smoking chips are available online at www.tailgatingplanks.com/chips.

4–5 medium tomatoes
1 cup (236 mL) uncooked long-grain rice (plus approx. 2 cups [472 mL] water)
½ cup (118 mL) finely grated onion
2 tablespoons (30 mL) butter, cut into pieces
1 tablespoon (15 mL) finely chopped fresh basil
Salt, to taste
Freshly ground black pepper, to taste
¼ cup (59 mL) freshly grated Parmigiano-Reggiano cheese
1 tablespoon (15 mL) minced fresh parsley

1. Cut the tomatoes in half and place them cut side up on a rack in a baking dish or shallow metal pan.

2. If using a smoker, set the smoker temperature to 180°F (80°C) to 200°F (95°C) and place the pan with tomatoes in the center of cooking grate. Close the lid and slow-smoke over hickory or other wood smoke for 30 minutes.

3. If using a barbecue, preheat it to 180°F (80°C) to 200°F (95°C). Cook the tomatoes over indirect heat, placing charcoal on one side of the barbecue and the pan on other side. Set a small foil pan filled with soaked Chef Locke Apple Smoking Chips on the bed of coals to smoke-grill the tomatoes.

4. Remove the tomatoes and allow them to cool slightly. Chop them into small cubes and add them to a rice cooker or saucepan. Add the rice, either 2 cups [472 mL] water or the amount of water or chicken stock recommended on the rice package, onion, butter, and basil and cook, stirring, until the rice is done. Add salt and pepper to taste.

5. Sprinkle with the cheese and parsley and serve.

Classic Mexican Rice

Yield: 4 servings

We like to soak the rice in chicken stock for an hour before cooking it in the saucepan. This gives it a bit more body and fullness. You could also use beef or vegetable stock.

3 tablespoons (45 mL) olive oil
1 cup (236 mL) uncooked long-grain rice
2¼ cups (532 mL) chicken broth
¼ cup (112 g) tomato sauce
1 onion, peeled and diced small
1 clove garlic, peeled and minced
1½ teaspoons (7.5 mL) salt
¼ teaspoon (1.25 mL) chili powder
¼ cup (59 mL) chopped adobo or chipotle chili peppers (optional)
1½ cups (354 mL) shredded Monterey Jack cheese

1. Preheat the barbecue to medium high (350°F [180°C] to 400°F [200°C]).

2. In a large cast-iron skillet on the barbecue grill or a side burner, heat the oil. Add the rice and cook until brown.

3. Add the broth, tomato sauce, onion, garlic, salt, and chili powder. Place the skillet in the barbecue and simmer, covered, over low heat for 25 minutes or until tender. Add the peppers, if desired.

4. Top with the Monterey Jack cheese and return the skillet to the barbecue. Heat until the cheese melts, remove the skillet from the heat, cool slightly, and serve.

Saffron–Raisin Rice

Yield: 6–8 servings

For an extra bit of color and flavor, substitute 1 cup (236 mL) each of dried cherries and dried apricots for the raisins, both cut into raisin-sized chunks.

4 cups (0.95 L) chicken or vegetable stock
¾ teaspoon (3.75 mL) saffron powder
2 cups (473 mL) uncooked long-grain basmati or Texmati rice, rinsed
1 tablespoon (15 mL) olive oil or butter
1 clove garlic, peeled and minced
Salt, to taste
Freshly ground black pepper, to taste
2 cups (473 mL) golden raisins, soaked in warm water for 20 minutes
3 tablespoons (45 mL) chopped chives

1. Preheat the barbecue to medium high (350°F [180°C] to 400°F [200°C]).

2. In a Dutch oven or roasting pan, bring the stock to a boil.

3. Stir the saffron powder into the boiling stock. Add the rice, oil or butter, garlic, salt, and pepper. Stir the rice once, and then cover the pot tightly and let the rice cook in the barbecue for about 25 minutes without opening the lid.

4. When the rice is cooked, remove the Dutch oven from the barbecue. Add the drained raisins and chives, let the rice sit for 2 minutes, fluff with a fork, and serve.

Curried Rice and Lentil Loaf

Yield: 4–6 servings

In all my seven years of hosting Barbecue America *on public TV, this, believe it or not, has been by far the most asked-for recipe. It's a great, healthful side dish, and although it's a bit tedious to make, it's obviously a favorite with my audience.*

1½ cups (354 mL) vegetable stock
¾ cup (177 mL) dried brown lentils
3 tablespoons (45 mL) soy sauce, divided
1 cup (236 mL) cooked wild rice
¼ cup (59 mL) barbecue sauce
½ cup (118 mL) oat bran
½ cup (118 mL) finely chopped celery
½ cup (118 mL) finely chopped carrot
½ cup (118 mL) finely chopped mushrooms, stems and caps
¼ cup (59 mL) finely chopped onion
½ cup (118 mL) chopped pecans or other nut
3–4 cloves garlic, peeled and minced
2 teaspoons (10 mL) curry powder
½ teaspoon (2.5 mL) dried savory
½ teaspoon (2.5 mL) dried sage
½ teaspoon (2.5 mL) freshly ground black pepper

1. Preheat the barbecue to medium high (350°F [180°C] to 400°F [200°C]). Grease a loaf pan.

2. In a saucepan, bring the vegetable stock to a boil. Add the lentils and 1 tablespoon (915 mL) of the soy sauce. Reduce the heat to low and simmer for 30 minutes, or until the lentils are tender. Do not drain.

3. Transfer the cooked lentils to a large bowl. Add the oat bran, celery, carrot, mushrooms, pecans, barbecue sauce, onion, wild rice, garlic, curry powder, savory, sage, and pepper and stir vigorously to help break down the lentils.

4. Pack the mixture firmly into the prepared loaf pan. Brush the top of loaf with the remaining soy sauce and bake it for about 45 to 50 minutes, or until it's crisp on the outside.

5. Let stand for 10 minutes before slicing and serving.

Lemongrass and Coconut Rice
Yield: 4 servings

Adding grilled shrimp, scallops, fish, lobster, or cooked crab to this side dish makes it into a delicious main course.

1 teaspoon (5 mL) butter
1 cup (236 mL) uncooked long-grain rice
1 cup (236 mL) water
½ cup (118 mL) coconut milk
1 tablespoon (15 mL) minced fresh lemongrass
1 teaspoon (5 mL) unsweetened dried coconut

1. Preheat the barbecue to medium high (350°F [180°C] to 400°F [200°C]).

2. In a Dutch oven, melt the butter. Add the rice and stir to coat each grain.

3. Add the water, coconut milk, lemongrass, and coconut. Put the Dutch oven in the barbecue or on a side burner and bring to a boil. Reduce the heat to the lowest setting and cover the Dutch oven.

4. If cooking on a side burner, transfer the Dutch oven to the barbecue. Cook for 25 minutes without stirring the rice.

5. Remove the Dutch oven from the barbecue and let it sit, covered, for 20 more minutes, again without stirring. Lift the lid and stir well. Scoop the rice into a serving bowl and serve immediately.

Rick's Rice Pilaf
Yield: 4 servings

If you wish, throw a couple tablespoons (30 mL) of uncooked wild rice into this dish and cook a bit longer. You can also add some chopped celery and chopped green onions.

¾ cup (177 mL) uncooked converted rice
3 tablespoons (45 mL) butter
¼ cup (59 mL) chopped onion
1¼ cups (295 mL) hot water
1 tablespoon (15 mL) chicken stock base
¼ teaspoon (1.25 mL) freshly ground black pepper
¼ cup (59 mL) diced green bell pepper
2 tablespoons (30 mL) diced red bell pepper

1. Preheat the barbecue to medium high (350°F [180°C] to 400°F [200°C]).

2. Rinse the rice with hot water.

3. In a saucepan, melt the butter. Add the onion and sauté for about 5 minutes, or until tender. Stir in the rice, coating it with butter.

4. In a small bowl, mix together the hot water, chicken stock base, and pepper. Pour this mixture over the rice and stir. Mix the bell peppers into the rice.

5. Transfer the mixture to a covered casserole or baking pan and bake in the barbecue for 25 to 30 minutes.

6. Remove the casserole from the barbecue, lift the lid, and stir the rice pilaf. Serve immediately.

Biscuits and Beans
Yield: 8–10 servings

Although I make this dish with one brand of beans, that doesn't mean it won't be a success if you use another brand. It's just that Bush's offers a huge variety and is available everywhere. Plus, they're darn good beans.

1 (15-ounce [425-g]) can Bush's original baked beans
1 (15-ounce [425-g]) can Bush's pinto beans, drained
1 (15-ounce [425-g]) can Bush's vegetarian beans, drained
1 (15-ounce [425-g]) can mandarin orange segments, undrained
1 cup (236 mL) golden raisins
1 pippin apple, unpeeled, minced
½ cup (118 mL) cane syrup or molasses
1 small onion, peeled and minced
½ cup (118 mL) ketchup
2 tablespoons (30 mL) orange juice
2 tablespoons (30 mL) prepared yellow mustard
½ teaspoon (2.5 mL) ground cinnamon
½ teaspoon (2.5 mL) ground nutmeg
1 (12-ounce [340-g]) tube Pillsbury refrigerator biscuit dough

1. Preheat the barbecue to medium high (300°F [150°C]).

2. In a large mixing bowl, gently combine the beans, mandarin oranges, raisins, apple, cane syrup, onion, ketchup, orange juice, mustard, cinnamon, and nutmeg.

3. Pour the mixture into a cast-iron skillet or Dutch oven, and cover it with aluminum foil or a lid. Put the pan in the barbecue and bake for 1 hour.

4. Remove the aluminum foil cover, then cover the beans with rounds of the biscuit dough and bake about 10 minutes longer, or until the biscuits puff up and turn brown.

5. Serve the beans at the table, giving each person a spoonful of biscuit and a heaping portion of beans.

Root Beer Barbecue Beans

Yield: 4–6 servings

The celery stalks aren't there as a garnish or vegetable addition; the stalks absorb some of the enzymes that cause the unpleasant side effect beans are known for. Really, it works.

5 slices bacon, diced
1 medium onion, peeled and diced
1 cup (236 mL) root beer (not diet)
2 tablespoons (30 mL) molasses
½ teaspoon (2.5 mL) dry mustard
¼ teaspoon (1.25 mL) garlic salt
¼ teaspoon (1.25 mL) lemon pepper
2–3 celery stalks, cut into 2-inch pieces
1 (36-ounce [1-kg]) can Bush's baked beans

1. Preheat the barbecue to medium high (350°F [180°C] to 400°F [200°C]).

2. In a cast-iron skillet set directly on the grill or on a side burner, cook the bacon and onions until the bacon is brown and crisp and the onions are just starting to brown and have become transparent.

3. Add the root beer, molasses, mustard, garlic salt, lemon pepper, and celery stalks and stir well.

4. Pour the beans into a Dutch oven or roasting pan with a lid. Add the mixture from the skillet and place the Dutch oven directly over the heated barbecue grill. Bring to a boil, reduce the heat, and simmer, stirring often, until the mixture is slightly thickened, about 20 minutes.

5. Remove the Dutch oven or roasting pan from the barbecue and serve.

Barbecued Lima Beans

Yield: 6–8 servings

You can make this into a barbecue succotash by adding 3 cups (708 mL) corn kernels, either freshly cut from the cob, frozen, or canned. Lima beans are sometimes called "butter beans," especially in the South.

4 slices bacon, cooked and crumbled
1 medium onion, peeled and diced
8 cups (1.9 L) lima beans, fresh or frozen (preferred)
1 cup (236 mL) ketchup
½ cup (118 mL) mustard-based barbecue sauce
¼ cup (60 mL) maple syrup
2 tablespoons (30 mL) dark brown sugar
2 tablespoons (30 mL) prepared yellow mustard
½ teaspoon (2.5 mL) dry mustard
¼ teaspoon (1.25 mL) salt
¼ teaspoon (1.25 mL) lemon pepper

1. Preheat the barbecue to medium high (350°F [180°C] to 400°F [200°C]).

2. In a saucepan set on the grill or a side burner, cook the bacon and onion until the bacon is brown and crisp and the onions are just starting to brown and have become transparent.

3. Transfer the onions and bacon to a 2-quart (1.9 L) casserole or Dutch oven, add the remaining ingredients, and stir to incorporate.

4. Place the covered casserole or Dutch oven in the barbecue and bake for 60 minutes. If the lima beans are not tender at that time, cook for another 15 to 20 minutes.

5. Remove the pot from the barbecue and serve.

Parmesan White Beans
Yield: 8–10 servings

You can easily make this side into a main dish just by adding chopped ham, turkey, or sausage when you add the tomatoes and paste. Serve this with a crusty bread (even a garlic bread from this book) to sop up the delicious juices in the beans.

2 tablespoons (30 mL) olive oil
2 medium carrots, peeled and diced
2 stalks celery, finely chopped
2 cloves garlic, peeled and minced
2 medium shallots, peeled and minced
1 onion, peeled and finely chopped
1 orange or yellow bell pepper, finely chopped
¼ cup (59 mL) minced fresh parsley
1 (28-ounce [784-g]) can diced tomatoes
1 (5½-ounce [154-g]) can tomato paste
¾ cup (177 mL) dry white wine
2 teaspoons (10 mL) sugar
1 teaspoon (5 mL) dried basil
1 teaspoon (5 mL) dried savory
1 teaspoon (5 mL) dried oregano
½ teaspoon (2.5 mL) sea salt
¼ cup (59 mL) grated Parmigiano-Reggiano cheese, divided
4 cups (0.95 L) cooked navy beans
1 cup (236 mL) fresh breadcrumbs
¼ cup (59 mL) chopped fresh parsley
2 tablespoons (30 mL) butter, melted
1 cup (236 mL) shredded mozzarella cheese

1. Preheat the barbecue to medium high (350°F [180°C] to 400°F [200°C]).

2. In a large pot or Dutch oven set on a side burner or on the grill over medium high heat, heat the olive oil until it just begins to smoke. Add the carrots, celery, garlic, shallots, onion, bell pepper, and parsley and sauté until the vegetables are just tender, about 8 to 10 minutes.

3. Add the tomatoes, tomato paste, wine, sugar, basil, savory, oregano, salt, and 2 tablespoons (30 mL) of the Parmesan cheese and bring the mixture to a boil. Reduce the heat and simmer for approximately 20 to 25 minutes, or until the mixture thickens.

4. Stir in the beans and cook for 15 minutes longer. While the beans are cooking, combine the breadcrumbs, parsley, butter, and the remaining Parmesan cheese in a small bowl and set aside.

5. Sprinkle the mozzarella cheese and the breadcrumb mixture evenly over the top of the beans. Bake in the barbecue for 20 to 30 minutes, or until the beans are bubbling.

Hawaiian Baked Beans

Yield: 6–8 servings

Storing pineapples at room temperature for 1 to 2 days before serving will make them softer and sweeter.

1 cup (236 mL) chopped Maui, Vidalia, or Walla Walla onion
1 tablespoon (15 mL) butter
½ pound (227 g) smoked bacon
1 pound (454 mL) boneless beef chuck steak, cut into ½-inch (1-cm) pieces
1 (28-ounce [784-g]) can baked beans
½ cup (118 mL) molasses
1 whole pineapple, stem and leaves left on
Sour cream, for garnish

1. Preheat the barbecue to medium high (350°F [180°C] to 400°F [200°C]).

2. Place a cast-iron skillet over a barbecue side burner or directly on the grill. Add the onion and butter and sauté until the onion is slightly browned. Remove the onion from the pan and set aside.

3. Add the bacon to the skillet and cook until it's crisp. Remove the bacon, drain it on paper towels, and chop the slices into 1–inch (2.5-cm) pieces. Pour out half of the bacon fat, leaving the rest in the pan.

4. Add the chuck steak to the skillet and brown the meat thoroughly over high heat. Add the bacon and stir well. Mix in the beans, molasses, and sautéed onion. Place the skillet on the grill over indirect heat and cook until the mixture boils. Reduce the heat to a simmer.

5. Cut the pineapple in half vertically, keeping the leaves attached. Lay each pineapple half on its round side and remove the core. Remove the pineapple flesh with a sharp knife or grapefruit spoon, leaving a ¼- to ½-inch shell. Chop the pineapple flesh you removed into ½- to 1-inch (1- to 2.5-cm) cubes.

6. When you are ready to serve the beans, gently fold 1 cup (236 mL) of the chopped pineapple into the bean mixture and divide that mixture between the two empty pineapple halves.

7. Garnish the beans with the remaining chopped pineapple and a few generous dollops of sour cream.

Dr. Pepper Baked Beans

Yield: 4–6 servings

You can substitute in any cola you prefer, but I first tasted this dish made with good old Dr. Pepper and have continued to use it when I make these beans. Do not use Diet Dr. Pepper or other diet colas, as they turn bitter when heated. If you can, buy original Dr. Pepper, which uses real cane sugar.

1 (28-ounce [784-g]) can pork and beans
1 onion, peeled and finely chopped
1 green bell pepper, finely chopped
1 tomato, chopped fine
½ cup (118 mL) packed dark brown sugar
⅓ cup (79 mL) Dr. Pepper
⅛ teaspoon (0.6 mL) ground cloves

1. Preheat the barbecue to medium high (350°F [180°C] to 400°F [200°C]).

2. Drain the liquid from the pork and beans and pour the beans into a large baking dish.

3. Gently mix in the onion, pepper, and tomato.

4. In as small saucepan, combine the brown sugar, Dr. Pepper, and cloves. Cook over low heat, stirring, until the sugar is dissolved. Pour the liquid evenly over the bean mixture.

5. Bake the beans in the barbecue, covered, for 30 minutes.

6. Remove the pan from the barbecue and serve.

Old-Fashioned Baked Beans

Yield: 6–8 servings

Baked beans are worth cooking from scratch because canned beans just can't match the rich, full taste. Ask your butcher for salt pork, because it's much better than bacon.

2 pounds (908 g) dry navy beans
1 teaspoon (5 mL) baking soda
1 pound (454 g) salt pork
1 large onion, peeled and diced
½ cup (118 mL) packed brown sugar
½ cup (118 mL) molasses
2 teaspoons (10 mL) dry mustard
2 teaspoons (10 mL) salt
½ teaspoon (2.5 mL) freshly ground black pepper

1. Place the beans in a large pot. Add water to cover and soak the beans overnight.

2. Preheat the barbecue to medium high (350°F [180°C] to 400°F [200°C]).

3. Add the baking soda to the beans and water and boil for 10 minutes. Drain the beans in a colander and rinse them with cold water.

4. With a sharp knife, cut the salt pork into 1-inch (2.5-cm) squares. Put half the pork in the bottom of a Dutch oven and add the diced onion.

5. Pour the drained beans into the Dutch oven and place the remaining salt pork on top.

6. In a large pot, mix 1 gallon (3.8 mL) of water with the brown sugar, molasses, mustard, salt, pepper. Pour the liquid over the beans, making sure they are just covered. Add more water if necessary.

7. Bake in the barbecue for 6 to 7 hours, adding water as needed to keep the beans moist.

Tom's Ranch Beans

Yield: 6–8 servings

One surefire method to prepare dry beans is to cover them with plenty of water, bring them to a boil for 2 minutes, turn off the heat, cover the pot tightly, and let them sit for 1 hour. Then drain and cook as usual. Or you can just soak them overnight, rinse, and cook. This recipe comes from Tom Perini from Buffalo Gap, Texas.

1 pound (454 g) dry pinto beans, soaked overnight or quick-soaked (see head note)
6 ounces (168 g) salt pork
3–4 cloves garlic, peeled and minced
1 tablespoon (15 mL) chili powder
Kosher salt, to taste
1 jalapeño pepper, sliced
½ cup (118 mL) chopped fresh cilantro

1. Rinse the beans and remove any stones or dirt. Cut the pork into thin strips and rinse.

2. In a large pot, combine the beans, pork, garlic, chili powder, and salt and add water to cover. Boil over medium heat on a barbecue side burner until the beans are tender, about 2 hours. Add hot water to keep the beans covered if necessary.

3. Add the jalapeño pepper and cilantro. Allow the beans to sit for about 30 minutes to absorb the flavors before serving.

Red Beans and Rice

Yield: 4–6 servings

Combine the creamy pink texture of pinto beans with a whole grain, such as rice, and you have a virtually fat-free, high-quality protein meal.

1 pound (454 g) dry pinto beans
7 cups (1.7 L) water
1 large onion, peeled and chopped
3 cloves garlic, peeled and minced
½ medium red bell pepper, chopped
1 medium ham hock
2 tablespoons (30 mL) tomato paste
2 teaspoons (10 mL) dried oregano
2 teaspoons (10 mL) dried thyme
½ teaspoon (2.5 mL) hot sauce
4 cups (946 mL) water (or chicken stock)
2 cups (473 mL) uncooked long-grain rice

1. Preheat the barbecue to medium high (200°F [95°C] to 250°F [120°C]).

2. Rinse the beans and pick out any stones or debris. Soak the beans overnight in the water. Or, to prepare them the same day, place the beans in a pot of water and bring them to a boil. Boil for 2 minutes and turn off the heat. Cover the pot and let the beans soak in the cooking water for 1 hour.

3. Add the onion, garlic, bell pepper, ham hock, tomato paste, oregano, thyme, and hot sauce to the soaked beans, cover, and bring to a boil. Reduce the heat to medium and cook for 1 hour.

4. Remove the ham hock, trim away the fatty skin, and remove the meat from the bone. Chop the meat into small pieces and return it to the pot. Place the pot in the barbecue, close the lid, and cook for 1 hour. The liquid will have boiled down to a thick, brown sauce, and the beans should be soft, but not mushy.

5. In a medium saucepan, combine the water and rice. Cover the pan and bring to a boil. Without lifting the lid, reduce the heat to a simmer and cook for 18 minutes. Turn off the heat and allow the rice to rest for 5 minutes.

6. Serve the beans over the rice.

Grilled Corn Salsa

Yield: 4–6 servings

The fresher the corn, the better, as fresh corn on the cob will lose up to 40 percent of its sugar content after 6 hours at room temperature. After you cut off kernels, use the back of the knife to milk the juice from the cob.

2 teaspoons (10 mL) olive oil
1 (16-ounce [454-g]) can black beans, drained and rinsed
2 large tomatoes, cut into chunks
1 avocado, pitted, peeled, cut into chunks
2 jalapeño peppers, minced
¼ cup (60 mL) fresh cilantro
2 tablespoons (30 mL) lime juice
½ teaspoon (2.5 mL) salt
Kernels from 2 ears grilled corn on the cob

1. Preheat the barbecue to medium high (350°F [180°C] to 400°F [200°C]).

2. In a large bowl, combine the oil, beans, tomatoes, avocado, jalapeño peppers, cilantro, lime juice, and salt.

3. Stir corn into the salsa. Let the mixture rest at room temperature for at least 30 minutes, stirring occasionally.

Apple-Peach-Apricot and Citrus Salsa

Yield: 4–6 servings

There are hundreds of salsas, most of which involve onions and/or tomatoes. This fruit salsa is especially good with fish and chicken. It's not grilled, but you could serve it with just about any grilled poultry or fish dish.

4 Granny Smith apples, unpeeled, finely diced
2 apricots, pitted and diced
1 large peach, pitted and diced
1 (8-ounce [227-g]) can jellied cranberries
¼ cup (60 mL) pineapple rum
¼ cup (60 mL) finely chopped fresh cilantro
6 green onions, green and white parts, diced
2 tablespoons (30 mL) cider vinegar
2 teaspoons (10 mL) finely chopped orange zest
1 teaspoon (5 mL) finely chopped lemon zest
1 teaspoon (5 mL) finely chopped lime zest
1 teaspoon (5 mL) finely minced jalapeño peppers
Salt, to taste
Freshly ground black pepper, to taste

1. In a large, nonreactive glass or ceramic bowl, combine all of the ingredients and mix thoroughly. Refrigerate for at least 30 minutes before serving.

Chipotle Salsa
Yield: 4–6 servings

Chipotle peppers are jalapeño chili peppers that have been smoked. The thick, fleshy, jalapeño is difficult to dry and prone to rot.

3 chipotle peppers, rinsed, drained, seeded, and finely chopped
6–8 fresh tomatillos
¼ cup (59 mL) chopped onion
1 tablespoon (15 mL) chopped fresh thyme
2 cloves garlic, peeled and minced
1 teaspoon (5 mL) brown sugar
¼ teaspoon (1.25 mL) salt

1. Slice the chipotle peppers in half and discard the stems and seeds. Chop the peppers into ¼-inch (0.5-cm) pieces. Place them in a small bowl and add boiling water to cover. Let stand for 45 to 60 minutes to soften the peppers, then drain well.

2. Remove and discard the husks from the tomatillos and rinse. Finely chop the tomatillos until you have 2 cups (473 mL).

3. In a mixing bowl, combine the soaked pepper pieces, tomatillos, onion, thyme, garlic, brown sugar, and salt. Cover the salsa and let it stand at room temperature for 30 minutes to blend the flavors. Serve as a dip or with grilled meat or fish.

Classic Salsa Fresca
Yield: 3–4 servings

You can do make this dish in a food processor, but you must pulse the vegetables to make a mixture of small chunks. Overprocess, and you get salsa soup.

2 cloves garlic, peeled
½ medium onion, peeled
1 jalapeño or other small, hot pepper, stemmed and seeded
¼ cup (59 mL) fresh cilantro sprigs
1 pound (454 g) ripe tomatoes, seeded and coarsely chopped
2 tablespoons (30 mL) vegetable or olive oil
Juice of 1 lime
Salt, to taste
Freshly ground black pepper, to taste

1. Using a sharp knife, mince the garlic, onion, and jalapeño pepper. Finely chop the cilantro.

2. Combine the vegetables in a nonmetallic bowl and mix well. Add the oil and the lime juice. Season with the salt and pepper.

Tomatillo Salsa Verde
Yield: 4–6 servings

This classic Veracruz-style salsa is great on chips and pita bread, but even better on grilled chicken, fish, or steaks! The avocado adds a smoothness to the bite of the hot peppers and onion.

2 cloves garlic, peeled and cut into chunks
1½ teaspoons (7.5 mL) salt
1 medium Spanish onion, peeled and coarsely chopped
2–3 serrano peppers, stems removed, cut into chunks
½ pound (227 g) tomatillos (about 6–8 medium), quartered
4–6 sprigs cilantro
1 ripe Hass or Fuerte avocado, pitted

1. In a food processor or blender, combine the garlic and salt and process to a paste.

2. Scrape down the sides, if necessary, with a rubber spatula. Add the onion, peppers, tomatillos, and cilantro and pulse to make a chunky puree.

3. Add the avocado and process to the desired smoothness. Serve within 1 hour (preferably at once).

Buttered, Baked, and Barbecued Potatoes
Yield: 4 servings

Use real butter in this dish, no substitutes, and don't skimp on the quality of the butter you buy. Only the best is good enough for this dish, and your hungry family, friends, and guests.

1½ pounds Yukon Gold fingerling potatoes (or freshly harvested new potatoes)
3 tablespoons (45 mL) butter, melted
½ teaspoon (2.5 mL) kosher salt
4 large sprigs rosemary
Freshly ground black pepper, to taste

1. Preheat the barbecue to medium high (350°F [180°C] to 400°F [200°C]) for direct and indirect heating.

2. Under running water, scrub the potatoes to free them of all soil, roots, or leaves. If the potatoes are very small you can use them whole; otherwise, cut them into 1½- to 2-inch (3.5- to 5-cm) pieces and set aside.

3. Place the potatoes in a single layer in a Dutch oven or roasting pan.

4. In a large bowl, combine the butter, salt, and rosemary and mix lightly.

5. Pour the butter and herbs over the potatoes and stir until they are well coated. Cover the Dutch oven or roasting pan tightly with a lid or aluminum foil.

6. Bake on the unheated side of the barbecue for 40 minutes, stirring several times, until the potatoes are tender.

7. Uncover the Dutch oven or pan and cook over direct heat for about 20 minutes, stirring often, until the potatoes are browned on all sides.

8. Add a healthy grind of pepper to the pan and serve piping hot.

Parmesan Garlic Spuds
Yield: 4–6 servings

We favor the soft, yellow Yukon Gold as one of the best potatoes, mainly for its buttery rich taste and smooth texture. Similar potatoes we've tried and liked include Red Gold and Yellow Finn. This recipe comes from Sandy Callon from Ridgefield, Wash.

6 large Yukon gold potatoes (or use russet potatoes)
5 cloves garlic, peeled and crushed
½ cup (118 mL) butter, melted
1 tablespoon (15 mL) chopped fresh basil
¼ teaspoon (1.25 mL) kosher salt
½ teaspoon (2.5 mL) ground white pepper
4 cups (0.95 L) chicken stock
4 cups (0.95 L) heavy cream
½ cup (118 mL) freshly grated Parmesan cheese

1. Preheat the barbecue to medium high (350°F [180°C] to 400°F [200°C]). Grease a roasting pan.

2. Halve the potatoes lengthwise. With the cut side lying flat on a cutting board, make cuts ¾ of the way through each potato half every ¼ inch (0.5 cm) along the length. Place the potatoes flat side down in the prepared roasting pan.

3. In a small bowl, mix together the garlic, butter, basil, salt, and pepper. Pour this mixture over the potatoes, making sure the butter gets in the cuts. Pour the chicken stock into the pan, *not* over the potatoes.

4. Cover the pan with aluminum foil and barbecue for about 35 minutes, or until the potatoes are soft.

5. Gently pour off the chicken stock. Pour in the cream and sprinkle the potatoes generously with the Parmesan cheese.

6. Bake in the barbecue for another 10 minutes, then serve.

New Potatoes in Garlic-Lemon Butter

Yield: 6–8 servings

Real new potatoes are immature red potatoes you dig yourself right out of the garden or a farmer's field. The best in the world come from the potato fields of Maine and are served with cream and freshly picked garden peas.

3 cloves garlic, peeled and finely minced
¾ cup (177 mL) butter, melted
3 pounds (1.3 kg) new potatoes, halved (about 24 potatoes)
2 lemons, quartered
1 tablespoon (15 mL) dried sage, divided
Salt, to taste
Freshly ground black pepper, to taste
2 tablespoons (30 mL) chopped fresh parley or dill

1. Preheat the barbecue to medium high (350°F [180°C] to 400°F [200°C]).

2. In a small bowl, stir the garlic into the melted butter.

3. Arrange half of the potatoes in a single layer on two layers of heavy-duty aluminum foil. Brush the cut side of the potatoes evenly with half of the butter mixture, squeeze the juice from 1 of the lemons over the potatoes, and drop the lemon quarters into the mixture.

4. Sprinkle the potatoes with half of the sage, the salt, and the pepper. Seal the foil package completely with a double fold.

5. Repeat with the remaining potatoes, butter, lemon, sage, salt, and pepper to form a second package.

6. Roast directly on hot coals or on the grill, turning the packages frequently, for 40 to 45 minutes, or until the potatoes are tender.

7. Remove foil packages from the barbecue and carefully open them, avoiding the escaping steam. Pour the potatoes into a serving bowl, remove the lemon wedges, sprinkle with the parsley, and serve.

Grilled Sweet Potatoes

Yield: 4–6 servings

Of the two varieties of sweet potato, I prefer the dark orange variety over the lighter yellow ones. The dark potatoes are sweeter and moister, and I think they are the best ones to barbecue.

2 pounds (908 g) sweet potatoes, peeled and cut lengthwise into ½-inch (1-cm) slices
4 tablespoons (60 mL) olive oil, divided
⅓ cup (79 mL) honey mustard
1 tablespoon (15 mL) minced fresh rosemary
Salt, to taste
Freshly ground black pepper, to taste

1. Make sure the grill is clean and generously sprayed with nonstick grilling spray. Preheat the barbecue to medium high (350°F [180°C] to 400°F [200°C]).

2. Bring a large pot of water to a boil. Drop the sweet potato slices into the water and boil for 2 to 3 minutes. Drain and pat dry.

3. Brush the potato slices with 2 tablespoons (30 mL) of the olive oil and place them directly on the hot grill. Cook for 2 to 3 minutes per side.

4. In a small bowl, combine the mustard, the remaining olive oil, and the rosemary. Brush both sides of the grilled sweet potato slices with this mixture and continue to cook them until they are fork-tender and nicely marked, turning 2 or 3 times and basting frequently. Lightly salt and pepper each side.

5. Serve on a heated platter.

Tequila Sweet Potatoes
Yield: 4–6 servings

This may be an unusual way to serve sweet potatoes, but the potato strands soak up the tequila, lime juice, and butter better than slices. However, you could make this dish using thin slices as well.

1 pound (454 g) dark orange sweet potatoes
1 cup (236 mL) butter, melted, divided
¾ cup (177 mL) tequila, divided
6 tablespoons (90 mL) brown sugar
6 tablespoons (90 mL) lime juice, divided
1 teaspoon (5 mL) salt

1. Preheat the barbecue to medium high (200°F [95°C] to 250°F [120°C]).

2. With a hand grater or a large grating disc on a food processor, grate the sweet potatoes into 2- to 3-inch (5- to 7.5-cm) long matchstick-sized strands.

3. Pour half the butter into a cast-iron skillet or roasting pan. Add the grated sweet potatoes.

4. Add ¼ cup (59 mL) of the tequila to the remaining melted butter. Add the brown sugar, 2 tablespoons (30 mL) of the lime juice, and the salt and stir. Pour this mixture over the sweet potatoes in the skillet.

5. Place the skillet in the barbecue and cook for about 1 hour.

6. Remove the pan from the barbecue and add another ¼ cup (59 mL) of the tequila and 2 more tablespoons (30 mL) of the lime juice. Stir and press the potatoes down. Return the skillet to the barbecue and continue cooking until the potatoes are tender and starting to brown around the edges.

7. Bring the pan to the table and drizzle the remaining tequila and lime juice over the top of the sweet potatoes. Stir and serve.

Consuela's Chipotle-Epazote Potatoes

Yield: 4 servings

Epazote is a popular herb in Mexico, often used in black bean dishes. Like cilantro, it is an acquired taste for some, but it's balanced here with the other herbs and chili peppers. This recipe comes from Consuela Lopez from Cancún, Mexico.

8 medium russet or Yukon Gold potatoes, washed and left unpeeled
2 sprigs rosemary
6 black peppercorns
1 sprig epazote
½ teaspoon (2.5 mL) ground chipotle pepper, divided
½ cup (118 mL) butter, melted
¼ teaspoon (1.25 mL) ground epazote
1 dash celery salt
¼ teaspoon (1.25 mL) chopped fresh rosemary
Freshly ground black pepper, to taste

1. Make sure the grill is clean and generously sprayed with nonstick grilling spray. Preheat the barbecue to medium high (350°F [180°C] to 400°F [200°C]).

2. Put the potatoes in a large pot with water to cover. Add the rosemary sprigs, peppercorns, epazote sprig, and ¼ teaspoon (1.25 mL) of the ground chipotle. Bring to a boil and cook the potatoes for 10 minutes, or until they are knife-tender. Drain, discarding the peppercorns and herbs.

3. With a sharp knife, cut the potatoes in half horizontally while they are still warm. Dip each potato half in the melted butter. In a large mixing bowl, combine the remaining ground chipotle, the ground epazote, the celery salt, the chopped rosemary, and the black pepper. Add the potatoes and turn them to coat with the seasonings.

4. Grill the potatoes until slightly crisp and not quite blackened, and serve.

Dish Pan Taters

Yield: 4–6 servings

This dish will liven any party, especially if you bring it right to the table and let people know you ran out of pots and had to cook this in Grandma's dish pan.

¼ cup (59 mL) butter
4 cloves garlic, peeled, crushed, and chopped
1 large Spanish or yellow onion, peeled and cut into chunks
4 carrots, cut into 1-inch (2.5-cm) pieces
4 stalks celery, cut into 1-inch (2.5 cm) pieces
2 tablespoons (30 mL) blackened seasoning
1 tablespoon (15 mL) garlic powder
1 tablespoon (15 mL) chili powder
1 teaspoon (5 mL) freshly ground black pepper
½ teaspoon (2.5 mL) kosher salt
4 large baking potatoes, unpeeled, cut into 1-inch (2.5-cm) chunks
1 tablespoon (15 mL) dried parsley flakes

1. Preheat the barbecue to medium high (350°F [180°C] to 400°F [200°C]).

2. In an old, deep pan, such as an aluminum or stainless steel dish pan, combine the butter, garlic, onion, carrots, celery, blackened seasoning, garlic powder, chili powder, black pepper, and salt and stir. Top with the potato chunks. (The steam from the veggies helps cook the potatoes on top of the mix.)

3. Cover the pan with a layer of heavy-duty aluminum foil, folding it around the rim of the pan to seal completely.

4. Place the pan on the grill for about 25 to 30 minutes, or until the potatoes are done and easily pierced with a fork.

5. Serve the dishpan at the table, scooping the potatoes and vegetables right from the pan onto plates.

Double-Cheese Foiled Potatoes

Yield: 6–8 servings

If you like this recipe, try adding crumbled bacon as another layer. You can also add some zest by sprinkling the dish with a small amount of red pepper flakes mixed with the salt instead of the black pepper.

10 large potatoes, sliced ¼-inch (0.5-cm) thick
5 medium onions, peeled, sliced, and separated into rings
1 pound (454 g) Tillamook aged white cheddar cheese, sliced
Sea salt, to taste
Freshly ground black pepper, to taste
¼ pound (112 g) blue cheese, crumbled
1 cup (236 mL) butter, cut into ¼–inch (0.5-cm) pats
6–8 tablespoons (90–120 mL) olive oil

1. Preheat the barbecue to medium high (350°F [180°C] to 400°F [200°C]).

2. Lay out a 12-inch (30-cm) square of foil and place a layer of the potatoes in the center of the foil. Top it with 3 or 4 rings of the onion, a slice of the cheddar cheese, salt and pepper, and a pat of the butter. Add another layer of potato, one of onion, and one of cheddar cheese. Sprinkle blue cheese on top, drizzle with olive oil, fold over twice, and seal the package.

3. Repeat with more foil sheets until you have used up all the ingredients. You should end up with 3 or 4 packages.

4. Place the foiled potatoes on the grill and cook, turning occasionally, for approximately 1 hour.

5. Remove foil packets and open them carefully so you don't get burned. Either serve 1 packet per couple or pour the contents into a large bowl and scoop onto plates.

Glazed Savory Sweet Potatoes

Yield: 6 servings

I learned this recipe during a recent visit to Ocho Rios, Jamaica, filming episodes for my TV series, Barbecue America. *They jerk everything and anything down there, and while I'm not a huge jerk fan, I love this spicy way of cooking sweet potatoes. Serve them with grilled flank or hangar steak, pork chops, chicken, or fish.*

4 large sweet potatoes, peeled and sliced ½-inch (1-cm) thick
1 tablespoon (15 mL) onion powder
2 teaspoons (10 mL) ground thyme
2 teaspoons (10 mL) salt
2 teaspoons (10 mL) sugar
1 teaspoon (5 mL) ground allspice
1 teaspoon (5 mL) coarsely ground black pepper
1 teaspoon (5 mL) cayenne pepper
¼ teaspoon (1.25 mL) ground nutmeg
¼ teaspoon (1.25 mL) ground cinnamon
1 pinch ground cloves
½ cup (118 mL) packed dark brown sugar
¼ cup (59 mL) molasses
¼ cup (59 mL) dark rum
2 tablespoons (30 mL) butter, softened

1. Preheat the barbecue to medium high (350°F [180°C] to 400°F [200°C]) for direct and indirect heating. Make sure the grill is clean and generously sprayed with nonstick grilling spray.

2. For the jerk seasoning, in a small bowl, stir together the onion powder, thyme, salt, sugar, allspice, black pepper, cayenne, nutmeg, cinnamon, and cloves.

3. Place the sweet potato slices in a plastic bag. Spray them with nonstick cooking spray. Reserve 1 teaspoon (5 mL) of the jerk seasoning for the glaze, add the rest to the potatoes in the bag, and toss well to coat.

4. Place the potato slices on the grill over direct heat and grill until they start to brown, about 4 minutes. Turn and grill the other side. When both sides are browned, move the slices to the indirect side of the grill and cook for another 10 to 12 minutes, or until they become fork tender.

5. In a small saucepan, combine the brown sugar, molasses, rum, and the remaining jerk seasoning and simmer for 10 minutes. Remove the saucepan from the heat and swirl in the butter.

6. Place the grilled sweet potatoes in a large mixing bowl and add the glaze, gently tossing the mixture to coat all the potato slices.

Smoke-Baked Spuds
Yield: 4–6 servings

While Americans love their potatoes, consuming an average of 145 pounds (20 kg) every year—much of that, unfortunately, as french fries—we are pikers compared with some Eastern Europeans, who gobble 420 pounds (191 kg) of spuds every year, almost none of which are french fries.

6 large russet or Yukon Gold potatoes
½ cup (118 mL) bacon grease
1 tablespoon (15 mL) kosher salt
1 tablespoon (15 mL) ground white pepper
1 tablespoon (15 mL) granulated garlic
1 tablespoon (15 mL) chopped fresh basil
1 tablespoon (15 mL) chopped fresh sage
1 tablespoon (15 mL) paprika

1. Soak a handful of wood chips (hickory, oak, apple, etc.) in water.

2. Preheat the barbecue to medium high (350°F [180°C] to 400°F [200°C]).

3. Place the soaked chips on a 12-inch (30-cm) square of aluminum foil, then fold the foil into an envelope and poke three holes in the top surface with a pencil. Have the foil packet ready to put directly on charcoal or gas flame when you begin to cook the potatoes.

4. Slice the potatoes in half lengthwise, but do not peel them. Brush the potatoes with the melted bacon grease, or use the more fun and much messier method—use your hands to massage the grease onto the potato halves. Put the greased potatoes in a bowl and set them aside.

5. In a wide, flat pan, combine the salt, pepper, garlic, basil, sage, and paprika. Roll each potato half in the spices until the spuds are well-coated on all sides.

6. Place the smoker packet directly on the coals or flame. Place the potatoes, cut side down, on the grill over direct heat and cook for 5 to 10 minutes, just long enough to get some browning and grill marks on the potatoes.

7. Using tongs, turn the potatoes and cook them skin side down over indirect heat for approximately 25 to 30 minutes, or until they are soft all the way through.

8. Turn potatoes flat side down for a few more minutes if they need more browning. Otherwise, remove them from the grill and place them on a heated platter.

9. Serve with butter, sour cream, and freshly chopped chives or green onions.

Salt-Packed Potatoes

Yield: 6–8 servings

If your casserole dish or Dutch oven is 4 inches (10-cm) deep or deeper, you can do this in two layers. Just add more salt and more potatoes.

1–2 pounds (454–908 g) small red potatoes, unpeeled
Kosher or sea salt (or a mix) as needed to completely cover the potatoes

1. Preheat the barbecue to medium high (350°F [180°C] to 400°F [200°C]).

2. Spread a ½-inch (1-cm) layer of salt in a Dutch oven or heavy casserole dish.

3. Place the potatoes on the salt and add more salt so that the potatoes are covered by at least ½ inch (1 cm).

4. Place the pot on the grill and cook for about 1 hour. Poke a knife through the salt, deep into the potatoes, to see if they are tender.

5. Dump the potatoes and salt onto a large baking sheet. Remove the potatoes and brush any clinging salt crystals from them. Reserve the salt to use the next time you make this dish.

6. Halve the cooked potatoes lengthwise and serve with sour cream, grated Swiss cheese, and melted butter.

Gratin Potatoes with Sweet Onions

Yield: 4 servings

The word "gratin" refers to any dish topped with cheese or breadcrumbs that browns and crisps during baking.

2 cups (473 mL) sliced, cooked peeled potatoes
1 cup (236 mL) chopped sweet Vidalia onions
⅓ cup (79 mL) butter or margarine
3 tablespoons (45 mL) all-purpose flour
1½ cups (354 mL) whole milk
2 teaspoons (10 mL) minced garlic
1 teaspoon (5 mL) freshly ground black pepper
¾ teaspoon (3.75 mL) salt
½ cup (118 mL) shredded cheddar cheese
½ cup (118 mL) shredded Gouda cheese
1 cup (236 mL) seasoned dry breadcrumbs
Paprika, for garnish
Chopped fresh parsley, for garnish

1. Preheat the barbecue to medium high (350°F [180°C] to 400°F [200°C]). Grease a 1-quart (0.95-L) casserole or Dutch oven.

2. Layer the sliced potatoes and onions in the prepared casserole or Dutch oven and set aside.

3. In a medium saucepan, melt the butter over medium heat. Add the flour and stir until smooth. Gradually add the milk, stirring constantly, until the mixture thickens and begins to bubble. Add the garlic, pepper, and salt. Gradually blend in the cheeses, stirring until the mixture is uniform and smooth.

4. Pour the cheese sauce over the potato and onion slices and stir once or twice to mix. Top with the seasoned breadcrumbs.

5. Place in the barbecue and cook for 40 minutes, or until the potatoes are fork-tender and the cheese is bubbly and beginning to brown on top.

6. Remove from the barbecue, sprinkle with paprika and parsley, and serve.

Hot German Potatoes
Yield: 4–6 servings

Try these once, and you'll be hooked on the interplay of tart and sweet, tender and crunchy, and overwhelmed by the scent of this dish as it comes to the table. Technically, they're not grilled or barbecued, but so what? They go wonderfully with any grilled or barbecued food.

8 medium potatoes
6–8 strips bacon
½–¾ cup (118–177 mL) chopped onion
2½–3 tablespoons (37.5–45 mL) all-purpose flour
1½ cups (354 mL) hot chicken broth or water
½ cup (118 mL) cider vinegar
1½ tablespoons (22.5 mL) sugar
1 teaspoon (5 mL) salt
1 teaspoon (5 mL) dry mustard
½ teaspoon (2.5 mL) freshly ground black pepper

1. Put the potatoes in a large pot and add cold water to cover. Set the pot on a barbecue side burner and bring to a boil. Reduce the heat and cook gently until just tender. Meanwhile, fry the bacon until crisp and drain the slices, reserving the bacon drippings. Crumble the crisp bacon and set it aside.

2. Measure ¼ cup (59 mL) of the bacon drippings and add to a skillet.

3. Add the chopped onion to the skillet and sauté until the onion is tender but not browned.

4. In a skillet or saucepan over a side burner, heat the ¼ cup (59 mL) of bacon drippings over low heat until very warm. Sprinkle in the flour (use more flour for a thicker dressing, less for a thinner dressing) and whisk for about 1 minute.

5. Whisk in the hot broth or water and the vinegar and continue cooking and whisking until the dressing is smooth and thickened. Add the sugar, salt, mustard, and pepper. Taste for seasoning, and correct as needed. Add a little warm vinegar or broth if needed to thin the dressing.

6. When the potatoes are cooked until just tender, drain and peel them while still warm. Slice the potatoes into a bowl, add the reserved crumbled bacon, and fold gently. Add the dressing and toss gently until the potatoes are well-coated with the dressing and well-blended. Serve hot or at room temperature.

New Potatoes and Fresh Peas in Cream
Yield: 4 servings

Not only does this classic Maine dish make a great side dish, it's also incredible as a whole meal. Just be sure to get the freshest-from-the-field potatoes and peas you can find, buy, grow, or harvest yourself. If you can't find fresh peas, you can substitute frozen peas, but it is against all culinary laws to use canned peas.

1 teaspoon (5 mL) salt, divided
1 pound (454 g) small new potatoes, washed and patted dry, unpeeled
2 cups (473 mL) fresh peas
⅔ cup (158 mL) heavy cream
½ cup (118 mL) butter, at room temperature
1 dash salt
1 dash freshly ground black pepper

1. On a barbecue side burner, bring 2 cups (473 mL) and ½ teaspoon (2.5 mL) of the salt to a boil. Halve the new potatoes and add them to the boiling water. Boil until the potatoes are almost tender.

2. In a separate pot of water with the remaining salt, cook the peas until they are just tender.

3. Serve bowls of peas and potatoes with the cream in a pitcher and slabs of the butter at the table. To eat, take 3 or 4 potatoes and roughly mash them on your plate. Dab the spuds generously with the butter, add 3 to 4 heaping tablespoons (67.5 to 90 mL) of cooked peas, drizzle cream over the plate, and add salt and pepper.

Low-Budget Au Gratin Taters
Yield: 4–6 servings

There are two memorable ways to use Velveeta cheese. The first way is in au gratin potatoes for the budget minded, and the second is in grilled cheese sandwiches. The creamy, easy-to-melt cheese is perfect for both.

1 teaspoon (5 mL) salt
5 cups (1.2 L) Yukon Gold potatoes, thinly sliced (5–6 medium potatoes)
8 ounces (227 g) Velveeta cheese, cut into chunks
½ cup (118 mL) milk
½ cup (118 mL) chopped onion
1 teaspoon (5 mL) dry mustard
¼ teaspoon (1.25 mL) freshly ground black pepper

1. Preheat the barbecue to medium high (350°F [180°C] to 400°F [200°C]). Butter or spray with nonstick cooking spray a Dutch oven or roasting pan.

2. Fill a large pot with water and add the salt. Bring the water to a boil, add the potatoes, and cook for 8 to 10 minutes, or until they are fork-tender. Drain.

3. In a bowl, stir together the cheese, milk, onion, mustard, and pepper. Toss the potatoes with the cheese mixture in the prepared Dutch oven or roasting pan. Cover the pan.

4. Cook in the barbecue for 22 to 25 minutes, or until the potatoes are tender. Stir gently before serving.

Creamy Coleslaw
Yield: 6–8 servings

This is another side dish that isn't grilled or barbecued, but it is irrefutably entwined with picnics and outdoor cooking. For a more vinegary dressing, reduce the mayonnaise to 2 tablespoons (30 mL), increase the sugar to ¼ cup (59 mL), and increase the vinegar to ¼ cup (59 mL).

¾ cup (177 mL) mayonnaise
⅓ cup (79 mL) olive oil
3 tablespoons (45 mL) sugar
1½ tablespoons (22.5 mL) white wine vinegar
1 tablespoon (15 mL) lemon juice
½ cup (118 mL) half-and-half
2 tablespoons (30 mL) grated sweet onion
¼ teaspoon (1.25 mL) salt
⅛ teaspoon (0.6 mL) dry mustard
⅛ teaspoon (0.6 mL) celery salt
1 dash freshly ground black pepper
1 large head green cabbage, finely shredded
½ head red cabbage, finely shredded
2 carrots, shredded with a vegetable peeler

1. In a large glass or plastic bowl, blend together the mayonnaise, olive oil, sugar, vinegar, and lemon juice.

2. Stir in the half-and-half, onion, salt, dry mustard, celery salt, and pepper.

3. In a separate large bowl, combine the shredded cabbages and carrots. Pour the dressing over the shredded vegetables and toss with your hands or large salad forks until the cabbage is well coated. Refrigerate the coleslaw until ready to serve.

Bean and Sweet Corn Salad

Yield: 4–6 servings

This is a very different way to serve beans at a barbecue: cold, with fruit. I developed this recipe for a certain bean company, and it became very popular when it showed up on their website.

1 (28-ounce [784-g]) can Bush's Original baked beans
1 (16-ounce [454-g]) can Bush's kidney beans, rinsed and drained
1(16-ounce [454-g])can Bush's garbanzo beans, rinsed and drained
1 (15.2-ounce [453-g]) can whole kernel corn, drained
1 (8-ounce [227-g]) can mandarin orange segments, drained
½ cup (118 mL) pineapple juice
2 tablespoons (30 mL) balsamic vinegar
1 pinch cinnamon

1. In a large saucepan, mix together all the ingredients. Stir gently and cook until the beans are hot and just beginning to bubble.

2. Serve hot or at room temperature as a side dish with your favorite burger, hot dog, grilled meat, or grilled fish dish.

Watermelon and Goat Cheese Salad

Yield: 6–8 servings

This refreshing salad was served to my wife and I on a trip to Cairns, Australia, several years ago. At a dinner party hosted by the owner of the internationally known Red Ochre restaurant, where they feature kangaroo, wallaby, alligator, and other local specialties, they served this delicious, palate cleansing, and perfectly marvelous salad.

8 cups (1.9 L) chopped seedless watermelon (1-inch [2.5-cm] cubes)
1 cup (236 mL) crumbled goat cheese
½ cup (118 mL) fresh raspberries
½ cup (118 mL) thinly sliced kiwifruit
2 tablespoons (30 mL) fresh lemon juice
2 tablespoons (30 mL) chopped fresh mint
1 teaspoon (5 mL) chopped fresh cilantro
Mint leaves, for garnish

1. In a large bowl, mix together the watermelon, goat cheese, raspberries, kiwifruit, lemon juice, cilantro, and chopped mint and toss lightly. Refrigerate until ready to serve.

2. Remove the salad from the refrigerator and let it come to just below room temperature. Decorate with whole mint leaves and serve.

Potato Salad with Bacon, Mustard, and Beer Vinaigrette
Yield: 6–8

Waxy moist potatoes, like the red ones used here, have a lower starch content and a higher sugar content than other varieties, so they are "stickier" and better for boiling and making scalloped potatoes and potato salad.

½ pound (227 g) lean, smoked bacon
3 pounds (1.3 kg) red potatoes
½ cup (118 mL) finely chopped red onion
⅓ cup (79 mL) chopped fresh herbs (basil, parsley, chives, rosemary)
1 cup (236 mL) beer
2 tablespoons (30 mL) butter
2 tablespoons (30 mL) all-purpose flour
1 tablespoon (15 mL) sugar
½ teaspoon (2.5 mL) dry mustard
½ teaspoon (2.5 mL) hot pepper sauce
2 tablespoons (30 mL) chopped fresh parsley
6 hard-boiled eggs, sliced

1. Cook the bacon until crisp and drain it on paper towels. Chop the pieces coarsely, place them in a bowl, and set aside.

2. Cook the potatoes in lightly salted water until tender but not mushy. Drain, cool slightly, and slice, unpeeled, into thick rounds.

3. In a large bowl, gently mix the potatoes with the reserved bacon, onions, and herbs.

4. In a separate bowl, mix together the butter, flour, mustard, sugar, beer, and hot sauce and pour this dressing over the potato–bacon–herb mixture. Fold gently to mix.

5. Sprinkle the salad with the parsley and sliced hard-boiled eggs and serve warm.

Gilroy-Style Garlic Bread
Yield: 4–6 servings

More garlic is grown in Gilroy, Calif., than anywhere else in the United States, so they know something about garlic bread. If you wish, you can add ½ teaspoon (2.5 mL) chopped parsley, savory, or fresh basil to make loaded garlic-herb bread. A lean, moist dough in a warm kitchen will probably rise in 45 minutes or less.

1 (¼-ounce [28-g]) package dry yeast
1 cup (236 mL) cottage cheese, warmed
6 cloves garlic, peeled, finely minced
1 large egg
1 tablespoon (15 mL) olive oil
1 tablespoon (15 mL) dried oregano
2 teaspoons (10 mL) sugar
1 teaspoon (5 mL) seasoned salt
½ teaspoon (2.5 mL) baking soda
2½ cups (591 mL) all-purpose flour

1. Soften the yeast in ¼ cup (59 mL) of warm water. Transfer this mixture to a large mixing bowl.

2. Add the cottage cheese, garlic, egg, oil, oregano, sugar, salt, and baking soda. Stir well.

3. Add the flour and, with your hands, work the mixture into a sticky dough. Put the bowl in a warm place and let the dough rise until doubled.

4. Preheat the barbecue to medium high (400°F [200°C]). Grease well or spray with nonstick cooking spray a bread pan.

5. Stir the dough down and turn it into the prepared bread pan. Let it rise another 30 minutes.

6. Bake in the barbecue for 40 minutes. Let the bread rest for 10 minutes, then slice it and serve warm.

Barbecue-Roasted Yorkshire Pudding

Yield: 6 servings

Instead of cooking one big pudding, you can make individual servings. Pour 1 tablespoon (15 mL) of the drippings into each cup of a muffin pan and brush it up the sides. Return the pan to the barbecue and heat it to smoking. Pour ¼ cup (59 mL) of batter into each cup, bake as you would with the large pan, and serve.

4 large eggs
1½ cups (354 mL) all-purpose flour
2 cups (473 mL) whole milk
½ teaspoon (2.5 mL) dried savory
¼ teaspoon (1.25 mL) garlic powder
Salt, to taste
Freshly ground black pepper, to taste
1 standing rib roast of beef, 1 crown roast of pork, or 1 rack of lamb, roasted

1. In a medium bowl, beat the eggs.

2. Sift the flour into a large bowl. Add the eggs and beat with a wooden spoon until elastic. Gradually whisk in the milk until the batter is smooth. Add the savory and garlic and season with salt and pepper.

3. When your roast is done, remove the meat from the barbecue. Remove the roast from the pan you cooked it in, cover the meat with aluminum foil, and let it stand to let the juices return to the center of the meat.

4. Return the roasting pan to the barbecue and heat the drippings to almost smoking.

5. Take the pan out of the barbecue and, using a heat-resistant brush, coat the sides of the pan (all the way to the top) with the hot grease. Pour the batter into the pan.

6. Bake for 25 to 30 minutes, or until the pudding is crispy and brown outside and soft and moist inside. The batter will have risen up the sides of the pan like a popover.

7. Immediately cut the large pudding into squares and serve with the roast.

Carolina Skillet Cornbread

Yield: 4–6 servings

When making cornbread, you should not use a hand-held or stand mixer as it's too easy to overmix. Instead, mix by hand, leaving a few lumps in the batter, which will break down when baked and will give the bread a rustic, homemade appearance. You can use frozen or canned (drained) corn, but neither has the taste and texture of fresh corn.

2 cups (473 mL) yellow cornmeal
½ cup (118 mL) all-purpose flour
1 tablespoon (15 mL) sugar
1 tablespoon (15 mL) brown sugar
1 tablespoon (15 mL) baking powder
1 teaspoon (5 mL) salt
½ teaspoon (2.5 mL) baking soda
2 cups (473 mL) buttermilk
2 large eggs, lightly beaten
2 tablespoons (30 mL) butter, melted
2 cups (473 mL) fresh corn kernels
¼ cup (59 mL) vegetable oil

1. Preheat the barbecue to medium high (350°F [180°C] to 400°F [200°C]).

2. In a mixing bowl, sift together the cornmeal, flour, sugars, baking powder, salt, and baking soda. Add the buttermilk, eggs, and butter and stir until just mixed. Add the corn kernels and stir.

3. Pour the vegetable oil into a seasoned skillet and place it in the barbecue until the oil is very hot. Remove the pan from the barbecue and pour off any excess oil.

4. Pour the batter into the hot skillet and return it to the barbecue. Bake until the cornbread is golden brown and a toothpick inserted into the center comes out clean.

5. Cool the cornbread on a wire rack for 5 minutes, then invert it onto a large plate and cut it into thick wedges.

Grilled Basil Tomatoes

Yield: 6 servings

Basil should only be cut at the last moment, and only with a very sharp knife to minimize bruising. It should be sprinkled on cooked food, as heat will negate its pungent essence.

6 firm medium tomatoes
¼ cup (59 mL) butter, melted
1 teaspoon (5 mL) granulated garlic
½ teaspoon (2.5 mL) kosher salt
Freshly ground black pepper, to taste
⅓ cup (79 mL) dry breadcrumbs
6 (¼-inch [0.5-cm] thick) slices mozzarella cheese
¼ cup (59 mL) finely chopped fresh basil

1. Make sure the grill is clean and generously sprayed with nonstick grilling spray. Preheat the barbecue to medium high (350°F [180°C] to 400°F [200°C]).

2. Halve the tomatoes horizontally. Brush each tomato half with melted butter and sprinkle with garlic, salt, a few grinds of black pepper, and the breadcrumbs.

3. Place the tomatoes on the barbecue and cook for 5 to 7 minutes, or until the crumbs begin to brown.

4. Place a slice of mozzarella cheese on each tomato and continue cooking until the cheese melts and begins to bubble.

5. With a spatula, transfer the tomatoes from the grill to a serving plate and sprinkle with the chopped basil. Serve each person 2 halves.

Mighty Fine Biscuits

Yield: 24 biscuits

Originally developed by the French, the word biscuit comes from "bis" (twice) and "cuit" (cooked). These were perfected on plantations in the southern United States. Since buttermilk is a by-product of churning butter, the plantation cooks used the "leftover" liquid to make their biscuits, and I can't image making great biscuits without using it.

1 (¼-ounce [7-g]) package active dry yeast
¼ cup (59 mL) warm water, at 110°F (43°C)
2 cups (473 mL) buttermilk, at room temperature
5 cups (1.2 mL) all-purpose flour
3 tablespoons (45 mL) sugar
1 tablespoon (15 mL) baking powder
2 teaspoons (10 mL) salt
1 teaspoon (5 mL) baking soda
¾ cup (177 mL) vegetable shortening

1. Preheat the barbecue to 425°F (220°C). Lightly grease 2 baking sheets.

2. In a small bowl, dissolve the yeast in the warm water. Let stand until foamy, about 5 minutes. Add the buttermilk and set aside.

3. In a large bowl, combine the flour, sugar, baking powder, salt, and baking soda. Cut in the shortening with a pastry blender until the mixture resembles coarse meal or flakes, then stir in the yeast mixture until the dry ingredients are moistened. Turn the dough out onto a floured surface, and knead gently for 10 to 12 strokes.

4. Roll the dough to ¾-inch (1.5 cm) thickness. Use a 2-inch (5-cm) round cutter to cut out biscuits, dipping the cutter in flour between cuts.

5. Arrange the biscuits on the prepared baking sheets, making sure they are not touching each other. Cover and let rise in a warm place free from drafts for 1 hour, or until the biscuits are almost doubled in size.

6. Bake for 10 to 12 minutes, or until browned.

Citrus and Buttermilk Hush Puppies

Yield: 6–8 servings

Hush puppies are a staple in the South, where few barbecue meals are without them. You can add flavorings as we did here (lemonade and orange zest) or leave them out.

2 cups (473 mL) yellow cornmeal
1 cup (236 mL) all-purpose flour
2 tablespoons (30 mL) brown sugar
1 teaspoon (5 mL) baking powder
¾ teaspoon (3.75 mL) seasoned salt
½ teaspoon (2.5 mL) baking soda
½ teaspoon (2.5 mL) freshly ground black pepper
2 large eggs, beaten
1½ cups (354 mL) buttermilk
¼ cup (59 mL) heavy cream
¼ cup (59 mL) lemonade
2 tablespoons (30 mL) minced orange zest
1 tablespoon (15 mL) corn oil
Vegetable oil, for frying

1. In a large bowl, mix together the cornmeal, flour, brown sugar, baking powder, seasoned salt, baking soda, and black pepper and stir well. Add the eggs, buttermilk, cream, lemonade, orange zest, and corn oil, and stir until thoroughly blended and you have a thick batter. Cover and set aside.

2. On a barbecue side burner, pour 3 inches (7.5 cm) of oil into a Dutch oven and heat it to 350°F (180°C). Drop a tablespoon (15 mL) of the batter at a time into the hot oil.

3. Fry the hush puppies until they are golden-brown on all sides, about 2 to 3 minutes per side.

Note: Hush puppies should begin floating when they are done; be careful not to overcook them.

Savory Baked Onion Pudding

Yield: 6–8 servings

Probably the most popular side dish I ever prepared on my TV series, Barbecue America, *this recipe came from my mother's cookbook in Canada. Serve with roast beef or pork, grilled leg of lamb, or roasted turkey (instead of stuffing).*

½ cup (118 mL) butter, divided
1 tablespoon (15 mL) olive oil
8 cups (1.9 L) thinly sliced onions
¼ cup (59 mL) dry vermouth
1 clove garlic, peeled and crushed
6 ounces (168 g) French bread, cut into chunks
2 cups (473 mL) grated Emmenthaler or Swiss cheese
3 large eggs
2 cups (473 mL) half-and-half
Sea salt, to taste
Freshly ground black pepper, to taste

1. Preheat the barbecue to 350°F (180°C) to 375°F (190°C) for direct and indirect heating, putting a water pan under the unheated side of the grill. Spray a cast-iron skillet or Dutch oven with nonstick cooking spray.

2. In a separate skillet, melt half (60 mL) of the butter with the olive oil over low heat. Add the onions, cover, and steam over low heat for 15 minutes.

3. Uncover the skillet, increase the heat to medium, and cook, stirring occasionally, until the onions caramelize and turn brown. Pour in the vermouth and boil, stirring constantly, until the liquid evaporates. Remove the skillet from the heat.

4. Add the bread chunks to the onions and stir well. Spread the mixture in the prepared skillet or Dutch oven. Melt the remaining butter and pour it over the bread-onion mixture. Sprinkle on the cheese.

5. In a medium bowl, beat the eggs lightly. Add the half-and-half. Pour this mixture evenly over the bread and cheese. Using a spoon, stir briefly to make sure liquid is infused into the bread; then salt and pepper to taste.

6. Bake over indirect heat for 30 to 40 minutes, or until the pudding is puffed and golden.

7. Remove the pan from the heat, cool slightly, and cut the pudding in large triangular pieces to serve.

Grilled Belgian Endive

Yield: 4 servings

In the United States, curly endive is sometimes called chicory, witloof, or witloof chicory, but it is really just Belgian endive, a member of the lettuce family.

2 small cloves garlic, peeled and smashed
1 teaspoon (5 mL) salt
½ cup (118 mL) olive oil
8 teaspoons (40 mL) balsamic vinegar
Freshly ground black pepper, to taste
4 heads fresh endive

1. Make sure the grill is clean and generously sprayed with nonstick spray. Preheat the barbecue to medium high (350°F [180°C] to 400°F [200°C]).

2. In a small bowl, mash the garlic and salt to a paste. Whisk in the oil and balsamic vinegar, season lightly with pepper, and set aside.

3. Slice the heads of endive in half lengthwise and brush them with the vinegar-and-oil mixture.

4. Place the endive halves cut side down on the grill and cook for about 4 minutes. Baste with the oil, turn, baste again, and grill for another 4 minutes on the second side, basting several times.

5. Serve each person 2 halves of the endive.

Asparagus with Lemon Marinade

Yield: 4 servings

You can use green or white asparagus for this dish. The only difference is that the white asparagus is grown under the soil, so the lack of sunlight prevents the plant from making the chlorophyll that produces the green color. Same plant, same taste, different color.

1 pound (454 g) fresh asparagus
½ cup (118 mL) butter, melted
Juice of 1 lemon
2 tablespoons (30 mL) honey
2 teaspoons (10 mL) olive oil
¾ teaspoon (3.75 mL) freshly ground black pepper
1 pinch kosher salt

1. Make sure the grill is clean and generously sprayed with nonstick grilling spray. Preheat the barbecue to medium high (350°F [180°C] to 400°F [200°C]).

2. Wash the asparagus thoroughly and peel the bottom ends of thicker stems with a hand peeler if they seem woody. Using a sharp knife, cut an X vertically from the bottom about ⅓ of the way up the stalk. Place the asparagus in a shallow glass baking pan.

3. In a small bowl, whisk together the butter, lemon juice, honey, oil, pepper, and salt. Pour this mixture over the asparagus and let it marinate for 15 to 30 minutes. Drain the asparagus, reserving the marinade.

4. Place the asparagus crosswise on the grill and cook until the stalks are lightly browned and tender, about 4 minutes, turning once with tongs.

5. Transfer the asparagus to a heated serving platter and drizzle the remaining lemon marinade over the asparagus spears. Serve immediately.

Barbecue-Baked Acorn Squash

Yield: 6 servings

If you wish to use pumpkins instead of acorn squash, look for the Jack Be Little, Little Boo, or Small Sugar varieties of miniature pumpkins and cook exactly the same way.

3 (1-pound [454-g]) acorn squash or small pumpkins, halved and seeded
3 tablespoons (45 mL) extra virgin olive oil
½ cup (118 mL) packed brown sugar
⅓ cup (79 mL) butter, melted
½ teaspoon (2.5 mL) ground allspice
½ teaspoon (2.5 mL) ground nutmeg
¼ teaspoon (1.25 mL) salt
½ cup (118 mL) golden raisins
2 tablespoons (30 mL) chopped pecans

1. Preheat the barbecue to medium high (350°F [180°C] to 400°F [200°C]).

2. Place each squash or pumpkin half, cut side up, on a piece of heavy-duty aluminum foil. Brush the cut sides and the inside of the halves with the olive oil.

3. In a small bowl combine the brown sugar, melted butter, allspice, nutmeg, and salt and stir. Divide this mixture equally among the squash halves. Sprinkle the raisins and chopped pecans inside the squashes.

4. Place the halves in a roasting pan. Pour ½ inch of water around the squash or pumpkins and cook directly on the grill for 40 to 50 minutes, or until the squash or pumpkins are tender when pierced and browned on top.

5. Dip a pastry brush into the melted butter mixture in the well of each squash and brush the mixture over the tops, which may appear dry.

6. Remove the pan from the barbecue with oven mitts and serve a squash half to each person.

Grilled Cabbage
Yield: 4 servings

Cooking cabbage outside negates the problem of "cabbage odor" that comes with boiling or steaming it in the kitchen. To remove the smell when boiling cabbage, put a whole, unshelled walnut in the cooking water.

1 head cabbage, quartered and cored
Olive oil, for brushing
½ cup (118 mL) butter, melted
Salt, to taste
Freshly ground black pepper, to taste
8 strips uncooked bacon, each strip halved crosswise
½ cup (118 mL) water

1. Preheat the barbecue to medium high (350°F [180°C] to 400°F [200°C]) for direct and indirect heating.

2. Brush both sides of the cabbage quarters with olive oil and place them directly on the hot side of the grill for 2 to 3 minutes per side, or just until the leaves are starting to brown at the edges.

3. Place the grilled cabbage in a roasting pan. Drizzle with the butter, season with the salt and pepper, and drape 4 half slices of bacon across each cabbage quarter. Pour in the water.

4. Place the pan on the unheated side of the grill and bake, uncovered, for 15 minutes. Cover the pan with a lid or aluminum foil and continue cooking until the bacon is crisp and the cabbage is soft, about 15 minutes more.

5. Remove the pan from the barbecue. Be careful when lifting the lid or removing the foil, as steam will escape. Serve 1 or 2 cabbage quarters per person.

Honey-Barbecue Grilled Vegetables
Yield: 4 servings

Instead of honey, you can use cane syrup, pure maple syrup, or, if you can find it, Indonesian kecap manis, a thick, sweet soy sauce that is the grandfather of today's ketchup. It is available online from several U.S. outlets.

½ cup (118 mL) butter, melted
⅓ cup (79 mL) cider vinegar
⅓ cup (79 mL) honey
2 cloves garlic, peeled and minced
1 teaspoon (5 mL) seasoned salt
½ teaspoon (2.5 mL) dry mustard
½ teaspoon (2.5 mL) dried marjoram
¼ teaspoon (1.25 mL) curry powder
Freshly ground black pepper, to taste
4 red bell peppers, cored, seeded, and cut into ½-inch (1-cm) wide vertical strips
1 large red onion, cut into ½-inch (1-cm) thick slices
2 yellow summer squash, cut into 3-inch (7.5-cm) long strips
4 large portobello mushrooms, cut into 1-inch (2.5-cm) wide strips

1. Make sure the grill is clean and generously sprayed with nonstick grilling spray. Preheat the barbecue to medium high (400°F [200°C] to 425°F [220°C]).

2. In a medium bowl, combine the butter, vinegar, honey, garlic, salt, mustard, marjoram, curry powder, and black pepper and mix thoroughly.

3. Drop the vegetables into a 1- to 2-gallon (3.8- to 7.6-L) resealable plastic bag, pour in the marinade, and marinate for 1 to 2 hours.

4. Remove the vegetables from the bag and drain them briefly, reserving the marinade. Place them on a baking sheet with a lip or in a shallow baking dish and bake for about 20 minutes, brushing several times with the marinade.

5. When the edges of the vegetables are getting a slight char, but while veggies are still al dente, transfer them to a heated platter. Serve with grilled meat, fish, or poultry.

Char-Grilled Corn
Yield: 6 servings

There is no vegetable better suited to a barbecue than corn on the cob. You can grill it, steam it, boil it, or even deep-fry it. But don't add salt while cooking, as it toughens the corn; use sugar instead.

6 ears corn, unshucked
¾ cup (177 mL) butter, melted
¼ cup (59 mL) olive oil
1 teaspoon (5 mL) dried dill weed
1 teaspoon (5 mL) brown sugar
½ teaspoon (2.5 mL) garlic powder
Freshly ground black pepper, to taste

1. Soak the unshucked corn in 1 gallon (3.8 L) of water with 2 tablespoons (30 mL) salt for several hours to moisten.

2. Make sure the grill is clean and generously sprayed with nonstick grilling spray. Preheat the barbecue to medium high (350°F [180°C] to 400°F [200°C]).

3. In a small saucepan, stir together the melted butter and olive oil. Add the dill, brown sugar, garlic powder, and pepper and whisk to thoroughly mix the flavors.

4. Peel the shucks back until most of the corn is exposed, but do not remove the shucks completely. Remove the silk. With a pastry brush, lavishly coat the corn with the spiced butter-oil.

5. Carefully close the shucks around the seasoned corn, tying the end with a piece of soaked twine.

6. Grill the corn, turning frequently, until done, about 30 minutes. The shucks may darken or turn black, but they will protect the corn. Carefully peel off the shucks and serve the corn with the remaining spice butter to brush on at the table with a pastry brush.

Garlic Fiddleheads

Yield: 4 servings

Young coiled leaves of the ostrich fern, fiddleheads are prized by New Englanders for their fresh, asparagus-like flavor. They appear in April and May and are gathered up by serious foodies, somewhat like the way truffles are harvested in Provence. Try them once, and you'll be hooked.

1 pound (454 g) fresh or frozen fiddleheads
¼ cup (59 mL) butter
3 cloves garlic, peeled and finely chopped
2 shallots, peeled and finely chopped
1 tablespoon (15 mL) soy sauce
1 tablespoon (15 mL) sugar
3 tablespoons (45 mL) dry white wine

1. If using fresh fiddleheads, put them in a paper bag and shake until the brown skins come off. Discard the skins.

2. Steam the fresh or frozen fiddleheads until just tender.

3. Meanwhile, melt the butter in a heavy skillet over medium heat on a barbecue side burner. Add the garlic and shallots and sauté until translucent. Blend in the soy sauce, sugar, and wine, and add the steamed fiddleheads, turning to coat them well. Serve at once.

Grilled Corn Salad

Yield: 4–6 servings

You can add cooked lima beans to this dish for a cold succotash salad, and even throw in some cooked, crumbled bacon for a more substantial side dish.

2 red bell peppers
1 green bell pepper
8 ears corn, shucked
2 tablespoons (30 mL) olive oil
Juice of 1½ oranges
Juice of 1 lime
½ cup (118 mL) thinly sliced green onion, green and white parts
⅓ cup (79 mL) chopped fresh cilantro
1 teaspoon (5 mL) brown sugar
½ teaspoon (2.5 mL) kosher salt
½ teaspoon (2.5 mL) freshly ground black pepper
⅛ teaspoon (0.6 mL) cayenne pepper

1. Make sure the grill is clean and generously sprayed with nonstick grilling spray. Preheat the barbecue to medium high (350°F [180°C] to 400°F [200°C]).

2. Remove the stems and seeds from the bell peppers, slice them into 1-inch (2.5-cm) strips, and set aside.

3. Brush the ears of corn with the olive oil and place them on the grill. Add the pepper strips and grill until the peppers begin to char and the corn barely begins to brown in a few places.

4. Remove the corn and peppers from the grill. Dice the peppers into ¼-inch (0.5-cm) pieces and put them in a medium bowl. Cut the kernels from the ears of corn and add them to the bowl. Add the juices, green onion, cilantro, brown sugar, salt, pepper, and cayenne pepper and stir well.

5. Serve warm, or refrigerate for 1 to 2 hours before serving.

Grilled Sweet Onion Steaks

Yield: 4–6 servings

If you like onions with a little more bite or kick, use Spanish or white onions in this dish. After all, we are already adding some sweetness.

2 large Walla Walla, Vidalia, or Maui onions, peeled
½ cup (118 mL) olive oil
¼ cup (59 mL) butter, melted
½ cup (118 mL) honey
½ cup (118 mL) prepared yellow mustard
1 tablespoon (15 mL) dried summer savory
1 tablespoon (15 mL) Worcestershire sauce
Kosher salt, to taste
Freshly ground black pepper, to taste
Paprika, for serving

1. Make sure the grill is clean and generously sprayed with nonstick grilling spray. Preheat the barbecue to medium high (350°F [180°C] to 400°F [200°C]).

2. Cut the onions in ½- to ¾-inch (1- to 1.5-cm) thick slices. Run 2 bamboo skewers sideways and parallel to each other through the slices to hold them together while grilling.

3. In a small bowl, mix together the olive oil and butter. Brush both sides of the onion steaks, then place them on a hot grill alongside ribs, steaks, or roasts.

4. In a separate small bowl, whisk together the honey, mustard, savory, Worcestershire sauce, salt, and black pepper. Brush this mixture on the onion steaks several times while they are cooking. Grill only until the onions begin to char on each side and the sauce is bubbling.

5. With a spatula, remove the onions from the grill. Sprinkle with paprika and serve on a heated platter.

Grilled Umami Eggplant

Yield: 6 servings

While the word "umami" usually describes a taste— it loosely means "delicious" in Japanese—we use it here to describe the delightful marriage of grilled eggplant and our homemade teriyaki sauce. There are dozens of varieties of soy sauces, in myriad colors, thicknesses, and flavors. We favor koikuchi (dark) varieties for most of our cooking.

1 cup (236 mL) dark soy sauce
½ cup (118 mL) water
¼ cup (59 mL) brown sugar
½ teaspoon (2.5 mL) ground ginger
1 teaspoon (5 mL) minced garlic
¼ cup (59 mL) minced green onion, green parts only
½ cup (118 mL) dry sake
2 medium-large eggplants, about 2–2½ pounds (908 g–1.1 kg) total
Salt, to taste
2 green onions, finely chopped, green parts only
½ yellow bell pepper, finely chopped
1 tablespoon (15 mL) olive oil
2 sprigs fresh parsley, chopped
½ teaspoon (2.5 mL) garlic salt
¼ teaspoon (1.25 mL) lemon pepper

1. In a small saucepan over medium heat, combine the soy sauce, water, sake, brown sugar, minced green onion, garlic, and ginger and stir well until the sugar dissolves. Set aside and keep warm.

2. Make sure the grill is clean and generously sprayed with nonstick grilling spray. Preheat the barbecue to medium high (350°F [180°C] to 400°F [200°C]).

3. Peel and cut the eggplant into ½-inch thick slices. Salt the slices and let them stand in a colander for 30 minutes, then quickly rinse and pat very dry.

4. In a medium saucepan, cook the chopped green onions and bell pepper in the olive oil over medium heat until until they are just tender. Cover the pan and set aside, keeping warm.

5. Brush the eggplant slices on both sides with the teriyaki marinade. Sprinkle the slices generously with the garlic salt and lemon pepper and place them on the grill. Cook for 5 to 7 minutes on each side, turning several times, and brushing on more marinade each time you turn the slices. Cook until they are nicely browned and tender.

6. Remove the slices from the grill and let them cool slightly on a cutting board. Cut them into strips and place them on a piping-hot serving platter. Spoon some of the green onion and peppers over the eggplant, and add enough additional teriyaki sauce to moisten and flavor the eggplant.

CB's Char-Grilled Veggies
Yield: 6–8 servings

When cooking vegetables on the grill, it's important not to overcook them. The idea is to get a nice char on some of the edges and to soften the vegetables, but to keep them al dente and crunchy. If you cook them too long, they droop, lose much of their vitamins, and don't' have a good mouth feel when you bite into them. This recipe comes from Chris Browne from Culver City, Calif.

½ cup (118 mL) dark soy sauce
¼ cup (59 mL) balsamic vinegar
2 teaspoons (10 mL) dried oregano
1 teaspoon (5 mL) dried thyme
1 tablespoon (15 mL) brown sugar
2 cloves garlic, peeled and minced
2 teaspoons (10 mL) olive oil
½ teaspoon (2.5 mL) freshly ground black pepper
½ teaspoon (2.5 mL) sea salt
2 bunches green onions, bottom 2–3 inches (5–7.5 cm), including the white root
2 small red bell peppers, cut into small bite-size pieces
2 small yellow bell peppers, cut into small bite-size pieces
4 small zucchini, quartered lengthwise, each quarter halved
2 small eggplants, cut into ¼-inch (0.5-cm) thick slices, each slice halved

1. In a small bowl, combine the soy sauce, vinegar, oregano, thyme, brown sugar, garlic, oil, black pepper, and salt and mix with a wire whisk.

2. Put the vegetables in a 1- to 2-quart (3.8- to 7.6-L) resealable plastic bag. Add the marinade, seal the bag, and marinate at room temperature for at least an hour (2 to 3 hours is even better). Drain the vegetables and reserve the liquid for basting.

3. Make sure the grill is clean and generously sprayed with nonstick spray. Preheat the barbecue to medium high (350°F [180°C] to 400°F [200°C]).

4. Coat a barbecue vegetable basket with cooking spray and add the veggies. Place the basket on the grill, close the lid of the barbecue, and cook for 5 minutes.

5. Baste or spray the vegetables with the remaining marinade, then turn the vegetables over and grill for an additional 5 minutes, or until tender.

6. Transfer the vegetables to a heated platted, drizzle them with the remaining marinade, and serve.

Buttered Bourbon Onions

Yield: 4–6 servings

For a different taste, substitute 1 tablespoon (15 mL) A1 steak sauce and 1 tablespoon (15 mL) lime juice for the balsamic vinegar in the butter sauce, and follow the same mixing and cooking directions.

4 large Vidalia, Maui, or Walla Walla onions
Garlic salt, to taste
Freshly ground black pepper, to taste
1 cup (236 mL) butter, melted
¼ cup (59 mL) bourbon
¼ cup (59 mL) packed brown sugar
1 tablespoon (15 mL) balsamic vinegar
1 cup (236 mL) corn kernels

1. Preheat the barbecue to medium high (350°F [180°C] to 400°F [200°C]).

2. Cut off a thin slice from the bottom (root end) of each onion so they can stand upright. Remove the outer skin and, using a grapefruit knife or a melon baller, remove the core almost to the bottom of each onion, leaving a ⅓-inch (0.8-cm) border around the hole.

3. Spray the outside of each onion with grilling spray. Sprinkle garlic salt and pepper over the outside and cavity of the onion and place each onion on a large piece of aluminum foil.

4. In a bowl, mix together the melted butter, bourbon, brown sugar, and balsamic vinegar. Reserving ⅓ cup (79 mL) of this mixture, fill the onion cavities with the corn, and drizzle the butter mixture over each cavity.

5. Bring the corners of the foil up over the onions and carefully twist at the top to seal the onions in the foil. Cook over indirect heat on the barbecue for 1½ hours.

6. Just before serving, warm the remaining butter sauce and drizzle over the onions.

Creamy Grilled Mac and Cheese

Yield: 4–6 servings

This makes a great side dish for hamburgers, tri-tip, or grilled chicken. It's easy to make, and the Huntsman cheese raises it far above ordinary macaroni and cheese.

2 cups (473 mL) water or chicken stock
1 (12-ounce [336-g]) can condensed cream of mushroom soup
1½ cups (354 mL) shredded cheddar cheese
3 cups (708 mL) cooked elbow macaroni
2 tablespoons (30 mL) chopped sweet yellow onion
1 tablespoon (15 mL) finely chopped pimiento
1 tablespoon (15 mL) finely chopped chives
1 tablespoon (15 mL) butter
¼ cup (59 mL) dry breadcrumbs
½ cup (118 mL) crumbled huntsman cheese

1. Preheat the barbecue to medium high (350°F [180°C] to 400°F [200°C]). Butter or spray with nonstick cooking spray a 1½-quart casserole dish.

2. Combine the water, soup, and cheese in the prepared casserole.

3. Stir in the macaroni, onion, pimento, and chives and barbecue for 30 minutes, or until the cheese is bubbling and starting to brown at the edges.

4. Melt the butter in a small saucepan and stir in the breadcrumbs. Sauté until all the butter is absorbed, and set aside.

5. Top the macaroni with the crumbled huntsman cheese and bread-crumbs and bake for 5 more minutes, or until the cheese melts and the breadcrumbs are browned.

Seared Green Beans

Yield: 4 servings

For a Latin touch, use tomatillos instead of tomatoes and add ½ teaspoon (2.5 mL) of chili powder to the bowl.

1 pound (454 g) fresh green beans, ends clipped
1 small onion, peeled and chopped
2 medium tomatoes, chopped
3 tablespoons (45 mL) prepared mustard
1 tablespoon (15 mL) brown sugar
1 teaspoon (5 mL) garlic salt
⅛ teaspoon (0.6 mL) cayenne pepper

1. Make sure the grill is clean and generously sprayed with nonstick grilling spray. Preheat the barbecue to medium high (400°F [200°C] to 450°F [220°C]).

2. Spray the green beans with grilling or nonstick spray and place them in a bowl.

3. In a medium bowl, mix together the onion, tomatoes, mustard, brown sugar, garlic salt, and cayenne pepper. Set aside.

4. Put the green beans directly on the grill and cook for 1 to 2 minutes per side to lightly char them. Stir the beans into the onion-tomato mixture.

5. Spray a 12-inch (30-cm) square of heavy-duty foil with nonstick cooking spray. Using a spoon, transfer the beans and vegetables to the foil, immediately folding up the edges to the juices don't run out. Seal the edges well so steam can't escape the foil package.

6. Cook the foil package on the hot grill for 20 to 25 minutes.

7. Carefully remove the foil package, open it carefully to make sure you aren't burned by the released steam, and pour the contents into a serving bowl. Serve immediately.

Barbecue-Roasted Root Vegetables
Yield: 4–6 servings

Turnips can be substituted for the parsnips, but buy the smaller ones because, as with rutabagas, the smaller they are, the sweeter their flavor.

1 head garlic
1 tablespoon (15 mL) olive oil, plus more, for drizzling
5 medium carrots, peeled and cut into 2-inch (5-cm) pieces
4 medium parsnips, peeled and cut into 2-inch (5-cm) pieces
1 small rutabaga, peeled and cut into 2-inch (5-cm) pieces
6 small potatoes, halved
8 small shallots, peeled
8 sprigs thyme, divided
1 tablespoon (15 mL) brown sugar
¼ teaspoon (1.25 mL) salt
¼ teaspoon (1.25 mL) freshly ground black pepper

1. Preheat the barbecue to medium high (375°F [190°C] to 425°F [220°C]).

2. Cut the top ¼ inch (0.5 cm) from the head of garlic. Drizzle the exposed cloves with olive oil and wrap the head of garlic in aluminum foil. Barbecue for about 45 minutes, or until the garlic is soft. Remove the foil pack from the barbecue, open it, and let the garlic head cool.

3. In a cast-iron skillet, toss the carrots, parsnips, rutabaga, potatoes, and shallots with the 1 tablespoon (15 mL) olive oil. Add 4 of the thyme sprigs, the brown sugar, the salt, and the pepper.

4. Squeeze the softened garlic cloves into the mixture and stir. Add about ½ cup (118 mL) water.

5. Roast in the barbecue for about 1 hour, or until the vegetables are tender and lightly browned.

6. Serve on a heated platter, using the remaining thyme sprigs as garnish.

Honeyed Veggies with Ginger
Yield: 4 servings

You can either julienne these vegetables by hand or use a julienne disk in a food processor. One method will take 3 minutes, the other 20. It's your choice.

1 red bell pepper, cut into thin julienne strips
1 carrot, cut into thin julienne strips
1 zucchini, cut into thin julienne strips
1 yellow squash, cut into thin julienne strips
10 green beans, halved lengthwise
3 tablespoons (45 mL) olive oil, divided
½ cup (118 mL) water
¼ cup (59 mL) dark soy sauce
¼ cup (59 mL) dry white wine
2 tablespoons (30 mL) honey
½ teaspoon (2.5 mL) ground ginger
¼ teaspoon (1.25 mL) dry mustard
1 large onion, peeled, thinly sliced, rings halved
3 cloves garlic, peeled and mashed
1 heaping teaspoon (7.5 mL) grated fresh ginger

1. In a large bowl, mix together the bell pepper, carrot, zucchini, yellow squash, and green beans. Drizzle with 2 tablespoons (30 mL) of the olive oil, stir several times, and set aside.

2. Make the sauce: In a medium bowl, combine the water, soy sauce, wine, honey, ground ginger, and mustard.

3. In a large skillet or wok, heat the remaining 1 tablespoon (15 mL) olive oil over low heat. Add the onion, garlic, and ginger and sauté until the onions become transparent. Add the sauce and bring to a gentle boil.

4. Increase the heat to the high and add the vegetables in the following order, waiting 1 minute after each addition: carrots, pepper, green beans, zucchini, and yellow squash. Cook until they are just *al dente* and serve immediately.

Veggie Kebabs
Yield: 2–4 servings

You can add mushrooms, green onions, cherry tomatoes, eggplant, and green beans to the skewers if you wish. Treat them the same as the peppers and squash.

2 red bell peppers, cut into 2-inch (5-cm) squares
2 small zucchini, cut into 2-inch (5-cm) squares
1 large white or red onion, peeled, halved and cut into 2-inch (5-cm) long wedges
¼ cup (59 mL) olive oil
2 tablespoons (30 mL) lemon juice
2 tablespoons (30 mL) white wine vinegar
2 tablespoons (30 mL) balsamic vinegar
1 teaspoon (5 mL) Italian seasoning
½ teaspoon (2.5 mL) salt

1. Place the peppers, zucchini, and onion into a 1-gallon (3.8-L) resealable plastic bag and set aside.

2. In a small bowl, combine the olive oil, lemon juice, vinegars, Italian seasoning, and salt and stir to mix well. Pour this mixture over the vegetables in the plastic bag, squeeze out the air, seal the bag, and marinate for 4 to 6 hours or overnight. Turn the bag over several times to distribute the marinade.

3. Make sure the grill is clean and generously sprayed with nonstick grilling spray. Preheat the barbecue to medium high (350°F [180°C] to 400°F [200°C]).

4. Soak 8 (6-inch [15-cm]) bamboo skewers in water overnight, weighting them with a bottle or can to keep them under the water.

5. Remove skewers from the water and the vegetables from the marinade. Reserve the marinade. Thread the vegetables onto the skewers.

6. Cook the kebabs directly on the grill, turning and brushing occasionally with the marinade, for 10 to 15 minutes, or until they begin to char slightly.

Grilled Artichokes Marinated with Honey and Basil
Yield: 6 servings

This recipe is a spin-off of the methods the Romans used to preserve artichokes way back in 77 A.D.

Juice of 1 lemon
3 artichokes
3 tablespoons (45 mL) balsamic vinegar
2 tablespoons (30 mL) honey
1 tablespoon (15 mL) minced fresh basil
1 clove garlic, peeled and minced
2 green onions, minced, green and white parts
1 teaspoon (5 mL) Dijon mustard
¼ teaspoon (1.25 mL) ground cumin
½ cup (118 mL) extra virgin olive oil
Salt, to taste
Freshly ground black pepper, to taste

1. Fill a Dutch oven with water and add the lemon juice. Trim the leaves from the top of an artichoke. Remove the outer layer(s) of leaves from the stem end and snip the spiky tips from the remaining outer leaves. Trim an inch (2.5 cm) from the bottom of the stem and use a vegetable peeler to remove the fibrous outer layer. As each artichoke is prepared, drop it into the lemon water to prevent it from turning brown.

2. When all the artichokes are prepared, cover the pan and bring to a boil. Boil until the base of the stem can be pierced with a fork, 12 to 15 minutes. Transfer the artichokes to a cutting board and let stand until cool enough to handle, about 10 minutes. Slice the artichokes in half lengthwise and scoop out the choke and the first few inner layers in the center until the heart is revealed.

3. Make sure the grill is clean and generously sprayed with nonstick grilling spray. Preheat the barbecue to medium high (350°F [180°C] to 400°F [200°C]).

4. In a small bowl, combine the vinegar, honey, basil, garlic, green onions, mustard, and cumin. Whisk to fully incorporate. Slowly whisk in the olive oil until smooth. Season with the salt and black pepper.

5. Put the cooked and halved artichokes in a 1- to 2-gallon (3.8- to 7.6-L) resealable plastic bag and pour the marinade over them. Marinate for 30 minutes to 1 hour. Remove the artichokes from the bag, reserving the marinade.

6. Place the artichokes on the hot grill, cut side down, and grill for about 5 minutes, turning after 3 minutes. Remove them from the grill, drizzle them with the leftover marinade, and serve.

Grilled Vegetable Soup

Yield: 4–6 servings

Yes, a grilled soup! You can add more grilled veggies than we're using here, such as cooked carrots, peas, or artichoke hearts. Serve this hot or cold. For a thicker soup, leave out the broth.

8 large tomatoes
2 medium red onions, peeled and sliced
2 zucchini, sliced
2 yellow squash, sliced
3 red bell peppers, roasted and skinned
2 cloves garlic, peeled and minced
1½ cups (354 mL) vegetable broth
Sour cream, for serving
Salt, to taste
Freshly ground black pepper, to taste
Juice of 1 lemon
2 tablespoons (30 mL) chopped fresh rosemary

1. Make sure the grill is clean and generously sprayed with nonstick grilling spray. Preheat the barbecue to medium high (350°F [180°C] to 400°F [200°C]).

2. Grill all the vegetables except the garlic until they begin to char and soften. Remove them from the grill.

3. Put all the grilled vegetables and the garlic in a food processor and pulse 2 to 3 times to coarsely chop them. Remove ½ cup (118 mL) of the mixed vegetables and set aside. Process the remaining vegetables until you achieve a smooth, thick soup. Add the vegetable broth and process until combined.

4. Pour the soup into a saucepan and heat until it begins to bubble. Divide it among individual bowls, add a spoonful of sour cream to each bowl, and sprinkle 1 to 2 teaspoons (5 to 10 mL) of the chopped vegetables on top of the sour cream. Season with salt, pepper, lemon juice, and rosemary and serve.

Grilled Stuffed Mushrooms

Yield: 4–6 servings

Crimini mushrooms are merely small Portobello mushrooms. When they get larger than 4 inches (10 cm), they get to call themselves by the new name.

24 medium crimini mushrooms
3 tablespoons (45 mL) butter, divided
¼ cup (59 mL) finely minced green onion, green and white parts
2 teaspoons (10 mL) all-purpose flour
½ teaspoon (2.5 mL) dried marjoram
Freshly ground black pepper, to taste
¼ cup (59 mL) dry white wine
½ cup (118 mL) ground sausage
1 tablespoon (15 mL) minced fresh parsley

1. Preheat the barbecue to medium high (350°F [180°C] to 400°F [200°C]).

2. Remove the stems from the mushrooms and reserve the caps. Finely mince the stems.

3. In a small skillet, melt 1 tablespoon (15 mL) of the butter over medium heat. Add the mushroom stems and green onion and sauté until just tender.

4. Stir in the flour, marjoram, and pepper. Add the wine and cook, stirring, until thickened and bubbly. Add the sausage and parsley and cook until sausage is browned.

5. Stuff the mushroom caps with the sausage–onion mixture.

6. Place the mushrooms on a 12-inch (30-cm) sheet of heavy-duty aluminum foil. Dot each mushroom with a bit of the remaining butter, then enclose the mushrooms in the foil, folding it all around to seal the edges.

7. Place the foil package on the grill and cook for 15 to 20 minutes.

Grilled Sweet Peppers

Yield: 2–4 servings

This dish, served hot or cold, is a great accompaniment to grilled roasts or chops. It can also be served as a cold appetizer with the aioli.

¼ cup (59 mL) red wine vinegar
2 tablespoons (30 mL) minced red onion
1 tablespoon (15 mL) Dijon mustard
4 cloves garlic, peeled and minced
Freshly ground black pepper, to taste
2 large red bell peppers, quartered
2 large green bell peppers, quartered
1 recipe Garlic Aioli (recipe follows)

1. Make sure the grill is clean and generously sprayed with nonstick spray. Preheat the barbecue to medium high (350°F [180°C] to 400°F [200°C]).

2. In a small bowl, combine the vinegar, onion, mustard, garlic, and pepper.

3. Place the bell peppers on the grill and brush them with the mustard mixture. Cook until lightly browned, then turn the peppers over. Brush the other side and cook until browned and slightly softened.

4. Serve hot or cold with the Garlic Aioli.

Garlic Aioli

1 clove garlic, peeled
⅛ teaspoon (0.6 mL) salt
2 egg yolks
1 tablespoon (15 mL) fresh lemon juice
½ cup (118 mL) olive oil
½ cup (118 mL) vegetable oil

1. Put the garlic clove through a garlic press, then put it in a mortar and pestle. Add the salt and grind it into a fine paste.

2. In a heavy mixing bowl, whisk the egg yolks with an electric mixer. Add the lemon juice and the garlic mixture, and keep mixing until well combined, about 1 minute.

3. Start adding the oils, drop by drop, beating constantly. You can add it a bit faster as you go along, but the key to success is going very slowly at the start.

Barbecued Broccoli Parmigiano-Reggiano
Yield: 4–6 servings

1 large stalk fresh broccoli, cut into 2-inch (5 cm) sections
1 teaspoon (5 mL) extra virgin olive oil
2 slices bacon, chopped
1 tablespoon (15 mL) minced garlic
1 pound (454 g) cooked penne, kept warm
1 cup (236 mL) grated fresh Parmigiano-Reggiano cheese
Salt, to taste
Freshly ground black pepper, to taste

1. In a saucepan on the grill or over a side burner, boil the broccoli pieces in a small amount of water for approximately 5 minutes, or until crisp-tender. Remove and drain well.

2. Preheat the barbecue to medium high (350°F [180°C] to 400°F [200°C]) for direct heating.

3. In a large cast-iron skillet over medium heat, heat the oil. Add the bacon and garlic and cook until the bacon is softened and the garlic is just starting to brown. Remove the bacon and garlic with a slotted spoon, drain, and set aside.

4. Add the broccoli to the bacon grease in the skillet and sauté for about 3 to 4 minutes, or until *al dente,* then drain off most of the grease.

5. Add the pasta and stir to combine. Mix in the cheese. Add salt and pepper to taste and serve.

Grilled Mozzy Tomatoes

Yield: 6 servings

You can use another variety of cheese in this recipe. Try aged sharp cheddar, imported Swiss, Gruyere, Gouda, or Pepper Jack cheese, each of which would add its own special flavor profile.

3 large ripe tomatoes
¼ cup (59 mL) balsamic vinegar and oil salad dressing
½ teaspoon (2.5 mL) kosher salt
Freshly ground black pepper, to taste
¼ cup (59 mL) julienned basil leaves
½ cup (118 mL) shredded mozzarella cheese

1. Preheat the barbecue to medium high (350°F [180°C] to 400°F [200°C]), making sure the grill has been well oiled or sprayed with a grilling spray.

2. Stem and wash the tomatoes. Cut them in half horizontally and drizzle each half generously with the salad dressing. Place the tomato halves cut side down on the grill and cook for about 3 minutes, until each half has grill marks on it.

3. Turn the tomatoes, season them with the salt and pepper, and sprinkle them with the basil leaves. Cover them with the shredded mozzarella cheese, close the barbecue lid, and grill for another 2 minutes, or until the cheese melts. Serve warm.

Seared Belgian Endive

Yield: 4 servings

Poor endive. It's grown in complete darkness, so it's leaves won't darken. Endives don't keep well once you bring them home, so eat them the day you buy them, or at least within two days.

2 tablespoons (30 mL) olive oil
1 tablespoon (15 mL) chopped fresh oregano
1 teaspoon (5 mL) dried savory
1 teaspoon (5 mL) dried tarragon
4 Belgian endives, halved lengthwise
1 tablespoon (15 mL) balsamic vinegar
Salt, to taste
Freshly ground black pepper, to taste

1. Preheat the barbecue to (350°F [180°C] to 400°F [200°C]) for indirect heating, putting a water pan under the unheated side of the grill.

2. In a small bowl, mix together the oil, oregano, savory, and tarragon and stir to incorporate.

3. Slice off the bottom of each endive, cutting away the woody part but leaving enough of the base for the leaves to stay connected. Place the endives on a plate or platter and brush the cut sides of the endives with the herb and oil mix.

4. Put the endives on the unheated side of the grill, cut side down, and grill until the edges are well browned and curled, 3 to 4 minutes.

5. Transfer them to a plate and drizzle them with the balsamic vinegar. Sprinkle with the remaining oil mixture, salt, and pepper, and serve hot (they will cool quickly).

Cheesed-Off Corn

Yield: 8–10 servings

If fresh corn isn't available, you can substitute 3 (10-ounce [280-g]) bags of frozen corn kernels (thawed and drained), or similar amount of canned corn (drained).

2 tablespoons (30 mL) butter
4 teaspoons (20 mL) all-purpose flour
¾ cup (177 mL) half-and-half or milk
1½ cups (354 mL) shredded cheddar cheese
1 (3-ounce [84-g]) package cream cheese, at room temperature
4 cups (0.95 L) fresh corn kernels (from about 8 ears)
1 tablespoon (15 mL) minced canned pimientos, drained
1 teaspoon (5 mL) minced fresh chives
½ teaspoon (2.5 mL) minced fresh garlic

1. Preheat the barbecue to (350°F [180°C] to 400°F [200°C]) for direct and indirect heating.

2. In a large, deep cast-iron skillet or roasting pan on the hot side of the grill, melt the butter. Add the flour and stir to blend into a roux. Add the half-and-half and stir until thick and bubbly. Add the shredded cheese and stir to mix, then add the cream cheese and stir.

3. Stir in the corn, followed by the pimientos, chives, and garlic, and stir to thoroughly combine. Cover the pan and move it to the unheated side of the grill. Cook for 20 to 25 minutes, or until the cheese is beginning to brown. Uncover and cook for 5 more minutes.

4. Remove the pan from the barbecue, let it cool for at least 5 minutes, and serve.

Kate's Spur-of-the-Moment Pumpkin

Yield: 4–6 servings

If you don't have French fleur de sel in your cupboard, too bad. It's the king of salt and offers an unrivaled gentle salt flavor to foods. You can substitute kosher or coarse sea salt, but use half the amount. Do not use regular table salt. This recipe comes from Kate Browne from Ridgefield, Wash.

3 (2–2½-pound [908 g–1.1 kg]) sugar pie pumpkins
2 tablespoons (30 mL) butter, melted
1 tablespoon (15 mL) olive oil
2 tablespoons (30 mL) chili powder
1 tablespoon (15 mL) dried oregano
3 tablespoons (45 mL) honey
1 tablespoon (15 mL) chopped fresh parsley
1 teaspoon (5 mL) fleur de sel

1. Preheat the barbecue to (350°F [180°C] to 400°F [200°C]) for direct heating, making sure the grill has been well oiled or sprayed with grilling spray.

2. Wash and cut the pumpkins horizontally into 1-inch (2.5-cm) thick slices (so there is a hole in the middle of each slice filled with seeds). Run a sharp knife around the inside of each slice, removing the seeds and stringy pulp. Discard the top and bottom slices, which don't have holes.

3. In a small bowl, mix together the butter and olive oil. Place the pumpkin circles on a plate or platter and brush each circle with this mixture. Sprinkle with the chili powder and oregano. Turn the slices over and repeat on the other side.

4. Place the pumpkin circles on the grill and cook until both sides are marked with grill marks, about 5 minutes per side.

5. Before you take the slices off the grill brush with the honey and sprinkle with the parsley and salt. Remove from the grill and serve.

Sweet Potato and Peanut Butter Cookie Casserole
Yield: 6 servings

There are many ways you could vary this recipe, including substituting coconut, white chocolate chip cookies, and marmalade; graham crackers and peanut butter; or even vanilla wafers and red currant jelly.

3½ pounds (1.6 kg) chopped cooked sweet potatoes
½ cup (118 mL) butter, melted, divided
½ cup (118 mL) packed brown sugar
¼ cup (59 mL) amaretto liqueur
½ teaspoon (2.5 mL) kosher salt
½ teaspoon (2.5 mL) ground ginger
⅛ teaspoon (0.6 mL) ground cinnamon
¼ cup (59 mL) peach preserves
¼ cup (59 mL) chopped peanuts
1 cup (236 mL) crumbled peanut butter cookies

1. Preheat the barbecue to 300°F (150°C) to 325°F (165°C) for direct heating. Grease a 2-quart (1.9-L) Dutch oven.

2. In a large mixing bowl, combine the sweet potatoes, ¼ cup (59 mL) of the butter, the brown sugar, the amaretto, the salt, the ginger, and the cinnamon and stir until smooth. Fold in the preserves and peanuts.

3. Spoon this mixture into the prepared Dutch oven. In a small bowl, mix the crumbled peanut butter cookies with the remaining butter. Sprinkle this mixture over the top of the sweet potatoes.

4. Place the Dutch oven in the barbecue and bake, uncovered, for 30 to 35 minutes, or until heated through.

5. Remove from the barbecue and let rest for 5 to 10 minutes. Serve.

FOURTEEN

Turkey

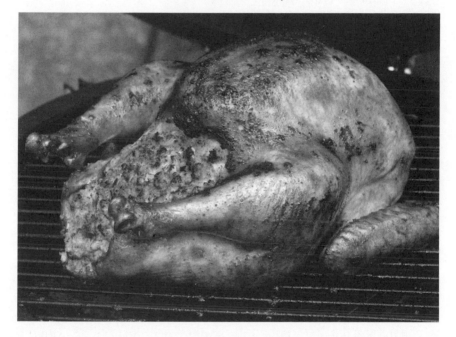

Apple Wood-Smoked Turkey with Maple Syrup–Apple Cider Brine

Yield: 8–10 servings

Turkey will only absorb smoke for about 20 minutes, the average duration of the smoke package you put on the hot coals. Any more smoke, and turkey will take on a bitter taste. The layer just under the skin may be pink, due to the smoke's effect on the meat. However, if it's pink from the bone out, it's undercooked.

2 gallons (7.6 L) hot water
½ cup (118 mL) kosher salt
2 cups (473 mL) apple cider
½ cup (118 mL) pure maple syrup
2 tablespoons (30 mL) maple sugar pepper
1 (12–14 pound [5.4–6.4 kg]) turkey, fresh or thawed
1 (10-pound [4.5-kg]) bag ice cubes
Extra virgin olive oil for rubbing
Salt, to taste
Freshly ground black pepper, to taste

1. In a large stockpot, heat the water until it is very warm. Add the kosher salt and stir with a long-handled spoon until the salt dissolves. Pour the water into a 5-gallon (19-L) plastic bucket. Add the apple cider, syrup, and pepper. Add the turkey and ice cubes, cover and let the turkey brine for at least 16 hours, stirring the water 2 or 3 times. Soak a handful of apple wood chips in water.

2. Preheat the barbecue to medium high (230°F [110°C] to 280°F [140°C]) for indirect heating, putting a water pan under the center of the grill, surrounded by the coals. If using gas, turn the outside burners to low and put the water pan over the center burner.

3. Make a smoker package by putting the soaked wood chips on a 12-inch (30-cm) square of heavy-duty aluminum foil, folding over the package, poking 3 or 4 holes in the top of the foil, and placing the package directly on the coals or open flame to add smoke to your grilling.

4. Pull the bird out of the brine, rinse it with water, and pat it dry with a paper towel. Rub the turkey with olive oil, season it with salt and pepper, and place it in the center of the grill.

5. Add charcoal or turn up gas as needed to keep a nice light flow of smoke coming out. Leave the exhaust vent all the way open to prevent too much smoke from building up in the grill. After 1½ hours, turn the bird 180 degrees to ensure even cooking. Cook for a total of 4½ to 5 hours, or about 25 to 30 minutes per pound (454 g).

6. The turkey is done when a thermometer inserted into the thick part of the breast reads 165°F (74°C), the thigh, 180°F (82°C). If the breast is done first, cover it with aluminum foil, shiny side up, while the thigh finishes cooking.

7. Remove the turkey from the barbecue, cover the entire bird with foil, and let it rest for 15 to 20 minutes to allow the internal juices to recirculate.

Carolina-Style Barbecued Turkey

Yield: 8–10 servings

Even folks who don't live in the Carolinas and are not familiar with the vinegar-sugar-red pepper sauce they favor in those parts love the flavor of this turkey—crisp, biting, tangy, yet tinged with sweetness.

1 (10–12 pound [4.5–5.4 kg]) turkey, fresh or thawed
½ cup (118 mL) peanut or olive oil
1½ pounds (681 g) hickory-smoked bacon
Salt, to taste
Freshly ground black pepper, to taste
1 tablespoon (15 mL) crushed red pepper flakes
2 cups (473 mL) apple cider vinegar
1 cup (236 mL) water

1. Cut the turkey in half and remove the spine. Rub the two halves with the oil, then lay strips of bacon over the skin side. (If the turkey is larger than 12 pounds [5.4 kg], use bacon substitute like turkey bacon as real bacon will burn. Frankly, I don't recommend doing a larger turkey with this method.)

2. Preheat the grill to 250°F [120°C] to 275°F [140°C] for indirect cooking. If you're using a three-burner gas grill, place a drip pan under the center of the grill, spray the grill with nonstick cooking spray, and turn on the outside two burners. If you're using a two-burner grill, heat one side and place the water pan on the other, then remember to rotate the turkey 180° halfway through the cooking time. If you're using a charcoal grill, place the coals around the outside edges of the grill, place a drip pan in the center, spray the rack, and light the charcoal.

3. Place turkey, breast side up, on the grill over drip pan. Cover the barbecue and grill the turkey for 2 to 2½ hours. Remove the bacon strips and continue cooking the turkey for 30 more minutes, or until a meat thermometer inserted into the deepest portion of the thigh reaches 180°F (82°C) and the leg bone will turn and separate from meat. The turkey should be golden brown, and the breast temperature will be around 165F (64°C) to 170°F (77°C).

4. Remove the turkey from the grill, cover it with foil, and allow it to rest for 15 minutes. Using heat-resistant gloves, remove the meat from bones and loosely chop it. Add salt and pepper, sprinkle with the red pepper flakes, and mix well. Combine the vinegar and water and sprinkle this mixture over the meat. Stir gently.

5. Serve with toasted, buttered rolls for North Carolina–style turkey sandwiches, and offer extra vinegar-pepper sauce on the side.

Blood Orange Turkey

Yield: 8–10 servings

If you can find them, blood oranges make a dramatic presentation here. If not, regular oranges will work fine. You can also put a few lemon or lime slices under the skin with the oranges, and garnish with slices of those as well.

1 (14-pound [6.4-kg]) turkey, fresh or thawed
3 carrots, roughly chopped
3 celery stalks, roughly chopped, leaves included
2 medium onions, peeled and quartered
3 large blood oranges, thinly sliced, divided
Turkey stuffing of your choice as needed
¾ cup (177 mL) orange juice
⅓ cup (79 mL) orange marmalade
¼ cup (59 mL) unsalted butter, softened
Salt, to taste
Freshly ground black pepper, to taste
Poultry seasoning, to taste
2 cups (473 mL) chicken broth

1. Preheat the barbecue to medium high (325°F [165°C] to 375°F [190°C]).

2. Rinse the turkey with cold water and blot it dry with a paper towel, including the cavity. Place the neck, giblets, carrots, celery, and onion in a large roasting pan, and arrange the turkey on top, breast side up.

3. Lift the skin up over the turkey breast, being careful not to tear it. Gently slide the slices from 2 of the oranges under the skin. Loosely pack the stuffing in the neck cavity and inside the body. Fold the wings back and under the body of the turkey. Fold the neck skin under to enclose the stuffing, and tie the legs together with butcher's twine.

4. In a medium bowl, combine the orange juice, marmalade, and butter. Season with the salt, pepper, and poultry seasoning. Pour the broth into the roasting pan around the turkey.

5. Roast for 3¾ to 4½ hours, basting frequently and tenting the turkey with aluminum foil two-thirds of the way through the cooking process. Test for doneness with a meat thermometer. The temperature in the thickest part of the turkey leg and thigh should be 180°F (82°C); in the thickest part of the turkey breast, 165F (74°C) to 170°F (77°C); and in the stuffing, 160°F (71°C). When turkey has cooked for 3½ hours, liberally brush the marinade on the turkey, and repeat when you take the turkey off the grill and just before you cover it with foil.

6. Transfer the stuffing to a bowl and cover it. Wrap the turkey loosely in foil and let the bird rest for 15 minutes before carving.

7. Carve the turkey and place the meat on a warmed platter. Garnish with the remaining orange slices and serve.

Barbecued Turkey Loaf

Yield: 4–6 servings

The white meat of turkey is generally considered much healthier than the dark meat because of its lower fat content, but the nutritional differences are small.

2 cups (473 mL) finely diced cooked turkey meat
1½ cups (354 mL) crumbled Ritz vegetable crackers
3 tablespoons (45 mL) butter, melted
3 tablespoons (45 mL) diced pimiento
2 tablespoons (30 mL) minced onion
½ teaspoon (2.5 mL) salt
½ teaspoon (2.5 mL) freshly ground black pepper
½ teaspoon (2.5 mL) celery salt
2 large eggs
¾ cup (177 mL) turkey broth (or chicken broth)
1 16 ounce (473 mL) can jellied cranberries

1. Preheat the barbecue to medium high (350°F [180°C] to 400°F [200°C]) for indirect heating, putting a water pan under the unheated side of the grill. Grease a metal loaf pan.

2. In a large bowl, combine the turkey, crackers, butter, pimiento, onion, salt, pepper, and celery salt.

3. In a small bowl, whisk the eggs to combine the yolks and white. Add the turkey broth and whisk again. Pour this mixture into the turkey mixture and stir until the crumbs are absorbed. Spoon the mixture into the prepared loaf pan.

4. Bake for 40 to 45 minutes, or until the loaf is lightly browned on top and the meat is firm.

5. Spread the jellied cranberries on top and return the pan to the barbecue for 5 minutes, or until the cranberries bubble and melt completely.

Katie's Smashed Bird

Yield: 4–6 servings

This is a perfect dish for turkey or chicken leftovers; just pick the meat from the carcass. The oysters are optional, but they add a wonderful flavor—if you like oysters, that is. This recipe comes from Kathleen Janice Welch from Hartford, Conn.

1 pound (454 g) turkey thighs, skin removed (about 6–8 thighs)
1 pint (473 mL) small oysters with juice
1 (12-ounce [336-g]) can condensed cream of celery soup
1 (12-ounce [336-g]) can condensed cream of mushroom soup
1 cup (236 mL) milk
1 (14-ounce [396-g]) bag Pepperidge Farm stuffing mix
1½ cups (354 mL) turkey broth
¼ cup (59 mL) butter, melted
½ cup (118 mL) grated Swiss cheese
Chopped parsley, for garnish

1. Preheat the barbecue to medium high (350°F [180°C] to 400°F [200°C]) for indirect heating, putting a water pan under the unheated side of the grill. Spray with nonstick cooking spray or butter a 9-inch (22.5-cm) square baking dish.

2. In a deep saucepan, boil the turkey until done, about 20 minutes. Pick the turkey meat from the bone and put it in the prepared baking dish. Add the oysters.

3. In a medium bowl, whisk together the soups and milk and pour this mixture over the turkey. Cover with the dry stuffing mix, pour on the melted broth and butter, and sprinkle with the grated Swiss cheese. Cook for 20 minutes, or until the cheese is melted and the top of the dish is nicely browned.

4. Sprinkle with the parsley, let sit for 5 minutes to cool slightly, and serve.

Beer-Butt Turkey
Yield: 8–10 servings

If you don't wish to use beer, you can substitute fruit juice, water, wine, cola, or soda. Do not use diet soft drinks, as they turn very bitter when cooked. But really—"water-butt turkey"? The best way to cook using this technique is to purchase a turkey beer can holder, a stainless steel frame that holds the beer can and the turkey at an angle so that it easily fits in most kettle barbecue grills.

2 teaspoons (10 mL) dried thyme
2 teaspoons (10 mL) poultry seasoning
4 tablespoons (60 mL) packed brown sugar
2 tablespoons (30 mL) paprika
2 tablespoons (30 mL) granulated garlic
1 tablespoon (15 mL) freshly ground black pepper
1 tablespoon (15 mL) celery salt
1 teaspoon (5 mL) cayenne pepper
1 (24-ounce [710-mL]) can beer, divided
¼ cup (59 mL) balsamic vinegar
1 cup (236 mL) apple cider
2 tablespoons (30 mL) olive oil
1 (12–15 pound [5.4–6.8 kg]) turkey

1. Preheat a gas or charcoal barbecue to medium high (250°F [120°C] to 275°F [140°C]) for indirect heating, putting a water pan under the unheated side of the grill.

2. In a small bowl, combine the thyme, poultry seasoning, brown sugar, paprika, garlic, pepper, celery salt, and cayenne pepper and set aside. In a spray bottle, mix together 12 ounces (355 mL) of the beer, the balsamic vinegar, the apple cider, and the olive oil and set aside.

3. Rub the surface of the turkey with the spice rub. Try to get as much as you can under the skin, particularly over the breast meat. Place the beer can with the remaining beer in the holder and slide the turkey rear-end first over the can and holder.

4. Make a smoker package by putting a handful of soaked hickory or oak chips on a 12-inch (30-cm) square of heavy-duty aluminum foil, folding over the package, poking 3 or 4 holes in the top of the foil, and placing the package directly on the coals or open flame to add smoke to your grilling.

5. Cook the turkey for about 6 hours, spraying it once or twice an hour with the basting spray. Turkey is done when the internal temperature in the thigh reaches 180°F (82°C); the breast should be at 165°F (74°C).

Trash Can Turkey
Yield: 8–10 servings

If you are using a new trash can, you must burn the galvanizing off first by heating the can over charcoal without any food in it before you cook anything. Place 10 to 15 lit briquettes on the ground, cover them with the can, add 10 to 15 hot briquettes on the top, and heat the can for 1 hour. Remove the briquettes, cool the can, and wash it out with a hose.

1 (12-pound [5.4-kg]) turkey

Trash Can Cooking Equipment
1 (20-pound [9-kg]) bag charcoal briquettes
Heavy-duty aluminum foil
Metal tube pan
1 (1½–2 inch [3.5–5 cm] diameter, 18–20 inch [45–50 cm] long) wooden dowel
1 (10-gallon [38-L]) metal can (seam must be crimped and rolled, not soldered)
Oven mitts

1. Using a barbecue chimney, light the briquettes so they are ready when you need them.

2. Place 3 (24 × 18-inch [60 × 45-cm]) sheets of heavy-duty aluminum foil on the dirt area where you will be cooking the turkey. (Do not cook on grass, unless you want to kill the grass.) Place the tube pan bottom down, in the center of the foil, and pound the dowel into the center hole of the pan through the foil. This will catch some of the grease from the cooking turkey.

3. Wrap the turkey wing tips in foil and tie the wing tips tightly to the body.

4. Lower the turkey onto the stick, legs down. The legs should rest on the edges of the pan.

5. Invert the garbage can over the turkey, making sure the can is tight to the ground all the way around, and place burning briquettes around the bottom of the can, approximately 3 rows high and deep. Cover the top of the can with burning briquettes.

6. The cooking time should begin when all the briquettes are in place. As the briquettes burn to ashes, add more to replace them. Follow the cooking times listed below. When the cooking time is up, gently remove the ashes from can and, using oven mitts, carefully remove can, being careful not to touch the turkey.

7. Cover the turkey with foil and let it rest for 15 to 20 minutes to let the juices recirculate. Remove the pan, skim off the fat, and use it to make turkey gravy.

Cooking Times

10 pounds (4.5 kg): 50 minutes.
12 pounds (5.4 kg): 1 hour
14 pounds (6.4 kg): 1 hour 25 minutes
16 pounds (7.3 kg): 1 hour 40 minutes
18 pounds (8.2 kg): 2 hours 5 minutes
22 pounds (10 kg): 2 hours 25 minutes

Grilled Osso Buco Bird

Yield: 6 servings

At one time, the turkey and the bald eagle were both considered as the national bird of the United States. Benjamin Franklin argued passionately on behalf of the turkey, saying that the turkey, although "vain and silly," was a better choice than the bald eagle, which he felt was "a coward." This recipe comes from Jack Lawrence from La Center, Wash.

½ cup (118 mL) all-purpose flour
1 teaspoon (5 mL) salt, plus more to taste
¼ teaspoon (1.25 mL) freshly ground black pepper, plus more to taste
2 turkey legs and 4 thighs
½ cup (118 mL) vegetable oil
2 large onions, peeled and chopped
2 large carrots, sliced
1 (8-ounce [227-g]) can tomato sauce
1 cup (236 mL) dry white wine
1 teaspoon (5 mL) dried oregano
½ teaspoon (2.5 mL) dried basil
½ teaspoon (2.5 mL) dried thyme
Juice of 1 lemon
3 tablespoons (45 mL) minced fresh parsley
Paprika, for garnish

1. Preheat the barbecue to medium high (350°F [180°C] to 400°F [200°C]) for indirect heating, putting a water pan under the unheated side of the grill.

2. In a paper bag, mix together the flour, salt, and pepper. One at a time, drop each turkey leg and thigh into the bag and shake until the pieces are completely coated.

3. In a large cast-iron skillet or roasting pan set on a barbecue side burner or a stovetop burner, heat the oil. Add the turkey, season with more salt and pepper, and cook until the meat is nicely browned. Remove the turkey from the skillet and set it aside.

4. Add the onions and carrots to the oil in the skillet and sauté until the onions are golden. Add the tomato sauce, wine, oregano, basil, and thyme and stir. Add the turkey and the lemon juice. Place the skillet on the indirect side of the barbecue grill, cover, and cook for about 2 hours, or until the turkey is tender.

5. Place the turkey on a warmed platter and spoon the sauce over the legs and thighs. Sprinkle with the parsley and paprika and serve.

Baked Honey–Molasses Turkey

Yield: 6–8 servings

There are dozens of varieties of honey, including clover (the most common), buckwheat (great for barbecue), blueberry (from Michigan and Maine), orange blossom (California, Arizona, Florida, and Texas), and tupelo (Georgia and Florida), all of which are wonderfully flavored.

¼ cup (59 mL) honey
¼ cup (59 mL) molasses
1 (12–14 pound [5.4–6.4 kg]) turkey, split in half
1 tablespoon (15 mL) poultry seasoning
1 teaspoon (5 mL) garlic salt
1 teaspoon (5 mL) freshly ground black pepper
1 pound (454 g) butter, melted
2 tablespoons (30 mL) balsamic vinegar
1 cup (236 mL) chicken stock
1 cup (236 mL) dry white wine
½ cup (118 mL) chopped onion
1 teaspoon (5 mL) dried parsley flakes

1. Preheat the barbecue to medium high (350°F [180°C] to 400°F [200°C]). Grease or spray with nonstick cooking spray a baking or roasting pan.

2. In a small bowl, mix together the honey and molasses. Microwave this mixture for 30 seconds until it melts together, and stir. Brush the skin side of the turkey halves with the molasses honey, and season generously with poultry seasoning, salt, and pepper.

3. Place the turkey skin side up in the prepared pan, and cook for 30 minutes. In a small bowl, combine the melted butter and balsamic vinegar. Add the remaining melted molasses honey to the melted balsamic butter, stir, and brush often over the turkey halves.

4. In a medium bowl, combine the chicken stock, wine, onion, and parsley. Pour this mixture around (not over) the turkey. Cover and bake, basting the turkey occasionally with the liquid from the pan, for 1 hour, or until the turkey is done. The turkey will be browned with a crispy skin, and a thermometer inserted into the thigh will read 180°F (82°C). Remove the turkey from the heat, cover it, and let it rest for 15 minutes. Carve and serve.

Barbecued Turkey Sandwiches

Yield: 6 servings

You could also add slices of Swiss or cheddar cheese, fresh lettuce, red onion slices, tomato slices, and, if you'd rather not add the small pieces to the mixture, full strips of crispy bacon.

2 teaspoons (10 mL) olive oil
1 medium onion, peeled and chopped
1 cup (236 mL) bottled chili sauce
3 tablespoons (45 mL) brown sugar
3 tablespoons (45 mL) water
2 tablespoons (30 mL) Worcestershire sauce
3 cups (708 mL) shredded cooked turkey, white and dark meat
¼ cup (59 mL) chopped cooked bacon
6 onion rolls or poppy seed buns
Coleslaw, for serving

1. In a large saucepan over a side burner, heat the oil over medium heat. Add the onion and sauté until tender. Stir in the chili sauce, brown sugar, water, and Worcestershire sauce. Bring to a boil, reduce the heat to low, and simmer, uncovered, for 5 minutes.

2. Stir in the turkey and add the bacon pieces.

3. Serve on toasted onion rolls or poppy seed buns with the coleslaw on the side, in case folks want to add it to their sandwiches.

Turkey-Stuffed Peppers

Yield: 6 servings

If you want to dress up this dish, you can use wild rice instead of the white, shallots instead of the onions, and chopped turkey breast medallions instead of the ground bird.

1 pound (454 g) ground turkey
1 cup (236 mL) cooked long-grain rice
2 tablespoons (30 mL) minced onion
1 tablespoon (15 mL) Worcestershire sauce
1 clove garlic, peeled and minced
¼ teaspoon (1.25 mL) freshly ground black pepper
½ teaspoon (2.5 mL) poultry seasoning
2 cups (473 mL) tomato sauce, divided
1 cup (236 mL) dry white wine, divided
6 medium red and green bell peppers, tops sliced off and seeds removed
¼ cup (59 mL) shredded mozzarella cheese

1. Preheat the barbecue to medium high (350°F [180°C] to 400°F [200°C]) for indirect heating, putting a water pan under the unheated side of the grill. Grease or spray with nonstick cooking spray a 2-quart (1.9 L) Dutch oven.

2. In a medium bowl, combine the turkey, rice, onion, Worcestershire sauce, garlic, pepper, poultry seasoning, ½ cup (118 mL) of the tomato sauce, and ¼ cup (59 mL) of the wine, stirring to incorporate all the ingredients.

3. Stand the peppers upright in the prepared Dutch oven. Fill the peppers with the turkey mixture, pour in the remaining tomato sauce and wine and stir. Cover and cook for 20 to 25 minutes. Remove the cover, sprinkle on the cheese, and cook, uncovered, for another 8 to 10 minutes, or until the cheese melts and begins to brown.

Turkey in the Orchard

Yield: 4–6 servings

This dish is also delightful served with chopped potatoes and sweet potatoes instead of the fruit. Do keep the pineapple, though. We could call this variation Turkey in the Field.

¼ cup (59 mL) butter, melted
½ teaspoon (2.5 mL) chopped fresh rosemary
½ teaspoon (2.5 mL) chopped fresh thyme
1 turkey half-breast, skin on
1 medium onion, peeled and cut into 1-inch (2.5-cm) pieces
1 medium green bell pepper, cut into 1-inch (2.5-cm) pieces
½ cup (118 mL) diced apples
½ cup (118 mL) chopped peaches
½ cup (118 mL) dried apricots
1 (8-ounce [227-g]) can pineapple chunks, drained, juice reserved
1 tablespoon (15 mL) brown sugar
½ cup (118 mL) dry red wine
2 tablespoons (30 mL) bottled chili sauce

1. Preheat the barbecue to medium high (425°F [220°C] to 450°F [240°C]) for direct and indirect heating, putting a water pan under the unheated side of the grill.

2. In a small bowl, combine melted butter, rosemary, and thyme. Brush the turkey breast with this mixture and place the turkey in a flat baking or roasting pan. Put the pan in the barbecue and cook, uncovered, for 25 minutes, or until the turkey is lightly browned.

3. In a large bowl, combine the onion, pepper, apples, peaches, apricots, and pineapple chunks. Stir this mixture and pour it around the turkey breast.

4. In a separate bowl, whisk together the reserved pineapple juice, brown sugar, wine, and chili sauce and pour this mixture over the turkey breast. Cover the pan with foil and place it on the unheated side of the barbecue for 1 hour. Close the vents to lower the temperature to about 350°F (180°C).

5. Remove the foil, baste the turkey with the sauce and fruit, and cook, uncovered, for 30 minutes, basting the turkey several times.

6. Remove the turkey from the barbecue and from the pot, cover it with foil, and let it sit for 10 minutes. Pour the fruit and sauce into a serving dish and serve it alongside the sliced turkey breast.

Smoked Turkey with Smoked Oyster Dressing

Yield: 6–8 servings

If you don't like oysters, don't add them. But you could substitute shrimp, which you treat the same way, but smoke them for just 30 minutes.

1 (10–12 pound [4.5–5.4 kg]) turkey
½ cup (118 mL) butter, melted
1 quart (0.95 L) fresh oysters, with liquid
1 cup (236 mL) cider vinegar
6–7 cups (1.4–1.7 L) water
1 stale loaf white bread, torn into chunks
1 medium red onion, peeled and diced
1 cup (236 mL) diced celery
1 tablespoon (15 mL) minced garlic
3 tablespoons (45 mL) Worcestershire sauce
1 tablespoon (15 mL) dark soy sauce
1 small jalapeño pepper, diced
1 teaspoon (5 mL) dried sage
1 teaspoon (5 mL) dried thyme
1 teaspoon (5 mL) dried basil
2 teaspoons (10 mL) poultry seasoning
Freshly ground black pepper, to taste

1. Preheat the smoker to 220°F (105°C) to 240°F (115°C). Put a water pan on the bottom of the smoker. If you don't have a smoker, you can use a gas or charcoal grill, although a gas grill is much easier to use. If it's a three-burner grill, turn off the middle burner and turn the outside two to their lowest setting. If it's a two-burner grill, turn one burner to the lowest and leave the other one off.

2. Make 3 smoker packages by putting a handful of soaked hardwood chips of your choice (I like a mixture of cherry, apple, and oak) on a 12-inch square of heavy-duty aluminum foil, folding over the package, poking 3 or 4 holes in the top of the foil, and placing the packages directly on the coals or open flame to add smoke to your grilling.

3. Put the turkey on the grill, brush it with the melted butter, close the lid, and cook for 6 hours. Drain the oysters, reserving the liquid, and pour them onto a baking sheet. Smoke the oysters beside the turkey to smoke for the first 2 hours. Remove the oysters from the smoker or grill and set aside.

4. At the end of the 6 hours, remove the turkey from the smoker and place it in a large roasting pan. Add the cider vinegar and water to the pan. You should have 1 inch (2.5 cm) of liquid in the bottom of the pan. Brush the turkey with more butter, cover it with foil, and return it to the smoker for another 2 hours, or until a meat thermometer placed in the thigh reads 180°F (82°C).

5. Butter a large baking pan or a 2 loaf pans.

6. In a large bowl, combine the bread, smoked oysters, onion, celery, garlic, Worcestershire sauce, soy sauce, jalapeño pepper, sage, thyme, basil, poultry seasoning, pepper, and reserved oyster liquor. Place this mixture in the prepared baking pan or loaf pans. If you have room, cook this mixture in the barbecue for the last hour the turkey is cooking. If you don't have room, cook it in your oven at 325°F (165°C) for about 45 minutes. In either case, cook until the top of the dressing is just slightly darker than golden brown. Remove the dressing from the barbecue or oven and serve it with the turkey.

Breaded Parmesan Gobbler Thighs

Yield: 4 servings

Using Parmigiano-Reggiano cheese is a bit of a luxury. You could also use another type of Parmesan cheese, but it is important to freshly grate it for this dish.

4 turkey thighs, about 3 pounds (1.3 kg) total
¼ cup (59 mL) butter, melted
1 clove garlic, minced
1 tablespoon (15 mL) Dijon mustard
1 teaspoon (5 mL) Worcestershire sauce
1½ cups (354 mL) panko
1 tablespoon (15 mL) dried rosemary
½ cup (118 mL) freshly grated Parmigiano-Reggiano cheese
¼ cup (59 mL) plus 2 tablespoons (30 mL) chopped fresh parsley
1 cup (236 mL) 1-inch (2.5-cm) pieces green onions, green and white parts
1 cup (236 mL) coarsely chopped carrots
1 cup (236 mL) coarsely chopped celery

1. Preheat the barbecue to medium high (350°F [180°C] to 400°F [200°C]).

2. In a small bowl, whisk together the butter, garlic, mustard, and Worcestershire sauce. In a shallow bowl, combine the panko, rosemary, cheese and parsley.

3. Dip the turkey in butter mixture and coat it with the panko mixture, pressing the turkey into the panko.

4. Place green onions, carrots, and celery in a glass dish. Arrange the thighs on top, drizzle with the remaining butter mixture, sprinkle with the remaining panko, and cook for 1 to 1½ hours, or until the turkey is browned and a little crisp. A thermometer inserted into the thigh should read 180°F (82°C).

5. Remove the turkey from the pan. Drain the vegetables and spoon them onto plates. Top the vegetables with the turkey thighs and serve.

Mushroom–Cranberry Turkey Burgers

Yield: 4 servings

For an entirely different taste, replace the cranberry sauce with a similar amount of fresh pesto or finely chopped tomato salsa.

2 pounds (908 g) ground turkey, thawed if frozen
¼ cup (59 mL) chopped whole-berry cranberry sauce
1 tablespoon (15 mL) chopped fresh parsley
1 tablespoon (15 mL) Worcestershire sauce
1 teaspoon (5 mL) garlic salt
1 tablespoon (15 mL) butter
1 cup (236 mL) sliced crimini mushrooms
4 hamburger buns, toasted and buttered

1. Preheat the barbecue to medium high (350°F [180°C] to 400°F [200°C]), and spray it well before cooking with a nonstick cooking or grilling spray.

2. In a medium bowl, combine the turkey, cranberry sauce, parsley, Worcestershire sauce, and garlic salt and stir well. Shape the turkey mixture into 4 (4-inch [10-cm]) patties, cover them with plastic wrap, and set them aside.

3. In a large skillet, melt the butter over medium heat. Add the mushrooms and cook, stirring, for 2 to 3 minutes, or until tender. Remove mushrooms and cover to keep warm

4. Cook the burgers on the hot grill, about 3 to 4 minutes per side, until the patties are nicely browned and have firmed up, turning several times. Serve them on the buns, topped with the sliced mushrooms.

Barbecued Turkey Divan

Yield: 6–8 servings

Chicken (and turkey) Divan was created at the Divan Parisienne restaurant in New York City. It is a casserole of sliced chicken or turkey breast and spears of broccoli, covered with cheese sauce and baked until the top is golden brown. We make a quick version here.

10 ounces (280 g) broccoli (about 1 large bunch)
2 cups (908 g) chopped or sliced cooked turkey
1 (8-ounce [227-g]) can condensed mushroom soup, diluted with ¼ cup (59 mL) heavy cream
½ teaspoon (2.5 mL) ground cumin
1 teaspoon (5 mL) dried oregano
½ cup (118 mL) shredded Parmesan cheese
¼ cup (59 mL) shredded Gruyère cheese
½ cup (118 mL) soft breadcrumbs
1 tablespoon (15 mL) butter, melted

1. Preheat the barbecue to medium high (350°F [180°C] to 400°F [200°C]). Grease a 9 × 13-inch (22.5 × 32.5-cm) baking pan.

2. Cook the broccoli in a large saucepan of boiling, salted water until tender; drain. Arrange broccoli stalks in the prepared pan. Add the turkey and pour on the diluted soup. Sprinkle with the cumin, oregano, Parmesan cheese, and Gruyère cheese.

3. In a small bowl, combine the breadcrumbs and butter and stir. Sprinkle this mixture over the shredded cheese.

4. Place the pan in the barbecue and bake for 25 to 30 minutes, or until the casserole is thoroughly heated and the top is lightly browned.

5. Remove the casserole from the barbecue and let it cool slightly, for about 5 minutes, then serve.

Turkey in a Brown Paper Bag

Yield: 8–10 servings

This recipe can't be done with a turkey weighing more than 16 pounds (7.3 kg). It should be golden brown and extremely moist when you carve it.

1 teaspoon (5 mL) freshly ground black pepper
2 teaspoons (10 mL) salt
1 tablespoon (15 mL) paprika
1 tablespoon (15 mL) poultry seasoning
4 teaspoons (20 mL) hot water
1 cup (236 mL) butter, melted, or vegetable oil
1 (12–14 pound [5.4–6.4 kg]) turkey

1. Preheat the barbecue to medium high (350°F [180°C] to 400°F [200°C]).

2. In a small bowl, combine the pepper, salt, paprika, poultry seasoning, and hot water and let stand for 10 minutes. Add the butter and whisk to mix completely. Wash and dry the turkey thoroughly inside and out. Brush the butter mixture generously onto the skin and inside the cavity of the turkey. Tie the legs together and tie the wings to the body. With the remaining butter, brush the top and sides of the bag until it is well covered.

3. Place the turkey, breast side up, on the rack of a deep ovenproof pan. Place the pan in the paper bag. Fold over the edges and staple shut.

4. Bake in the barbecue over a double layer of heavy-duty aluminum foil or a large baking sheet, so that no part of the bag is directly over the flames or open heat. Cook for 2½ to 3 hours (12 minutes per pound [454 g]).

5. Open the bag carefully to avoid the steam that will escape. If the turkey isn't browned enough, brush it with more butter or oil and return it to the barbecue for 15 minutes.

White Castle Hamburger Stuffing

Yield: 9 cups (2.1 L), enough for 1 (10–12 pound [4.5–5.4 kg]) turkey

You could also use White Castle cheeseburgers. Or, if you're really daring, chop up five double bacon cheeseburgers for the stuffing. Allow one burger or half of a double cheeseburger for each pound (454 g) of turkey, which will be equivalent to ¾ cup (177 mL) of stuffing per pound.

10 White Castle hamburgers with buns and grilled onions, pickle removed
2 orders White Castle onion rings, chopped
1 cup (236 mL) diced celery
1 teaspoon (5 mL) poultry seasoning
1 teaspoon (5 mL) ground sage
1 teaspoon (5 mL) freshly ground black pepper
¼ cup (59 mL) chicken broth

1. On a cutting board, chop the hamburgers into small chunks and place the chunks in a large bowl. Add the chopped onion rings, diced celery, poultry seasoning, sage, and pepper.

2. With serving forks, toss to combine. Add the chicken broth and mix until all the ingredients are combined. Stuff the cavity of the turkey just before roasting.

Apple-Onion Turkey Stuffing

Yield: 4½ cups (1.1 L)

I make this recipe using stale onion hamburger rolls. They stay relatively firm and add extra onion flavor to the stuffing.

¼ cup (59 mL) butter, melted
1 cup (236 mL) diced onion
2 cups (473 mL) dry breadcrumbs
2 cups (473 mL) chopped pippin apples
1 cup (236 mL) dry white wine
2 tablespoons (30 mL) lemon juice
¼ teaspoon (1.25 mL) ground nutmeg
1 teaspoon (5 mL) onion salt
¼ teaspoon (1.25 mL) ground allspice
¼ cup (59 mL) chopped fresh parsley

1. In a large nonstick frying pan, melt the butter. Add the onions and sauté until they are translucent. Add the breadcrumbs, apples, and wine, and cook for 5 minutes. Add the breadcrumbs, apples, and wine.

2. Add the lemon juice, nutmeg, onion salt, allspice, and parsley. Stuff this mixture into the turkey neck and body cavities just before you put it in the barbecue.

Apricot Stuffing for Turkey

Yield: 5–6 cups (1.2–1.4 mL)

This recipe can also be made ahead, up to the point of cooking, and stuffed into a turkey (or chicken) just before you roast it.

1 cup (236 mL) dried apricots
1½ cups (354 mL) chicken stock
18 slices dry bread, torn into small pieces
¼ cup (59 mL) chopped pine nuts
1 cup (236 mL) chopped celery
1 cup (236 mL) chopped onions
1 teaspoon (5 mL) salt
2 teaspoons (10 mL) dried sage
1 teaspoon (5 mL) dried oregano

1. Preheat the barbecue to medium high (350°F [180°C] to 400°F [200°C]). Oil or butter a 9-inch (22.5-cm) square baking pan.

2. In a saucepan, combine the apricots and chicken stock. Bring to a boil, remove from the heat, and let stand for 15 minutes.

3. Pour the cooked apricots into a large bowl. Add the bread, pine nuts, celery, onions, salt, sage, and oregano and toss lightly to moisten the bread and blend the ingredients. Spoon the stuffing into the prepared baking pan and cover with foil.

4. Bake in the barbecue for about 40 minutes. Remove the cover during the last 10 minutes of baking to brown the top of the stuffing.

Italian-Style Turkey Stuffing

Yield: 6–8 servings

This recipe will stuff a 10- to 12-pound (4.5- to 5.4-kg) turkey nicely. It can also be used for chicken, whole fish, or bell peppers.

2 cups (473 mL) uncooked long-grain rice
1¾ cups (413 mL) chicken broth
1¾ cups (413 mL) water
3 tablespoons (45 mL) olive oil
2 cloves garlic, peeled and minced
2 large onions, peeled and diced
12 cups (2.8 L) washed and chopped fresh spinach
1 teaspoon (5 mL) dried oregano
½ cup (118 mL) grated Parmigiano-Reggiano cheese
½ teaspoon (2.5 mL) salt
½ teaspoon (2.5 mL) freshly ground black pepper
½ pound (277 g) cooked Italian sausage
3 large eggs, beaten

1. Place the rice in a saucepan with a tight-fitting lid. In a separate saucepan, bring the broth and water to a boil. Pour the liquid over the rice, stir, and cover. Cook over low heat for 15 minutes or until all the liquid is absorbed and the rice is tender. Uncover and fluff with a fork.

2. While the rice is cooking, heat the olive oil in large skillet over medium heat. Add the garlic and cook until fragrant, about 2 to 3 minutes, but don't let it brown. Add the onions and cook, stirring often, until they are softened and starting to turn light brown. Add the spinach and cook until just done, about 5 minutes. Remove the skillet from the heat and add the cooked rice, oregano, Parmigiano-Reggiano, salt, pepper, and sausage.

3. Taste and adjust the seasonings, then stir in the eggs. Let the mixture cool and stuff it into the neck and body cavity of the turkey.

Lemon Turkey Kebabs
Yield: 4–6 servings

You could substitute peeled peaches, nectarines, cantaloupe, or pitted large plums for the mango and honeydew melon.

1 pound (454 g) turkey tenderloins, cut into 1-inch (2.5-cm) cubes
1 (6-ounce [168-g]) can frozen lemonade concentrate, thawed
3 tablespoons (45 mL) soy sauce
3 tablespoons (45 mL) olive oil
1 generous dash hot sauce
1 ripe but firm mango, pitted, peeled, and cut into 1½-inch (3.5-cm) chunks
¼ large honeydew melon, peeled and cut into 1½-inch (3.5-cm) chunks

1. Place the turkey in a 1- to 2-gallon (3.8- to 7.6-L) resealable plastic bag. In a small bowl, combine the lemonade, soy sauce, olive oil, and hot sauce. Reserve ¼ cup (59 mL) of this marinade and pour the rest over the turkey. Seal the bag and refrigerate for 4 hours or overnight.

2. Preheat the barbecue to medium high (350°F [180°C] to 400°F [200°C]) for grilling, making sure the grilling rack has been sprayed heavily with nonstick cooking or grilling spray.

3. Place mango and honeydew melon in the reserved ¼ cup (59 mL) of marinade and marinate for 20 minutes, turning the fruit often.

4. Remove the turkey from the marinade and thread it onto 10- to 12-inch (25- to 30-cm) metal skewers (or bamboo skewers you've soaked in hot water for an hour). Thread the fruit chunks, alternating fruits, onto separate skewers.

5. Grill the turkey kebabs for 10 to 12 minutes, or until the turkey is beginning to brown, there is no pink showing and the internal temperature of the turkey is 170°F (77°C). Grill the fruit kebabs for about 5 minutes.

6. Remove the kebabs from the grill and place them on a serving platter.

Bacon-Wrapped Turkey Burgers
Yield: 6 servings

Instead of the bacon you could grill slices of Canadian bacon while you cook the burgers. Add one slice each of Swiss cheese and beefsteak tomato for a delicious and hearty sandwich.

12 slices bacon
6 slices pineapple
1 pound (454 g) ground turkey
½ cup (118 mL) fine breadcrumbs
1 teaspoon (5 mL) Worcestershire sauce
½ teaspoon (2.5 mL) garlic salt
Salt, to taste
Freshly ground black paper, to taste
6 sesame seed hamburger buns, toasted

1. Preheat the barbecue to medium high (350°F [180°C] to 400°F [200°C]).

2. In a roasting pan, cook the bacon just until the fat starts to become translucent and set it aside. Grill the pineapple slices alongside the bacon until both sides have grill marks. Cover the pineapple with foil and set it aside.

3. In a large bowl, mix together the turkey, breadcrumbs, Worcestershire sauce, and garlic salt. Season with salt and pepper. Shape the mixture into 6½-inch (1-cm) thick patties. Criss-cross 2 slices of bacon on each patty, tucking the ends under. Secure the bacon with wooden picks stuck into the sides of the patties.

4. Grill the patties until the turkey springs back when touched and is no longer pink, about 4 minutes on each side.

5. Place a slice of pineapple and a bacon-wrapped patty on each toasted bun and serve.

Turkey–Noodle Barbecue Casserole
Yield: 4 servings

I like to use wide noodles in this dish, but you can use just about any pasta, including macaroni, ziti, spaghetti, fettuccine, bow tie, capellini, or fusilli.

1 (8-ounce [227-g]) can condensed cream of mushroom or cream of celery soup
½ cup (118 mL) milk
2 cups (473 mL) cooked egg noodles
2 cups (473 mL) cooked turkey (smoked preferred)
1 cup (236 mL) cooked peas and carrots
2 tablespoons (30 mL) chopped red bell pepper
2 tablespoons (30 mL) chopped green onions, green and white parts
Salt, to taste
Freshly ground black pepper, to taste
2 tablespoons (30 mL) butter, melted
¼ cup (59 mL) fresh breadcrumbs

1. Preheat the barbecue to medium high (350°F [180°C] to 400°F [200°C]). Butter a casserole dish.

2. In the prepared casserole, combine the soup and milk. Stir in the noodles, turkey, peas and carrots, bell pepper, and green onions. Season with salt and pepper. Bake, uncovered, for 25 minutes, or until the top of the casserole is starting to brown. Stir.

3. Meanwhile, in a small bowl, pour melted butter over the breadcrumbs and stir to combine. Spoon this mixture on top of the casserole, bake for 5 minutes more, and serve.

Thai Turkey Wings
Yield: 4 servings

Sriracha is made from ground chilies and garlic. It is probably the most popular hot sauce in Asia, which is funny, since it's made in and distributed from Southern California.

8 turkey wings
½ cup (118 mL) smooth peanut butter
½ cup (118 mL) water
3 tablespoons (45 mL) light soy sauce
3 tablespoons (45 mL) fresh lemon juice
2 tablespoons (30 mL) brown sugar
2 green onions, green and white parts, chopped
1 teaspoon (5 mL) fish sauce
3 drops Sriricha hot sauce

1. Discard the wing tips and separate the wings into 2 pieces.

2. Place the wings in a large saucepan and add water to cover. Bring to a boil, reduce the heat, and simmer for 20 minutes.

3. Meanwhile, in a small saucepan, combine the peanut butter, water, soy sauce, lemon juice, brown sugar, green onions, fish sauce, and Sriracha. Cook over medium heat, stirring well to dissolve the sugar. Let cool.

4. Remove the turkey from the water, allow it to cool, and place it in a 1- to 2-gallon (3.8- to 7.6-L) resealable plastic bag. Pour in the marinade, seal, shake the bag, and refrigerate for 4 to 6 hours or overnight, turning several times.

5. Preheat the barbecue to medium high (350°F [180°C] to 400°F [200°C]).

6. Remove the wings from the marinade. Pour the marinade into a saucepan and boil it for 10 minutes while the wings come to room temperature.

7. Grill wings for 15 to 20 minutes, turning and basting them often.

Athenian Roasted Turkey
Yield: 6–8 servings

The lemons, raisins, pine nuts, and sage are all key ingredients to Greek cooking, a style which was documented in the world's first cookbook, written by Archestratos in 330 B.C.

1 (10–12 pound [4.5–5.4 kg]) turkey
Juice of 1 lemon
3 tablespoons (45 mL) olive oil
1 cup (236 mL) chopped onion
¾ pound (336 g) ground beef
¾ cup (177 mL) uncooked long-grain rice
½ cup (118 mL) pine nuts
⅓ cup (79 mL) raisins
½ cup (118 mL) chopped fresh parsley
2 teaspoons (10 mL) ground oregano
Salt, to taste
Freshly ground black pepper, to taste
1 cup (236 mL) water
2 tablespoons (30 mL) all-purpose flour
1½ cups (354 mL) milk, heated

1. Preheat the barbecue to medium high (400°F [200°C] to 425°F [220°C]) for direct and indirect heating, putting a water pan under the unheated side of the grill. Spray a roasting pan with nonstick spray.

2. Remove the giblets from the turkey, finely chop them, and set them aside. Wash the turkey inside and out and dry it thoroughly with towels. Rub the turkey all over, inside and out, with the lemon juice and set it aside to absorb the juice.

3. In a large skillet, heat the olive oil over medium heat. Add the onion and cook until it is translucent. Add the giblets and cook, stirring constantly, until their red color has disappeared. Add the ground beef and cook, stirring constantly, until it crumbles. Add the rice and stir. Stir in the pine nuts. Add the raisins, parsley, oregano, salt, pepper, and water.

4. Cook, uncovered, until the water is absorbed and the rice is half cooked, about 15 minutes. Remove the stuffing from the heat and let it cool.

5. Stuff the turkey with the stuffing. Turn the tips of the wings backward and tie the legs together. Place the turkey in the prepared roasting pan and put the pan over direct heat for 30 minutes. Move the pan to the unheated side of the grill, close the vents to lower the temperature, and cook for 2 to 2½ hours, or until the legs pull away from the body easily. Transfer the turkey to a warm platter.

6. To make gravy from the pan juices and drippings, heat the roasting pan on the grill over medium heat until the drippings sizzle. Add the flour, stirring until it is absorbed by the drippings. Add the hot milk and cook, stirring constantly, until the gravy comes to a boil. Reduce the heat and simmer, stirring, until the gravy thickens. Season the gravy with salt and pepper and serve it with the turkey and the stuffing.

Mango Grilled Turkey Tenderloins

Yield: 3 servings

You could also spread homemade or store-bought pesto on the tenderloins before grilling.

2 teaspoons (10 mL) mango preserves
4 green onions
4 cloves garlic, peeled
1 teaspoon (5 mL) hot pepper sauce
¼ teaspoon (1.25 mL) freshly ground black pepper
1 teaspoon (5 mL) salt
2 teaspoons (10 mL) lime juice
1 teaspoon (5 mL) chopped lime peel
1 teaspoon (5 mL) soy sauce
1 (½-pound [227-g]) package turkey breast tenderloins

1. Preheat the barbecue to medium high (350°F [180°C] to 400°F [200°C]) for direct heating, putting a water pan under the unheated side of the grill. Cover the heated side of the grill with a 12-inch (30-cm) square piece of aluminum foil and spray the foil with nonstick grilling spray.

2. In food processor, purée the preserves, green onions, garlic, hot sauce, pepper, salt, lime juice, lime peel, and soy sauce into a thick paste. With a table knife, spread the paste onto the tenderloins.

3. Place the tenderloins on the foil and grill for 6 to 8 minutes. Turn the tenderloins, brush the second side with the purée, and grill for another 6 to 8 minutes, or until the tenderloin reaches 160°F (71°C) on a meat thermometer.

4. Remove the tenderloins from the grill and serve them with side dishes or as sandwiches on toasted, buttered hamburger buns or French bread rounds.

Oven-Barbecued Turkey Legs

Yield: 6 servings

I use one particular brand of soup base for making gravy—they offer ham, beef, chicken, pork, and vegetable flavors—because the first ingredient in each of these concentrated seasonings is the meat or poultry they are named for, and they contain less salt than bouillon cubes.

¼ cup (59 mL) all-purpose flour
½ teaspoon (2.5 mL) chili powder
¼ teaspoon (1.25 mL) freshly ground black pepper
6 turkey legs
¼ cup (59 mL) corn oil
½ cup (118 mL) barbecue sauce
½ cup (118 mL) water
½ teaspoon (2.5 mL) Penzeys turkey soup base

1. Preheat the barbecue to medium high (350°F [180°C] to 400°F [200°C]). Spray a roasting pan with nonstick cooking or grilling spray.

2. In a shallow bowl, combine the flour, chili powder, and pepper. Dredge the turkey legs in this mixture.

3. In a large skillet, heat the oil. Add the turkey legs and sauté, turning several times with tongs to brown all sides. Transfer the turkey to the prepared roasting pan.

4. In a medium bowl, combine the barbecue sauce, water, and soup base. Stir until the soup base is dissolved. Spoon this mixture over the turkey.

5. Cover the pan with foil and bake for 1 hour.

6. Uncover the pan and bake, turning and basting the legs often, for 1 hour, or until the turkey is tender. Serve with garlic mashed potatoes and grilled vegetables.

Grant's Turkey Potpie

Yield: 6 servings

For a variation on this recipe, add mushrooms (try fresh sliced morels), boiled pearl onions, and chopped hard-boiled egg, and finish with handfuls of grated cheese before you add the crust. This recipe comes from Grant Browne from Kimberly, British Columbia.

1 (10¾-ounce [301-g]) can condensed cream of mushroom soup
1 (5-ounce [140-g]) can evaporated milk
¼ cup (59 mL) chopped fresh parsley
½ teaspoon (2.5 mL) dried thyme
3 cups (708 mL) cubed cooked turkey, light and dark meat
1 (10-ounce [280-g]) bag frozen mixed vegetables, thawed and drained
½ teaspoon 2.5 mL) freshly ground black pepper
¼ teaspoon (1.25 mL) garlic salt
⅛ teaspoon (0.6 mL) hot sauce
¾ cup (177 mL) instant mashed potato flakes
¾ cup (177 mL) all-purpose flour
¼ cup (59 mL) grated Parmigiano-Reggiano cheese
⅓ cup (79 mL) cold butter
¼ cup (59 mL) ice water
1 egg yolk
2 tablespoons (30 mL) milk

1. Preheat the barbecue to medium high (350°F [180°C] to 400°F [200°C]) for indirect heating, putting a water pan under the unheated side of the grill. Grease a 7 × 11-inch (17.5 × 26.5-cm) baking dish or roasting pan.

2. In a large bowl, combine the soup, evaporated milk, parsley, and thyme and stir well. Add the turkey, mixed vegetables, pepper, garlic salt, and hot sauce and stir to mix. Spoon the mixture into the prepared baking dish or roasting pan.

3. In a medium bowl, combine the potato flakes, flour, and cheese. Using a fork or a pastry cutter, cut in the butter and mix until crumbly. Add the water, 1 tablespoon (15 mL) at a time, mixing lightly with a fork after each addition, until the dough forms a ball.

4. Place the dough on a lightly floured surface. Roll it out into a rectangle large enough to cover the top of the baking dish. Place the dough over filling and flute the edges. Cut vents in the pastry. In a small bowl, combine the egg yolk and milk. Brush the crust with the egg wash mixture. Bake for 25 to 30 minutes, or until the crust is golden brown and the filling is bubbling. Halfway through the baking time, cover the outer edges of the crust with strips of aluminum foil to prevent the edges from burning.

Grilled Turkey Steaks with Pineapple Sauce
Yield: 4–6 servings

Pineapple plants give their lives for us—literally. Each pineapple plant produces one fruit and then dies. However, the top leaves, which are removed in the processing of the fruit, can be planted, and a new plant will grow.

1 (6-pound [2.7-kg]) full turkey breast (2 halves), with skin
1 cup (236 mL) honey
1 cup (236 mL) plus ¼ teaspoon (1.25 mL) salt, divided
1 tablespoon (15 mL) dried basil
1 tablespoon (15 mL) dried thyme
6 cups (1.4 L) cold water
½ cup (118 mL) rice wine vinegar
3 cups (708 mL) pineapple juice
¼ teaspoon (1.25 mL) freshly ground black pepper
½ teaspoon (2.5 mL) ground cumin
½ teaspoon (2.5 mL) ground coriander
⅛ teaspoon (0.6 mL) ground cloves
½ teaspoon (2.5 mL) crushed red pepper flakes
2 tablespoons (30 mL) brown sugar
2 tablespoons (30 mL) fresh lemon juice
½ cup (118 mL) minced sweet onion

1. With a sharp knife, remove the turkey breast from the bone by gently pulling the meat from bone. Separate the breast into 2 halves. Slice the turkey breasts into steak-size portions, ¾-inch (1.5-cm) thick and ¼ pound (112 g) each. In a saucepan, combine the honey, 1 cup (236 mL) of the salt, the basil, the thyme, the water, and the vinegar and bring the mixture to a boil.

2. Cool the marinade. Place the turkey steaks in a 1- to 2-gallon (3.8- to 7.6-L) resealable plastic bag and pour in the marinade. Seal the bag, shake to coat, and refrigerate for 4 to 6 hours or overnight, turning several times.

3. Preheat the barbecue to medium high (350°F [180°C] to 400°F [200°C]) for direct grilling. Heavily spray the grill with nonstick grilling spray.

4. Remove the turkey from the bag and let it come to room temperature. Discard the marinade.

5. In a saucepan, combine the pineapple juice, the remaining salt, the pepper, the cumin, the coriander, the cloves, the red pepper flakes, the brown sugar, the lemon juice, and the onion. Bring to low boil, stirring. Reduce the heat and simmer for 20 to 30 minutes, stirring occasionally. Remove the pan from the heat, cover, and set aside.

6. Grill the turkey steaks for about 8 to 10 minutes. Turn and grill for another 8 to 10 minutes, or until the internal temperature of the steaks reaches 170°F (77°C).

7. Serve the steaks on a heated platter, drizzled with the pineapple sauce.

Last-Minute Turkey and Stuffing Pie

Yield: 6 servings

Most baby corn sold in the United States is grown in Asia, especially in Taiwan, China, and Thailand, where cooks use it frequently in stir-fry meals. It's great in salads and pasta dishes as well, as the small ears readily absorb whatever sauce they're cooked in. This recipe comes from Dr. Robert Browne from Indianapolis, Ind.

2 cups (473 mL) diced cooked turkey
½ teaspoon (2.5 mL) seasoned salt
1 cup (236 mL) prepared turkey stuffing
½ cup (118 mL) cooked green peas
½ cup (118 mL) canned whole baby corn (or fresh, if you can find it)
¼ cup (59 mL) sliced green onions, green and white parts
1 cup (236 mL) whole milk
2 large eggs
½ cup (118 mL) Bisquick baking mix

1. Preheat the barbecue to medium high (400°F [200°C] to 425°F [220°C]) for indirect heating, putting a water pan under the unheated side of the grill. Spray a 9-inch (22.5-cm) square baking dish with nonstick cooking or grilling spray

2. Arrange the diced turkey in the prepared dish and sprinkle it with the seasoned salt. Separate the stuffing into small pieces and arrange it on top of the turkey. Top with the peas, baby corn, and onions.

3. In a mixing bowl, beat together the milk, eggs, and baking mix until the batter is smooth. Pour this batter over the turkey, stuffing, and vegetables. Bake in the barbecue over the unheated side of the grill for approximately 30 to 35 minutes, or until a knife inserted in the center comes out clean.

4. Let the pie cool for 5 minutes, and serve with hot turkey gravy, mashed sweet potatoes, and cranberry sauce.

Fruit-Stuffed Turkey Breasts

Yield: 10–12 servings

If these fruits don't ring your bell, you can chop up equal amounts of apples, pears, and peaches and use those to stuff the breasts.

2 boneless turkey breast halves
1 (10-ounce [280-g]) package pitted dates
1 (6-ounce [168-g]) package dried apricots
2 cups (473 mL) dry white wine
1 cup (236 mL) cashew pieces
½ teaspoon (2.5 mL) ground cinnamon
¼ teaspoon (1.25 mL) freshly ground black pepper
¼ teaspoon (1.25 mL) ground ginger
¼ teaspoon (1.25 mL) ground nutmeg
¼ teaspoon (1.25 mL) ground cloves

1. Preheat the barbecue to medium high (350°F [180°C] to 400°F [200°C]). Butter or spray with nonstick cooking spray a roasting pan.

2. Cut 3 parallel, lengthwise, 1-inch (2.5-cm) deep slits 2–3 inches (5–7.5 cm) apart in each turkey breast half. Place the turkey breast halves flat in the prepared pan, cover, and set aside.

3. Cut the fruit in small chunks and place them in a saucepan. Add the wine, cashews, cinnamon, pepper, ginger, nutmeg, and coves. Cook over medium heat, stirring constantly, until the mixture boils. Reduce the heat and simmer, stirring, for 2 minutes. Let cool slightly.

4. Spoon the cooled fruit into the slits in turkey. Place the roasting pan in the barbecue and cook for 2 hours.

5. Remove the pan from the barbecue and let the meat rest for 10 minutes. Slice each breast half into 5 to 6 thick slices and serve with the pan juices dribbled over the turkey.

Sauced Drumsticks

Yield: 4 servings

Do not use diet colas here, as they turn bitter when cooked. If you don't wish to use a soft drink you can substitute apple, orange, or cranberry-apple juice for the cola.

4 (1–1½ pound) turkey drumsticks
¼ cup (59 mL) melted bacon drippings
Salt, to taste
Freshly ground black pepper, to taste
½ cup (118 mL) barbecue sauce
½ cup (118 mL) orange marmalade
½ cup cola (RC Cola preferred)
¼ teaspoon (1.25 mL) cayenne pepper
1 tablespoon (5 mL) butter

1. Preheat the barbecue to medium high (350°F [180°C] to 400°F [200°C]) for indirect heating, putting a water pan under the unheated side of the grill. Spray a roasting pan with nonstick cooking spray.

2. Brush the drumsticks with the bacon drippings, season them with salt and pepper, and place them in the prepared roasting pan. Cover the pan and cook for 1 to 1¼ hours, or until tender, turning and basting occasionally with pan drippings during cooking.

3. In small saucepan, combine the barbecue sauce, marmalade, cola, and cayenne pepper. Cook until the sauce just barely begins to bubble. Add the butter and stir to melt. Brush this mixture over the drumsticks 2 or 3 times as they cook for 20 minutes more.

4. Serve the drumsticks with the pan juices and any remaining sauce.

Grilled Cajun Turkey

Yield: 4–6 servings

You can also cook this recipe using a half turkey; just increase the oil by 2 tablespoons (30 mL) and double the rub ingredients. The cooking time will be about the same.

1 (3-pound [1.3-kg]) boneless turkey breast, thawed
2 tablespoons (30 mL) olive oil
1 tablespoon (15 mL) onion flakes
1 tablespoon (15 mL) garlic powder
½ teaspoon (2.5 mL) dried thyme
¼ teaspoon (1.25 mL) cayenne pepper
¼ teaspoon (1.25 mL) anise seed
¼ teaspoon (1.25 mL) ground cloves
¼ teaspoon (1.25 mL) ground allspice
1 bay leaf, crushed

1. Preheat the barbecue to medium high (350°F [180°C] to 400°F [200°C]) for indirect heating, putting a water pan under the unheated side of the grill. Make sure you've generously sprayed the grill with nonstick grilling spray.

2. Brush the turkey with the olive oil. In a small bowl, combine the onion flakes, garlic powder, thyme, cayenne pepper, anise seed, cloves, allspice, and crushed bay leaves and mix well. Sprinkle this mixture on the turkey, rubbing it well into the meat and under the skin wherever possible.

3. Place the turkey on the indirect side of the grill and cook for approximately 45 minutes, turning often.

4. When the temperature in the breast reaches 165°F (74°C), wrap the meat in foil and let it stand for 10 to 15 minutes. The juices will recirculate and the temperature will rise to 170°F (77°C). Slice the turkey and serve.

Lemon-Barbecued Turkey

Yield: 4–8 servings

If you don't want to use lemons, try mandarin orange juice with grated mandarin orange zest, or lime or grapefruit juices (adding ½ cup [118 mL] sugar to the grapefruit juice) with their corresponding grated zests. Or, mix a couple of them together.

4 small cloves garlic, peeled and crushed
2 teaspoons (10 mL) celery salt
1¾ cups (413 mL) lemon juice
½ cup (118 mL) grated lemon zest
1 cup (236 mL) vegetable oil
½ cup (118 mL) chopped onion
2 teaspoons (10 mL) ground thyme
2 teaspoons (10 mL) lemon pepper
1 (10–10½ pound [4.5–4.7 kg]) turkey, quartered

1. In a medium bowl, combine the garlic, celery salt, lemon juice, lemon zest, oil, onion, thyme, and pepper and mix well. Place the turkey in a 2-gallon (7.6-L) resealable plastic bag and pour the marinade in over it. Seal the bag and marinate overnight in the refrigerator.

2. Preheat the barbecue to medium high (350°F [180°C] to 400°F [200°C]).

3. Remove the turkey from the marinade. Pour the marinade into a saucepan and boil for 10 minutes while the turkey comes to room temperature.

4. Place the turkey, skin side down, on the grill. Cook for about 2 hours, turning every 15 minutes and brushing often with the sauce. Turkey is ready when it's nicely browned all over, firm to the touch, and the juices that run out when a knife is inserted into the thigh are clear, not pink.

Tied Thai Thighs

Yield: 4–6 servings

While living in Thailand for 4 months, I watched this being made at a cooking school in Chiang Mai. They used a very fiery red chili paste. I suggest a milder version for American palates. This recipe comes from Rick and Jennifer Browne from Oxford, Ohio.

2 (¾-pound [336-g] boned turkey thighs
¼ cup (59 mL) chopped fresh basil
¼ cup (59 mL) chopped fresh cilantro
¼ cup (59 mL) chopped fresh mint
4 cloves garlic, peeled and minced
1 tablespoon (15 mL) brown sugar
1 tablespoon (15 mL) soy sauce
2 teaspoons (10 mL) grated fresh ginger
2 teaspoons (10 mL) Asian fish sauce (nuoc mam or nam pla)
2 teaspoons (10 mL) vegetable oil
½ teaspoon (2.5 mL) Asian red chili paste
Lime wedges, for serving
Kosher salt, for serving

1. Preheat the barbecue to medium high (350°F [180°C] to 400°F [200°C]) for indirect heating, putting a water pan under the unheated side of the grill.

2. Rinse and pat dry the turkey thighs.

3. In a small bowl, combine the basil, cilantro, mint, garlic, brown sugar, soy sauce, ginger, fish sauce, oil, and chili paste and mix well.

4. Spread about 2 tablespoons (30 mL) of the mixture evenly over the boned side of a turkey thigh. Set the remaining thigh, boned side down, over the first thigh, and tie them together at 1-inch (2.5-cm) intervals with cotton string to create a piece of meat about 3 inches (7.5 cm) wide by 7 inches (17.5 cm) long. Spread the remaining paste all over the thighs.

5. Place the thighs on the indirect side of the grill, over the water pan, and roast for 40 to 45 minutes, or until a thermometer inserted in the center of the meat reads 175°F (79°C).

6. Transfer the thighs to a platter and, keeping them warm, let them rest for 5 to 10 minutes.

7. Cut the thighs into ½-inch (1-cm) thick slices to serve. Squeeze the lime wedges over the slices and lightly sprinkle them with salt.

8. Serve with coconut rice and steamed vegetables.

Rotisserie Tea and Orange Turkey

Yield: 6–8 servings

This is a small turkey. Keep in mind that most rotisserie units included with grills are not able to accommodate a turkey larger than 12 to 14 pounds (5.4–6.4 kg).

1 (8–10 pound [3.6–4.5 kg]) turkey
4 cups hot water
5 black tea bags (orange pekoe preferred)
Grated zest of 1 large orange
¼ cup (59 mL) frozen orange juice concentrate, thawed
2 teaspoons (10 mL) grated fresh ginger
2 teaspoons (10 mL) salt
3 tablespoons (45 mL) olive oil
2 tablespoons (30 mL) kosher salt
1 tablespoon (15 mL) garlic pepper

1. Clean and dry the turkey and place it in a 2-gallon (7.6-L) resealable plastic bag. In a large bowl, combine the hot water, tea bags, orange zest, orange juice concentrate, ginger, and 2 teaspoons salt. Pour this mixture into the bag over the turkey. Seal the bag, turn it to distribute the marinade, and refrigerate overnight, turning several times.

2. Remove the turkey from the bag. Pour the marinade into a saucepan and boil for 10 minutes while the turkey comes to room temperature.

3. Preheat the barbecue to medium high (350°F [180°C] to 400°F [200°C]) for indirect heating, putting a water pan under the unheated center of the grill. If you're using charcoal, mound it around the water pan; if you're using gas, turn on the outside gas jets only, leaving the center jet closed.

4. Truss the turkey, place it on the rotisserie, and secure it. Brush the turkey with the olive oil and sprinkle it with the 2 tablespoons kosher salt and garlic pepper.

5. Place the turkey on the rotisserie base and cook until the breast reaches an internal temperature of 170°F (77°C) and the thighs reach 180°F (82°C), about 10 to 15 minutes per pound

6. Remove the turkey from the grill and rotisserie bar, cover it with foil, and let it rest for 20 minutes before carving.

Barbecue Pit Turkey Pizza
Yield: 8 servings

You may wish to include chunks of the dark meat (thighs and leg) so that you have a mixture of turkey on the pizza. We cook this using a Big Easy Pizza Plank, which is available at barbecue or grocery stores or online at www.tailgatingplanks.com/chef. You'll need a bread machine to make this recipe.

1 cup (236 mL) warm water (70°F [21°C] to 80°F [27°C])
2 tablespoons (30 mL) olive oil
1 tablespoon (15 mL) sugar
1 teaspoon (5 mL) salt
3 cups (708 mL) all-purpose flour
2 teaspoons (10 mL) active dry yeast
¾ cup (177 mL) sweet, smoky barbecue sauce, divided
1½ cups (413 mL) cubed cooked turkey breast
½ cup (118 mL) canned baby corn
1 small red onion, peeled and cut into thin rings
1 small green bell pepper, cut into thin rings
1 clove garlic, peeled and finely minced
1 cup (236 mL) (4 oz.) shredded part-skim mozzarella cheese
½ cup (118 mL) shredded cheddar cheese
¼ cup (59 mL) freshly grated Parmigiano-Reggiano cheese
1 cup (236 mL) thinly sliced mushrooms

1. Preheat the barbecue to medium high (400°F [200°C] to 425°F [220°C]) for direct and indirect heating, putting a water pan under the unheated side of the grill. Brush the top of the Big Easy Pizza Plank with olive oil.

2. In a bread machine pan, place the water, olive oil, sugar, salt, flour, and yeast in the manufacturer's suggested order. Select the dough setting. Check the dough after 5 minutes of mixing and add 1 to 2 tablespoons (15 to 30 mL) of water or flour if needed. When the cycle is complete, turn the dough out onto a lightly floured surface. Punch it down; cover it and let it stand for 10 minutes. Roll the dough into a 14-inch (35-cm) circle. Transfer it to the prepared pizza plank and build up the edges slightly.

3. Spread all but 2 tablespoons (30 mL) of the barbecue sauce over the crust. Add the turkey, corn, onion, green pepper, garlic, and cheeses. Drizzle the top with the remaining barbecue sauce, and add the mushrooms. Bake for 25 to 30 minutes over indirect heat, or until the crust is golden brown and the sauce is bubbling.

4. Remove pizza from the plank and cook for additional 10 minutes directly on the grill to crisp up the bottom.

5. Let the pizza rest for 3 to 4 minutes, then slice and serve.

Turkey and Sweet Potato Loaf

Yield: 4–6 servings

To make this a bit more substantial, you can use ½ cup (118 mL) ground beef or ground sausage instead of the ½ cup (118 mL) of turkey.

2 large sweet potatoes, peeled and sliced
1½ pounds (681 g) ground turkey breast
2 large eggs
1 medium onion, peeled and finely chopped
1 tablespoon (15 mL) chopped chives
½ teaspoon (2.5 mL) poultry seasoning
3 cloves garlic, peeled and minced
¼ cup (59 mL) honey
½ cup (118 mL) ketchup
3 tablespoons (45 mL) Dijon mustard
4 slices wheat bread, torn into fingertip-size pieces
1 teaspoon (5 mL) freshly ground black pepper
1½ teaspoons (7.5 mL) lemon salt

1. Preheat the barbecue to medium high (350°F [180°C] to 400°F [200°C]) for direct heating. Lightly grease a 2-quart (1.9-L) loaf pan.

2. In a large saucepan, boil the sweet potato in water until tender, about 10 minutes. Drain thoroughly and whip with a hand-held mixer until very fluffy.

3. In a large bowl, fold the turkey together with the eggs, onion, chives, poultry seasoning, garlic, honey, ketchup, mustard, and breadcrumbs. Season with lemon salt and pepper, add the sweet potatoes, and stir until well mixed. If the mixture seems too wet, add more pieces of torn bread.

4. Spoon the mixture into the loaf, making sure there are no air pockets. Place the pan in the barbecue and cook for 1 hour.

5. Remove the pan from the barbecue, cover it, and let it cool slightly. Slice and serve.

Cedar-Planked Turkey Tenderloins

Yield: 6 servings

Turkey tenderloins are the tender, long strip of white meat hidden under the breast. This strip of meat is quite devoid of fat and excellent for recipes. It doesn't take long to cook, and cooking it on a soaked plank ensures that it stays moist. This recipe comes from Russ Falk from Kalamazoo Outdoors.

1 large clove garlic, peeled
2–3 tablespoons (30–45 mL) olive oil
6 turkey tenderloins
12 fresh sage leaves
6 fresh thyme sprigs
Fine sea salt, to taste

1. Soak a ⅜-inch (1-cm) thick wood cedar plank large enough to hold all 6 tenderloins for at least 4 to 6 hours.

2. Preheat the grill to 400°F (200°C) for direct grilling. To help kill bacteria, place the plank on the preheated grill for 1 minute with the side you want to put the turkey on facing down, and then remove it.

3. Cut the garlic clove in half, and rub the cut side of half of the clove into the plank. Rub 1 tablespoon (15 mL) of the olive oil into the plank.

4. Arrange the turkey tenderloins on the plank with 2 sage leaves and 1 sprig of thyme under each tenderloin (between the turkey and the plank). Rub the other garlic clove half into the tops of the tenderloins, and then very lightly brush them with the remaining olive oil. Sprinkle each tenderloins with a pinch of fine sea salt.

5. Place the loaded plank in the center of the direct grilling zone and close the grill. Cook until the juices run clear, about 30 minutes. Check the plank every 5 minutes to see if it is burning. Have a squirt bottle of water ready to douse any flames that may erupt from the plank.

6. Remove the plank and turkey from the grill. Discard the herbs from the bottoms of the tenderloins. Replace the tenderloins on the plank, and place the plank on a platter in the middle of the table for serving.

FIFTEEN

Wild Game

Teriyaki Buffalo Burgers

Yield: 4 servings

This recipe also works well with ground venison, elk, or moose. But please cook to medium-rare or medium only, as buffalo, like most game meats, is very lean and becomes dry and tough when overcooked. Burgers are medium-rare when internal temperature is 140°F and medium at 150°F. They should take about 4 to 5 minutes per side.

¼ cup (59 mL) pineapple juice
2 tablespoons (30 mL) brown sugar
1 tablespoon (15 mL) chopped sweet onion, such as Vidalia
1 teaspoon (5 mL) ground ginger
1 teaspoon (5 mL) finely chopped garlic
Thin slices fresh pineapple, for garnish
Olive oil or cooking spray
1 pound (454 g) ground buffalo meat
4 hamburger buns

1. Preheat a gas or charcoal grill to 350°F (180°C) to 400°F (200°C) for direct grilling.

2. In a small saucepan, mix together the pineapple juice, brown sugar, onion, ginger, and garlic. Bring to a boil, stir until well mixed, and set aside.

3. Brush the pineapple slices with olive oil or spray them with cooking spray. Grill the slices until they are marked on both sides, about 2 minutes per side, remove them from the grill, and set them aside for garnish.

4. Form the buffalo meat into 4 equal-sized patties. Using half the marinade, marinate the burgers for 30 minutes, turning several times.

5. Grill the burgers until done (no more than medium), turning once and brushing with the remaining marinade. Brush with more marinade just before removing them from the grill.

6. Remove the burgers from grill. Place each burger on a bun, add a full slice of grilled pineapple to each burger, and serve.

Venison, Bacon, and Sage Burgers

Yield: 4 servings

If you can't get venison you can try buffalo, elk, moose, or antelope in this recipe. All make great burgers. Be careful not to overcook any wild game meats, as they are much leaner than beef.

1½ pounds (681 g) venison steak, cut in 1-inch (2.5-cm) chunks
5 slices hickory-smoked bacon, chopped
1 large onion, peeled and minced
2 cloves garlic, peeled and roughly chopped
1 tablespoon (15 mL) ground sage
1 tablespoon (15 mL) ketchup
1 large egg, beaten
1 tablespoon (15 mL) Worcestershire sauce
Salt, to taste
Freshly ground black pepper, to taste

1. Make sure the grill is clean and generously sprayed with nonstick grilling spray. Preheat the barbecue to medium high (350°F [180°C] to 400°F [200°C]).

2. In a food processor, combine the venison, bacon, onion, garlic, sage, ketchup, egg, Worcestershire sauce, salt, and pepper and process to a coarse grind.

3. Divide the mixture into 4 portions and shape each portion into a burger a little less than 1-inch (2.5-cm) thick.

4. In a cast-iron skillet on a side burner or on the barbecue, grill the burgers for about 3½ to 4 minutes per side, turning once, until the meat is cooked to your preference. Medium-rare or medium is as far as you should go with wild game meats.

5. Serve with your favorite condiments and fresh tomato and onion slices.

Blackberry Venison Tenderloin

Yield: 4–6 servings

This recipe works best if the venison is fresh, or, if frozen, very well thawed.

1 cup (236 mL) soy sauce
½ cup (118 mL) sweet red wine
¼ cup (59 mL) olive oil
¼ cup (59 mL) butter, melted
2 tablespoons (30 mL) balsamic vinegar
1 (3-pound [1.3-kg]) venison (or elk) tenderloin
2¼ cups (590 mL) fresh (preferred) or frozen blackberries, divided
¼ cup (59 mL) rice wine vinegar
2 tablespoons (30 mL) dark brown sugar
1 teaspoon (5 mL) lemon pepper
1 teaspoon (5 mL) garlic salt
½ teaspoon (2.5 mL) ground nutmeg
¼ teaspoon (1.25 mL) ground cinnamon
¼ teaspoon (1.25 mL) ground cloves
Fresh parsley or sage, for garnish

1. Place 2 handfuls of hickory or fruit wood chips in water to soak overnight.

2. In a small bowl, combine the soy sauce, wine, olive oil, butter, and balsamic vinegar. Place the tenderloin in a resealable plastic bag with this marinade. Seal and refrigerate overnight. Remove the meat from marinade, wipe if off, and let the meat sit for about 20 minutes to come to room temperature. Boil the remaining marinade for 10 minutes so it can be used to baste the meat.

3. Preheat a gas or charcoal grill to 350°F (180°C) to 400°F (200°C) for direct grilling.

4. Push 2 cups of the blackberries through a fine sieve or use a food mill to separate the juice from the pulp and seeds. Pour the juice into a small saucepan and add the rice wine vinegar, brown sugar, lemon pepper, garlic salt, nutmeg, cinnamon, and cloves and cook for approximately 10 minutes, or until the sauce is slightly thickened. Remove the pan from the burner and set it aside to cool.

5. Scatter the soaked wood chips over the coals. Place the tenderloin on the grill and baste it with the marinade. Close the lid and cook for 10 minutes. Turn the tenderloin and baste again. Close the lid and cook for another 10 minutes, or until the internal temperature reaches approximately 135°F (57°C) for medium-rare or 145°F (63°C) for medium. Remove the meat from the grill, cover it with foil, and let it rest for 10 minutes. The temperature will rise 5°F (2°C) to 10°F (4°C) during this time.

6. Place the roast on a heated platter, garnish it with parsley or sage, and remaining ¼ cup blackberries, and serve the sauce on the side.

Boone and Crockett Venison Chili
Yield: 4–6 servings

Lots of ingredients make this a very complex and tasty chili. It tastes great the first day and even better reheated the next day.

4 pounds (2.2 kg) boneless venison, cubed
¼ cup (60 mL) bacon grease
2 onions peeled and chopped
2 jalapeño peppers, seeded and chopped
½ cup (118 mL) chopped green bell pepper
½ cup (118 mL) chopped red bell pepper
2 cloves garlic, chopped
12 ounces (354 mL) beer
2 tablespoons (30 mL) whiskey
2 cups (473 mL) stewed tomatoes
1 (8-ounce [224-g]) can tomato sauce
1 cup (236 mL) dry red wine
5 tablespoons (75 mL) ground cumin
5 tablespoons (75 mL) chili powder
3 tablespoons (45 mL) soy sauce
½ teaspoon (2.5 mL) salt
½ teaspoon (2.5 mL) cayenne pepper
2 tablespoons (30 mL) masa harina (tortilla flour)

1. In a large cast-iron skillet or Dutch oven over the barbecue side burner, brown the venison in bacon grease. Remove the venison from the pan and set it aside. To the remaining grease, add the onions, jalapeño peppers, green and red bell peppers, and garlic and sauté until the onions start to become transparent.

2. Preheat the barbecue to medium high (350°F [180°C] to 400°F [200°C]). Move the Dutch oven to the grill. Return the meat to the pan and stir. Stir in the beer and whiskey, bring to a boil, and boil for 5 to 7 minutes. Reduce the heat to medium.

3. Add the tomatoes, tomato sauce, wine, cumin, chili powder, soy sauce, salt, and cayenne pepper. Cook, stirring occasionally, for 30 minutes. Add the masa harina and stir well. Reduce the heat to a simmer and cook for 1 hour more.

4. Serve with chopped onions, shredded cheddar cheese, and very cold beer.

Venison Medallions with Mushrooms

Yield: 8 servings

You can use any mushroom in this dish, such as button or crimini, but if you really want to dress it up, go for chanterelles, morels, or oyster mushrooms. The taste difference is spectacular.

3½ tablespoons (52.5 mL) butter, divided
¼ cup (59 mL) diced carrot
¼ cup (59 mL) diced celery
¼ cup (59 mL) diced onion
1 bay leaf
½ teaspoon (2.5 mL) dried thyme
½ teaspoon (2.5 mL) cracked black peppercorns
⅔ cup (158 mL) brandy
½ cup (118 mL) honey
1 teaspoon (5 mL) ground sage
⅔ cup (158 mL) beef stock
8 (1-inch [2.5-cm] thick) venison filets
Salt, to taste
Freshly ground black pepper, to taste
2 cups ¼-inch-thick sliced mushrooms

1. Preheat the barbecue to medium high (350°F [180°C] to 400°F [200°C]), making sure grill is well oiled or sprayed with non-stick grilling spray.

2. In a cast-iron skillet, melt 2 tablespoons (30 mL) of the butter over low heat. Add the carrots, celery, and onions, cover, and cook until tender. Add the bay leaf, thyme, and peppercorns. Add the brandy, honey, and sage, and flambé. When the flames go out, add the beef stock. Cook until the sauce is reduced by two-thirds, then whisk in the remaining butter.

3. Sear the filets on the hot grill for 2 minutes per side. Add them to the sauce in the skillet, ladling the sauce over the meat. Season with salt and freshly ground black pepper. Cover with the mushrooms and place the skillet in the barbecue for 20 minutes, or until the mushrooms are softened and browned.

4. Remove the pan from the barbecue. Top each filet with a large spoonful of mushrooms and the remaining sauce.

Venison Loin Chops with Apricot-Mango Chutney
Yield: 4 servings

This dish is best served with a full-bodied, robust red wine, such as a domestic Cabernet Sauvignon, Pinot Noir, or Shiraz; an Argentinean Malbec; or an Italian Barolo.

2 cups (473 mL) white wine vinegar
1¼ cup (233 g) golden raisins
4 medium apricots, diced
3 medium mangoes, peeled, pitted, and diced
1⅛ cup (230 g) sugar
½ red onion, finely diced
1 red bell pepper, finely diced
1 teaspoon (5 mL) ground cardamom
1 teaspoon (5 mL) ground ginger
1 teaspoon (5 mL) salt
1 teaspoon (5 mL) ground white pepper
½ cup (118 mL) olive oil
2 cloves garlic, peeled and chopped
1 sprig rosemary, leaves only
1 sprig thyme, leaves only
2 teaspoons (10 mL) black peppercorns
8 (4-ounce [112-g]) venison loin chops
1 teaspoon (5 mL) kosher salt

1. In a saucepan, combine the vinegar, raisins, apricots, mangoes, sugar, red onion, bell pepper, cardamom, ginger, salt, and white pepper. Bring to a simmer and cook, uncovered, for 45 minutes, stirring often. If you're making it ahead, let the chutney cool, then transfer it to clean jars and refrigerate. Warm it up to use with meat recipes.

2. In small frying pan, heat the oil over very low heat. Add the garlic, rosemary, thyme, and cracked peppercorns and heat through. Stir and cook for 10 minutes to let the flavors mix.

3. Preheat the barbecue to medium high (350°F [180°C] to 400°F [200°C]).

4. Brush the venison chops with the olive oil mixture and sprinkle them with the kosher salt. Place them on the heated grill and cook for 4 to 5 minutes per side, or until the meat is cooked the way you like it, basting every time you turn it. Let the loin chops rest, covered, for 2 minutes before serving.

5. Serve each person 2 grilled chops with 1 to 2 generous tablespoons (15 to 30 mL) of the warm chutney.

Venison-Stuffed Bell Peppers

Yield: 4–8 servings

If you wish to add a little more character to this recipe, use diced cubes of venison instead of the ground meat, or use half ground and half cubed. You could also use elk, or mix venison with bear, wild boar, or moose.

1 large yellow onion, peeled and diced
4 tablespoons (60 mL) olive oil, divided
1 cup (236 mL) diced mushrooms
3 tablespoons (45 mL) balsamic vinegar, divided
1 tablespoon (15 mL) minced garlic
1½ teaspoons (7.5 mL) freshly ground black pepper, divided
1 teaspoon (5 mL) dried oregano
1 teaspoon (5 mL) dried basil
1 teaspoon (5 mL) celery salt
1 pound (454 g) ground venison
1 (14-ounce [396-g]) package Pepperidge Farm cornbread stuffing
1 cup (236 mL) (salt free) chicken broth or water
1 pound (454 g) broccoli, broken into 1-inch (2.5-cm) florets
1 pound (454 g) yellow squash, sliced
1 (15.25-ounce [432-g]) can corn
½ pound (227 g) fresh sliced mushrooms
1 (8-ounce [226-g]) bottle artichoke hearts, drained and diced
1 teaspoon (5 mL) salt
4 medium red bell peppers
4 medium green or yellow bell peppers
3 (15-ounce [420-g]) cans tomato sauce
1 (6-ounce [168-g]) can tomato paste

1. Preheat a gas or charcoal grill to medium high (350°F [180°C] to 400°F [200°C]) for direct grilling. Spray with nonstick cooking spray or grease a 6-quart (5.7-L) Dutch oven.

2. In a cast-iron skillet, cook the onion in 2 tablespoons of olive oil over medium heat until translucent. Add the diced mushrooms, 1 tablespoon (15 mL) of the vinegar, the garlic, ½ teaspoon (2.5 mL) of the black pepper, the oregano, the basil, and the celery salt and heat through. Add the ground venison and cook, stirring, until the meat is browned all over. Add the stuffing and broth and stir well, set aside to cool.

3. In a medium bowl, combine the broccoli, squash, sliced mushrooms, corn, and artichokes. Add the salt. Add the remaining vinegar and oil and stir to mix well. Cut off the tops off the bell peppers and remove the seeds and membranes. Fill the bell peppers with the meat filling, packing down lightly so the peppers are well-filled.

4. Pour the cans of tomato sauce and tomato paste into the prepared Dutch oven and stir. There should be 1½ inches (3.5 cm) of liquid in the bottom of the pan; add water if you are a bit shy of this measurement. Place the peppers upright in the pot, making them snug. Place the Dutch oven on the grill and cook for 25 minutes, or until the vegetables are just beginning to get tender and the meat is well browned on top.

Scott's Venison Goulash
Yield: 4–6 servings

The High Lonesome Ranch is one of Colorado's—and America's—premier hunting ranches for black bear, cougar, wild turkeys, pheasant, chukkar, partridges—and more deer and elk than I've ever seen in one spot. For the fisherman, there are browns, rainbows, cutthroats, brooks, and cut bows lurking in the ponds and surrounding rivers. This recipe comes from Scott Hutchinson from High Lonesome Ranch in DeBeque, Colo.

2 pounds (908 g) venison flank meat
2 tablespoons (30 mL) olive oil
3 large onions, peeled and thinly sliced
3 tablespoons (45 mL) mild Hungarian paprika
1 teaspoon (5 mL) salt
1 large red bell pepper, thinly sliced
½ cup (118 mL) water
¼ cup (59 mL) sweet red wine

1. Preheat the barbecue to medium high (350°F [180°C] to 400°F [200°C]).

2. Cut the venison into 1-inch (2.5-cm) cubes. In a deep cast-iron pot or Dutch oven, heat the olive oil. Add the venison cubes and cook until all the pieces are well browned.

3. Add the onions, paprika, and salt and continue cooking, stirring often, until the onions have softened. Add the red pepper slices, water, and wine, cover, and cook over medium-low heat for 1½ hours, or until the venison is fork tender.

4. Serve with cooked wide noodles or dumplings.

Venison Lasagna
Yield: 4–6 servings

I've also made this dish using ½ pound (227 g) of ground elk in addition to the venison sausage, but you could use just about any ground game meat, including moose, rabbit, wild turkey, duck, buffalo, or goose breast.

1 pound (454 g) spicy or mild venison sausage
2 teaspoons (10 mL) onion salt
2 teaspoons (10 mL) garlic salt
1 (16-ounce [454-g]) can whole tomatoes
1 (15-ounce [420-g]) can tomato sauce
3 tablespoons (45 mL) chopped fresh parsley, divided
1 teaspoon (5 mL) brown sugar
1 teaspoon (5 mL) minced fresh basil
1½ teaspoons (7.5 mL) seasoned salt, divided
1 (8-ounce [227-g]) package sliced mushrooms
6 lasagna noodles, uncooked
16 ounces (454 g) ricotta cheese
½ cup (118 mL) grated Parmesan cheese, divided
1½ teaspoons (7.5 mL) dried oregano
2 cups (473 mL) shredded mozzarella cheese, divided

1. Preheat the barbecue to medium high (350°F [180°C] to 400°F [200°C]).

2. In a cast-iron skillet, cook the sausage, onion salt, and garlic salt until the sausage is lightly browned. Drain off the grease. Add the tomatoes with their juice, the tomato sauce, 2 tablespoons (30 mL) of the parsley, the brown sugar, the basil, ½ teaspoon (2.5 mL) of the seasoned salt, and the mushrooms to skillet. Bring to a boil, stirring occasionally. Reduce the heat and simmer, uncovered, until mixture has thickened, about 1 hour. Measure out ½ cup (118 mL) of the sauce and set it aside.

3. Cook the lasagna according to the package directions.

4. In a medium bowl, mix together the ricotta cheese, ¼ cup (59 mL) of the Parmesan cheese, the remaining parsley, the remaining seasoned salt, and the oregano.

5. In an ungreased 6 × 10-inch (15 × 25-cm) baking pan, layer half the noodles, half the sauce mixture, ⅔ cup (158 mL) of the mozzarella cheese, and half the ricotta cheese. Repeat with a second layer, using another ⅔ cup (158 mL) of mozzarella cheese. Spoon the reserved sauce on top, sprinkle with the remaining parmesan and mozzarella cheeses, and cook, uncovered, in the barbecue for 45 minutes. Let stand for 15 minutes before serving.

Grilled Bison Ribeye Steaks with Roquefort Butter
Yield: 4–6 servings

If Roquefort is too strong for you, use a good-quality blue cheese or Stilton instead.

1 tablespoon (15 mL) extra virgin olive oil
4 or 6 (8–10 ounce [224–280 g]) buffalo ribeye steaks, 1 to 1¼ inches (2.5 to 3 cm) thick
1½ teaspoons (7.5 mL) salt, divided
¼ teaspoon (1.25 mL) freshly ground black pepper, plus more to taste
½ cup (118 mL) unsalted butter, at room temperature
4–6 tablespoons (60–90 mL) crumbled Roquefort cheese
2 teaspoons (10 mL) brandy
½ teaspoon (2.5 mL) finely minced shallots
Freshly ground black pepper, to taste

1. Preheat the barbecue to medium high (350°F [180°C] to 400°F [200°C]) for direct and indirect heating, putting a water pan under the unheated side of the grill.

2. Rub the olive oil onto both sides of the steak. Generously sprinkle each side of each steak with 1 teaspoon (5 mL) of the salt and ¼ teaspoon (1.25 mL) of the pepper.

3. Place the steaks on the grill and cook until well browned on both sides, 2½ minutes per side. Turn the steaks and transfer them to the cooler side of grill for 5 to 6 minutes for rare (120°F [49°C] on an instant-read thermometer), 7 to 8 min. for medium-rare (130°F [54°C]), or 8 to 9 minutes for medium (135°F [57°C] to 140°F [60°C]).

4. While the steaks are cooking, mash together the butter, Roquefort cheese, brandy, and shallots. Season with the remaining salt and pepper.

5. Remove the steaks from the pan and place them on a heated platter. Top each cooked steak with a generous portion of the Roquefort–brandy–butter mixture, cover the steaks with foil, and let the meat rest for 5 minutes before serving.

Elk and Moose Cheese Pie
Yield: 4–6 servings

If you don't have both elk and moose, you can use 1 pound (454 g) of either, but the varied textures and flavors of the two meats is the best for this dish.

1 tablespoon (15 mL) olive oil
1 cup (236 mL) chopped white onion
½ pound (227 g) ground elk
½ pound (227 g) ground moose
½ cup (118 mL) ketchup
1 tablespoon (15 mL) prepared mustard
½ teaspoon (2.5 mL) seasoned salt
Freshly ground black pepper, to taste
2 (8-ounce [227-g]) cans crescent roll dough
1½ cups (354 mL) shredded cheddar, jack, or Swiss cheese
2 eggs, beaten
1 egg yolk
1 teaspoon (5 mL) milk

1. Preheat the barbecue to medium high (350°F [180°C] to 400°F [200°C]).

2. In a skillet, heat the oil. Add the onions, cover the pan, and cook for 10 minutes. With a slotted spoon, remove the onions and set them aside. Add the meat to the skillet and cook it until browned. Remove the pan from the heat, drain off the grease, and stir in the ketchup, mustard, salt, and pepper.

3. Unroll the dough from both cans and roll each out on a floured surface to a 15-inch (37.5-cm) square. Put one sheet into a 10-inch square baking dish and set the other sheet aside. Spoon the meat mixture onto the dough in the dish and sprinkle it with the cheese and onion. Pour the beaten eggs over the filling.

4. Lay the remaining sheet of dough over the top and press the edges of both layers of pastry together. In a small bowl, beat together the egg yolk and milk. Brush this mixture over the top of the pastry. Cut 3 small vents in the pastry to let steam escape.

5. Bake the pie in the barbecue for 30 to 35 minutes, or until the crust is browned all over and the filling is bubbling.

Teriyaki Buffalo Ribeyes

Yield: 4–8 servings

This is about the best steak money can buy—tender, flavorful, and marbled with a fat that nutritionists says is very similar to the oil and fat in cold-water fish, an omega-based fat, so it's actually healthy to eat.

2 tablespoons (30 mL) soy sauce
1 clove garlic, peeled and minced or pressed
2 tablespoons (30 mL) brown sugar
2 tablespoons (30 mL) lemon juice
2 tablespoons (30 mL) vegetable oil
1 tablespoon (15 mL) dried minced onion
1 teaspoon (5 mL) ground ginger
¼ teaspoon (1.25 mL) freshly ground black pepper
4 (8–9 ounce [224–252 g]) buffalo ribeye steaks

1. In a medium bowl, combine the soy sauce, garlic, brown sugar, lemon juice, oil, onion, ginger, and pepper. Pour this marinade over the steaks, cover, and refrigerate for 6 hours or, preferably, overnight.

2. Preheat the barbecue to medium high (350°F [180°C] to 400°F [200°C]) for direct grilling.

3. Lift steaks from marinade and drain them briefly. Boil the remaining marinade for 10 minutes in a small saucepan. Place the ribeyes on the barbecue and grill for 6 to 8 minutes for medium-rare, turning once and basting with the marinade.

4. Serve with barbecued beans, barbecued corn on the cob, and Indian fry bread.

Elk Medallions with Rhubarb–Port Wine Sauce

Yield: 4 servings

This very simple but rich sauce can be made in larger batches then frozen or canned for later use. It's also great with any game bird or chicken.

2 cups (473 mL) peeled and chopped rhubarb (about 1 pound [454 g])
1¼ cups (295 mL) red currant jelly
1 tablespoon (15 mL) balsamic vinegar
¼ cup (59 mL) plus 1 tablespoon (15 mL) port, divided
1 tablespoon (15 mL) arrowroot
4 (6–7 [168–196 g]) elk loin steaks
2 tablespoons (30 mL) peanut oil
2 tablespoons (30 mL) freshly cracked black peppercorns

1. In a saucepan, combine the rhubarb, red currant jelly, and the balsamic vinegar and cook over medium heat until the mixture is reduced by about a third.

2. Pour the mixture into a fine sieve, pressing down with a spoon to extract all the juice. If there is more than 1 cup (236 mL), reduce it to that amount in a saucepan. Combine 1 tablespoon (15 mL) of the port and the arrowroot to the fruit purée and whisk out any lumps. Add the remaining port to the boiling rhubarb sauce and stir vigorously for 1 minute, then add the port-arrowroot and stir to thicken. Simmer for 2 minutes and keep warm until ready to serve. Refrigerate the cooked rhubarb overnight.

3. Preheat a gas or charcoal grill to medium high (350°F [180°C] to 400°F [200°C]) for direct grilling.

4. Rub the steaks with the peanut oil and then press the peppercorns into the meat on both sides.

5. Grill the loin steaks for about 4 to 5 minutes per side, or until done to medium or medium-rare. Remove the steaks from the grill, cover, and let them rest for 5 minutes. Pour the sauce over the meat, spoon some of the rhubarb puree alongside, and serve.

Grilled Ostrich Medallions
Yield: 6–8 servings

You can substitute emu medallions easily; they cook exactly the same way and have a similar taste. Remember both emu and ostrich meat are very red, like good-quality beef.

2 pounds (908 g) ostrich tenderloin medallions, cut 1-inch (2.5 cm) thick
½ cup (118 mL) soy sauce
¼ cup (59 mL) lime juice
¼ cup (59 mL) orange juice
¼ cup (59 mL) chopped green onions, green and white parts
2 tablespoons (30 mL) rice wine vinegar
1 tablespoon (15 mL) brown sugar
1 tablespoon (15 mL) honey
1 teaspoon (5 mL) olive oil
1 teaspoon (5 mL) minced garlic
½ teaspoon (2.5 mL) ground ginger
1 pinch nutmeg
Sea salt, to taste
Citrus pepper, to taste
2 to 3 tablespoons (30 to 45 mL) chilled butter, cut in cubes

1. Place the sliced tenderloins on a cutting board, cover them with plastic wrap, and pound lightly to flatten them to ½- to-¾-inch (1- to 1.5-cm) thick medallions and to tenderize the meat. In a large bowl, whisk together the soy sauce, lime juice, orange juice, green onions, vinegar, brown sugar, honey, olive oil, garlic, ground ginger, nutmeg, salt, and citrus pepper. Pour this marinade into a 1-gallon resealable plastic bag, add the ostrich, and marinate the medallions for 8 to 10 hours in the refrigerator, turning the bag several times.

2. Preheat a gas or charcoal grill to medium high (350°F [180°C] to 400°F [200°C]) for direct grilling, making sure the grill is well-oiled or sprayed with nonstick grilling spray.

3. Drain the meat, reserving the marinade. Place the meat on a platter, cover it with plastic wrap, and let it come to room temperature.

4. In a medium saucepan over high heat, boil the remaining marinade for 10 minutes. Reduce the heat to the lowest setting to keep the marinade warm.

5. Make a smoker package by putting a handful of soaked hickory or oak chips on a 12-inch (30-cm) square of heavy-duty aluminum foil, folding over the package, poking 3 or 4 holes in the top of the foil, and placing the package directly on the coals or open flame to add smoke to your grilling. When the wood chips begin to smoke, put the medallions on the grill.

6. Grill the ostrich for approximately 1 to 2 minutes per side. Do not overcook, as ostrich is very lean.

7. Place the medallions on a heated platter, cover them with foil, and let the meat rest for 2 to 3 minutes. Whisk the cold butter into the warm marinade/sauce until melted, pour into a sauce boat, and serve on the side.

Buffalo Rib Roast with Orange-Molasses Glaze

Yield: 6–8 servings

Do not use diet root beer in this recipe. Diet drinks turn bitter when they are cooked and will spoil this delicious dish. This recipe comes from Dave Hentosh from Presque Isle, Maine.

1 (7–9 pound [3.2–4.1 kg]) buffalo rib roast or top sirloin roast
1 tablespoon (15 mL) olive oil
1¼ cups (295 mL) finely minced red onion
3 tablespoons (45 mL) finely minced garlic
1¼ cups (295 mL) fresh orange juice
1 cup (236 mL) root beer
½ cup (118 mL) balsamic vinegar
⅓ cup (79 mL) molasses
¼ cup (59 mL) yellow mustard seeds
1 tablespoon (15 mL) grated orange zest
1 tablespoon (15 mL) cracked black pepper
1 tablespoon (15 mL) ground coriander
1 tablespoon (15 mL) chili powder
2 cups (473 mL) beef stock
1 cup (236 mL) dry red wine
Salt, to taste
Freshly ground black pepper, to taste

1. Carefully trim the roast to remove all but a thin layer of fat. Tie it securely and set it aside on a rack in a roasting pan or Dutch oven.

2. In a cast-iron skillet, heat the oil. Add the onion and garlic and sauté until they just beginning to color. Add the orange juice, root beer, vinegar, molasses, mustard seeds, orange zest, pepper, coriander, and chili powder and bring to a boil. Reduce the heat and simmer for 8 to 10 minutes, or until the glaze is thickened.

3. Generously brush the roast with the glaze and allow it to sit for at least 2 hours at room temperature, turning until all sides are coated. Refrigerate overnight, but bring back to room temperature before cooking. Reserve any remaining glaze to baste the roast during cooking.

4. Preheat the barbecue to medium high (350°F [180°C] to 400°F [200°C]) for direct and indirect heating, putting a water pan under the unheated side of the grill.

5. Roast the meat for 15 minutes over direct heat. Move the pan to the un-heated side of the grill, close the vents, and continue to cook until a meat thermometer inserted into the roast registers 130°F (54°C). Baste the roast occasionally with the remaining glaze.

6. Remove the roast from pan and keep it warm. Add the stock and wine to the pan and bring to a boil, scraping up any browned bits. Reduce this mixture slightly, and then strain. Add salt and pepper as desired.

Antelope Medallions with Grand Marnier
Yield: 4–6 servings

If you don't want to use the orange-flavored liqueur in this dish, you can substitute a favorite beer, white wine, ginger ale, lemon-lime soda, or fruit juice as the main marinade ingredient. Do not use colas, as the acid in them can make the meat mushy.

1 pound (454 g) antelope tenderloin medallions, sliced ½-inch (1-cm) thick
¼ cup (59 mL) plus 2 tablespoons (30 mL) Grand Marnier, divided
4 tablespoons (60 mL) olive oil, divided
2 cloves garlic, peeled and minced, divided
4 shallots, peeled and minced, divided
½ teaspoon (2.5 mL) seasoned salt
¼ teaspoon (1.25 mL) ground cinnamon
⅛ teaspoon (0.6 mL) freshly ground black pepper
1 pinch ground cloves
1 cup (236 mL) beef stock
3 tablespoons (45 mL) sour cream

1. Place the meat in a 1- to 2-gallon (3.8- to 7.6-mL) resealable plastic bag. In a medium bowl, combine 2 tablespoons (59 mL) of the Grand Marnier, 1 tablespoon (15 mL) of the oil, half the garlic, half the shallots, the seasoned salt, the cinnamon, the black pepper, and the cloves. Pour this marinade into the bag over the meat and refrigerate for 2 to 4 hours.

2. Preheat the barbecue to medium high (350°F [180°C] to 400°F [200°C]) for direct and indirect heating, putting a water pan under the unheated side of the grill.

3. Remove the meat from the bag and discard the marinade. Pat the me-dallions dry with paper towels. Place a cast-iron skillet on the grill, add the remaining oil, and heat until it begins to smoke. Add the medallions and sear for 2 to 3 minutes per side. Remove the meat from the pan. Add the remaining shallots and garlic and fry for 2 minutes.

4. Return the medallions to the pan. Add the remaining liqueur and flambé by holding a charcoal lighter near the edge of the pan to ignite the alcohol fumes. When the flames have subsided, remove the meat, wrap it in foil, and place it over the unheated side of the grill.

5. To the same skillet, add the stock. Increase the heat to high and boil until it is reduced to about ¾ cup (177 mL), about 3 to 5 minutes. In a small bowl, mix 1 tablespoon (15 mL) of the reduced stock into the sour cream, then stir this mixture into the hot sauce. Return the meat to the skillet and roast it on the unheated side of the barbecue for 4 to 5 minutes, covered.

6. Serve 2 to 3 antelope medallions and 3 tablespoons (45 mL) of the sauce to each person.

Plum Good Antelope Roast
Yield: 4–8 servings

For a thicker sauce in this recipe, mix 1 tablespoon (15 mL) cornstarch with enough water to create a paste. Then add this mixture to the saucepan and stir to blend and thicken the sauce.

1 (4–6 pound [1.8–2.7 kg]) antelope roast
¼ cup (59 mL) olive oil
1 tablespoon (15 mL) freshly ground black pepper
2 teaspoons (10 mL) ground allspice
Juice of ½ lemon
2 stalks celery, chopped
1 medium onion, peeled and chopped
2 carrots, peeled and chopped
1 bay leaf
1¼ cups (295 mL) water, divided
2 cups (473 mL) whole plums, pitted
¼ cup (59 mL) plum jam
1 tablespoon (15 mL) capers
1 tablespoon (15 mL) butter
2 teaspoons (10 mL) Dijon mustard
Salt, to taste
Freshly ground black pepper, to taste

1. Preheat the barbecue to medium high (350°F [180°C] to 400°F [200°C]). Spray a roasting pan with nonstick cooking or grilling spray.

2. Brush the roast generously with the olive oil, season it with the pepper and allspice, and drizzle it with the lemon juice.

3. Place the celery, onion, and carrots in the prepared roasting pan. Add the bay leaf, 1 cup (236 mL) of the water, and the roast. Cook for approximately 16 minutes per pound (454 g), basting frequently with the pan drippings.

4. Approximately 30 minutes before the roast is done, add the plums, plum jam, and remaining water to the roasting pan. When the roast is done, remove the pan from the grill, remove the meat from the pan, cover the meat with foil, and let it rest for 10 minutes.

5. While the meat is resting, discard the bay leaf in the pan drippings. Pour the contents of the pan into a food processor or blender and mix or pulse to a thick sauce. Pour the sauce into a medium saucepan and simmer for 3 minutes. Add the capers, butter, mustard, salt, and pepper and simmer for 2 minutes longer.

6. Thinly slice the antelope roast and serve it with the plum sauce.

One-Shot Antelope Steaks
Yield: 6–8 servings

I picked up this recipe while attending the Lander, Wyo., One-Shot Antelope Hunt with former Secretary of the Interior James Watt, a really nice guy in person. At this event, hunters are given one bullet and must bag their buck antelope with only one shot.

1 (2–3 pound [908 g–1.3 kg]) antelope steak, 1½ inches (3.5 cm) thick
⅔ cup (158 mL) fresh lemon juice
⅓ cup (79 mL) dry white wine
¼ cup (59 mL) vegetable oil
¼ cup (59 mL) chopped white onion
1 tablespoon (15 mL) soy sauce
1 tablespoon (15 mL) minced garlic
½ teaspoon (2.5 mL) celery salt
½ teaspoon (2.5 mL) onion powder
½ teaspoon (2.5 mL) dried rosemary
¼ teaspoon (1.25 mL) dried oregano

1. Place the steak in a 2-gallon (7.6-L) resealable plastic bag. In a small bowl, whisk together the lemon juice, wine, oil, onion, soy sauce, garlic, celery salt, onion powder, rosemary, and oregano. Pour this mixture into the bag over the meat and turn several times to coat the steak well. Refrigerate for 6 to 8 hours, turning the bag occasionally.

2. Preheat a gas or charcoal grill to medium high (350°F [180°C] to 400°F [200°C]) for direct and indirect heating, putting a water pan under the unheated side of the grill.

3. Remove the meat from the marinade. Pour the marinade into a saucepan and boil for 10 minutes while the meat comes to room temperature.

4. Place the steak on the grill over direct heat and cook for 5 minutes, brushing with the marinade several times. Turn the steak over and grill for another 5 minutes, again brushing generously with the marinade. Move the steak to the unheated side of the grill and cook for 10 to 12 minutes per side, again brushing with the marinade several times. Cook until the internal temperature is between 130°F (54°C) and 140°F (60°C) for medium-rare. Cover the steak and let it rest for 10 minutes (the temperature will rise about 5°F [2°C] to 10°F [4°C]).

5. Put the steak on a platter and cut it against the grain into ¼-inch (0.5-cm) thick slices. Drizzle with the remaining sauce and serve.

Grilled Chocolate Moose

Yield: 4 servings

When serving, present the sauce in stemmed dessert glasses with a dollop of sour cream on top to make it look like chocolate mousse.

4 dried pasilla peppers, stems and seeds removed
4 dried red New Mexican peppers, stems and seeds removed
2 medium tomatoes, peeled, seeded, and chopped
1 medium onion, peeled and chopped
2 cloves garlic, peeled and chopped
½ cup (118 mL) almonds
¼ cup (59 mL) raisins
2 tablespoons (30 mL) sesame seeds
¼ teaspoon (1.25 mL) ground cloves
¼ teaspoon (1.25 mL) ground cinnamon
¼ teaspoon (1.25 mL) ground coriander
3 tablespoons (45 mL) vegetable shortening or vegetable oil
1 cup (236 mL) chicken broth
1–2 bars Mexican bitter chocolate (or more to taste)
¼ cup (59 mL) butter
¼ cup (59 mL) olive oil
4 moose steaks
¼ cup (59 mL) plus 2 tablespoons (30 mL) all-purpose flour
¼ cup (59 mL) honey
½ teaspoon (2.5 mL) salt
¼ teaspoon (1.25 mL) freshly ground black pepper

1. In a blender, combine the peppers, tomatoes, onion, garlic, almonds, raisins, 1 tablespoon (15 mL) sesame seeds, cloves, cinnamon, and coriander and process until smooth.

2. In a skillet, melt the shortening. Add the puree and sauté for 10 minutes, stirring frequently. Add the chicken broth and chocolate and reduce the heat to very low. Cook, stirring often, for 45 minutes. The sauce should be very thick. If you wish to make it thicker, add a corn tortilla and blend until mixed into the sauce.

3. Preheat the barbecue to medium high (350°F [180°C] to 400°F [200°C]).

4. Heat a cast-iron skillet. Melt the butter with the olive oil. Dredge the moose steaks in ¼ cup (59 mL) of the flour. Brown the meat on both sides, then drain the meat, discarding the oil. Return the browned moose steak to the skillet. In a small bowl, mix together the honey, salt, and pepper. Pour this mixture over the top of the steak.

5. Roast the steaks, covered, in the barbecue until tender, about 2 hours. Remove the skillet from the oven and transfer the steaks to warmed plates. Serve with the chocolate mole sauce.

Mickey Moose Pie

Yield: 4–6 servings

This is a delicious way to serve tougher cuts of moose. Prepare the steak by pounding it on both sides with the side of a plate or a meat tenderizing mallet.

⅓–½ cup (79–118 mL) all-purpose flour
1 (1½-pound [681-g]) moose steak, cubed
2 tablespoons (30 mL) bacon grease
1 medium onion, peeled and chopped
1 clove garlic, peeled and minced
2 cups (473 mL) sweet red wine
2 tablespoons (30 mL) Worcestershire sauce
1 teaspoon (5 mL) dried marjoram
1 teaspoon (5 mL) dried thyme
1 teaspoon (5 mL) celery seed
1 teaspoon (5 mL) salt
½ teaspoon (2.5 mL) freshly ground black pepper
1 bay leaf
1 cup (236 mL) diced potatoes
1 cup (236 mL) diced carrots
1 cup (236 mL) frozen peas
Refrigerated pie dough for a two-crust pie

1. Preheat the barbecue to medium high (350°F [180°C] to 400°F [200°C]) for direct heating.

2. Put the flour in a plastic bag. Add a few cubes of steak at a time and shake to coat.

3. On the barbecue grill or a side burner, heat the bacon grease in a cast-iron skillet. Add the onions and garlic and cook just until onions become translucent. Remove the onions with a slotted spoon, leaving the drippings in the skillet.

4. If the skillet is on a side burner, move it to the barbecue. Add the moose steaks and sear them until the meat is browned on both sides. Add the wine, Worcestershire sauce, marjoram, thyme, celery seed, salt, pepper, and bay leaf and bring to a boil. Reduce the heat and simmer for 1½ hours.

5. Add potatoes and carrots, and stir to incorporate the vegetables and meat. Cook for approximately 30 minutes. Stir in the peas.

6. Line a pie pan with pastry dough, and add the filling. Cover it with the top crust and press the edges together to seal. Flute the edges and cut vents in the top. Bake for 20 to 25 minutes, or until the crust is nicely browned.

7. Remove the pie from the barbecue and let it rest for 10 minutes to cool slightly.

Grilled Rabbit

Yield: 4 servings

The U.S. Department of Agriculture states that rabbit meat is the most nutritious meat known to man, with only 795 calories per pound (454 g). (Beef has 1,440, chicken has 810, and turkey has 1,190.)

1½–2½ pounds (681g–1.1 kg) rabbit, cut into pieces
1 (16-ounce [454-g]) bottle Italian dressing
1 lemon, quartered
1 leek, chopped, white part only
Thin lemon slices, for garnish
Paprika, for garnish

1. Pierce the rabbit pieces with a barbecue fork to allow the marinade to penetrate deeply into the meat. Place the pieces in a 2-gallon (7.6-L) resealable plastic bag. In a medium bowl, combine the Italian dressing, lemon, and leek. Pour the marinade into the bag with the rabbit and refrigerate for 24 to 48 hours. Remove the meat from the marinade. Pour the marinade into a saucepan and boil for 10 minutes while the rabbit comes to room temperature.

2. Preheat the barbecue to medium high (350°F [180°C] to 400°F [200°C]).

3. Place a soaked Chef Locke Smoke Bomb (I love the cherry wood in this recipe) directly on the coals or open flame to add smoke to your grilling. When the package is smoking put the rabbit on the grill.

4. Grill the rabbit, turning frequently and basting generously with the boiled marinade, until it's browned nicely and the meat near the bone turns white. Do not overcook.

5. Serve on a heated platter, drizzled with the remaining sauce, garnished with the lemon slices, and sprinkled with paprika.

Farmer McGregor's Rabbit

Yield: 6 servings

Well, Farmer McGregor finally caught Peter purloining his pea pods and parsley and came up with a tasty recipe to share with his friends. You can substitute chicken in this recipe if you wish.

2 pounds (908 g) rabbit pieces
1 cup (236 mL) fresh lemon juice
¼ cup (59 mL) fresh lime juice
½ cup (118 mL) all-purpose flour
Salt, to taste
Freshly ground black pepper, to taste
3 tablespoons (45 mL) olive oil
¼ pound (112 g) salt pork, diced
1 tablespoon (15 mL) chopped fresh rosemary
1 teaspoon (5 mL) dried savory
2½ cups (591 mL) coarsely chopped onions
1 cup (236 mL) dry white wine
1 cup (236 mL) frozen peas
1 tablespoon (15 mL) dark brown sugar
Freshly chopped parsley, for garnish

1. Preheat the barbecue to medium high (350°F [180°C] to 400°F [200°C]).

2. Place the rabbit in a 2-gallon (7.8-L) resealable plastic bag and add the lemon and lime juices. Marinate at room temperature for 30 minutes, turning the bag often. Remove the rabbit, discarding the marinade and pat the pieces dry.

3. In a brown paper bag, combine the flour, salt, and pepper. Drop in the rabbit pieces one at a time and shake to coat each piece. Place the coated pieces on a plate while you finish flouring the remaining pieces.

4. In a large cast-iron skillet, heat the olive oil over medium-high heat. Add the rabbit pieces and brown them on all sides. Add the salt pork and sauté for 2 minutes. Sprinkle with the rosemary and savory, stir, and remove the pan from the heat.

5. Spread the onions over the bottom of a roasting pan or Dutch oven and arrange the rabbit pieces and salt pork on top of the onions. Add the wine, peas, brown sugar, and salt and pepper to taste. Cover the pan with a lid or aluminum foil and bake for 35 minutes, or until the rabbit is tender.

6. Place the rabbit pieces on a heated serving platter, spoon the onion and pea mixture over the meat, sprinkle with parsley, and serve.

Roasted Wild Pig

Yield: 4–6 servings

You may wish to sear the meat directly on the heated grill before putting it in the bag. To do so, cook it for 5 to 6 minutes on each side until the pork is nicely browned and marked, then follow through with the rest of the recipe.

1 6 to 6½ pound pork shoulder or butt roast
1 teaspoon (5 mL) garlic salt
1 teaspoon (5 mL) dried oregano
1 teaspoon (5 mL) paprika
1 teaspoon (5 mL) cracked black pepper
1 (16-ounce [454-g]) can crushed pineapple in syrup
½ cup (118 mL) lemon juice

1. Trim any exposed fat from the roast. Rub the garlic salt, oregano, paprika, and cracked pepper into the meat. Place the meat into a 2-gallon (7.6-L) resealable plastic bag. Pour the can of pineapple and the lemon juice in over the meat. Remove all the air from the bag, seal, and refrigerate overnight.

2. Remove the pork from the marinade. Pour the marinade into a saucepan and boil for 10 minutes, while the roast comes to room temperature.

3. Preheat the barbecue to medium (250°F [120°C] to 275°F [140°C]) for direct heating.

4. Place the meat in a roasting pan or Dutch oven, cover, and cook for 8 to 10 hours, basting once an hour with the marinade. It is done when an instant-read thermometer inserted into a thick part of the roast registers 160°F (71°C).

5. Remove the pan from the barbecue. Let it stand for 10 minutes to recirculate the meat juices inside the roast.

6. Slice the meat into thick slices and serve it with the sauce in the pan. If you wish, you can thicken the sauce by combining 1 tablespoon (15 mL) of cornstarch with 1 tablespoon (15 mL) of the juices from the pan; stir to form a paste and and whisk it into the pan juices. Cook, stirring constantly, until thickened.

Korean Wild Boar Meatballs

Yield: 4–6 servings

These are also wonderful served with an Asian hoisin sauce or teriyaki sauce, or cooked in your favorite tomato sauce and served over spaghetti.

Dipping Sauce

¼ cup (60 mL) soy sauce
¼ cup (60 mL) vinegar
2 tablespoons (30 mL) finely chopped green onion, green and white parts
1 tablespoon (15 mL) grated fresh ginger
2 teaspoons (10 mL) honey or firmly packed brown sugar
2 teaspoons (10 mL) toasted sesame seeds
¼ teaspoon (1.25 mL) Sriracha sauce

Meatballs

1 pound (454 g) ground wild boar
2 tablespoons (30 mL) soy sauce
1 clove garlic, peeled and minced
1 green onion, chopped, white and green parts
1 tablespoon (15 mL) toasted sesame seeds
Freshly ground black pepper, to taste
½ cup (118 mL) all-purpose flour
1 egg, beaten with 1 tablespoon (15 mL) water
2 tablespoons (30 mL) vegetable oil

1. Preheat the barbecue to medium high (350°F [180°C] to 400°F [200°C]).

2. In a small saucepan, combine the dipping sauce ingredients. Bring to a boil, stirring often. Set aside to cool.

3. In a large bowl, combine the ground wild boar, soy sauce, garlic, green onion, sesame seeds, and pepper. Shape the mixture into 1½- to 2-inch (3.5- to 5-cm) balls. Roll them in the flour, dip them into the egg mixture, and dredge them again in the flour.

4. Place a cast-iron skillet in the barbecue, add the oil, and heat until the oil just begins to smoke. Add the meatballs and bake for 20 minutes, turning them several times, until they are browned on all sides.

5. Cool slightly and serve with the dipping sauce.

Sixty-Cloves-of-Garlic Wild Boar

Yield: 6–8 servings

The cloves of garlic will brown, soften, and sweeten as they cook and will taste like sweet buttery nuts. You can remove them from the meat and serve them at the table with a knife to spread on slices of French or Italian bread.

1 (5-pound [2.3-kg]) javelina or wild boar roast
60 cloves garlic, peeled
3 cups (708 mL) dry red wine
1 teaspoon (5 mL) ground ginger
½ teaspoon (2.5 mL) ground cinnamon
⅛ teaspoon (0.6 mL) ground cloves
1 teaspoon (5 mL) freshly ground black pepper
3 cups (708 mL) chicken or beef stock
½ cup (118 mL) sweet rice wine vinegar
1 (10-ounce [280-g]) bottle honey-mustard barbecue sauce
1 tablespoon (15 mL) cornstarch

1. Preheat a barbecue to high (450°F [240°C] to 500°F [260°C]) for indirect grilling, putting a water pan under the unheated side of the grill.

2. With a small sharp knife, cut small slits all over the roast. Fill each slit with a whole garlic clove. In a large bowl, whisk together the wine, beef stock, vinegar, ginger, pepper, cinnamon, and cloves.

3. Place the roast in a deep roasting pan or Dutch oven and generously mop it with the wine sauce. Put the pan in the barbecue and immediately turn the gas down to 350°F (180°C). If you are using charcoal, place the meat on the heated side of the grill and cook for 20 minutes, turning once, then move it to the indirect side of the grill, over the water pan; close down the vents to lower the heat.

4. Roast the meat for 4 hours, basting every 30 minutes with the pan juices.

5. After 3½ hours, pour the barbecue sauce over the meat and continue cooking.

6. Remove the roast from the barbecue and place it on a cutting board. Cover it with foil and let it rest for 15 to 20 minutes to let the meat juices recirculate. Return the pan to the barbecue. In a small bowl, combine the cornstarch with 1 tablespoon (15 mL) of the juices from the pan and stir to form a paste. Whisk the paste into the pan and cook, stirring, until a thick gravy forms.

7. Slice the roast and serve with the sauce.

Wild Boar Scaloppini with Raspberry–Mushroom Gravy
Yield: 6–8 servings

Wild boar is similar to domestic pork, but it's slightly stronger and sweeter, and the meat is darker and redder. Properly cooked, it's as good as any domestic pork roast.

8 (6-ounce [168-g]) wild boar tenderloin medallions
2 cups (473 mL) all-purpose flour
1 teaspoon (5 mL) garlic powder
1 teaspoon (5 mL) dried savory
1 teaspoon (5 mL) celery salt
1 teaspoon (5 mL) paprika
½ cup (118 mL) olive oil
24 mushroom caps, cleaned
1½ quarts (1.5 L) veal (or vegetable) stock
¼ cup (59 mL) raspberry vinegar
1 cup (227 g) unsalted butter
2 tablespoons (30 mL) finely chopped fresh parsley
Salt, to taste
Freshly-ground black pepper, to taste
1 pint (473 mL) red or golden raspberries

1. Preheat a gas or charcoal grill to medium high (350°F [180°C] to 400°F [200°C]) for direct and indirect grilling, putting a water pan under the unheated side of the grill.

2. Place the boar medallions in a plastic bag and pound them with a tenderizing mallet or the bottom of a wine bottle to flatten to ¼-inch (0.5-cm) thickness and to tenderize them.

3. In a brown paper bag, combine the flour, garlic powder, savory, celery salt, and paprika. Add the pounded medallions and shake to coat all sides.

4. In a hot skillet, heat the olive oil. Add the boar fillets and sauté until they are brown on both sides. Remove them from the pan, wrap the meat in aluminum foil, and place it on the indirect side of the grill.

5. Add the mushroom caps to the drippings remaining in the pan (you may need to add 1 to 2 tablespoons [15 to 30 mL] more olive oil) and cook until they are brown and softened. Transfer the mushrooms to a saucepan on the unheated side of the grill, beside the meat.

6. Deglaze the skillet by adding the stock and stirring up the browned bits from the bottom of the pan. Add the raspberry vinegar, increase the heat, and cook at a high simmer to reduce the liquid by half. Add the butter, parsley, salt, and pepper and whisk until well combined.

7. Return the meat to the pan and cover it with the gravy. Add the mushrooms, cover the skillet, and return the skillet to the barbecue. Cook over direct heat for 20 minutes. Remove the skillet from the barbecue; add the berries to the warm gravy, and serve.

Braised Bear Roast

Yield: 6–8 servings

There are several secrets to cooking bear meat. First, cut off all visible fat, as it turns rancid and bitter when cooked. Second, you must cook bear to medium. Do not eat bear meat that's still pink or even light red inside; it must be brown all the way through.

¼ cup (59 mL) bacon grease
3–4 pounds (1.3–1.8 kg) young bear roast
½ cup (118 mL) bottled chili sauce
⅓ cup (79 mL) water
⅓ cup (79 mL) cider vinegar
¼ cup (59 mL) soy sauce
2 large carrots, finely chopped
1 large onion, peeled and minced
3 cloves garlic, peeled and mashed
2 tablespoons (30 mL) dry mustard
2 tablespoons (30 mL) brown sugar
1 tablespoon (15 mL) lemon juice
2 teaspoons (10 mL) celery salt
½ teaspoon (2.5 mL) chili powder
½ teaspoon (2.5 mL) cayenne pepper
¼ teaspoon (1.25 mL) freshly ground black pepper
2 bay leaves

1. Preheat the barbecue to medium high (350°F [180°C] to 400°F [200°C]).

2. Pour the bacon grease into a Dutch oven or roasting pan and heat it in the barbecue for 10 minutes. Add the meat and the brown it on all sides, turning it every 5 minutes for 20 minutes.

3. In a large saucepan, combine the chili sauce, water, vinegar, soy sauce, carrots, onion, garlic, mustard, brown sugar, lemon juice, celery salt, chili powder, cayenne pepper, black pepper, and bay leaves and whisk until well mixed.

4. Open the barbecue and pour the cooking sauce over the meat. Cover and cook for 3 to 4 hours. Baste 2 or 3 times an hour until the roast is done.

5. Remove the roast from the barbecue, cover it, and let it sit for 15 to 20 minutes so the juices re-circulate. Pour the pan drippings into a sauce boat, skim off any fat, and serve at the table. Serve with garlic mashed or roasted potatoes and grilled green beans or asparagus.

Smoky Bear Meatloaf

Yield: 4–6 servings

No, not Smokey the Bear. This is a recipe for bear meat smoke-baked in a barbecue.

1 egg, beaten
1 cup (236 mL) ketchup
1 cup (236 mL) chopped canned potatoes
½ cup (118 mL) minced red bell pepper
½ cup (118 mL) chopped onion
½ cup (118 mL) minced carrots
1 teaspoon (5 mL) dried marjoram
1 teaspoon (5 mL) ground cumin
Salt, to taste
Freshly ground black pepper, to taste
1½ pounds (681 g) ground bear meat
¼ pound (112 g) ground pork
¼ cup (59 mL) chopped bacon

1. Preheat a gas or charcoal grill to medium high (350°F [180°C] to 400°F [200°C]) for indirect grilling. Grease or spray with nonstick cooking spray a metal loaf pan.

2. Make a smoker package by putting a handful of soaked Chef Locke hickory or oak chips on a 12-inch (30-cm) square of heavy-duty aluminum foil, folding over the package, and poking 3 or 4 holes in the top of the foil.

3. In a large bowl, combine the egg, ketchup, potatoes, bell pepper, onion, carrots, marjoram, cumin, salt, and pepper. Add the bear meat, pork, and bacon. Mix well with your hands.

4. Scoop the meatloaf mixture into the prepared loaf pan and place it on the unheated side of the grill. At the same time, place the smoke package on the coals or gas flame. Cook for about 1 hour, or until the meatloaf is firm, browned on top, and reaches an internal temperature of 160°F (71°C).

5. Let the loaf rest for 10 minutes and then slice and serve.

Blackened Alligator Steaks

Yield: 4 servings

Do not prepare this recipe in your kitchen unless you want to have to wipe down the walls and ceiling to remove the smoky soot that will be deposited there when you cook these steaks.

1 teaspoon (5 mL) salt
1 tablespoon (15 mL) paprika
1 teaspoon (5 mL) garlic powder
1 teaspoon (5 mL) cayenne pepper
½ teaspoon (2.5 mL) freshly ground black pepper
½ teaspoon (2.5 mL) freshly ground white pepper
½ teaspoon (2.5 mL) dried thyme
½ teaspoon (2.5 mL) dried oregano
½ teaspoon (2.5 mL) dried chives
4 (1½-inch [3.5-cm] thick) alligator steaks, from the tail
3 tablespoons (45 mL) butter, melted

1. Preheat the barbecue to high (450°F [240°C] to 500°F [260°C]).

2. In a small bowl, mix together the salt, paprika, garlic powder, cayenne pepper, black pepper, white pepper, thyme, oregano, and chives. Pour this mixture into a shallow baking pan.

3. Brush the steaks lightly with the melted butter and coat both sides of each steak with the seasoning mix.

4. Place a dry, heavy cast-iron skillet or Dutch oven directly on the grill over high heat or on the side burner for 5 to 7 minutes. Place the steaks in the pan and sear for 2 minutes. Turn, brush with the remaining melted butter, and cook for 1 to 2 minutes.

5. Place the pan with steaks in the barbecue and bake for 5 to 6 minutes. Remove the pan from the barbecue and serve the steaks on warmed plates with grilled corn and fried potatoes.

Barbecue-Baked Rattlesnake Chili

Yield: 6 servings

Rattlesnake is light and chewy, with a delicate flavor similar to that of chicken. Rattlesnake chili is a favorite dish at a number of restaurants in the Southwestern United States.

2 pounds (908 g) rattlesnake meat, deboned or partially deboned
6 cups (1.4 L) water
Juice of ½ lemon
1 (28-ounce [784-g]) can diced tomatoes
1 (28-ounce [784-g]) can chili beans
1 (15-ounce [420-g]) can tomato paste
1 large onion, peeled and chopped
1 red bell pepper, chopped
1 jalapeño pepper, seeded and diced
3 large cloves garlic, peeled and minced
¼ cup (59 mL) chili powder
1 tablespoon (15 mL) ground cumin
1 teaspoon (5 mL) garlic salt
1 teaspoon (5 mL) freshly ground black pepper

1. Simmer the rattlesnake in the water and lemon juice for 1 hour. Remove the rattlesnake from the liquid and separate the meat from any bones.

2. Preheat the barbecue to medium high (230°F [110°C] to 250°F [120°C]) for direct and indirect heating.

3. In a cast-iron Dutch oven, combine the meat with the remaining ingredients. Place the pot on the heated side of the grill and bring it to a boil. Cook for 5 minutes. Move the pot to the unheated side of the grill and simmer for 2 hours.

4. Serve with the traditional chili accompaniments of diced onion, cheddar cheese, and sour cream. Grilled garlic bread is a nice addition as well.

SIXTEEN

Desserts

Barbecued Ice Cream

Yield: 6–8 servings

I introduced this recipe to national television with a live appearance on Live with Regis and Kelly *in 2001. Since then, I've repeated the demonstration of this fun dish on the* Today Show, FOX & Friends, CBS Good Morning, *and many other popular daytime TV shows.*

8–10 egg whites
1 cup (236 mL) sugar
1 teaspoon (5 mL) cream of tartar
1 (1-pound [453-g]) Sara Lee pound cake, thawed
1 (8-ounce [227-g]) jar raspberry or apricot jam (or other favorite)
3 Klondike ice cream bars (your favorite flavor or a mix of flavors)
1 (8-ounce [227-g]) jar chocolate-mint fudge sauce
1 small bunch fresh mint leaves, for garnish
Chocolate sprinkles, for garnish

1. Wrap a 12-inch (30-cm) square, ½-inch (1-cm) thick wooden plank in 2 or 3 layers of heavy-duty aluminum foil.

2. Get a good, hot (600°F [315°C] to 700°F [370°C]) fire going in a grill or smoker. If you use charcoal or briquettes in a grill, use enough to cover the bottom of the grill pan. If you use a gas grill, turn all the burners to high.

3. Using an electric mixer, whip together the egg whites, sugar, and cream of tartar into a very stiff meringue, so that when you pull the beaters away, sharp points stand up. Refrigerate the mixture until ready to use.

4. Set the foil-wrapped plank on the counter. Use a sharp, serrated knife to cut the pound cake in half horizontally, and lay one half on the foil.

5. Spread the jam on one side of each cake half. Place the Klondike bars on the bottom layer of the cake, then cover it with the second cake.

6. Using a rubber spatula, completely cover the cake on all sides with the meringue, being sure to spread the meringue all the way down to the foil all around the cake. If you leave any gaps between the meringue and foil, the ice cream may melt and spoil the dessert.

7. Place the plank in the center of the grill and immediately close the cover. Check it after 2 minutes, and as soon as you see the peaks of meringue turning brown, remove the dessert from the cooker.

8. Spoon a generous pool of fudge sauce on each serving plate. With an electric knife (an ordinary knife could crush the meringue and ice cream, ruining the look of the dish), cut vertical slices through the dessert, and put the slices on the plates. Garnish with the fresh mint leaves, shake chocolate sprinkles over the meringue, and serve immediately.

Dorothy and Kate's Barbecued Butter Tarts

Yield: 4–6 servings

This recipe comes from my mother, who got it from her mother, so it's more than 100 years old. It's still one of the best desserts my friends and I have ever eaten. My wife, Kate, is the latest tart practitioner. I suggest making a double batch, as these vanish very quickly.

5 cups (1.2 L) all-purpose flour
1½ cups (354 mL) plus 2 tablespoons (30 mL) packed brown sugar, divided
1 teaspoon (5 mL) baking powder
1 teaspoon (5 mL) plus 1 pinch salt, divided
1 pound (454 g) lard
1 large egg, beaten, with enough water added to make 1 cup (236 mL)
1 cup (236 mL) raisins
½ cup (118 mL) currants
2 large eggs
½ cup (118 mL) corn syrup
3 tablespoons (45 mL) butter, melted
2 teaspoons (10 mL) distilled white vinegar
½ teaspoon (2.5 mL) vanilla extract

1. In large bowl, mix together the flour, 2 tablespoons (30 mL) of the brown sugar, the baking powder, and 1 teaspoon (5 mL) of the salt. Cut in the lard. Make a well in the center and pour in the water/egg mixture. Stir well until the dough forms a ball, cover, and chill for at least 2 hours.

2. Remove the dough from the refrigerator and roll it out. Cut out 4-inch (10-cm) circles of dough.

3. Preheat the barbecue to 350°F (180°C). Spray a muffin pan with non-stick baking spray.

4. Place the raisins and currants in a bowl, add boiling water to cover, and soak for 5 minutes. Drain on paper towels.

5. Beat the eggs well. Add the remaining brown sugar, the corn syrup, and the melted butter and beat again. Add the raisins, currants, vinegar, vanilla, and the remaining pinch of salt and mix vigorously.

6. Place the circles of pie dough in the sprayed muffin pan. Fill the shells ⅔ full and bake until the pastry is light brown, about 20 minutes.

Barbecue Sweet Potato Pie

Yield: 6–8 servings

A favorite Southern dessert, this pie could easily be mistaken for pumpkin pie. Indeed, many people prefer the consistency of this pie to that of the traditional holiday pie.

1 pound (454 g) sweet potatoes
1 teaspoon (5 mL) plus 1 pinch salt, divided
3 large eggs, divided
1½ cups (354 mL) evaporated milk
1 cup (236 mL) packed brown sugar, divided
1½ teaspoons (7.5 mL) ground cinnamon, divided
½ teaspoon (2.5 mL) ground nutmeg
3 tablespoons (45 mL) butter, melted
1 prepared 9-inch (22.5-cm) deep-dish pie crust
2 tablespoons (30 mL) butter, softened
1 cup (236 mL) chopped pecans
½ cup (118 mL) cane syrup (Steen's preferred)
1½ teaspoons (7.5 mL) grated orange zest

1. Preheat the barbecue to 425°F (220°C), with one side of the grill unheated. If you're using charcoal, place all the briquettes on one side. If you're using gas, light one set of burners only.

2. Peel and wash the sweet potatoes and cut them into 1-inch (2.5-cm) pieces. Put the sweet potatoes in a medium saucepan and add enough water to cover and add ½ teaspoon (2.5 mL) of the salt. Bring to a boil and reduce the heat to low. Cover the pot and simmer for 20 minutes, or until the sweet potatoes are tender. Drain the sweet potatoes and mash them in a large bowl. In a small bowl, beat 2 of the eggs with a fork. Add the beaten eggs, evaporated milk, ½ cup (118 mL) of the brown sugar, 1 teaspoon (5 mL) of the cinnamon, the nutmeg, the melted butter, and ½ teaspoon (2.5 mL) of the remaining salt to the sweet potatoes. Mix well, and pour the mixture into the prepared pie crust.

3. For the praline topping, in a large bowl, cream together the remaining brown sugar and the softened butter. Add the remaining egg and, with a wire whisk, beat until the mixture is light and fluffy. Add pecans, cane syrup, orange zest, the remaining cinnamon, and the remaining pinch of salt and blend well.

4. Place a 10-inch (25-cm) square of aluminum foil, shiny side down, on the hot side of the grill. Place the pie on the foil and bake it for 10 minutes. Pour the praline topping over the pie. Move the pie to the cool side of the grill and bake for 50 minutes, or until a toothpick inserted into the pie comes out clean.

Grilled Ice Cream Oranges

Yield: 4–6 servings

This is a fun, surprising, and quite refreshing dessert. You can use tangelos instead of oranges and fill them with any flavor ice cream, sherbet, or gelato you like.

4 large oranges
1 cup (236 mL) water
3 cups (708 mL) packed brown sugar
2 cups (473 mL) granulated sugar
4 egg whites
½ cup (118 mL) confectioners' sugar
1 teaspoon (5 mL) cream of tartar
4 scoops chocolate ice cream

1. Preheat the barbecue to its highest temperature (600°F [315°C] to 700°F [370°C] degrees is best). Cover an 8 × 12-inch (20 × 30-cm) wooden plank with 2 layers of aluminum foil.

2. Cut the oranges in half horizontally. Remove and discard the juice and pulp keeping the orange-peel shells intact. Bring a medium saucepan of water to a simmer. Place the orange shells in the simmering water and cook for 5 minutes. Remove the orange shells and drain thoroughly.

3. In a large saucepan, bring the 1 cup water to a boil. Add the brown sugar and bring the mixture to a rolling boil. Reduce the heat to low and add the orange shells. Simmer for about 30 minutes, turning each shell over several times.

4. Using tongs, remove the shells from the syrup and place them, cut side down, on sheets of aluminum foil or waxed paper to cool. Sprinkle the granulated sugar over the shells while they cool.

5. With a hand-held mixer, whip the egg whites until they form stiff peaks, adding the confectioners' sugar and cream of tartar as you whip.

6. Fill the orange shells with the ice cream and cover the ice cream with meringue, making sure to spread the meringue down to the edges of the orange shells all the way around. Place the shells on the aluminum-covered board and place the board in the center of the hot barbecue. Cook for 2 to 3 minutes, or until the meringue is just starting to brown. Remove the oranges from the heat and serve immediately.

Raspberry–Rhubarb Tart

Yield: 8 servings

If you can't find fresh rhubarb and raspberries you can use either one frozen. Frozen rhubarb holds up better than frozen raspberries, but either one works fine in this recipe.

Pastry dough for a double-crust pie
2 cups (473 mL) rhubarb cut in ¼- to ½-inch (0.5- to 1-cm) pieces
1 cup (236 mL) raspberries (or strawberries)
¾ cup (177 mL) granulated sugar
3 large eggs
1 egg yolk
½ cup (118 mL) heavy cream
⅓ teaspoon (1.5 mL) pure vanilla extract

1. Preheat the barbecue to medium high (350°F [180°C] to 400°F [200°C]).

2. Roll out half of the dough, large enough to fit into a 10-inch (25-cm) tart or pie pan. Fit rolled dough into the tart or pie pan. Roll out the second half of dough and set aside.

3. Distribute the rhubarb evenly in the tart shell, then sprinkle with the raspberries.

4. In a mixing bowl, whisk together the sugar, eggs, and egg yolk. Add the cream and vanilla and stir to mix well.

5. Pour the egg mixture over the fruit in the pie shell. Cover the filling with the second crust and press the edges of the crusts together to seal. Cut 3 or 4 vents in the top crust to allow steam to escape.

6. Bake in the barbecue for 20 to 25 minutes, or until the top crust is lightly browned.

7. Remove the tart from heat, let it cool slightly, and serve.

Grampa's Grilled Apple Crisp

Yield: 6–8 servings

One of my all-time favorite desserts, this is probably one of the simplest to make. It doesn't take much time, and the smell of the baking apples, cinnamon, and nutmeg will drive everyone crazy.

1 (20-ounce [560-g]) can apple pie filling
⅓ cup (79 mL) packed brown sugar
2 tablespoons (30 mL) lemon juice
1 teaspoon (5 mL) molasses
½ teaspoon (2.5 mL) ground cinnamon
¼ teaspoon (1.25 mL) ground nutmeg
½ box (approximately 2 cups [473 mL]) yellow cake mix
½ cup (118 mL) butter or margarine, cut in pieces

1. Preheat a gas grill to medium (350°F [180°C] to 400°F [200°C]) for 10 minutes, then turn off one side of the grill and invert a baking pan on the unheated side. If you're using charcoal, pile the charcoal on one side of barbecue only. Spray a 9-inch (22.5-cm) baking pan or cast-iron pan with nonstick spray.

2. Pour the pie filling into the prepared pan. Stir together the brown sugar, lemon juice, molasses, cinnamon, and nutmeg, and sprinkle over the apple filling. Drizzle the molasses over the mixture. Sprinkle the cake mix over the pie filling to cover, and dot with the butter pieces.

3. Place the prepared baking pan on top of the inverted pan. Close the lid of barbecue and bake for 55 to 60 minutes, or until the apple crisp is browned and bubbly.

4. Let the apple crisp cool, and serve it with whipped cream or ice cream.

Berry Good French Toast

Yield: 10 servings

Yes, French toast for dessert. After all, you like bread pudding, right? This is a festive and different dessert that the kids and most adults will love.

⅔ cup (158 mL) strawberries
⅔ cup (158 mL) raspberries
2 tablespoons (30 mL) granulated sugar
3 large eggs
½ cup (118 mL) half-and-half
½ teaspoon (2.5 mL) pure vanilla extract
¼ teaspoon (1.25 mL) ground cinnamon
10 (½- to 1-inch [1- to 2.5-cm] thick) slices pound cake
Confectioners' sugar, for serving
Ground nutmeg, for serving

1. Preheat the barbecue to medium, making sure the grill has been well greased.

2. Wash, hull, and roughly chop the berries. Place them in a medium bowl and use a wooden spoon to mash them to jam consistency. Add the sugar, stir well, and set aside at room temperature.

3. In a shallow glass baking dish, whisk together the eggs, half-and-half, vanilla, and cinnamon until they are well mixed.

4. Using a spatula, dip the pound cake slices, one at a time, into the liquid for about 12 seconds per side. Drain slightly, and transfer each slice to the grill. Cook for 2 to 3 minutes per side, or until the slices are lightly browned.

5. Pour 3 to 4 tablespoons (45 to 60 mL) of the fruit sauce on each warmed serving plate, and top each with a slice of the grilled pound cake. Sprinkle each serving with confectioners' sugar and nutmeg.

Smokin' Chocolate Cake
Yield: 8 servings

A gentle smoky flavor adds a nice dimension to this moist and hearty cake. The smoked chocolate icing is a perfect finishing touch.

¾ cup (177 mL) all-purpose flour
1 ounce (28 g) unsweetened cocoa
1 teaspoon (5 mL) baking powder
5 ounces (140 g) packed brown sugar
2 large eggs, separated
6 tablespoons (90 mL) vegetable oil
¼ cup (60 mL) heavy cream
6 tablespoons (90 mL) Grand Marnier
1 teaspoon (5 mL) pure vanilla extract
1 recipe Smoky Chocolate Frosting (recipe follows)

1. Preheat the smoker or barbecue to 350° F (180°C) for indirect cooking. Thoroughly grease an 8-inch (20-cm) round cake pan.

2. In a mixing bowl, sift together the flour, cocoa, and baking powder. Stir in the brown sugar. Add the egg yolks, oil, cream, Grand Marnier, and vanilla and beat to a smooth batter.

3. In a separate bowl, whip the egg whites until soft peaks form. Using a rubber spatula, fold the egg whites into the batter. Pour the batter into the prepared cake pan and bake for 1¼ hours, or until the cake has fully risen and is golden and a skewer or toothpick inserted into the middle comes out clean.

4. Remove the cake from the barbecue. Let it cool for 10 minutes, and then turn it out onto a wire rack to cool completely.

Smoky Chocolate Frosting
1 pound (454 g) semisweet chocolate, grated
1 pound (454 g) milk chocolate, grated
1 pint (473 mL) heavy cream
¾ cup (177 mL) Grand Marnier
1 tablespoon (15 mL) butter

1. Preheat the smoker to 220°F (105°C).

2. In a medium stainless-steel mixing bowl, combine the grated chocolates. Add the cream and stir.

3. Place the bowl in the smoker and smoke for 30 minutes, stirring halfway through the cooking time. For a heavier smoke flavor, increase the smoking time by 15 minutes. If the chocolate mixture is not completely melted after 30 minutes, place it over a pot of boiling water and bring it up to 160°F (71°C). Whisk the mixture until smooth. Add the Grand Marnier and whisk again until smooth.

4. When the frosting is smooth, remove the bowl from the heat and stir in the butter. Let the frosting cool thoroughly. When you are ready to frost the cake, beat the frosting until fluffy with a hand-held mixer and spread it over the cake.

Grilled Avocados with Strawberry–Mango Salsa
Yield: 4 servings

Yes, avocado is a fruit, so serving it as a dessert is OK—a bit surprising to most folks, but OK. This recipe is delightful on a hot summer evening after a barbecue dinner.

4 avocados, not ripe but just turning soft
¼ cup (59 mL) honey
¼ cup (59 mL) olive oil
1 medium mango, peeled, pitted, and cut into ½-inch (1-cm) cubes
½ pound (277 g) strawberries, cut into ½-inch (1-cm) cubes
⅓ cup (79 mL) orange juice
2 tablespoons (30 mL) lemon juice
1 tablespoon (15 mL) balsamic vinegar
Lettuce leaves, for serving

1. Preheat the barbecue to medium high (300°F (150°C) to 400F (200°C), making sure the grill is well oiled.

2. Slice the avocados in half lengthwise and carefully remove the seeds. In a small bowl, mix together the honey and olive oil. Brush the exposed flesh with the honey–olive oil mixture, cover with plastic wrap and set aside in a cool place (do not refrigerate).

3. In a medium bowl, combine the mango, strawberries, orange juice, lemon juice, and balsamic vinegar. Let the fruit sit for at least 20 minutes, stirring occasionally, so the flavors can blend.

4. Grill the avocados, skin side down, for 2 to 3 minutes, or until the skin begins to lightly char and take on grill marks. Brush the flesh side of the avocados again with the honey-oil mixture and place them flesh side down on the grill for 2 to 3 minutes.

5. With a spatula, carefully remove the avocados from the grill and place them on beds of lettuce on warm serving plates, 2 halves per person. Fill the seed cavity of each avocado half with the mango-strawberry salsa. Serve with spoons to scoop out the avocado flesh and salsa.

Black and Blue Burning Berries
Yield: 4–6 servings

Quick and easy to prepare, this dessert can also be served for breakfast or brunch. At that hour you could leave out the liquor . . . or maybe not.

¼ cup (59 mL) unsalted butter
¼ cup (59 mL) packed brown sugar
1 (16-ounce [454-g]) bag frozen blueberries
1 (16-ounce [454-g]) bag frozen blackberries
½ cup (118 mL) Grand Marnier
1 tablespoon (15 mL) whiskey
Chocolate-mint ice cream (or your favorite flavor), for serving

1. Preheat the barbecue to medium high (350°F [180°C] to 400°F [200°C]) for direct heating.

2. In a large cast-iron skillet on the grill, melt the butter. Add the sugar, swirl and stir until it is melted, then add the berries.

3. Cook until the berries release their liquid and the blueberries begin to break apart, approximately 8 minutes. Stir a few times, mashing a few berries as you do so.

4. Add the Grand Marnier and whiskey and, using a charcoal lighter, light the liquid quickly. Serve carefully by scooping flaming berries over the ice cream with a long metal spoon or ladle.

Charred Hazelnut Pears
Yield: 8 servings

If you can buy or make hazelnut or cashew nut butter, please use it in this recipe. It's quite unlike peanut butter and will put this dessert on the "we've got to make this again" list.

4 Anjou, Bartlett, or Comice pears
2 tablespoons (30 mL) lemon juice
1 tablespoon (15 mL) butter
1 cup (236 mL) packed brown sugar
½ cup (118 mL) hazelnut liqueur
1 tablespoon (15 mL) hazelnut butter (or smooth peanut butter)
¼ cup (59 mL) coarsely chopped toasted hazelnuts
Confectioners' sugar, for serving

1. Preheat the barbecue to medium high (400°F [200°C]).

2. Peel the pears, halve them lengthwise, and scoop out the cores. Place them in a resealable plastic bag. Add the lemon juice, turn to coat the pears with the juice, and set aside.

3. In a Dutch oven or cast-iron frying pan large enough to hold the pears in single layer, melt the butter. Add the sugar and cook, swirling the pan to melt the sugar evenly, for 5 minutes or until the sugar is a deep golden color.

4. Carefully add the pears, cut side down, in a single layer. Cover the cast-iron pan and cook for 20 minutes, or until the pears are tender.

5. With a slotted spatula or spoon, transfer the pears to a warmed platter, cut side up, and cover them with aluminum foil to keep them warm.

6. Stir liqueur and nut butter into the pan. Stir in the hazelnuts. Bring the mixture to a boil and cook, stirring, for 3 minutes, or until the sauce is slightly thickened.

7. Pour the sauce over the platter of pears and serve warm.

Peanut Butter Cup Tartlets

Yield: 36 cookies

These are rich, perfect for a cold rainy day, and sure to be a favorite with your children or your spouse.

36 Reese's Peanut Butter Cups
1 (1-pound [454-g]) package refrigerated sugar cookie dough
Confectioners' sugar, for garnish

1. Preheat the barbecue to 350°F (180°C).

2. Refrigerate the candies for 15 to 20 minutes.

3. Unwrap each peanut butter cup and cut them into quarters. If the cookie dough is packaged in a roll, cut it into ½-inch (1-cm) thick rounds. Otherwise, roll the dough into 1½-inch (3.5-cm) balls. Place each portion of dough in the bottom of a miniature muffin pan.

4. Put the muffin pan in the barbecue for 8 to 10 minutes, or until each cookie puffs up but is still very raw.

5. Push a peanut butter cup section into the middle of each cookie-filled cup. The cookie will deflate and form around the candy.

6. Bake for another 5 minutes, then remove the pan from the barbecue. Let the tartlets cool and either serve them immediately or refrigerate them for eating later. Sprinkle with confectioners' sugar before serving.

Three Ps Strudel

Yield: 8 servings

You can substitute just about any fruit here for the pears, peaches, and prunes, including strawberries, blueberries, apples, apricots, or plums.

6 tablespoons (90 mL) butter, divided
¼ cup (59 mL) packed brown sugar
1 teaspoon (5 mL) ground nutmeg
2 medium Elberta peaches, peeled and sliced
2 medium Comice pears, peeled and sliced
10 prunes, soaked in hot water and drained
¼ cup (59 mL) ground vanilla wafers
4 sheets phyllo dough, thawed
1 tablespoon (15 mL) granulated sugar
1 teaspoon (5 mL) ground cinnamon

1. Preheat the barbecue grill to medium high (300°F [150°C] to 350°F [180°C]) for indirect heating. Line a baking sheet with parchment paper.

2. In a large saucepan, melt 2 tablespoons (30 mL) of the butter. Stir in the brown sugar and nutmeg then add the peaches, pears, and prunes and and sauté for 7 to 10 minutes, or until the peaches and pears are soft. Remove the fruit from the pan, drain, and chill completely.

3. In a flat sauté pan, melt 2 more tablespoons (30 mL) of the butter. Add the vanilla wafer crumbs and sauté until they are golden brown. Add them to the chilled pear mixture and mix thoroughly.

4. In a small saucepan, melt the remaining butter. Place a sheet of phyllo dough on a clean work surface and lightly brush the sheet with the melted butter. Place a second sheet of phyllo on top of the first and brush it with melted butter. Repeat with the remaining sheets.

5. Spread the chilled peaches, pears, and prunes along one of the long sides of the phyllo and carefully roll the dessert into a strudel by folding the short ends over filling and rolling the dough up along the long end.

6. Brush the roll with melted butter and sprinkle it with the sugar and the cinnamon. Place the roll seam side down on the lined baking sheet. Place the baking sheet on the indirect side of the barbecue and cook for 20 to 30 minutes, or until the phyllo roll turns golden brown.

7. Allow the roll to cool for 10 to 15 minutes to firm up the fruit filling before cutting and serving. Sprinkle with confectioners' sugar and serve with freshly whipped cream.

Baby Pecan Tartlets
Yield: 48 tarts

If you wish, you can substitute walnuts or just about any other nut for the pecans.

6 ounces (168 g) cream cheese
1 cup (236 mL) butter
2 cups (473 mL) all-purpose flour
2 large eggs
1¾ cups (413 mL) packed light brown sugar
2 tablespoons (30 mL) butter, melted
1 teaspoon (5 mL) pure vanilla extract
1 pinch salt
¾ cup (177 mL) chopped pecans

1. Preheat the barbecue to medium high (350°F [180°C] to 400°F [200°C]).

2. In a small bowl, cream together the cream cheese and butter. Add the flour. With your hands, roll the mixture into 48 balls. Put each ball into a cup in mini cupcake pans or mini tart pans, and press the dough into bottom and up the sides of the cup.

3. In a medium bowl, beat the eggs lightly with a fork. Add the sugar, melted butter, vanilla, and salt. Add the nuts. Add about ¾ teaspoon (3.75 mL) of the filling (maybe a little more) to each tart. Bake for 30 minutes.

4. Remove the pans from the barbecue and cool before serving.

Raspberry-Blueberry Turnovers

Yield: 4–8 servings

These are easy to make and taste much better than the frozen ones that have a mere couple of teaspoons (10 mL) of filling. You can fill these up with much more fruit.

2 sheets frozen puff pastry, thawed
½ cup (118 mL) raspberry jam
¼ cup (59 mL) blueberry preserves
6 ounces (177 mL) cream cheese
8 (2-inch [5-cm]) squares milk or semisweet chocolate
1 egg
1 teaspoon (5 mL) milk
1½ tablespoons (22.5 mL) confectioners' sugar

1. Preheat the barbecue to 425°F (220°C) for indirect heating.

2. On a lightly floured surface, roll out each sheet of pastry into a 12-inch (30-cm) square and cut each square into 4 (6-inch [15-cm]) squares. In a small bowl, mix together the jam and preserves together.

3. Put one very full tablespoon (15 mL) of cream cheese in the center of each pastry square. Add a very full tablespoon (15 mL) of the fruit jam mixture. Add a square of chocolate. Lightly brush the edges of each pastry square with water.

4. Fold the pastry squares in half diagonally to form triangles, pressing the edges together firmly with the tines of a fork dipped in milk to seal the edges well.

5. Mix the egg with the milk and brush the top of each turnover with the egg wash. Sprinkle a baking sheet with a tablespoon (15 mL) of water and arrange the turnovers on the baking sheet. With a sharp knife, cut several vents in the top of each turnover. Sprinkle them with the confectioners' sugar and bake on the unheated side of the barbecue for 12 to 15 minutes, or until they are puffed and golden.

6. Remove the turnovers from the barbecue and sprinkle them with more confectioners' sugar. Serve them warm with ice cream if you wish.

Kate's Tangerine Popovers with Tangerine Butter

Yield: 6 servings

Popovers are the Yorkshire puddings of the dessert world and are almost a forgotten dessert. They're light, they can by served with all sorts of syrups and toppings, and they're fun to make in the barbecue.

1 tablespoon (15 mL) vegetable oil or nonstick cooking spray
3 large eggs
1¼ cups (177 mL) milk, at room temperature
1¼ cups (177 mL) all-purpose flour
1 teaspoon (5 mL) grated tangerine zest
1 pinch salt
6 tablespoons (90 mL) Tangerine Butter (recipe follows)

1. Preheat the gas barbecue to high (400°F [200°C] to 450°F [220°C]) for indirect heating, putting a water pan under the unheated side of the grill. Lightly oil or spray with nonstick cooking spray all surfaces of a popover tin or muffin tin.

2. In a medium bowl, beat the eggs with a whisk or hand-held mixer until they are lemon-colored and foamy. Add the milk and blend well, but do not overbeat. Add the flour, zest, and salt. Beat until foamy and smooth on top.

3. Pour the popover batter into a pitcher so that it can be easily poured, and fill each popover cup ¾ full with the batter. (If you're using a muffin tin, fill every other cup, so that when the popovers puff they will not touch each other.)

4. Bake for 15 minutes. Turn down the burner(s) by ⅓ to reduce heat to 350°F (180°C) and bake for 30 minutes more. Do not open the lid of the barbecue while the turnovers are baking (you can lose up to 15 minutes of cooking time with each lifting of the lid).

5. When the popovers are slightly browned and have risen properly, remove the pans from the barbecue. Using a sharp knife remove the popovers from the pans and serve them with a large pat of the Tangerine Butter on each plate.

Tangerine Butter

Yield: 2¾ cups (650 mL)

½ cup (118 mL) unsalted butter, at room temperature
2 cups (473 mL) confectioners' sugar
2 teaspoons (10 mL) grated tangerine zest

1. Using an electric mixer, beat the butter until creamy. Beat in the sugar and zest until smooth.

2. Cover the mixture and refrigerate until thoroughly chilled. Roll the butter into logs, wrap them well, and freeze. Bring the logs to room temperature before using.

AnnTerCal's Grilled Bread Pudding

Yield: 4–6 servings

A lovely Canadian couple shared this recipe when I visited them in Victoria, British Columbia. They both love to cook and love to eat, and this recipe proves both statements.

10 (½-inch [1-cm]) slices French bread
6 large egg whites
1¼ cups (295 mL) packed brown sugar
2 tablespoons (30 mL) unsalted butter, melted
1½ teaspoons (7.5 mL) pure vanilla extract
1¼ teaspoons (6.25 mL) ground nutmeg
1¼ teaspoons (6.25 mL) ground cinnamon
½ teaspoon (2.5 mL) grated lemon zest
1 cup (236 mL) skim milk
1 cup (236 mL) whole milk (or, if you're feeling decadent, 1 cup [236 mL] heavy cream)
½ cup (118 mL) dried apricots
½ cup (118 mL) golden raisins
Pure maple syrup, for drizzling
Ice cream, for serving (optional)

1. Grill the French bread directly over medium heat until grill marks appear, about 2 minutes, turning once halfway through the grilling time. Cut the bread into cubes (you should end up with approximately 5 cups [1.2 L]) and set aside.

2. In a large bowl, beat the egg whites until they are frothy, about 2 minutes. Add the brown sugar, melted butter, vanilla, nutmeg, cinnamon, and zest. Beat until the mixture is well blended. Add the skim and whole milk, and stir in the apricots and raisins. Add the bread cubes and toss until mixed well. Let the bread rest for about 45 minutes, patting it down into the liquid occasionally.

3. Preheat the barbecue to medium high (350°F [180°C] to 400°F [200°C]), leaving one side unheated. Butter well a 5 x 9-inch (12.5 x 22.5-cm) loaf pan.

4. Pour the bread and egg mixture into the prepared loaf pan. Place the pan on the unheated side of the barbecue and cook for 50 to 60 minutes, or until the top of the dessert is well browned and puffy. Slice, drizzle with maple syrup, and serve warm with a scoop of your favorite ice cream.

Saucy Mango Chimichangas

Yield: 4 servings

I recently made this dish and added 1 teaspoon (5 mL) of chili powder, and I was blown away by the wonderful flavor it added to the sweet dessert.

6 ripe mangoes, peeled, pitted, and diced
2 tablespoons (30 mL) sugar
2 tablespoons (30 mL) Triple Sec
Juice of 2 limes, divided
⅓ cup (79 mL) finely ground toasted almonds
2 teaspoons (10 mL) butter
4 (7-inch [17.5-cm]) flour tortillas
Confectioners' sugar, for serving
Whipped cream, for serving

1. Preheat the barbecue to medium high (350°F [180°C] to 400°F [200°C]) for indirect heating, putting a water pan under the unheated side of the grill. Make sure the grill is well greased.

2. In a large saucepan on a side burner, combine the mangoes and sugar over medium-low heat. Add the Triple Sec and half the lime juice, and bring to a boil. Simmer until the mixture is very thick, stirring constantly toward the end. Stir in the almonds, butter, and the remaining lime juice. Remove the pan from the heat and set the mixture aside to cool.

3. Warm the tortillas for a few seconds on the grill, then transfer them to a plastic bag to keep them soft and moist. Spoon a quarter of the fruit mixture onto the center of a tortilla, fold in the sides, and roll it up into a tight package, securing the chimichangas with wooden toothpicks. Repeat with the remaining tortillas and fruit.

4. Grill the chimichangas until they are lightly browned on both sides and charred on the edges. Remove them from the barbecue and sprinkle them with confectioners' sugar shaken through a sieve. Serve immediately, topped with whipped cream.

Banana and Pineapple Crêpes

Yield: 14 crêpes

You'll love this taste sensation!

2½ cups (354 mL) milk
2 cups (473 mL) all-purpose flour
3 large eggs
2 tablespoons (30 mL) butter, melted, plus more for brushing
2 tablespoons (30 mL) sugar
1 pinch salt
1 (3–5 pound [1.3–2.3 kg]) whole pineapple
3 large green bananas
Vegetable oil for the pan

1. In a medium bowl, whisk together the milk, flour, eggs, 2 tablespoons (30 mL) of the melted butter, the sugar, and the salt. Refrigerate the batter up to an hour before making the crêpes.

2. Preheat the grill to medium high.

3. Twist the crown off the pineapple and cut the pineapple into halves and then quarters. Trim the ends, remove the core, and carefully slice off the skin with a sharp knife. Cut the pineapple into slices and brush them lightly with melted butter. Grill for about 4 minutes on each side, then chop the grilled slices into small pieces. Peel the bananas, cut them in half lengthwise, brush the cut sides with melted butter, and grill for about 3 minutes on each side. Mix the bananas with the grilled pineapple, drain well, and set aside.

4. Heat an 8-inch (20-cm) skillet over medium-high heat, drizzle a small amount of oil in the hot pan, and spread it around with a paper towel. Pour about ½ cup (118 mL) of batter into the pan and quickly swirl it so the batter evenly coats the bottom of the pan. Cook until batter starts to set along the edges and the bottom turns light golden and slightly crisp. Carefully turn the pancake with a spatula and cook the other side until light golden. Remove the crêpe to a warm plate and repeat the process with the remaining batter.

5. When all the crêpes are made, spoon 2 tablespoons (30 mL) pineapple-banana mixture along the center of each crêpe, fold over, roll up, and serve.

Grilled Pound Cake with Chocolate–Orange Sauce
Yield: 4–6 servings

There is no substitute for the Grand Marnier liqueur in this sauce. The orange marmalade and hazelnut essences mixed with the scent of orange flowers simply can't be beat for adding a distinguished and sophisticated taste to this dish.

¾ cup (177 mL) heavy cream
1 tablespoon (15 mL) pure maple syrup
6 tablespoons (45 mL) Grand Marnier, divided
8 ounces (227 g) bittersweet baking chocolate, grated
1 tablespoon (15 mL) finely grated orange zest
1 (11.75-ounce [329-g]) frozen Sara Lee pound cake, thawed
2 tablespoons (30 mL) orange juice

1. Preheat the barbecue to high (450°F [240°C] to 500°F [260°C]).

2. In a small saucepan, combine the heavy cream and maple syrup and bring to a boil. Stir in 3 tablespoons (45 mL) of the Grand Marnier and remove the pan from the heat. Add the grated chocolate and let stand for 1 minute, then whisk until all of the chocolate is melted and the mixture is smooth and creamy. Stir in the orange zest, cover, and keep warm.

3. Cut the pound cake into 6 (1-inch [2.5-cm] thick) slices and poke each slice several times with a fork. In a measuring cup, mix together the orange juice and the remaining Grand Marnier, stir, and drizzle this mixture evenly over the cake slices.

4. Place the cake slices directly on the heated grill and cook for 2 to 4 minutes, turning once, until both sides have nice grill marks on them.

5. Serve the grilled cake slices lavishly drizzled with the orange-chocolate sauce.

Barb's Apricot Pie
Yield: 6 servings

Ninety-five percent of all apricots sold in the United States are grown in California, but many of them migrate each year to the East Coast, where my sister-in-law regularly turns them into an incredible dessert pie. This recipe comes from Barb Smith from Southington, Conn.

5 cups (1.2 L) apricot halves
2 teaspoons (10 mL) lemon juice
¾ cup (177 mL) sugar
¼ cup (59 mL) all-purpose flour
¼ teaspoon (1.25 mL) ground cinnamon
¼ teaspoon (1.25 mL) ground nutmeg
Pastry dough for double-crust pie
2 tablespoons (30 mL) butter

1. Preheat the barbecue to medium high (350°F [180°C] to 400°F [200°C]).

2. In a large bowl, combine the apricots and lemon juice. Add the sugar, flour, cinnamon, and nutmeg and toss lightly to mix.

3. Fit one of the crusts into a pie pan. Scoop the mixture into the pastry, dot with butter, and cover the filling with the top crust. Press the edges of the crusts together to seal and flute the edges. Cut 3 vents in the top crust. You may want to cover the edge of the pie with strips of aluminum foil to prevent them from browning too much or too quickly.

4. Bake on the grill for 35 to 40 minutes, or until the juice begins to bubble through the slits in the crust and the crust is lightly browned.

Dorothy's Lemony Boston Cream Pie
Yield: 8–10 servings

Some folks, including my wife, Kate, think the filling in this dessert should be vanilla custard. I, however, grew up with a mom who used lemon flavoring and zests to make the filling lemony. If you choose the vanilla way, use 2 teaspoons (10 mL) vanilla extract in the filling instead of the lemon extract, and omit the zest. This recipe comes from Dorothy Browne from Battle Creek, Mich.

Cake
3 large eggs, separated
1 teaspoon (5 mL) pure vanilla extract
½ cup (118 mL) sugar, divided
1 pinch salt
¾ cup (177 mL) cake flour

Filling
½ cup (118 mL) sugar
¼ cup (59 mL) all-purpose flour
1½ cups (354 mL) milk
6 large egg yolks
Finely minced zests from 2 large lemons
2 teaspoons (10 mL) lemon extract
1 pinch salt

Icing
½ cup (118 mL) sugar
3 tablespoons (45 mL) light corn syrup
2 tablespoons (30 mL) water
4 ounces (112 g) semisweet chocolate, coarsely chopped
Confectioners' sugar, for sprinkling

1. Preheat the barbecue to medium high (300°F [150°C] to 320°F [165°C]). Grease a 9-inch (22.5-cm) round cake pan and line it with a round of waxed paper.

2. Make the cake. In a mixing bowl, use a hand-held mixer on medium to beat together the 3 egg yolks and the vanilla until well blended. Add half the sugar and beat until very thick and pale. In a separate bowl, using clean, dry beaters, beat together the 3 egg whites and salt at medium speed until very soft peaks form. Gradually beat in the remaining sugar until stiffer peaks form. With a rubber spatula, fold the yolk mixture into the egg whites. Sift the flour over the mixture and fold it in gently. Do not overmix.

3. Pour the batter into the prepared cake pan and bake in the barbecue until the top springs back when lightly pressed, about 25 minutes. Let the cake cool partially. Loosen it from the sides of the pan by running a sharp knife around the edges. Invert the cake onto a wire rack. Remove the cake pan but leave the waxed paper on the cake. Turn the cake right-side up, with the paper again at the bottom, and cool it completely on the rack.

4. Make the filling. In a small saucepan, mix together the sugar and flour. Gradually whisk in the milk. Whisk in the egg yolks, lemon zest, lemon extract, and salt. Bring to a boil over medium heat and cook for 1 minute, whisking constantly. Strain through a fine sieve into a bowl. Press plastic wrap onto the surface top keep it from forming a skin, and chill for 30 minutes.

5. Using a serrated knife, carefully cut the cake in half horizontally, and carefully remove the waxed paper. Place the bottom layer on a serving plate, cut side up. Spread this layer evenly with the filling, then top it with the remaining layer.

6. Make the icing. In a small saucepan, combine the sugar, corn syrup, and water and bring to a boil over low heat. Cook, stirring constantly, until the sugar is dissolved, and remove the saucepan from the heat. Add the chocolate pieces and let stand for 1 to 2 minutes, until they look like they're beginning to melt. Whisk the icing until smooth. While the icing is still very warm, slowly pour it over the cake, allowing it to drip down the sides. Let the cake stand until the glaze sets. Sprinkle it with confectioners' sugar just before taking it to the table to serve.

Chocolate–Maraschino Cherry Tarts
Yield: 4–6 servings

Real maraschino cherries were first formulated in Italy, where a sweet liqueur was developed from the juice and ground pits of bitter wild cherries and used to preserve the local Marasca cherries. U.S. cherry growers couldn't afford this pricey process, so they developed their own variety of maraschino cherries.

2 tablespoons (30 mL) butter, softened
1 cup (236 mL) sugar, divided
1 ounce (28 g) semisweet chocolate, melted
2 large eggs, divided
½ teaspoon (2.5 mL) pure vanilla extract
1¼ cups (295 mL) all-purpose flour
¼ teaspoon (1.25 mL) salt
⅛ teaspoon (0.6 mL) baking soda
8 ounces (227 g) cream cheese
½ cup (118 mL) maraschino cherries, coarsely chopped
20 maraschino cherry halves, for garnish

1. Preheat the barbecue to medium high (350°F [180°C] to 400°F [200°C]). Spray with nonstick cooking spray or butter 20 tartlet pans.

2. In a mixing bowl, cream together the butter and ½ cup (118 mL) of the sugar. Add the melted chocolate and blend until it's completely incorporated. Add 1 of the eggs and vanilla and beat well.

3. In a separate bowl, sift together the flour, salt, and baking soda. Blend this mixture into the chocolate mixture.

4. Scoop the pastry onto a floured pastry cloth and roll it to ⅛-inch (0.25-cm) thickness. Using a 3-inch cookie cutter, cut out circles of the dough and place them in the prepared tartlet pans.

5. In a small bowl, blend together by hand the cream cheese, the remaining sugar, and the remaining egg. Fold in the chopped cherries. Spoon 1 tablespoon (15 mL) of the cherry filling into each tart.

6. Bake for 10 to 12 minutes. Remove the tartlets from the heat, top each with a cherry half, chill, and serve cooled.

Tangy Rhubarb Crunch
Yield: 4–6 servings

Funny fact: Rhubarb is a close relative to (of all things) buckwheat, and it is actually considered a vegetable, except by those of us who treasure it for rhubarb pie.

1 cup (236 mL) all-purpose flour
1 cup (236 mL) packed brown sugar
¾ cup (177 mL) rolled oats
½ cup (118 mL) butter, melted
4 cups (0.95 L) chopped rhubarb (½-inch [1-cm] pieces)
1 cup (236 mL) sugar
2 tablespoons (30 mL) cornstarch
1 cup (236 mL) water
1 teaspoon (5 mL) pure vanilla extract

1. Preheat the barbecue to medium high (350°F [180°C] to 400°F [200°C]). Grease a 9-inch (22.5-cm) square glass baking dish.

2. In a medium bowl, mix together the flour, brown sugar, oats, and butter until crumbly. Press half of this mixture into the prepared dish.

3. Add the rhubarb to the pan.

4. In a small saucepan, cstir together the sugar and cornstarch; stir in the water and vanilla and cook over medium heat until the mixture becomes thick and clear.

5. Pour the sauce over the rhubarb in the baking pan, then sprinkle on the rest of the crumb mixture.

6. Bake for 45 minutes, or until the top is browned and the filling is bubbling.

7. Remove the pan from the barbecue. Cool partially before serving, as the filling can be scaldingly hot.

Plum Cinnamon Tart

Yield: 4–6 servings

If you want to be adventurous, you can add 1 cup (236 mL) of chopped, rehydrated dried apricots to the plum mixture before you add the filling, making sure the apricots are are very moist and soft.

8 large purple plums, pitted and quartered
1 prebaked 9-inch (22.5-cm) pie shell
1 cup (236 mL) heavy cream
2 large eggs
1 egg yolk
½ cup (118 mL) granulated sugar
Juice of 2 lemons
2 teaspoons (10 mL) ground cinnamon, divided
3 tablespoons (45 mL) brown sugar

1. Preheat the barbecue to medium high (350°F [180°C] to 400°F [200°C]), making sure the grill is clean and generously sprayed with nonstick spray.

2. Arrange the quartered plums in the pie shell, skin side up.

3. In a medium bowl, beat together the cream, eggs, egg yolk, sugar, lemon juice, and 1 teaspoon (5 mL) of the cinnamon, mixing thoroughly.

4. Pour the custard over the plums, place the tart in the barbecue, and cook for 20 to 25 minutes, or until the plums give easily when probed with a knife. Remove the tart from the barbecue.

5. In a small bowl, stir together the brown sugar and the remaining cinnamon. Sprinkle this mixture over the tart. Return the pie to the barbecue and bake for about 10 minutes, or until the top becomes crusty. Serve warm with vanilla ice cream.

Mark's Maker's Mark Peachtarines

Yield: 4 servings

This works as either a dessert or a side dish. It's great on a hot summer night after a barbecue dinner, or as a side dish with a smoked country ham or a succulent butterflied leg of lamb. This recipe comes from Mark Mathias from Vancouver, Wash.

1 pound (454 g) fresh peaches, peeled, pitted, and cut into thin slices
1 pound (454 g) fresh nectarines, peeled, pitted, and cut in thin slices
2 cups (473 mL) packed brown sugar
2 cups (473 mL) water
½ cup (118 mL) plus 2 tablespoons (15 mL) Maker's Mark (or your favorite whiskey), divided
1 stick cinnamon
Ground nutmeg, for garnish

1. In a heavy saucepan, combine the peaches, nectarines, brown sugar, water, ½ cup (118 mL) of the Maker's Mark, and the cinnamon stick. Bring the mixture to a high boil and reduce the heat to a low boil. Cook until the fruit can be pierced easily but is not too soft, about 5 minutes.

2. Remove the pan from the heat, discard the cinnamon stick, and pour the fruit and syrup into a sealable container. Fill the container to the top so no air gets to the fruit, or weigh the fruit down with a small bowl so it stays immersed in the syrup. Refrigerate for at least 12 hours.

3. Just before serving, stir the remaining 2 tablespoons (30 mL) Maker's Mark into the fruit.

4. Serve the fruit at room temperature over ice cream or cake, sprinkled with a few shakes of nutmeg.

Southern Cracker Pie

Yield: 6 servings

Sometimes called "Mock Apple Pie," this Southern-inspired pie was first published in 1863 in the Confederate Receipt Book. *(And yes, it's the "Receipt" book, not the "Recipe" book.) It has been made through the years, reaching a peak when Ritz Crackers were introduced in 1934.*

20 Ritz original flavor crackers
½ cup (118 mL) walnuts, chopped
3 egg whites
1 cup (236 mL) sugar
1 teaspoon (5 mL) pure vanilla extract
½ teaspoon (2.5 mL) baking powder
Whipped cream, for serving
Grated sweet chocolate, for serving

1. Preheat the barbecue to medium high (350°F [180°C] to 400°F [200°C]).

2. In a small bowl, crush the crackers coarsely. Add the walnuts and set aside.

3. In a medium bowl, beat the egg whites until stiff peaks form, gradually adding the sugar, vanilla, and baking powder. Fold in the crackers and nuts, and fold this mixture into a pie plate.

4. Bake for 20 to 25 minutes. Remove the pie from the barbecue and let it cool.

5. Cover the top of the pie with whipped cream and sprinkle it with grated sweet chocolate.

6. Cut into generous slices and serve.

Awesome Dutch Babies

Yield: 2–4 servings

If you have a deep cake tin, use it to make these. The batter should climb all the way to the top of the pan, giving you a deeper well for the butter, lemon juice. and powdered sugar. Yum. This recipe comes from Tabbatha Hornowski from Ridgefield, Wash.

3 eggs
½ cup (118 mL) bread flour
½ cup (118 mL) milk
2 tablespoons (30 mL) butter, melted
¼ teaspoon (1.25 mL) salt
¼ cup (118 mL) minced lemon zest
¼ cup (118 mL) butter, softened
2 tablespoons (30 mL) confectioners' sugar
8–10 lemon wedges

1. Preheat the barbecue to medium high (400°F [200°C] to 450°F [240°C]). Spray 2 (9-inch [22.5 cm]) pie plates heavily with nonstick cooking spray.

2. In a medium bowl, beat the eggs. Mix in the flour, 2 tablespoons (30 mL) at a time, beating just until smooth. Add the milk, melted butter, salt, and lemon zest and stir to mix well.

3. Divide the batter between the prepared pie plates. Bake for 10 minutes.

4. Lower the heat to around 350°F [176°C], if using charcoal close vents and/or prop open the barbecue lid, and bake for 5 more minutes. Remove the pans from the barbecue.

5. Using a spatula, spread half of the soft butter on the inside walls and bottom of both pastries. Squeeze 2 to 3 lemon wedges into each pie shell and sprinkle with confectioners' sugar. Serve with the remaining lemon wedges.

The Best Quick Dessert Ever

Yield: 4–6 serving

You can whip up this easy and quick dessert in 25 minutes, less if you have a pre-baked pie shell handy. This recipe comes from Kate Browne from Ridgefield, Wash.

1½ cups (354 mL) graham cracker crumbs
1 cup (236 mL) chopped pecans
½ cup (118 mL) margarine, melted
1 (8-ounce [227-g]) package cream cheese, softened
1 cup (236 mL) confectioners' sugar
4 cups (0.95 L) Cool Whip, divided
3 ounces (84 g) chocolate pudding mix
3 ounces (84 g) instant vanilla pudding
3 cups (708 mL) milk
1 ounce (28 g) unsweetened chocolate, melted

1. Preheat the barbecue to medium high (350°F [180°C] to 400°F [200°C]). Butter a 9 × 13-inch (22.5 × 32.5-cm) baking pan.

2. In a small bowl, combine the graham cracker crumbs, pecans, and melted margarine. Place this mixture into the bottom of the prepared baking pan. Bake in the barbecue for about 20 minutes, or until it begins to brown. Cool completely.

3. In a medium bowl, beat together the cream cheese, confectioners' sugar, and 1 cup (236 mL) of the Cool Whip. Spoon this mixture onto the graham cracker crust.

4. In a separate medium bowl, mix together both puddings and the milk and beat per the package directions. Let the pudding almost thicken and pour it over the cream cheese layer. Add the remaining Cool Whip on top, and swirl the melted chocolate throughout the topping.

5. Let the mixture cool, then slice and serve.

Moroccan Date Cake
Yield: 6–8 servings

There are six varieties of dates available in most U.S. markets, all hailing originally from the Middle East. In addition to the "king" of dates—the glorious Medjool, which was brought to California from Morocco in 1927—look for the Deglet Noor, Halaway, Khadrawy, Zahidi, and Thoory varieties.

½ cup (118 mL) butter, at room temperature
½ cup (118 mL) packed brown sugar
4 eggs
1 cup (236 mL) all-purpose flour
1 teaspoon (5 mL) baking powder
1½ teaspoons (7.5 mL) ground cinnamon, divided
1 teaspoon (5 mL) ground nutmeg
½ teaspoon (2.5 mL) ground cloves
½ cup (118 mL) heavy cream
½ teaspoon (2.5 mL) pure vanilla extract
1 cup (236 mL) pitted, chopped Medjool dates
½ cup (118 mL) chopped walnuts
¼ cup (59 mL) dried apricots, soaked in water and drained
Freshly whipped cream, for serving
Confectioners' sugar, for garnish

1. Preheat a charcoal or gas grill to 325°F (165°C) for indirect cooking. Butter and flour a 9-inch (22.5-cm) cake pan.

2. In a large bowl, beat together the butter and sugar with an electric mixer on medium-high speed until pale and fluffy, 3 to 5 minutes. Beat in the eggs, 1 at a time, until completely incorporated.

3. In a small bowl, combine the flour, baking powder, 1 teaspoon (5 mL) of the cinnamon, the nutmeg, and the cloves. Add the dry ingredients to the wet ingredients and beat for 1 minute, until just combined. Add the heavy cream and vanilla, and continue beating for 1 to 2 minutes more, or until the cream is thoroughly mixed with the dry ingredients. Add the dates, walnuts, and apricots, and stir well with a spatula to combine.

4. Pour the batter into the prepared pan and place it on the grill rack over indirect heat. Lower the lid and cook for about 30 minutes, or until a knife inserted in the center of the cake comes out clean. Serve with lots of freshly whipped cream, dusted with the remaining cinnamon and some confectioners' sugar.

Grilled Fruit
Yield: 4 servings

Lots of people love grilled fruit as a side dish or dessert. This recipe is quick to pre-pare, and the lovely sauce sets off the fruit perfectly. It also goes very well with roast chicken and grilled white fish, such as trout or cod.

2 Fuji or Granny Smith apples, cored and quartered
2 small, ripe Bosc or Comice pears, cored and quartered
2 large, ripe peaches, pitted and quartered
10 ripe red plums, pitted and quartered
Juice of 1 lemon
5 tablespoons (75 mL) brown sugar, divided
3 large egg yolks
5 ounces (148 mL) dry cider

1. Preheat the barbecue to medium high (350°F [180°C] to 400°F [200°C]). Make sure the grill is clean and generously sprayed with nonstick grilling spray.

2. Place the cut fruit in a bowl. Add the lemon juice and toss to coat. Re-serve any juices that leak out of the fruit.

3. Place fruit on the hot grill and sprinkle it with 1 tablespoon (15 mL) of the sugar. Grill for about 15 to 20 minutes, or until the fruit caramelizes and the edges brown. As the fruit finishes grilling, transfer it to a heated platter.

4. In the top pot of a double boiler, combine the egg yolks and the re-maining sugar. Whip the mixture with a balloon whisk until it starts to thicken. As the sauce thickens, trickle in the cider and reserved fruit juices and place the pot over 1 to 2 inches (2.5 to 5 cm) of simmering water and cook, stirring continually, until the sauce thickens to a fluffy consistency.

5. Drizzle the warm sauce over the fruit and serve.

Li'l Anne's Butterscotch Pie

Yield: 6–8 servings

You should never refrigerate pies with meringue, as the cold, moist air causes the meringue to weep. Instead, cover them and store them in a cool place.

3 tablespoons (45 mL) butter
2 cups (473 mL) packed brown sugar
2 cups (473 mL) milk, divided
3 large eggs, separated
¼ cup (59 mL) all-purpose flour
½ teaspoon (2.5 mL) salt
1¼ teaspoons (6.25 mL) pure vanilla extract
1 prebaked 9-inch (22.5-cm) pie crust
3 tablespoons (45 mL) granulated sugar

1. Preheat the barbecue to medium high (350°F [180°C] to 400°F [200°C]).

2. In a large cast-iron skillet, melt the butter. Add the brown sugar and ½ cup (118 mL) of the milk and mix well. Bring to a boil and cook for 5 minutes, stirring constantly.

3. In a medium bowl, beat the egg yolks. Stir in the remaining milk. In a separate bowl, combine the flour and salt. Add the flour and salt mixture to the egg and milk mixture. Gradually add to this combined flour-salt-egg-milk mixture about a third of the hot brown sugar mixture. Stir.

4. Pour all of the mixture into the skillet containing the butter, brown sugar, and milk. Cook over low heat, stirring constantly, until thickened. Cool slightly. Blend in 1 teaspoon (5 mL) of the vanilla. Pour the mixture into the pie crust.

5. In a medium bowl, beat the egg whites until stiff peaks form. Slowly add the granulated sugar and continue to beat until the sugar is dissolved. Fold in the remaining ¼ teaspoon (1.25 mL) vanilla.

6. Spoon the meringue on top of the pie, spreading it to the edges all the way around.

7. Bake for about 10 to 15 minutes, or until the meringue is lightly browned. Serve warm or cold.

Orange–Pine Nut Cake

Yield: 6–8 servings

Pine nuts are ivory in color, shaped like torpedoes, and have a sweet, delicate flavor. If you can't get them, you can substitute chopped walnuts for a fairly similar taste. This is a thin cake and will only rise 1- to 1½-inches.

¾ cup (177 mL) unsalted butter, melted
1 cup (236 mL) cane sugar or granulated sugar
⅔ cup (158 mL) packed brown sugar
2 extra-large eggs, at room temperature
Juice of 3 oranges
2 teaspoons (10 mL) pure vanilla extract
2 cups (473 mL) all-purpose flour
½ teaspoon (2.5 mL) salt
3 tablespoons (45 mL) pine nuts

1. Preheat the barbecue to medium high (350°F [180°C] to 400°F [200°C]). Generously butter or spray with nonstick cooking spray a 9-inch (22.5-cm) round cake pan. Dust the inside with flour and shake off the excess. Cut a round piece of parchment paper to fit the bottom of the pan. Butter the parchment and place it in the pan, butter side up.

2. Pour the melted butter into a large bowl. Add the sugars and stir with a rubber spatula until thoroughly blended.

3. One at a time, whisk the eggs into the butter mixture, scraping down the sides of the bowl with a spatula as you go. The mixture will look curdled as the eggs are added, but it will smooth out. Add the orange juice and vanilla and stir to blend.

4. In a medium bowl, sift together the flour and salt. Add this to the butter mixture in 3 batches, stirring well after each addition.

5. Transfer the batter to the prepared cake pan. Use a rubber spatula to spread it evenly into the pan, and scrape all the batter from the bowl. Sprinkle the pine nuts evenly over the top.

6. Bake for 35 to 40 minutes, or until a knife inserted into the center of the cake comes out clean.

7. Remove the pan from the barbecue and place it on a rack to cool completely. Invert the pan to remove the cake, peel off the parchment paper, and invert the cake onto a serving plate. Cut into wedges and serve at room temperature.

South Carolina Peach Pizza

Yield: 4–6 servings

It's a little known fact that South Carolina produces more peaches than Georgia (you know—the Peach State?). Actually, South Carolina is the second largest producer in America. But every other state pales in relation to California, which produces more clingstone and freestone peaches than the other 49 states combined.

½ cup (118 mL) butter, softened
¼ cup (59 mL) confectioners' sugar
1 cup (236 mL) all-purpose flour
2 tablespoons (30 mL) granulated sugar
1 tablespoon (15 mL) cornstarch
¼ teaspoon (1.25 mL) ground nutmeg
¼ teaspoon (1.25 mL) ground cinnamon
½ cup (118 mL) orange juice
½ cup (118 mL) red currant jelly
5 cups (1.2 L) fresh peach slices
½ pint (236 mL) blueberries
Whipped cream, for serving

1. Preheat the barbecue to medium high (350°F [180°C] to 400°F [200°C]).

2. In a small bowl, cream together the butter and confectioners' sugar. Stir in the flour. Pat the mixture into a 12-inch (30-cm) pizza pan, filling the pan edge to edge. Prick the bottom with a fork and bake for 10 minutes, or until the edges are brown. Let the crust cool.

3. In a small saucepan, combine the sugar, cornstarch, nutmeg, and cinnamon and stir. Add the orange juice and jelly and cook, stirring, until the mixture boils and thickens. Set aside to cool.

4. Arrange the peach slices and blueberries on the pizza crust and spoon the sauce over the fruit.

5. Refrigerate until the glaze is set. Serve with whipped cream.

P-ig Strudel (Pear and Fig)

Yield: 8–10 servings

The only way to serve strudel is to accompany it with freshly whipped real cream—not ice cream, not canned whip cream, not refrigerated petroleum-based whipped topping. Use heavy cream, add a bare minimum of sugar, whip just before serving, and serve very cold.

1 pound (454 g) figs, stems removed
1⅔ cups (158 mL) unsweetened pear juice
10 ripe pears
1 teaspoon (5 mL) ground cinnamon
½ teaspoon (2.5 mL) ground allspice
1 (1-pound [454-g]) box frozen phyllo dough, thawed overnight in the refrigerator
½ cup (118 mL) butter, melted
1 cup (236 mL) toasted whole-wheat breadcrumbs
½ cup (118 mL) honey
½ cup (118 mL) chopped hazelnuts

1. Preheat the barbecue to medium high (350°F [180°C] to 400°F [200°C]). Butter a 9 × 13-inch (22.5 × 32.5-cm) baking dish.

2. In a large saucepan, combine the figs and pear juice and bring to a boil. Reduce the heat and simmer for 25 minutes, or until the figs are very tender. Transfer the figs to a blender, purée, and set aside.

3. Peel and core the pears, chop them into bite-sized pieces, and place the pieces in a small bowl. Add the fig purée, cinnamon, and allspice and stir lightly.

4. Cover the bottom of the prepared baking dish with 10 phyllo sheets, brushing every second sheet with the melted butter and sprinkling each buttered layer with breadcrumbs.

5. Using a spatula, spread the pear filling evenly over the last sheet. Cover with another 10 sheets of phyllo, layering as before with the butter and breadcrumbs. The phyllo dough will be too long to fit in the pan, so fold the ends down inside the pan.

6. Bake for 35 to 40 minutes in the barbecue. Remove the pan from the barbecue and allow the strudel to cool for 15 minutes.

7. In a small saucepan, heat the honey until it gets very fluid and warm, then drizzle it over the strudel. Sprinkle the strudel with the hazelnuts.

8. With a sharp knife, cut the strudel into 3-inch (7.5-cm) squares and serve warm.

Creamy Apricot Pie

Yield: 6 servings

If you prefer, you can make this with peaches, nectarines, or pluots (a plum-apricot hybrid). If you use peaches, make sure to peel them.

1 (3-ounce [85-g]) package vanilla pudding mix (not instant)
⅔ cup (158 mL) all-purpose flour
1 teaspoon (5 mL) baking powder
½ teaspoon (2.5 mL) salt
1 egg, beaten
½ cup (118 mL) milk
3 tablespoons (45 mL) butter, softened
1 (15.5-ounce [434-g]) can apricot halves in syrup
8 ounces (227 g) cream cheese
½ cup (118 mL) plus 1 tablespoon sugar, divided
½ teaspoon (2.5 mL) ground cinnamon

1. Preheat barbecue to 350°F (180°C). Grease well or spray with nonstick cooking spray a deep-dish pie plate.

2. In a medium bowl, combine the pudding mix, flour, baking powder, and salt; stir in the egg, milk, and butter. Whisk together for 2 to 3 minutes and pour it into the prepared pie plate.

3. Drain the apricots, reserving 3 tablespoons (45 mL) of the syrup, and arrange the halves on top of the batter.

4. In a medium bowl, whisk together the cream cheese, ½ cup (118 mL) of the sugar, and the reserved apricot syrup. Spoon this mixture on top of the fruit, leaving a 1-inch (2.5-cm) border around the outside edge of the pie.

5. In a small bowl, combine the remaining sugar and the cinnamon and mix well. Sprinkle this mixture on top of the pie.

6. Place the pie in the barbecue and cook for 25 to 30 minutes, or until the top is browned. Remove the pie from the barbecue, let it cool for 10 to 15 minutes, and serve.

Quick Pecan Surprise

Yield: 6–8 serving

This is a light dessert. After all, it's mainly meringue and whipped cream, both of which are 90 percent air bubbles. It's also a tasty, quick dessert that kids will love.

3 egg whites
1 cup (236 mL) sugar
1 teaspoon (5 mL) pure vanilla extract
¼ teaspoon (1.25 mL) baking powder
1 sleeve Ritz crackers (about 30), crushed
1 cup (236 mL) finely chopped pecans
Whipped cream, for serving

1. Preheat the barbecue to medium high (350°F [180°C] to 400°F [200°C]). Grease or spray with nonstick cooking spray a 9-inch (22.5-cm) glass pie plate.

2. In a mixing bowl, use a hand-held beater to beat the egg whites until they begin to stiffen. Fold in the sugar, vanilla extract, and baking powder and continue beating until stiff.

3. Fold in the cracker crumbs and chopped pecans. Pour the mixture into the prepared pie plate.

4. Bake for 20 minutes. Remove the pan from the barbecue heat, let it cool for 10 minutes, top with the freshly whipped cream, and serve.

Ginger Ale Apple Dumplings
Yield: 6 servings

This recipe comes from Angel Ripp from Vancouver, Wash.

1 package refrigerated double-crust pie dough
6 small pippin apples, cored
¼ cup (59 mL) butter, cut into 6 equal pieces
¾ cup (177 mL) packed brown sugar
1 teaspoon (5 mL) ground cinnamon
½ teaspoon (2.5 mL) ground nutmeg
3 cups (708 mL) water
2 cups (473 mL) granulated sugar
¼ cup butter
1 tablespoon (15 mL) dark rum

1. Preheat the barbecue to medium high (375°F [190°C] to 425°F [220°C]) for direct heating. Generously butter a 9 × 13-inch (22.5 × 32.5-cm) piece of parchment paper and put it in the bottom of a 9 × 13-inch (22.5 × 32.5-cm) pan.

2. On a floured surface, unroll the pastry. Cut it into 6 square pieces. Place an apple on each pastry square with the cored opening facing upward. Slip a piece of butter into the core of each apple.

3. In a small bowl, mix together the brown sugar, cinnamon, and nutmeg. Divide the spiced brown sugar into 6 portions, spoon some into each apple core, and sprinkle the rest under and around each apple on the pastry. Brush all four corners of the pastry with cold water. Bring the pastry up around the apples, press the edges together, and pinch to seal.

4. Place the pastries on the parchment paper in the baking pan, then put the pan in the barbecue and bake for 45 minutes.

5. While the dumplings are baking, combine water, granulated sugar, butter, and rum in a saucepan. Bring to a boil and cook, stirring, for 5 minutes. Remove the pan from the heat.

6. Remove the baking pan from the barbecue, pour two-thirds of the sugar-rum sauce over the apples, and return the pan to the barbecue for 10 to15 minutes, or until the pastries are browned all over and the sauce is bubbling.

7. Place each apple dumpling in a dessert bowl, and spoon the remaining sauce over the top of each dumpling. Serve with freshly whipped cream.

Blueberry Gingerbread
Yield: 8–10 servings

We've tried other berries, and most just melt into the batter. But we did find that a mixture of golden raisins and black currants works very well in place of the blueberries.

1 cup (236 mL) plus 2 tablespoons (30 mL) sugar, divided
½ cup (118 mL) vegetable oil
3 tablespoons (45 mL) molasses
½ teaspoon (2.5 mL) salt
1 large egg, beaten
2 cups (473 mL) all-purpose flour
1 teaspoon (5 mL) baking soda
1 teaspoon (5 mL) ground cinnamon
½ teaspoon (2.5 mL) ground ginger
½ teaspoon (2.5 mL) ground nutmeg
1 cup (236 mL) fresh blueberries (or frozen, thawed, drained blueberries)
1 cup (236 mL) buttermilk

1. Preheat the barbecue to medium high (350°F [180°C] to 400°F [200°C]). Grease and flour a 9 × 13-inch (22.5 × 32.5-cm) baking dish.

2. In a large mixing bowl, beat together 1 cup (236 mL) of the sugar, the oil, the molasses, and the salt, then beat in the egg.

3. In a separate large bowl, combine the flour, baking soda, cinnamon, ginger, and nutmeg. Put the blueberries in a small bowl, add 2 tablespoons (30 mL) of the flour mixture, and stir well. Add the rest of the flour mixture to the oil mixture and stir. While stirring, add the buttermilk.

4. Fold in the floured blueberries and pour the batter into the prepared baking dish. Sprinkle the top with the remaining sugar and bake for 35 to 40 minutes.

5. Remove the gingerbread from the barbecue and let it cool for 20 minutes. Cut it into squares and serve warm with freshly whipped cream.

Goat Cheese–Blueberry–Strawberry Pizza

Yield: 8–10 servings

Pizza isn't just an entrée anymore. This fruit variety is a real crowd pleaser, and you can customize it further with sweetened sour cream, whipped cream, raspberries, sliced bananas, or just about any fruit you like.

1 (13.8-ounce [386-g]) package Pillsbury Classic refrigerated pizza dough
1 pint (473 mL) blueberries
½ pound (227 g) fresh strawberries, thinly sliced
¼ cup (59 mL) Grand Marnier
2 tablespoons (30 mL) sugar
8 ounces (227 g) goat cheese, at room temperature
3 tablespoons (45 mL) plus 2 teaspoons (10 mL) honey
1 cup (236 mL) strawberry jam

1. Preheat the barbecue to medium high (450°F [240°C] to 500°F [260°C]).

2. With your hands, shape and stretch the thawed dough in a 8 × 12-inch (20 × 30-cm) baking dish.

3. In a medium bowl, combine the sliced blueberries, strawberries, Grand Marnier, and sugar and toss to coat evenly. Let the mixture sit for 10 minutes. Drain the berries in a colander, reserving the liquid.

4. In a small bowl, combine the reserved Grand Marnier liquid, goat cheese, and 3 tablespoons (45 mL) of the honey and mix together with a spoon until smooth. Brush or spoon the strawberry jam over the pizza, covering it completely with a thin layer. Spoon the goat cheese mixture over the jam, spreading lightly so as to not disturb the jam.

5. Place the pizza on the grill and cook until golden brown, rotating after 3 or 4 minutes. The topping should be bubbling when the pizza is done.

6. Slice the pizza and place the slices on serving plates. Drizzle each piece with a scant amount of the remaining honey and serve.

Brandied Pecan Pie

Yield: 6–8 servings

First created by French settlers who came to New Orleans, pecan pie has become the classic pie of the South. Local orchards produce upwards of 250 million pounds (113 million kg) of the flavorful nuts every year, and they gotta do something with them.

¼ cup (59 mL) butter, warm
1 cup (236 mL) sugar
3 large eggs
1 cup (236 mL) light corn syrup
¼ cup (59 mL) brandy
1 unbaked 9-inch pie shell
1 cup (236 mL) whole pecans
¼ cup (59 mL) honey, warm

1. Preheat the barbecue to medium high (350°F [180°C] to 400°F [200°C]).

2. In a medium bowl, beat the butter with an electric mixer to soften it. Gradually blend in the sugar, then the eggs, one at a time, until well blended. Beat in the corn syrup and brandy until well blended. Pour this mixture into the pie shell and completely cover it with the pecans.

3. Bake for 45 to 50 minutes, or until the pie is set around the edges. The filling will be puffy. Brush the nuts with the warm honey.

4. Cool on a wire rack and serve with ice cream or freshly whipped cream.

German Chocolate Soufflé

Yield: 4–6 servings

No kidding, a soufflé on a barbecue grill. Why not? A barbecue is merely an oven you take outside. Anything you can do in your oven, you can do in a barbecue.

1 (8-ounce [118-mL]) jar cherry preserves (do not use jam)
5 eggs, separated, at room temperature
1 teaspoon (5 mL) cream of tartar
½ cup (118 mL) sweetened coconut flakes
¼ cup (60 mL) confectioners' sugar
3 tablespoons (45 mL) unsweetened cocoa

1. Preheat the barbecue to 375°F (190°C) to 400°F (200°C) for indirect cooking. Generously butter and sugar the sides and bottom of a 6-cup (1.4-L) soufflé dish. Tap out the excess sugar. Add a triple-thick collar of waxed paper or parchment that reaches from the bottom of the dish to 3 inches (7.5 cm) above the top. Butter and sugar the inside of the paper; then tie the collar onto the soufflé dish.

2. Spread the cherry preserves over the bottom of the prepared soufflé dish.

3. Using a balloon whisk or the balloon whisk attachment on an electric mixer, beat the egg whites until they form stiff peaks. Add the cream of tartar as you begin to whip the egg whites.

4. In a medium saucepan, beat the egg yolks. Gradually add the coconut, sugar, and cocoa and beat until well mixed.

5. Fold the whites into the egg yolk mixture, very gently incorporating the whites and yolks so as to not break up the bubbles in the egg whites. Gently spoon the soufflé mixture over the cherry preserves.

6. Bake for 24 to 26 minutes, or until the soufflé rises and turns brown on top, but is still jiggly in the middle. Carefully remove the pan from the barbecue and serve immediately.

Browne-Bag Apple Pie

Yield: 6–8 servings

This pie is cooked over a baking sheet or several sheets of heavy-duty aluminum foil in a large brown paper bag. I like to bring the bag right to the table on a serving tray, tear open the bag, and enjoy the reaction. Note: This works best with a metal pie pan (inside the bag). If all you have are disposable aluminum tins, put one inside another so you have two layers of aluminum.

3½ cups (826 mL) plus 2 tablespoons (30 mL) all-purpose flour, divided
½ teaspoon (2.5 mL) salt
½ cup (118 mL) vegetable shortening
5 tablespoons (75 mL) ice water
¼ cup (59 mL) granulated sugar
2 tablespoons (30 mL) freshly squeezed lemon juice
1 teaspoon (5 mL) ground cinnamon
½ teaspoon (2.5 mL) ground nutmeg
⅛ teaspoon (0.6 mL) ground cloves
8 cups (1.9 L) sliced apples
½ cup (118 mL) packed brown sugar
⅓ cup (79 mL) unsalted butter
Vanilla ice cream, for serving (optional)
Extra-sharp cheddar cheese, sliced thickly, for serving (optional)

1. Preheat a charcoal or gas grill to 300°F (150°C) to 350°F (180°C).

2. In a mixing bowl, combine 1½ cups (354 mL) of the flour, the salt, and the shortening. Using an electric mixer, beat until the mixture resembles coarse crumbs. Stir in the ice water, a little at a time, until the dough forms a ball. On a lightly floured surface, roll out the dough to an 11- or 12-inch (27.5- or 30-cm) round and fit it into a 9-inch (22.5-cm) pie plate, fluting the edges.

3. In a large bowl, combine the granulated sugar, 2 tablespoons (30 mL) of the remaining flour, the lemon juice, the cinnamon, the nutmeg, and the cloves. Add the apples and stir to coat. Transfer the apple mixture to the pie plate, smooth out the filling, and set aside.

4. In a medium bowl, combine the brown sugar and the remaining ½ cup (118 mL) flour. Using 2 knives or a pastry blender, cut in the butter until the mixture resembles coarse crumbs. Sprinkle this topping evenly over the apple filling.

5. Place the pie in the bottom of brown paper bag and transfer the bag to a large baking sheet. Fold the top of the bag and staple it shut. Transfer the baking sheet to the grill rack over direct heat. If you don't have a large baking sheet, cut 3 large pieces of heavy-duty aluminum foil and cover the grill rack with this triple layer. It's important that no area of the paper bag is over direct flames or hot coals. Close the barbecue lid and cook the pie until the apples are tender, 50 to 60 minutes.

6. Carefully remove the pie from the bag, avoiding the hot steam when you open the bag. Serve with generous scoops of ice cream and slices of extra-sharp cheddar cheese, if desired.

Balsamic Grilled Peaches

Yield: 4 servings

This dessert can easily be turned into a side dish for ham, pork roast, or barbecued chicken by putting a scoop of cottage cheese in the peach halves instead of the ice cream.

1 cup (236 mL) balsamic vinegar
½ cup (118 mL) honey
4 ripe peaches, pitted and halved
Ice cream of your choice, for serving
1 cup (236 mL) candied walnuts, for sprinkling

1. Make sure the grill is clean and generously sprayed with nonstick grilling spray. Preheat the barbecue to medium high (300°F [150°C] to 350°F [180°C]).

2. In a shallow bowl or baking dish, combine the balsamic vinegar and honey and stir. Add the peach halves and soak for 5 to 10 minutes.

3. Drain the peaches and put them flesh side down on the grill. After a few minutes, turn the peaches and cook for an additional 2 to 3 minutes.

4. Remove the peaches from the grill and place two halves each, flesh side up, in individual serving bowls. Scoop ice cream into each peach half. Sprinkle the candied walnuts on the ice cream and around the bowl.

Pepsi and Peanut Butter Cake

Yield: 8–10 servings

2 cups (473 mL) unbleached all-purpose flour
2 cups (473 mL) granulated sugar
1 cup (236 mL) Pepsi
2 tablespoons (30 mL) unsweetened cocoa
½ cup (118 mL) buttermilk
2 large eggs, beaten
1 teaspoon (5 mL) baking soda
1 teaspoon (5 mL) pure vanilla extract
1½ cups (354 mL) miniature marshmallows
1⅓ cups (315 mL) butter, divided
1 cup (236 mL) packed dark brown sugar
⅔ cup (158 mL) smooth peanut butter
¼ cup (59 mL) heavy cream
⅔ cup (158 mL) chopped peanuts

1. Preheat the barbecue to medium high (300°F [150°C] to 350°F [180°C]). Butter or spray with nonstick cooking spray and flour a 9 × 13-inch (22.5 × 32.5-cm) baking pan.

2. In a large bowl, combine the flour and granulated sugar. Melt the 1 cup butter, add the Pepsi and cocoa, and pour this mixture over the flour-sugar mixture. Stir until well blended. Add the buttermilk, beaten eggs, baking soda, and vanilla and stir to mix well. Mix in the miniature marshmallows.

3. Pour the batter into the prepared pan and bake for 35 to 40 minutes. Remove the cake from the barbecue and after 5 minutes remove from the baking pan.

4. In a medium saucepan over medium heat, heat the brown sugar, peanut butter, and ⅓ cup butter until smooth. Stir in the heavy cream. When the mixture just begins to bubble, remove the pan from the heat and pour the frosting over the still-warm cake, so it drips down the sides. Sprinkle on the peanuts and spread the frosting over the cake.

5. Let the cake cool to room temperature, slice, and serve.

Upside-Down Apple–Raisin Gingerbread
Yield: 8–10 servings

Gingerbread tastes best when it's served fresh from the oven (or barbecue). The heat brings out the ginger flavor, and the warm cake teamed with cold whipped cream is heaven on a plate.

¼ cup (59 mL) butter, melted
2 large apples, peeled, cored, and sliced
⅔ cup (158 mL) packed brown sugar, divided
½ cup (118 mL) margarine, melted
½ cup (118 mL) dark molasses
½ cup (118 mL) granulated sugar
1 large egg
2 cups (473 mL) all-purpose flour
1 teaspoon (5 mL) baking soda
1 teaspoon (5 mL) ground cinnamon
1 teaspoon (5 mL) ground ginger
½ teaspoon (2.5 mL) salt
½ teaspoon (2.5 mL) ground allspice
¼ teaspoon (1.25 mL) ground cloves
¼ teaspoon (1.25 mL) ground nutmeg
1 cup (236 mL) golden raisins
¾ cup (177 mL) hot dark tea

1. Preheat the barbecue to medium high (300°F [150°C] to 350°F [180°C]).

2. Pour the ¼ cup melted butter into a 9-inch (22.5-cm) square baking pan. Scatter the apples over the butter. Sprinkle with ⅓ cup (79 mL) of the brown sugar and set aside.

3. In a mixing bowl, combine the margarine, molasses, granulated sugar, and egg. Using a hand-held mixer, whip until smooth. Add the flour, baking soda, cinnamon, ginger, salt, allspice, cloves, and nutmeg; stir in the raisins and tea and mix well. Pour the batter over the apples.

4. Place the baking dish in the barbecue and cook for 45 to 50 minutes, or until the cake tests done. Cool for 3 to 5 minutes, loosen the sides with a sharp knife, and invert the cake onto a serving plate. Serve warm with freshly whipped cream.

White Chocolate Crème Brulée
Yield: 4 servings

This is a more delicate tasting dish than than a brulée made with milk or dark chocolate. White chocolate contains cocoa butter instead of the cocoa solids that are in the other two varieties, making the taste subtler and milder.

5 large egg yolks
½ cup (118 mL) plus 2 tablespoons (30 mL) sugar, divided
2 cups (473 mL) heavy cream
3 ounces (84 g) white chocolate, chopped
¼ teaspoon (1.25 mL) pure vanilla extract

1. Preheat the barbecue to medium high (350°F [180°C] to 400°F [200°C]).

2. In a medium bowl, whisk together the egg yolks and ¼ cup (59 mL) of the sugar.

3. In a heavy medium saucepan, combine the cream and ¼ cup (59 mL) of the remaining sugar and bring to a simmer. Reduce heat to low and gradually add the chopped chocolate, whisking until smooth.

4. Gradually whisk the hot chocolate mixture into the egg yolk mixture. Add the vanilla, stir, and spoon the cooked custard into 4 (10-ounce [280-g]) crème brulée cups. Place the cups in a wide, flat baking or roasting pan and add enough hot water to the pan to come halfway up the sides of the cups.

5. Cook in the grill until the custards are set in the center, about 60 to 70 minutes. Carefully remove the custards from the water and let them cool.

6. Cover and refrigerate overnight. Sprinkle 1½ teaspoons (7.5 mL) sugar over each custard and, using a kitchen propane torch, brown the sugar. Serve the custards hot, or return them to the refrigerator and serve them cold.

Milk Chocolate Fondue

Yield: 2–4 servings

You can make two batches of the fondue, one milk chocolate and one dark, and swirl them together at the last moment for a bittersweet flavor. I know this isn't grilled, but we do use flame in this recipe, so hush up and dip your marshmallows.

12 ounces (336 g) milk or dark chocolate
1 cup (227 g) heavy cream
2 tablespoons (29 mL) Kirschwasser or cherry brandy

1. In the top of a double boiler set over a barbecue side burner, combine the chocolate and cream and whisk until the chocolate melts completely into a creamy mixture. Do not overcook.

2. Add the Kirschwasser and pour the mixture into a fondue pot over a warm flame to keep the chocolate warm.

3. Serve with strawberries, apples, fresh apricots, mandarin orange segments, kiwi fruit, bananas, graham crackers, pound cake, shortbread cookies, or Rice Krispie bars to dip into the chocolate.

Blueberry and Soda Cracker Pie

Yield: 6–8 servings

The crackers in this pie form a crust during baking as they absorb the butter and sugary blueberry filling piled above and below the cracker layers.

1 cup (236 mL) sifted all-purpose flour
¼ teaspoon (1.25 mL) baking soda
⅛ teaspoon (0.6 mL) salt
1 cup (236 mL) sugar
1 pinch ground cinnamon
1 pinch ground nutmeg
1½ cups (354 mL) crushed soda crackers
½ cup (118 mL) butter, melted
1 (21-ounce [588-g]) can blueberry pie filling
2 teaspoons (10 mL) lemon juice

1. Preheat the barbecue to medium high (350°F [180°C] to 400°F [200°C]). Lightly butter a 9-inch (22.5-cm) pie plate.

2. In a medium bowl, combine the flour, baking soda, salt, sugar, cinnamon, nutmeg, crackers, and melted butter, in that order.

3. Spread half of this mixture in the prepared pie plate. In a separate bowl, combine the pie filling and lemon juice. Pour this mixture over the mixture in the pie plate. Cover with the remaining soda cracker mixture.

4. Cook in the barbecue for 25 to 30 minutes.

5. Remove the pie from the barbecue and let it cool on a rack. Serve with whipped cream or your favorite ice cream.

Tyrolean Baked Apples

Yield: 6 servings

You can also make this recipe with pears. Core them from the bottom, cutting off ¼ inch (0.5 cm) of the skin end of the core, fill the pears, then replace the piece of core, like a cork, to help keep the filling in the pears.

6 large Rome Beauty apples (or your favorite variety)
¼ cup (60 mL) butter
½ cup (118 mL) seedless raspberry jam
½ cup (118 mL) finely chopped pecans
Grated zest of ½ orange
3 tablespoons (45 mL) light brown sugar, divided

1. Preheat the barbecue to high (450°F [240°C] to 500°F [260°C]) for direct and indirect heating. Make sure the grill is clean and generously sprayed with nonstick grilling spray.

2. Core the apples and pierce the skin all over with a fork to lessen wrinkling and splitting. Place the apples in a large, deep pan with a tight-fitting cover and add water to a depth of ¼ inch (0.5 cm). Place the butter in the water.

3. In a small bowl, mix together the jam, pecans, and orange zest. Spoon this mixture into the center of each apple, then sprinkle 2 tablespoons (30 mL) of the sugar over the top.

4. Place the pan directly over the hottest part of the grill until the water comes to a boil. Cover the pan, close down the barbecue vents, and move the apples to the unheated side of the grill to simmer for 20 to 30 minutes, basting several times with the pan juices.

5. Remove the pan from the barbecue, uncover, and let the apples cool. Sprinkle the tops of the apples with of the remaining sugar and place them under a broiler, 3 inches (7.5 cm) from the heat, until lightly browned. Watch closely, as they brown very quickly. Serve warm or cooled.

Barbecued Honey and Whiskey Cake

Yield: 6–8 servings

If you prefer rum to whiskey, by all means substitute it here. You can also substitute maple or cane syrup for the honey.

¾ cup (177 mL) packed brown sugar
½ cup (118 mL) plus 2 tablespoons (30 mL) butter, at room temperature, divided
5 teaspoons (25 mL) minced orange zest (from about 3 large oranges), divided
3 large eggs, beaten
¾ cup (177 mL) self-rising flour, divided
¼ cup (59 mL) whiskey
3 tablespoons (45 mL) clear honey
2 tablespoons (30 mL) freshly squeezed orange juice
¾ cup (177 mL) confectioners' sugar
¼ cup (59 mL) slivered almonds, toasted

1. Preheat the barbecue to medium high (300°F [150°C] to 350°F [180°C]) for indirect heating. Liberally butter or grease 2 (7-inch [17.5-cm]) cake pans.

2. In a large mixing bowl with an electric mixer on medium-high speed, beat together the brown sugar and ½ cup (118 mL) of the butter until pale and fluffy, 3 to 5 minutes. Add 2 teaspoons (10 mL) of the zest and beat in the eggs one at a time until combined, about 3 to 4 minutes longer.

3. Sift in half of the flour, pour in the whiskey, and fold it in with a spatula. Sift in the remaining flour, again folding it in with the spatula.

4. Divide the batter evenly between the prepared pans, smoothing the tops with a rubber spatula. Transfer the pans to the barbecue over indirect heat, and cook for 20 to 25 minutes, or until the cake is a light golden color. Transfer the cakes to a wire rack to cool.

5. In a mixing bowl, combine the remaining 2 tablespoons (30 mL) butter, the honey, the orange juice, and 1 teaspoon (5 mL) of the remaining zest, beating with a wooden spoon. Slowly sift in the confectioners' sugar, stirring until the mixture is well blended and smooth.

6. Spread half the frosting on top of 1 cake layer. Top with the second layer and frost the top only. Sprinkle with the almonds and the remaining zest.

Bubba's Giant Chocolate Chip Cookies
Yield: 18 cookies

You could also make these with just one kind of chocolate but I like to mix the semisweet and milk chocolate flavors here.

2 cups (473 mL) all-purpose flour
1 teaspoon (5 mL) baking soda
1 teaspoon (5 mL) salt
1 cup (236 mL) butter, softened
1½ cups (354 mL) sugar
1 large egg, beaten
1 teaspoon (5 mL) pure vanilla extract
6 ounces (168 g) semisweet chocolate chips
6 ounces (168 g) milk chocolate chips
Confectioners' sugar, for serving

1. Preheat the barbecue to medium high (300°F [150°C] to 350°F [180°C]).

2. In a small bowl, mix together the flour, baking soda, and salt.

3. In a large bowl, cream the butter with an electric hand-held mixer until fluffy. Gradually add the sugar, egg, and vanilla, beating until the mixture is fluffy. Stir in the flour mixture and chocolate chips.

4. Shape the dough into 1½- to 2-inch (3.5- to 5-cm) balls. Arrange the balls 3 inches (7.5 cm) apart on ungreased baking sheets.

5. Cook in the barbecue for 25 to 30 minutes. Remove the pans from the barbecue and let the cookies cool on the baking sheets. Sprinkle with confectioners' sugar and serve.

Honeycrisp Apple Enchiladas
Yield: 4–6 servings

If you can't find Honeycrisp apples, substitute Granny Smith, Rome Beauty, or Gala. If you use Gala, reduce the sugar in the first part of the recipe to 1 tablespoon (15 mL), as these apples are very sweet. Sometimes I sprinkle the filling with grated cheddar cheese before rolling up the tortillas.

2½ cups (591 mL) chopped unpeeled Honeycrisp apples
2 tablespoons (30 mL) lemon juice
2 tablespoons (30 mL) granulated sugar
1 teaspoon (5 mL) ground cinnamon
½ teaspoon (2.5 mL) ground nutmeg
⅛ teaspoon (0.6 mL) ground cloves
6 (8-inch [20-cm]) four tortillas
1 cup (236 mL) apple juice or cider, or as needed
½ cup (118 mL) packed light brown sugar
⅓ cup (79 mL) butter
½ teaspoon (2.5 mL) ground allspice

1. Preheat the barbecue to medium high (300°F [150°C] to 350°F [180°C]). Butter or spray with nonstick cooking spray a 2-quart (1.9-L) baking dish.

2. Put the apple chunks in a medium bowl. Drizzle the chunks with lemon juice while stirring. Add the sugar, cinnamon, nutmeg, and cloves. Drain the apples in a colander set over a bowl for 10 minutes. Reserve the juices that collect in the bowl.

3. Spoon the fruit down the center of each tortilla. Roll up the tortillas and place them seam side down in the prepared baking dish.

4. Pour the reserved apple juices into a measuring cup, then add enough apple juice or cider to make 1 cup (236 mL). Pour the liquid into a small saucepan. Add the brown sugar, butter, and allspice and bring to a boil over medium-high heat. Reduce the heat and simmer, stirring, for 3 to 4 minutes. Pour this mixture over the enchiladas and let them stand for 30 minutes.

5. Cook in the barbecue for 20 minutes. Remove the pan and let the enchiladas cool. Serve each enchilada with freshly whipped cream or a generous scoop of vanilla ice cream.

Old-Fashioned Apple and Pear Browne Betty
Yield: 4–6 servings

This is a recipe favored by my sister-in-law, Betty Browne—hence the unconventional spelling. You can use other varieties of apples or pears, but we've used this combination to great success.

3 Granny Smith apples
3 ripe Anjou pears
1 tablespoon (15 mL) lemon juice
¼ cup (59 mL) butter, melted
5 slices whole-wheat bread, crusts removed
1 tablespoon (15 mL) granulated sugar
⅔ cup (158 mL) packed brown sugar
½ teaspoon (2.5 mL) grated lemon zest
½ teaspoon (2.5 mL) chili powder
¼ teaspoon (1.25 mL) ground cinnamon
⅛ teaspoon (0.6 mL) ground nutmeg

1. Preheat the barbecue to medium high (375°F [190°C] to 400°F [200°C]).

2. Peel and thinly slice the apples and pears. Place them in a medium bowl and toss them with the lemon juice so the fruit doesn't discolor. Set aside.

3. Put the melted butter in a separate bowl. With your hands, tear the bread slices into ½-inch (1-cm) pieces. Add the bread pieces to the butter, stirring as you add the bread to moisten every piece. Sprinkle with the granulated sugar.

4. In a small bowl, combine the brown sugar, lemon zest, chili powder, cinnamon, and nutmeg. Set aside.

5. With a rubber spatula, spread half of the apple-pear mixture in a 9-inch (22.5-cm) square baking dish. Cover with half of the bread cubes and then half of the spiced sugar. Repeat with another layer of fruit, another of bread, and the remaining sugar. Cover and bake for 30 minutes in the barbecue.

6. Uncover and bake for 30 minutes more. Remove the dessert, let it cool slightly, and serve with whipped cream or ice cream.

Pomme (Apple) Lasagna
Yield: 8–10 servings

This is an adaptation of an Italian dish made for my brother and I by a lovely Canadian neighbor in the mid 1950s. I never forgot her or this unique, crowd-pleasing recipe. This recipe comes from Marie Chenevert from Montreal, Québec.

¼ cup (59 mL) plus 2 tablespoons (30 mL) butter or margarine, divided
6 Granny Smith or pippin apples, thinly sliced
½ cup (118 mL) packed brown sugar, divided
½ cup (118 mL) toasted walnuts
1 teaspoon (5 mL) ground cinnamon
½ teaspoon (2.5 mL) ground nutmeg
1 (8-ounce [227-g]) package cream cheese, softened
1 large egg, beaten
1 teaspoon (5 mL) pure vanilla extract
1 cup (236 mL) firmly whipped cream
1 cup (236 mL) fresh breadcrumbs
½ cup (118 mL) granulated sugar, divided
9 lasagna noodles, cooked according to the package directions
⅛ teaspoon (0.6 mL) ground cloves

1. Preheat the barbecue to medium high (300°F [150°C] to 350°F [180°C]). Spray a wide baking dish with nonstick cooking spray.

2. In a large saucepan, melt ¼ cup (59 mL) of the butter over medium heat. Add the apples, stir several times, cover, and cook for 10 minutes, or until the apples are tender, stirring occasionally. Remove the pan from the heat. Add 3 tablespoons (45 mL) of the brown sugar, the toasted walnuts, the cinnamon, and the nutmeg. Stir several times, and set aside.

3. In a large bowl, combine the cream cheese and the remaining brown sugar. With a hand-held mixer, beat for 3 to 4 minutes, or until the mixture is light and fluffy. Add the egg and vanilla and beat until well mixed. Using a rubber spatula, slowly fold the whipped cream into the cream cheese mixture and set it aside. In a small saucepan, melt the remaining butter and pour it into a small bowl. Stir in the breadcrumbs and granulated sugar.

4. Spread half of the apple mixture in the prepared baking dish. Cover with 3 of the lasagna noodles. On top of the noodles, spread half of the cream cheese mixture. Layer with 3 more noodles, then spread the remaining apple mixture over the noodles. Cover with the last 3 noodles. Cover these with the remaining cream cheese mixture. Sprinkle with the breadcrumbs, and very lightly sprinkle with the ground cloves.

5. Place the baking pan in the barbecue and cook for 30 minutes, or until the top is browned and the lasagna is bubbling. Remove the pan from the barbecue and let it cool for 20 minutes before serving.

Caramel-Strawberry Tortillas

Yield: 4 servings

If you wish, you can substitute peaches and cherries, nectarines and raspberries, blueberries and kiwi fruit, or any combination of these for the banana-strawberry mixture.

2 (10-inch [25-cm]) tortillas
2 tablespoons (30 mL) butter, softened
2 medium bananas, peeled and thinly sliced
1 cup (236 mL) strawberries, thinly sliced
3 tablespoons (45 mL) brown sugar
1 teaspoon (5 mL) ground cinnamon
⅓ cup (79 mL) heavy cream
2 tablespoons (30 mL) granulated sugar
½ teaspoon (2.5 mL) pure vanilla extract
¼ cup (59 mL) sour cream or plain yogurt

1. Preheat the barbecue to high (400°F [200°C] to 550°F [290°C]). Spray a large baking sheet with nonstick cooking spray.

2. Place the tortillas on the prepared baking sheet. Butter the top of each tortilla.

3. In a medium bowl, combine the bananas, strawberries, brown sugar, and cinnamon.

4. Spoon half of the fruit mixture into the center of each tortilla, roll them up, and return them to the baking sheet. Bake for 10 minutes.

5. With a whisk or an electric hand-held mixer, whip the cream with the granulated sugar and vanilla until stiff peaks form. Fold in the sour cream.

6. Remove the tortillas from the baking sheet and cut them into quarters. Serve 2 quarters on each dessert plate, topped with the whipped cream.

Barbecue Maple Squares

Yield: 6 servings

I have fond memories of my Aunt Mary's baking when we visited her in Ontario while growing up. This is her original recipe, but sometimes she added golden raisins or black currants to the mix. This recipe comes from Mary Browne from Scarborough, Ontario.

3 large eggs, beaten
⅔ cup (158 mL) vegetable oil
1 cup (236 mL) dark maple syrup
1 teaspoon (5 mL) pure vanilla extract
1 teaspoon (5 mL) baking powder
½ teaspoon (2.5 mL) salt
¾ cup (177 mL) dark chocolate chips
½ cup (118 mL) chopped cashews (or pecans or peanuts)
2 cups (473 mL) all-purpose flour

1. Preheat the barbecue to medium high (300°F [150°C] to 350°F [180°C]). Butter well or spray with nonstick cooking spray a 9 × 13-inch (22.5 × 32.5-cm) baking pan.

2. In a medium bowl, mix together the eggs, oil, maple syrup, vanilla, baking powder, salt, chocolate chips, chopped cashews, and flour, in that order. Pour this mixture into the prepared baking pan, and cook in the barbecue for 30 minutes.

3. Remove the pan from the barbecue and let it cool before cutting the dessert into 2-inch (5-cm) squares.

Blackberry–Blueberry Charlotte

Yield: 6 servings

This charlotte can be frozen for up to 3 months. Thaw it slowly in the refrigerator and serve it chilled, but not frozen.

20 lady finger cookies (or 30 vanilla wafers)
3 cups (708 mL) blackberries, rinsed and dried
2 cups (473 mL) blueberries, rinsed and dried
3 large eggs, beaten
1 cup (236 mL) granulated sugar
½ cup (118 mL) all-purpose flour
¼ cup (59 mL) packed brown sugar
½ cup (118 mL) butter
½ teaspoon (2.5 mL) pure vanilla extract
Whipped cream, for serving

1. Preheat the barbecue to medium high (300°F [150°C] to 350°F [180°C]) for indirect heating. Heavily butter the bottom and sides of an 8-inch (20-cm) round baking dish.

2. Arrange the lady fingers on the bottom and around the sides of the prepared baking dish. Fill the dish with the blackberries and blueberries and set the dish aside.

3. In a small bowl, whisk together the eggs, granulated sugar, flour, and brown sugar and set aside.

4. In a small saucepan, heat the butter over medium heat until it foams and turns a nutty brown color. Remove the pan from the heat and slowly pour the butter into the egg-flour mixture, stirring continuously. Add the vanilla extract and pour the mixture over the berries; do not stir.

5. Place the baking dish on the unheated side of the barbecue and bake for 35 to 40 minutes, or until the top is crusty and the inside is smooth but not runny. A toothpick inserted into the center should come out fairly clean.

6. Let cool completely before serving. Invert the charlotte onto a plate, cut it into generous slices, and serve with generous dollops of freshly whipped cream.

Blueberry–Raspberry–Strawberry Lasagna

Yield: 6–8 servings

Lasagna? For dessert? You betcha! This dessert will blow your guests' minds.

1 (8-ounce [227-g]) package lasagna noodles
15 ounces (420 g) ricotta cheese
⅔ cup (158 mL) granulated sugar
1 large egg
1 cup (236 mL) all-purpose flour
1 cup (236 mL) packed brown sugar
1 teaspoon (5 mL) ground cinnamon
½ teaspoon (2.5 mL) ground nutmeg
1 pinch ground cloves
1 pinch chili powder
½ cup (118 mL) butter, melted
1 pint (473 mL) blueberries
1 pint (473 mL) raspberries
1 pint (473 mL) strawberries, sliced
Whipped cream, for serving

1. Preheat the barbecue to 350°F (180°C) for indirect heating. Butter a 9 × 13-inch (22.5 × 32.5-cm) glass or metal baking pan.

2. Bring a large pot of water to a boil and cook the noodles for 1 minute. Drain the noodles and put them into a bowl of ice water to stop the cooking. Drain them again and lay on paper towels to dry. Lay 3 noodles in the bottom of the prepared glass or metal baking pan.

3. In a mixing bowl, combine the ricotta, granulated sugar, and egg and beat until almost smooth. In a separate bowl, combine the flour, brown sugar, cinnamon, nutmeg, clove, chili powder, and butter and mix well.

4. In a third bowl, gently toss together the berries, being careful not to crush the raspberries.

5. Top the first layer of lasagna noodles with one-third the berry mixture, one-third the ricotta mixture, and one-third of the flour mixture. Add 2 more layers of all 3 components. Cook in the barbecue over indirect heat for 45 minutes. Remove the pan from the heat, let the lasagna cool, and serve with a dollop of whipped cream on each plate.

Old-Fashioned Brown Sugar Pie

Yield: 8–10 servings

This down-home dessert, this can be soft and almost creamy in the center, but that's the way it's supposed to be.

1 cup (236 mL) packed brown sugar
3 tablespoons (45 mL) all-purpose flour
1 pinch ground cloves
1 pinch salt
1 unbaked 8-inch (20-cm) pie shell
1 (12-ounce [336-g]) can evaporated milk
2½ tablespoons (37.5 mL) butter
¼ teaspoon (1.25 mL) ground cinnamon
Whipped cream, for serving
Ground nutmeg, for serving

1. Preheat the barbecue to 350°F (180°C).

2. In a small bowl, mix together the brown sugar, flour, cloves, and salt. Transfer this mixture to the pie shell. Pour the evaporated milk over the sugar mixture, but do not stir or mix it in.

3. Dot the filling with pats of the butter, and sprinkle the cinnamon over the top.

4. Cook in the barbecue for 50 minutes, or until the filling just bubbles up in the middle. Don't be worried if the filling never completely sets.

5. This pie is best eaten at room temperature. Do not serve it cold; instead warm it up in an oven (or barbecue) for 15 minutes before serving. Do not warm it in the microwave, as this will set the filling and you'll lose the creamy character of the pie. Serve with freshly whipped cream sprinkled with nutmeg.

Fire-Seared Bananas

Yield: 2–4 servings

This is an easy imitation of bananas foster. You can substitute dark rum for the Grand Marnier. Use ripe bananas; green ones will take too long to cook. Be very cautious when making this recipe; do not pour alcohol into the pan while it's over a flame.

½ cup (118 mL) sugar
2 tablespoons (30 mL) butter
2 tablespoons (30 mL) lemon juice
2 tablespoons (30 mL) freshly squeezed orange juice
2 large ripe bananas
¼ cup (59 mL) Grand Marnier
Vanilla ice cream, or your favorite flavor, for serving

734   *1,001 Best Grilling Recipes*

1. In a sauté pan over medium-high heat on the grill or a side burner, melt together the sugar and butter. Cook until the mixture turns light brown, being careful not to burn the sugar.

2. Add the juices and simmer over high heat until the mixture has reduced to a thin syrup.

3. Peel and halve the bananas and sauté them in the syrup. When they start to get soft, remove the pan from the flames and add the Grand Marnier. Ignite the alcohol with a long charcoal lighter. Light the vapors on the side of the pan; never reach over the pan to light.

4. Serve over a scoop of your favorite ice cream.

Grilled Peaches and Blueberries

Yield: 4 servings

Grilled fruit adds a nice touch to roasted meats, fish, and poultry. Replace starch dishes with fresh fruits for a healthy and flavorful meal that is easy to prepare and that will surprise your guests.

4 large ripe peaches
1 pint (473 mL) fresh blueberries (use frozen if fresh are not available)
¼ cup (60 mL) packed brown sugar
¼ cup (60 mL) lemon juice
8 pinches ground cloves

1. Preheat the barbecue to medium high (350°F [180°C] to 400°F [200°C]) for indirect heating, putting a water pan under the unheated side of the grill.

2. Wash and halve the peaches, removing the pits. Spray 8 double-thick squares of heavy-duty aluminum foil with nonstick cooking spray. Place each peach half on a foil square.

3. Fill the peach halves generously with blueberries. Sprinkle equal amounts of brown sugar and lemon juice on each peach, then add a pinch of ground cloves to each—just a pinch though, as too much will overpower the fruit flavors.

4. Wrap the fruit securely, sealing the foil packages well, and cook on the unheated side of the grill for 20 to 25 minutes without turning.

5. With a spatula, remove the peach halves from the foil and place them, berry side up, on individual plates.

Quick Mexican Cheesecake Flan

Yield: 4 servings

The chili powder adds a wonderful flavorful, but you can substitute the same amount of finely ground instant coffee. The propane step at the end is optional, but it adds a professional restaurant touch.

½ cup (118 mL) sugar
3 tablespoons (45 mL) water
8 ounces (227 g) cream cheese, softened
3 large eggs
1 teaspoon (5 mL) pure vanilla extract
¼ teaspoon (1.25 mL) chili powder
1 (13–ounce [384-mL]) can sweetened condensed milk
1 (13–ounce [384-mL]) can evaporated milk

1. Preheat the barbecue to 350°F (180°C).

2. In a medium skillet or saucepan, combine the ½ cup sugar and water and cook over medium heat until the sugar just begins to turn brown. Pour the caramelized sugar into a 9-inch (22.5-cm) round baking pan.

3. In a blender, combine the cream cheese, eggs, vanilla, and chili powder and blend until smooth.

4. Add the condensed milk and blend again. Add the evaporated milk and blend once more. Pour this mixture over the caramelized sugar and set the baking pan in a larger pan with about 1 inch (2.5 cm) of water in it.

5. Cook in the barbecue for 1 hour, or until the custard is set and a knife inserted in the middle comes out clean. Refrigerate.

6. Just before serving, sprinkle 1 tablespoon (15 mL) granulated sugar over the dish and use a hand-held kitchen butane or propane torch to caramelize the sugar until it's golden brown and crusty. Cool briefly and serve.

Chocolate Chip and Cherry Cookie Pizza

Yield: 8–10 servings

An easy way to warm the cream cheese is to put an unwrapped bar on a plate and microwave it for 20 to 30 seconds.

2 tablespoons (30 mL) all-purpose flour
1 (16-ounce [454-g]) package Nestlé's Toll House Cookie Dough, at room temperature
2 (8-ounce [227-g]) packages cream cheese, warmed to soften
¼ cup (59 mL) confectioners' sugar
1 (21-ounce [588-g]) can cherry pie filling
Chocolate or multi-colored sprinkles, for garnish
Sweetened coconut flakes, for garnish

1. Preheat the barbecue to medium high (300°F [150°C] to 350°F [180°C]). Spray a 12-inch (30-cm) pizza pan liberally with nonstick baking spray.

2. Sprinkle the prepared pizza pan with the flour. Press the cookie dough onto the pizza pan, spreading it with a rolling pin and your hands so it reaches to the pan edges.

3. Cook in the barbecue for 7 minutes, or until the cookie is golden brown. Remove the pan from the barbecue and let it cool to room temperature. (You can put it in the refrigerator or freezer to speed this process.)

4. In a large bowl, combine the cream cheese and confectioners' sugar and stir to mix well.

5. Spread the sweetened cream cheese over the cooled cookie crust, leaving a ½-inch (1-cm) border around the edges.

6. Spoon the cherry pie filling over the cream cheese layer.

7. Slice the pizza into wedges and serve, offering a shaker of chocolate or colored sprinkles and a shaker of sweetened coconut flakes to your guests to add to their slice (instead of the red pepper flakes and Parmesan cheese for traditional pizza).

Sour Cherry Crispy Crumble
Yield: 6–8 servings

You can also make this dessert with canned plums, peaches, or berries.

1 (16–ounce [454-g]) can sour red pitted cherries
4 teaspoons (20 mL) granulated sugar
1½ tablespoons (22.5 mL) cornstarch
¼ teaspoon (1.25 mL) pure vanilla extract
½ cup (118 mL) quick-cooking oats
3 tablespoons (45 mL) cashew pieces or chopped walnuts
1 tablespoon (15 mL) brown sugar
1 tablespoon (15 mL) butter or margarine, melted

1. Preheat the barbecue to medium high (300°F [150°C] to 350°F [180°C]). Spray an 8-inch (20-cm) square baking pan with nonstick cooking spray.

2. Drain the cherries, reserving ¾ cup (177 mL) of the juice.

3. In a saucepan, combine the cherry juice, granulated sugar, and cornstarch and stir to incorporate. Cook over medium heat, stirring constantly, until the liquid is thickened and clear. Remove the pan from the heat, add the cherries and vanilla, and stir lightly to mix. Spread on the bottom of the prepared baking pan.

4. In a small bowl, combine the oats, cashews, and brown sugar. Add the butter or margarine and mix well with a fork until the mixture is crumbly. Sprinkle the oat-nut topping over the cherries.

5. Cook in the barbecue for 20 minutes, or until the topping is browned. Serve warm with whipped cream or ice cream, or refrigerate for 30 minutes before serving.

Chocolate Brulée with Bananas

Yield: 8 servings

This is not a diet dessert, but it will satisfy the most serious sweet tooth. You can substitute milk chocolate or white chocolate, but the cream and half-and-half are mandatory.

2 cups (473 mL) heavy cream
2 cups (473 mL) half-and-half
8 ounces (227 g) dark chocolate, finely chopped
8 large egg yolks
⅓ cup (79 mL) plus 3 tablespoons (45 mL) sugar, divided
1 large banana, peeled and sliced into ¼-inch (0.5-cm) rounds

1. Preheat the barbecue to medium high (300°F [150°C] to 350°F [180°C]) for direct and indirect heating. Butter 8 (6-ounce [168-g]) custard cups or ramekins.

2. In a large saucepan over a barbecue side burner or stovetop burner, combine the cream and half-and-half. Cook over medium heat until the liquid just begins to bubble, then reduce the heat to low. Add the chocolate and whisk until the chocolate is melted and the mixture is smooth. Remove the pan from the heat and set it aside.

3. In a large bowl, whisk together the yolks and ⅓ cup (79 mL) of the sugar. Blend well until the yolks turn light yellow and become thick and syrupy. Gradually whisk in the hot chocolate mixture.

4. Divide the chocolate custard among the prepared ramekins or custard cups and place the cups in a large, shallow baking pan. Add enough hot water to the pan to come halfway up the sides of the cups. Bake in the barbecue until the custards are just set, about 45 minutes. The custards will be mostly solid, but they may still jiggle a bit as you move them.

5. Place 3 or 4 banana slices on top of each cup, then sprinkle the top with the remaining sugar. Using a propane or butane kitchen torch, caramelize the sugar. Serve immediately.

Grilled French Bread Pudding
Yield: 4–6 servings

Don't throw away those last few stale slices of French or sourdough bread. Save and use them to make bread pudding. Just for fun, we've also thrown in two slices of raisin bread.

8 (½-inch [1-cm] thick) slices French bread
2 slices raisin bread
6 large egg whites
1¼ cups (295 mL) packed brown sugar
2 tablespoons (30 mL) unsalted butter, melted
1½ teaspoons (7.5 mL) pure vanilla extract
1¼ teaspoons (6.25 mL) ground nutmeg
1¼ teaspoons (6.25 mL) ground cinnamon
½ teaspoon (2.5 mL) grated lemon zest
1 cup (236 mL) skim milk
1 cup (236 mL) heavy cream
½ cup (118 mL) dried apricots
½ cup (118 mL) golden raisins
Pure maple syrup, for drizzling

1. Preheat the barbecue to medium high (300°F [150°C] to 350°F [180°C]), leaving one side unheated. Butter well a 5 × 9-inch (12.5 × 22.5-cm) loaf pan.

2. Grill the French bread until it is toasted and grill marks appear, about 2 minutes, turning once halfway through the grilling time. Grill the raisin bread the same way. Cut all the bread into cubes (you should end up with approximately 5 cups [1.2 L]) and set aside.

3. In a large bowl, beat the egg whites until they are frothy, about 2 minutes. Add the brown sugar, butter, vanilla, nutmeg, cinnamon, and lemon zest. Beat until the mixture is well blended. Add the milk and cream. Stir in the apricots and raisins. Add the bread cubes and toss until mixed well. Let the bread rest for about 45 minutes, occasionally patting the bread cubes down into the liquid.

4. Pour the bread and egg mixture into the prepared loaf pan. Place the pan on the unheated side of the grill and bake for 50 to 60 minutes, or until the top of the dessert is well-browned and puffy.

5. Remove the pan from the barbecue and let the pudding cool slightly. Cut it into 3- to 4-inch (7.5- to 10-cm) squares, drizzle with real maple syrup, and serve warm with a scoop of your favorite ice cream.

Bing Cherry Fritters

Yield: 4–6 servings

Peaches, blueberries, raspberries, apricots, apples, or pineapple may be used instead of cherries.

Vegetable oil, for frying
1 cup (236 mL) all-purpose flour
1 teaspoon (5 mL) baking powder
½ teaspoon (2.5 mL) salt
1 tablespoon (15 mL) butter, melted
1 large egg, beaten
⅓ cup (79 mL) milk
¼ cup (59 mL) loosely chopped pitted Bing cherries
2 tablespoons (30 mL) confectioners' sugar

1. Pour 1½ to 2 inches (3.5 to 5 cm) of vegetable oil into a deep pot. Heat the oil on the grill or a side burner until a deep-frying thermometer reads 350°F (180°C).

2. In a large bowl, mix together the flour, baking powder, and salt. Add the melted butter, egg, and milk and stir to mix completely.

3. Gently fold the cherries into the batter. Drop the batter by tablespoon-fuls (15 mL) into the hot oil and fry the fritters for 2 to 4 minutes, or until they are nicely browned.

4. Drain the fritters and dust them with the confectioners' sugar. Serve very warm with ice cream.

Peanut Butter and Banana Pizza

Yield: 6–8 servings

You can use any nut butter for this: almond, cashew, hazelnut, and so on. But good old-fashioned peanut butter is best by far. Do not use organic varieties, as they are too oily to make a good crust.

2¼ cups (552 mL) smooth or chunky peanut butter, divided
⅔ cup (158 mL) packed brown sugar
¼ cup (59 mL) vegetable shortening
2 eggs, lightly beaten
½ teaspoon (2.5 mL) pure vanilla extract
1½ cups (354 mL) all-purpose flour
3 barely ripe bananas
1 cup (236 mL) semisweet chocolate chips
1 cup (236 mL) miniature marshmallows
Sweetened coconut flakes (optional)

1. Preheat the barbecue to 375°F (190°C). Grease a 10½ × 15-inch (26 × 37.5-cm) pizza pan or baking sheet.

2. In a large mixing bowl, use a hand-held mixer to cream together, ¾ cup (177 mL) of the peanut butter, the brown sugar, and the shortening.

3. Add the beaten eggs and vanilla and mix well. Stir in the flour and mix well.

4. Spoon the dough onto the prepared pizza pan or baking sheet, and spread it with your hands, leaving a 1-inch (2.5-cm) border around the sides. Cook in the barbecue for 12 minutes, or until the crust is lightly browned.

5. While the crust is baking, slice the bananas ¼-inch (0.5-cm) thick and put the slices in a bowl. Drizzle them with the lemon juice and fold gently to distribute the juice without mushing or breaking up the slices.

6. Remove the pizza from the barbecue. Spread the remaining peanut butter on top. Cover the top with banana slices and sprinkle generously with the chocolate chips. Scatter the marshmallows over the pizza so that it is nicely covered.

7. Return the pan to the barbecue and cook until the marshmallows are browned to your liking. Watch carefully, as the marshmallows can easily burn.

8. Remove the pizza from the grill and sprinkle it with the coconut flakes, if using. Let the pizza cool slightly and cut it into wedges. Serve with whipped cream on the side.

Maple Crème Caramel
Yield: 4 servings

Crème caramel is simply a custard made with heavy cream and eggs usually cooked in a sugar syrup. Maple syrup makes this recipe even tastier, but only if you use real maple syrup, not the watery imitation sold at many grocery stores.

4 cups (0.95 L) whole milk
¼ cup (59 mL) chopped orange zest
1 teaspoon (5 mL) chopped fresh rosemary leaves
3 extra-large or 4 large eggs
4 tablespoons (60 mL) superfine sugar
1 tablespoon (15 mL) pure vanilla extract
3 cups (708 mL) hot water
4 tablespoons (60 mL) pure maple syrup (amber grade, if you can find it)
1 fresh rosemary sprigs, for garnish
Confectioners' sugar, for serving

1. Preheat the barbecue to medium high (300°F [150°C] to 350°F [180°C]). Spray 4 individual soufflé dishes or ramekins with nonstick cooking spray.

2. In a large saucepan over the grill or a side burner, heat the milk, orange zest, and chopped rosemary until just about to boil.

3. Strain the milk into a large bowl, discarding the rosemary and orange zests. Cool the milk. Stir in the eggs, sugar, and vanilla. Pour the custard into the prepared soufflé dishes or ramekins.

4. Place a 9-inch (22.5-cm) square baking dish on the grill rack. Place the filled soufflé dishes in the baking dish and pour the hot water into the large dish so that it comes ¾ of the way up the sides of each individual dish. Cover the baking dish loosely with aluminum foil, shiny side up, and bake for 1 hour, or until the custards are well set and a knife inserted into one comes out clean.

5. Remove the dishes from the water bath and let them cool for about 40 to 45 minutes.

6. Loosen the custards from the soufflé dishes or ramekins by running a knife around the edge. Invert the dish over an individual serving plate and gently shake the custard out.

7. Spoon 1 tablespoon (15 mL) of the maple syrup over the top of each and garnish with a sprig of rosemary and a few shakes of confectioners' sugar. Serve warm or chilled.

Chocolate–Raspberry–Peanut Butter Quiche

Yield: 4–6 servings

My granddaughter Emi said this was like a "peanut butter and jam sandwich for dessert." Yup, and just about anyone who loves PB&J sandwiches will love this dessert. I prefer smooth peanut butter in this dish, but you can use chunky if you like.

1 prebaked 9-inch (22.5-cm) pie shell
1¼ cups (295 mL) smooth or chunky peanut butter
1 cup (236 mL) packed brown sugar, divided
1½ cups (354 mL) heavy cream, chilled, divided
4 egg yolks, divided
½ cup (118 mL) raspberry or apricot jam
3 ounces (78 g) semisweet chocolate, chopped
3 ounces (78 g) unsweetened chocolate, chopped

1. Preheat the barbecue to medium high (350°F [180°C] to 400°F [200°C]).

2. In a medium bowl, mix together the peanut butter, ½ cup (118 mL) of the brown sugar, 1 cup (236 mL) of the cream, and 1 of the egg yolks. Using a rubber spatula, spoon the filling into the pie shell. Dot with the jam. Refrigerate while you prepare the rest of the dessert.

3. In a double-boiler over low heat, combine the remaining cream, the semisweet chocolate, and the unsweetened chocolate. Add the remaining brown sugar and cook, stirring, until everything is melted together.

4. Beat the remaining egg yolks until frothy. Add them to the chocolate mixture, stirring vigorously until completely mixed. Pour the topping over the peanut butter mixture in the pie shell and spread it with a spatula.

5. Bake until a knife inserted in the center comes out clean. Refrigerate until firm and serve with freshly whipped cream.

Dad's Deep-Dish Peach Pie

Yield: 6–8 servings

Perhaps there is no fruit more suited to pie than the peach. If you can get just-picked ripe peaches from a farm, you-pick-it location, or fruit stand, you can make the best peach pie ever. Plus, you will be supporting a local farmer, orchard, or fruit stand owner, helping to keep them in business. This recipe comes from Arnold Browne from Battle Creek, Mich.

1½ pounds (681 g) fresh peaches, sliced (6 cups [1.4 L] sliced)
2 tablespoons (30 mL) lemon juice
1¼ cups (295 mL) plus 2 tablespoons (30 mL) sugar, divided
3 tablespoons (45 mL) all-purpose flour
½ teaspoon (2.5 mL) ground cinnamon
¼ teaspoon (1.25 mL) ground allspice
⅛ teaspoon (0.6 mL) salt
4 tablespoons (60 mL) butter
1 package rolled refrigerated pie dough, at room temperature
1 tablespoon (15 mL) peach schnapps
1 cup (236 mL) heavy cream

1. Preheat the barbecue to high (400°F [200°C] to 450°F [240°C]) for direct and indirect heating. Generously spray a large, well-seasoned cast-iron pan with nonstick cooking spray.

2. Put the peach slices in a large bowl and sprinkle them with the lemon juice. in a medium bowl, combine 1¼ cups (295 mL) of the sugar, the flour, the cinnamon, the allspice, and the salt. Sprinkle this mixture over the peaches and toss until evenly coated. Pour the peaches into the prepared cast-iron pan. Dot with the butter.

3. Roll out the pastry large enough to cover the dish with 1½ inches (3.5 cm) of overhang. Place the dough over the pan, fold the extra dough under, and press the pastry to the edge of the dish. Flute the edges. Cut 3 or 4 vents in the crust. Sprinkle with the remaining sugar.

4. Bake for 10 minutes on the heated side of the grill. Move the pie to the unheated side, close the vents to lower the temperature, and bake for 30 minutes, or until the top is browned and the filling is bubbling through the vents.

5. Remove the pie from the barbecue and let it cool slightly.

6. Add the schnapps to the cream and whip until you have soft peaks. Serve a big spoonful of the whipped cream with each slice of the warm pie.

Argentine Sugar Cookies

Yield: 20 cookies

Meaning "milk candy" in Spanish, dulce de leche is a caramel-like candy syrup seen everywhere in Argentina and, for that matter, all over South and Central America. It is used to make these popular cookies, candy, frosting, ice cream, flan, and cakes, and it is even spread on toast for a sweet treat.

1 cup (236 mL) sugar
½ cup (118 mL) butter, softened
1 large egg
2 egg yolks
2 teaspoons (10 mL) grated lemon zest
1 teaspoon (5 mL) pure vanilla extract
1½ cups (354 mL) cornstarch
½ cup (118 mL) all-purpose flour
1 teaspoon (5 mL) baking powder
¼ teaspoon (1.25 mL) salt
1½ cups (354 mL) dulce de leche

1. Preheat the barbecue to medium high (300°F [150°C] to 350°F [180°C]). Grease or spray with nonstick cooking spray a large baking sheet.

2. In a large mixing bowl, combine the sugar and butter and beat with an electric mixer until pale and fluffy, about 5 minutes. Add the egg and egg yolks, one at a time, beating well after each addition. Beat in the lemon zest and vanilla until well blended.

3. In a separate mixing bowl, sift together the cornstarch, flour, baking powder, and salt. Add this to the butter mixture and mix well.

4. Drop the batter by spoonfuls (about 2 inches [5 cm] in diameter) onto the prepared baking sheet. Transfer the baking sheet to the barbecue over direct heat and bake until the cookies begin to turn golden, about 15 minutes.

5. Remove the sheet from the barbecue and immediately transfer the cookies to a cutting board or large platter. Spoon 1 tablespoon (15 mL) of the dulce de leche over half of the cookies. Top each of these cookies with a second cookie, making a sandwich.

Yummy Crescent Roll S'Mores

Yield: 4–6 servings

A quick and fun dessert for a summer evening . . . or a fall, winter, or spring evening. You don't need a campfire or long sharpened sticks. Grill up these delights right on your back deck.

1 (16–ounce [454-g]) package Pillsbury refrigerated crescent roll dough
16 large marshmallows (regular or chocolate flavor)
1 Caramello milk chocolate candy bar
½ cup (118 mL) butter or margarine, melted
1 cup (236 mL) graham cracker crumbs

1. Preheat the barbecue to high (450°F [240°C] to 500°F [260°C]).

2. Separate the crescent roll dough into 16 triangles. Place a large marshmallow on the wide end of each triangle. Top with 2 squares of the chocolate bar. Fold the corners of the dough over the marshmallow and chocolate and roll toward the opposite point, completely covering the marshmallow and chocolate. Seal well.

3. Brush each roll with melted butter and then gently roll them in the graham cracker crumbs.

4. Place the rolls in 16 ungreased muffin cups and bake in the barbecue for 10 to 12 minutes, or until the rolls are golden brown. Immediately remove them from the barbecue. Cool slightly and serve warm, not hot.

Barbecued Pineapple

Yield: 4–6 servings

Pick fresh pineapples that are golden in color, have a pleasant sweet scent, and are firm to the touch. Use the top of the pineapple, with the sharp leaves, as a garnish.

½ cup (118 mL) butter
½ cup (118 mL) packed dark brown sugar
2 tablespoons (30 mL) Worcestershire sauce
1 pinch salt
1 pinch freshly ground black pepper
½ cup (118 mL) dark rum, plus more for serving if desired
1 medium pineapple, peeled, cored, and sliced into ½-inch (1-cm) thick circles

1. Preheat the barbecue to medium high (300°F [150°C] to 350°F [180°C]).

2. In a medium saucepan over a side burner, combine the butter, brown sugar, and Worcestershire sauce. Add the salt and pepper. Bring the liquid to a boil, stirring constantly.

3. Reduce the heat and simmer until the sauce begins to thicken, about 10 minutes. Remove the pan from the heat and allow it to cool. Stir in the rum.

4. Brush the pineapple pieces with the cooled sauce and place them on the hot grill. Cook for about 5 minutes, turning occasionally, until the pineapple just begins to brown on all sides.

5. Remove the pineapple from the grill and let cool slightly. Serve warm with additional rum, if you wish.

Grilled Plantains with Spicy Brown Sugar Glaze

Yield: 4 servings

Plantains are a staple food in the tropical regions of the world. They are treated in much the same way as potatoes and have a similar, neutral flavor and texture when unripe. Cooked, they have a wonderful banana-like flavor and texture.

4 very ripe plantains, peeled and sliced lengthwise in long ½-inch (1-cm) thick slices
2 tablespoons (30 mL) vegetable oil
¼ cup (60 mL) packed light brown sugar
2 tablespoons (30 mL) fresh orange juice
1 tablespoon (15 mL) honey
1 teaspoon (5 mL) lime juice
½ teaspoon (2.5 mL) ground allspice
Salt, to taste
Freshly ground black pepper, to taste

1. Preheat the grill to medium high (350°F [180°C] to 400°F [200°C]).

2. Brush the plantains with the oil and grill them until they become caramelized, about 2 minutes on each side.

3. In a small bowl, combine the brown sugar, orange juice, honey, lime juice, and allspice. Season with salt and pepper.

4. Transfer the plantains to a heated platter and pour the glaze over the fruit.

5. Keep the platter and fruit warm until you are ready to serve.

Fired-Up Mangoes

Yield: 4–6 servings

Mangoes can be difficult to cut, but with some patience, you'll get the hang of it. It doesn't matter if the pieces you cut off are uneven or of different sizes, as you will eventually chop them into relatively similar pieces.

4 fresh mangoes
1 teaspoon (5 mL) butter
2 cups (473 mL) orange juice
¼ cup (60 mL) packed brown sugar
1 teaspoon (5 mL) ground cinnamon
½ teaspoon (2.5 mL) ground nutmeg
1½ cups (354 mL) tequila (or dark or light rum)
Ice cream, for serving

1. Preheat the barbecue to medium high (300°F [150°C] to 350°F [180°C]).

2. Wash and peel the fresh mangoes. Cut each into slices and chop the slices into ½- to 1-inch (1- to 2.5-cm) chunks.

3. In a nonstick skillet on the grill or a side burner, heat the butter over medium heat. Add the mango chunks. Pour the orange juice over the fruit and sprinkle with the brown sugar, cinnamon, and nutmeg. Bring to a simmer, stirring gently to dissolve the sugar and thoroughly coat the fruit. Cook for 3 to 4 minutes.

746   *1,001 Best Grilling Recipes*

4. Remove the pan from the heat and add the tequila. Return the pan back to the heat.

5. Scoop the ice cream into serving bowls and keep nearby.

6. Wearing a barbecue glove, use a barbecue lighter to flame the liquor sauce, igniting the vapors at the edge of the skillet, not in the middle.

7. Immediately pour the flaming liquid and mangoes over the ice cream and serve.

Oh Mon! Barbecue Banana Bread Custard
Yield: 6–8 servings

We had this incredible rum bread custard on a recent visit to Montego Bay, Jamaica, and although we were stuffed with jerk chicken and bammy (a sweet fried cornbread), we greedily devoured every scrumptious bite.

5 tablespoons (75 mL) butter, divided
⅔ cup (158 mL) packed brown sugar, divided
6 slices white bread, crusts removed, torn into ½-inch (1-cm) pieces
6 slices light wheat bread, crusts removed, torn into ½-inch (1-cm) pieces
1 pound (454 g) ripe bananas, split lengthwise
3 tablespoons (45 mL) dark rum
3 tablespoons (45 mL) apricot or raspberry preserves
3 ounces (89 mL) condensed milk
8 egg yolks, beaten
6 large eggs, beaten
2½ cups (591 mL) milk
3 tablespoons (45 mL) granulated sugar
½ teaspoon (2.5 mL) ground allspice
¼ teaspoon (1.25 mL) ground ginger

1. Preheat the barbecue to high (300°F [150°C] to 350°F [180°C]). Butter the bottom and sides of an 8-inch (20-cm) square baking pan with 1 tablespoon (15 mL) of the butter. Sprinkle the bottom and sides with 2 tablespoons (30 mL) of the brown sugar.

2. Cover the bottom of the prepared pan with the bread pieces. Dot with the remaining butter and sprinkle with the remaining brown sugar.

3. Place the bananas on top of the bread and sprinkle with the rum.

4. Drop spoonfuls of the apricot preserves evenly over the bread and bananas. Drizzle the condensed milk over the mixture.

5. In a medium bowl, whisk together the egg yolks and whole eggs.

6. In a saucepan over a stovetop burner or barbecue side burner, combine the milk and granulated sugar and cook until the mixture begins to simmer. Pour the milk slowly into the eggs, whisking constantly until well blended. Pour this mixture over the bread and bananas in the pan. Sprinkle with the allspice and ground ginger. Let the mixture sit for 15 minutes to thoroughly soak the bread.

7. Bake in the barbecue for 25 to 30 minutes, or until a knife inserted into the custard comes out clean.

Lemon-Lime Bread

Yield: 4–6 servings

If you wish, you can add or substitute orange, tangelo, or tangerine zests, but change the juice in the glaze accordingly (i.e., orange juice with orange zests or grapefruit with grapefruit zests [increasing the sugar for this fruit by ⅓]).

1½ cups (354 mL) sugar, divided
½ cup (118 mL) milk
6 tablespoons (90 mL) unsalted butter, softened
2 large eggs, beaten
1½ cups (354 mL) all-purpose flour
3 tablespoons (45 mL) grated lemon zest, divided
2 tablespoons (30 mL) grated lime zest, divided
1 teaspoon (5 mL) baking powder
¼ teaspoon (1.25 mL) ground cardamom
⅛ teaspoon (0.6 mL) salt
¼ cup (59 mL) fresh lemon juice

1. Preheat the barbecue to medium high (300°F [150°C] to 350°F [180°C]). Grease or spray with nonstick cooking spray and flour a 9 × 5-inch (22.5 × 12.5 cm) loaf pan.

2. In a medium bowl, combine 1 cup (236 mL) of the sugar, the milk, the butter, and the eggs and mix well. Add the flour, 2 tablespoons (30 mL) of the grated lemon zest, 1 tablespoon (15 mL) of the lime zest, the baking powder, the cardamom, and the salt and stir to fully incorporate.

3. Turn the mixture into the floured pan and cook in the barbecue for 1 hour. Cool the bread slightly, then remove it from the pan and set it on serving plate.

4. While bread is cooling, prepare the glaze. In a saucepan, combine the remaining sugar and the lemon juice. Add the remaining lemon and lime zest and cook, stirring, over low heat until the sugar dissolves and the glaze is hot.

5. Pour the hot glaze slowly over the surface of bread. Let the bread cool completely before slicing.

Pennsylvania Dutch Apple–Cheese Tart

Yield: 8–10 servings

Since the Pennsylvania Dutch specialize in family-style serving, you can place this bowl on the table with a big spoon and let folks help themselves. But be careful as this will go quickly and you want to make sure everyone gets some.

1 frozen 9-inch (22.5-cm) rolled pie crust
3 large pippin apples peeled, cored, and thinly sliced
5 tablespoons (75 mL) golden raisins
1 teaspoon (5 mL) ground cinnamon
½ teaspoon (2.5 mL) ground nutmeg
¼ cup (60 mL) sugar
½ cup (118 mL) skim milk
½ cup (118 mL) cottage cheese
2 large eggs, beaten
2 tablespoons (30 mL) honey
2 teaspoons (10 mL) pure vanilla extract
1 teaspoon (5 mL) fresh lemon juice
1 teaspoon (5 mL) grated lemon zest

1. Preheat the barbecue to medium high (300°F [150°C] to 350°F [180°C]) for direct and indirect heating.

2. Allow the pie crust to defrost at room temperature. Unroll it into a nonstick 9-inch (22.5-cm) round cake pan. Center the dough in the pan and press it with your fingertips to fit, starting in the center and working outward, using gentle pressure to stretch the crust up the sides of the cake pan as far as you can.

3. In a large bowl, combine the apples, raisins, cinnamon, and nutmeg and mix lightly.

4. Spoon the fruit into the pan and sprinkle with the sugar.

5. In a food processor, combine the milk, cottage cheese, eggs, honey, vanilla, lemon juice, and zest and blend until smooth. Pour this mixture over the apple filling.

6. Bake, uncovered, on the bottom rack of the barbecue for 15 to 20 minutes.

7. Close vents or lower the gas flame, move the pan to the unheated side of the grill and bake for an additional 25 to 30 minutes, or until the cheese topping is set.

Garden and Orchard Cake

Yield: 10–12 servings

Even though there are a ton of fruits and vegetables in this dish, you can still substitute—for instance, currants for the raisins, peaches for the apricots—and still come up with a wonderfully flavored, unique cake.

1 cup (236 mL) dark raisins or currants
½ cup (118 mL) golden raisins
½ cup (118 mL) dried apricots, minced
1 cup (236 mL) hot water
3 cups (708 mL) all-purpose flour
1 tablespoon (15 mL) ground cinnamon
2 teaspoons (10 mL) baking soda
½ teaspoon (2.5 mL) salt
¼ teaspoon (1.25 mL) ground nutmeg
⅛ teaspoon (0.6 mL) ground cloves
1 cup (236 mL) vegetable oil
1 cup (236 mL) granulated sugar
1 cup (236 mL) packed brown sugar
4 large eggs, beaten
1½ cups (354 mL) finely grated carrots (from about 2 large carrots)
1 medium zucchini, grated
½ cup (118 mL) canned crushed pineapple, drained
2 ripe bananas, mashed
¼ cup (60 mL) dark rum
8 ounces (227 g) cream cheese, at room temperature
1½ cups (354 mL) confectioners' sugar
1 teaspoon (5 mL) pure vanilla extract
1 tablespoon (15 mL) chopped orange zest
1 tablespoon (15 mL) chopped lemon zest
1 tablespoon (15 mL) chopped lime zest

1. Preheat the barbecue to medium high (300°F [150°C] to 350°F [180°C]) for indirect heating. Grease or spray with nonstick grilling or baking spray a 9 × 13-inch (22.5 × 32.5-cm) baking pan. Flour the pan.

2. In a small bowl, combine the raisins, apricots, and hot water and let stand for 15 minutes to hydrate them.

3. In a medium bowl, whisk together the flour, cinnamon, baking soda, salt, nutmeg, and cloves. Set aside.

4. In a large bowl, using an electric mixer set on medium, beat together the vegetable oil, granulated sugar, brown sugar, and eggs until combined. Stir in the carrots, zucchini, pineapple, and bananas.

5. Add the dry ingredients to the wet ingredients, ½ cup (118 mL) at a time, and stir until incorporated. Drain the raisins and apricots then fold in along with the rum.

6. Pour the batter into the prepared pan and spread it evenly. Bake in the barbecue over indirect heat for 40 to 45 minutes, or until a toothpick inserted in the center of the cake comes out clean. Cool to room temperature.

7. Make the frosting. In a medium bowl, beat together the cream cheese, confectioners' sugar, vanilla, and orange, lemon and lime zests until well mixed. Using a spatula, spread the frosting over the cake.

Rainbow Fudge Pudding Pie

Yield: 8 servings

This colorful and fun dessert is great for kids or adults. Add candles, and you've got a birthday pudding pie! If you want to be more conservative, garnish with plain chocolate sprinkles or chocolate curls that you make yourself, using a vegetable peeler on a bar of chilled bittersweet chocolate.

1½ cups (354 mL) graham cracker crumbs
1 tablespoon (15 mL) vegetable oil
¼ cup (59 mL) semisweet chocolate chips
1 (3-ounce [85-g]) package fat-free vanilla pudding mix
2 tablespoons (30 mL) minced orange zest
1 cup (236 mL) heavy cream
1 teaspoon (5 mL) Grand Marnier
Multi-colored sprinkles, for garnish

1. Preheat the barbecue to medium high (300°F [150°C] to 350°F [180°C]). Generously spray a 9-inch (22.5-cm) square baking pan with nonstick spray.

2. In a small bowl, combine the graham cracker crumbs and oil. Press this mixture into the bottom and sides of the prepared pan. Sprinkle with the chocolate chips.

3. Bake in the barbecue for 10 minutes, or until the chocolate chips are slightly melted. Using a rubber or plastic spatula, spread the softened chocolate chips evenly over the graham crust. Set the crust aside.

4. Using an electric mixer, prepare the vanilla pudding according to the package directions. Stir in the orange zest.

5. When the pudding is just beginning to set, spread it over the chocolate crust. Whip the cream with the Grand Marnier. Cover the pie with the freshly whipped cream and liberally decorate it with the sprinkles.

Baked Red Cherries in Sauce

Yield: 6 servings

If you wish, you can add ¼ cup (59 mL) of brandy or other liquor at the end and ignite it just before you pour it over the cherries at the table.

1 cup (236 mL) dry red wine
¾ cup (177 mL) sugar
Zest of 1 large lemon
1 (3-inch [7.5-cm]) stick cinnamon
⅛ teaspoon (0.6 mL) ground cloves
2 pounds (908 g) Bing or Rainier cherries, stemmed and pitted Confectioners' sugar, for serving (optional)

1. Preheat the barbecue to 350°F (180°C).

2. In a saucepan, combine the wine, sugar, lemon zest, cinnamon, and cloves and bring to a boil. Reduce the heat and simmer for 5 minutes. Remove and discard the cinnamon stick.

3. Place the cherries in a shallow baking dish. Pour the syrup over the cherries and bake in the barbecue for about 30 minutes, or until the cherries are soft and just beginning to brown on top.

4. Let the cherries cool a bit in the syrup. Serve warm or at room temperature, spooning the mixture over ice cream or pound cake. If you're using cake, sift confectioners' sugar over the dish before you serve.

Grilled Raspberry–Chocolate Pound Cake
Yield: 4–6 servings

Chocolate + raspberries = the perfect dessert. You can, however, substitute blackberries, in which case we suggest using blackberry brandy instead of the Framboise. This recipe comes from Brigida Diggs from Ridgefield, Wash.

1 pint (473 mL) fresh raspberries or blackberries
1 tablespoon (15 mL) confectioners' sugar
2 tablespoons (30 mL) Framboise liqueur
1 (11.75-ounce [329-g]) frozen Sara Lee pound cake, thawed
5 tablespoons (75 mL) butter, melted
⅓ cup (79 mL) miniature semisweet chocolate chips
Fresh raspberries, for garnish
Fresh mint leaves, for garnish

1. Preheat the barbecue to medium high (300°F [150°C] to 350°F [180°C]).

2. In a food processor, purée the raspberries. Add the sugar and blend well. Add the Framboise and set aside.

3. Cut the cake into 8 (¾-inch [3.75-cm]) slices and brush both sides of each slice with the melted butter. Place the slices on the grill and grill until lightly browned on one side, about 1 to 2 minutes.

4. Turn the slices of cake and immediately sprinkle about 2 teaspoons (10 mL) of the miniature chocolate chips on top of each slice. As the chips melt, use a metal or plastic spatula to gently spread the chips over the slices.

5. Prepare dessert plates by putting 2 to 3 tablespoons (30 to 45 mL) raspberry purée on each plate.

6. Grill the cake slices until the second sides are lightly browned, about 1 to 2 minutes longer. Set the slices on the prepared dessert plates and garnish with the raspberries, the mint, or both.

Maine Wild Blueberry Cobbler
Yield: 4–8 servings

If you can get Maine wild blueberries, this dish will soar into the heavens, but ordinary blueberries are wonderful as well. You could also substitute huckleberries or other berries.

1 pint (473 mL) Maine wild blueberries (or a local substitute)
1 cup (236 mL) granulated sugar, divided
⅓ cup (79 mL) water
1 teaspoon (5 mL) grated lemon zest
1 cup (236 mL) all-purpose flour
¼ cup (59 mL) packed brown sugar
1½ tablespoons (22.5 mL) ground cinnamon
1 teaspoon (5 mL) baking powder
1 pinch ground ginger
⅓ cup (79 mL) butter

1. Preheat the barbecue to 350°F (180°C). Generously spray a 9-inch (22.5-cm) square baking dish with nonstick cooking spray.

2. In a saucepan, combine the blueberries, ¾ cup (177 mL) of the granulated sugar, the water, and the lemon zest. Bring to boil and simmer for 2 minutes.

3. In a medium bowl, mix together the remaining granulated sugar, the flour, brown sugar, cinnamon, baking powder, and ginger. Using two forks, cut in the butter until the mixture is crumbly.

4. Pour the blueberry mixture into the prepared baking dish.

5. Evenly sprinkle the crumbs over the blueberry mixture and bake for approximately 25 minutes, or until the top is browned and bubbly. Serve warm with whipped cream, heavy cream, or vanilla ice cream.

Fresh-From-Scratch Pumpkin Pie
Yield: 8–10 servings

This pie is lighter than most pumpkin pies and surprisingly easy to make. One very important note: Do not boil the pumpkin, or it will soak up the water and make a watery pie. Instead, steam or bake it.

1 (5–8 pound [2.3–3.6 kg]) pumpkin
1 unbaked 9-inch (22.5-cm) pie crust
¾ cup (177 mL) packed dark brown sugar
¼ cup (59 mL) granulated sugar
2 tablespoons (30 mL) all-purpose flour
1 tablespoon (15 mL) molasses
1½ teaspoons (7.5 mL) ground cinnamon
1 teaspoon (5 mL) ground ginger
½ teaspoon (2.5 mL) ground nutmeg
¼ teaspoon (1.25 mL) salt
⅛ teaspoon (0.6 mL) ground cloves
3 large eggs
1¾ cups (413 mL) heavy cream

1. Preheat the barbecue to 350°F (180°C) for direct and indirect heating.

2. Cut off the top of the pumpkin and scrape out all the seeds and membranes (a large metal serving spoon works well for this). With a paring knife, carefully cut the pumpkin into sections. Cut the skin off the flesh. Steam or bake the flesh until tender. Transfer the cooked pumpkin to a food processor or blender and purée until smooth. Measure out 2 cups (473 mL) and set it aside. Discard any remaining purée or save it for another use.

3. In a large bowl, combine the brown sugar, granulated sugar, flour, molasses, cinnamon, ginger, nutmeg, salt, and cloves. Stir in the pumpkin puree. Beat 2 of the eggs and add them to the pumpkin mixture, along with the heavy cream. Break the remaining egg into the unbaked pie crust, swish it around to cover the entire surface with egg white, and pour the egg out into the pumpkin mixture. Mix well.

4. Pour the filling into the unbaked pie crust. Bake the pie in the middle of barbecue for 15 minutes. Reduce the barbecue temperature to 325°F (165°C) by closing the vents and moving the pie to the unheated side of the grill. Bake for 45 minutes longer, or until a knife inserted in the center comes out clean. Cool completely and refrigerate until 20 minutes before you're ready to serve. Serve each slice with a dollop of sweetened whipped cream, if desired.

Grilled Peach and Blueberry Pie

Yield: 4 servings

If you wish, you can substitute nectarines for the peaches here, but peaches provide the best results, especially if they are fresh from the farm or produce stand. You can peel the peaches if you wish, but as with most fruits, the skin is very nutritious.

2 ripe peaches, each sliced into 14–16 wedges
1 pint (473 mL) blueberries
¼ cup (59 mL) sugar
4 tablespoons (60 mL) all-purpose flour, divided
Zest of 1 lemon, minced
¼ teaspoon (1.25 mL) ground ginger
1 refrigerated rolled 9-inch (22.5-cm) pie crust, at room temperature
1 large egg
1 tablespoon (15 mL) milk

1. Preheat the barbecue to 350°F (180°C) for indirect heating.

2. In a large bowl, combine the peaches, blueberries, sugar, 2 tablespoons (30 mL) of the flour, the lemon zest, and the ginger and mix well.

3. Lay a double layer of aluminum foil large enough to fit under the pie crust on your work surface. Dust the foil with the remaining flour and lay the pie crust on top.

4. Place the fruit mixture in the middle of the crust and fold the sides up around it. The crust will not cover the fruit completely, but it should cover a couple of inches (about 5 cm) of the fruit around the edges.

5. In small bowl, beat the egg with the milk. Using a pastry brush, cover all sides of the dough with this egg wash.

6. Transfer the pie and foil to the unheated side of the grill, away from the coals or gas burners.

7. Close the lid and cook for 30 to 40 minutes, or until the dough is beautifully browned and the fruit has softened.

8. Serve at room temperature with freshly whipped cream or your favorite ice cream.

Blueberry–Sour Cream Coffee Cake

Yield: 8–10 servings

The smell of this cake cooking in the morning will just about drive you crazy, but be patient and wait. You can also serve this as a brunch, lunch, or even dinner dessert. If you're serving it after dinner, you may want to accompany it with a scoop of ice cream.

2 cups (473 mL) all-purpose flour
1 tablespoon (15 mL) baking powder
½ teaspoon (2.5 mL) salt
1 cup (227 g) plus 1 teaspoon (5 mL) unsalted butter, at room temperature, divided
1½ cups (354 mL) plus 1½ tablespoons (22.5 mL) sugar, divided
2 large eggs
1 cup (236 mL) sour cream
3 tablespoons (45 mL) dark rum, divided
¾ cup (177 mL) plus 3 tablespoons (45 mL) blueberry jam
½ teaspoon (2.5 mL) ground cinnamon)

1. Preheat the barbecue to 350°F (180°C). Butter and flour a 10-inch (25-cm) fluted tube pan.

2. In a large bowl, sift together the flour, baking powder, and salt. Set aside.

3. In a large bowl, use a hand-held mixer to beat 1 cup (227 g) of the butter until soft and creamy. Add 1½ cups (354 mL) of the sugar and beat until fluffy. Add the eggs, one at a time, beating well after each addition. Add the sour cream and 1 tablespoon (15 mL) of the rum and beat until the mixture is smooth. Turn the mixer to low, add the flour mixture, and beat just until incorporated.

4. Pour half of the batter into the pan and set it aside. To the remaining batter, add ¾ cup (177 mL) of the blueberry jam and beat until thoroughly combined. Pour this batter into the cake pan over the other batter.

5. Cook in the barbecue for 1 hour, or until the cake begins to pull away from the edges of the pan and a skewer inserted in the center of the cake comes out clean. Cool the cake in the pan for 15 minutes, then invert the cake onto a wire rack to cool completely.

6. In a small bowl, melt the remaining blueberry jam with the remaining butter in the microwave on medium for 10 to 15 seconds. Add the remaining rum and stir to mix.

7. Drizzle the cake with the melted blueberry jam. In a small bowl, combine the remaining sugar and the cinnamon. Sprinkle this mixture over the jam and serve warm.

Grilled Pears and Apples with Mango Relish
Yield: 4 servings

This is a great dessert for a warm summer evening. Kids love these, and they'll eat just about any fruit you can put on a skewer. They usually like just the fruit, but we dress it up with relish for moms and dads.

2 large pears, ripe but firm, cut into 1-inch (2.5-cm) chunks
2 apples, each cut into 8 wedges
½ cup (120 mL) preserved ginger syrup
¼ cup (60 mL) rice wine vinegar
¼ cup (60 mL) plus 2 teaspoons (10 mL) olive oil, divided
2 mangoes, diced
2 tablespoons (30 mL) chopped shallots
2 tablespoons (30 mL) chopped fresh mint
¼ teaspoon (1.25 mL) ground ginger

1. Make sure the grill is clean and generously sprayed with nonstick grilling spray. Preheat the barbecue to high (400°F [200°C] to 450°F [260°C]).

2. Thread the pears and apples onto soaked wooden skewers. In a small bowl, combine the ginger syrup, vinegar, and ¼ cup (60 mL) of the oil. Grill skewers, brushing them frequently with the ginger syrup mixture, until lightly browned and crisp.

3. Remove the fruit from the skewers and divide the chunks among individual serving bowls.

4. In a separate small bowl, combine the mangoes, shallots, fresh mint, ground ginger, and the remaining oil. Set the bowl on the table for spooning on the grilled fruit.

Barbecued Raspberry Pie

Yield: 4–6 servings

This could also be made with blackberries, Marion berries, or huckleberries, but raspberries have a balance of sweetness, delicate flavor, and beautiful color that will wow your dinner guests. I suggest baking two pies at once and hiding the second one for yourself.

1 (9-ounce [252-g]) package pie crust mix
4 cups (0.95 L) fresh raspberries
1 cup (236 mL) plus 1 teaspoon (5 mL) sugar, divided
¼ cup (60 mL) all-purpose flour
1 tablespoon (15 mL) lemon juice
1 teaspoon (5 mL) grated lemon zest
⅛ teaspoon (0.6 mL) salt
1 pinch cinnamon
1 teaspoon (5 mL) butter
1 egg yolk
1 cup (236 mL) half-and-half or milk

1. Preheat the barbecue to 350°F (180°C) for direct and indirect heating.

2. Prepare the pie crust according to the package directions. Line a 9-inch (22.5-cm) pie plate with the bottom crust. Set the pie plate and the top crust aside.

3. In a large bowl, gently toss together the raspberries, 1 cup (236 mL) of the sugar, the flour, the lemon juice, the lemon zest, the salt, and the cinnamon. Gently spoon the mixture into the pie shell. Dot with the butter.

4. Either cover the pie with the top crust and cut 3 to 4 vents into the top to release steam, or cut the remaining pastry into ½- to 1-inch (1- to 2.5-cm) wide strips and interlace them across the top of the pie. Pinch the edges together with a fork that has been dipped in water.

5. In a small bowl, combine the egg and cream. Brush the pastry with the egg-cream wash.

6. Sprinkle the top of the pie with the remaining sugar and place the pie on a sheet of aluminum foil or a baking sheet to prevent any spillage from burning. Bake in the barbecue for 10 minutes.

7. Reduce the heat to 325°F (165°C) by closing the vents and moving the pie to the unheated side of the grill. Bake for 50 to 60 minutes, or until the crust is golden brown.

8. Let the pie cool, and serve it with ice cream or freshly whipped cream.

Chocolate–Apricot Quesadillas

Yield: 4 servings

This easy, fun-to-make dessert takes about 6 to 8 minutes per person. If you wish, you can have your guests assemble their own.

4 flour tortillas
1 cup (236 mL) shredded mozzarella cheese
1 cup (236 mL) apricot preserves (or substitute raspberry, strawberry, or another flavor of your choice)
Confectioners' sugar, for serving
Milk chocolate sauce, for serving

1. Preheat the barbecue griddle to high (300°F [150°C] to 350°F [180°C]). If you don't have a barbecue griddle, heat a large nonstick skillet over medium heat on the grill. If you use a griddle, you can do several quesadillas at once; in a skillet, you can probably only do one at a time.

2. Place a tortilla on the griddle or in the skillet and cook until warmed on one side. Turn the tortilla and spoon on 1 tablespoon (15 mL) of the cheese, 2 tablespoons (30 mL) of the preserves, and another tablespoon (15 mL) of the cheese. Cook until the cheese starts to melt.

3. With tongs, fold the tortilla in half, hold it down for a moment, and continue cooking for 2 to 3 minutes, or until the tortilla is browned and all the cheese has melted.

4. Transfer the tortilla to a plate, sprinkle it with confectioners' sugar, drizzle it with warm milk chocolate sauce, and serve. Repeat with the remaining ingredients.

Blackberry–Blueberry–Raspberry Pie

Yield: 6–8 servings

Not only does this taste great, it presents beautifully, especially with a dollop of freshly whipped cream perched on top as you place the slices in front of your guests.

1½ cups (354 mL) granulated sugar
⅓ cup (79 mL) all-purpose flour
2 cups (473 mL) blackberries
2 cups (473 mL) raspberries
1 cup (236 mL) blueberries
1 medium cooking apple, peeled and coarsely shredded
1 refrigerated rolled 9-inch (22.5-cm) pie crust
Whipped cream, for serving

1. Preheat the barbecue to 375°F (190°C).

2. In a large mixing bowl, stir together the sugar and flour. Stir in the blackberries, raspberries, blueberries, and apple.

3. On a floured cutting board, roll the pastry into a 12-inch (30-cm) circle. Place the fruit in the middle of the circle and lift the edges up and around the filling, leaving the pastry open at the top. Cover the top edges with foil. Bake in the barbecue for 15 to 20 minutes, or until the top is golden and the fruit is tender.

4. Cool on a wire rack for at least 20 minutes before serving.

Banana–Rum Pot Stickers

Yield: 4–6 servings

I prepared these for Martin Yan's Yan Can Cook *television series in Toronto, Canada. He and the audience loved them. You can add raisins to the mix for a different texture.*

4 egg yolks
2 cups (473 mL) half- and-half
¼ cup (59 mL) granulated sugar
¼ teaspoon (1.25 mL) salt
2 tablespoons (30 mL) plus 2 teaspoons (10 mL) dark rum, divided
¾ cup (177 mL) finely chopped ripe banana
¼ cup (59 mL) packed brown sugar
1 teaspoon (5 mL) lemon juice
¼ teaspoon (1.25 mL) ground nutmeg
16 round wonton skins
1 large egg, beaten
¼ cup (59 mL) vegetable oil
Confectioners' sugar, for serving

1. In the top of a double boiler over hot water, beat together the egg yolks, half-and-half, granulated sugar, and salt. Cook, stirring until the mixture is thick enough to coat a spoon. Strain the custard. Add 2 tablespoons (30 mL) of the rum, then let the custard cool to room temperature.

2. In a medium bowl, use a rubber spatula to gently mix the bananas, brown sugar, the remaining rum, the lemon juice, and the nutmeg, taking care not to mash the bananas. If using raisins, add them here.

3. Lay the wonton skins on a work surface and brush the edges with the beaten egg. Spoon 1½ heaping teaspoons (8.75 mL) of banana filling onto the center of each pastry. Fold the wonton skins diagonally over filling and press the edges with a fork to seal.

4. Place the pot stickers on a baking sheet lined with plastic wrap. Cover with plastic and refrigerate (for up to 6 hours) until you are ready to cook them.

5. Preheat the barbecue to medium high (350°F [180°C] to 400°F [200°C]).

6. Spoon 1 to 2 tablespoons (15 to 30 mL) of the oil onto a well-seasoned griddle or a large cast-iron skillet (or add ¼ cup [59 mL] of the oil to a wok over a barbecue side burner). Working in batches, add the pot stickers, cooking them until they are golden brown, about 45 seconds per side, adding more oil as needed. Using a slotted spoon, transfer the cooked pot stickers to a dish lined with paper towels to drain. Keep the pot stickers warm until ready to serve.

7. Spoon a generous 1 to 2 tablespoons (15 to 30 mL) of custard into the center of each serving plate then arrange the pot stickers around the rum custard. Dust with confectioners' sugar and serve.

Tricia's Barbecued Apricot and Peach Cobbler
Yield: 8–10 servings

My daughter, Tricia, has a sweet tooth the size of Mount Rushmore, so I created this dish in her honor. Add a scoop of fresh peach ice cream, and even the guys on Mount Rushmore would smile.

½ cup (118 mL) butter
1 (15-ounce [443-mL]) can peaches
1 (15-ounce [443-mL]) can apricots
1 cup (236 mL) peach brandy
2 cups (473 mL) all-purpose flour
1 cup (236 mL) half-and-half
¼ cup (59 mL) packed dark brown sugar
¼ teaspoon (1.25 mL) ground cloves
¼ teaspoon (1.25 mL) ground allspice

1. Preheat the barbecue to medium high (300°F [150°C] to 350°F [180°C]) for indirect heating.

2. In an 8 × 11-inch (20 × 27.5-cm) pan, melt the butter. Add the peaches, apricots, and brandy. In a medium bowl, whisk together the flour and half-and-half. Pour this mixture into the pan over the fruit, stir once, and put the pan into the barbecue over indirect heat.

3. Bake for 1½ to 2 hours, or until a toothpick inserted into the batter comes out clean and the top is nicely browned.

4. In a small bowl, combine the brown sugar, cloves, and allspice. Sprinkle this mixture over the top of the dessert and put under the broiler for 1 minute. Serve warm, with chocolate or peppermint ice cream.

White Chocolate and Orange Soufflé
Yield: 4–6 servings

We've also made this with milk chocolate, lemon and lime zests, and Ke Ke Beach Key Lime Cream Liqueur (available online or at some liquor stores) for a tropical dessert.

½ cup (118 mL) heavy cream
¼ cup (59 mL) plus 2 tablespoons (30 mL) sugar, divided
8 ounces (227 g) white chocolate (such as Lindt), coarsely chopped, divided
5 large eggs, separated, at room temperature
1 tablespoon (15 mL) grated orange zest
4 teaspoons (20 mL) Grand Marnier
1 pinch cream of tartar
Confectioners' sugar, for serving

1. Preheat the barbecue to 350°F (180°C) to 375°F (190°C). Generously butter a 6- to 8-cup (1.4- to 1.9-L) soufflé dish. Sprinkle the dish with sugar; roll the dish around to coat all surfaces, and tap out the excess. Add a buttered and sugared aluminum foil collar that extends 2 to 3 inches (5 to 7.5 cm) above the rim of the dish and tie with butchers' twine.

2. In a medium saucepan, combine the cream and ¼ cup (59 mL) of the sugar over medium heat. Cook, stirring, until the sugar dissolves. Add 6 ounces (168 g) of the white chocolate and stir until the chocolate dissolves. Whisk in the egg yolks and orange zest and cook, stirring constantly, until the mixture thickens slightly, about 5 minutes. Do not boil. Remove the pan from the heat and whisk in the Grand Marnier. Transfer the mixture to a large bowl.

3. In a separate large bowl, using an electric mixer, beat the egg whites and cream of tartar until soft peaks form. Add of the remaining 2 tablespoons sugar and beat until stiff peaks form.

4. Mix the remaining chopped chocolate into the warm egg yolk mixture, then fold in the egg whites in 2 batches. Transfer this mixture to the prepared soufflé dish. Bake in the barbecue over indirect heat for about 35 minutes, or until the soufflé is puffed and the top is golden brown. Dust with confectioners' sugar and serve. Offer snifters of orange liqueur with a mandarin orange segment and a cherry on a toothpick floating inside, to sip.

Triple-Chocolate Marshmallow Cake
Yield: 10–12 servings

Cowboys used to cook everything in their Dutch ovens, and here we present an incredibly decadent chocolate cake cooked in a Dutch oven using nothing but charcoal briquettes. Let me say that again: This dessert is baked using only charcoal briquettes placed on top of and below a Dutch oven.

½ cup (118 mL) butter
1 cup (236 mL) packed brown sugar
2 tablespoons (30 mL) unsweetened cocoa
2 cups (473 mL) water
1 cup (236 mL) mini marshmallows, divided
2 (1.5-pound [680-g]) boxes double-chocolate cake mix
Eggs as called for in the cake mix instructions
1 (12-ounce [355-mL]) can cola
2 Cadbury Caramello bars, broken into squares

1. Generously spray the bottom, sides, and inside of the lid of an 8-quart (7.6-L) cast-iron Dutch oven with nonstick grilling or baking spray.

2. Melt the butter in a saucepan over medium heat on a barbecue side burner or stovetop and pour into the bottom of the Dutch oven. Stir in the brown sugar and cocoa. Pour in the water, stir, and layer on half of the marshmallows.

3. In a bowl, whisk together the cake mixes, eggs, and cola. Pour half of this over the marshmallows and scatter the chocolate pieces over the batter. Add the remaining marshmallows and cover with the remaining cake batter. Do not mix. Sprinkle the remaining chocolate bits over top of the cake.

4. Cover the Dutch oven and bake by placing 7 hot briquettes on the bottom and 14 hot briquettes on the top of the oven for 25 to 30 minutes. (Or bake at approximately 350°F (180°C) in a gas or charcoal barbecue grill.)

5. Serve warm, with freshly whipped cream.

Grilled Banana Splits
Yield: 4 servings

You can make these at home, at a campsite, in your RV, or on the beach. Prepare the ingredients in your kitchen and throw them on the fire or grill or in the fireplace and cook quickly.

½ cup (118 mL) unsalted butter
½ cup (118 mL) packed brown sugar
8 ripe bananas
Vanilla ice cream, for serving
Hot fudge sauce (or caramel, butterscotch, or your favorite dessert sauce), for serving
Whipped cream, for serving
Chopped nuts, for serving

1. Preheat your barbecue to 350°F (180°C) to 400°F (200°C).

2. In a small saucepan, combine the butter and brown sugar. Cook over medium to low heat until the butter is completely melted and the sugar is dissolved. Remove the pan from the heat.

3. With a sharp knife, cut each banana in half lengthwise, leaving the peel on the halves. Brush the cut sides of the banana halves with the sugar mixture and place the bananas, cut side down, on the grill. Grill until golden brown and caramelized, about 2 minutes. Turn the banana halves and brush with more glaze. Grill for 2 to 3 minutes longer, or until tender.

4. To serve, place two grilled banana halves in a sundae dish or shallow bowl. Top with 2 scoops of vanilla ice cream, drizzle with sauce, and top with whipped cream and chopped nuts.

Raspberry Puff Pastries
Yield: 6 servings

This elegant dessert couldn't be easier to make. Plus, you have puff pastry, cream, Grand Marnier, milk chocolate, and raspberries—all components of some of the greatest desserts ever gulped down.

1 (10-ounce [282-g]) package frozen puff pastry shells, thawed
2 cups (473 mL) heavy cream
¼ cup (59 mL) grated orange zest
1 tablespoon (15 mL) Grand Marnier
15 (1-ounce [28-g]) squares milk chocolate, chopped
1 pint (473 mL) fresh raspberries or blackberries

1. Preheat the barbecue to 375°F (190°C).

2. Place the pastry shells on a baking sheet and bake in the barbecue for the time instructed on the package. When the shells are cooked, remove the centers and return the shells to the barbecue as directed to firm up the inside of the puff pastry. Cool on a wire rack.

3. In a medium saucepan set over a barbecue side burner, combine the cream, orange zest, and Grand Marnier and heat the mixture to a boil. Remove the pan from the heat and let it stand for 5 minutes. Place the chocolate in a bowl. Pour the cream mixture over the chocolate and let it stand 10 minutes, or until the chocolate melts. Whisk the chocolate and cream until smooth.

4. Fill each pastry shell with raspberries and place each filled shell on a dessert dish. Pour the orange and milk chocolate sauce around the filled pastry, drizzling some over the berries. Garnish the dessert with a few loose berries and a mint sprig.

Rum and Coca-Cola Cake

Yield: 10–12 servings

You can make this with other colas, such as RC, Pepsi, or Dr. Pepper. But since I made this while filming Barbecue America *in Atlanta, Georgia, that just wouldn't be right.*

Cake

2 cups (473 mL) self-rising flour
1¼ cups (295 mL) granulated sugar
3 tablespoons (45 mL) unsweetened cocoa
1½ cups (354 mL) miniature marshmallows
1 cup (236 mL) Coke, at room temperature, flat
1 cup (236 mL) butter
¼ cup (59 mL) dark rum
2 large eggs, beaten
½ cup (118 mL) whole milk
1¼ teaspoons (6.25 mL) baking soda
1 teaspoon (5 mL) rum extract

Frosting

½ cup (118 mL) butter
5 tablespoons (75 mL) Coke, at room temperature, flat
1 tablespoon (15 mL) unsweetened cocoa
1 tablespoon (15 mL) dark rum
1 (1-pound [454-g]) bag confectioners' sugar
1 cup (236 mL) miniature marshmallows
2 tablespoons (30 mL) grated lime zest

1. Preheat the barbecue to medium high (325°F [165°C] to 375°F [190°C]). Butter and flour a 9 × 13-inch (22.5 × 32.5-cm) cake pan.

2. Make the cake. In a large bowl, combine the flour and sugar and mix well.

3. In a large saucepan, combine the marshmallows, Coke, butter, rum, and cocoa and bring to a boil, stirring constantly. Pour this mixture over the flour mixture and whisk to fully incorporate all the ingredients.

4. In a separate bowl, whisk together the eggs, buttermilk, baking soda, and rum extract. Pour this mixture into the batter and stir to combine. Pour the batter into the prepared pan and bake in the barbecue for 30 to 35 minutes, or until a toothpick inserted into cake comes out clean. Place the cake on a rack to cool slightly.

5. Make the frosting. In a large saucepan on the grill or on a side burner, melt the butter. Add the Coke, cocoa, and rum and bring to a boil. Stir in the confectioners' sugar and mix well. Cool slightly and stir in the marshmallows.

6. Immediately spread the frosting over the still-warm cake. Sprinkle with the grated lime zest and let the cake cool.

Lavender-Apricot-Peach Pie
Yield: 6–8 servings

Instead of the pie crust you could use sheets of phyllo dough. Brush 3 sheets with melted butter and place them in the foil container. Place 3 more buttered sheets crosswise over the first sheets, fold all of the sheets loosely over the pie filling, and brush with more melted butter.

1 rolled refrigerated 9-inch (22.5-cm) pie crust
¼ cup (59 mL) packed brown sugar
1 tablespoon (15 mL) dried lavender blossoms, divided
2 teaspoons (10 mL) all-purpose flour
½ teaspoon (2.5 mL) chili powder
¼ teaspoon (1.25 mL) ground cinnamon
1 (15-ounce [420-g]) can unpeeled apricot halves in light syrup, drained
1 (15-ounce [420-g]) can peach halves in light syrup, drained
¾ cup (177 mL) granola with raisins
2 tablespoons (30 mL) chopped gingersnap cookies

1. Preheat the barbecue to medium high (300°F [150°C] to 350°F [180°C]) for indirect heating. Spray a disposable aluminum 8- or 9-inch (20- or 22.5-cm) pie plate with nonstick grilling or baking spray. Remove the pie crust from the package, unroll it, and let it come to room temperature.

2. In a medium bowl, combine the brown sugar, 2 teaspoons (10 mL) of the lavender, the flour, the chili powder, and the cinnamon and stir well. Add the apricots and peaches and gently fold them into the flour until the fruit is well-coated.

3. In a small bowl, mix together the granola and chopped gingersnap cookies. Set aside.

4. Unfold the crust into the prepared pie plate, allowing the edges the of the crust to hang over the edges.

5. Spoon the apricot–peach mixture over the crust. Sprinkle with the granola–gingersnap mixture and the remaining lavender. Fold the crusts over the filling. Some of the filling will be left uncovered; this is OK.

6. Place the pie directly on the grill on the unheated side of the barbecue. Cover it loosely with a sheet of aluminum foil and bake for 40 minutes, or until the filling is bubbly and the crust is golden brown.

7. Remove the pie from the barbecue and let it cool for 15 to 20 minutes. Using a large serving spoon, serve generous scoops of pie in individual bowls. Accompany with freshly whipped cream.

Grilled Peppered Cantaloupe

Yield: 4 servings

This is a light and simple-to-prepare dessert. But you can also serve this as a side dish with grilled pork chops, halibut steaks, salmon fillets, or grilled chicken breasts.

1 large cantaloupe
¼ cup (59 mL) honey
¼ cup (59 mL) lemon juice
2 tablespoons (30 mL) cracked black pepper

1. Preheat the barbecue to medium high (300°F [150°C] to 350°F [180°C]).

2. In a shallow dish, stir together the honey and lemon juice. Set aside.

3. Cut the melon into ½-inch (1-cm) round slices. Remove the seeds and cut the slices in half so you have half-moon slices.

4. Place the slices directly on the hot grill, brush with the honey-lemon mixture, and cook just long enough to get good grill marks on the bottom side. Turn and brush again with the honey-lemon mixture. Remove the slices from the grill after 2 to 3 minutes.

5. Place the slices on a serving platter, brush the better-marked side with more honey and lemon, and sprinkle with the cracked black pepper.

Index

Metric Guidelines

With the tables below and a little common sense, you'll have no trouble making these recipes using metric measuring instruments. We have rounded off the liters, milliliters, centimeters, and kilos to make conversion as simple as possible.

Some Benchmarks—All You Really Need to Know
Water boils at 212°F
Water freezes at 32°F
325°F is the oven temperature for roasting
Your 250 mL measure replaces one 8 oz cup
Your 15 mL measure replaces one tablespoon
Your 5 mL measure replaces one teaspoon
A 20 cm x 20 cm baking pan replaces a U.S. 8" x 8"
A 22.5 cm x 22.5 cm baking pan replaces a U.S. 9" x 9"
A 30 cm x 20 cm baking pan replaces a U.S. 12" x 8"
A 22.5 cm pie pan replaces a 9" pie pan
A 21.25 cm x 11.25 cm loaf pan replaces an 8" x 4" loaf pan
A 1.5 liter casserole, sauce pan, or soufflé dish replaces a 1 ½ qt dish
A 3 liter casserole, sauce pan, or soufflé dish replaces a 3 qt dish
5 cm is about 2 inches
1 pound is a little less than 500 gm
2 pounds is a little less than 1 kg

Oven Temperatures

175°F............80°C	350°F..........180°C
200°F..........100°C	375°F..........190°C
225°F..........110°C	400°F..........200°C
250°F..........120°C	425°F..........220°C
275°F..........140°C	450°F..........240°C
300°F..........150°C	500°F..........260°C

Fahrenheit to U.K. Gas Stove Marks

275°F........mark 1	425°F.........mark 7
300°F........mark 2	450°F.........mark 8
325°F........mark 3	475°F.........mark 9
350°F........mark 4	
375°F........mark 5	
400°F........mark 6	

Volume

¼ cup...50 mL	4 cups (1 quart)...........................0.95 L
½ cup.......................................125 mL	1.06 quarts.....................................1 L
1/3 cup ....75 mL	4 quarts (1 gallon).......................3.8 L
¾ cup.......................................175 mL	
1 cup...250 mL	1 teaspoon ....5 mL
1 ¼ cups ....300 mL	½ teaspoon ....2 mL
1 ½ cups ....375 mL	¼ teaspoon ....1 mL
2 cups ....500 mL	1 tablespoon ....15 mL
2½ cups ....625 mL	2 tablespoons ....25 mL
3 cups ....750 mL	3 tablespoons ....50 mL

Weight

1 oz..25 gm
2 oz..50 gm
¼ pound ....125 gm (4 oz)
1 pound ....500 grams
2 pounds...1 kg
5 pounds ....2½ kg

Length

½ inch..1 cm
1 inch..2.5 cm
4 inches..10 cm

**Sayville Library
88 Greene Avenue
Sayville, NY 11782**